USA

D0833377

Hints for using the guide

Following the tradition established by Karl Baedeker in 1846, buildings, places of natural beauty and sights of particular interest are distinguished by one ★ or two ★★ stars.

To make it easier to locate the various places listed in the Sights from A to Z section of the guide, their coordinates on the large map included with the guide are shown in red at the head of each entry.

Coloured strips down the outside edge of the right-hand pages are an aid to finding the different sections of the guide. Blue indicates the introductory material, red the descriptions of sights, and yellow the practical information at the end of the book.

Only a selection of hotels and restaurants can be given: no reflection is implied, therefore, on establishments not included.

In a time of rapid change it is difficult to ensure that all the information given is entirely accurate and up to date, and the possibility of error can never be entirely eliminated.

Although the publishers can accept no responsibility for inaccuracies and omissions, they are always grateful for corrections and suggestions for improvement.

Preface

This guide to the USA is one of the new generation of Baedeker guides. These guides, illustrated throughout in colour, are designed to meet the needs of the modern traveller. They are quick and easy to consult, with the principal places of interest described in alphabetical order, and the information is presented in a format that is both attractive and easy to follow.

The guide is in three parts. The first part presents a general survey of the country, its geography, climate, flora and fauna, population, original inhabitants and modern society, economy, history, famous people, and culture. A

*Above:
paddleboats on
the Mississippi
Left: view of the
Grand Canyon*

selection of quotations and suggested itineraries lead on to the second part, in which the individual sights and features of interest – states, towns and cities, national parks, historic sites – are described. The third part contains a variety of practical information. Both the Sights and the Practical Information sections are in alphabetical order.

Baedeker guides are noted for their concentration on essentials and their convenience of use. They contain numerous colour illustrations and specially drawn plans, and at the end of the book is a fold-out map, making it easy to locate the various places described in the Sights from A to Z section.

Contents

Introduction
8–131

Sights
from A to Z
132–539

Practical
Information
from A to Z
540–613

Baedeker Specials

God's own

A country straight out of the cinema. Limousines cruising along apparently endless highways; lonely filling stations on roads shimmering in the heat; and of course, ice-cold coke to slake your thirst, all just like in a road movie. Streets like canyons, peopled by characters from some big-city melodrama, downing

thin coffee and doughnuts in neighbourhood coffee bars. The chink of spurs along dusty Main Streets, and boundless expanses of prairie, the epitome of countless Westerns. Glittering façades and displays of wealth to match anything in "Dallas", "Denver" or "Miami Vice". Sultry southern belles, and melancholy work songs wafting gently on the breeze. Cinderella's castle, Mickey Mouse and Donald Duck. Vast works of nature, and a desert, still surviving.

Confronted by one such experience or another in the course of your travels through the United States, it is sometimes necessary to pinch yourself to confirm that it is all real. So much is

History

In the former British colony of Virginia

familiar from the silver screen – whether it be America's immense natural splendour, the skyscrapers of huge cities, or the make-believe of Disney World and Universal Studios.

Forget for a moment the world of make-believe: the real-life United States is fantastic enough – a country made for holidays, from the pages of a picture book, with everything you could want of a tourist destination. Scenery to take your breath away, from the glaciers of Alaska in the far north to the stupendous Grand Canyon in the arid

The Charm of the South

Displayed in the old mansions and plantations

Country

south-west, the Rocky Mountains, the tropical everglades of Florida and Louisiana, and the forests of the Appalachians. And towns and cities that, as well as being open-air museums of modern architecture, are cultural centres rich in history: Chicago, New York City, San Francisco, Philadelphia, New Orleans and many others. Here too there is entertainment and diversions to suit every taste: fantasy in Hollywood and Orlando, gambling in Las Vegas and Atlantic City, bathing, swimming, diving and surfing in the Atlantic and Pacific, skiing, climbing and trapping in the Rockies. There is the world of the North American Indian to explore in Navajo country, and the life of the cowboy on the vast plains of Wyoming.

The cinema however is misleading in at least one respect: Americans do not gather in the evening around checked cloth covered tables to consume hamburgers and near-frozen beer. Real American cuisine has little in common with this stereotyped image. The country is, after all, a melting pot of cultures and local specialities, each contributing to the long menu on offer – Chinese in San Francisco, Italian in New York, gumbo and grits in New Orleans, ham in Virginia, and wine from California.

No one, though, can travel round the United States, eyes open, without realising that this glorious picture book also has blemishes. The land of the American Dream is a land of harsh social contrasts. Even so, whether the Almighty would agree or not, every American considers his homeland to be God's own Country, and most of them, including the less affluent, make an open display of their patriotism, something visitors quickly become accustomed to – or are already well acquainted with, from the movies.

Mickey Mouse
Well-known American friend

New York
City of cities

Nature's wonders
The Arches National Park in Utah

Indian Summer in Acadia National Park, Maine

ft), near Denver, and Pikes Peak (14,110 ft) at Colorado Springs in the Front Range.

The entire Pacific coastal rim is an area of tectonic disturbance, still active and manifesting itself in frequent earthquakes (St Andreas Fault) and volcanic eruptions (Mt Rainer). Deeply indented with fiords and islands, the west coast from the Alaskan peninsula to Puget Sound (Olympic National Park) and the mouth of the Columbia River, is of outstanding scenic beauty. South of this, down to the United States–Mexican border and the Baja California peninsula, there are few harbours but endlessly long sandy beaches. The chain of mountains running north-south parallel to the coast is only breached in the Golden Gate area, behind which extends the long fertile Californian valley.

Intermontane regions

The arid intermontane regions in the rain shadow of the Pacific mountain system offer impressive steppe and desert landscapes. With scanty vegetation cover, the geological structure is revealed with great clarity, for example in the multi-coloured strata of the sedimentary rocks.

This can be seen at its most impressive in the world-famous Grand Canyon, which the Colorado River has cut through the horizontally bedded Palaeozoic strata of the Colorado Plateau.

Similar erosional forms can be seen in the basaltic lavas of the Columbia Plateau.

The particularly arid southern section of the intermontane region, most of it without any drainage to the sea, is known as the Basin and Range Province, in which basins alternate with short, steep ranges of hills. The largest of these basins, much ramified, is the Great Basin, on the eastern edge of which is the Great Salt Lake and in its south-western part Death Valley, the lowest point in the United States (282 ft below sea level).

Central Lowlands

The Central Lowlands, between the Appalachians and the Cordilleras, consist of horizontally bedded Mesozoic rocks. The steep edge of the High Plains facing the Missouri plateau, the Pine Ridge Escarpment, is – like the Coteau du Missouri and many other similar features – a scarp formed by the differing resistance to erosion of the horizontally bedded sedimentary rocks. Although much of the landscape of the Central Lowlands is monotonous, there are occasional features offering a little variety, particularly resulting from the glaciation of the Canadian Shield. Great areas of recent morainic landscape in the north, with rounded hills and numerous lakes, alternate with absolutely flat and featureless areas of alluvial deposits occupying former glacial lakes.

In the five Great Lakes (Superior, Huron, Michigan, Erie and Ontario), formed by the melting of the inland ice, the United States possesses a substantial share (60,600 sq. mi.) of one of the largest freshwater systems in the world, with a total area, including the Canadian section, of some 96,500 sq. mi.

    The Great Lakes play a very important part in the North American system of inland waterways. They are linked with the open sea (the North Atlantic) by the St Lawrence Seaway, opened in 1959, and have various connections with the navigable Mississippi–Missouri river system.

Great Lakes

To the south the Central Lowlands merge into the Gulf Coast Plain, which extends inland for some 560 mi. along the Mississippi and in Florida runs into the Atlantic Coast Plain. Both of these plains consist of geologically recent deposits (Tertiary and Quaternary). Along their coasts, fringing the Atlantic and the Gulf of Mexico, are numerous spits of land, which have frequently been cut off to form islands, as in the Sea Islands of Georgia. The coastal lagoons within the spits of land Intracoastal Waterway in the Gulf Coast Plain form the important Intracoastal Waterway.

Coastal Plains

The "Goosenecks" of the San Juan River near Mexican Hat, Utah

Along the Atlantic coast, where the sea has encroached on the land, the wide funnel-shaped estuaries of the rivers, particularly the Delaware, Susquehanna and Potomac, give access for shipping to the inner reaches of Delaware Bay and Chesapeake Bay. The endless sandy beaches in both coastal plains offer ample scope for bathers; in the south bathing is possible throughout the year.

Minerals

Oil, gas

The United States occupies a leading place in the world in the exploitation of its mineral resources, particularly oil and natural gas. There are large oilfields in the western Gulf Coast plain (Texas), providing the basis for a massive petro-chemical industry. There are also rich deposits of oil and gas in the Central Lowlands (Texas, Oklahoma), on the eastern edge of the Rockies (Colorado) and in the intermontane basins (e.g. the Wyoming basin). Oilfields of some size have also been found in the Central Valley of California, and in the early 1980s considerable reserves of oil were discovered off the southern Californian coast. Since the completion of the Trans-Alaska Pipeline in 1977 oil has also been worked in the northern coastal plain of Alaska, on the Arctic Ocean. The Prudhoe field in this area is at present the largest working oilfield in North America.

Coal

The United States has the richest coal resources in the world, with 27 per cent of total world reserves, and the coal can be extracted at a much more economic rate than in Europe, since the seams lie in relatively undisturbed rock and are close to the surface. In 1992 some 860 million tons of hard coal and 80 million tons of brown coal were extracted. Considerable reserves of hard coal have been discovered in the Appalachian plateaux and in the west (particularly in Colorado and Wyoming). The coal is worked by opencast methods (30 per cent) and by horizontal shafts (70 per cent), which can be easily driven in from the slopes of the hills. The oldest-established coalfield is round Pittsburgh, which in the 19th c. developed into the main centre of the American iron and steel industry. The large deposits of brown coal in the Central Lowlands (particularly North Dakota, Montana and Wyoming) are still being worked.

Iron ore

The largest reserves of iron ore are in the Canadian Shield, which is rich in minerals of all kinds and extends into the United States in the Great Lakes area. This area yields over 90 per cent of national production (in 1996 over 62 million tons). The high-grade haematite ores of the Mesabi Range (in the Superior Upland Range to the west of Lake Superior), with an iron content of 56 per cent, established the world reputation of American iron ore. Following the gradual exhaustion of these stocks of high-grade ore since the end of the Second World War the lower-grade taconite ores, with an iron content of 20–35 per cent, found in northern Minnesota have increasingly been worked. These ores can be brought up to a competitive level of quality by a concentration process. The ore is shipped from the port of Duluth to the centres of the steel industry on the Great Lakes and in the Appalachian region – earning the Great Lakes the name of the "inland ocean" of North American heavy industry. In spite of its rich deposits of ore, however, the Superior Upland region cannot meet the enormous demands of American industry, and considerable quantities of iron have to be imported.

Other minerals

Other important reserves of minerals are to be found mainly in the Cordilleras. There are large fully mechanised opencast copper-mines and associated non-ferrous metal smelting works in the states of Utah, Arizona and Montana. Uranium is worked mainly in the southern Rockies. Outside the Cordilleras the principal minerals worked are

metals and industrial minerals. Gold is mined in Alaska and the Black
Hills, and also in the Cordilleras (Rocky Mountains, Sierra Nevada).
Large quantities of silver are worked in the Rockies. Lead comes mainly
from the Ozark plateaux. Phosphate is worked in Florida and bauxite in
Arkansas.

Rivers and lakes

The United States shares with Canada the largest continuous area of
fresh water in the world, the five Great Lakes, and much of the country
is drained by the Mississippi and its tributaries. The Mississippi – "Old
Man River" – is one of the longest and most abundantly flowing rivers
in the world.

The largest catchment area among the river systems of the United   Rivers
States – with a length of over 3700 mi. and an area of 1.25 million sq. mi.
– is that of the Mississippi and Missouri, which drains into the Gulf of
Mexico. Its most important tributaries are the Arkansas and the Ohio,
with the Allegheny and the Tennessee. The Mississippi–Missouri river
system plays an important part as an inland waterway: along with the
Illinois Waterway it provides a link between the industrial regions of the
Great Lakes and the Gulf of Mexico.

The Rio Grande, with a total length of 1885 mi. and a catchment area
of 220,000 sq. mi., also flows into the Gulf of Mexico.

The Colorado River, which flows through the arid region of the south-
west, is 1450 mi. long, with a catchment area of 165,000 sq. mi. It flows
into the Gulf of California, and in the course of its passage through the
south-western United States has carved out a grandiose valley through
the rock (see Sights from A to Z, Grand Canyon National Park).

The 1240 mi. Columbia River, with an abundant flow of water, rises in
the Canadian Rockies and in its lower course flows through the north-
western United States into the Pacific. It has a catchment area of 258,000
sq. mi. Its most important tributary within the United States is the Snake
River, whose source streams tumble down from the mountains of the
Yellowstone and Grand Teton region.

Among the rivers draining into the Atlantic the St Lawrence, which
flows out of Lake Ontario (length 800 mi.; catchment area, including the
Great Lakes, 398,000 sq. mi.), occupies a special position. As the St
Lawrence Seaway, opened in 1959, it enables large ocean-going ships to
reach the ports of the manufacturing belt on the Great Lakes, far inland

The river systems of the United States have been turned to good
account. **Dams** have been constructed on most of the rivers, including
some (on the Colorado, Columbia and Missouri) that are among the
largest in the world. The prototype for all later developments was the
Tennessee Valley project, begun in 1933. The dams provide protection
against flooding, produce hydro-electric power and, in the arid regions,
supply water for irrigation. Two important schemes in the Pacific West
are the Central Valley Project and the California State Water Project,
which supply the densely populated arid region of southern California
with water from the wetter north. To ensure that water will be available
to meet the steadily increasing needs of the arid regions, schemes such
as the Snake River-Colorado Project (to provide increased resources for
the irrigation of the Columbia plateau) and the North American Water
and Power Alliance (to supply the Central Valley of California) have been
developed. The basic idea of such large-scale projects is to convey the
surplus water resources of the northern Pacific states, with their abundance of rain, to the drought regions of the south.

As already noted, the five Great Lakes lying on the frontier with Canada   Lakes
are the largest continuous area of fresh water in the world. They influ-

ence the climate of the surrounding regions of the United States and are of predominant importance as an inland waterway for the transport of raw materials to the great industrial centres. The individual lakes are Lake Superior (area 31,820 sq. mi.), Lake Huron (23,000 sq. mi.), Lake Michigan (22,400 sq. mi.), Lake Erie (area 9940 sq. mi.) and Lake Ontario (7540 sq. mi.). Containing as they do 20 per cent of the world's supply of fresh water, the Great Lakes are of immense importance as a natural reservoir. Yet they are at risk precisely for this reason. The 33 million Canadians and Americans living round the lakes have the highest water consumption in the world. If this trend continues the outflow into the St Lawrence will be reduced by a quarter, to avert which danger water extraction must be halved.

The Great Salt Lake, which has no outlet, lies in a huge intermontane basin in the western United States at an altitude of 4200 ft, with an area of some 1500 sq. mi. and a maximum depth of 35 ft. The water level is subject to sharp variations depending on weather conditions.

Climate

Apart from Alaska and southern Florida the United States lies within the temperate zone. The larger northern part is within the cool temperate climatic zone.

In most of the United States the weather pattern is determined by cyclones (areas of low pressure) that travel throughout the year, bringing an alternation between cold and warm air masses and between overcast and clear skies and producing wide differences in rainfall.

Pacific coast

On the Pacific coast the mountains striking north-south form a barrier that gives the area an oceanic climate and high rainfall. In the coastal regions of the north-western United States the annual rainfall is frequently over 80 in.

Southern California

Southern California has a climate of Mediterranean type, with dry summers and winter rain.

West

The maritime influence, however, does not reach far inland. The intermontane region of the Cordilleras and the western parts of the Central Lowlands (the plains and prairies) are areas of marked aridity where the only period of precipitation of any quantity occurs in the hills. The leeward slopes of the hills have an annual rainfall of under 20 in. In the south-western United States there are areas of extreme aridity in which there is only sporadic rainfall.

East

The eastern United States, on the other hand, have plenty of rain, since the masses of warm air moving north from the Gulf of Mexico are charged with moisture. The Gulf Coast and the Appalachians have annual precipitations of over 60 in. The boundary between the wetter east and the drier west runs roughly along the 98th degree of longitude. This important climatic frontier is clearly reflected in the different agricultural patterns in the transition from the humid to the arid regions. Since the level of precipitations varies widely from year to year the boundary of the arid zone moves this way or that way within a broad corridor.

South-east

The climate of the south-eastern United States is influenced by the masses of hot, moist air coming in from the Gulf of Mexico. Its characteristics are mild winters, hot summers and high rainfall.

"Father of the Water", "Wide River", "Ol Man River" – the ▶
Mississippi has many names

Climate

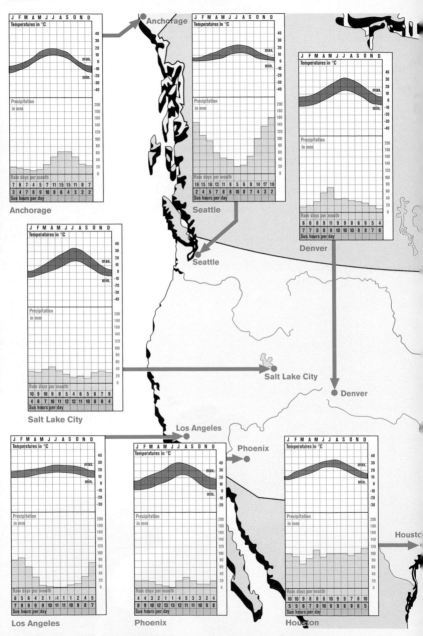

Anchorage

J F M A M J J A S O N D	
Temperatures in °C	
Precipitation in mm	
Rain days per month	7 6 7 4 5 7 11 15 15 11 8 7
Sun hours per day	3 4 7 8 9 10 8 6 4 3 2 2

Seattle

J F M A M J J A S O N D	
Temperatures in °C	
Precipitation in mm	
Rain days per month	19 15 16 13 11 9 5 6 8 14 17 19
Sun hours per day	2 4 5 7 8 8 10 9 7 4 3 2

Denver

J F M A M J J A S O N D	
Temperatures in °C	
Precipitation in mm	
Rain days per month	6 6 8 9 11 9 9 9 6 6 5 4
Sun hours per day	7 7 8 8 9 10 10 9 8 7 6

Salt Lake City

J F M A M J J A S O N D	
Temperatures in °C	
Precipitation in mm	
Rain days per month	10 9 10 9 8 5 4 6 5 6 7 9
Sun hours per day	4 6 7 10 11 12 12 11 10 8 6 4

Los Angeles

J F M A M J J A S O N D	
Temperatures in °C	
Precipitation in mm	
Rain days per month	6 5 6 4 2 1 >1 1 1 2 4 5
Sun hours per day	7 8 9 9 10 11 11 11 10 9 8 7

Phoenix

J F M A M J J A S O N D	
Temperatures in °C	
Precipitation in mm	
Rain days per month	4 4 3 2 1 4 5 3 3 2 4
Sun hours per day	8 9 10 12 13 13 12 11 11 10 9 8

Houston

J F M A M J J A S O N D	
Temperatures in °C	
Precipitation in mm	
Rain days per month	10 10 9 6 8 9 9 9 7 8 10
Sun hours per day	5 5 7 8 9 10 9 9 8 8 6 5

Regional climates in the USA

Designed by
H. Linde

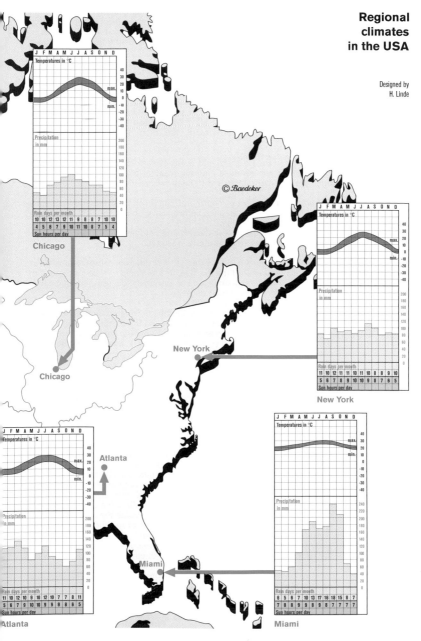

© Baedeker

Chicago

J	F	M	A	M	J	J	A	S	O	N	D
Temperatures in °C

Precipitation in mm

Rain days per month
10 10 12 12 13 11 9 8 8 7 10 10
Sun hours per day
4 5 6 7 9 10 11 10 8 7 5 4

New York

J	F	M	A	M	J	J	A	S	O	N	D
Temperatures in °C

Precipitation in mm

Rain days per month
11 10 12 11 11 11 10 11 9 8 9 10
Sun hours per day
5 6 7 8 9 10 10 9 8 7 6 5

Atlanta

J	F	M	A	M	J	J	A	S	O	N	D
Temperatures in °C

Precipitation in mm

Rain days per month
11 10 12 9 10 12 12 10 7 7 8 11
Sun hours per day
5 6 7 9 10 9 9 9 8 8 6 5

Miami

J	F	M	A	M	J	J	A	S	O	N	D
Temperatures in °C

Precipitation in mm

Rain days per month
6 5 6 7 10 13 17 16 18 15 8 7
Sun hours per day
7 8 8 9 9 8 9 8 7 7 7 7

23

Flora and Fauna

Continental climate

The continental character of the climate, particularly in the central regions of the United States, means that visitors from Europe must be prepared for very high temperatures in summer and very low ones in winter. In the south-east the high humidity of the air frequently produces an unpleasant mugginess.

Air masses

Since the mountain ranges run north-south there is a practically unhindered exchange of air masses between arctic and tropical latitudes. Cold air coming from Canada gives the north-eastern states extremely cool winters and springs, even though New York, for example, lies in the same latitude as central Italy. In summer, on the other hand, warm, moist air masses from the Gulf of Mexico can be carried to the north-eastern United States, bringing with them long periods of sultry weather.

Blizzards

Particularly in the northern and north-eastern states inflows of cold air from Canada can produce extreme weather conditions in the form of unpleasant winter blizzards with heavy snowfalls.

Northers

The cold winds known as "northers" can reach far south and frequently cause considerable damage to subtropical crops on the Gulf Coast, particularly in Florida in winter.

The rapid change between warm and cold air leads to extreme variations in temperature, particularly in winter.

Tornadoes

The collision between air masses at very different temperatures gives rise, particularly east of the Rockies, to tornadoes – violent storms with winds whirling round a small area of extremely low pressure that cause considerable damage in their passage.

Hurricanes

Hurricanes travelling in from the Caribbean in late summer and early autumn also cause great devastation, not so much from the high winds as from the tidal waves, heavy rain and flooding that they bring with them. Only the Gulf Coast plain and the Atlantic coastal plain lie in the path of these storms, against which there is now a well organised tracking and early warning system.

Flora and Fauna

Flora

Northern regions

Apart from the arid western regions and the sub-Arctic tundra in Alaska the territory of the United States has a natural cover of forest. The boreal coniferous forest (spruce, fir, larch and pine) characteristic of great expanses of Canada extends far south into the United States only in the Cordilleras. Between the 60th and the 40th degrees of latitude there extends parallel to the coast the 90–180 mi. wide belt of coniferous forest of the Pacific coastal regions (Douglas fir, Sitka spruce, western red cedar, western hemlock), giving place towards the east to the pine forests and the sub-alpine coniferous forests of the mountain regions. These in turn are succeeded by the grassland of the Plains, the short-grass prairie, which around the 100th degree of longitude merges into the tall-grass prairie. Further east the north-eastern mixed forest (hemlock, red pine, hickory, beech, yellow birch and maple species) extends by way of the oak-hickory deciduous forest of the Midwest and the Appalachian deciduous forest to the Atlantic coast.

Southern regions

Below the 40th degree of latitude, about the level of San Francisco, a narrow strip of sequoia forests gives place to the macchia and sclerophyllous (hard-leaved) forests of the Chaparral and beyond this the sagebrush region of the Great Basin. Further east extend the plains and prairies, followed by the oak-pine mixed forests reaching to the Atlantic coast.

Other regions with characteristic vegetation patterns are the creosote bush area, a subtropical steppe with succulents, Covillea tridentata, cactuses, yuccas and agaves on the high plateaux of eastern Arizona and New Mexico, and the subtropical pine forests between New Orleans and Florida. In the swampy region of southern Florida (the Everglades) there are great expanses of palmetto scrub.

Fauna

The relatively late (in geological terms) separation of the American from the Eurasian continent has led to remarkable correspondences between the fauna of the two continents. Nevertheless a number of endemic species developed, among them the bison, pronghorn antelope, prairie dog, turkey and some amphibians and reptiles, the best known of which are the various species of rattlesnakes. At the end of the 19th c. large nature reserves began to be established in order to preserve native species that had been decimated by human settlement.

Endemic species

In the hills of the north-eastern and eastern United States are found the Virginia or white-tailed deer, the raccoon, the opossum and the chipmunk; the black bear is now rare. The birds of the Atlantic coast are numerous and varied – various species of terns, the laughing gull, the American grey heron, the great white egret and the pelican.

Eastern regions

The swamplands of the south-east are the habitat of the Mississippi alligator, once common but now found only in nature reserves. The few manatees living off the coast of Florida are now threatened with extinction.

The herds of bison (buffaloes) that once roamed the prairies are now represented only by a few survivors. They share this territory with prairie dogs, pronghorn antelopes and the American badger. Typical birds are the prairie chicken, the prairie falcon and the burrowing owl.

Prairies

The coyote now prefers to live in the cultivated land of the open grassland steppe.

The mountains of the north-west and west and the northern forests are the home of the black and grizzly bears. Here too are found the bighorn sheep, the elk and the wapiti. There are small numbers of pumas (cougars) in the Rockies. The population of some species of lynx and of the wolf has shown an increase. The white-tailed eagle, the heraldic bird of the United States, lives along the edges of the waterways. Along the Pacific coasts of Oregon and California are found the Californian sealion, the grey whale and the sea elephant.

Western regions

Alaska is the home of the Arctic fox, the wolverine and the otter. In the adjoining Bering Sea and the North Pacific there are bottle-nosed dolphins and various species of whale and seal.

Environment

Although claimed to be the "land of unlimited possibilities" and "God's own country", the United States – like every other country in the world – is threatened with the continuing destruction of the balance of nature by the activities of man. The process began when the traditional way of life of the native Indian inhabitants, living close to nature, was disturbed and displaced by the first settlers from the Old World, and reached a peak in the 19th c., when whole tribes were forced to leave their home territories, the buffaloes that roamed the prairies were almost completely wiped out and forests were ruthlessly cleared (involving the decimation of the giant redwoods of the Pacific West).

Erosion

In farming country the crops are threatened by soil erosion and dust storms, and in order to increase yields recourse is had to dry farming (in which the land is regularly cultivated but not sown every year) and strip farming (in which strips of land of varying width are alternately sown with grain and left fallow). In some areas marginal land has been abandoned.

Overfelling

The logging industry, which formerly supplied building timber and firewood, is now geared to paper and cellulose production. A common practice has been to clear whole areas of forest – leading, particularly in upland areas of high rainfall, to wholesale erosion of the soil. The practice of selective felling, accompanied by reafforestation, is only gradually becoming established.

Pollution

The problem of acid rain has not yet been solved, and much damage has been caused to the terrestrial eco-system (vegetation, soil structure, water quality), particularly in the north-eastern United States and round large cities. To this is added the pollution of rivers and lakes, mainly by agriculture but also by mining, industry, transport and urban development. In Florida and other parts of the country, for example, pesticides and fungicides have seeped into the ground-water, threatening the supply of drinking water. Round the Great Lakes much damage to the forests and dramatic changes in the stocks of freshwater fish have been reported, no doubt mainly due to the emission of harmful substances from the gigantic industrial concentrations in the Chicago-Indianapolis-Pittsburgh area.

Mining

Further dangers to the environment are the large-scale development of opencast mining, the creation of huge spoil heaps and the uncontrolled

No mountain is too steep for the snow goats in the Rockies

prospecting for oil in ecologically sensitive areas. Some tracts of land already have the aspect of a lunar landscape.

The use of irrigation in agriculture and extensive building development in the sunshine states of Florida, Arizona and California have led not only to dramatic changes in the water table but also to the destruction of the balance of nature over a wide area. As a result of the expansion of agriculture, the demand for more houses and the growth of leisure activities more and more species of flora and fauna are threatened with extinction.

Agriculture

The uncontrolled growth of building development, industry and transport has led to serious air pollution in many areas. The problem is particularly acute in Los Angeles, whose blanket of smog, caused mainly by its huge numbers of private automobiles, has become proverbial.

Air pollution

The native fauna of the United States was decimated, and in some cases completely destroyed, from an early stage in the country's development by the white man. In the latter part of the 19th c., however, a beginning was made with the establishment of large national parks and nature reserves in order to limit human intrusion and provide refuges for the native flora and fauna. Pioneers in this development were the Scottish immigrant John Muir and the bird painter John James Audubon. In 1864 the Yosemite Valley and the surrounding forests of giant redwoods were given statutory protection by the Californian government, and in 1872 Yellowstone National Park was established.

Conservation

Many particularly sensitive natural regions have now been scheduled as protected zones, managed either by the federal government (National Park Service) or by individual states (usually by the Department of Resources). Among them are the Everglades of Florida, the redwood forests of the Pacific coast, stretches of the Atlantic, Gulf and Pacific coasts and beautiful mountain regions like the Grand Teton, Yosemite and Mount Rainier areas. Recently numbers of individual natural features, recreation areas, cycling and hiking trails and historic sites have also been given statutory protection.

The various protected areas have their own administrations, and there are strict regulations for visitors, with park rangers to secure their observance. The park rangers are also a source of information about the region, and in some cases organise nature excursions. All the protected areas have visitor centres that provide a wide range of information, literature and maps, together with audio-visual shows and exhibitions focussing on problems specific to the area.

In many parks – for most of which there are admission charges – there are refreshment facilities, campgrounds and picnic areas, and sometimes also hotels and motels. The most important of the National Parks are described in the Sights from A to Z section of this guide, the remainder being listed under "Practical Information".

Population

At the last census (1997) the United States had a population of 267 million, with a density of 73.8 per sq. mi. Density is very much higher in the highly urbanised Atlantic coastal region, where more than a fifth of the total population live in the Boswash (Boston-Washington) megalopolis. The highest density is found in Washington, DC, with 10,132 inhabitants per sq. mi. The east coast states containing the great urban concentrations also show high densities: New Jersey 987 per sq. mi., Rhode Island 826, Massachusetts 728, Connecticut 655, Maryland 453, New York State 363. There are also large concentrations of population in the highly industrialised areas round the Great Lakes, on the Pacific coast

27

(particularly in California) and on the west coast of the Gulf of Mexico. At the other end of the scale are the arid regions of the Plains and the intermontane areas of the Cordilleras, the boreal forests and the sub-Arctic tundra in Alaska. In the arid regions of the west the population density falls below 5 per sq. mile; in Alaska it is only 0.9.

Growth

The United States population has risen by 6 per cent since 1996, with larage variations between individual states due to the high level of mobility. There is a clear trend in internal migration within the United States from the predominantly agrarian regions to the urbanised industrial ones.

Thus there has for several decades been a steady movement of population to the Pacific coast, and there has been a continuing migration of coloured people from the south into the industrial regions of the Atlantic coast and the Midwest. The greatest increase of population is in the Sun Belt, the climatically favoured stretch of country in the south between the Atlantic and the Pacific.

Urbanisation

The population of the United States is highly urbanised. In 1990 80 per cent of the population lived in towns of over 2500 inhabitants (compared with 64 per cent in 1950); in the areas round the Atlantic megalopolises and in California the figure was over 90 per cent. Urbanisation is proceeding at a great rate in these areas, though not so much in the city centres as on the urban fringes. There are in the United States 174 large cities with a total of some 60 million inhabitants, compared with 132 in 1960; 970 middle-size towns (25,000–100,000 inhabitants) with just under 45 million inhabitants (633 in 1960); and 1770 small towns (10,000–25,000 inhabitants) with 28 million inhabitants (1134 in 1960). There are now eight cities with over a million inhabitants (New York, Los Angeles, Chicago, Houston, Philadelphia, San Diego, Phoenix and Dallas) and 15 cities with over 500,000.

Immigrants from Europe

From the early 17th c. onwards some 47 million Europeans left their old homes and found new ones in North America. Some were refugees from religious persecution or political oppression, but most of them came to seek a better life. The first mass movement was started by immigrants from England who landed in the territory of the Powhatan Indians in 1607 and founded the colony of Virginia. By then, however, Scots, Germans, Irishmen, Dutch, Swedes, Swiss and French were also crossing the Atlantic. After the formation of the United States a certain hostility to foreigners began to develop, but this declined during the Presidency of Thomas Jefferson (1801–9). In the hundred years between the Congress of Vienna (1815) and the outbreak of the First World War almost 30 million Europeans entered the United States in three great waves of immigration.

1815–60

Between 1815 and 1860 there were some 5 million immigrants – more than the total population of the United States at that time. Most of them came from Ireland (2 million), England, Wales and Scotland (a quarter of a million each) and Germany (1.7 million). The most influential group was the Irish, who were almost exclusively Catholic; almost all of them settled in the large towns of the north, particularly New York, where they soon came to dominate the unskilled labour market and developed into a powerful political force. During the heyday of Irish "boss rule" between 1870 and 1920 every town with a high proportion of Irish in its population had an Irish political leader and an Irish mayor. Many old-established Americans, predominantly Protestant, saw the "papists" as a threat and organised themselves in such activities as the Nativist Movement. In 1844 there were riots in Philadelphia during which Roman Catholic churches were set on fire and Irishmen were killed.

During the second wave of immigration, between 1860 and 1890, a further 10 million Europeans came to the United States, again predominantly British, Irish and German. Again, too, they settled mainly in the cities of the north: at this period half the population of New York, Chicago, Cincinnati, Milwaukee and Detroit had been born outside the United States. 1860–90

The third wave of immigration, between 1890 and 1914, brought another 15 million people to the United States, but this time they came from southern, south-eastern and eastern Europe. They were less rapidly assimilated than their predecessors, and tended to live in separate districts of their own and to follow particular trades (Italians in the construction industries, Poles in heavy industry). 1890–1914

The increase in the number of immigrants gave rise to a new "nativist" movement and led finally to the Johnson Read Act of 1924, which restricted the number of immigrants to 150,000 a year and set quotas for different nationalities. In spite of this legislation, however, the United States was during the 1930s the country that took in the largest numbers of refugees from Nazi persecution from all over Europe, particularly German Jews. Restrictions

African-Americans

The 1997 census showed that 33.8 million coloured people lived in the United States, representing 13 per cent of the total population. In recent

In East Village, New York

years the discriminatory term "negro" has fallen out of use, the terms "coloured" or "black" people being used instead. Increasingly, too, the black citizens of the United States like to refer to themselves as African-Americans. With the exception of the District of Columbia, where blacks make up 66 per cent of the population, most of them live in the southern states of Mississippi (35.6 per cent of the population), Louisiana (30.8 per cent), South Carolina (29.8 per cent) and Georgia (27 per cent). The lowest proportions are in the states of Idaho and Montana (0.3 per cent).

Slavery

The first blacks arrived in Jamestown, in the British colony of Virginia, in 1619. They came not as slaves but as indentured labourers, who had bound themselves to pay the cost of their passage from Africa out of their wages, after which their earnings would be their own – an arrangement that also applied to many white workers. The bringing in of slaves began about 1660, and in the course of the 17th and 18th centuries the slave trade increased by leaps and bounds. By 1790 there were 610,000 slaves in Virginia, Georgia and North and South Carolina; in the other nine states there were only 40,000. Their numbers had doubled by 1808, when the import of slaves was banned; and thereafter the need for additional labour was met by the children of slaves. The contrast between North and South was highlighted on the admission of Missouri to the Union in 1820, when under the Missouri Compromise slave-owning was prohibited north of latitude 36°30'. The Californian constitution of 1850 banned slave-owning, but it was permitted in other new territories. Federal officials were obliged by law to arrest runaway slaves and return them to their owners. In 1854 the Kansas-Nebraska Bill was passed, allowing slavery in these two states in spite of the fact that they lay north of the boundary line. This led to bloody riots and to the foundation of the Republican Party with its anti-slavery policy. The Republican victory in an election in 1860 sparked off the movement for secession.

Free blacks

In 1860 there were some 4 million black slaves in the southern states, owned by 384,000 whites. In addition there were in the United States 482,000 blacks who were not slaves, half of them in the slave-owning states. Neither in the south nor in the north, however, were these "free" blacks treated as equal with whites. In the south they were required by statutory restrictions to live as quasi-slaves, and in the north they were subject to discrimination, abuse and violence. During this period there was no public discussion of any change in their legal status: even the country's intellectual leaders, like Thomas Jefferson, who saw "natural and indelible lines of difference" between the white and black races, and Abraham Lincoln, in whose opinion blacks and whites could not be considered on the same level, had no thought of change.

Civil War

The Civil War (1861–5) began as a political conflict over the maintenance of the Union but ended as a war for the abolition of slavery. This war aim – if indeed it was one – was based primarily on pragmatic grounds. With the idea of weakening the economy of the south, attracting increased numbers of blacks into the army of the Union and stirring up unrest and risings among the blacks of the south, Lincoln issued in 1863 his proclamation of emancipation, which declared all black slaves in the southern states to be free. Some 190,000 slaves fled to the north, where they became competitors in the labour market. This led from 1863 onwards to the "draft riots", mainly involving Irish immigrants, in the course of which an orphanage for black children in New York was burned down.

Progressive developments

After the Civil War there were some progressive developments for the benefit of the black population. On December 18th 1865 the ban on slavery was incorporated in the Constitution under the 13th Amendment, and further constitutional amendments guaranteed the civil rights of blacks (1868) and granted them the vote (1870). Thus, theoretically, the liberation of blacks was achieved; but it was to be many years before further statutory measures were introduced to give them full equal rights. It was mainly from the 1950s that they were granted rights that had been denied them since 1875 – the abolition of racial segregation in the armed forces between 1950 and 1955, the Civil Rights Acts of 1857 and 1964, the Voting Rights Act of 1965 and the Fair Housing Act of 1968. But all this still did not go far enough. As Martin Luther King declared, the black man was not fighting for some vague abstract rights but for a concrete and immediate improvement in his living conditions. What good did it do him if he could send his children to an integrated school if he had no money to buy school clothing, and what did he gain from permission to move into any part of his town if he could not afford it? Blacks not only wanted the right to make use of any institution open to the public: they had to be fitted into the economic system in such a way that they were able to exercise that right.

In spite of the bussing boycott of 1955 in Montgomery, Alabama, and the sending in of the National Guard in 1957 to end racial segregation in schools, not much had changed in the situation of the black population. They were more poorly housed, their wages were lower and they were frequently unemployed. The road to equality led by way of demonstrations in Birmingham, Alabama, in 1962, the march on Washington and the murder of Martin Luther King to the race riots of 1965–9, which brought the state to the brink of a new civil war. Martin Luther King had sought by his Peace Movement to achieve integration, while Malcolm X and Eldridge Cleaver, leaders of the Black Power movement, aimed at racial segregation, the separation of the black from the white population, each with the same rights, and were prepared to use violence to attain their ends.

Civil-rights movement

The social situation of black Americans has undoubtedly improved, but openly racist discrimination has now given place to social discrimination. 28.4 per cent of all blacks live below the poverty line, compared with 11.2 per cent of whites, and the unemployment rate among black workers is twice as high as for whites. Visitors to the United States cannot but observe the high proportion of blacks among beggars and the homeless, and will notice how many blacks buying food in a supermarket pay for it with coupons. The slums of the cities are mainly occupied by blacks, for although the separation of black and white residential areas is banned it still happens in practice. Resistance to continuing discrimination still leads to violent outbreaks like the riots in Los Angeles in the summer of 1993. The United States is still a long way away from a solution of the problem.

Hispano-Americans

The second largest minority group in the United States, after the African-Americans, is the Hispano-Americans (29 million, or 11 per cent of the total population), with their roots in the Latin American countries. 13.5 million of them are "Chicanos" (Americans of Mexican/Indian descent); the rest are mainly from Puerto Rico, an American territory since 1848, and, over the last thirty years, from Cuba – refugees from the economic difficulties of Castro's Cuba, now numbering something like a million. The states with the largest numbers of Mexican Americans are New Mexico (39.4 per cent of the population), California (25.8 per cent) and Texas (25.5 per cent). The Puerto Ricans make up a high proportion (12 per cent) of the population of New York; the Cuban exiles have settled mainly in Miami.

A major problem is presented by illegal immigration from Mexico, which the American authorities can barely control even with the aid of a fence along the frontier and increased patrols.

Asians

Americans of Asian origin (10 million, or 4 per cent of total population) are the third largest ethnic minority in the United States. The largest group is the Chinese (1.6 million), with large Chinatowns in New York and San Francisco, followed by Filipinos (1.4 million) and Japanese (0.8 million). Subsequent to the Vietnam War, the United States has opened its doors to 140,000 Vietnamese.

Chinese

Between 1850 and 1866 increased numbers of Chinese crossed the Pacific to the west coast of the United States, where they played a part in building up the state of California. Many of them worked on the construction of the transcontinental railroad, competing with European workers. In 1877 an Irishman founded the Working Man's Party, with the object of denying jobs to Chinese workers, and in 1880 there were anti-Chinese riots in Denver, Colorado. During the last thirty years of the 19th c. the Chinese were permitted to live only in certain areas in the United States, and they were not allowed to become American citizens. The Chinese Exclusion Act of 1882 put a stop to further immigration and prevented those born abroad from obtaining naturalisation. The ban on immigration was not finally done away with until 1943.

Settlements

Towns

The 8000 or so towns of the United States show a considerable degree of uniformity, mainly because they were new foundations laid out on similar plans. Except in the towns of New England a regular grid is the norm. In the larger cities the centre (Downtown, the City, the Central Business District) is an area of high-rise blocks. The widespread erection of skycrapers in all the larger towns is one manifestation of the increased importance of the service sector.

The rapid growth of cities and the steady increase in the services sector have led not only to traffic problems but also to a radical change in the structure of cities. The more prosperous families have moved from districts near the centre to the outer fringes, and have been replaced by families lower in the social scale, particularly blacks. As a result the districts round the centre – severely overcrowded and mostly much dilapidated – have degenerated into slums. The result of the development of the cities has thus been to create social and ethnic ghettos.

The **town planners** have tried to counter the negative developments resulting from continuing urbanisation. The separation of traffic into several levels and the provision of freeways into the central area have been achieved in many cities. The rehabilitation of areas round the centre, in a process of urban renewal, is well under way. The construction of tower apartment blocks is proceeding, with the object of restoring to the city centre its residential function. On the outskirts of the cities, where there is more space, carefully planned shopping centres (plazas) and industrial parks are being developed. In the great conurbations the planning of "strip cities" along the main highways is designed to obviate the spreading of development over large areas of the countryside. As a result, even in quite small towns, seemingly endless rows of filling stations, shops, second-hand car dealers and hamburger stalls are encountered before the town centre is finally reached.

Rural settlement

Only a small proportion of the rural population of the United States live in towns, and villages of European type are almost non-existent. The settlements that have grown up at road intersections are centres providing essential facilities such as schools, churches, post offices, police stations, filling stations and garages, shops and cooperative institutions. Some 20 per cent of the rural population live in settlements of this kind.

Most of the farmers live in separate farmsteads. The regular layout of the fields and farms, like the grid plan in towns, reflects the original allocation of the territory of the states on the basis of "townships", square in plan and measuring 6 mi. each way. The townships are divided into 36 "sections" with an area of 1 sq. mi. (640 acres), and the sections into "quarter sections" with an area of 160 acres. The quarter section was originally intended to be worked by an individual farmer; but with the move of workers away from the land and the reduction in the number of separate farms the average size of farms has steadily increased and is now around 445 acres. The development of fully mechanised "farming factories" is illustrated by the fact that 3 per cent of the total number of farms (with an average area of 2000 acres) work some 46 per cent of the total agricultural land in the United States. In spite of this development the regular layout of the original division of the land is still reflected in the agricultural landscape. The roads, farm tracks and local government and state boundaries still run north–south and east–west, like the street grids of the cities. The featurelessness of the topography is thus paralleled by the monotony of the field pattern.

Indians of North America

For many people the term "Indian" calls up a picture of redskins with eagle feathers in their hair roaming over the prairies on their mustangs. This is a romantic cliché that originated in the 18th c. and has little to do with the indigenous inhabitants of North America. The very name "Indian" is misleading, derived from Columbus's erroneous belief that he had landed in India. The real "discoverers" of North America, the Indian peoples who occupied an immense area in more than a hundred different tribal groups and even more different languages and cultural forms, had no general sense of community or name for themselves. The tribal names like Sioux, Cheyenne and Comanche that came into use in the 18th and 19th centuries were either devised by whites or used by neighbouring tribes. As seen by the whites the Tsis-tsis-tas, Numenoi and Lakota, for example, were merely Cheyennes, Comanches and Sioux, referred to collectively as Indians; and, following traditional prejudices, denied their common humanity, for it was easier to make war on them, drive them from their territories, exterminate them and deceive them if they were not recognised as having human attributes. This treatment of the peoples of North America began with the European colonisation and left a bloody trail over the centuries. It is only in our own day that there has been some attempt to recognise the separate identity of these peoples.

Origins

When it was realised that the natives of North America were not Indians in the sense of inhabitants of India, speculation began about their origins. Since they were not mentioned in the Bible their membership of the human race was at first denied. It was only in 1512 that Pope Julius II declared publicly that the "Indians" of the New World were true descendants of Adam and Eve and must thus have come out of the Garden of Eden. One of the earliest theories to which this declaration gave rise was that they were descended from the "ten lost tribes of Israel".

In 1590, 150 years before the discovery of the Bering Strait, José de Acosta, a Jesuit, came astonishingly close to the answer to the problem of American Indian origins: "It is not probable that there was a second Noah's Ark that transported men to East India or that the first men were

José de Acosta

carried to this new world by an angel ... I come to the conclusion, therefore, that the first men came to this new world of America as the result of a shipwreck and foul stormy weather." But since a shipwreck could not explain the presence of animals in the New World he concluded that there must be, somewhere to the north, a piece of America "which was not completely separated and cut off, over which the animals travelled."

Edward
Brerewood

In the 17th c. the English antiquary Edward Brerewood observed that the Indians "showed little interest in the arts, science and culture of Europe, nor in those of China and civilised Asia" and because of their colour could not be descended from Africans. The only remaining possibility was the "Tartars", the term applied to the inhabitants of northern and central Asia. Brerewood believed that he had found in them cultural parallels with America. He concluded that there must be a land connection, which he thought would be "in that north-eastern part of Asia where the Tartars dwell". Although he was wrong in identifying Indian with Tartar culture, some of his conclusions were correct. 200 years later the German traveller Alexander von Humboldt drew attention to a "striking similarity between the Americans and the Mongol race". Modern scholarship has confirmed this view: it is now accepted that there is a close genetic relationship between the American Indians and the peoples of north-east Asia.

Settlement of the American continent

The time of arrival of the first modern men in America was determined by the possibility of crossing the land bridge between Asia and America – somewhere in the region of the Bering Strait – and by the ability of men to exist for any length of time in Arctic cold. Thus the arrival of man in America cannot be set further back than 40,000 years ago, for the land bridge has been crossable (that is, not covered by either water or ice) only twice during the last 40,000 years – some 32,000–26,000 years ago and, probably, 16,000–13,000 years ago. The most favourable route for further migration was through the valleys of the Yukon and Mackenzie Rivers and then south down the east side of the Rockies into the Dakotas. This line of separation between the eastward-flowing glaciers of the Pacific mountain system and those flowing down from the Laurentian Shield was no more than 25 mi. wide at some points, and before 20,000–13,000 years ago was completely impassable and ice-covered. After the retreat of the glaciers, for thousands of years, small groups of hunters followed the herds of mammoths, caribou and bison that ranged over these territories. Generation after generation men spread over the new land, while the land bridge from Asia was gradually reclaimed by the sea. Thus, cut off from their past, after their arduous journey over the Mackenzie watershed, the "Indians" from Asia settled the American continent.

Cultural phases

It is now believed that with high probability the advance of man into America took place in two phases – before 22,000–21,000 years ago and before 15,000–10,000 years ago. In the early days of settlement, the Palaeo-Indian period, men lived mainly by hunting large mammals and by about 9000 BC, at the peak of this cultural phase, had spread over the whole of North America. The following Archaic period, which reached its greatest extension about 4000 BC, was characterised by a semi-sedentary way of life in limited areas of settlement where men lived by hunting and gathering. This phase was gradually superseded by farming cultures, and there was a transition to the Formative phase, with settled communities living in villages and towns that were continuously occupied throughout the year and might have populations of several thousands. Around AD 100 this way of life was predominant down the whole of the east coast as far as Florida, round the Great Lakes and along the great rivers of the American prairies. The two other cultural phases, however, continued to coexist.

The succession, co-existence and constant change of ways of life down to the end of the 18th c. created a cultural variety in the American continent that found expression not only in

more than a hundred different languages but also in a wide range of social and state structures. The course of settlement in North America, however, cannot yet be conclusively established, since our information is based on archaeological evidence that is continually being supplemented by new material and may thus have to be reinterpreted. The evidence so far points to an early settlement of the east and west coasts, the river deltas along these coasts, the territory on the Pacific side of the Rockies and the Arctic regions. Traces of settlement have also been discovered round the Great Lakes, on the borders of the Canadian forest country and along the

Mandan feather headress

great rivers. Temporarily occupied hunting camps have been found at Folsom and Bascombe, fishing settlements on the east and west coasts, farming settlements in the Mississippi delta. In the south-west there are the remains of two large farming settlements: the ruins of Cliff Palace in the Mesa Verde National Park (see illustration p. 582), which in its heyday was occupied by over 400 people in its 200 rooms, and Pueblo Bonito in the valley of the Charco River in New Mexico, built between AD 900 and 1100, which could accommodate some 1200 families in its 800 rooms. From western New York State to Nebraska, along the Gulf Coast from Florida to Texas and all over the interior of the United States there are thousands of conical mounds shaped into the form of birds, human figures and snakes. In the Ohio valley alone 10,000 artifacts have been found belonging to a people that had created a civilisation in the forests of the Midwest and built up a community of over 10,000 people living mainly by intensive farming and producing a wide range of luxury and utility articles. The valleys of the Mogollon range in New Mexico were settled from around 300 BC by a farming people, ancestors of the present-day Zuni Indians. The valleys of the Salt and Gila rivers were occupied by Mandan feather headdress about 100 BC by farming communities of the Hohokam, ancestors of the Papago and Pima. North of this were the Anasazi, among whose descendants are the Hopi Indians. Their villages are found from about AD 1200 in the Four Corners area where Arizona, New Mexico, Utah and Colorado meet. Comparable with historic sites in the Old World are the city states of the Mississippi Indians, who by AD 1200 had developed the most important culture so far found in North America. Their largest settlement at Cahohia, near present-day East St Louis in southern Illinois, had a population of over 20,000, whose cultural inheritors were the Natchez. Around the turn of the millennium there were primitive farming communities round the Great Lakes, forerunners of the Lakota-speaking tribes and the Algonquins. Within the Arctic Circle the Athabaskans and Inuits lived by hunting.

When the first Europeans arrived most of the North American subcontinent had long been occupied by flourishing cultures totalling some 10 million people that had attained a high degree of economic wellbeing. Excluded from this development, however, were the prairies, since with the then available means of movement – on foot, with dogs as transport animals – their vast expanses formed a natural barrier to settlement.

Discovery of America

Whether the Phoenicians actually had trading bases in what is now the United States and whether the lost tribes of Israel, Breton fishermen or Irish monks played a part in the discovery of America are matters of pure speculation. What is historically established is the landing in Newfoundland about AD 1000 of the Viking Leif Eriksson, followed about 1005 by the first attempt to establish a settlement in "Vinland" (probably Newfoundland) by a group of Vikings led by Thorfinn Karlsefni. They brought back the first accounts of the indigenous inhabitants of America, whom they called Skraelings – probably Eskimos. The relationship between the two groups, originally reserved but friendly, soon developed into conflict, and the Vikings were compelled to abandon their settlement at L'Anse aux Meadows in Canada. Thereafter the American continent disappeared from the consciousness of the Old World for almost 500 years: then on October 12th 1492 Columbus "discovered" America for the Spanish crown. From their base in Central America the Spaniards also prospected the new land to the north. Cabeza de Vaca's two-year journey through the southern part of North America was followed by military settlement by the Spaniards, whose objects, under the sign of the Cross, were to bring Christianity to the natives and to bring back gold and slaves to their royal masters.

Spain was followed by other powers. England established settlements on the east coast, moving from north to south, while the French occupied Louisiana and part of the Mississippi valley. Under this pressure the Indian societies were forced into movement and began to restructure themselves.

Iroquois League

Between 1559 and 1570 the Seneca, Onondaga, Cayuga, Mohawk and Oneida Indians founded the Iroquois League, a confederation of five nations bringing together both farming and hunting tribes that achieved such a high level of social and political progress that some of its democratic ideas influenced the American constitution. With the arrival of settlers in the territory of the Powhatan confederacy of the twenty Algonquin tribes (now Virginia) and the foundation of Jamestown in 1607 Britain established a foothold in North America; and in 1620 the Pilgrim Fathers landed in the territory of the double Algonquin tribe of the Wampanoags and Pokanokets at Cape Cod in the present-day state of Massachusetts. Their settlement was preserved from starvation during its first two years only by massive help from the Indians. Metacomet, son of the Wampanoag chief, known to the British as King Philip, saw the only future for his people in the expulsion of the whites and, allying himself with the Narragansett Indians of Rhode Island and other tribes, in 1675 King Philip's War launched "King Philip's War", which lasted two years and resulted in the destruction of twelve British settlements. The colonists struck ruthlessly back; Metacomet was killed and his Pontiac wife and son sold into slavery. In 1754 the Ottawa chief Pontiac rose against the British, and in 1763 formed an alliance of several tribes. This "Red Man's Revolution" was, from the Indian point of view, the greatest and most successful war of the 18th c.

The War of American Independence put an end to the Iroquois League, which in 1722, thanks to the influence of Hiawatha, had been enlarged to include the Tuscarora. The league was broken up as a result of shrewd negotiations and empty promises by both sides, and the individual tribes were set at odds with one another and reduced to insignificance. The Miami chief Little Turtle defeated the American general Arthur St Clair in the Ohio valley in 1791; but from 1830 onwards the flood of immigrants increased the pressure for the movement of settlement to the west. A policy of Indian resettlement was initiated under the

Indian Removal Act, and during the 1830s and 1840s the "five civilised tribes" (Cherokee, Choctaw, Creek, Chickasaw, Seminole) were transported to distant Oklahoma (the "Trail of Tears"), though the Seminoles continued their resistance in a guerrilla war in the swamps of Florida until 1842.

Indians of the prairies and plains

The European colonisation and settlement also led to dramatic changes in the heart of the continent. Until about the middle of the 17th c. the prairies and plains of the Midwest and south-west were occupied by Indian tribes practising simple arable farming only on the fringes and in areas with a water supply – on the southern edge of the grassland plain small groups of Apaches, known as Paducahs; in the north-west, in present-day Oregon, Cayuse; Comanche in Wyoming; Cheyenne, Arapaho and Absaroka round the Great Lakes. Blackfoots (Piegan) lived on the Canadian frontier and Sioux-speaking tribes hunted in the forest country of the north-west. For all these tribes the plains, with their immense empty expanses, were a closed territory, although these great areas of grassland supported millions of buffaloes, which were hunted only on a very modest scale. Two "technical innovations" changed this situation radically.

Around 1620, through the agency of the Hudson Bay Company, firearms began to come into the hands of the Indian tribes round the Great Lakes. Originally intended to increase the yield of the fur-hunters, they were used by the Ojibway to attack smaller tribes in the area, which were compelled to move further west to escape from their better armed neighbours.

In the Spanish occupied South the Indians were, until the Pueblo Revolution that began in 1680, forbidden to own horses. After the expulsion of the Spaniards the numbers of horses living in freedom increased; they now became objects of trade, and were also distributed over the country by the widespread practice of horse-stealing. Herds of horses roamed over the prairies, and horses from Californian settlements found their way up the coast to Oregon. The Cayuse Indians were noted horse-breeders, rearing the famous Appaloosa breed; and these tribes carried the horse further east. The first horsemen on the fringes of the plains were the Paducahs, who used their new power to raid the territory of their neighbours the Pawnees and other Cadda tribes. In the middle of the 18th c. the horse reached the Uto-Aztec Comanches, who then left their homeland in Wyoming, advanced into the plains and drove out the Paducahs. The Cheyenne and Arapaho Indians moved westward, as did the Crow (Absarokee) and the related Mandan tribe. By about 1785 the way of life of the Sioux-speaking Lakota was centred on the horse. Somewhat later the Kiowa moved from Montana into the region between Texas and Oklahoma and from there, along with the Comanches, attacked Spanish and Pueblo Indian settlements. The Paducahs moved into the south-west and joined up with the related Apaches.

Apart from the Mandan and the Pawnees all the Indian tribes now gave up their traditional farming life and developed a hunting culture centred on the horse and the buffalo. For the prairie tribes buffaloes were the very basis of life: they provided food, clothing and dwellings and imposed on the Indians the rhythm of their existence. Wars – often bloody wars – were fought over hunting grounds, and for their own protection the nomadic tribes developed social structures involving warrior communities, special rites and complicated personal relationships. The struggle for survival always depended on the horse and the buffalo, and the slightest changes – for example if the herds of buffalo failed to appear after a hard winter – might lead to famine, while the loss of many

Hunting culture

men in battle might mean the ruin of a tribe. On the other hand the possession of horses and buffaloes brought great wealth and reputation to a tribe, a family group or an individual warrior, and wealth was used for lavish display.

It is an error to believe that this prairie culture was in harmony with nature. The Indians' herds of horses, some of them of great size, devastated great areas of pastureland, and there was often mass destruction of the buffalo herds. Even without the intervention of the whites this culture of warriors and hunters would probably have brought about its own destruction, particularly since almost all its essential elements – horses, firearms, metal – came from the world of the white man. The stylisation of fighting into a sport or a game, too, was a further indication that this type of civilisation had little chance of surviving. For many family groups and tribes the whole basis of life was destroyed by war; and the numbers were so small, and the ratio between numbers of men and women so unequal, that the prairie culture was unlikely to continue for any length of time.

In its variety and colour as well as in its freedom, however, this culture was unique in the world. Six different language families, with a total of 22 languages between them, were nevertheless able, in times of peace, to communicate with one another, discuss complicated matters and carry on trade with the help of a sign language developed for the purpose. In course of time the prairie tribes grew increasingly similar in their dress, their tools and implements and their dwellings, and many tribes developed similar forms of organisation. The chief of a tribe might be elected or might have inherited his title, but in either case, in almost all tribes, he could only advise and not command. Everywhere there were counselling and control organisations designed to guarantee peaceful coexistence and settle conflicts. The view of the majority of the tribe was always decisive. Only during major hunting expeditions or when there was danger of war did the Indians submit to a severe and strictly policed discipline.

Campaign against the Indians

As early as 1763 a British decree confirmed the Indians' right to their hereditary homeland, and settlers were prohibited from acquiring land beyond the Appalachians. The United States followed a similar line after achieving independence. At the beginning of the 19th c. the noted lawyer and federal judge John Marshall expressly confirmed the status of the Indian tribes as nations and their natural right to the possession of the lands they occupied. Dealings with the Indians, he declared, must be conducted with the greatest possible honesty; land and property should never be taken from them without their agreement; and they should never be injured or restricted in their possessions and their rights and freedoms except in legally justified wars authorised by Congress. On this basis the United States concluded treaties with the Indians almost all of which were later broken.

Removal and resistance

From 1837 and in subsequent decades, under the Indian Removal Act, almost the entire Indian population of the eastern United States was moved, sometimes with violence, to Indian territory in what is now Oklahoma. This territory was administered by the Ministry of War, and its area was repeatedly reduced. In 1889 part of it was opened to whites, and in 1907 it was incorporated in the state of Oklahoma.

In the south-west the Indians had been able, from 1680 onwards, to hold up the Spanish advance, and from 1760 the Comanches and Apaches went over to the attack, in a war that was so murderous that after Spain was compelled to give up Mexico in 1824 most of the whites, after suffering huge losses, left New Mexico and New Spain. After the foundation of the state of Texas the extermination or expulsion of the

Hidatsa dog dancer, c. 1830

Indians was seen there as the best solution, and a ruthless campaign was launched against them, until by 1855 all the Indian tribes had left the region; and in the following year Texas was declared "Indian-free". Only the Comanches were able to maintain their bare existence, withdrawing, with numerous rearguard actions, into the remote deserts of the Texas panhandle. In New Mexico and Arizona the resistance of the Apache guerrilla fighters was not finally broken until 1886.

The interest of the Europeans in the furs of the prairies and of the Plains Indians in the weapons and implements of the whites led to relatively peaceful trading activity between the two peoples during the fur-trading era of 1740 to 1840. From 1783, with the ending of the colonial period, the Indians had ever more frequent dealings with the American Fur Company of John Jacob Astor, who was ruthless in establishing his

Conquest of the plains

monopoly, undercutting the firms that supplied the independent traders until his competitors were bankrupted and the Indians were dependent on him alone. He also contrived to have competitors put out of business by accusing them of selling whiskey to the Indians, while if the Indians sold to rival firms the American Fur Company itself began to sell alcohol, leading inevitably to riots and to disciplinary measures by the government. The company thus succeeded in bringing a huge area under its control, in making the Indians dependent on it and in playing them off against each other.

Under treaties between the American government and various Indian tribes all the land west of the Mississippi-Missouri line had been confirmed as Indian territory in perpetuity. In order to ensure safe transit on the country's new roads, however, the Bureau of Indian Affairs that had been established in 1824 called a peace council of all the prairie tribes in 1841. Gifts to the value of 100,000 dollars were distributed, and the boundaries of the Indian hunting grounds were fixed by treaty: for the southern Dakota, Cheyenne and Arapaho tribes the area between the Arkansas and North Platte Rivers, the whole of Colorado east of the Rockies, part of present-day Kansas and the whole of southern Nebraska; for the northern Dakota, Cheyenne and Arapaho the whole of the Big Bend area on the northern Missouri; for the Crow, Assiniboin, Gros Ventre and Minnetaree Indians Montana and half of Wyoming. The Indians for their part pledged themselves to peaceful and friendly relations between the tribes, recognised the right of the United States to build roads and establish posts on their territory and declared themselves ready in future to make good any damage caused by Indians to citizens of the United States or to their property. In return the United States promised to protect the Indians "so long as grass grows and water runs".

Beginning of conflict

The American government kept a close watch on the observance of the treaty. When two Teton Dakota Indians stole a cow at Fort Laramie in 1854 a small army detachment moved into their encampment but was wiped out. The Dakotas now began to attack wagon trains on the roads, and in response the army marched into the valley of the Platte River and destroyed the village of the Brulé chief Little Thunder. For a time the roads were safe to travel – until 1862, when the government opened a new road through Indian territory, the Bozeman Trail to the goldfields of Montana. The Santee Indians led by Little Crow, who had for many years been cheated by traders and agents of the Bureau of Indian Affairs and had been thrust back ever further into their reserve, rose in rebellion but were defeated in the battle of Cone Tree Lake on September 24th 1862. The survivors fled to the related Plains tribes, and their accounts of their experience led the northern Plains Indians – the Arapaho, Cheyenne and Dakota – to draw closer together. As a result of the gold and silver boom the Cheyenne were driven out of the territory that had been assigned to them under the 1851 treaty. Thereafter there were frequent conflicts, continuing until 1864.

Sand Creek massacre

Thanks to two shrewd chiefs, Black Kettle and White Antelope, the southern Cheyenne were able until that year to live undisturbed. Faced with the alternatives of living in peace with the United States and obtaining regular food or choosing war and winning their food by raids on the settlers, they put themselves under the protection of Fort Lyon, accepting the directions of the fort commandant that they should establish their camp on Sand Creek, hand in their arms and ammunition and live on prisoners' rations. In return they received confirmation in writing that they were "peaceful Indians under the protection of the United States" and an American flag that they flew prominently in their encampment. On November 29th 1864, when "no grass grew and no water ran", Colonel John M. Chivington, a former Methodist pastor, appeared with the 1st and 3rd Colorado Cavalry and a battery of howitzers. The 500 inhabitants of the camp, among whom were practically no warriors, were attacked by 700 soldiers who had orders to take no prisoners and not to spare even children. 26 warriors and 274 women, children and old people were brutally murdered. The Sand Creek massacre became a rallying cry for the Indian wars.

From 1866 onwards the Oglala chief Red Cloud successfully resisted the government's attempts to drive a road through Indian territory to the Montana goldfields. After forcing the abandonment of three military outposts on the Bozeman Trail he and Gall, on behalf of Sitting Bull, signed a treaty in 1868 under which all of South Dakota to the west of the Missouri, the Powder River hunting grounds and the territory round the Bighorn Mountains were closed to whites. Soon afterwards, however, in 1872, a railway line for the North Pacific Railroad was surveyed through this territory.

Red Cloud

In 1874 Col. Custer prospected the Black Hills, the sacred land of the Dakota, Paha Sapa, and when gold was discovered there a number of American settlements were established, contrary to treaty. On December 3rd 1875 the Department of the Interior ordered all tribes in the area to report to their agencies by January 31st 1876. The Indians were unwilling to expose their women, children and old people to the bitter cold of a particularly severe winter, but the government ultimatum was enforced by military units. The year of the Indian wars had begun.

The Indian wars

In March General Crook attacked an Oglala and Cheyenne village near the Powder River, but counter-attacks by Crazy Horse forced his 1400 men to retreat. In June, though warned against it, he crossed the Tongue River with fresh troops, and his 1400 men became involved in a one-day battle on the Rosebud River with equal numbers of Cheyenne, Arapaho and Oglala Indians led by Crazy Horse. On June 26th Colonel Custer, with 600 soldiers and 44 scouts, came on a huge camp of Dakota and Cheyenne and, without any reconnaissance to establish their numbers, attacked and was annihilated.

The campaign against the Indians had been a failure, but the Indians could not regard themselves as victors, for the deliberate slaughter of the buffalo herds had deprived them of their food stocks. Some Indian chiefs, among them Crazy Horse and Dull Knife, returned with their tribes into the reservations; Crazy Horse was killed in Camp Robinson, and the Cheyenne were sent to the reservation in Oklahoma. Some 800 of them fled from the catastrophic conditions there and sought to return to their old homeland but were hunted down and captured. Sitting Bull and Gall fled to Canada; then five years later, in 1881, Sitting Bull returned to the United States with the last 187 members of his tribe and gave himself up at Fort Buford. The General Allotment Act of 1887 divided the territory of the reservations among the Indians, making it their personal property. Then the Indian owners, driven by poverty, sold their land to white speculators at knockdown prices.

The last flare-up of Indian feeling was the Ghost Dance religion promoted by a young Paiute Indian, Wovoka, in the 1890s. He saw in a vision that a great flood would sweep away the whites, the buffaloes would return and the Indians would again be able to live as they had in past times. Until these events occurred the Indians were to dance and be ready to greet their ancestors and relatives on their return from the Beyond. 60,000 Indians of many different tribes joined the movement. The Dakota dressed in

Ghost Dance

Bow and quiver of the Crow

41

"bullet-proof" Ghost Dance shirts, and their medicine-men foretold the expulsion of the whites. The Indians armed themselves, and there were battles with the whites. Sitting Bull was killed by Indian police officers in Standing Rock. A group of 146 men, women and children led by chief Bigfoot were massacred with the most modern weapons at Wounded Knee. The last military unit in Indian territory, a cavalry detachment, left Fort Yates on September 3rd 1903, at which time there remained in the United States only about 250,000 of Indian origin.

Indian policy in the 20th century

After the abolition of collective Indian ownership of land under the General Allotment Act of 1908 further portions of the reservations were opened up to whites by government decree. It was not until June 1924 that Congress passed a law making all Indians born in the American citizens with equal rights. Under the Indian Reorganisation Act of 1934 the tribes were granted the right to self-government and it was provided that all tribal territory not sold to whites was to be returned. This land, however, continued to be administered by the Bureau of Indian Affairs on behalf of the Indians. The Indian Claims Commission, a body independent of the Bureau, was set up in 1946 to establish Indian claims based on treaty undertakings that had not been fulfilled. So far over 1000 claims have been submitted; some have been accepted but many are still pending, including a million-dollar claim from the Sioux for the Black Hills, which were guaranteed to them by treaty. In the United Tribes Corporation, founded in 1967, tribes that were formerly opposed to one another are seeking to establish industry in the North Dakota reservations. In 1969 a family training centre was established in a joint

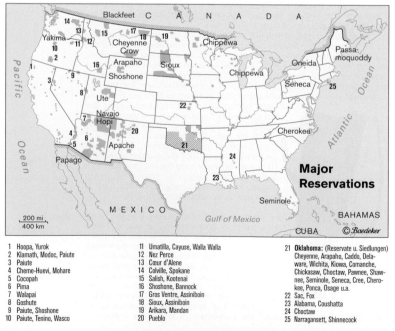

1 Hoopa, Yurok
2 Klamath, Modoc, Paiute
3 Paiute
4 Cheme-Huevi, Mohave
5 Cocopah
6 Pima
7 Walapai
8 Goshute
9 Paiute, Shoshone
10 Paiute, Tenino, Wasco

11 Umatilla, Cayuse, Walla Walla
12 Nez Perce
13 Cœur d'Alene
14 Colville, Spokane
15 Salish, Kootenai
16 Shoshone, Bannock
17 Gros Ventre, Assiniboin
18 Sioux, Assiniboin
19 Arikara, Mandan
20 Pueblo

21 **Oklahoma:** (Reservate u. Siedlungen) Cheyenne, Arapaho, Caddo, Delaware, Wichita, Kiowa, Comanche, Chickasaw, Choctaw, Pawnee, Shawnee, Seminole, Seneca, Cree, Cherokee, Ponca, Osage u.a.
22 Sac, Fox
23 Alabama, Coushatta
24 Choctaw
25 Narragansett, Shinnecock

operation by the United Tribes Corporation and the Bureau of Indian Affairs with the idea of preparing Indian families for entry into the world of the whites.

Against progress of this kind must be set evidence of continuing dis- Indian resistance crimination against the Indian tribes and continuing exploitation of their natural resources. There have been harmful results from the abolition of the ban on alcohol in the reservations in 1951. Indians still, as in the 19th c., are exposed to further loss of land and destruction of their environment, for the reservations are rich in minerals. Thus the world's largest deposits of lead and zinc (85 million tons) are being worked in the territory of the Inupiah-Inuits, while the compensation promised by way of jobs and training facilities is slow in coming. Copper is worked on a large scale in the territory of the Courte Oreille Chippewa; and an attempt by the Chippewa to halt the extension of the workings by an action in the Wisconsin courts was frus trated by the high legal costs. 70 per cent of world reserves of uranium lie within Indian territories, and the Lakota and Navajo tribes are opposed to mining operations.

Today the number of Americans with a claim to Indian origin has risen Indians today to some 1.9 million. Of these only a fifth live on the reservations, the largest of which is the Navajo Reservation in New Mexico, Arizona and Utah (population 134,000, not all of them Navajo) followed by the much smaller Pine Ridge Reservation at Wounded Knee, home of 11,000 Sioux. The greatest number of Indians (252,000) are found in the state of Oklahoma, after which come California (242,000), Arizona (203,000), New Mexico (134,000) and Alaska (86,000). The largest tribes are the Cherokee (369,000), the Navajo (225,000), the Chippewa (105,000) and the Sioux (107,000). One third of Indians live below the poverty line, the situation on the reservation being especially bad.

Religion

Churches and religious communities in the United States have some 157 million members, in a wide variety of denominations and sects that reflects the pattern of settlement of the United States. Their influence on different parts of the country is related to their socio-economic structures, varying life styles, mentalities, marriage connections and international relationships.
In view of the largely European origins of the population the Christian churches are predominant, the largest groups being Protestants in various denominations, Catholics and Orthodox.

The largest of the Protestant denominations, which have a total of some Protestants 87 million members, are the Baptists, Methodists, Lutherans and Presbyterians. In addition there are some 4.7 million Mormons, 1.6 million members of the Churches of Christ, 2.4 million members of the United Church of Christ, 2½ million members of the Pentecostal churches and several hundred thousand Mennonites, Amish and Hutterites.

Just under 60 million Americans profess the Catholic faith, which is Catholics strongly represented in the north-east, Midwest and particularly in the west. There are around half a million Old Catholics.

Roughly half of the 4 million members of the eastern churches are Greek Orthodox Orthodox, while the various American communities form the second largest group.

Some 5.3 million Americans profess the Jewish faith. There are three Jews congregations, whose main strongholds are New York and Florida.

Religion and Agriculture

Many Christian movements have found a home in the United States. Some are of very old tradition brought from Europe; another, the Mormon Church, was founded in America.

Soon after the beginning of Luther's Reformation the Baptist movement came into being. The term "Baptist" or "Anabaptist" reflected the belief that the only valid baptism was the baptism of an adult. The Anabaptist movement developed first in Switzerland, and by 1525 there was already a community of "Evangelical Baptists" in Zurich. The new teaching found many adherents, particularly among peasants and craftsmen, and spread from the Alpine region into Saxony and Moravia. From an early stage, however, the Baptists were exposed to ruthless persecution.

The **Mennonites**, a Baptist sect founded by a Frisian priest named Menno Simons (1497–1561), flourished mainly in North Germany and the Netherlands. There were also Mennonite groups in South Germany, from which the Amish (see below) later split off. The Mennonites, who had close affinities with Calvinism, rejected infant baptism, military service and state compulsion in matters of faith and sought to follow Christ in the spirit of the Sermon on the Mount. Their pacifism and opposition to the power of the state frequently brought them oppression and persecution, and as early as the 17th c. some of them emigrated to the United States. Towards the end of the 18th c. numbers of European Mennonites moved into the Ukraine. In the late 19th and early 20th c. many Mennonites emigrated from Central Europe and the Ukraine to the United States.

In the late 17th c. an Anabaptist from Switzerland named Jakob Ammann moved to Alsace, then liberal in matters of belief. He achieved his first great success as a preacher of his faith in 1692 at Markirch (Sainte-Marie-aux-Mines), where he called for a strict belief in Scripture and a chaste and virtuous

An Amish family

community. Any who did not live in accordance with his prescriptions were to be expelled from the bed and board of members of the community. Ammann's followers, the Amish, could also be distinguished by their hair and dress (long beards for men, woven fabrics with no buttons). Ammann's rigorous demands drew criticism from other communities and led some to split off from the mainstream of Anabaptism. When Louis XIV decreed the expulsion of the Anabaptists from Alsace in 1712 they moved first into the Palatinate (particularly round Zweibrücken) and Hesse (particularly in the Kassel area). By this time a number of Mennonites had settled in America (Pennsylvania), and gradually this example was followed by some Amish families. The first Amish settlement was established at Northkill in Pennsylvania about 1738. From 1817 onwards several groups of Amish moved from Hesse to Ohio, and in subsequent years there was a regular emigration movement from Alsace, the Palatinate, Hesse and Bavaria to Ohio, Indiana, Illinois, Maryland, New York and Iowa.

There are now some 100,000 **Amish** living in 20 states of the Union. They adhere strictly to their traditions and reject the amenities of modern life – machinery, electricity, automobiles, insurance. They pay their taxes but no social security contributions, since they care for their own members. They speak their old South German dialects and send their children to their own schools. The period of schooling lasts only eight years: in addition to reading, writing and arithmetic the children learn only what is necessary for their life on the farm, and further study is regarded as superfluous. A thorough knowledge of the Bible, however, is essential. The tradition established by Jakob Ammann of excluding from the community all who do not believe in its tenets is still maintained. All who live in sin – that is, those who infringe any of the Ten Commandments or bring discord into the community – are thus banned. The Amish, as the "enlightened", hold themselves apart from the "worldly" and live independently in their own world.

To the Amish work in the fields is the right way to fulfil the charge laid on them by the Bible, and particularly by the Sermon on the Mount. Through their old-world way of life the Amish avoid idleness. Children are of course involved in the work of the community, and the individual farms are of such a size that they can be worked by a family. The houses must be big enough to accommodate religious services once or twice a year for up to 200 members. The principal means of transport is a horse-drawn buggy, and horses are also used in the fields.

There are some 33,000 **Hutterites** in the United States, all sharing a small number of family names. They too are descended from the early Anabaptists and adhere to a fundamentalist view of Christianity. Their founder, Jakob Hutter, established a Baptist community based on common ownership of property in the manner of the early Christians at Nikolsburg (Mikulov) in Moravia in 1529. He was persecuted and burned at the stake in Innsbruck in 1536, and thereafter the Hutterites were driven out of their homeland to Hungary and then to Transylvania and Russia. In 1874 many Hutterites emigrated to the United States. Like the Amish, they maintain the traditions of their forebears and live an ascetic life working in the fields. They too have preserved their old South German dialect; they are convinced that, after the children of Israel, they are God's chosen people and daily await the Second Coming of Christ.

The **Mormons** maintain that their community was brought into being directly by God and was not merely an offshoot of an existing Christian church. They believe that their founder Joseph Smith (1805–44) was God's prophet, charged to restore the primitive church. From a collection of writings revealed to him by an angel he compiled a new Revelation, the "Book of Mormon", which he published in 1830. This is the sacred book of the Mormons. It contains accounts of the various peoples who have moved to America since the building of the tower of Babel and enjoyed Old Testament experiences of salvation with prophets, revelations and the appearance of Christ. In the Mormon view European Christians have fallen away from the true faith but the Mormons in America have restored the original Christian church with its offices and sacraments.

From Fayette in New York State the Mormon movement travelled west, and its first temple was built in Ohio in 1844. Others followed in Missouri and Illinois. In 1844 Joseph Smith was killed by a mob after the rumour that the Mormons practised polygamy proved to be true. A new leader and prophet was elected in the person of Brigham Young, who decided, in view of the severe persecution to which the Mormons were exposed, that they must move further west. In 1847 some 15,000 Mormons, exhausted by their arduous journey, reached the valley of the Great Salt Lake, where they created a thriving agricultural community. Finally in 1896, after they had given up polygamy, their territory, centred on their capital of Salt Lake City, was admitted to the Union as the state of Utah.

The Mormon church has a priesthood on several levels, with differing powers and rituals, including sealing and the baptism of the dead. The unique practice of baptising the dead led to the Mormons' interest in genealogical research. The dead may also be sealed by proxy. The Mormons have a positive conception of man and believe in progress.

Society

Other religions   The varied population structure means that almost all the world's leading religions are represented in the United States. The largest non-Christian communities are Muslims (5.1 million), Buddhists (780,000), Baha'i (113,000), Taoists, Confucians, Shintoists, Sikhs and Hindus.

Sects   Alongside the old-established religious denominations numerous sects have developed in the United States, particularly since the Second World War; many of them have split off from various evangelical communities. In addition there are a number of bizarre sects, many of them highly militant, which have come to considerable prominence in recent years. Notable for their missionary zeal and good organisation have been Jehovah's Witnesses and the Scientologists, who have achieved a considerable increase in membership in the last few years.

Natural and tribal religions   The number of believers in natural and tribal religions – predominantly various Indian cults and religions – is estimated at about 40,000.

Society

National flag    The national flag of the United States, the Stars and Stripes, consists of seven red and six white horizontal bands, symbolising the original thirteen states of the Union, with fifty white stars on a blue ground in the top left-hand corner, representing the present fifty states. As first adopted in 1777, during the War of Independence, the flag originally showed a circle of thirteen stars. The coat of arms of the United States is a blue, white and red shield borne by the American heraldic bird, the white-headed sea eagle (the "bald eagle") – a former imperial symbol taken over by the American revolutionaries – holding in its beak a ribbon with the motto "E pluribus unum" ("Out of the many comes one"). The national motto "In God we trust" goes back to the American Civil War, but was only officially adopted by Congress in 1956.

National anthem   The text of the national anthem, the "Star-Spangled Banner", which was officially adopted only in 1931, was written by Francis Scott Key in 1814. It describes how, on the morning of September 14th 1814, the American flag was still flying over Fort Henry, near Baltimore, after a 25-hour bombardment by the British (see Quotations).

Federal structure   The United States of America consist of the fifty states of the Union, the Federal District of Columbia round the national capital, Washington, and the four associated territories of Puerto Rico, United States Virgin Islands, Guam and American Samoa.

Constitution

The American constitution of 1787 was based on the then revolutionary premise that the best possible democratic government was ensured by a state ruled by law and not by a ruler's personal will ("government of laws and not of men"). The structure of American democracy is therefore based on separation of powers and a system of checks and balances. In order to counter the danger of any form of absolute power each of the three branches of the state – the executive (the President and his ministers), the legislature (Congress) and the judiciary (with the Supreme Court as the highest instance) – has certain defined powers of control over the other two. The Supreme Court, for example, decides on the legality of laws put forward by Congress; the President has a power of veto on laws passed by Congress; and the Senate, as part of Congress, can refuse to confirm government appointments by the President. Congress and the President in particular are compelled by political realities to work together in mutual dependence on one another. In the tension-ridden relationship between the two members of this "antagonistic partnership" lies the core of the American political system, which in this respect is very different from the parliamentary system.

When the "founding fathers", the creators of the Constitution, met in Philadelphia in May 1787 the first attempt, in the Articles of Confederation of 1777, to formulate a state organisation had already been shown to be inadequate. Out of fear of a powerful central authority – a fear inherited from the period of British colonial rule – the thirteen founding states had left the central government with practically no powers, not even the right to levy taxes. The new constitution of 1787 strengthened federal authority, but still held its rights to be derived from the original rights of the states. The primary competence of the states in certain fields is now much less extensive than in the early days of the Republic, but is still very considerable, mainly because their powers extend to all matters not expressly assigned to the federal government. Visitors travelling through the United States will frequently come up against striking examples of the independence of the states in a variety of everyday concerns – the supply or sale of alcoholic liquor, the import of certain foodstuffs, the regulation of Summer Time, the interpretation of marriage law. Police, electoral law and education all fall within the competence of the states.

Federal authority

Since the 1787 Constitution contained no statement of basic human rights the first ten Amendments to the Constitution, adopted in 1791, constituted a Bill of Rights. Although the Bill of Rights is not formally part of the Constitution, for many representatives its passage was a necessary precondition for the ratification of the Constitution. The first two Amendments guarantee such basic rights as freedom of religion, speech, the press and assembly and the right to carry weapons. With the

Bill of Rights

CT = Connecticut ; DE = Delaware ; MA = Massachusetts ; MD = Maryland ; NH = New Hampshire ; NJ = New Jersey ; RI = Rhode Island ; VT = Vermont ; WV = West Virginia

present high crime rate in the United States this last provision has been called in question; but any proposal for a more restrictive gun law is represented by the interest groups concerned – headed by the manufacturers and the National Rifle Association (NRA) – as an attack on a basic right and has therefore little chance of success. The 3rd and 4th Amendments are concerned with the security of private property, the 5th to 8th with the guarantee of the prosecution of offences in accordance with law. The 9th Amendment guarantees various rights of the citizen not mentioned in the Constitution, the 10th the rights of the states. Other important Amendments deal with the abolition of slavery (13th Amendment, 1865), the prohibition of any restriction on basic rights or electoral right on the grounds of race (14th, 1868; 15th, 1870) and the vote for women (19th, 1920). An attempt in the 1980s, mainly promoted by the feminist movement, to incorporate the principal of sexual equality in the Constitution (the Equal Rights Amendment) failed because the bill was not ratified by a sufficient number of states.

President and the government

The President of the United States is elected by indirect popular vote every four years, on the Tuesday after the first Monday in November in a leap year. The President's term of office begins on January 20th in the year following the election and ends on the same day four years later. Under the 22nd Amendment (1951) a President can be re-elected only once (Franklin D. Roosevelt had served for four successive terms). If the President dies in office or resigns he is automatically succeeded by the Vice-President, who serves until the end of the current term.

Elections

The election of the President is a two-stage process. Most states hold primary elections in the spring of election year that decide which candidates in the two main parties will run against one another in the main election. Depending on voting results, the individual states send delegates to the National Congress of each of the parties, where the candidates will finally be selected. The primaries are as a rule open to all voters, though voters can take part only in the congress of one party. In some states the function of the primaries is taken over by party meetings ("caucuses") in which delegates are chosen by voters and party members. Candidates for other offices – e.g. state governors and Congressmen – are also selected in primaries. A candidate for the Presidency does not have to be put forward by one of the parties: independent candidates may submit themselves for election, but such candidates usually lack the financial resources and the organisation to make them serious contenders.

In the main stage of the election voters formally choose the members of the Electoral College, which in practice amounts to the direct election of the President. The number of members a state sends to the Electoral College depends on its representation in Congress (reckoned as the number of its representatives in the House of Representatives plus two for its Senators). The candidate who wins a majority of votes in a state thereby wins the votes of all the state's members of the Electoral College – a provision that can produce a landslide victory even though the numbers of votes for the individual candidates are not so very far apart.

Presidents

Although the President possesses great authority and influence, it is misleading to call the American system of government a presidential system, given the pattern of relationships between the President and Congress. The President alone appoints the ministers in his Cabinet; but the Senate are required to confirm his appointments and may refuse to do so. Moreover the President has no right to propose legislation and, apart from his annual "State of the Union" message, can speak in Congress only by invitation. On the other hand, since members of

Presidents of the USA

1.	George Washington	1789–1797	22.	S. Grover Cleveland	1885–1889
2.	John Adams	1797–1801	23.	Benjamin Harrison	1889–1893
3.	Thomas Jefferson	1801–1809	24.	S. Grover Cleveland	1893–1897
4.	James Madison	1809–1817	25.	William McKinley	1897–1901
5.	James Monroe	1817–1825	26.	Theodore Roosevelt	1901–1909
6.	John Quincy Adams	1825–1829	27.	William H. Taft	1909–1913
7.	Andrew Jackson	1829–1837	28.	T. Woodrow Wilson	1913–1921
8.	Martin Van Buren	1837–1841	29.	Warren G. Harding	1921–1923
9.	William H. Harrison	1841	30.	Calvin Coolidge	1923–1929
10.	John Tyler	1841–1845	31.	Herbert C. Hoover	1928–1933
11.	James K. Polk	1845–1849	32.	Franklin D. Roosevelt	1933–1945
12.	Zachary Taylor	1849–1850	33.	Harry S. Truman	1945–1953
13.	Millard Fillmore	1850–1853	34.	Dwight D. Eisenhower	1953–1961
14.	Franklin Pierce	1853–1857	35.	John F. Kennedy	1961–1963
15.	James Buchanan	1857–1861	36.	Lyndon B. Johnson	1963–1969
16.	Abraham Lincoln	1861–1865	37.	Richard M. Nixon	1969–1974
17.	Andrew Johnson	1865–1869	38.	Gerald R. Ford	1974–1977
18.	Ulysses S. Grant	1869–1877	39.	James E. Carter	1977–1981
19.	Rutherford B. Hayes	1877–1881	40.	Ronald R. Reagan	1981–1989
20.	James A. Garfield	1881	41.	George H.W. Bush	1989–1993
21.	Chester A. Arthur	1881–1885	42.	William J. Clinton	1993–2000

Congress are not bound by party directions, the President can exert considerable influence on them; and important decisions now tend to be preceded by long telephone calls from the President to undecided members. In addition to the members of the Cabinet (with the title of Secretary), at present sixteen in number, the President appoints considerable numbers of advisers and advisory bodies, among the most important and influential of which are the National Security Council and the staff of the White House.

Formally, the Vice-President has no decisive function in the government, and his position as President of the Senate is not one of great influence. His importance lies in his role as successor to the President if he should die or be removed from office.

Vice-President

Congress

The traditional counterpart of the President in the political process in the United States is Congress, which consists of two houses, the Senate and the House of Representatives. The Senate consists of two representatives of each state (irrespective of the state's population), who are elected for a six-year term. A third of the Senate retire every two years, so that the terms of office of individual senators overlap. The members of the House of Representatives are also elected in each state by majority voting for a two-year term, their number being determined in theory by the population of the various states as recorded in the census; in practice, however, the number of representatives has remained at 435 since 1912.

Since there is no control by the parties over the actions of their members, even a President whose party is in a minority in Congress can still obtain a majority for a proposal he desires to put forward. Much more frequent, however, is the "gridlock" situation in which neither the President nor the opposing party is prepared to give way, thus holding up the work of government. Another consequence of the American system of checks and balances is that both houses of Congress must cooperate in the legislative process and that the President must sign all laws but has power to veto them – though his veto can be overridden by a two-thirds majority vote in both houses. Although the President is supreme commander of the armed forces only Congress can declare war. Congress is also responsible for the granting of budgetary funds and can initiate the procedure for the impeachment and removal from office of members of the executive, including the President, and the judiciary. The Senate has a key position mainly in foreign affairs, for the President can sign international treaties only with its approval by a two-thirds majority; he can, however, act independently in entering into agreements that are not classed as treaties.

Judiciary

Alongside the legislature (Congress) and the President as head of the executive the third element in the American government structure is the judiciary. American law is based on English common law, a system of uncodified rules derived from judicial decisions in particular cases that are accepted as precedents. Judicial interpretation takes precedence over actual legislation – in complete contrast to the system of civil law, which attached greater importance to the examination and interpretation of legal texts by jurists. There is no such thing as a code of criminal or civil law in the United States.

Supreme Court

The highest legal instance is the United States Supreme Court, which sits in Washington, DC and has as one of its principal responsibilities the final decision on the constitutionality of legislation. The nine judges of the Supreme Court are appointed by the President for life, subject to confirmation of appointments by the Senate; and a President can thus influence the character of the court for many years after his period of

US Supreme Court, Washington, DC

office. Depending on its composition, the Supreme Court has frequently handed down judgments – on freedom of opinion, on race questions, on criminal law – which have had political implications and have given rise to controversy, for example on the abolition (1972) and reintroduction (1976) of the death penalty and on the right to abortion (1973).

As a result of the federal structure of the United States there are two judicial systems, the federal courts and the state courts, running side by side. In contrast to the federal judges, who are appointed, the judges in the states are elected and thus frequently lose their political independence.

Two judicial systems

The states

The federal structure of the United States makes it difficult to generalise about the situation in the various states. The American states have wider powers than, for example, the länder in the German federal system: in a country of such vast extent the case for strong local decision-making authorities is still valid.

Each of the states is headed by a Governor. As at federal level, there is a legislature, the Congress, consisting of a Senate and a House of Representatives. Although the position of the Governor is politically important he is still bound by the decision of his Congress. This is seen, for example, in Congress's right to exercise a decisive voice in the appointment of officials. A veto by the Governor on a decision of Congress can be overridden by a simple majority vote. On the other hand a Governor's power to call out the National Guard to reinforce the state police in the event of riots or other disturbances has on occasion been a factor of great importance.

Governor

Parties

Since the Civil War and the election of Abraham Lincoln, a Republican, as President in 1860 the dominant parties in the United States have been the Republicans and the Democrats. There have been a number of other parties, but none of them has ever produced a President. There have been remarkable changes, however, in the two great parties. While it was the Republicans who originally stood for the freeing of the slaves, in opposition to the Democrats, and thereafter campaigned for civil rights for blacks, it is now the Democratic Party that tends to represent the interests of minorities.

For outside observers it is sometimes difficult to see much difference between the two great parties; but in view of the heterogeneous character of the electorate and the system of election by majority vote a high degree of flexibility and readiness to compromise is required of the parties. If a party moves too far from the centre its chances of gaining or retaining power are reduced. Although differences between the two parties are often difficult to detect, it can be observed that in the present political landscape the Republicans tend to appear conservative and to represent mainly economic interests. The Democrats have the reputation of being more in favour of reform, and appeal more to minorities, women and workers.It is also difficult to assign the parties to any particular political trend because no party discipline is exercised in Congress.

Party programmes

The organisation of the American parties is much looser than in Europe. There are no organised arrangements for party membership, no formal procedures for admission to the party and no regular subscriptions. To

Organisation

belong to a party a voter has only to declare himself a Republican or a Democrat by entering his name on the electoral register. This procedure is necessary for the primary elections, for only registered "members" of a party can take part in the primary within their party, and a voter automatically becomes a member of his party by taking part in the primary election.

Education

The educational system of the United States is neither centrally organised nor uniform throughout the country, for under the constitution education is a function of the individual states, Management of the educational system at local level is the responsibility of elected boards.

The public school system of the states ("public school" being used in a very different sense from the British public school), provided free of charge, comprises kindergartens, pre-school classes, primary schools, high schools, colleges and universities, together with various special types of school. Alongside the public schools are numerous private schools, run either by foundations or by churches. The Roman Catholic church is particularly active in this field, but Lutherans, Mormons, Jews, Quakers, Adventists and other religious communities also have their own schools. Renowned universities like Harvard, Yale and Stanford demonstrate the quality of private educational establishments, though because of their high costs they tend to be accessible only to students from better-off families. There are recurring complaints that the nation's educational level is steadily falling and that the 10 per cent of the national income spent on education and training is too little in comparison with other fields.

The American educational system consists of three main stages: elementary or primary education, with the elementary or primary schools; secondary education in high schools; and higher education in colleges, technical colleges and universities. School attendance is obligatory for twelve years – six years of elementary school and six of high school.

High schools

The high schools are divided into two stages, junior high schools (7th–9th years) and senior high schools (10th–12th years), which are usually separate establishments. In addition to a general stream and an academic (pre-college) stream there is also a vocational stream preparing pupils for future careers. The curricula of the three streams are interchangeable, and the core subjects (literary, scientific and social

High-school student in Chicago

studies and sport) are common to all three streams. At the end of their final year pupils of high schools receive a high school diploma, which is granted without any special final examination and merely certifies that the pupil has regularly completed the obligatory twelve years' schooling. Unlike European school-leaving certificates, it does not necessarily qualify the pupil for admission to a university.

The American school year is one of the shortest in the western world – 180 teaching days (differently regulated in different states). The school week has five days, each with six hours of teaching.

Half of all high school leavers continue to higher education, beginning with a higher education college. The conditions for admission to these colleges are laid down by the state authorities, or in the case of private colleges in the statutes of the college; in general they are related to the standard of achievement evidenced by the high school diploma. Although there is a free choice of subjects the teaching is on the same lines as in schools. The college course leads to a bachelor's degree (Bachelor of Arts or Bachelor of Science). The college year runs from September to June and is divided into two semesters, each lasting four and a half months, or into three "quarters" of three months each. The cost of a college education varies considerably; it is cheapest in a city or state college. In 1996 15 million students were enrolled at some 3800 colleges of higher education.

Higher education colleges

Advanced higher education ("graduate studies"') is provided by universities and professional schools of similar status (e.g. in technology or law). A master's degree (MA, Master of Arts; MS, Master of Science) can be obtained after a year's further study and the presentation of a thesis on some special subject. The doctorate is usually sought only by students aiming at a professional career as a scientist or scholar, college professor or physician.

Universities

The United States have numerous universities of world fame and high academic reputation, in particular the seven "Ivy League" universities in the north-eastern states – so named after the venerable ivy-clad walls of the oldest of them (Harvard, in Cambridge, Mass., founded in 1636). The other members of the Ivy League are Yale University, in New Haven, Connecticut; Princeton University, in Princeton, New Jersey; Columbia University in New York; the University of Pennsylvania in Philadelphia; Brown University, in Providence, Rhode Island; and Cornell University, in Ithaca, New York State. Newer universities of world reputation are the University of California in Berkeley, the Leland Stanford Junior University in Palo Alto, California, the University of Chicago, the State University of Michigan in Ann Arbor, the Massachusetts Institute of Technology in Cambridge and the California Institute of Technology in Pasadena. Berkeley University alone has produced eleven Nobel Prize winners since the Second World War.

Ivy League

Economy

Favoured by variety of topography, rich reserves of raw materials and a climatic range in which both temperate and subtropical crops can be grown, and with a domestic market that is the largest in the world, the United States has developed an economy that in numerous fields is one of the leading and most innovative economies in the world. The country's gross national product of 27,500 dollars (1996) per head of the population is one of the highest in the world.

The economy of the United States is a fully free market economy, characterised by the concentration of production and of services in large firms and organisations. The state plays a notably small part in the total economy, and so far has made only very minor contributions to social welfare spending.

It is difficult, therefore, to compare the economy of the United States with that of other states; and the extraordinary economic successes that in this setting can be achieved by individuals show that the United States is still the "land of unlimited possibilities" that exerts such a powerful attraction.

The variety of topography, found even within the main natural regions, the varying climatic conditions and the vast extent of this great country produce both the opportunities and the problems of economic development. With a total area of 3.61 million sq. mi. (3.02 million sq. mi. in the mainland United States, excluding Alaska and Hawaii), the development of transport and communications was an important strategic factor and stimulus for the economy. New technologies were developed and new industries grew up, which played their part in making the United States in the 20th c. the world's leading economic power.

Economic history

The roots of American economic history go back to the country's earliest days. The immigrants who came from the Old World, often from a narrow feudal social order, to the possibilities and opportunities of the New World were filled with a sense of mission and a drive to make good. They were deterred neither by the unaccustomed climate nor by the hardships that they had to endure. The first great economic centres developed first in the temperate North-East, then in the Midwest and California and finally, towards the end of the 19th c., in the prairies.

In the first place maritime trade began to develop, starting from the

Hectic activity in New York's Stock Exchange

ports on the Atlantic coast. Peasants and craftsmen from Europe found an abundance of land and a steadily increasing market for products of all kinds. The combined skills of the new settlers, coming from different countries and backgrounds, made possible rapid technological progress.

In the east of the country metal processing and metalworking, mechanical and precision engineering made particularly rapid progress. Numerous inventions, like Samuel Colt's repeating revolver, John Deere's steel plough and Samuel Morse's telegraph that permitted communication over long distances, responded to the challenge of the land.

The first overland communications – the building of new roads and the establishment of postal services – were developed by private enterprise, as were shipyards, shipping services and canals. The most important contribution to the opening up of new territories was made by the private railroad companies, of which there were some 300 by about 1840. During the 19th c. the railroads were the greatest stimulus to development, and at the end of the century something like two-thirds of all dealings in American stock exchanges were concerned with the shares of railroad companies. Railway construction and continuing technological advance were the basis on which great fortunes were amassed, including those of Cornelius Vanderbilt and Andrew Carnegie.

Transport and communications

All this promoted the development of mining and steel production in the northern states, contributing to their economic superiority over the predominantly agricultural southern states and leading to one of the causes of the Civil War. The freeing of the slaves that was one of the consequences of the Civil War speeded up rationalisation and increased the use of machinery in agriculture.

North/south divide

An important spur to further economic development came from the use of electricity and the inventions of Thomas Alva Edison (including the light bulb, the phonograph and the ciné camera) and Graham Bell (the telephone). The discovery of oil and the monopolistic development of the new form of energy by John D. Rockefeller and his Standard Oil Company (Esso), together with the rapid spread of the automobile – promoted by the cheap mass production methods introduced by Henry Ford – gave a great boost and a further technological lead to the American economy. The consumption of energy per head of the population grew enormously, and later was still further increased by the large-scale use of refrigerators and air conditioning.

Energy

A further increase in mobility was brought by the development of aircraft. The first regular air services were started in 1926.

The north-eastern United States developed into the country's industrial heartland, with a particular concentration in the area bounded by New York, Detroit, Chicago and St Louis. After the Second World War there was a further expansion of the "manufacturing belt" to the west and south.

Industrial heartland

On the Gulf Coast new branches of industry (e.g. the manufacture of synthetic fibres) developed out of the traditional cotton and textile industries. The steel industry, which originally was mainly concentrated round Pittsburgh, established new centres on Lake Michigan and in the Detroit and Cleveland areas. The rich reserves of oil in Texas led to the establishment of gigantic petro-chemical plants in the Gulf Coast plain. Major industrial areas also grew up on the Pacific coast, particularly round Los Angeles, San Francisco and Seattle. Then from the 1940s onwards "Silicon Valley" in California became the world centre of computer technology. And almost everywhere industrial development was followed by supply and service industries.

Economic and social policy

The essential foundation of the United States as a leading economic power in the 20th c. has been its massive resources of the fossil fuels (coal, oil and natural gas). For many years the United States accounted for almost a quarter of world national product. Since the 1970s, however, the economic situation of the United States in many fields has changed dramatically. Its self-sufficiency in many raw materials has declined; agricultural production has entered a phase of stagnation; and manufacture of capital and consumer goods has likewise suffered. Only in the armaments and high-tech industries has there been buoyant investment. At the same time, the service sector of the economy has shown substantial growth.

Balance of trade

The deficit on the American balance of trade has grown steadily, and even President Reagan's economic policy ("Reaganomics") was unable to halt the trend. During the 1980s there was indeed an economic upswing; but this was soon seen to be a false dawn. Stock exchange quotations of American shares rose to unheard heights, only to fall through the floor in the October 1987 crash. The rate of exchange of the dollar also fell: worth 3.47 German marks in 1985, it was valued at only 1.58 marks two years later. And while the deficit on the balance of trade continued to increase, the budgetary deficit grew steadily larger, and the United States now became the greatest debtor nation in the world.

Jobs miracle USA

Bill Clinton took office in an America buoyed by optimism. And indeed, in the course of his presidency the dollar has not only stabilised but regained its unchallenged position as the world's leading reserve currency (the euro notwithstanding). Furthermore, Clinton is committed to reducing the country's internal deficit by the year 2002. Of much greater importance at this stage of his presidency however is that the United States economy is once again booming. All the talk is of an employment miracle, which in the last five years has seen the creation of 13 million jobs. The vast majority though have been in small- to medium-sized businesses in the service sector, requiring few if any qualifications. In contrast the number of new jobs created in large companies is measured only in thousands. The average wage today is actually lower than in 1988, reflecting on the one hand the low level of education and on the other the attitudes prevailing in the United States, where people would rather take a poorly paid job than live off social security.

While unemployment as a whole has fallen to 4.5 per cent, youth unemployment remains substantial, with young Afro- and Hispano-Americans particularly affected.

Prosperity gap

The gap between rich and poor has continued to widen. In 1996 the average annual income for a family of four was $40,611. The middle-income group (earnings between $30,000 and $50,000) is progressively shrinking, and has been for some years, whilst those in the upper income bracket and the "rich" are increasing in number.

Poverty

At the other end of the scale, the number of poor families (annual income below $13,000) is rising, and now comprises almost 14 per cent of the population. Many of these are low waged rather than unemployed, with African-Americans and Hispanics disproportionately represented. The high levels of consumption evident especially in the large cities, contrast sharply with the neediness away from the centres of commerce. The poorest states are in the south: New Mexico (25.4 per cent of households below the poverty line), Mississippi (22.1 per cent) and Louisiana (20 per cent).

Welfare spending

Many Americans lack both health and unemployment insurance. State spending on welfare has reduced in recent years to a bare 8 per cent of

GDP. Although President Clinton came to office armed with proposals
for reform, his plans have been thwarted by the Republican majority in
Congress. Social assistance is currently restricted to a maximum of five
years, no more than two of which may be consecutive. Substantial cuts
have also been made in the health care programme and supplementary
food aid (soup kitchens, ration coupons).

In comparison with Europe, trade unionism has never been a mass
movement in the United States, and the unions have anyway had their
day. Labour disputes are generally limited in scale. At most 20 per cent
of employees nationally are members of AFL.CIO, an umbrella organisation founded in 1955. Even so it has considerable influence when it
comes to protecting jobs and negotiating improvements in the welfare
system.

Trade unions

Agriculture

The contribution of agriculture, forestry and fishing to the gross domestic product is declining: some 3 per cent in 1976, by 1996 it has fallen to
1.7 per cent. At the same time, the number employed in agriculture and
forestry as a proportion of the national workforce has fallen from 4 per
cent in 1976 to 2.5 per cent in 1996.

Share of GDP

Of the total area of the United States, three quarters is in use for agriculture or forestry. The largest areas under agriculture are Montana,
Kansa and Texas. The average farm size in 1996 was 470 acres. The old
division of the cultivated land into belts characterised by different mono-
cultures is no longer so clearly recognisable as a result of increasing dif-
ferentiation, but a number of classic production zones can still be
distinguished:

Land use

The North-East and the region round the Great Lakes belong to the **dairy
belt**, in which dairy farming and the growing of fodder crops are predominant. Fruit and vegetables are now also grown in these areas, helping to feed the megalopolises on the east coast.

Immediately south of the dairy belt, mostly in the states of Ohio, Indiana,
Illinois, Iowa and Missouri, is the **corn belt**, in which maize ("corn" in the
United States) is the principal crop. The maize is used to feed cattle, pigs
and poultry. A quarter of all American cattle and half of all American pigs
are reared in the corn belt.

In the **cotton belt**, which extends across the southern states, the once
dominant cotton crop has to a considerable extent given way to the
growing of soya beans and peanuts. Tobacco is now also a crop of some
importance.

The **wheat belt** extends uninterruptedly northwards from Texas to the
Canadian frontier.

The **arid areas** further west, mainly in the states of Colorado and
Wyoming, are devoted to extensive cattle rearing.

In the west and south-west great expanses of land have been irrigated
since the beginning of the 20th c. The largest such areas are in the Great
Plains and on the edge of the Rockies (particularly in the state of
Colorado), along some rivers in Arizona, on the lower course of the
Colorado River (Imperial Valley) and in the Central Valley of California. In
these areas elaborate irrigation systems have made it possible to grow
various special crops, including citrus and other fruits, rice, sugar-cane,
vegetables, cotton and fodder plants.

Irrigation
agriculture

Farm in the mountains of Virginia

Productive crops are also grown on the Atlantic coast, under the influence of the warm Gulf Stream, and on the Gulf Coast. In addition to fruit and vegetables in the northern regions there are citrus fruits in Florida and sugar-cane plantations in Florida and along the Gulf Coast; and in some areas (e.g. in the Napa Valley) there are vineyards and a flourishing wine-making industry.

Mixed farming

In the upland regions of the east, which were settled at an early stage, the traditional mixed farming is still practised, with intensive market-oriented livestock rearing (particularly poultry) in some areas.

Production and export

Following restructuring and modernisation American agriculture has taken a leading place in the world in terms of productivity and yield. The value of agricultural and forestry exports in 1996, at $59.9 billion, is considerably more than the export value of computers and office machinery or of aircraft and aircraft parts, and is roughly on the same level as the export value of motor vehicles. The United States accounts for more than a third of world wheat exports, about two-thirds of world maize exports, some three-quarters of world soya bean exports, just under 30 per cent of world cotton exports, a quarter of world production of citrus fruits, a fifth of world rice exports and a fifth of world meat production.

Forestry

With 1 million sq. mi. of forests, the United States has one of the largest expanses of forest in the world. Two-thirds of this area are worked for timber; most of it is in private ownership, often in the hands of large timber companies and cellulose concerns.

Fishing

The United States has rich fishing grounds, mainly off the Gulf and Pacific coasts but also in the Arctic Ocean and in inland waters. In 1976 the American government introduced a 200 mi. exclusion zone round its coasts to protect its fishing grounds. The American fishing fleet, however, can supply only half the nation's needs; the rest must be imported.

Mining

The United States has numerous large deposits of almost all useful minerals, and American output of coal, natural gas, oil, iron, copper, zinc, molybdenum, lead, gold, silver, uranium, bauxite, potassium, phosphates, sulphur and salt represents a high proportion of world production. The mining industry accounts for some 0.75 per cent of gross domestic product.

With an output of around 850 million tons – roughly a quarter of total world output – the United States ranks after the People's Republic of China as the world's largest producer of coal. There are huge reserves of coal in the states of Wyoming and Colorado and elsewhere.

Coal

This "black gold" lies for the most part near the surface in rich continuous seams. This, combined with a high degree of mechanisation, makes for low mining costs, so that in spite of high transport charges American coal can be sold in Europe more cheaply than the native product.

With an annual output of 400 million tons of oil (1996), the United States took second place only to Saudi Arabia and the Gulf States. In spite of the opening-up of new oilfields, however, American output is insufficient to meet domestic needs and 40 per cent of national requirements must be imported. The largest oilfields in the United States are on the Gulf Coast, in Texas, Oklahoma and Louisiana, the eastern foreland of the Rockies (Colorado, Wyoming), the Wyoming Basin, southern California and above all in northern Alaska.

Oil

The United States is the world's largest producer of natural gas after Russia, with an output that is ample to meet domestic needs.

Natural gas

Energy

Of the total amount of energy consumed in the United States two-thirds is met by oil and natural gas, a quarter by coal and just over a tenth by nuclear power; the rest is provided by hydro-electric power, geo-thermal power and other alternative sources. The United States is the country with the highest rate of energy consumption per head in the world. A few years ago over a third of total world energy production was consumed in the United States, and appeals to save energy had no effect. More recently, however, there has been an increasing realisation of the need for economy.

Industry

In spite of the problems of industrial development that arose in the late 1980s and early 1990s the United States is still one of the world's leading industrial nations, with six of the ten largest industrial concerns in the world. In 1996, however, industry accounted for no more than 18 per cent of the gross domestic product.

The traditional heartland of American industry is the north-east, with the densest industrial concentration in the "manufacturing belt", occupying the triangular area between the cities of New York, Chicago and St Louis. Nowadays, however, this area, apart from some centres round Boston and the renowned New England universities, is a region of industrial stagna-

Industrial
heartland

Boeing in Seattle, the world's largest manufacturer of airplanes

tion, now known as the "rust belt". This is particularly evident in the partial decline of Detroit, the legendary centre of the American automobile industry. Many places show evidence of the "de-industrialisation" process and the increasing movement into the services sector. The number of workers employed in industry in this area has been falling steadily for years.

Sun Belt

Over the last two decades, with a speed and dynamism barely conceivable in Europe, new industrial regions have developed in the south and west, mainly in the "Sun Belt" that extends from Georgia (particularly round Atlanta) by way of Florida, Alabama, Texas, New Mexico and Colorado to California, on the Pacific coast. Numerous firms, mainly engaged in the aircraft and space industries, electronics, petrochemicals, chemicals and pharmaceuticals, have been established here, and half the workers employed in industry now work in the Sun Belt.

Industrial products

The most important branch of manufacture is the automobile industry: a fifth of world automobile production is based in the United States. The highest growth rate, however, by a considerable margin, is in high-tech industry. The aircraft and space industry produces three-quarters of world production of aircraft, while the United States is unsurpassed in computer technology and software production. The increase in refinery capacity has enabled the United States to achieve a leading place in the manufacture of petro-chemical products and synthetic fibres. Other flourishing branches of industry – mainly in the Great Plains and the south – are tyre manufacture, textiles and clothing, paper and cellulose, and the foodstuffs and associated industries.

Service industries

For many years the services sector of the American economy has been developing with particular dynamism. A survey in the year 1978 showed that two-thirds of the working population of the United States were employed in the services sector of the economy. Now three-quarters of the working population are in the services sector, which accounts for just under 75 per cent of GDP. It is in services that the so-called employment "miracle" of recent years has had the greatest impact.

The United States has a high potential in research and innovation. Industry and the universities, public and private research institutes work closely together with no barriers or hang-ups. Elites are deliberately fostered, and the large number of Nobel Prize winners in the United States suggests that the liberal American economic system has advantages over the less flexible Japanese or even European set-up. American scientific research, with its sights set on practical application, is now the real motive force behind the world economy. The American system has shown how it is possible to harness to development an extraordinarily high proportion of the gross domestic product and of the working population.

Foreign trade

The United States still occupies a leading place among the commercial nations of the world. In 1996 it exported goods to the value of 625 billion dollars, mainly machinery, electrical and electronic products, motor vehicles, petro-chemicals and other chemical products, maize, soya beans, wheat, fruit and vegetables, meat, coal and iron and steel. The main customers for American goods are Canada, the European Union (particularly Britain and Germany), Mexico, Japan, Taiwan and South Korea.

Exports

In 1996 the United States imported goods to the value of well over 795 billion dollars, principally motor vehicles, machinery, electrical and electronic equipment, oil and oil products, iron and steel, non-ferrous metals, chemicals, agricultural produce, fish and foodstuffs and related products. The main suppliers were Japan, Canada, the European Union (particularly Germany, Britain, Italy and France), Taiwan, South Korea, Hong Kong, the People's Republic of China, Mexico and Brazil.

Imports

The North American Free Trade Agreement (NAFTA) came into force in 1994, established a common market with a population of some 365 million and an annual economic product of some 6 billion dollars.

NAFTA

Tourism

Over the last twenty years or so the United States has developed into a popular long distance holiday destination. Served by all the leading airlines and with the largest hotel and motel chains in the world, it is well equipped to meet demand. In 1996 this magical country attracted more than 46 million visitors. Most came from neighbouring Canada and Mexico, followed by Japan in third place, then Britain and Germany.

The importance of tourism as an economic factor is indicated by a single figure: in 1996 alone foreign visitors spent 69 billion dollars. The main beneficiaries from tourism are the states of California, Florida, New York, Nevada (Las Vegas), Arizona and Texas.

Transport

The United States has an excellent transport and communications system to meet the needs of its economy and its great geographical extent. Its communications make use of the most modern technology: in this respect the United States is a world leader. Passenger transport is shared between the automobile and air services. In traffic in and around cities and regional traffic the automobile is predominant; for longer distances aircraft take over. Public transport for local travel, including buses and tram or rail systems, is well developed only in a few large cities (e.g. New York, San Francisco, Chicago and Miami). The railroads play only a subordinate part in passenger transport but are dominant in freight transport. Internal shipping services are of little importance.

Roads

The United States has well over 3.8 million mi. of roads. Its highways (motorways) and national, regional and local roads are used by more than 136 million automobiles, 41 million lorries (trucks) and buses and some 5.5 million motorcycles. This is the most highly motorised nation in the world, with just under 600 automobiles per 1000 inhabitants.

Rail services

The private railroads, which in the 19th c. made such a major contribution to the opening up of the country and its economic development, still run a network of 154,000 mi. The bulk of passenger revenue accrues to AMTRAK, an amalgamation of 13 different rail companies. Of all journeys in the United States however, only 1 per cent are made by rail (a figure which has been falling for years). Consequently AMTRACK needs considerable financial support from government. Though the railways' many critics now believe them to be superfluous, the transportation of goods by rail continues to be of some significance.

Air services

Almost half the world's air traffic is handled in the United States. In 1996 the number of passengers totalled some 581 million. The busiest airports are those of New York (John F. Kennedy, Newark and La Guardia), Chicago, Atlanta, Dallas and Los Angeles. In 1996 Chicago–O'Hare alone handled over 69 million passengers, making it the busiest airport in the

Close encounter of the lonely kind

world. Both Atlanta and Dallas also exceeded London Heathrow, which tops the list outside the United States. These vast numbers of passengers are transported by the largest civil air fleet in the world. In addition to some 2200 commercial aircraft there are around 275,000 other aircraft (including light and sporting aircraft).

Inland shipping in the United States serves predominantly to carry freight traffic. The most important inland waterways are the Mississippi–Missouri river system, including the Tennessee and Ohio Rivers, the Great Lakes, the St Lawrence Seaway and the Intracoastal Waterway. There are some tourist steamboats and passenger ships on the Mississippi, Missouri, Ohio and Tennessee Rivers and on the Great Lakes.

Shipping

The United States has a seagoing fleet of some 495 vessels, with a total capacity of over 13 million tons. The principal seaports are South Louisiana, Houston, New York, Corpus Christi, Austin, New Orleans, Baton Rouge, Norfolk and Baltimore. The most important import is oil; the principal exports are agricultural produce (wheat, maize), coal and petro-chemical products.

Pipelines are increasingly being used for the transport of gaseous and fluid raw materials and basic industrial materials. They have been installed not only in the oil states of Texas and Oklahoma but also in distant Alaska. There are now special networks for natural gas, oil and refinery products; and some 7 billion barrels of oil and over 4.5 billion barrels of refinery products annually are now pumped through long-distance pipelines.

Pipelines

With the exception of the postal service telecommunications are in the hands of fiercely competitive private companies. Rapid communication is provided by six communications satellites and 26 cable systems, and there are some 130 million telephone subscribers. Telephone corporations have efficient communications networks that carry radio and television programmes and electronic data communications as well as telephone calls.

Tele-
communications

History

The ethnic origins of the earliest inhabitants of the North American sub-continent are still the subject of controversy, but the generally accepted view is that the indigenous inhabitants of North America, wrongly identified by Columbus as Indians, came from northern Asia in two waves some 25,000–20,000 and 12,000–11,000 years ago, travelling over the land bridge that then still existed in the area of the Bering Strait. For their further spread and subsequent history see the chapter on the Indians of North America (p. 33).

c. 1000   The Viking Leif Eriksson, coming from Greenland, lands on the coast of Newfoundland and calls the country Vineland. A first attempt at settlement led by Thorfinn Karlsefni is a failure.

1492   Christopher Columbus, looking for the western seaway to India, lands on October 12th 1492 on the small island of San Salvador (Guanahani, Watling Island) in the Bahamas. Between 1492 and 1504, on this and three subsequent voyages, he reconnoitres the West Indies, the north coast of South America and the Central American coast. Although he never set foot on the territory of the United States, his fame outshines that of the other discoverers.

1497–8   John Cabot (Giovanni Caboto), a Venetian in the service of the English crown, sails along the coasts of Newfoundland and Delaware.

1507   After the much-travelled Florentine Amerigo Vespucci claims in his writings that the New World is a continent the German cartographer Martin Waldseemüller names the continent America in Vespucci's honour.

1513   The Spanish navigator Juan Ponce de León discovers Florida.

Colonisation

Spain   Spain becomes the first European nation to establish a colonial empire in the New World. The ruthless conquistadors, seeking rapid success and wealth for themselves and their country, destroy the flourishing empires of the Aztecs and the Incas in Central and South America. The southern regions of North America also attract their interest.

1539–43   Hernando de Soto, starting from Florida, explores the coast of the Gulf of Mexico as far as the Mississippi and presses on into Arkansas and Oklahoma.

1540   Francisco Vásquez de Coronado leads an expedition into the territory of Arizona and New Mexico. Hernando de Alarcón reaches the Colorado River. García López de Cardenas discovers the Grand Canyon.

1565   Pedro Menendez founds the first enduring Spanish colony in North America at what is now St Augustine in Florida.

France   While Spanish and Portuguese colonising activity is mainly in Central and South America, the French establish their colonial empire of Nouvelle France in North America, extending from Canada to the Mississippi.

Giovanni da Verrazano, a Florentine in the French service, reconnoitres the east coast of North America. He is probably the first European to sail into the estuary of the Hudson River, now the port of New York.	1524
Jacques Cartier discovers the river St Lawrence.	1534
Samuel de Champlain (1570–1635) founds the first French colony in the New World at Québec.	1608
The Jesuit Jacques Marquette and Louis Joliet advance south to the Mississippi and claim the whole river for France.	1673
René Robert Cavelier, Sieur de la Salle, reaches the Mississippi delta and takes possession of the whole river basin in the name of Louis XIV, calling it Louisiana.	1682
Jean-Baptiste Le Moyne, Sieur de Bienville (1680–1768), founds Nouvelle Orléans (New Orleans).	1718
France thus theoretically controls the whole of known North America. Towards the end of the 17th c. it becomes involved in war with Britain (King William's War). During the War of the Spanish Succession (1704–13) France and Britain are also at war in North America (Queen Anne's War). Under the treaty of Utrecht in 1713 Britain receives the territory round Hudson Bay, Nova Scotia and Newfoundland. After King George's War (1744–8) and the French and Indian War (1754–63), during the Seven Years' War, France loses Canada and the territory east of the Mississippi.	Conflicts with Britain
In the Louisiana Purchase the United States buys the French colony of Louisiana.	1803
Dutch interest in the New World is concentrated on the area round New York and New Jersey.	**Holland**
Henry Hudson, an Englishman in the service of the Dutch East India Company who is looking for the North-West Passage, sails up the Hudson River and claims the territory for Holland.	1609
The area round Long Island Sound is named Nieuw Holland.	1614
Peter Minuit buys the island of Manhattan from the Indians – it is said with trinkets worth 24 dollars – and founds Nieuw Amsterdam.	1626
British forces occupy Nieuw Amsterdam, of which Peter Stuyvesant is governor, and rename it New York.	1664
Britain is the last of the great powers to establish a colonial empire in North America. Around 1700 there are some 2500 British settlers; by 1750 two-thirds of the inhabitants have been born in the colonies.	**Britain**
Sir Walter Raleigh founds the first English settlements on Roanoke Island in North Carolina. They are later abandoned.	1584
British colonisation of North America begins in earnest with the arrival of 105 settlers led by Captain John Smith. Their settlement of Jamestown is the nucleus of the colony of Virginia.	1607
The first black Africans, voluntarily engaged as indentured labourers, arrive in Jamestown.	1619
In November 102 Puritans, the Pilgrim Fathers, land from the	1620

"Mayflower" at Cape Cod in Massachusetts, after signing the Mayflower Compact, an agreement promising obedience to the laws and ordinances introduced by the leaders of the enterprise. This government by the people is seen as foreshadowing one of the basic principles of American democracy. The Pilgrims' first harvest in 1621 is still commemorated on Thanksgiving Day.

1623	Foundation of the colony of New Hampshire.
1629	Robert Heath receives from King Charles I the originally Spanish colony of Carolina (later, in 1730, divided into North and South Carolina).
1634	Foundation of the Catholic colony of Maryland.
1635	Foundation of the colony of Connecticut.
1636	Foundation of the colony of Rhode Island. Harvard College founded in Boston.
1650	Slave-owning is officially permitted.
1664	British forces occupy Nieuw Amsterdam, Nieuw Holland and Delaware.
1676	The Wampanoag and Narragansett Indians, living on the east coast, rebel against the British (King Philip's War).
1681	The Quaker William Penn founds the colony of Pennsylvania. Its capital, Philadelphia, is founded in 1683.
1704	The first newspaper in the colonies, the "Boston News Letter", appears.
1732	James Oglethorpe founds Georgia, the thirteenth and last British colony in North America.

The American Revolution

The colonists, increasingly self-confident, their trade restricted by the Navigation Act of 1660, without any political weight in London and governed from there, with ever new regulations and taxes, strive to achieve independence.

1764–7	The Currency Act prohibits the colonies from issuing their own currency. The Sugar Act reintroduces a tax on sugar. The Stamp Act (repealed in 1766) requires all documents and printed works to be stamped. The Quartering Act obliges the colonies to meet the cost of reinforcing the British garrisons. The Townshend Acts impose import duties on tea, paint, glass, paper and other items. The colonists' resentment is expressed in passive resistance and soon also in a demand for representation in Parliament ("No taxation without representation"), made at a congress of representatives from nine colonies at New York in November 1767.
1770	During a riot in Boston on March 5th three civilians are killed by British troops. This "Boston Massacre" further alienates the colonists from the mother country.
1773–4	The Boston Tea Party. In protest against the banning of trade with other countries a party of Boston citizens disguised as Indians throw several cargoes of tea into Boston harbour. The British government introduces a series of restrictive Acts (the "Intolerable Acts") and closes Boston harbour.

Representatives of all the colonies except Georgia meet in Philadelphia in the first Continental Congress and resolve to break off all commercial relations with Britain and with other British colonies throughout the world.

The first clashes between British "redcoats" and American "minutemen" (patriots ready for action at a moment's notice) occur at Concord and Lexington, near Boston. This marks the beginning of the War of American Independence. On June 15th the second Continental Congress appoints George Washington commander in chief of American forces. On June 17th the patriots are defeated in the battle of Bunker Hill. — 1775

On July 4th 1776 the Congress in Philadelphia proclaims the independence of the colonies from Britain in the Declaration of Independence. This day, the foundation date of the United States of America, is now a national holiday (Independence Day). — 1776

The military situation is characterised by varying fortunes. Washington drives the British out of Boston, but is defeated on Long Island in August. In December, after crossing the frozen Delaware River, he defeats British forces at Trenton. British troops, with mercenaries from Hesse and Brunswick, occupy New York.

1777   The British occupy Philadelphia, but are defeated at Saratoga on October 17th. On December 17th France recognises the independence of the thirteen colonies.

1778–80   On February 6th 1780 France concludes an assistance pact with the United States and sends a fleet to support the American patriots. In June the British leave Philadelphia. In 1779 Washington is condemned by shortage of men to inactivity in his camp at West Point. On May 12th 1780 British forces take Charleston in what is now South Carolina.

1781   The British army, commanded by General Cornwallis, withdraws to Yorktown, Virginia. A French fleet under the command of Admiral de Grasse then closes the Hampton Roads, and the combined American and French forces, commanded by Washington and General Rochambeau, defeat the British army and force Cornwallis to surrender (October 19th). This victory decides the war in favour of the Americans.

1782   On November 30th Britain and its former colonies sign a preliminary peace treaty in Paris.

1783   On September 3rd the independence of the thirteen American states is recognised in the treaty of Versailles. Canada, the American north-west and Nova Scotia remain in British hands, but the western frontier of the United States moves west to the Mississippi, incorporating the territories ceded by France in 1763. Some 100,000 pro-British Loyalists flee to Canada or join the British army to escape the hatred and revenge of the patriots.

Foundation, consolidation and extension of the Union

1787   In the Northwest Ordinance of July 13th the Continental Congress establishes the territory west of New York and north of the Ohio River as a state. On September 17th the Constitutional Convention approves the Constitution of the Union.

1789   The first Congress of the United States meets in Federal Hall in New York and elects Washington unanimously as first President of the Union. On March 4th the Constitution comes into force, and on April 30th the Supreme Court is established.

1791   The Bill of Rights, promulgated on December 15th, guarantees basic rights such as freedom of religion, assembly and the press and the inviolability of persons and property.

1792   The United States Mint is established in Philadelphia on April 2nd.

1793   The invention of the cotton gin by Eli Whitney leads to the extension of cotton monoculture. A direct consequence is a rapid increase in the slave trade.

1796   Washington ends his second term of office with the Farewell Address of September 19th, in which he warns against long-term alliances with other powers and against high state debts.

1800   The population of the United States, with around a third of its present-

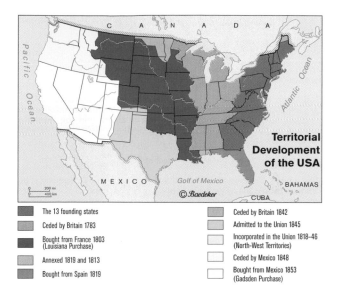

Territorial Development of the USA

The 13 founding states	Ceded by Britain 1842	
Ceded by Britain 1783	Admitted to the Union 1845	
Bought from France 1803 (Louisiana Purchase)	Incorporated in the Union 1818–46 (North-West Territories)	
Annexed 1819 and 1813	Ceded by Mexico 1848	
Bought from Spain 1819	Bought from Mexico 1853 (Gadsden Purchase)	

day territory, is about 4 million. There are only five towns of more than 10,000 inhabitants. Washington, DC becomes the official residence of the President and the seat of Congress.

In the Louisiana Purchase the United States acquires the largely unexplored French territory of Louisiana and thus doubles its area.   1803

On May 14th 1804 Meriwether Lewis and William Clark set out from St Louis on a 2½ year expedition in the course of which they explore the territory now occupied by the states of the north-west and reach the Pacific coast.   1804–6

Maiden trip of Robert Fulton's steamboat.   1807

Congress bans the import of slaves.   1808

Napoleon's Continental System, British counter-measures that seriously injure American trade and British support of a rebellion by the Shawnees lead to war with Britain. The American attempt to take Canada fails; British troops occupy Washington and burn down the Capitol and the White House. The status quo is restored by the treaty of Ghent on December 24th 1814. In the battle of New Orleans in January 1815 – fought before news of the peace treaty is received – there are heavy losses, particularly on the British side.   1812–14

The United States buys Florida from Spain.   1819

The Missouri Compromise permits slave-owning in the new state of Missouri but prohibits it in all territories west of the Mississippi and north of latitude 36°30′N.   1820

President James Monroe sets out the Monroe Doctrine: the United States renounces any idea of exerting American influence in Europe and   1823 rejects any intervention by European powers in the western hemisphere ("America for the Americans").

1825	The Erie Canal is opened on October 26th.
1829	Andrew Jackson becomes President – the first representative of the farmers of the west to reach the highest office.
1830s	During the 1830s there is a threat of secession from the Union by the farming and slave-owning Southern states because of the introduction of taxes favouring the industrial Northern states and the northern demand for the abolition of slavery. The dispute is settled for the time being by new tax laws.
1830	Joseph Smith founds the Mormon sect in Fayette, New York State.
1832	War against the Sac and Fox Indians in Illinois and Wisconsin. The Democrats hold their first party convention in Baltimore.
1833	William Lloyd Garrison founds the radical Antislavery Society.
1835	The Seminole Indians of Florida launch a war against the whites that lasts eight years. Texas declares its independence from Mexico.
1836	Mexican troops occupy San Antonio in Texas and wipe out the defenders of the Alamo mission there. Six weeks later Texan forces, with the battle-cry "Remember the Alamo!", defeat the Mexicans at San Jacinto.
1838	The Cherokee Indians are deported from their hereditary territory in the Smoky Mountains to Oklahoma (the "Trail of Tears").
1840	75,000 slaves escape to Canada on the secret "underground railway".
1841	On May 1st 1841 the first wagon trek sets out from Independence, Missouri, for California. A year later the Oregon Trail is opened.
	In 1841 the American government guarantees various Indian tribes possession of the territory west of the Mississippi "so long as grass grows and water runs".
1844	On May 24th Samuel Morse sends the first message by telegraph from Washington to Baltimore.
1845	Texas is admitted to the Union.
1846	After the signature of a frontier agreement with Britain the north-western Territories are incorporated in the Union.
	In the war with Mexico that is sparked off by the incorporation of Texas in the Union American troops occupy Veracruz and Mexico City. The war ends in 1847 with an agreement by Mexico, in return for compensation, to renounce any claim to Texas, New Mexico, Colorado, Arizona, Utah, Nevada and northern California.
	In July 1847 the Mormons, led by Brigham Young, travel to Utah.
1848	Gold is found on the American River in California, and by 1849 80,000 gold-seekers have made their way to California. In July the world's first conference on women's rights is held in Seneca Falls, New York State.
1850	The Southern states prevent the banning of slavery in the territories acquired from Mexico except California.
1852	Harriet Beecher Stowe publishes her novel "Uncle Tom's Cabin", the success of which exacerbates the conflict between North and South.

The Kansas-Nebraska Bill permits the inhabitants of these states to own slaves – in effect abrogating the Missouri Compromise. There are conflicts in Kansas and Nebraska between the supporters and opponents of slavery; the opponents are members of the Republican Party.   1854

The first transcontinental mail service reaches the Pacific coast.   1858

John Brown attacks the military post at Harpers Ferry in Virginia in order to get arms for the fight against slavery.   1859

Abraham Lincoln, a Republican, is elected President.   1860
    The population of the United States passes the 30 million mark.

Civil War

The election of Lincoln as President brings the conflict between the south and the north to crisis point. At the end of 1860 South Carolina withdraws from the Union, to be followed in 1861 by Mississippi, Florida, Alabama, Georgia, Louisiana, Texas, Virginia, Arkansas, North Carolina and Tennessee. Representatives of these states, meeting in Montgomery, Alabama, form the Confederate States of America, with Richmond, Virginia, as capital and Jefferson Davis as President. On April 12th 1861 the Confederates open hostilities with the bombardment of Fort Sumter in the harbour of Charleston, South Carolina; thereupon Lincoln calls up 75,000 volunteers. From April 19th the ports of the southern states are blockaded. In the first battle of the war, at Bull Run (Manassas, Virginia), the Union forces are defeated.   1860
    The first transcontinental telegraph line comes into operation.

Union troops win successes in the west and occupy New Orleans. In the East there are no decisive results. A naval battle in the Hampton Roads (Williamsburg, Virginia) is the first encounter in history between two armour-clad warships, the "Monitor" on the Union side and the Confederacy's "Virginia". A seven-day battle at Mechanicsville, Virginia, ends in the retreat of the Union forces. The Confederates win another victory at Bull Run and advance on Washington, but after the battle of Antietam (Sharpsburg, Maryland) are compelled to retreat. At Fredericksburg, Virginia, the Union army is again defeated.   1862

On January 1st, in the Emancipation Declaration, Lincoln declares all slaves in the rebel Southern states to be free. The Civil War now becomes a war for the liberation of the slaves, though this is a subsidiary war aim in comparison with the maintenance of the Union. On the same day the Homestead Act comes into force, enabling any citizen of full age to acquire land, subject to an obligation to build a homestead and cultivate the land.   1863
    On July 1st, at Gettysburg, Union troops commanded by General Meade defeat the Confederate army, which, under the command of General Lee, has advanced into Pennsylvania and Maryland. Thereafter the Southern army is in more or less continuous retreat. On July 4th, in the Gettysburg Address, Lincoln sets out his ideas on the future form of the Union. Union forces under the command of General Grant take Vicksburg, the principal Confederate base on the Mississippi.

Grant throws Lee's Confederate army back to Richmond and Petersburg, Virginia. A Union army led by General Sherman takes Atlanta and then drives through Georgia to Savannah, leaving a trail of devastation.   1864
    On November 29th, at Sand Creek, a cavalry unit shoots down some 300 peaceable Cheyenne Indians (the Sand Creek Massacre).

The Confederates abandon Columbia and Charleston in South Carolina   1865

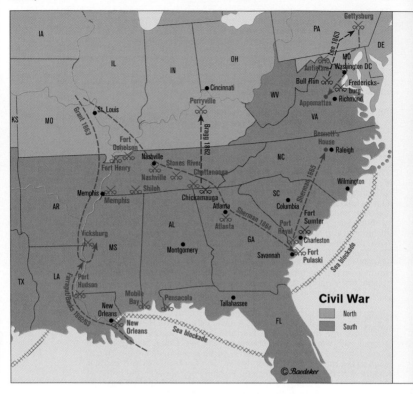

Civil War

North

South

© Baedeker

and Petersburg and Richmond in Virginia. On April 9th, at Appomattox, Virginia, the main Confederate army, commanded by Lee, surrenders unconditionally to Grant. At the end of the war, which has cost 385,000 dead and 282,000 wounded, the Union is restored to its unity, the slaves are, formally, freed and the South is devastated. Tensions remain, however, between the South, whose pride has been wounded, and the "progressive" North, and indeed are exacerbated by the social and economic differences between North and South as well as by the race question.

On April 14th Lincoln is shot in Ford's Theatre in Washington by John Wilkes Booth, a fanatical Southerner.

With the adoption of the 13th Amendment to the Constitution on December 18th slavery is abolished throughout the United States and some 3 million blacks are formally granted their freedom.

Reconstruction and the rise to world power

The two decades after the Civil War are an unsettled period in which events are dictated by war profiteers and speculators. In the second half of the 19th c. the population of the United States grows at a tremendous rate (from 23 million in 1850 to 76 million in 1900), and technological development proceeds at a breathtaking pace. Commercial trusts are formed, and the magnates of the oil and steel

⚔ **Victories of the Union**

⚔ **Victories of the Confederates**

Fort Sumter, April 12–14th 1861: The American Civil War starts with the bombardment of Fort Sumter outside Charleston by the Confederates.

Bull Run, July 21st 1861: In the first Battle of Bull Run/Manassas, the southern states under the leadership of Lee put the northern states to flight.

Atlantic and Gulf Coast, 1861–62: During the first year of the war the Union captures the important ports and fortifications at Port Royal, Fort Pulaski near Savannah, St Augustine (March 9th 1862) and Pensacola, thus allowing an effective sea blockade.

Fort Donelson, February 6th 1862, and **Fort Henry, February 16th 1862:** These two forts are the first fortifications in Tennessee to be conquered by General Grant. His victory at Shiloh April 6–7th 1862 and the capture of Memphis on June 5th 1862 followed.

Bull Run, August 29–30th 1862: Lee remains successful in the second Battle of Bull Run, and prevents the Union's attempt to conquer Richmond.

Antietam, September 17th 1862: Lee's first attempt to take the war to the north ends in his defeat and 25,000 dead in his army.

Perryville, October 8th 1862: General Bragg's army, which had penetrated into the north, is stopped.

Fredricksburg, December 13th 1862 and May 1st–4th 1863: In the winter, the southern states score another victory at Fredericksburg. Half a year later they again repel the Union troops in nearby Chancellorsville.

Gettysburg, July 1st–4th 1863: The army of the southern states under Lee is finally defeated in its attempt to carry the war to the north. This, the largest battle in the war, has a death toll of 55,000.

Mississippi, 1863: Following his successful campaigns in Tennessee, General Grant marches along the Mississippi towards the south in May 1863. His most important objective is Vicksburg, which falls on July 4th 1863 after a siege that lasted nearly two months. From the south, General Banks marches towards him. General Farragut had already taken New Orleans on May 1st 1862.

Chickamauga, September 19–20th 1863: After their earlier successes at Stones River, at the turn of 1862, the progress of the Union troops is halted.

Chattanooga, November 24–25th 1863: In the Battle of Chattanooga, Union troops regain the upper hand. This leaves General Sherman free to move south.

Mobile Bay, August 5th 1864: Another important southern port falls to the Union.

Atlanta, September 2nd 1864: On their way to the coast, Sherman's troops raze the capital of Georgia to the ground. On December 21st they reach Savannah on the Atlantic coast. Now the Confederate area is divided.

The north, 1864 and 1865: General Grant, now Supreme Commander of the Union, has been advancing from Washington since the spring of 1864. On April 8th 1865, General Lee and the main body of the Confederates capitulate at Appomattox; on April 14th General Johnston and the rest of the army follow suit at Bennett's House near Raleigh.

industries lay the foundations of their fortunes. At the same time social contrasts become more acute, leading, particularly in the industrialised cities of the north, in strikes and sometimes in violent riots. Trade unions are now formed.

By the end of the 19th c. the United States has established itself as a world power that does not hesitate to intervene in other countries' affairs, particularly in Latin America (the policy of the "big stick").

Foundation of the Ku Klux Klan in the southern states. It commits its first atrocities.	1866
The United States acquires Alaska from Russia for 7.2 million dollars.	1867
The Sioux, headed by their chief Red Cloud, successfully resist an attempt to drive the Bozeman Trail through their territory.	1866–8
The Central Pacific and Union Pacific Railroads meet in Promontory, Utah, completing the transcontinental line.	1869
The 15th Amendment to the Constitution gives blacks the vote.	1870
The Yellowstone National Park is established – the first National Park in the United States.	1872

May 10th 1869: the completion of the first transcontinental railway

1876	The centenary of the foundation of the United States is marked by the World's Fair in Philadelphia. On June 15th Sioux and Cheyenne Indians wipe out the 7th United States Cavalry, commanded by George Custer, on the Little Bighorn River in Montana.
1877	During the Presidency of Rutherford B. Hayes Carl Schurz, Secretary of the Interior, builds up a professional civil service.
1881	President James A. Garfield, who had taken up office in January, dies on September 19th from the consequences of an attack on his life in Washington on July 2nd.
1886	In May eleven people are killed in eight days of fighting between anarchists, workers and the police in Chicago (the Haymarket Riot). On December 8th the American Federation of Labour is founded.
	In September the Apache rebel leader Geronimo surrenders to the police.
1887	The General Allotment Act divides collectively owned Indian land into individual holdings. The Indians, to whom this form of land ownership is unknown, become the victims of speculators.
1889	Oklahoma, hitherto guaranteed Indian territory, is opened up for settlement by whites.
1890	The Sherman Anti-Trust Law is the first of a series of laws against the formation of cartels that restrict competition.
	The Ghost Dance movement makes rapid headway among the Indians. The government seeks to control its spread by repressive measures. On December 29th American troops kill Chief Bigfoot and 200

of his followers at Wounded Knee – the last battle between Indians and whites.

The Federal Bureau of Census officially records the end of the "frontier" period in the history of the United States, the three hundred years of continuing acquisition of land.

The declared aim of the United States in the war with Mexico during the Presidency of William McKinley is to free Cuba from Spanish rule. After annihilating defeats of the Spanish fleet in naval battles at Cavite (Manila Bay, Philippines) and Santiago de Cuba Spain cedes to the United States in the treaty of Paris the Philippines (in return for a payment of 20 million dollars), Puerto Rico and Guam. Cuba's independence is guaranteed. 1898

Congress annexes the Hawaiian Islands.

The United States sends an auxiliary corps to China to assist in the crushing of the Boxer rebellion. 1900

President McKinley dies on September 14th after being shot by an anarchist on September 6th. He is succeeded by Theodore ("Teddy") Roosevelt, who restricts the power of the trusts and makes a name as a "trust buster". 1901

The independent state of Panama is established, under American protection, to safeguard work on the Panama Canal. 1903

Henry Ford founds his first automobile factory. The brothers Orville and Wilbur Wright make the first powered flight in history on the coast of North Carolina (December 17th).

San Francisco is destroyed by an earthquake and a great fire on April 18th and 19th. 1906

The Federal Reserve Act establishes twelve federal reserve banks to mobilise banking reserves and issue currency notes. 1913

On August 15th 1914 the first ship passes through the Panama Canal. The United States continues its policy of intervention in its own back yard, landing troops in Haiti in July 1915, intervening in the Mexican civil war and installing a military government in the Dominican Republic in 1917. 1914–18

On the outbreak of the First World War in Europe President Woodrow Wilson declares the neutrality of the United States. The sinking of two British passenger ships, the "Lusitania" and the "Arabic", by German submarines in May 1915 sparks off a wave of violent protests against Germany, which apologises. After an unsuccessful attempt at mediation in 1916 the United States begins to rearm and increases its relief supplies to the Allies. When Germany declares unrestricted submarine warfare in February 1917 the United States breaks off diplomatic relations, and on April 6th declares war on Germany. Universal military service is introduced on May 18th. By the summer of 1918 the American expeditionary corps is in action on the Western Front, and by the end of the war it amounts to over a million men and has had 116,000 men killed and 204,000 wounded. The "Fourteen Points" put forward by President Wilson at the beginning of 1918 as the basis for a lasting peace prepare the way for an armistice on November 11th 1918. The Senate refuses to ratify the treaty of Versailles or to join the League of Nations.

Prosperity and Neo-Isolationism

By the end of the First World War the United States has become the world's leading economic power. After a brief period of readjustment the American economy enjoys an unprecedented boom. Technological progress combined with new methods of rationalisation and an apparently irrepressible optimism brings in an era of extraordinary prosperity – counterbalanced, however, by the inadequate purchasing power of the mass of the people, the bootlegging that flourishes during the period of Prohibition and an alarming increase in gangster activity. Uncontrolled speculation increasingly endangers the liberal economic system, and the Stock Exchange crash of 1929 not only leads to the collapse of the American capital market but triggers off one of the world's worst economic crises. By the end of the 1930s the crisis appears to be over, and even after the outbreak of the Second World War the American people favour pacifism and neutrality. After Hitler comes to power in Germany the United States takes in great numbers of refugees from the Nazis.

1920	During the period of Prohibition, which continues until 1933, the production, sale, transport, import and export of alcoholic drinks are banned. The first radio programmes are transmitted. The 19th Amendment to the Constitution gives American women the vote. The trial for murder of two anarchists, Sacco and Vanzetti, and their execution in 1921 create a worldwide sensation.
1921	On August 25th the United States concludes a separate peace with Germany, Austria and Hungary that takes over only some of the provisions of the treaty of Versailles. After many years of inactivity the Ku Klux Klan resumes its acts of violence against blacks in the southern states.
1922	A miners' strike in Herrin, Illinois, leaves 36 dead.
1924	All Indians are granted full civil rights. The Johnson Read Act drastically restricts the number of immigrants and puts a total ban on Chinese and Japanese immigrants.
1927	Charles Lindbergh makes the first non-stop flight across the Atlantic. The first talking film, the "Jazz Singer", is shown.
1929	A great Stock Exchange crash on October 29th ("Black Friday") ends the period of prosperity.
1930–1	There are 8 million unemployed in the United States. President Hoover tries to counter the depression by great construction projects (the Hoover Dam), the granting of credits, tax increases and a moratorium on international payments.
1932	The number of unemployed reaches 15 million.
1933	President Franklin D. Roosevelt announces his New Deal, a programme for recovery that involves a series of far-reaching measures (declaration of a state of national emergency, agricultural subsidies, the huge Tennessee Valley construction project).
1934	The devaluation of the dollar by 41 per cent leads to a considerable increase in exports. The United States gives up its special rights in Cuba and its protection of Haiti.
1935	A new social programme gives workers extensive rights and lays the basis of a pension scheme.
1936–8	The law on the permanent neutrality of the United States comes into force on April 1st, but by the following year the government shows signs

of departing from its isolationist policy. Roosevelt threatens states that
endanger world peace with "political quarantine".

Second World War

The first splitting of the atom is achieved at New York's Columbia   1939
University. When the Second World War breaks out in Europe the United
States again declares its neutrality and bans the export of war materials.
Soon, however, Britain is excepted from the embargo and receives mili-
tary equipment from the United States.

In spite of its neutrality the United States embarks on comprehensive   1940
rearmament, particularly of the navy. Roosevelt is re-elected President
for an unprecedented third term and a National Defence Council is
established.

In a speech to Congress Roosevelt sets out the "four freedoms" that he   1941
sees as the foundations of a future world order: freedom of speech, free-
dom of religious belief, freedom from want and freedom from fear. The
Lend-Lease Act enables Britain, and later the Soviet Union, to acquire
American war materials. In July American troops land in Greenland and
Iceland. On August 14th Roosevelt and the British prime minister,
Winston Churchill, agree on the Atlantic Charter, which is to become the
basis for the creation of the United Nations. The Japanese air attack on
the American base of Pearl Harbor on the Hawaiian island of Oahu on
December 7th 1941 sparks off the war in the Pacific. On December 11th
Germany and Italy declare war on the United States. On December 12th
universal military service is introduced. 120,000 Japanese living in the
United States, two-thirds of them American citizens, are interned.

The Japanese conquer the Philippines, but suffer heavy losses in sea   1942
and air battles in the Coral Sea and Midway Islands. At the beginning of
November American and British troops land in French North Africa.
    On December 2nd Enrico Fermi achieves the first nuclear chain reac-
tion at the University of Chicago.

At the Casablanca Conference in January Roosevelt and Churchill   1943
resolve to carry on the war until the unconditional surrender of the
enemy. After bitter fighting (begun in August 1942) American troops
capture the Japanese air base of Guadalcanal in the south-western
Pacific. In September Allied troops land in Sicily. The air war against
Germany, based mainly in Britain, is stepped up and continues on an
increased scale until 1945. At the Teheran Conference Roosevelt and
Churchill meet with Stalin for the first time and discuss common military
action and cooperation after the end of the war.

On June 6th ("D-Day") Allied forces land in Normandy: the opening of   1944
the second front called for by Stalin. Paris is freed in August, and in
October Aachen is taken by the Americans – the first German city to fall
to the Allies. In the same month American troops land in the Philippines.
    Roosevelt is re-elected President for a fourth term.

At the Yalta Conference in February Roosevelt, Churchill and Stalin   1945
agree on guidelines for the further conduct of the war and the occupation of Germany. On April 12th Roosevelt dies and is succeeded by the
Vice-President, Harry S. Truman. On April 25th American and Soviet
troops meet at Torgau on the Elbe. On May 7th the German Wehrmacht
surrenders unconditionally.
    The tactic of "island-hopping" has brought American forces in the
Pacific steadily closer to Japan. Iwo Jima falls in February, Okinawa in
April. On July 16th the first atom bomb is detonated at the Alamogordo

test site in New Mexico. On August 6th and 9th two atom bombs are dropped on Hiroshima (killing between 80,000 and 200,000) and Nagasaki (killing between 39,000 and 74,000). Japan surrenders on September 2nd. Of the 16 million American soldiers involved in the war 292,000 have been killed and 671,000 wounded.

On June 26th representatives of 51 states meet in San Francisco and found the United Nations. During the last two years of the war there have been ever clearer signs of the power-political trends that lead after the war to the split between the western capitalist and the eastern socialist camps.

Cold War to détente

1947   Under the "Truman doctrine" the United States gives military and economic aid to Greece and Turkey in order to prevent a Communist takeover.

The controversial Taft-Hartley Labor Act curtails the authority of trade unions.

1948   The Soviet blockade of West Berlin is broken by the American and British airlift. The Marshall Plan for the rebuilding of western Europe, initiated by Secretary of State George Marshall in 1947, begins to operate.

1949   Truman, re-elected President, outlines a 21-point domestic programme that comes to be known as the Fair Deal. The United States is the leading power in the North Atlantic Treaty Organisation (NATO) that is established on April 4th.

1950   In January President Truman gives approval to the development of the hydrogen bomb.

Senator Joseph McCarthy launches his first attack on "Communists" in the country's political and cultural life. The following years are marked by anti-Communist hysteria and an atmosphere of denunciation and mistrust.

After North Korea's invasion of South Korea American troops commanded by General MacArthur intervene on behalf of the United Nations. In October they reach the frontier with China and clash with Chinese troops.

1951   Truman recalls MacArthur, who wants to carry the war into Chinese territory. Negotiations on a cease-fire begin.

Australia, New Zealand and the United States conclude the ANZUS pact in San Francisco.

1952   The United States, Britain and France sign a peace treaty with the German Federal Republic.

On November 1st the first hydrogen bomb is detonated on Eniwetok atoll in the Marshall Islands.

1953   On July 27th an armistice in the Korean War is signed at Panmunjong. Of the 5.7 million American soldiers engaged more than 54,000 were killed and 103,000 wounded.

1954   Senator McCarthy's pursuit of Communists reaches a final peak in a series of televised hearings; at the end of the year, however, his activities are condemned by the Senate. The Supreme Court declares racial segregation in public schools unconstitutional.

ANZUS is replaced by the wider SEATO (South-East Asia Treaty Organisation).

1955   The two largest American trade unions, AFL and CIO, join to form AFL-

CIO, with a total of 15 million members. In Montgomery, Alabama, a black woman refuses for the first time to give up her seat to a white; the buses are boycotted by blacks; and a federal court declares segregation in buses unconstitutional.

The first military advisers are sent to South Vietnam.

In September troops of the National Guard are called out by the 1957 Governor of Arkansas to prevent nine black children from entering the previously white Central High School in Little Rock. President Eisenhower sends federal troops to enforce the Supreme Court's declaration that racial segregation in public schools is unconstitutional.

The successful launch on October 4th of the Soviet satellite "Sputnik 1" is a shock to Americans' belief in their technological superiority.

On January 31st the first American earth satellite, "Explorer", is put into 1958 orbit.

American troops land in Lebanon to forestall an attempted coup d'état.

Alaska and Hawaii are admitted to the Union as the 49th and 50th states. 1959 On April 25th the St Lawrence Seaway is opened, giving the ports on the Great Lakes a direct link with the Atlantic.

Nikita Khrushchov becomes the first Soviet head of state to visit the United States.

On May 1st an American U 2 reconnaissance aircraft is shot down over 1960 the Soviet Union. As a result a planned summit conference in Paris is called off.

Black and white students demonstrate against racial discrimination with sit-ins all over the country. The Democrat John F. Kennedy, a Roman Catholic, is elected President by a narrow majority over the Republican Richard Nixon. Kennedy's "New Frontier" programme shakes up the nation and makes him the idol of a new and more hopeful era.

The "Sugar War" between the United States and Fidel Castro's Cuba 1961 leads in January to the breaking off of diplomatic relations. The invasion of Cuba, with American support, by Cuban exiles landing in the Bay of Pigs is a fiasco.

On April 12th the Soviet cosmonaut Yuri Gagarin becomes the first man to fly into space. He is followed on May 5th by the first American in space, Alan B. Shepard.

President Kennedy strengthens American presence in South Vietnam. In 1962 October the Cuban missiles crisis brings the world to the verge of a third world war, when the Soviet Union stations troops and medium-range rockets on the island. The United States calls for them to be dismantled and mounts an air and sea blockade of Cuba. After days of worldwide tension the Soviet Union gives way on condition that the United States withdraws its rockets from Turkey. Kennedy's successful handling of the crisis is his greatest foreign policy achievement.

On August 5th the United States, Soviet Union and Britain sign a nuclear 1963 test-ban treaty.

At the end of August some 200,000 people, mainly coloured, demonstrate in Washington against racial discrimination. They are led by Martin Luther King, who makes his famous speech, "I have a dream". On November 22nd President Kennedy is shot in Dallas, Texas.

At the end of the year there are 15,000 American troops in South Vietnam.

A new civil rights law is directed against racial discrimination in employ- 1964 ment, housing and political actiivity.

Martin Luther King and the March on Washington, August 28th 1963

On August 2nd two American warships are attacked by North Vietnamese torpedo-boats in the Gulf of Tonkin. Congress thereupon gives President Lyndon Johnson unlimited authority for action in South-East Asia. The Vietnam War now officially begins.

1965 President Johnson orders the bombing of North Vietnam north of the 20th parallel. By the end of the year the number of American troops in South Vietnam has risen to 184,000.

Martin Luther King leads thousands of civil rights supporters in a protest march from Selma to Montgomery, Alabama. In race riots in Los Angeles in August 35 people are killed.

1966 The strength of American forces in Vietnam, Laos and Thailand has risen to 480,000.

1967 President Johnson and the Soviet prime minister, Kosygin, meet in Glassborough, New Jersey, in June and agree that an atomic war must be avoided at all costs.

During the summer the National Guard is called in to quell violent race riots in Newark and Detroit that leave 66 dead and thousands of injured. Thurgood Marshall becomes the first black judge in the Supreme Court.

Protests against the war in Vietnam increase. On October 21st and 22nd 35,000 people demonstrate in Washington.

1968 The Tet offensive by the Vietcong and the North Vietnamese causes heavy American and South Vietnamese losses. The bombing of North Vietnam is called off, and peace negotiations begin in Paris.

On April 4th Martin Luther King is shot in Memphis, leading to race riots in many states. On June 5th Senator Robert Kennedy is shot in Los Angeles. The Republican Richard Nixon is elected President.

The Supreme Court recognises the right of objection to military service   1969
on moral as well as on religious grounds.

In April there are 534,000 American servicemen in Vietnam. Their
withdrawal begins in July. On November 15th 250,000 people demonstrate in Washington against the Vietnam war. On the following day
there is news of the My Lai massacre, in which American troops are said
to have killed several hundred South Vietnamese civilians.

Climaxing the series of manned space flights that have been carried
out since 1961 (Mercury, Gemini, Apollo), Apollo 11 lands on the moon
on July 20th, with the two astronauts Neil Armstrong and Edwin Aldrin.

SALT negotiations, aimed at the limitation of American and Soviet
strategic arms, begin in Helsinki. Relationships between the two superpowers enter a period of détente.

Crisis and new hope

From the beginning of his term of office President Nixon is faced with a
variety of problems – racial discrimination, poverty, economic stagnation and the fall of the dollar, unemployment, environmental pollution,
increasing protests against the war in Vietnam – which raise doubts
throughout the world about the "land of unlimited possibilities". The
state of shock in America at the end of the Vietnam War – the realisation
that the world's mightiest military machine had been defeated by poorly
equipped jungle fighters, the split in the nation between opponents and
supporters of the war, the gradual revelation of the real reasons for
American involvement – shatters the collective consciousness of the
United States for years if not decades to come. The Watergate scandal
and the deplorable behaviour of President Nixon increase doubts about
the "American dream".

The nuclear weapons non-proliferation treaty comes into force on March   1970
5th.

On Earth Day (April 22nd) millions of Americans demonstrate in a call
for effective protection of the environment.

President Nixon authorises American forces to enter Cambodian territory. During protests against this action at Kent State University in Ohio
four students are shot by the National Guard.

The voting age is reduced to 18.   1971

On June 13th the "New York Times" begins to publish the "Pentagon
Papers", which reveal the deliberate intervention of the United States in
Vietnam at an early stage and sparks off a violent controversy. The
number of American servicemen in Vietnam is reduced to 140,000.

At the end of February President Nixon pays a "friendly" visit to the   1972
Chinese People's Republic, and in May travels to Moscow. The United
States and the Soviet Union sign the SALT 1 agreement in Moscow.

Nixon orders the mining of North Vietnam ports. The last American
troops leave Vietnam on August 11th.

An Amendment to the Constitution declares discrimination against
women unconstitutional, and the Supreme Court declares the death sentence unconstitutional. In June there is a break-in at the Democratic
Party's headquarters in the Watergate building in Washington. Nixon
wins the Presidential election with a large majority.

An armistice in the Vietnam War is signed in Paris on January 24th.   1973
United States losses in the war are 56,000 dead and over 303,000
wounded. Universal military service is abolished on June 30th.

Militant Indians occupy the hamlet of Wounded Knee and hold it for
ten weeks in protest against the continuing discrimination.

In the course of the year the direct involvement of President Nixon's closest advisers in the Watergate break-in and the President's attempts to hush the matter up become increasingly clear. After the resignation of Vice-President Spiro Agnew, accused of tax evasion, Gerald Ford becomes Vice-President.

In October the oil-producing Arab states put an oil embargo on the United States because of its support for Israel in the Yom Kippur War.

The Supreme Court declares abortion during the first six months of pregnancy to be legal.

1974   During the further course of the Watergate affair impeachment proceedings are started against Nixon. He resigns on August 8th. He is granted a pardon by the new President, Gerald Ford, in spite of strong public protests.

1975   After the capture of Saigon by North Vietnamese forces Vietnam capitulates on April 30th. The last American citizens are evacuated from the roof of the American embassy by helicopter. The United States take in 140,000 refugees from South Vietnam. In September SEATO is dissolved.

1976   The 200th anniversary of the Declaration of Independence is celebrated in July. The Supreme Court, reversing its previous decision, declares the death sentence to be constitutional. In the Presidential election on November 2nd Jimmy Carter, a Democrat from Georgia, wins a narrow victory over his Republican opponent, President Gerald Ford.

1977   President Carter grants a pardon to some 10,000 objectors to service in Vietnam.

1979   A peace treaty between Egypt and Israel is signed in Washington on March 26th. On June 18th the United States and the Soviet Union sign the SALT 2 treaty in Vienna. On November 4th Iranian revolutionaries storm the American embassy in Teheran and take 63 diplomats hostage; their object is to secure the return to Iran of the Shah, who has taken refuge in the United States.

There is a nuclear accident, classed in the highest category, in the Three Miles Island reactor at Harrisburg, Pennsylvania.

1980   Following the Soviet intervention in Afghanistan (1979) the United States imposes a grain embargo on the Soviet Union. In subsequent years the policy of détente suffers setbacks. The United States boycotts the Olympic Games in Moscow. An attempt to free the Teheran hostages by military means ends in fiasco.

Mount St Helens, a volcano in Washington state, erupts on May 18th with a force equal to 500 bombs of Hiroshima type.

Ronald Reagan, a Republican, wins the Presidential election.

1981   On January 20th, the day on which President Reagan takes up office, the Teheran hostages are released. Reagan's economic programme ("Reaganomics") is based on reductions in taxes and government expenditure and an increase in the defence budget; his aim is to restore American self-confidence and overcome the trauma of Vietnam.

The space shuttle "Columbia", the first reusable spacecraft, is launched on April 12th. Sandra Day O'Connor is appointed assessor to the Supreme Court, the first woman to join the court.

1982   The Peace Movement is formed and, with the slogan "Freeze nuclear arms!", calls for an end to nuclear weapons. On June 12th half a million people demonstrate in New York.

Over 12 million Americans are unemployed.

1983   In a television address President Reagan puts forward his idea of an anti-rocket defence system based in space, the "Strategic Defence Initiative".

241 American soldiers, part of an international peace-keeping force in Lebanon, are killed in a bomb attack in Beirut on October 23rd.

On October 25th American troops land on the Caribbean island of Grenada, an independent Commonwealth state, to overthrow the left-wing Military Council.

The Olympic Games in Los Angeles are boycotted by the countries of the Eastern Bloc. Ronald Reagan has a triumphal victory in the Presidential election. The Democratic candidate for the Vice-Presidency is Geraldine Ferraro, the first woman to be nominated for the post.   1984

President Reagan and the Soviet leader, Mikhail Gorbachov, meet in Geneva. A fresh boost is given to the policy of détente.   1985

The space shuttle "Challenger" blows up soon after its launch on January 28th, killing all seven of its crew.   1986

After terrorist attacks in Europe the United States accuses Libya of being responsible, and American aircraft bomb Tripoli and Benghazi.

At the end of the year details of the "Irangate" affair, in which the proceeds of arms sales to Iran went to the Contra rebels in Nicaragua, begin to leak out.

On June 12th official sources draw attention for the first time to the threat from AIDS.

On October 19th the fall in share prices on the New York Stock Exchange brings heavier losses than on "Black Friday" in 1929.   1987

Presidents Reagan and Gorbachov sign an agreement in Washington on the destruction of land-based medium-range missiles.

Republican George Bush is elected President.   1988

A new world order?

After the dissolution of the Soviet Union the United States, in President Ford's view, is the only real world power, whose task is to defend and protect the free world. It must be ready, therefore, to intervene militarily in international crisis areas – in the Third World and where it is necessary to defend American interests.

The wreck of the supertanker "Exxon Valdez" on the coast of Alaska in March leads to catastrophic oil pollution. On October 17th the strongest earthquake since 1906 hits San Francisco, causing over 59 deaths. The Supreme Court restricts the right to abortion.   1989

In December 25,000 American troops occupy Panama and arrest the President, General Noriega, who is suspected of drug dealing.

After the occupation of Kuwait by Iraq American troops are sent to Saudi Arabia.   1990

Under United States command, American, British, French, Saudi and other troops attack Iraq and liberate Kuwait.   1991

After the collapse of the Eastern Bloc the United States begins to reduce its military presence in Europe and Asia and to cut down its atomic weaponry.

Serious race riots in Los Angeles following the acquittal of four white policeman who maltreated a black motorist: 58 people are killed and damage estimated at a billion dollars is caused.   1992

President Bush announces the creation of the North American Free Trade Area (NAFTA), which comes into force at the beginning of 1994 and removes restrictions on trade between Mexico, the United States and Canada.

A Democrat, Bill Clinton, wins the Presidential election, ending 12 years of Republican Presidency that have seen severe cuts in expenditure on social welfare and raising the hopes of millions of socially disadvantaged Americans.

In December American troops land in Somalia as part of a UN peacekeeping force aimed at ending the civil war in the country.

1993

The Clinton administration brings forward proposals for health service reform, but these are rejected by Congress. In the following years substantial cuts are made in the social services budget. Devastating floods in the Mississippi/Missouri valley. In November a referendum in Puerto Rico produces a majority against incorporation in the United States as the 51st state. Congress approves the establishment of NAFTA. In December President Clinton signs a law making it more difficult to buy guns.

In September representatives of Israel and the Palestine Liberation Organisation, meeting in Washington, agree on the peace process.

1994

At the beginning of 1994 the NAFTA agreement comes into force, bringing together the United States, Canada and Mexico in a free trade area.

In January a severe earthquake shakes the northern districts of Los Angeles causing many deaths and much destruction.

In April there is a meeting between the President and all the Indian chiefs, the first such meeting in American history.

In November the mid-term elections to the Senate and House of Representatives result in a landslide victory for the Republicans. The Democrat President Clinton is now confronted by Republican majorities in both Houses.

1995

February and March see the withdrawal of American troops from Somalia.

In Dayton, Ohio, the two sides in the Bosnian civil war finally reach agreement on a peace accord. The United States sends 20,000 soldiers to the Balkans as part of the peace keeping force set up to oversee the settlement.

In the same month the dollar falls to an all-time low against the Deutschmark, threatening its status as a key international currency.

The partial insolvency of the United States administration precipitates a serious economic crisis; almost half the civil service are put on temporary unpaid leave.

In April right-wing extremists carry out a bomb attack on a government building in Oklahoma City, leaving 168 dead and more than 800 injured.

In October Louis Farrakhan, leader of the black Muslim society, the Nation of Islam, heads the largest demonstration seen in Washington, DC since Martin Luther King (1963).

1996–9

The United States economy is booming; unemployment falls and the dollar stabilises. Bill Clinton, however, faces problems of a different kind as Independent Counsel Kenneth Starr doggedly pursues allegations of corrupt property deals and sexual affairs. Clinton's reputation, however, remains undamaged as far as the voters are concerned. In the mid-term elections in November 1998, the Democrats actually improve their position, the first time in more than 60 years that the party of the incumbent president does not lose support mid-term. Neither this nor the still growing popularity of the president, who in December 1998 orders the bombing of Iraq, prevents the Republicans from initiating proceedings to remove him from office. But in February 1999 the process concludes without impeachment and the matter is quickly forgotten.

Famous People

The jazz trumpeter and singer Louis Armstrong, born in New Orleans, made a name for himself at the age of 18 with his new-style solos and husky voice, performing in small jazz spots in the south. In the early 1920s he played in the bands of "King" Oliver and Fletcher Henderson, and later was equally successful as soloist in various smaller groups. With his extraordinary virtuosity and infectious musicality "Satchmo" became a central figure in the world of jazz and had a decisive influence on its development.

Louis Armstrong (1900–71)

Leonard Bernstein, born in Lawrence, Mass., studied composition under Walter Riston and conducting under Fritz Reiner and Serge Koussevitzky. His brilliant career as a conductor took off when he stood in at the last minute for Bruno Walter in 1943. From 1958 to 1969 he was permanent conductor of the New York Philharmonic – the first occupant of the post to have been born and trained in the United States. He composed symphonies, ballet music, musicals and chamber music. Among his best known works are the Jeremiah Symphony (1942), the ballet "Fancy Free" (1944) and above all the very popular musical "West Side Story" (1957) with its catchy tunes. He also wrote a number of works on the theory and appreciation of music.

Leonard Bernstein (1918–90)

William H. Bonney, known as Billy the Kid, was born in New York. He is said to have committed his first murder at the age of 12 (the victim had insulted his mother), and by 1877 was credited with eleven other murders. When the Cattle War broke out in Lincoln County, New Mexico in 1878 he became leader of a band that murdered a sheriff and his deputy and was ruthlessly hunted down by Pat Garrett, a former friend of Billy's. Billy was captured and condemned to death but managed to escape from prison. Three months later, however, Garrett cornered him in Fort Sumner, New Mexico, and shot him. Billy the Kid is said to have killed a total of 21 people. Why he committed the murders even Pat Garrett, who wrote the first biography of him, was unable to explain.

Billy the Kid (1859–81)

The great opponent of slavery, born in Torrington, Connecticut, believed that he had a divine mission to fight slavery, by violent means if necess-

John Brown (1800–59)

Famous People

ary. In 1858 he founded an organisation of both coloured people and whites that set about establishing a refuge for runaway slaves in the mountains of Maryland and Virginia and forming an armed force. He led his men in an attack on a military post at Harpers Ferry in West Virginia with the object of seizing arms for a nationwide rising of the slaves. After a bloody battle, however, Brown's men were overpowered by a force of United States Marines commanded by Robert E. Lee. Brown was condemned to death and hanged in Charles Town, West Virginia. Although his plan to bring about a general rising of the slaves had failed, the battle of Harpers Ferry underlined the conflict between North and South that finally led to the Civil War. John Brown is commemorated by the song "John Brown's Body".

Al Capone
(1899–1947)

Al (Alfonso) Capone, the most famous of American gangsters, was born in Naples and grew up in a New York slum. In 1920 he moved to Chicago, where he became a much feared underworld boss, establishing his position by bootlegging during the period of Prohibition. Although he was suspected of being involved in numerous murders and attacks he was never brought to court, due to fear of reprisals. Finally in 1931 he was sentenced to eleven years in prison for tax evasion, but in 1939 was released on health grounds and retired to Miami.

William F. Cody
"Buffalo Bill"
(1846–1917)

The most celebrated Wild West hero of them all was born in Scott County, Iowa. After working in his youth as a Pony Express rider he became a gold-hunter in Colorado, fought against the Indians and served in the Civil War in the forces of Tennessee and Missouri. During the construction of the Kansas–Pacific Railroad he contributed to the food supply of the construction workers by – according to his own account – killing over 4000 buffaloes in 17 months. This exploit and his fights with the Sioux and Cheyenne Indians were recounted by Ned Buntline in "Buffalo Bill", published in popular form, which brought the hero of the stories world fame and established the mythology of the Wild West. In 1883 Cody organised his Wild West show, with performers who included the markswoman Annie Oakley and chief Sitting Bull, and travelled with it throughout the United States and Europe. In 1890 he retired to a ranch near the township of Cody, Wyoming, which he had founded. Despite his fame as a hero of the Wild West, he must also bear a share of the blame for the extinction of the buffalo and thus for the destruction of the basis of Indian life.

Jefferson Davis
(1808–89)

Jefferson Davis, born in Abbeville, Kentucky, served in the American-Mexican War in 1845–7 and then became a Senator and from 1853 to 1857 Secretary of War. Originally a supporter of an expansionist federal policy, after the election of Abraham Lincoln as President he fought for the secession of the southern states from the Union. In 1861 he was elected President of the Confederate States of America, and along with General Lee was the driving force on the Southern side during the Civil War. After the surrender of the South in April 1865 he was imprisoned but was pardoned in 1868. He died in Beauvoir, Mississippi.

Miles Davis
(1926–91)

When the jazz trumpeter Miles Davis (born in Alton, Illinois) was asked by a politician's wife at a party in Washington what he had achieved in life he replied that he had five or six times changed something in music and asked in return what she had achieved apart from being white. He had some justification for his claim; for Miles Davis, the "man with the horn", had since 1945, when he first performed in Charlie Parker's quintet, influenced or initiated all the various schools of jazz. His greatest hit was the combination of jazz, rock and African rhythms in the album "Bitches' Brew" (1970), which was a powerful stimulus to almost all the leading jazzmen of the day, including Herbie Hancock, Wayne Shorter and Tony Williams.

Walt Disney, a native of Chicago, laid the foundations of his fame with the creation and animation, along with his brother Roy, of Mickey Mouse in 1925. The appearance of Mickey Mouse in "Steamboat Willie" (1928) established the popularity of the animated cartoon film. It was followed by the first feature-length cartoon film, "Snow White and the Seven Dwarfs" (1937) and then by "Fantasia" (1940) and "Bambi" (1942) – all classics of the cartoon film. Then came adventure films ("20,000 Leagues under the Sea", 1955), documentary nature films ("The Living Desert", 1953; "The Vanishing Prairie", 1954) and television films ("Mickey Mouse Club",

Walt Disney (1901–66)

"Davy Crockett", "Walt Disney's Wonderful World of Color"). Disney's modest original studio in a garage developed over the years into a great film production company and finally into an international entertainment corporation, running Disneyland in Anaheim, near Los Angeles (established 1955), Disney World at Orlando, Miami (1971) and Euro Disney Resort, near Paris (1992).

Donald Duck can claim to be the most famous duck in the world. He first appeared in the film "The Wise Little Hen" in 1934, and since then has not only improved his appearance but has launched a whole series of (usually unsuccessful) attempts to achieve fame and fortune – as an auxiliary fireman, a sales representative, Emperor of America, a scientist (investigating, for example, the hens in the Andes that lay square eggs) and Sheriff of Bullet Valley. Although bad-tempered by nature, he is kind and affectionate to his nephews Louie, Huey and Dewey; but his relationship with his immensely rich Uncle Scrooge is marred by profound differences of view, largely based on difference in social standing. Nevertheless he is immensely popular: his portrait appears on stamps (for example in San Marino) and he is internationally known – as Paperino in Italy, Donald Furioso in Spain, Pato Donald in Brazil, Kalle Anka in Sweden and Anders And in Denmark. It has not been possible to establish his new Russian name.

Donald Duck (b. 1934)

Amelia Earhart, born in Atchison, Kansas, became the first woman to fly solo across the Atlantic. After studying at Columbia University, New York, she took up flying as a hobby and in 1928 was the first woman passenger on a transatlantic flight. Thereafter she flew only on her own: in 1932 across the Atlantic from Newfoundland to Ireland, in 1935 on the first solo flight from Hawaii to the American mainland. In 1937 she set out with her navigator Frederick J. Norman on a flight round the world, but after completing two-thirds of the distance her plane disappeared near Howland Island in the Pacific.

Amelia Earhart (1897–1937)

Wyatt Earp, born in Monmouth, Illinois, became one of the great figures of the Wild West and the hero of numerous films – though it is still not clear whether he should be remembered as an upholder of the law or as a gun-happy criminal. Somewhere on the way from Kansas, where he is known to have been an upholder of law and order in a number of towns, to Arizona he and his two brothers seem to have crossed the boundary

Wyatt Earp (1848–1929)

Famous People

Wyatt Earp

between the status of marshal and that of outlaw. At any rate the event that made him a legend, the shoot-out with the Clanton gang at the O.K. Corral in Tombstone, Arizona, was regarded by many contemporaries as cold-blooded murder. But Earp survived this and later shoot-outs and died peacefully in Los Angeles. His legendary ally Doc Holliday died of consumption and heavy drinking.

Thomas Alva
Edison
(1847–1931)

Thomas Alva Edison, a native of Milan, Ohio, ranks as one of the world's most productive inventors – in spite of the fact that he had only three months regular schooling. He was active throughout his life as an experimenter and inventor, patenting over a period of 50 years something like 1100 inventions, including the carbon filament lamp, the phonograph (using wax records) and the Ediphone, a dictating machine, motion-picture cameras and projectors and a ready-mixed concrete process.

Henry Ford
(1863–1947)

The automobile manufacturer Henry Ford, born in Dearborn, Michigan, started life as a mechanic and engineer; then in 1892 he built his first automobile and in 1903 founded the Ford Motor Company in Detroit. He was the first to introduce assembly-line manufacture, an idea that revolutionised industrial production. Within 25 years the Ford works grew into an industrial giant, whose legendary Model T, 15 million of which were produced, dominated the roads of the United States in the 1920s. The firm continued to be family-owned until the thirties. The Ford Foundation, established in 1936, is now one of the wealthiest American foundations, active particularly in the educational field in the United States and in promoting technical aid programmes in developing countries.

Benjamin Franklin
(1706–90)

Benjamin Franklin – statesman, scientist and publicist, a man learned in many fields – was born in Boston, Massachusetts, the 17th child of a soapmaker and candlemaker who had emigrated to the United States from Oxfordshire. As a printer and publisher, he soon began to take an interest in politics. In 1732 he founded the influential "Pennsylvania Gazette", and between 1753 and 1758 published "Poor Richard", a witty annual almanac. He was also concerned for his fellow-men in practical life, and was involved in the foundation of Pennsylvania's first university, the first hospital in the North American colonies and a learned society that became the American Philosophical Society. He earned a place in the history of science with his invention of the lightning conductor (1752) and of binoculars, and was also responsible for numerous discoveries and publications in the most varied fields – education and science, international relations and the public service, engineering, medicine and health services, printing, publishing and graphic art, finance and insurance, religion and freemasonry, agriculture and botany, music. In spite of all this activity he refused to take out patents for any of his inventions, for he believed that all inventions should be for the public benefit. He supported the strivings of the colonies for independence from an early stage, and as their ambassador in France from 1776 to 1785 exerted so powerful an influence that the French support for the Americans must be attributed to him. He was one of the signatories of the Declaration of Independence, the alliance with France against Britain, the peace treaty with Britain and the Constitution of 1787. In 1788 he was elected president of the first society for the abolition of slavery. He died in Pennsylvania.

Clark Gable, born in Cadiz, Ohio, established his reputation as one of the great screen heart-throbs in his role as Rhett Butler in "Gone with the Wind" – a part that he was at first disposed to turn down. At that time (1939) he was already an established Hollywood figure, having won an Oscar for his part in the comedy "It Happened One Night". After serving as a pilot in the Second World War he returned to Hollywood, but he was not in great demand and was unable to repeat his previous successes. He put up a brilliant performance in John Huston's "Misfits" (1960), alongside Marilyn Monroe and Montgomery Clift, but it was too late for a comeback. Soon after the shooting of the film he died of a heart attack.

Clark Gable
(1901–60)

The New Yorker George Gershwin, creator of so many marvellous tunes, grew up without any contact with music; later he had piano lessons, and finally studied music. At first he was drawn to jazz, and wrote popular songs and musicals; then, beginning with "Rhapsody in Blue" (1924), he turned away from light music and developed his own conception of classical music, in which he mingled elements of the everyday music of the 1920s, jazz and serious music: Piano Concerto in F Major (1925); the tone poem "An American in Paris" (1928); "Of Thee I Sing" (1931), a satire on the American political system; and the still popular opera "Porgy and Bess" (1935). He died of a brain tumour in Hollywood at the height of his fame.

George Gershwin
(1898–1937)

Ernest Miller Hemingway, born in Oak Park, Illinois, ranks as the principal representative of the "lost generation" after the First World War, with which his first novel "The Sun Also Rises" ("Fiesta"), published in 1926, was concerned; it was also a celebration of Spanish machismo. "A Farewell to Arms", a novel of love and war, appeared in 1929. "For Whom the Bell Tolls" (1940) dealt with the Spanish Civil War from the point of view of an American – like himself – fighting on the Republican side. His short novel "The Old Man and the Sea" (1952) was another international success, and in 1954 he was awarded the Nobel Prize for literature. Hemingway's novels are written in a spare, laconic and virile style. Writing in the novels of strong-willed men facing a variety of challenges, he tried to act the same part in his own life, with bullfighting, big game hunting and deep-sea angling as his favourite recreations. Unable to face his greatest challenge – dealing with his own personality and with alcohol – he finally shot himself.

Ernest
Hemingway
(1899–1961)

One of the most eccentric figures in the history of the United States was the billionaire, aviator and film producer Howard Hughes, a native of Houston, Texas. In 1924 he inherited his father's tool factory, the large profits from which he invested in film productions, airlines and aircraft production. In his factory were built the first retractable undercarriage and the "Spruce Goose", a huge wooden seaplane – the largest aircraft then in existence – that he himself piloted. In 1938 he made a record 91-hour flight round the world. After a series of legal proceedings against him for various commercial offences he became increasingly reclusive, and from 1958 onwards never appeared in public. He became a legend the subject of speculation by the press, which regularly carried reports of his death or his appearance somewhere in the world. In fact he continued to run his financial empire from various hiding-places. He died in 1976 on a flight from Mexico to Texas.

Howard Hughes
(1905–76)

Legend and reality were so mingled in the life of Jesse Woodson James, the son of a Baptist preacher in western Missouri, that many people,

Jesse James
(1847–82)

seeing him as a kind of Robin Hood of the Wild West, refused to believe in his death. On February 13th 1866 Jesse, his brother Frank and their gang raided a bank in Liberty, Montana – the first bank robbery in the United States in time of peace but by no means the last. The brothers meanwhile continued to live peacefully on their mother's farm, until information pointing to them began to emerge in 1869. Thereafter they were blamed for a wide range of other hold-ups and robberies, to such an extent that Jesse disclaimed responsibility in the press. The legend, however, was born. The gang then specialised in train robbery, pursuing their activities in Texas, Arkansas, Montana and Colorado. Jesse James was never caught, for he was always able to return to an ordinary quiet existence. He settled with his wife and two children in St Joseph, Montana, living under a false name, but was tracked down by Robert Ford, a member of the gang, and shot for the sake of the reward. He it was who died as a hero, while Ford was the villain.

Thomas Jefferson (1743–1826)

Thomas Jefferson, third President of the United States (1801–9), was a man of universal learning. Born in Shadwell, Virginia, he attended William and Mary College and began his career as a lawyer and politician in Virginia. A brilliant polemical writer, he came to prominence in 1774 with a broadside directed against Britain, "A Summary View of the Rights of British America", and in 1776 was one of the drafters of the Declaration of Independence. He succeeded Benjamin Franklin as American ambassador in France (1784–9), and thereafter became Secretary of State under Washington. Jefferson's party of Democratic Republicans (forerunners of the Democrats) was opposed by the Federalists led by Alexander Hamilton, and in 1793 the disagreements became so acute that Jefferson resigned. Under John Adams, however, he became Vice-President, and in 1801 became President – the first to be inaugurated in Washington, DC. As President he sought to achieve simplicity in administration and the restriction of federal powers to foreign affairs but to maintain close control on Congress. His greatest foreign policy success was the acquisition of the French territory of Louisiana (the Louisiana Purchase). At the end of his term of office he retired to his well-managed estate and country house, Monticello, which he had designed himself and developed for forty years. In 1819 he founded the University of Virginia in Charlottesville.

John F. Kennedy (1917–83)

John Fitzgerald Kennedy, scion of a wealthy Massachusetts family and great-grandson of an Irishman who emigrated to the United States about 1850, was the first Roman Catholic President of the United States. After studying at the best universities in the country (Princeton, Harvard and Stanford) he commanded a torpedo-boat in the Pacific during the Second World War. In 1946 he entered the House of Representatives as a Democrat, and in 1952 was elected to the Senate. Eight years later, after narrowly defeating Richard Nixon, he became the 35th President of the United States. His inaugural address – "Ask not what your country can do for you: ask what you can do for your country" – appealed to Americans and raised high hopes for his Presidency. John F. Kennedy, who had constantly to take strong drugs for a severe kidney disease and back problems, was murdered on November 22nd 1963 in Dallas, Texas. Since then there has been much speculation about the motives for the shooting.

With hindsight it is astonishing to see how the Kennedy myth grew up. His foreign policy was marked by more misjudgements than successes. During his period of office 16,000 American servicemen were sent to Vietnam, the Bay of Pigs invasion was a fiasco and even the success of his tough stance in the Cuba missiles crisis was bought at the price (which was kept secret) of the withdrawal of American missiles from Turkey and an undertaking not to intervene in Cuba. In domestic policy the moving spirits in such matters as reform and civil rights were his brother Robert and Vice-President Johnson rather than the President himself.

The President's younger brother Robert, his closest adviser and Attorney General in his government, was murdered on June 8th 1968 while running for the Presidency.

Coloured Americans still revere the memory of the theologian and Baptist preacher Martin Luther King Jr, a native of Atlanta, Georgia, who was murdered in April 1968. He was one of the first to oppose racism in his country: in 1955–6 he organised a boycott of the public transport system in Montgomery, Alabama, in protest against racial segregation in public buses. Through this and similar actions and above all through his speeches and preaching, expressing a charisma that captivated his listeners, he made racial discrimination a matter of public concern – leaving no doubt, however, about his insistence on non-violence in the struggle for civil rights. The high point of his work was the peaceful march on Washington in 1963, when he made his famous "I have a dream" speech. In 1964 he became the youngest recipient of the Nobel Peace Prize. He was shot by a Southern racist in Memphis, Tennessee.

Martin Luther
King Jr (1929–68)

General Robert E. Lee was the hero of the south during the American Civil War – in spite of the fact that he had been appointed commander in chief of the Confederate army rather against his will. Yet there is no doubt that he felt more strongly bound to his home state of Virginia than to the Union in which he had begun his military career. He inflicted heavy losses on the northern army, particularly at Fredericksburg, but suffered a decisive defeat at Gettysburg. Thereafter the Confederates could fight only delaying actions, and Lee was finally compelled to surrender to Ulysses S. Grant on April 9th 1865. After the war he supported the cause of reconciliation, and his name is now honoured both in the south and the north.

Robert E. Lee
(1807–70)

Abraham Lincoln, son of a poor family of farmers and craftsmen, was born in a small township in Kentucky and spent much of his early life, which was marked by hard work and study of the Bible, in Illinois. He trained as a lawyer in Springfield, Illinois, and was active in politics as a Democrat. Then, believing that slavery was irreconcilable with the principles of freedom and equality, he went over to the Republicans and was elected to the Senate in 1858. In 1860 he was elected President, and soon after he took up office the Civil War broke out. From the beginning he insisted that the Union must be preserved, and called up a citizens' militia, strengthened the army and suspended Habeas Corpus in the southern states. After the Northern victory at Antietam, Maryland, in 1862 he made the liberation of all slaves in those states that on January 1st 1863 were still "in rebellion" one of the objectives of the war. The Civil War thus became also a war for the liberation of the slaves. Only five days after General Lee's surrender Lincoln was shot in Ford's Theatre in Washington by an actor named John Wilkes Booth.

Abraham Lincoln
(1809–65)

Famous People

Lincoln owes his place in American history to the abolition of slavery (under the 13th Amendment to the Constitution, December 18th 1865) and his determination to preserve the Union. His vision of "government of the people, by the people, for the people" was given its clearest expression in his Gettysburg Address on November 19th 1863.

Charles Lindbergh (1902–74)

Abraham Lincoln statue at the Lincoln Memorial, Washington, DC

On May 20th and 21st 1927 Charles Lindbergh, a native of Detroit, made the first non-stop solo flight across the Atlantic from west to east. His plane, the "Spirit of St Louis", took 33½ hours to fly from Long Island, New Jersey, to Le Bourget near Paris. In 1932 his son was kidnapped and murdered. Lindbergh opposed America's entry into the Second World War in 1941, and was rehabilitated only in 1954. He died on the island of Maui (Hawaii).

Joe Louis (1914–81)

The "Brown Bomber" of Lafayette, Alabama, was one of the most successful boxers of all time: in 71 professional fights between 1934 and 1951 he suffered only three defeats, and between 1937 and 1949, when he retired, he successfully defended his title 25 times.

Malcolm X (1925–65)

Malcolm Little of Omaha, Nebraska, left school early and thereafter went to the bad, spending the years 1946–52 in prison. There he was converted to the Nation of Islam (Black Muslim) faith and began to call himself Malcolm X (as an ex-smoker, ex-drinker, ex-Christian and ex-slave). As spokesman for the radical militant blacks he preached black nationalism in a way that went too far for the Black Muslim leader Elijah Muhammad, who ordered him in 1963 to call a halt to his preaching. Thereupon Malcolm X left the Black Muslims (1964) and founded the Muslim Mosque. Soon afterwards he established the Organisation for African-American Unity, the object of which was to combine the fight of black Americans and that of the oppressed peoples of the Third World. Malcolm X was murdered in Harlem by three blacks.

Mark Twain (1835–1910)

Samuel Langhorne Clemens, born in Florida, Missouri, made an international name for himself, under the pseudonym Mark Twain, with his two principal novels, "Tom Sawyer" (1876) and "Huckleberry Finn" (1884), which rank as the finest works of American prose of the later 19th c. He started his working life as apprentice to a local printer, but then became an apprentice steamboat pilot on the Mississippi (hence his pseudonym, from the call of the man sounding the depth of the river) and an unsuccessful gold prospector. Finally he became a newspaper reporter and began his career as a writer with a series of humorous and sometimes grotesque sketches. It is easy to forget, however, that Mark Twain also saw himself as a critic of social conditions.

Glenn Miller (1904–44)

The band leader Glenn Miller, a native of Clarinda, Iowa, wrote a series of catchy tunes that are still popular, notably "Tuxedo Junction", "Moonlight Serenade" and above all "In the Mood". A trombonist, he spent years as an ordinary member of various bands until in 1937 he realised his dream of founding his own band, which soon became by far the most popular group of the big band era. During the Second World War he conducted the United States Air Force Band in Europe. He disappeared without trace on a flight from England to Paris.

Marilyn Monroe (real name Norma Jean Baker) was born in Los Angeles, an illegitimate child, and grew up in various foster homes. In films such as "Gentlemen Prefer Blondes" and "How to Marry a Millionaire" she acquired a reputation as an attractive but dumb blonde, and soon became known as the "sex goddess of the fifties". She herself disliked this image and tried to establish herself as a serious actress with a great gift for comedy; and indeed achieved this in the very successful films "The Seven Year Itch" and "Some Like It Hot". She never managed, however, to get her anxieties and depression under control, either through her three marriages (to such varied husbands as the baseball player Joe Di Maggio and the dramatist Arthur Miller) or by recourse to the bottle. Her constant absences from the set led to her dismissal from the film "Something Has Got to Give". Soon afterwards she died of an overdose of sleeping pills.

Marilyn Monroe (1926–62)

Edgar Allan Poe, born in Boston, Massachusetts, achieved his first great literary success with his "Tales of Ratiocination", published between 1841 and 1845. These tales, including "The Murders in the Rue Morgue", made him the creator of the modern detective story – in Arthur Conan Doyle's words, "the master of us all". His fame was enhanced by the publication of a collection of poems ("The Raven and Other Poems", 1845) on fantastic and frightening themes – themes found also in his tales ("The Fall of the House of Usher"). As the leading member of the American Romantic movement Poe had great influence on European literature. Throughout his life, however, he was always short of money, lonely and given to the use of alcohol and later, in consequence of a serious nervous illness, of opium. His death might have come from one of his stories: he was found unconscious in a bar in Baltimore and the cause of his death remained a mystery.

Edgar Allan Poe (1809–49)

Elvis Aron Presley, born in Tupelo, Mississippi, was mainly employed as a truck driver before the meteoric rise to a mega-star of the rock and roll era, the "King", which began between 1956 and 1958. The songs that he moaned into the microphone – usually expressing an innocent teenage eroticism – and the gyrations that accompanied them (earning him the name of Elvis the Pelvis) drove his young audiences into a kind of mass hysteria. Unusually for a white singer, he drew from the style of black performers, giving it his own interpretation. His first hit "Love Me Tender", the later "In the Ghetto" and many other songs are still popular. In the course of his career Elvis Presley sold over half a million records, and his satellite television show "Aloha from Hawaii" on January 14th 1973 drew a worldwide audience of a billion viewers. By then – without any future artistically or, after a failed marriage, in his private life – he was addicted to alcohol and drug misuse. He died wretchedly in his mansion of Graceland in Memphis, Tennessee.

Elvis Presley (1935–77)

Famous People

Red Cloud
(1822–1909)

One of the bitterest and most effective opponents of the expansion of the whites in North America was Red Cloud, a chief of the Oglala Sioux, whose Indian name was Che-ton-waka-wa-mani ("The hawk who hunts on foot"). In 1866 and 1867 he opposed the government's plan to drive the Bozeman Trail through what is now Wyoming to the goldfields of Montana and to establish three forts. The route ran through the richest Sioux hunting grounds east of the Bighorn River. Under Red Cloud's leadership a combined Sioux and Cheyenne force launched one of the most celebrated raids of the Indian Wars, the attack on Colonel Fetterman's force at Fort Phil Kearny in December 1866. The Indians' activities inflicted such heavy losses on the whites that in 1868 the government signed a treaty with Red Cloud and gave up the idea of the Bozeman Trail. Red Cloud observed the treaty for the rest of his life; but in the 1880s his tribe was moved to the Pine River reserve in South Dakota, where he died.

Rockefeller dynasty

Perhaps no other family was more archetypal of the "land of unlimited possibilities", in which it is possible to rise from dish-washer to millionaire, than the Rockefellers. The founder of the family was John D. Rockefeller (1839–1937), who made his fortune in the oil and steel industries. He founded the Standard Oil Company in 1870, and by 1882 controlled practically the whole American oil industry. Retiring from business in 1896, he devoted himself to the Rockefeller Foundation he had established, which is mainly active in the medical field. His only son, John D. Rockefeller Jr (1874–1960), made over to the United Nations the site on New York's East River now occupied by its headquarters (1947), founded the Museum of Primitive Art in New York (1957) and financed the reconstruction of Williamsburg, one-time capital of the colony of Virginia. Two of his sons, Republicans, became Governors – Nelson Aldrich Rockefeller (1908–79) in New York State and Winthrop Rockefeller (1912–73) in Arkansas; and Nelson Aldrich was Vice-President of the United States from 1974 to 1977. Winthrop's grandson John D. Rockefeller IV was Democratic Governor of West Virginia from 1977 to 1985.

Franklin Delano Roosevelt
(1882–1945)

The greatest President of the United States in the 20th c., Franklin Delano Roosevelt, was born in Hyde Park, New York State. After studying law at Harvard and the Columbia Law School he worked as a lawyer for some time and then entered politics. Although stricken with polio in 1921 he remained politically active, and in 1932 became the 32nd President of the United States. During his four successive terms of office he helped by the reforming policies of his "New Deal" to overcome the country's economic crisis and took the United States well prepared into the Second World War, in which he fought the Axis powers with great determination. He also played a major part in the formulation of the Atlantic Charter, which led to the foundation of the United Nations. His sudden death came as a shock to the nation. His wife Eleanor (1884–1962) saw her role as First Lady as more than a background figure and played an active part in politics.

Babe Ruth
(1895–1948)

George Herman Ruth, the great hero of American baseball, was born in Baltimore, Maryland. Playing for the New York Yankees, he revolutionised the game, putting the emphasis on power rather than speed. With his tremendous strength, he drove the ball across the field and frequently out of the ground altogether, enabling him to make his home runs at leisure. In the 1927 season he established a record of 60 home runs in 154 games that was not beaten until 1960.

The statesman and reformer Carl Schurz was born near Cologne. As a student at Bonn University he was involved in the 1848 Revolution and was obliged to leave Germany. In 1852, with his wife, he emigrated to the United States, where he soon felt himself an American and became a firm supporter of the Republicans. In 1861 he was sent to Spain as the American ambassador, but on the outbreak of the Civil War returned to the United States to become a general in the Union forces. As editor of the "Detroit Post" and the German language "St Louis Westliche Post" he advocated a policy of reconstruction and opposed the expansionist trends in American foreign policy. As Secretary of the Interior under President Hayes (1877–81) he promoted reforms and a humaner treatment of Indians. After retiring from politics he wrote for "Harper's Weekly", still showing himself an eloquent advocate of political morality and the principles of freedom. His wife Margarethe Meyer-Schurz established the first kindergarten in the United States.

Carl Schurz (1829–1906)

Frank Sinatra's career was the archetypal American career. Sinatra, "the voice", born in Hoboken, New Jersey, to a family of poor Italian immigrants went on to become an icon of American show business. And from a singing head waiter to the best entertainer in the world he experienced all the highs and lows of life. In the first half of the 1940s he was the pop star incarnate, who delighted his fans, the "swooners", with his amazing timbre. Illness and alcoholism almost brought him down but he climbed back to the top with his supporting role as Angelo Maggio in the 1953 film "From Here to Eternity", for which he received an Oscar. And from hereon Sinatra remained on top. Even when he was hitting the bars between New York and Las Vegas with the "rat pack" – Dean Martin, Sammy Davis Jr and Peter Lawford – or was seen with the Mafia boss Lucky Luciano and other shady personalities, the critics couldn't care less; Ol' Blue Eyes certainly "did it my way", as the refrain goes in his most popular song. Sinatra died on May 14th 1998, in Los Angeles.

Frank Sinatra (1915–98)

Sitting Bull (in the Sioux language "Tatanka Yotanka"), of the Hunkpapa Sioux tribe, is perhaps the most legendary of the Indian chiefs. Born on the Grand River in South Dakota, by his refusal to move with his tribe into the reservation assigned to them he brought about the greatest defeat suffered by the United States Army in the Indian Wars, the annihilation of a detachment of the 7th United States Cavalry led by George Custer in the battle of the Little Bighorn on June 25th 1876. He himself took no direct part in the battle, for as medicine-man he had the task of seeking "good medicine" (that is, the support of the spirits for the warriors). The military victory was mainly due to the tactical skill of Crazy Horse. In spite of this success Sitting Bull was compelled to flee to Canada, but in 1881, after an amnesty, he was able to return to the Standing Rock reservation. Then, for reasons that are obscure, he allowed himself to be persuaded to take part for a year

Sitting Bull (?1834–1890)

Famous People

in Buffalo Bill's Wild West show. When in 1890 the Ghost Dance movement led to the threat of unrest among the Indians the American government, still fearing his popularity among the Indians, ordered his arrest by the Indian police. In the affray that followed Sitting Bull and his son Crow Foot were shot. His grave is in Mobridge, South Dakota.

Joseph Smith (1805–44)

Joseph Smith, a farm worker of Windsor County, Vermont, claimed that God had appeared to him in 1823 and charged him to form a religious community that should exceed all others in perfection; in the same revelation he had been instructed where to find a number of gold plates inscribed with the "Book of Mormon", recording the history of an elect people that had emigrated from Israel to America. Joseph Smith maintained that he had received the gold plates from an angel called Moroni in 1827 – though no one has ever set eyes on the plates themselves. At any rate Smith became priest and prophet of the new faith and in 1830 founded in Fayette, New York State, the Church of Jesus Christ of Latter Day Saints – the Mormons. After a number of unsuccessful attempts he founded a settlement at Nauvoo, Illinois, in 1841. The new sect attracted much criticism and hostility, particularly on account of its practice of polygamy, to which Smith reacted intransigently and violently. After the destruction of the premises of a local newspaper that had attacked him Joseph Smith and his brother Hyrum were arrested and lynched in prison by an angry mob. His successor Brigham Young (1801–77) led the Mormons from Illinois by way of Missouri to Utah.

John Sutter (1803–80)

John Sutter, "King of New Helvetia", was a character who could have come to the fore only in the pioneering days of the United States. Originally called Johann August Sutter, he was of Swiss origin but was born in Germany. Fleeing from bankruptcy, he emigrated to North America in 1834, and within a short time had acquired a vast area of land (50,000 acres) in California, then almost uninhabited. He named the territory New Helvetia and styled himself its king. In 1848 the first Californian gold was found near its capital, Sacramento, which Sutter had founded, and during the subsequent gold rush Sutter's model farming settlement of New Helvetia was totally devastated. After California joined the Union he was unable to establish a legal claim to his territory and spent the rest of his life in poverty, a ruined man.

George Washington (1732–99)

The leading figure in American history, commander in chief during the War of Independence and first President of the United States, was born on the estate of Pope's Creek in Virginia, the son of English immigrants. After working for some time as a land surveyor he served in the British forces against the French in the Ohio valley (1753) and in securing the western frontier of Virginia (1755). In 1774–5 he was a delegate at the first Continental Congress in Philadelphia, and on the outbreak of the War of Independence was appointed commander in chief of the "continental" forces. In spite of inferior numbers and inadequate equipment he won the victory at Yorktown, Virginia, in 1781 that decided the war in favour of the Americans. Nominated by the Constitutional Convention in 1787, he was appointed first President of the United States in 1789. During his two terms of office he established a national currency and a national bank, a postal service, a customs system and patent and copyright protection, reorganised the army and the fleet, founding the West Point Military Academy in New York State, and ordered the construction of fortifications on the east coast and the western frontier. In 1796 he withdrew to his Mount Vernon estate, setting out his political testament in his farewell address.

The film actor John Wayne was born Marion Michael Morrison, the son of a chemist in Winterset, Iowa, but was given the name under which he became famous by the film director Raoul Walsh. His break-through came with "Stagecoach" (1939). Thereafter, in a succession of films like "Red River", "El Dorado", "Rio Grande" and "The Sons of Katie Elder", under such directors as Howard Hawks, John Ford and Henry Hathaway Wayne, known as the "Duke", became the archetypal man of the west. He was less successful in excursions into other fields (as Genghis Khan, as Police Officer Brannigan, or as an officer in the super-patriotic Vietnam film "The Green Berets", which was panned by the critics), for without cowboy gear it became clear that John Wayne's best role was the hard-hitting tough guy – himself.

John Wayne
(1907–79)

The Wright brothers of Dayton, Ohio, had a fac-tory manufacturing printing machinery and bicy-cles, but after learning about Otto Lilienthal's gliding experiments began to experiment with gliders, carrying out their first flights at Kitty Hawk, on the Outer Banks of North Carolina, in 1901 and 1902. Their real ambition, however, was to construct and fly the first powered aircraft. On December 17th 1903 they achieved the first powered flight in history, in which their plane covered a distance of 118 feet in 12 seconds – not a great distance, but nevertheless a revolutionary technological achievement. The brothers were finally granted a patent for their flying machine in 1906. In 1908 Wilbur Wright carried out a series of exhibition flights in Europe; in 1909 Orville Wright passed the first official flying test; and in the same year the brothers won a United States Army con-tract for the world's first military plane.

Wilbur Wright
(1867–1912)
Orville Wright
(1871–1948)

Culture

Art

Apart from the art and the crafts of the indigenous Indian peoples American art is as young as the nation itself. The Puritan founding fathers, who tended in any event to be disapproving of art, had their hands full in the early days of settlement with the practical requirements of everyday life. The first artistic products were therefore purely utilitarian objects. Nevertheless American painting has a considerably longer history than is generally believed in Europe, where it is generally identified with art since the Second World War, when American artists began to set the tone in the international art scene with Abstract Expressionism, Pop Art and Minimal Art: that there was any American art before then is not commonly realised.

American art achieved a first flowering in the 19th c., when the structures of the state were being consolidated and the towns were growing rapidly. During this period landscape painting – influenced by the great expanses of unspoiled natural landscape in North America – developed as a genre in its own right. American sculpture, on the other hand, remained traditional, becoming of greater interest only in the 20th c. The earliest American paintings, in the late 18th c., took the form of portraits, mainly representing the sitters as they liked to see themselves.

Painting

Most painters of the 18th and early 19th centuries either came from Britain or at any rate were strongly influenced by British art. In art as in other fields the mother country only gradually lost its influence. The artistic centre of the United States in this period was Boston. The leading painters were John Singleton Copley (1738–1815), John Trumbull (1756–1843), Charles Wilson Peale (1741–1827), Benjamin West (1738–1820) and Gilbert Charles Stuart (1755–1828), who painted several portraits of Washington (including the one that appears on the one-dollar bill). J.S. Copley ranks as the "father of American painting", and some of his pictures, like the portrait of the American hero Paul Revere, are familiar to every schoolchild in the United States. On the outbreak of the War of Independence, in 1775, Copley and his family moved to London, where he lived for the rest of his life. Benjamin West, well known as a historical painter, moved to Britain in 1763 and in 1792 succeeded Sir Joshua Reynolds as President of the Royal Academy. It is symptomatic of early American painting that its best known representatives were more successful in Europe than in their home country.

Landscape

Landscape painting became of increasing importance in the 19th c. After the War of Independence Americans were concerned in art as in other matters to cut loose from Europe and in particular from Britain. The new genre of landscape painting satisfied the American need for artistic independence. (In Europe too landscape painting developed as a separate genre in the 19th c.) The unspoiled American wilderness was depicted as a kind of Garden of Eden in which the ideal society could be brought into being. Favoured compositions were mountain and lake landscapes, panoramas of the American wilderness, forest scenes and coastal

Albert Bierstadt: "The Last of the Buffallo"

scenery. Representations of everyday life and pictures of Indians also began to appear. The artists who practised this last type of genre painting, rather in the manner of naïve art, were mostly self-taught. Among them were Edward Hicks (1780–1849), George Caleb Bingham (1811–79) and Charles Wimar (1818–62).

Landscape painting was practised particularly by the Hudson River school, with its artistic centre in New York (which lies on the Hudson). It established itself around 1825 and reached its peak in the middle of the century. The "father of American landscape painting" was Thomas Cole (1801–48), an Englishman who emigrated to the United States at the age of 18. He studied at the Pennsylvania Academy of Fine Arts while working in his father's business but was otherwise self-taught, like many American artists. In 1825 he moved to New York, where his paintings of scenery on the Hudson River – which were to give the school its name – soon attracted attention. Cole was friendly with two other important representatives of the Hudson River school, Asher B. Durand (1796–1886) and Frederic Edwin Church (1826–1900). Durand's painting "Kindred Spirits" (1849), one of his best known pictures, is a memorial to Thomas Cole: it shows Cole and the writer William Cullen Bryant contemplating a grandiose landscape. "Mount Katahdin" (the highest peak in the state of Maine; 1853) and "Niagara Falls" (1857) are two of F.E. Church's best known works.

Fritz H. Lane (1804–65), the best known American seascape painter, was, like Church, trained exclusively in America: he regarded study visits to Europe as unnecessary. Although artists of this period were fascinated by the American west, most of their landscapes were painted in their own part of the country, the east coast. Albert Bierstadt (1830–1902) was the first artist to concentrate, in the 1860s and 70s, on the landscapes of the west. Of German origin, he came to the United States with his parents at the age of two, and apart from two years at the Düsseldorf Academy was self-taught. In 1859 he took part in an expedition to the Rocky Mountains that produced a rich harvest of landscape paintings. The success of his landscapes brought him a commission for two historical paintings in the Capitol in Washington,

"Discovery of the Hudson" and "Landing of the Vizcaino Expedition in Monterey, 1601".

Towards the end of the 19th c. American landscape painting once again came under European – mainly French – influence, from the Barbizon school and from the Impressionists. One member of the group was George Innes (1825–94), who had been trained in Europe. William Merritt Chase (1849–1916) and above all Mary Cassatt (1844–1926), a close friend of Degas, had a particular affinity with the Impressionists. The development of abstract painting is foreshadowed in the landscapes of James McNeill Whistler (1834–1903), one of the most innovative and most controversial painters of his time. Although an American, he was trained in Paris

Andy Warhol: "Ethel Scull"

and spent much of his life in London. Another London resident was the American painter John Singer Sargent (1856–1925), who received numerous commissions in the United States, including murals in Harvard's Wildener Library and the Boston Museum of Fine Arts and Public Library.

Ash-can school

In the early years of the 20th c. the Ash-can school – so called because its members frequently depicted the poverty and misery of life in the slums in a spirit of social criticism – grew up round Robert Henri (1865–1929).

The Ashcan school reached its culmination in the Hard Realism of the 1930s. In addition to Max Beckmann, an immigrant from Germany, the members of this school included Ben Shan (1898–1969), Philip Evergood (1901–73) and Jack Levine (b. 1915). A realism of a very distinctive type is seen in the pictures of Edward Hopper (1882–1967), who frequently took as his subject the loneliness of man in modern society.

Abstract Expressionism

After 1945 Abstract Expressionism came to the fore, with Jackson Pollock as its leading representative. The picture was now not only the expression of an artistic idea but was also affected by the accidental combination of painting technique, colour and technical aids. Other members of this school were Robert Rauschenberg, Willem de Kooning, Arshile Gorky and Franz Kline.

Minimal Art

Abstract Expressionism was succeeded by Minimal Art, which sought to reduce the various art forms to a minimum.

Pop Art

Perhaps the most controversial art trend of the post-war period was Pop Art, whose best known exponent was Andy Warhol. Other practitioners of Pop Art included Roy Lichtenstein with his outsize pictures in the style of the comic strip, Jasper Johns, Richard Lindner, Claes Oldenburg and George Segal. Oldenburg and Segal became best known for their sculpture.

During the 1970s there developed, in reaction against total artistic freedom, the school of Hyperrealism, which aimed at a photographically exact reproduction of reality. Among its best known representatives were Richard Estes and Howard Kanovitz.

Hyperrealism

Sculpture

Right into the 20th c. American sculptors showed a marked predilection for realistic monumental sculpture. The best known example is the Statue of Liberty (1871–84), by the Alsatian sculptor Frédéric-Auguste Bartholdi. Others are the Jefferson Memorial (by Daniel Chester French, 1943) and the Lincoln Memorial (by Rudolph Evans, 1915–22). The climax of this trend is to be seen at Mount Rushmore, South Dakota, where from 1927 onwards Gutzom Borglum and his son Lincoln hewed from the living rock figures of Presidents George Washington, Thomas Jefferson, Abraham Lincoln and Theodore Roosevelt. This tradition ontinues to this day. In South Dakota sculptors have been working on a gigantic carving of the Sioux chief Crazy Horse. Larger than Mount Rushmore or the Sphinx, the idea and design for it came from Korzcak Ziolowski, who died in 1982.

Under the influence of émigrés from Europe American sculpture enjoyed a considerable upswing in the course of the 20th c. and produced a number of new native sculptors. Among the most important émigrés were the Russians Naum Gabo (1890–1977) and Alexander Archipenko (1887–1964).

Emigré art

The moving spirit of modern American sculpture was Alexander Calder (1898–1976), who achieved world fame with his mobiles. David Smith (1906–65) became known for his metal sculpture. Among more recent sculptors are Edward Kienholz and George Segal. Asian influence can be seen in the work of the Los Angeles sculptor Isamu Noguchi. Jeff Koons, meanwhile, has made a name for himself with his colourfully-kitschy-to-semi-pornographic works. A very special position is occupied by Christo, famous for his spectacular "packaging" of whole areas of landscape, bringing his work into the category of Land Art, the foremost representative of which is Walter de Maria.

Modern

Photography

With the invention of photography a new art form soon developed. By the 1920s photography had been recognised in the United States as an artistic genre in its own right; among its most notable exponents were Alfred Stieglitz, lifetime companion of the famous painter Georgia O'Keeffe, and Edward Streichen, who together ran in New York one of the first galleries devoted to photography. Man Ray, Duane Michals, Paul Strand and Walter Evans were among other artistic personalities who worked in the new medium. The history of photography is now taught in the universities as part of the history of art – a situation that is still exceptional in Europe – and there are photographic collections in many American museums.

Architecture

While American painting and sculpture have been for the most part influenced by Europe, architecture has become the distinctively

Architecture

American form of artistic expression. During the second half of the 19th c. in particular many cities in the United States were in process of rapid growth and accordingly attracted gifted young architects. A new type of building, the skyscraper, now came into being. Among the most lucrative commissions for young architects were the huge new office and commercial blocks now required, for the exteriors of which a whole new language of forms was developed.

Domestic

Residential buildings, on the other hand, remained for many years traditional in style, following neoclassical or neo-Gothic models. Typical examples are the shingle-clad façades of the frequently bizarre wooden buildings on the north-east coast (the "shingle style") and the neoclassical imitations in the tradition of Thomas Jefferson's buildings in Virginia, in particular the University of Virginia in Charlottesville and Jefferson's own mansion of Monticello. Houses of this type still set the pattern of many American residential areas.

Frank Lloyd Wright

A distinctive modern architecture began to emerge only about 1900 with the houses built by Frank Lloyd Wright in Chicago. He remained, however, an isolated figure: most people preferred houses in eclectic styles. Nevertheless Frank Lloyd Wright is one of the few architects of his period whose influence has continued into our own time. His houses establish a unity between nature and architecture: a striking example of this is the house Falling Water at Bear Run, Pennsylvania, built in 1936. He was not afraid to leave natural materials like stone and timber visible and to use them as a stylistic feature – an idea that is now taken as a matter of course but at the beginning of the 20th c. was revolutionary. He was one of the most creative architects in history. One of his late works of the mid 20th c., the Guggenheim Museum in New York, is more like a work of sculpture than a building; and the interior likewise bears witness to its architect's very personal interpretation of architecture.

Skyscrapers

An important development in the history of architecture was the appearance of the skyscrapers that have become such characteristic features of American cities. Their construction was made possible by a number of technological innovations, new building methods like the use of steel and concrete, and Elisha Otis's invention of the passenger lift (elevator). The steel-frame structure made possible the construction of higher buildings than did traditional methods and materials. The earliest high-rise buildings were erected in New York in the 1870s. Rising to heights of between 245 ft and 295 ft, they were still, by present-day standards, relatively low. Among the first such skyscrapers were the Tribune Building and Western Union Building in New York City, neither of which has survived.

The first half of the 20th c. saw the erection of such famous skyscrapers as the Empire State Building and the Chrysler Building. Later there was a move away from the type of tower block tapering towards the top in favour of square or slab-shaped buildings. The Sears Tower in Chicago (1453 ft; 110 floors) and the twin towers of the World Trade Center in New York (1368ft; 110 floors) are at present the highest office blocks in the world.

Architectural centres

As with painting and sculpture, the main architectural centres were originally Boston and New York. Towards the end of the 19th c., however, Chicago took over as the capital of American architecture, with such architects as Daniel H. Burnham (1846–1912), John Wellburn Root (1850–91), William LeBaron Jenney (1832–1907), Louis H. Sullivan (1856–1924) and his pupil Frank Lloyd Wright (1867–1959) all working there. After a great fire in 1871 and the construction of the railroad

Chicago – the Wrigley Building and Tribune Tower ▶

Architecture

Chicago became an important traffic junction and a commercial centre of major importance, and the population of the city doubled within ten years. The rapidly growing city attracted many young and talented architects, including the young Louis H. Sullivan, who had received his architectural training in Boston. His famous statement that "form follows function" was later much quoted and is said to have influenced the Bauhaus school. In contrast to later Bauhaus buildings, however, Sullivan's buildings have rich floral ornament and can be seen as a Chicago version of art nouveau. Five or six years before art–nouveau ornament appeared in Europe Sullivan used similar forms of ornament. One of his best known buildings, designed in association with his partner Dankmar Adler, is the Wainwright Building in St Louis (1890–1). In spite of its ornament the building is much more modern in effect than Sullivan's Auditorium Building in Chicago, built a few years earlier, which still shows neo-Romanesque stylistic influences.

One of the most important American architects of the 19th c. was Henry H. Richardson (1838–86). He worked for some time for Théodore Labrouste, brother of the more famous Henri Labrouste. Labrouste was one of the first architects to use steel-framing. Richardson's buildings were technically innovative but still employed traditional forms, mainly Romanesque as in the Marshall Field Wholesale Store in Chicago (not preserved).

Architecture of the 1930s

American architecture received important new impulses in the 1930s that led to the formation of new schools and gave the United States a leading place in modern architecture. Great architects like Mies van der Rohe, Walter Gropius, Richard Joseph Neutra and the Finns Eliel and Eero Saarinen emigrated to the United States and gave the International Style almost a monopoly position in American architecture over the next two decades. From 1938 Mies van der Rohe taught at the Illinois Institute of Technology in Chicago and built a number of high-rise buildings in Chicago and New York.

Postwar: the International Style

The influence of Mies van der Rohe can be detected particularly in the work of Philip Johnson, Gordon Sunshaft and Eero Saarinen. Johnson was associated with Mies van der Rohe in the design of the Seagram Building (1956–8) in New York, and he made his name with his "Glass House" in New Canaan, Connecticut, with walls of huge steel-framed glass panels on a clinker-brick base. Johnson's design is very clearly in the tradition of Mies van der Rohe's buildings. The almost exactly contemporary Farnsworth House in Plano, Illinois, shows how the two architects each inspired the other.

Walter Gropius taught at Harvard University and influenced such architects as Paul Rudolph, Hugh Stubbins and his pupil I.M. Pei. The Graduate Center in Harvard was built to his design.

One of the largest architectural firms of the postwar period was Skidmore, Owings and Merrill, who established their reputation in the design of complex office and commercial buildings and through the development of a particular type of steel construction for high-rise buildings (Lever Building, New York, 1952; Sears Tower, Chicago, 1972–4).

New trends

In the mid-1950s, with the exhaustion of the reduced language of forms of the International Style, there was a quest for new possibilities of expression – for example in the work of Minoru Yamasaki, who along with Emery Roth and Sons built the World Trade Center (1966–73) in New York, and I.M. Pei, who designed the remarkable East Wing of the National Gallery in Washington, DC, a building that has something of the effect of sculpture with its simple forms and smooth, luxurious-seeming surface treatment. In sharp contrast are the buildings of Paul Rudolph, an exponent of the New Brutalism, who experimented with concrete as a building material. Characteristic of this school were the rough surface treatment of the concrete buildings and their often fortress-like aspect.

One of the pioneers of postmodernism was Robert Venturi, who in the 1960s had rejected the principles of modern architecture and argued for the separation of function and decoration. Postmodern architecture, like the Historicism of the late 19th c., returned to traditional forms (columns, porticoes) and admitted the use of colour and decoration. A characteristic feature, however, was the playful and sometimes almost ironic application of traditional forms, which thus were given a fresh interpretation. The former AT & T Building (1984) in New York, designed by Philip Johnson, is considered the first example of postmodern architecture.

Postmodernism

In sharp contrast to postmodernism, in the late 1960s and early 70s, were the "New York Five", a group of young architects led by Richard Meier who were influenced by the rationalism and functionalism of the 1920s and in particular by Le Corbusier. For their elegant buildings, invariably faced in white (hence their nickname of the "Whites", in opposition to the "Greys"), they favoured the use of glass, steel and concrete.

New York Five

In the 1980s the German-born architect Helmut Jahn, who from 1981 headed the Murphy and Jahn partnership, revolutionised the construction of high-rise buildings, combining the technological advances in steel-framing with a playful use of postmodern forms. His design for the Frankfurt Exhibition Tower extended his reputation outside the United States, especially in his native Germany, Jahn thus maintains the tradition of United States architects whos imprint spans the globe – whether in the Potsdamer Platz in Berlin or the Basque city of Bilbao, where Frank Gehry's spectacular Guggenheim Museum breaks new ground.

Helmut Jahn

Literature

The myths and legends of the Indians were transmitted by word of mouth. Written literature first appeared at the time of British colonisation, at the beginning of the 17th c. It mainly comprised theological works, such as the first book published in the Puritan colonies, the "Bay Psalm Book" (1640).

When the ideas of the Enlightenment reached the American colonies in the 18th c. the subject matter of books became increasingly political. Alexander Hamilton (1757–1804), Thomas Paine (1737–1809) and Thomas Jefferson (1743–1826; see Famous People), one of the authors of the Declaration of Independence, wrote polemical works supporting the American striving for independence. Benjamin Franklin (1706–90; see Famous People), whose autobiography, with its stress on rationalism and individualism, was one of the most important works of the revolutionary period, promoted the development of an independent American literature by establishing and supporting magazines and newspapers. The first American theatres were built in Philadelphia, New York and Charleston before the Revolution, though their repertoire consisted mainly of works by British authors.

19th-century prose

It was only after the Revolution that a few American authors were able to make a living by writing – in each case only for a short time. The first professional writer in the United States was Charles Brockden Brown (1771–1810), whose Gothic novel "Wieland" was published in 1799. The first American works to achieve success in Europe were the fairytale-like stories of the early Romantic writer Washington Irving (1783–1859) and the adventure novels of James Fenimore Cooper (1789–1851).

The first major literary movement in the new country was

Transcendentalism

105

The first page of the manuscript of "Uncle Tom's Cabin

Transcendentalism, an influential representative of which was the essayist and philosopher Ralph Waldo Emerson (1803–82). Although Emerson regarded himself as a thoroughly religious man he rejected organised religion, believing instead in a "super-reality", the presence of God in man and nature. With his conviction that the individual must rely on intuitive knowledge and reject any adaptation to the ideas of society he reflected on an intellectual level the individualistic trend of American ideology. He created a philosophy in which the individual and not religious doctrine, tradition or society is the measure of all things.

Another Transcendentalist was Henry David Thoreau (1817–62), whose idea of civil disobedience – the doctrine of peaceful resistance – influenced such leading 20th c. figures as Gandhi and Martin Luther King Jr. Margaret Fuller (1810–50), a pioneer of the feminist movement, was editor of the Transcendentalist journal the "Dial" and an inspirer of other writers of the period. Nathaniel Hawthorne (1804–64) is believed to have taken her as the model for Zenobia in "The Blithedale Romance" (1852). With this generation of writers the United States achieved its first literary flowering and began to distance itself from English literature. Nathaniel Hawthorne, one of the leading literary figures of his day, stressed in the foreword to "The House of the Seven Gables" the writer's entitlement to go beyond the purely realistic treatment of reality. He argued for a literature that should represent individual truths in symbolic and allegorical fashion.

Edgar Allan Poe (see Famous People) was another writer who detached himself from the English tradition in tales and poems that draw their horror from extreme conditions of the human psyche. Both in practice and in theory he made a major contribution to the development of the short story.

The greatest literary achievement of this period was the novel by Herman Melville (1819–91), "Moby Dick" (1851), a masterpiece in which the mythic theme of Captain Ahab's obsession with the capture of the White Whale is set against a realistic contemporary background of whaling. In his own time Melville was better known for his South Seas novels, and "Moby Dick" was rediscovered only at the beginning of the 20th c.

The publication of the famous novel by Harriet Beecher Stowe (1811–96), "Uncle Tom's Cabin", in 1852 was not a purely literary event; it also gave a decisive stimulus to the move for the abolition of slavery. With its moving depiction of the life of slaves it made a major contribution to public awareness of the miseries of slavery and thus to the course of the conflict between Northern and Southern states. The novel occupies a unique situation in American literary history and must rank as one of the most influential works of the 19th c.

After the Civil War the angle of vision of American literature became narrower and sharper. The subject matter was now regional, not transcendental; the treatment was predominantly realist, not allegorical. Every part of the country had its chroniclers, who mostly depicted the life, the people and the dialect of a particular region. Sarah Orne Jewett (1849–1909) and Mary E. Wilkins Freeman (1852–1930) concentrated on depicting the life of small New England towns in short stories.

Kate Chopin (1851–1904) described the life of people of French origin, Cajuns and Creoles, in Louisiana. Her novel "The Awakening" (1899), the story of a married woman who slowly discovers her sexuality, caused a scandal from which she never recovered. Bret Harte (1836–1902) depicted the rough life of California for curious readers in the East. Mark Twain (1835–1910; see Famous People) wrote stories about the west and life on the Mississippi; his most famous work, the "Adventures of Huckleberry Finn" (1884), is a classic of American literature.

With the beginnings of industrialisation after the Civil War the first forerunners of the great novels of social criticism of the turn of the 19th c. began to appear, like "Life in the Iron Mills" by Rebecca Harding Davis (1831–1910) and "The Silent Partner" by Elizabeth Stuart Phelps (1844–1911). These two writers belonged to a realist tradition that had more in common with the works of their European contemporaries than with Hawthorne and Melville.

Among the leading figures of this period was Henry James (1843–1916) who, however, felt himself more at home in the intellectual atmosphere of Europe than in his own country, and a year before his death became a British citizen. Although he made his name as a realist, his works became increasingly experimental in the course of his career. His narrative and technical innovations paved the way for the development of the modern psychological novel; and some of the great English and Irish writers of recent times, like Virginia Woolf and James Joyce, owe a great deal to Henry James.

In the second half of the 19th c. American lyric poetry also turned in new directions. In his "Leaves of Grass" Walt Whitman (1819–92) revealed a completely new form and subject matter reflecting the immeasurable landscapes of America and the individualism of Americans. Emily Dickinson (1830–86), on the other hand, led the life of a hermit and wrote poems that with their brief, precise observations were at the opposite extreme from Whitman's excesses.

While American poetry, novels and short stories had towards the end of the 19th c. established their place in the literature of the world, American drama remained of little significance until the early years of the 20th c. Around the turn of the 19th c., however, William Vaughn Moody (1869–1910) wrote plays that had a decisive influence on later developments. Before the success of his play "The Great Divide" the dramatic repertoire in North America consisted mainly of English imports and

Regionalism

Social criticism

Realism

Poetry

Drama

adaptations of successful prose works. The works of dramatists like David Belasco (1859–1931), who in 1905 founded the Belasco Theater in New York, and Susan Glaspell (1882–1948), who was particularly concerned with the studio theatre, made possible the development of an independent theatrical culture in subsequent decades.

20th-century Naturalists

The economic upswing of the late 19th c. and the peopling of the whole continent, now largely completed, gave American literature round the turn of the 19th c. a new character. The problems of industrialisation, the flood of new immigrants and the consequent formation of slums provided material for novels of social criticism by the "Naturalists" Theodore Dreiser (1871–1945), Stephen Crane (1871–1900), Frank Norris (1870–1902) and Jack London (1876–1916). Influenced by Zola and a philosophy of determinism, the Naturalists mostly depicted the dark side of the American dream.

The critical attitude displayed in the satirical novels of Sinclair Lewis (1885–1951), the first American to win the Nobel Prize for literature, and the denunciatory works of Upton Sinclair (1878–1968) is derived from the Naturalists. A more temperate realism is seen in the works of Willa Cather (1873–1947), Ellen Glasgow (1874–1945) and John O'Hara (1905–70).

Lost Generation

The results of industrialisation and the events of the First World War shattered American optimism. A new cynicism found expression in the works of writers of the "Lost Generation", as Gertrude Stein (1874–1946) called them. Among them were F. Scott Fitzgerald (1896–1940), with his depictions of the wild but empty social life of the 1920s, and Ernest Hemingway (1898–1961; see Famous People), whose rootless heroes sought to preserve their dignity in defeat. Henry Miller (1891–1980) wrote novels of such meticulous detail in the depiction of sexual encounters that for many years they were banned in the United States and Britain.

Imagists

This generation of writers, to which the poets Ezra Pound (1885–1972) and T.S. Eliot (1888–1965) also belonged, was born in the last decades of the 19th c. and grew up in isolationist prewar America, only to be confronted with the reality of the First World War. The disillusion expressed in the works of these writers is encapsulated in Eliot's "Waste Land". Harriet Monroe's journal "Poetry", in which Eliot's first works were published, proclaimed a revolution in the art of poetry. As an element of

Ernest Hemingway

the Modern movement in literature, the poetry of the Imagists – an important member of whom, in addition to Pound and Eliot, was H.D. (Hilda Doolittle, 1886–1961) – was deliberately experimental. These poets explored new directions, particularly in the form of their poetry. Carl Sandburg (1878–1967) and Robert Frost (1874–1963), although belonging to the same generation, were less concerned with form than with their subject matter – the language, life and dreams of America and its people.

The novelist William Faulkner (1897–1962), a pioneer of modern narrative technique, also belongs to the Modern movement. In his novels he depicts, with sympathetic insight and philosophical depth, the history and life of the southern states and assesses the consequences of slavery.

While the Modern movement was essentially apolitical – T.S. Eliot was a conservative, Pound a convinced fascist – John Dos Passos's (1896–1970) trilogy of novels "U.S.A." was driven by socialist commitment. During the 1930s – the "Red Decade" – political commitment was widespread in the literary scene. Red Decade

American drama in particular, which with Eugene O'Neill (1888–1953) at last attained international significance, was imbued with social consciousness. O'Neill's plays marked the beginning of a flowering of the drama in the United States; after him came Thornton Wilder (1897–1975) and Tennessee Williams (1911–83).

A conservative reaction against left-wing trends in the intellectual scene was expressed during the 1930s by a group of writers from the southern states who published mainly in a journal called "The Fugitive" and accordingly were known as the Fugitives. Writers belonging to the school of "New Criticism", particularly John Crowe Ransom (1888–1974) and Robert Penn Warren (1905–89), exerted influence on academic circles. Eliot's theory of the autonomy of the poetical imagination, which reflected a profound disillusion with politics and social reality, was the basis of the New Criticism, which for many years determined the intellectual climate in America. New Criticism

Partly as a result of the regional pride that the New Critics were concerned to promote, and also because of Faulkner's reputation, the southern states became in the 1940s an important centre of literary production. Led by Katherine Anne Porter (1890–1980), a group of women writers came to the fore who depicted predominantly grotesque and abnormal aspects of life; among them were Eudora Welty (b. 1909), Carson McCullers (1917–67) and Flannery O'Connor (1925–64). Other representatives of this "Southern Gothic" school were Walker Percy (1916–90) and Truman Capote (1924–84). Southern Gothic

The quest for meaning in modern American life became the most important theme for the writers of the 1950s and 60s. In 1958 Vladimir Nabokov (1899–1977), who had emigrated from Russia in 1919 and lived in the United States since 1940, published his novel "Lolita", a satirical consideration of American society that brought him worldwide success and scandal. Other works of social criticism were the early novels of Norman Mailer (b. 1923) and Ken Kesey (b. 1935), two writers who returned in their writings to the individualist trends of American ideology. The writers of the "Beat Generation" – Jack Kerouac (1922–69) in prose and Alan Ginsberg (b. 1926) in poetry – also saw the only possibility of individual fulfilment outside the compulsions of society. Many publications of this period were lightly fictionalised autobiography. The important thing was the "authenticity" of the work, and the writers were concerned to achieve an exact reproduction of their experiences. The process of adolescence became a genre on its own, and weltschmerz an everyday matter. The prototype in this field was J.D. Salinger's (b. 1919) Postwar period

Literature

"Catcher in the Rye". While Saul Bellow (b. 1915), Bernard Malamud (1914–86) and Philip Roth (b. 1933) gave expression to the problems of (usually Jewish) intellectuals, John Updike (b. 1932) and John Cheever (b. 1912) depicted the monotony of everyday life from the viewpoint of the white middle classes. Joyce Carol Oates (b. 1938) repeatedly depicted the violence of life at all levels of American society.

Black writers

Like some of the Jewish writers mentioned above, many black writers also produced autobiographical novels. The novel "Invisible Man" by Ralph Ellison (b. 1914) describes how attempts by black Americans to live in the white culture finally end in the "invisibility" of the protagonist. Richard Wright (1908–60), James Baldwin (1924–87) and Maya Angelou (b. 1928), in both fictional and non-fictional confessions, all made the quest for their own identity the central theme of their writing.

Women's writing

In the 1970s Erica Jong (b. 1943) and Marilyn French (b. 1929) did for women what Bellow and Updike had done for their own particular social class: with light self-irony they gave expression to weltschmerz from a very particular, feminine, point of view.

New Journalism

Truman Capote and Norman Mailer carried the quest for authenticity to its extreme, combining journalism and fiction in an experimental fashion. Tom Wolfe (b. 1931), one of the leading representatives of the so-called "New Journalism", sought to achieve a new type of social novel through the mingling of fiction and reportage in his hugely successful novel "The Bonfire of the Vanities".

Irrealism

In parallel to the "non-fictional novels" there developed another trend, marked by unashamed delight in story-telling, in which the authors explore unrealistic and even unreal premisses. Thomas Pynchon (b. 1937), John Barth (b. 1930), John Hawkes (b. 1925), Kurt Vonnegut Jr (b. 1922), Joseph Heller (b. 1923) and Don DeLillo (b. 1936) depict a world in which paranoia is normal, logic is turned on its head and black humour is the only possible reaction to the lunacy of everyday life.

Black women writers

A new generation of black women writers were not content with autobiographical accounts of the miseries of life. The works of Toni Morrison (b. 1931) and Alice Walker (b. 1944) do not disregard historic and social injustices but still find some hope of a better future. With best-sellers like Walker's "The Color Purple" and Morrison's "Beloved" the African-American experience and literature move into the mainstream of American culture.

Current trends

It is inevitably difficult to categorise contemporary literature. Among the trends of the moment are postmodernism, minimalism, magical realism and metahistory; but if there is one overall trend it is perhaps the turning away from traditional realist forms. Of the movements just mentioned only minimalism is thoroughly realist. John Barth takes the impossibility of reproducing reality as a ground for concerning himself mainly with other literary phenomena, and thus deliberately draws attention to the fictional character of the novel. John Gardner (1933–82), in his "Grendel", retells the Old English epic "Beowulf" from the point of view of the monster Grendel. The crazy fictional games of Tom Robbins (b. 1936) appear repeatedly in the best-seller lists. In E.L. Doctorow's (b. 1931) "Ragtime" the traditional cultural history of the turn of the 19th c. is rewritten from top to bottom. "The Woman Warrior", by Maxine Hong Kingston (b. 1940), blurs the boundary between fiction and autobiography. Lisa Alther (b. 1944) parodies the autobiographical novel in "Kinflicks". During the 1980s some authors who hitherto had traditionally been realists joined this trend. John Updike's "The Witches of Eastwick" was a farce about witches in New England in the sixties, and Joyce Carol Oates took over ideas from

Magical Realism and played with the literary conventions of the family saga in her novel "Bellefleur".

Recent American plays, on the other hand, have been traditional in form, though not in content: for example Harvey Fierstein's (b. 1954) depiction of the dangerous life of a transvestite in the "Torch Song Trilogy" and Marsha Norman's shattering account of a mother-daughter relationship in "Night Mother". In Tony Kushner's play on AIDS, "Angels in America", however, the provocative plot is combined with a new form. Sam Shepard (b. 1943) is one of the most productive and most important contemporary playwrights in America.

Drama

And finally homage must be paid to the crime story representing a major United Statets contribution to literature, though perhaps not its most popular with their protagonists Sam Spade and Philip Marlowe, Dashiell Hammett (1894–1961), founder of the "hard boiled school", and Raymond Chandler (1888–1959), gave birth to the figure of the hard-bitten city detective whose only weapon against the criminal underworld is cynicism – not hard to recognise as a vehicle for social criticism. Such novels, and the films based on them, especially the ones starring Humphrey Bogart ("The Maltese Falcon", "The Big Sleep"), shaped the genre which lives on in the United States today through authors like Kinky Friedman.

Crime fiction

Music

American popular music

The history of popular music was for decades identical with the history of 20th c. American music. Light music produced outside the United States was usually a mere imitation of American originals. This dominance was challenged only in the mid-1960s by the Beatles, but even they originally copied Chuck Berry, Buddy Holly and Little Richard.

Surprisingly, the genuinely American music, the music of the indigenous inhabitants, played no part in the development of the different styles. The origins of the music of the United States lie mainly in Europe, Africa and the Caribbean – brought by immigrants and slaves. A musical identity had first to emerge from the crucible of cultures alien to one another. Most of the immigrants brought with them their own folk music, which had frequently to be shielded from alien influences. Only when the Irish, the British, the Poles and the Germans felt themselves to be Americans and the former slaves were also permitted to become Americans could an independent American musical tradition develop.

The distinction made in Europe between serious music and light music could not establish itself in the United States, at any rate so far as the styles that had developed in America were concerned. It was not until rock'n'roll came along that the strict separation between "normal" music and "race music" could be relaxed. Until then records by black performers were produced only for a market of black people – though the labels established for the purpose were still subsidiaries of white record companies. "Jungle music", with its frequent sexual allusions, was regarded as inferior and suspect. This cultural racism compelled the blacks to seek their own musical identity. They themselves were much less narrow-minded: they had an ear for European harmonies, they adopted many of the European instruments that had previously been unknown to them and combined them with their own favourite instrument, the drum. There thus came into being a form of music that for the first time combined rhythm and melody on an equal basis.

Black music

It don't mean a thing, if it ain't got that swing: Jazz

Jazz was not "invented" solely by black musicians, though the performers who formed its various styles were mainly coloured. The frequently cited characteristic "blue notes" were the result of an attempt to reconcile the five-note scale of the African savanna with the European eight-note scale. In addition racial segregation gave rise to hybrid forms like spirituals and the blues – in effect the earliest independent styles produced in North America. Spirituals, already popular in the early 19th c., expressed the deep religious feeling of the blacks. A hundred years later the blues grew out of the spirituals and the work songs or "field-hollers" sung by blacks at work in the fields.

Ragtime

A forerunner of jazz was ragtime, which became popular about the turn of the 19th c.; its characteristic feature was syncopation, and any type of music, from operetta to marches, was grist to its mill. Its outstanding exponent was Scott Joplin, who as early as 1899 had sold more than 400,000 scores of his "Maple Leaf Rag".

New Orleans

Jazz, which is said to have originated in New Orleans, was played about the same time in other parts of the United States – in Memphis (Tennessee) and in Indiana, Texas and Oklahoma. New Orleans, however, is of importance in the history of traditional jazz because it got its name there. Apparently in the mixed French-English language of the Creoles the Biblical Jezebel (a female of very questionable repute) became the "Jazz Belle"; and the bars and brothels of the New Orleans district of Storyville, in which prostitution was legalised in 1898 in order to keep the rest of the city "clean", were the only places where black musicians could find paid employment. Originally only pianists were employed, like Jelly Roll Morton, later famous as a band leader; but the marching bands (still employed to accompany funeral corteges) soon gave rise to small jazz combos that also sought to exploit this lucrative market. The most popular bands were those of Kid Ory and King Oliver, who employed musicians like Louis Armstrong (see Famous People) and Sidney Bechet. The characteristic division of the band into the rhythm group and the wind players who provide the melody was soon accomplished.

Dixieland

The first group to make a record, in 1917, was a white ensemble, the Original Dixieland Jazz Band; and Dixieland is still the name applied to the white interpretation of New Orleans jazz. The compositions of the Dixieland Band, however, were invariably longer than the three minutes' capacity of the wax matrix and had to be reduced in length by being played at a breakneck tempo. This technical problem is the main reason why Dixieland music is still played at such a cracking pace.

The move north

During the First World War large numbers of impoverished land workers moved into the industrial cities of the north and the east coast, and many jazz musicians followed the same route. The new jazz centres were Kansas City (with Count Basie), New York (with Fletcher Henderson and Duke Ellington) and above all Chicago. Here most of the New Orleans musicians met, including Louis Armstrong, who as early as 1928 had preferred his small group, the Hot Five, to the big bands that were steadily growing bigger. In the Prohibition era a small group also had practical advantages: it could be more easily accommodated in a small and crowded speakeasy, it made less noise and so attracted less attention, and in the event of a police raid the instruments could be quickly spirited away.

The big bands

During the 1930s jazz was dominated by big band swing, with Benny Goodman, Woody Herman and Tommy Dorsey among the best known white band leaders. Also very popular was the almost improvisation-free dance music of Paul Whiteman and Glenn Miller (see Famous People), which can only with difficulty be regarded as jazz at all. The more exciting jazz was mostly played by black bands under such leaders as Duke Ellington or Count Basie, who were readier to experiment, allowed more scope for improvisation and solo performances and engaged fine singers like Billie Holiday, who sang with Count Basie before embarking on her solo career.

During the 1940s many performers, finding their creativity restricted by membership of a big band, founded their own small combos. Charlie Parker (saxophone), Dizzy Gillespie (trumpet) and Thelonious Monk (piano) were the best known exponents of bebop, which with its complex rhythms, breakneck tempo and apparently unconnected shreds of melody was totally unsuited for dancing and for many people was difficult to take. Accordingly jazz came increasingly to be regarded as an elite form of music for intellectuals. The cool jazz of the 1950s – a gentler style with relaxed rhythms and a mood of melancholy created by such musicians as Lester Young, Gerry Mulligan and Miles Davis (see Famous People) – did little to change this view. This was followed by the free jazz of such as Ornette Coleman, Cecil Taylor, John Coltrane and Albert Ayler, which broke completely away from all accepted styles and was met with a general lack of appreciation. Jazz now lost its leading role in popular music.

Bebop, cool and free jazz

Jazz lives on, however, in the big bang rock of Blood, Sweat and Tears and the jazz rock of Chick Corea, Herbie Hancock and Pat Metheny, who learnt from the great master Miles Davis. In the mid-eighties, while musicians like the Wynton brothers, Branford Marsalis and the British saxophonist Courtney Pine achieved success with a return to the earliest forms of jazz, established avant-garde artists such as Don Cherry and Pharoah Sanders continued undaunted to record far more exciting albums. With little new impetus being provided by rock music, younger musicians have increasingly turned in recent years to classical jazz. Recordings under the Blue Note label in particular have acquired cult status with the release of many so-called "Rare Grooves" – made possible by advances in computer technology.

Jazz today

How blue can you get?: Blues

In contrast to jazz, which was a city music, the blues were the form of musical expression of the blacks who had remained in the rural South – not only in the Mississippi delta but all over the region; they are better referred to, therefore, as country blues rather than Delta blues. The structure of the blues is simple and relatively inflexible: a system of "call and response" in a pattern that is always the same. The first line of the song, usually a cry or a question, is repeated in the second line and then receives an answer in the third. This structure is similar to that of the spirituals and work songs, in which the audience responded to the soloist or the workers to the foreman.

In the mid-1920s the first records were produced of blues singers like Blind Lemon Jefferson, Tampa Red and Son House, who accompanied themselves on the acoustic guitar. The finest interpreter of this style, ten years later, was Robert Johnson, who legend said had sold his soul to the devil in order to become the leading singer and guitarist of the blues. Unlike his contemporaries, Johnson sang not so much of the injustices of life as of the irrepressible craving for luxury, sex and alcohol and the fear that this would mean literally going to the devil ("Hellhound on my Trail"); and in fact Johnson himself died of poisoning at the age of 25 in mysterious circumstances. Among the many other singers with big and expressive voices and sparse guitar accompaniment were Big Bill

Acoustic blues

113

City Blues played in the clubs of Chicago

Broonzy, Skip James, Leadbelly and Mississippi John Hurt, who travelled around the south singing of unrequited love, hard times and the misfortune of being born with the wrong colour of skin.

Barrelhouse

At the same time there developed out of the boogie-woogie of Meade Lux Lewis and Pinetop Smith a version of the blues that was soon to be heard in every bar and dive. Pianists like Roosevelt Sykes, Memphis Slim and Champion Jack Dupree introduced a fast tempo and demonstrated in the Barrelhouse style that blues did not always need to sound melancholy.

City blues

During the Second World War many blacks again moved north, looking for jobs in the armaments and automobile industries. Chicago now became the centre of modern city blues. Among the musicians who settled there were Muddy Waters, Howlin' Wolf and Elmore James, who recorded classics such as "Hoochie Coochie Man", "Little Red Rooster" and "Dust my Broom".

Rhythm and blues

In order to make themselves heard in the din of the great city they reinforced their music electrically. With bass, percussion, guitar, piano and mouth organ they produced a hard sound: rhythm and blues. B.B. King and T-Bone Walker became famous as virtuosos of the solo guitar. John Lee Hooker demonstrated with items like "Boom Boom" that a stamping boot could be an impressive rhythm instrument.

Orchestral blues and soul

From the mid-1950s it became almost impossible to assign particular performers to this or that school. Most of them followed musicians like Ray Charles and Bo Diddley, who performed blues, rhythm and blues and black rock'n'roll. With the blacks' increasing self-confidence they lost taste for the blues, now seen as antiquated and uncultivated, and too reminiscent of their country origins. In the 1960s the more sophisticated orchestral style of Ray Charles and Sam Cooke was enriched with Gospel elements and developed into soul by Otis Redding and James Brown.

Had it not been for the success of young whites like Alexis Korner and John Mayall in Britain and Johnny Winter, Paul Butterfield and Canned Heat in the United States in winning a new audience, the blues might have fallen into oblivion. Of the grand old men of the blues only B.B. King (b. 1924) and John Lee Hooker (b. 1917) still regularly perform, and hardly a year passes without news of the death of another veteran. Musicians like Robert Cray, Eric Clapton and Stevie Ray Vaughan, the latter dying young, have ensured that the blues do not completely disappear from the hit parade. Happily most of the classics from leading labels such as Chess, Vee Jay, Arhoolie and Bluesway have been reissued on CD. As a result it is now easy to appreciate the extent to which the Rolling Stones for example – who took their name from Muddy Waters – are indebted to Slim Harpo, Jimmy Reed or Willie Dixon.

The blues today

Take me home country roads: Country Music

In 1904 "Harper's Magazine" drew attention to a breed of men living hidden in the hills of Kentucky, Tennessee and Carolina whose music was not only distinctive but, like the men themselves, distinctively American. There, in the recesses of the Appalachians, settlers of Anglo-Saxon origin, mocked as "hillbillies", played their old folksongs, though usually forced by poverty to make do with home-made fiddles, banjos and mandolines. The themes of this "mountain music", like the performers, were ultra-conservative, inspired by the Bible and anti-pleasure. In 1927 Ralph Peer discovered the Carter family and recorded their songs, celebrating their life on the land and the fear of God, often with something of the musical style of Christian chorales. The records sold astonishingly well, and the Carters' style was carried on by singers like Ernest Tubb and Roy Acuff.

Country music at the Grand Ole Opry

Instrumentalists like Bill Monroe, Lester Flatt and Earl Scruggs soon began to play this music at double the normal tempo, creating in items like "Orange Blossom Special" and "Foggy Mountain Breakdown" the bluegrass style, which became the very epitome of traditional country music. It owed its wide popularity to the radio: although the Grand Ole Opry programme transmitted by station WSM in Nashville, Tennessee, was not the earliest radio show devoted to country music it was undoubtedly the most important. First presented in 1925, it gave the

Bluegrass

white music of the southern states a wider audience; it launched many leading performers on their careers (though the young Elvis Presley's appearance on the show was a flop); and it made Nashville "Music City USA", the capital of country music.

Storytellers

Only two days after the Carter family the itinerant white singer Jimmy Rodgers, who had travelled all over the south as a railway worker and had thus seen more of life than the sedentary Carters, made his first record. His "Blue Yodel" sold half a million copies right off the reel. His example was followed by the "Storytellers", from Hank Williams, Johnny Cash and Merle Haggard to the "Outlaws", Willie Nelson and Waylon Jennings.

Middle-class music

The leading song-writer in this field was Hank Williams, who contrived in the early 1950s to free country music from its rustic backwoods image and make it the music of middle-class America. The whimpering sound of the pedal steel guitar was soon heard across the United States, from California to Alaska. In 1973 there were more than 800 radio stations that played nothing but country music and were able to make stars: Dolly Parton has been for decades the female Number 1, Charley Pride has achieved fame as the only black in this field, and Chet Atkins is not only an exceptional guitarist but one of the most successful producers of country music.

Country rock

In the mid-1970s young bands like the Flying Burrito Brothers and the Nitty Gritty Dirt Band combined rock'n'roll with country music, and the style, though criticised as reactionary, found a sympathetic audience in the Woodstock generation. Townes van Zandt and Dong Sahm remain outsiders, though outsiders of great talent, while the ancestral line of superstars is continued in the 1990s by Dwight Yoakam and Garth Brooks, the latter of whom sold more discs in 1992 than megastar Michael Jackson.

Offspring of the blues: Rock'n'Roll

So at least assert renowned blues musicians like Willie Dixon, though Johnny Cash maintains that country music must have had a share in its paternity. The principal characteristic (and the recipe for success) of rock'n'roll, however, was not so much the mingling of black and white styles as the age and comportment of its interpreters. In the eyes of their distraught elders, who wanted a quiet life after the depression and the war to enjoy their unaccustomed prosperity, it was pure rebellion. Bill Haley with his "Rock Around the Clock" was nerve-racking but was not seen as a sex symbol for teenagers or a figure for them to identify with; but swinging-hips Elvis Presley with his bedroom eyes was a potential threat to domestic peace.

Elvis Presley

Musically Elvis Presley was no innovator, but he was the right man at the right time, who showed millions of adolescents that there was another attitude to life than that of their parents, and that it found expression in music rather different from that of Bing Crosby, Frank Sinatra and Perry Como. Presley got his first chance from Sam Phillips, owner of Sun Records in Memphis, Tennessee, who was convinced that a good-looking young white man who could play black rhythm and blues was bound to be a success – and a look at contemporary photographs of his competitors shows why Elvis became king of rock'n'roll. After his first successes Sam Phillips sold him to RCA Records for 50,000 dollars, thinking that he had made the best deal of his life; then when "Heartbreak Hotel" and "Hound Dog" reached the top of the charts he began to wonder. The whole entertainment industry wondered likewise, and then tried des-

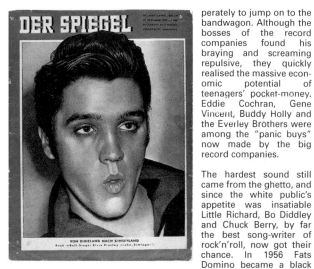

Elvis, "Der Spiegel", 1956

perately to jump on to the bandwagon. Although the bosses of the record companies found his braying and screaming repulsive, they quickly realised the massive economic potential of teenagers' pocket-money. Eddie Cochran, Gene Vincent, Buddy Holly and the Everley Brothers were among the "panic buys" now made by the big record companies.

The hardest sound still came from the ghetto, and since the white public's appetite was insatiable Little Richard, Bo Diddley and Chuck Berry, by far the best song-writer of rock'n'roll, now got their chance. In 1956 Fats Domino became a black rock star with his comfortable "Blueberry Hill", and hardly anyone knew that he had been performing hard numbers like "The Fat Man" since 1949 – when Elvis Presley was 14 years old. Characteristic of black rock'n'roll were vocal groups of several voices, with a repertoire that ranged from the rough Gospel music of the Coasters ("Poison Ivy") by way of the refined harmonies of the Drifters ("Under the Boardwalk") to the schmaltzy doo-wop style of the Platters ("Only You").

Black rock'n'roll

The wild time of rock'n'roll, however, was soon over. In the early 1960s the aggressive sound of "Tutti Frutti", "Summertime Blues", "Roll Over, Beethoven" and "Great Balls of Fire" was toned down. Although musical "fabric-softeners" like Fabian, Paul Anka and Frankie Avalon still took after Elvis Presley, it was after "Love Me Tender" rather than "Jailhouse Rock". It was a black lookout for fans of hard rhythms: Buddy Holly and Eddie Cochran were dead, Gene Vincent was crippled, Elvis was in the army and Chuck Berry in prison, Little Richard had become a convert to Gospel and Jerry Lee Lewis to country music. Bert Kaempfert and Billy Vaughn now dominated the hit parade: the young people of America seemed to have been domesticated.

The end of rock'n'roll

The beat goes on

Friday October 5th 1962 was the day that changed the world, or at any rate the world of pop music. On that day the Beatles published their first official single, "Love Me, Do", and thereafter Beatlemania overran the American entertainments industry so rapidly and violently that to this day it has still not completely recovered. Between February and June 1964 the Beatles had four successive hits at the top of the charts. In September they were displaced by another British band, the Animals ("House of the Rising Sun"), and in October by Manfred Mann; but the main thrust of the British invasion was still to come, with the Rolling Stones, the Kinks and The Who – to name only the best known. American dominance was broken, and the imitation of American models was replaced, with increasing self-confidence, by the independent style of British beat groups, though the most important of these still had their roots in the blues and rock'n'roll.

Apart from the "surf sound" of the Beach Boys, which had enjoyed success since 1962, the United States had little to oppose to the British bands. New groups were founded almost daily, hoping to become the American Beatles; and the Lovin' Spoonful, the Turtles, the Monkees, the Young Rascals, Sam the Sham, the Pharoahs and many others had hits selling a million records.

Motown

In the middle of the "crisis" the first independent record company run wholly by blacks was established. The leading exponents of what came to be known as Motown sound (after the automobile town of Detroit) included Stevie Wonder, Marvin Gaye, the Supremes and the Temptations. Tamla Motown soul was a successful attempt to appeal to a mass white public with black music. It was catchier and more light-weight than the soul music of Otis Redding, Aretha Franklin and Wilson Pickett produced in Memphis and Harlem.

Folk rock

Bands like Mamas and Papas, Buffalo Springfield and above all the Byrds married beat music with the American folksong tradition to pro-duce folk rock. Its leading representative, apart from Arlo Guthrie and Pete Seeger with their protest songs and trade union songs, was Bob Dylan, who had just discovered the electric guitar and published his first long-playing record just six months before the Beatles. Accompanying himself on mouth-organ and guitar, he denounced war profiteers, racial discrimination and social abuses, and became the voice of "the other America", the spokesman of all those who had not found the fulfilment of their dreams in the American way of life. When he appeared for the first time with a fully electric band in 1965 he put off some of his hear-ers but won a wider audience through a combination of intelligent texts,

Woodstock 1969: "Three days of Peace and Music"

elements of social criticism and rough rock music. He prepared the way for the increasingly rebellious attitudes of American schoolchildren and students from 1966 onwards.

From the "Summer of Love" in 1967 to the Woodstock Festival of 1969 the rebellious youth of America was very much in the news, with love-ins, experiments with LSD, hippies, Flower Power and anti-Vietnam demonstrations. Terms like the Underground, psychedelic, acid rock and progressive music were coined to describe the music that was to lead to an enlargement of consciousness and to revolution. The contribution of British groups like Cream, Pink Floyd and the Jimi Hendrix Experience (though Hendrix himself was an American) was no less important than that of the San Francisco scene, with the Grateful Dead and Jefferson Airplane, Janis Joplin, plagued by alcohol, drugs and loneliness, New York's uncompromising and illusionless Velvet Underground, Detroit's radical socialist MC5, the Doors group led by the egomaniac Jim Morrison, who left no taboo unbroken, from incest to exhibitionism, and Frank Zappa's Mothers of Invention, who made such inimitable fun of Mr and Mrs America. As had happened with rock'n'roll, the industry resolved to follow the principle "If you can't beat them, join them"; and by the early 1970s most of the important bands were under contract and thus stripped of their wildness.

Summer of Love to Woodstock

The 1970s were not quite so boring as was often claimed. Iggy Pop and the Stooges, the New York Dolls and the Dictators dedicated themselves to hard city rock'n'roll, swimming stubbornly against the stream. Neil Young took his fans aback with his astonishing variety of styles and his fireworks with the guitar, which could have been equalled only by Jimi Hendrix, who had died in 1970. Bob Dylan, The Band, Randy Newman, Lou Reed, Little Feat, the Eagles and many others still continued to produce fine music, and in 1973 the superstar of our own day, Bruce Springsteen, made his first record, which was hailed by the critics as "the future of rock'n'roll".

Boring seventies

The entertainment industry, however – now consisting of billion-dollar international corporations – managed to establish its idea of "adult-oriented rock", which was more a marketing strategy than a musical style. It changed the image of rock music, so that the average young American, newly married and with a good job, could still identify with it. The result of these efforts was the bombast rock, dominated by keyboard instruments, of Boston, Kansas and Styx. In Britain this was the heyday of Supertramp, Yes, Genesis and Queen. Country and rock'n'roll elements had almost completely disappeared from this music.

Bombast rock

Where to now?

The term "punk", which cropped up in American slang in the 1960s, meant the kind of young hooligan who would trip his grandmother up rather than help her across the street. Punk as a musical style achieved world notoriety in 1977 when British groups like the Sex Pistols, The Clash and the Stranglers, in deliberately shocking rig-out and with provocative texts and ear-shattering volume, bellowed their contempt for the Establishment and the rock music that was inherent in the system. Their slogan "No future" was an expression of frustration with a society that could not offer its young people enough jobs, even as labourers. A similarly radical political line appeared in the United States only in 1980 with the Dead Kennedys, and their protest expressed their disgust with superfluity. But Punk as a form of musical expression was nothing new in America. Johnny Thunder's Heartbreakers had branched off from the New York Dolls; Patti Smith had published their debut in 1975; and the first album of the Ramones was on the market in 1976, before the Sex Pistols had produced even a single.

Punk

Music

Mixture of styles

The industry was not much taken with these violent sounds, but it had learned from experience. It soon had everything that could be called punk under contract, and coined the term New Wave for a more polished and rather less coarse version of the new music. Numbers of groups with a readiness to experiment and with very varying styles now got their chance. Talking Heads, Blondie, the B 52s, even Tom Petty and Mink de Ville took advantage of the fresh wind and put the fear of death in the dinosaurs of rock. They also found inspiration in rock'n'roll and the music of the sixties; and the electric guitar came back into favour. The number of new bands that were now founded was huge, and many of them established their own labels. The Independent scene that resulted is now a well of talent for the record firms, constantly producing new bands that are brought under contract and so lose their independence.

Instead of being caught unawares and overrun by new waves the industry, equipped with large advertising budgets, now creates them itself. Market research is used to identify target groups, to which the latest new trend can be "sold" by the massive use of videos on cable television. Thus the fusion of punk and heavy metal produced a style from which a steadily increasing number of groups have hived off – Hardcore, Grunge, Speed Metal, Grindcore, Thrash and Death Metal – which are often easier to distinguish from one another by the type of fans than by musical criteria.

Rap and hip hop

The rap of the angry young men from the ghetto like Tone-Loc, Run D M C, Public Enemy and Ice Cube was soon declared the sound of the nineties. What appealed was not so much the hard mechanical rhythm – copied from the likes of George Clinton – but the rap itself, the rapid-fire speech-song denouncing society's evils in clever rhymes and the directest of language. What a pity then that a form of lyric so fitted to the close of the millenium should have become increasingly sullied by the sexism and glorification of violence of Ganster Rap. But in any case, the appearance of rap adverts for washing power and peanut butter signal that Hip Hop has already had its day, likewise the misture of rock, punk and rap which brought success to the Beastie Boys and Red Hot Chilli Peppers. Nor can much except a proliferation of forms be expected from "crossover", the synthesizing of different styles made possible by modern sampling techniques, fabricating "new" from old.

The most charismatic name of the most recent past are already fading. Guns n' Roses quarrel rathern than make music, REM have apparently retired, and Kurt Cobain's suicide has killed off the rest of grunge along with Nirvana.

Taming of the Shrew

Since the end of the beat era there has been no single dominating style in popular music. Pop and rock have become part of everyday life throughout the world. Nowadays even the mainstream accommodates such very different artistes as Prince, Dire Straits, Madonna, Michael Jackson, Bruce Springsteen and Tina Turner. The old guard, in so far as it has not been carried off by sex and drugs or by rock'n'roll, is still (or is back) in business. Paul Simon, Paul McCartney and Eric Clapton have no need to worry about paying the rent, the Beach Boys are still busily touring, Bob Dylan after a long lean period, re-emerged in 1997 with a new masterpiece, which Bruce Springsteen might well envy, and the Rolling Stones have not yet found a stadium big enough to ensure that it will not be sold out over night. A spectacular video seems nowadays to be a more effective way of selling records and discs than a song of above-average quality. Now that rock music is no longer the privilege of youth, the battle between the generations is no longer fought in the musical field and the entertainment industry is almost unshockable, we can only wait for the next great revolution. At present, however, no Elvis, no Beatles, no Sex Pistols are in sight. The Americans are lucky though; techno is not that big in the United States.

Serious music

In comparison with the great prominence of "popular" music, "serious" music occupies a relatively modest position. James W. Johnson and Randall Thompson, for example, took over themes and techniques from jazz and country music and formed them into appealing symphonic music, which George Gershwin (see Famous People) stylised into music of serious artistic quality in "Rhapsody in Blue" and above all in "Porgy and Bess". Leonard Bernstein (see Famous People) and Paul Creston were more strongly influenced by European music. John Philip Sousa, inventor of the sousaphone and composer of "The Stars and Stripes Forever", wrote popular march music.

New York's Broadway is the home of the musical, the American coun-   Musicals
terpart to the European operetta. Its most important representatives, composers of many immortal tunes, are Frederick Loewe ("My Fair Lady"), Irving Berlin ("Annie Get Your Gun") and Leonard Bernstein ("West Side Story"), and in more recent times Galt McDermot ("Hair") and Marvin Hamlisch ("A Chorus Line"). Since then London has replaced New York as the musicals capital of the world, particularly with Andrew Lloyd Webber's productions ("Jesus Christ Superstar", "Cats").

Serious music was produced in the second half of the 19th c. by such   Classical
American composers as John Knowles Paine and Arthur William Foote – though this "New England school" looked to European models. The breakaway began with Charles Edward Ives, who, along with colleagues like Walter Piston, took up themes from American folklore. Emigrants from Europe brought new impulses to American music, in particular Arnold Schînberg, who brought the twelve-tone system with him and influenced Ross Lee Finney, Milton Babbitt and other American composers. Breaking away from all traditions, Edgar Varese composed pure background music, while Henry Dixon Cowell was the creator of "tone clusters". John Cage ranks as the father of the avant-garde composers and Nestor of the experimentalists. In recent years Philip Glass has attained an international reputation as an exponent of "minimal music".

Cinema

When Mr and Mrs Horace Wilcox bought land in southern California in the 1880s and called it Hollywood they could not foresee that this area would develop into the largest and mightiest centre of production of moving pictures in the world and that the name Hollywood would become a synonym for the American film industry. A strictly Puritan couple, they would probably not have approved of what later happened to Hollywood, either as to the content of the films produced or the life led by the stars in their luxury villas.

But when Hollywood first received its name all this was in the future. The cinematograph had to be invented by Thomas Alva Edison in 1891 and further developed by the French Lumière brothers before the first public film show could be held in New York in 1895. A popular feature in fairgrounds for many years was the nickelodeon, a machine operated by inserting a five-cent coin that allowed one person to look at a one-minute film strip that might depict, for example, a man sneezing. Thereafter the film developed with giant strides into a mass medium. The small shops in which films were originally shown gave place to proper cinemas and later to huge and showy film palaces. For many years the middle classes remained sceptical about the cinema, but from the outset they were immensely popular with the masses, including new immigrants who had little English but could follow the pictures.

At first the film makers were content to film actual events – sometimes frightening their audiences with the sight of a train heading straight for them – but they soon began to experiment with the language of film. There is still room for argument about which film can claim to be the first; but current histories of the cinema assign that honour to an 11 minute western, Edwin S. Porter's "The Great Train Robbery", shot in 1903. Thus American film history begins with that characteristically American genre, the western.

Pioneering days

In the pioneering days of the American cinema, before the First World War, businessmen began to take an interest in the new medium. Edison, whose patent rights were not absolutely watertight, spent some time fighting with his competitors before deciding to form a trust with the biggest of them, which then proceeded to pursue all the others in the courts, and sometimes also by sending in hired thugs to interrupt the shooting of the rivals' films and destroy the cameras. (In order to escape such attacks some of the independent producers moved their operations for the first time to California.) The trust was never able, however, to cut out completely the independent producers, among whom were William Fox and Carl Laemmle. Moreover in comparison with the cheeky newcomers the trust was too inflexible, for example in holding to the usual ten-minute one-acters after innovative producers had been experimenting for some time with longer films.

D.W. Griffith

This led D.W. Griffith, the greatest producer-director of his time, to leave Edison's firm in 1913, and two years later he shot a film in which the cinema finally found its own language: "The Birth of a Nation". Griffith, who in his revolutionary innovations (e.g. parallel editing, in which he cuts in and out of different settings) was inspired by Dickens's technique in the novel, made the cinema respectable: henceforth good middle-class citizens could be seen at the movies.

Hollywood as Babylon

In the years after the First World War Hollywood became the main centre of the film industry. There was enough room for the studios, the weather made open-air shooting almost risk-free and the variety of scenery provided the settings. During the 1920s, when the American economy was booming, huge sums of money flowed into the cinema. By then, too – although the producers were at first reluctant to reveal the names of their actors and only did so after massive pressure from the public – a star system had developed. It was this system, which enabled actors to live a life of luxury, that led finally to Hollywood's reputation as "Sin City". After a series of scandals about orgies, murders and other killings the Puritan element in American society imposed a form of self-censorship on the film industry. The Hays Code prescribed exactly what the stars – at least in their films – could do and not do. One film-maker described the effect of the code in these words: "Hollywood buys a good story about a bad girl and turns it into a bad story about a good girl". Nevertheless resourceful directors found plenty of ways of making good films in spite of the code.

The greats

By the mid-1920s the big producing and distributing companies had been established: Paramount, First National and Metro-Goldwyn-Mayer, followed by Fox, Universal and United Artists, formed by stars like Charlie Chaplin, Mary Pickford and Douglas Fairbanks along with D.W. Griffith to avoid being too dependent on the big companies. The young Irving Thalberg (later portrayed by Scott Fitzgerald in "The Last Tycoon") became production manager at MGM and in that capacity was able to oversee the shooting of the company's films. Production managers were soon appointed in other studios, leading to constant friction with directors concerned for their artistic freedom. During the 1920s a great variety of genres developed in Hollywood to satisfy almost every public taste: Rudolph Valentino, Gloria Swanson and Lilian Gish provided the love interest in melodramas, Douglas Fairbanks fought his way through adventure films, Tom Mix and company rode in the west, and in a series of slapstick comedies ("The Gold Rush", 1925) Charlie Chaplin's tramp became celebrated throughout the world. Since Hollywood offered the world's best production facilities, European directors like Friedrich Wilhelm Murnau, Ernst Lubitsch and Viktor Sjîström made their way there, producing such masterpieces as Erich von Stroheim's "Greed" (1923), King Vldor's "The Crowd" (1928) and Murnau's "Sunrise" (1927).

The talkies

There had been earlier experiments with sound film, but the breakthrough came only on October 6th 1927, when Al Jolson spoke a few sentences and sang a few songs in "The Jazz Singer". Many stars, unable to cope with the requirements of the new medium, became unemployed; actors with theatrical experience were now in demand, and many were recruited from Broadway. The technical teething troubles of the sound film were soon overcome, and new film genres developed such as the revue and the musical, in which Busby Berkeley in particular made a name for himself with his mass choreographies. The 1930s saw the beginning of the fabulous career of Fred Astaire and Ginger Rogers, who danced their way through a series of successful musicals.

Ernst Lubitsch, who had begun his career in Germany, seized on the new possibilities of the sound film with enthusiasm and developed a type of elegant drawing-room comedy with polished dialogue that was unmistakably his own (the "Lubitsch touch"). This was also the great age of the screwball comedy, in which masterful women angle for shy and eccentric men, with quick-fire verbal sparring between the two. In Howard Hawks's "Bringing Up Baby" (1938), a classic of the genre, an energetic Katharine Hepburn snaps up an awkward Cary Grant. Finally Walt Disney (see Famous People) established a highly specialised studio and in 1937 produced "Snow White", the first feature-length animated cartoon film. *Screwball comedy*

These light entertainment films reflect only indirectly the years of the American depression during which they were produced. They offered entertainment and an escape from an existence that for most cinemagoers was very different from that depicted on the screen. During the early years of the depression at least Hollywood, the dream factory, was one of the few industries that increased their turnover. *Dream factory*

In parallel with these films – which reached the extreme of remoteness from reality and of kitsch in the films constructed round the child star Shirley Temple – Hollywood also turned out films that dealt directly and robustly with reality, including the darker sides of life: the first gangster films and the first "films noirs" were now produced. Films like "Scarface" (1932), "Little Caesar" (1932) and "The Public Enemy" (1931), in which a violent James Cagney crushes a grapefruit on the face of his female opposite number, depict the rise and fall of the gangster and, as the critic Robert Warshow observed, give the audience the double satisfaction of joining in the gangster's sadism by proxy and seeing how this sadism is directed against the gangster himself. *Gangster films*

On the eve of the Second World War the rigidly organised studios had achieved a high degree of efficiency. The year 1939 marked a high point in the history of Hollywood. The 15,000 American movie houses had a weekly *Hollywood's high point*

audience of 85 million (four times the present figure), and more than 400 films were produced during the year, including some of the most famous in the history of the cinema. John Ford shot the classic western "Stagecoach", which gave John Wayne his big break; William Wyler earned rave notices with his filming of "Wuthering Heights", with Laurence Olivier and Merle Oberon; Greta Garbo laughed for the first time in Lubitsch's "Ninochka"; Judy Garland sang "Somewhere Over the Rainbow" in the fairy-tale musical "The Wizard of Oz"; and Vivien Leigh and Clark Gable pursued their love and hate affair through "Gone with the Wind", perhaps the greatest melodrama of them all and claimed by the posters as "the most magnificent picture ever".

Light and shadow
During the Second World War and immediately after it gangster and detective films and thrillers grew ever bleaker. Many German directors who had emigrated from Hitler's Third Reich were now working in America. Fritz Lang ("Fury", 1936), Robert Siodmak ("The Spiral Staircase", 1945), Billy Wilder ("Double Indemnity", 1944) and others produced pessimistic films with a shadowy atmosphere and often with a shady hero. John Huston's "Maltese Falcon" (1941) and Howard Hawks's "The Big Sleep" (1946), both starring Humphrey Bogart in the principal role, paint the picture of a morally corrupt America. The other side of the picture was presented by Frank Capra ("Mr Smith Goes to Washington", 1939), whose heroes – usually James Stewart or Gary Cooper – at first almost fall victim to political machinations and intrigues but then pull themselves together and courageously save democracy.

Hollywood in crisis

Citizen Kane
In 1941 the multi-talented Orson Welles, aged only 25, produced his first film, "Citizen Kane", which opinion polls among critics repeatedly rate as the finest film of all time. In the postwar years, however, Hollywood, like Welles's career, slid into crisis. An anti-trust law aimed at separating production from distribution compelled the large film corporations to divest themselves of their chains of movie houses. At the same time Senator McCarthy launched a campaign against "unAmerican activities" that in the early 1950s led to a witch-hunt directed against all who were or might be "left-wing". Stars, directors and script-writers were summoned to appear before investigating committees; black lists were drawn up that amounted to a ban on the employment of those who appeared on them; and an atmosphere of mutual suspicion and denunciation built up. Charlie Chaplin was driven out of the country (taking his revenge in 1957 with his malicious comedy "A King in New York") and the famous "Hollywood Ten" were imprisoned for their convictions, while others betrayed their best friends.

Even as this was going on, however, a new cohort of young actors were embarking on careers which were to end with them as veteran Hollywood campaigners – Kirk Douglas, Robert Mitchum and Burt Lancaster to name only the most prominent. Others came to personify rebellion: Marlon Brando ("The Wild One"), who has always stood aloof from the cauldron of Hollywood; and above all James Dean, whose early death after just three films turned him into the idol of his generation.

As if this was not trouble enough, the film industry was now faced with competition from television – competition that, in spite of technical innovations such as the wide screen (e.g. Cinemascope) and the 3-D film, they were never to shake off. Between 1946 and 1952 the number of cinema-goers was almost halved, and although the downward trend later slowed it could not be halted. The industry was compelled to reach an accommodation with its competitor: it sold transmission rights on older feature films, hired out studios that could no longer be fully used and finally bought into television. Soon, however, television was able to make some return to the cinema: directors like Sidney Lumet ("Twelve Angry Men", 1957), Martin Ritt ("Hombre", 1967), Arthur Penn ("Bonnie and Clyde", 1967) and later Robert Altman ("Nashville", 1975) and Sam Peckinpah ("The Wild Bunch", 1969), who had all learned their trade in television studios, brought a fresh wind to Hollywood.

Television

The decline of the old studio and star system offered – and still offers – opportunities to independent directors, new talents and outsiders. In 1969 Dennis Hopper produced "Easy Rider", a tale of two motorcyclists trekking across the country to a meaningless death that created the genre of the road movie. Others who now achieved success included the directors Peter Bogdanovich ("What's Up, Doc?", 1972), Francis Ford Coppola ("The Godfather", 1972) and Martin Scorsese ("Taxi Driver",

New talents

James Dean and Elizabeth Taylor in "Giant"

125

1976) and the stars Jack Nicholson, Robert de Niro and Al Pacino. The greatest successes of the seventies, however, were achieved by George Lucas and Steven Spielberg with their fantasy and science fiction spectaculars "Star Wars" (1977) and "Close Encounters of the Third Kind" (1977), later followed by "Star Wars" 2 and 3 and "E.T." (1982), which is claimed to be the most successful film of all time.

Hollywood today

Hollywood no longer lives by maintaining a healthy level of production, or even by producing good average films, but almost exclusively by turning out increasingly expensive blockbusters, from the success of which the whole future of the company sometimes depends. When Michael Cimino's epic of immigration "Heaven's Gate" reached the movie houses in the eighties, at a time when Ronald Reagan was spreading an atmosphere of optimism, audiences were not interested in such a critical view of America; and the flop of "Heaven's Gate" meant ruin for United Artists.

The merry-go-round of Hollywood personalities is now revolving at a frantic rate, in an industry now supported by much foreign, particularly Japanese, capital. Directors are appointed who have rarely any special commitment to the subject of the film but are more familiar with book-keeping and financial management. They try to meet the public taste but have no clear idea of what they want to do. In consequence directors are often sacked as suddenly as they are appointed. (Robert Altman's film "The Player", issued in 1992, on which many stars worked without pay, is a sarcastic account of the present climate in the dream industry.) Hollywood now seldom produces films for adults but aims mainly at the youth market. Films by Woody Allen, Quentin Tarrantino ("Pulp Fiction") and other independent film-makers reach only a restricted audience and are often more popular in Europe than in their country of origin. Films that devote time to their subject, like the melodrama "Out of Africa" (1985) or the Indian epic "Dancing with Wolves" (1992) or "Forrest Gump" (1994), are increasingly becoming the exception. The common feature that distinguishes almost all new Hollywood productions from the films of twenty or more years ago is the great pace at which they run. Not only action films like the Schwarzenegger vehicles "Total Recall" (1991) and "Terminator II" (1992) but thrillers and comedies move at full speed compared with their counterparts of yesteryear.

Hollywood has thus become a little more childish and, in its attempt to track down the latest trends, rather short-winded. Nevertheless it still controls the world market. One reason for this is that film production in every other country is in crisis; another, perhaps, is that – as in the case of the two "Batman" films (1992), and the dinosaur film "Jurassic Park" (1993), "Titanic" (1997) or the new production of "Star Wars" (1999) – the film itself is almost fading into the background in comparison with the huge marketing campaign for film-related products like stickers, T-shirts, caps and models. The fact remains, however, that Hollywood still sets the standards – perhaps now not so much the artistic standards, but certainly the entertainment standards. It still celebrates the annual presentation of Oscars with the usual razzmatazz as if nothing had happened, while the world looks on in fascination, and perhaps also with a touch of envy.

Quotations

Maestoso

Oh,___ say, can you see, by the dawn's ear - ly light, what so
proud - ly we hailed at the twi - light's last gleam-ing? Whose stripes and bright
stars, thro' the per - il - ous fight, o'er the ram - parts we watch'd, were so
gal - lant - ly stream-ing? And the rock - et's red glare, bombs burst-ing in
air, gave___ proof thro' the night that our flag was still there. Oh,___
energico
say, does the___ star - span - gled ban - ner___ still___ wave___ o'er the
piu lento
land _____ of the free and the home of the brave?

Text of the national anthem by Francis Scott Key (1780–1843), written after the British siege of Fort Henry, Baltimore, on September 14th 1814; tune by John Stafford Smith (1750–1836), after the English song "To Anacreon in Heaven".

National anthem

And, truly, the scene was of a nature deeply to impress the imagination of the beholder. Towards the west, in which direction the faces of the party were turned, and in which alone could much be seen, the eye ranged over an ocean of leaves, glorious and rich in the varied but lively verdure of a generous vegetation, and shaded by the luxuriant tints that belong to the forty second degree of latitude. The elm, with its graceful and weeping top, the rich varieties of the maple, most of the noble oaks of the American forest, with the broad leafed linden, known in the parlance of the country as the bass-wood, mingled their uppermost branches, forming one broad and seemingly interminable carpet of foliage, that stretched away towards the setting sun, until it bounded the horizon, by blending with the clouds, as the waves and sky meet at the base of the vault of Heaven. Here and there, by some accident of the tempests, or by a caprice of nature, a trifling opening among these giant members of the forest, permitted an inferior tree to struggle upward toward the light, and to lift its modest head nearly to a level with the surrounding surface of verdure. Of this class were the birch, a tree of some account in regions less favored, the quivering aspen, various generous nut-woods, and divers others, that resembled the ignoble and vulgar, thrown by circumstances into the presence of the stately and great. Here and there, too, the tall, straight trunk of the pine pierced the vast field, rising high above it, like some grand monument reared by art on the plain of leaves.

James Fenimore Cooper
American writer
(1789–1851)

Quotations

It was the vastness of the view, the nearly unbroken surface of verdure, that contained the principle of grandeur. The beauty was to be traced in the delicate tints, relieved by gradations of light and shadow, while the solemn repose induced a feeling allied to awe.

"The Pathfinder", 1840

Chief Seattle

Every part of this soil is sacred in the estimation of my people. Every hillside, every valley, every plain and grove, has been hallowed by some happy or sad event in days long vanished. Even the rocks, which seem to be dumb and dead as they swelter in the sun along the silent shore, thrill with memories of stirring events connected with the lives of my people ... Our departed braves, fond mothers, glad, happy-hearted maidens, and even our little children who lived here and rejoiced here for a brief season, will love these sombre solitudes and at eventide they greet shadowy returning spirits. And when the last Red Man shall have perished, and the memory of my tribe shall have become a myth among the White Men, these shores will swarm with the invisible dead of my tribe ... At night when the streets of your cities and villages are silent and you think them deserted, they will throng with the returning hosts that once filled them and still love this beautiful land.

Speech during the negotiations in 1850 on the division of the Oregon Territory.

Abraham Lincoln
President of the
United States
(1809–65)

Four score and seven years ago our fathers brought forth on this continent a new nation, conceived in Liberty, and dedicated to the proposition that all men are created equal.

Now we are engaged in a great civil war, testing whether that nation, or any nation so conceived and so dedicated, can long endure. We are met on a great battlefield of that war. We have come to declare a portion of that field, as a final resting place for those who here gave their lives that that nation might live. It is altogether fitting and proper that we should do this.

But, in a larger sense, we can not dedicate – we can not consecrate – we can not hallow – this ground. The brave men, living and dead, who struggled here, have consecrated it, far above our poor power to add or detract. The world will little note, nor long remember what we say here, but it can never forget what they did here. It is for us the living, rather, to be dedicated here to the unfinished work which they who fought here have thus far so nobly advanced. It is rather for us to be here dedicated to the great task remaining before us – that from these honoured dead we take increased devotion to that cause for which they gave the last full measure of devotion – that we here highly resolve that these dead shall not have died in vain – that this nation, under God, shall have a new birth of freedom – and that government of the people, by the people, for the people, shall not perish from the earth.

Address delivered at the dedication of the cemetery at Gettysburg, November 19th 1863

William Archer

The great advantage, it seems to me, that America possesses over the Old World is its material and moral plasticity. Even among the giant structures of this city, one feels that there is nothing rigid, nothing oppressive, nothing inaccessible to the influence of changing conditions. If the buildings are Cyclopean, so is the race that reared them. The material world seems as clay on the potter's wheel, visibly taking on the impress of the human spirit; and the human spirit, as embodied in this superbly vital people, seems to be visibly thrilling to all the forces of civilisation.

"America Today", 1900

In a great many ways travelling in the United States is, to one who under- Fritz Baedeker
stands it, more comfortable than in Europe. The average Englishman will
probably find the chief physical discomforts in the dirt of the city streets,
the roughness of the country roads, the winter overheating of hotels and
railway cars (70–75°F being by no means unusual), and (in many places)
the habit of spitting on the floor; but the Americans themselves are now
keenly alive to these weak points and are doing their best to remove
them ... Throughout almost the whole country travelling is now as safe
as in the most civilised parts of Europe, and the carrying of arms, which
indeed is forbidden in many states, is as unnecessary here as there. – No
limit is placed on the number of passengers admitted to public con-
veyances, and straps are provided in the cars of tramways and elevated
railways to enable those who cannot obtain seats to maintain their equi-
librium. – Indoor clothing for American use should be rather thinner in
texture than is usual in England, but winter wraps for outdoor use require
to be much thicker. The thick woollen gowns that English ladies wear in
winter would be uncomfortably warm in the ordinary winter temperatures of American hotels and railway carriages; and a thin soft silk will,
perhaps, be found the most comfortable travelling dress on account of its
non-absorption of dust. Overshoes ("arctics" and "rubbers") are quite
necessary in winter and are worn almost as much by men as by women.

"The United States, with an Excursion to Mexico. Handbook for
Travellers", 1893

I have fallen in love with American names, Stephen Vincent
The sharp names that never get fat, Benét
The snakeskin titles of mining claims, American poet
The plumed war-bonnet of Medicine Hat, (1898–1943)
Tucson and Deadwood and Lost Mule Flat.

Seine and Piave are silver spoons,
But the spoonbowl-metal is thin and worn.
There are English counties like hunting-tunes,
Played on the keys of a postboy's horn,
But I will remember where I was born.

I will remember Carquinez Straits,
Little French Lick and Lundy's Lane,
The Yankee ships and the Yankee dates
And the bullet-towns of Calamity Jane.
I will remember Skunktown Plain.

I will fall in love with a Salem tree
And a rawhide quirt from Santa Cruz,
I will get me a bottle of Boston sea
And a blue-gum nigger to sing me blues.
I am tired of loving a foreign muse.

Rue des Martyrs and Bleeding-Heart-Yard,
Senlis, Pisa, and Blindman's Oast.
It is a magic ghost you guard
But I am sick for a newer ghost,
Hamburg, Spartanburg, Painted Post ...

I shall not rest quiet in Montparnasse.
I shall not lie easy at Winchelsea.
You may bury my body in Sussex grass,
You may bury my tongue at Champmedy.
I shall not be there. I shall rise and pass.
Bury my heart at Wounded Knee.

"American Names", 1931

Quotations

A.G. Macdonell
English writer

The truth of the matter is, and I record it with misgiving, reluctance, and a sense of imminent calamity, that the American does not like strangers to say that America is a new country. He himself will say it, over and over again, but it is as much as your life is worth to say it yourself. It is risky even to agree with him when he says it. In fact it is safer either to say nothing at all in answer to him, or to confine yourself to a muttered reference to Karlsefne or Leif Ericson.

It is a peculiar business, the American attitude to Antiquity. Of all the citizens of the world there is no one so alive as the American to the values of modernity, so fertile in experiment, so feverish in the search for something new. There is nothing, from Architecture to Contract Bridge, from the Immortality of the Soul to the Ventilation of Railroad Cars, from Golf to God, that he does not pounce upon and examine critically to see if it cannot be improved. And then, having pulled it to pieces, mastered its fundamental theory, and reassembled it in a novel and efficient design, he laments bitterly because it is not old.

"A Visit to America", 1935

Woody Guthrie
American folk
singer
(1912–67)

This land is your land, this land is my land.
From California to the New York Island,
From the redwood forest to the Gulfstream Waters
This land was made for you and me.

As I went walking that ribbon of highway
I saw above me that endless skyway,
I saw below me that golden valley.
This land was made for you and me.

I've roamed and rambled and I followed my footsteps
To the sparkling sands of her diamond deserts,
And all around me a voice was sounding.
This land was made for you and me.

When the sun comes shining and I was strolling
And the wheatfields waving and the dust clouds rolling
A voice was chanting and the fog was lifting.
This land was made for you and me.

Martin Luther
King Jr
Civil rights activist
(1929–68)

I am not unmindful that some of you have come here out of excessive trials and tribulation. Some of you have come fresh from narrow jail cells. Some of you have come from areas where your quest for freedom left you battered by the storms of persecution and staggered by the winds of police brutality. You have been the veterans of creative suffering. Continue to work with the faith that unearned suffering is redemptive.

Go back to Mississippi; go back to Alabama; go back to South Carolina; go back to Georgia; go back to Louisiana; go back to the slums and ghettos of the northern cities, knowing that somehow this situation can, and will be changed. Let us not wallow in the valley of despair.

So I say to you, my friends, that even though we must face the difficulties of today and tomorrow, I still have a dream. It is a dream deeply rooted in the American dream that one day this nation will rise up and live out the true meaning of its creed – we hold these truths to be self-evident, that all men are created equal.

I have a dream that one day on the red hills of Georgia, sons of former slaves and sons of former slave-owners will be able to sit down together at the table of brotherhood.

I have a dream that one day even the state of Mississippi, a state sweltering with the heat of injustice, sweltering with the heat of oppression, will be transformed into an oasis of freedom and justice.

I have a dream my four little children will one day live in a nation where they will not be judged by the colour of their skin but by the content of their character. I have a dream!

From a speech in Washington on August 28th 1963

**Sights
from A to Z**

Suggested Routes

The best way of seeing the United States is by car or motorcycle. All the major scenic beauties are accessible by road. Municipal tourist offices and the visitor centres of National Parks and State Parks (see Practical Information, National Parks) are well supplied with good maps and descriptions of the area. With the help of the map of the United States at the end of this guide it is easy to work out individual routes and round trips. In the main part of the guide (Sights from A to Z) a number of particularly attractive routes are briefly described: for example the Blue Ridge Parkway in Virginia (see entry) and North Carolina, the Needles Skyway in the Black Hills (see entry) and the Skyway to the Sun in the Waterton-Glacier International Peace Park (see entry). In the following pages a number of the most interesting routes and round trips for visitors with several weeks at their disposal are briefly sketched.

Route 66

Route 66, 2448 mi. long, was opened in 1926, the first transcontinental highway with an all-weather surface. It linked Chicago, the pulsating economic metropolis on Lake Michigan, with Los Angeles, the then still relatively young boom town on the Pacific.

In the 1930s Route 66 became a legend when, after a number of rainless years in the Middle West, tens of thousands of farmers left the dust bowl of the prairies (particularly in Oklahoma) and made their way to the "golden land" of California. In his famous novel "The Grapes of Wrath" John Steinbeck pictured the life of these victims of drought and their journey along Route 66.

During the Second World War military transports and the training camps in the Mojave Desert increased the importance of Route 66, and after the war Nat King Cole's interpretation of Bobby Troup's song "Get your kicks on Route 66" made the road world-famous.

In the early 1950s the federal government launched a roads programme designed to give the United States a modern highway network, and by 1984 the old US 66 had been replaced, section by section, by new roads. The modern interstate highways I 55, I 44 and I 40 took over its functions, and the old road was left to itself.

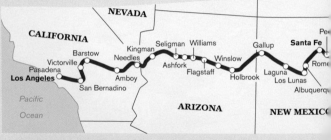

◀ *One of America's greatest natural sights – Niagara Falls*

Its gas stations, snack bars, restaurants, motels and hotels remained, but were now in the backwoods. The legend, however, still lives on.

Course of Route 66

Between Chicago and St Louis only sections of the old Route 66, running parallel to I 55, survive as rather bumpy country roads. South of Bloomington U 66 serves as a local link road or "business loop". Interesting relics of better days are Funk's Grove, the old maple syrup factory south of Shirley, the Dixie Truckers' Home in McLean, Mort's Roadhouse in Glenarm, now a bikers' rendezvous, and the Ariston Café in Lichfield.

Illinois

In the state of Missouri, particularly in the south-west, round Springfield and between Lebanon and Joplin, Route 66, here running parallel to I 44, is well preserved. Many little townships founded in the heyday of Route 66 are visibly in decline. From Stanton a side trip can be made to the Meramec Caverns, where the bank robber Jesse James and his gang are said to have concealed themselves.

Missouri

Between Joplin, Missouri, and Quapaw, Oklahoma, Route 66 cuts across the southernmost tip of Kansas. The road runs on a zigzag course with many right-angled bends, following old district and farm boundaries. In Baxter Springs is Murphy's Restaurant, in which Jesse James stayed when there was still a bank here.

Kansas

In the state of Oklahoma Route 66 has memories of the more recent past, when in the 1930s thousands of impoverished farmers ("Okies") travelled along it on their way to the west. The road is still well preserved and carries considerable traffic – a paradoxical result of modern road development. The people of Oklahoma were in the forefront of the movement for the construction of the new highways, calling as early as the 1950s for the building of new freeways, to be financed by tolls; and because the new I 44 is still a toll road many drivers branch off into the old US 66, which here is still in excellent condition. Features of interest on the route are the Lincoln Hotel in Chandler, the Cowboy Hall of Fame in Oklahoma City and Pop Hicks Hotel in Clinton.

Oklahoma

©Baedeker

135

Coast to Coast

Texas

Early travellers over the dreary plateau of the High Plains in Texas were dismayed rather than impressed. On the Llano Estacado stakes were driven into the ground to mark the route. On the western outskirts of Amarillo ten old Cadillacs, half buried in the ground on Cadillac Farm, which belongs to the art collector Stanley Marsh III, now perform the same function – marking, as it were, the frontier of the motorised society.

New Mexico

Between Santa Rosa and Albuquerque, where I 40 now cuts across the barren plateau, US 66 formerly followed a winding course to Santa Fe. West of Albuquerque, in the neighbourhood of Laguna and between Grants and the continental watershed at Thoreau there are very fine scenic stretches of the old Route 66, now state road NM 122. In the centre of Gallup there are many old buildings reminiscent of earlier days; and the town's 1st Street is part of the old US 66.

Arizona

In western Arizona, between Ashfork and the boundary with California, a 160 mi. stretch of Route 66 is preserved. Particularly fine is the section between Seligman and Kingman. The road here is dead straight, as if drawn by a ruler. The road between Kingman and the Californian border, on the other hand, is a real challenge for the driver, even in a cross-country vehicle. Travellers who are not put off by rough roads and the Sitgreave Pass, the steepest parts of which could be negotiated by the automobiles of the 1930s only in reverse, can see a Wild West show in the gold-mining town of Oatman and visit the hotel in which Clark Gable spent his wedding night with Carole Lombard.

California

There is another fine stretch of Route 66 between Essex and Ludlow, California. The road runs through the Mojave Desert for some 60 mi., passing a salt lake and the crater of an extinct volcano at Ambay. It runs through the godforsaken township of Bagdad, where scenes from the film "Out of Rosenheim" were shot, and the little settlement of Siberia, where the temperatures are very far from Siberian. There is also a well preserved section of the road between Barstow and Victorville to the south. At San Bernardino Route 66 turns west again and follows the Foothill Boulevard (CA 66) to Pasadena. From there it continues on the Colorado Boulevard to Glendale and from there on the Los Felíz Boulevard to Hollywood. The last few miles are on the Santa Monica Boulevard through Beverly Hills and Santa Monica, and so down to the Pacific.

Coast to Coast

Highlights of the United States

Boston to San Francisco

Distance: 5000 mi. Duration: at least 4 weeks.
Boston – Cape Cod – New York – Philadelphia – Baltimore – Washington, DC – Gettysburg – Pennsylvania Dutch Country – Niagara Falls – Toronto (Canada) – Detroit – Chicago – Sioux City – Badlands National Park (side trip to Wounded Knee) – Rapid City – Mount Rushmore – Black Hills (side trip to Hot Springs and Devil's Tower) – Buffalo, Wyoming – Bighorn Mountains – Ten Sleep – Cody – Yellowstone National Park – Grand Teton National Park – Jackson – Idaho Falls – Salt Lake City – Bryce Canyon National Park – Grand Canyon National Park – Lake Mead National Recreation Area – Las Vegas – Los Angeles (side trip to San Diego) – Hollywood – Beverly Hills – Santa Monica – Malibu – Santa Barbara – San Luis Obispo – Monterey – San Francisco.

Northern route

Distance: 4350 mi. Duration: at least 4 weeks.
Boston – Cape Cod – New York (side trip to Niagara Falls) – Philadelphia
– Baltimore – Washington, DC – Pittsburgh – Cleveland – Detroit –
Chicago – Milwaukee – Minneapolis/St Paul – Sioux Falls – Badlands
National Park (side trip to Pine Ridge Indian Reservation, with Wounded
Knee) – Rapid City – Mount Rushmore – Black Hills (side trip to Devil's
Tower) – Buffalo, Wyoming – Bighorn Mountains – Cody – Yellowstone
National Park – Grand Teton National Park – Idaho Falls – Butte –
Waterton-Glacier National Park (Skyway to the Sun) – Spokane – Seattle.

Middle route

Distance: 3400 mi. Duration: at least 4 weeks.
Washington, DC – Allegheny Mountains (Spruce Knob) – Charleston,
West Virginia – Lexington, Kentucky (side trip to Cincinnati) – Louisville
– St Louis – Kansas City – Denver – Rocky Mountain National Park –
Cheyenne – Laramie – Medicine Bow Mountains – Rock Springs –
Flaming Gorge National Recreation Area – Dinosaur National Monument
– Uintah Mountains – Salt Lake City – Great Basin – Reno – Carson City
– Lake Tahoe – Sacramento – Oakland – San Francisco.

Washington, DC
to San Francisco

Southern route

Distance: 3400 mi. Duration: at least 3 weeks.
Miami – Miami Beach (side trip to Florida Keys, with Key West) –
Everglades National Park – Naples – Fort Myers (side trip to
Sanibel/Captiva) – Sarasota – Bradenton – Sunshine Skyway – St
Petersburg (side trip to Tampa and Orlando, with Walt Disney World) –
Pinellas Suncoast – Tallahassee – Panama City – Gulf Islands National
Seashore – Pensacola – Mobile – Biloxi – New Orleans – Baton Rouge –
Lafayette – Houston (side trip to Galveston and Texas Gulf Coast) – San
Antonio – El Paso (side trip to El Paso National Monument) – Tucson –
Phoenix (side trip to Montezuma Castle) – Joshua Tree National
Monument – Palm Springs – San Bernardino – Los Angeles.

Miami to Los
Angeles

Atlantic Coast

Distance: 2100 mi. Duration: at least 14 days.
Boston – Cape Cod – New York (side trip to valley of Hudson River and
Niagara Falls) – Philadelphia (side trip to Atlantic City) – Baltimore –
Washington, DC – Norfolk – Outer Banks, Cape Hatteras – Wilmington –
Myrtle Beach – Charleston – Savannah (side trip to Hilton Head Island) –
Amelia Island – Jacksonville – St Augustine – Daytona Beach – Cape
Canaveral (Kennedy Space Center; side trip to Orlando and Walt Disney
World) – Palm Beach – Fort Lauderdale – Miami/Miami Beach – Florida
City (side trip to Everglades National Park) – Key West.

Boston to Key
West

Pacific Coast

Distance: 1600 mi. Duration: at least 14 days.
Seattle – (side trip to Olympic National Park and Mount Rainier National
Park) – Portland (possible side trip to Mount St Helens) – Salem – Eugene
– Oregon Dunes National Recreation Area – Crescent City – Redwood
National Park – Eureka – Point Reyes National Seashore – San Francisco
– Monterey – Big Sur – San Luis Obispo – Santa Barbara – Malibu – Santa
Monica – Los Angeles (with Hollywood, Beverly Hills and

Seattle to San
Diego

Anaheim/Disneyland) – Huntington Beach – San Clemente – San Diego (side trip to Tijuana in Mexico).

Special Interest Tours

Historic Heartland

Round trip: 2300 mi. Duration: at least 14 days.
New York – Philadelphia – Baltimore – Washington, DC – Williamsburg – Richmond – Charlottesville – Shenandoah National Park – Gettysburg – Pennsylvania Dutch Country – Niagara Falls – Rochester – Syracuse – Albany – Boston – Cape Cod – New York.

The Historic East and Old South

Distance: 2000 mi. Duration: at least 14 days.
Boston – Cape Cod – Philadelphia (side trip to Amish Country) – Baltimore – Washington (side trip to Gettysburg) – Williamsburg – Durham – Cherokee Indian Reservation – Great Smoky Mountains – Knoxville – Nashville – Memphis – Natchez – Vicksburg – New Orleans.

The South-East

Distance: 2000 mi. Duration: at least 14 days.
Atlanta – Birmingham – Tuscaloosa – Jackson – Vicksburg – Natchez – Baton Rouge – Lafayette – New Orleans – Biloxi – Mobile – Tallahassee – Wakulla Springs – St Augustine – Orlando – Tampa – Naples – Everglades National Park – Miami (side trip to Key West).

Florida Sunshine Circle

Round trip: 1100 mi. Duration: at least 7 days.
Miami – Miami Beach – Fort Lauderdale – Palm Beach – Space Coast (with Cape Canaveral, Kennedy Space Center and Cape Canaveral National Seashore; side trip to Daytona Beach and St Augustine) – Orlando (side trip to Walt Disney World) – Ocala National Forest – Crystal River – Weeki Wachee Spring – Pinellas Suncoast – Tampa – Sarasota – Venice – Fort Myers (side trip to Sanibel/Captiva) – Naples – Port Everglades – Everglades National Park – Florida City (side trip to Florida Keys, with Key West) – Miami.

Land of Dixie

Distance: 2200 mi. Duration: at least 14 days.
Charleston – Savannah – Atlanta – Chattanooga – Nashville – Memphis – Natchez – New Orleans – Baton Rouge – Houston (side trip to Galveston and Texas Gulf Coast National Recreation Area) – San Antonio – Austin – Dallas.

Rose of Texas

Round trip: 2500 mi. Duration: 14 days.
Dallas – Oklahoma City – Amarillo – Las Vegas – New Mexico – Santa Fe – Albuquerque – White Sands National Monument – El Paso – Guadalupe Mountains National Park – Carlsbad Caverns – Pecos – Balmorhea – Big Bend National Park – Fort Stockton – Fort Lancaster National Historic Site – San Antonio – Corpus Christi (side trip to Padre Island National Seashore) – Houston – Dallas.

Rocky Mountains

Round trip: 2400 mi. Duration: at least 14 days.
Denver – Idaho Springs – Mount Evans – Rocky Mountain National Park – North Platte River – Medicine Bow Peak – Laramie – Laramie Mountains – Casper – Wind River Indian Reservation – Thermopolis – Cody – Yellowstone National Park – Grand Teton National Park – Idaho Falls – Wasatch Range – Salt Lake City – Provo – Price – Green River – Capitol Reef National Park – Glen Canyon National Recreation Area – Canyonlands National Park – Arches National Park – Grand Junction – Black Canyon of the Gunnison – Aspen – Mount Elbert – Florissant Beds National Monument – Colorado Springs (side trip to Pikes Peak) – Denver.

Canyons and Indian Country

Round trip: 2300 mi. Duration: at least 3 weeks.
Denver – Colorado Springs – Black Canyon of the Gunnison – Silverton

– Mesa Verde National Park – Durango – Santa Fe (side trip to Taos) – Albuquerque – Window Rock – Canyon de Chelly – Kayenta – Monument Valley – Navajo Indian Reservation – Grand Canyon National Park – Sedona (Montezuma Castle) – Phoenix/Scottsdale (side trip to Tucson, Tombstone and Yuma) – Las Vegas – Zion National Park – Bryce Canyon National Park – Capitol Reef National Park – Moab – Grand Junction – Vail – Denver.

Round trip: 2300 mi. Duration: at least 2½ weeks.
Los Angeles – Anaheim (Disneyland) – San Diego – Palm Springs – Phoenix (side trip to Tucson and Tombstone) – Montezuma Castle – Flagstaff – Grand Canyon National Park – Monument Valley – Navajo Indian Reservation – Lake Powell – Page – Bryce Canyon National Park – Zion National Park – Las Vegas – Death Valley – Mono Lake – Yosemite National Park – Lake Tahoe – San Francisco – Monterey – San Luis Obispo – Santa Barbara – Los Angeles.

Pacific Coast and Canyon Country

Round trip: 3800 mi. Duration: at least 4 weeks.
San Francisco – Sacramento (side trip to Lake Tahoe) – Lassen Volcanic National Park – Mount Shasta – Lava Beds National Monument – Crater Lake National Park – Bend – Portland – Mount Rainier National Park – Seattle (side trip to Olympic National Park) – North Cascades National Park – Spokane – Kalispell – Waterton-Glacier National Park (Skyway to the Sun) – Great Falls – Butte – Bozeman – Yellowstone National Park – Grand Teton National Park – Jackson – Salt Lake City – Bryce Canyon National Park – Zion National Park – Grand Canyon National Park – Lake Mead National Recreation Area – Las Vegas – Death Valley – Mono Lake – Yosemite National Park – San Francisco.

Western Highlights

Other Scenic Routes

Arkansas Highway 7 runs through the magnificent scenery of the Ouachita Mountains west of Little Rock and the cave country on the Buffalo River, near the boundary with Missouri. It begins in Diamond City, on Bull Shoals Lake, in the north, and ends in the little artists' town of El Dorado in the south.

Arkansas Highway 7

From Portland there is an attractive trip to the wild and romantic valleys that the Columbia River has carved through the Cascade Range and the Coast Range. Particularly impressive is the gorge with its tumbling white water between Mount St Helens in the north and Mount Hood (11,240 ft) to the south.

Columbia River and Gorge, Oregon

From the little town of Twin Falls on I 84 a very rewarding excursion can be made – first north-eastward to the Craters of the Moon, an extraordinary lunar landscape created by volcanic activity and erosion; then through the Lost River Range into the valley of the Salmon River. In the Sawtooth region are two gold-mining ghost towns, Bonanza and Custer. Further south are the two well-known winter sports resorts of Ketchum and Sun Valley and the Shoshone ice cave.

Craters of the Moon/Salmon River/Sawtooth, Idaho

There is very attractive country round the Finger Lakes, in a landscape created in the last ice age. It is particularly fine south of Seneca Falls (Seneca Lake, Cayuga Lake and Watkins Glen State Parks, Montour Falls, Ithaca, Buttermilk Falls).

Finger Lakes

From Chicago the route runs north along the western shores of the lake to Milwaukee and on to Sturgeon Bay. From there the narrow peninsula to the north, with its beautiful State Parks, can be explored. The route then continues up the west side of Lake Michigan to Escanaba and Lake

Lake Michigan Circle

Superior; then east to the great locks at Sault Ste Marie, on the Canadian frontier. A few miles to the south the road crosses the narrow channel between Lake Michigan and Lake Huron. The north-eastern shore of Lake Michigan, with its little offshore islands, is particularly beautiful. The Sleeping Bear Dunes are now a nature reserve. Traverse City is widely famed for its cherries. Further south are the little towns of Holland and Saugatuck, from which a short excursion can be made to Grand Rapids. At the southern tip of the lake, near Michigan City, is the Indiana Dunes National Lakeshore.

Oregon Trail

A very interesting and beautiful part of the Oregon Trail is the prairie region traversed by the North Platte River, in the border area between the states of Wyoming and Nebraska. The imposing rock formations of Chimney Rock (near Bridgeport) and Scotts Bluff were prominent landmarks for settlers moving west in the 19th c. Along the trail there are many places scheduled as historic monuments. The area round Crescent Lake is one of the largest resting places for migrant birds in North America.

Ozark Mountains

In the border region between the states of Arkansas and Missouri is a particularly beautiful part of the Ozark Mountains centred on Table Rock Lake and Beaver Lake. In this area, with numerous springs and caves, there are a number of State Parks and two National Forests. A good base for excursions is the town of Eureka Springs.

Vermont Highway 100

Vermont's Highway 100 runs through the beautiful upland scenery of Green Mountain National Forest, which lies between the valley of the Connecticut River and the border with New York State.

Through the United States by Rail

The section on rail travel in the Practical Information part of this guide shows the main railroad lines in the United States and lists the most important express trains. It also lists a selection of the best known old-time railroads.

Steamboat on Old Man River

A very special holiday experience is a trip on one of the old-style paddle steamers that run cruises on the Mississippi, the Arkansas and the Ohio River and its tributaries the Tennessee and Cumberland Rivers. The steamers operate on three stretches of the Mississippi: from Minneapolis/St Paul to St Louis, from St Louis to Memphis, and from Memphis to New Orleans. River stations on the Arkansas River include Little Rock and Tulsa, and on the Ohio River Pittsburg, Cincinnati and Louisville. Others are Nashville on the Cumberland River and Chattanooga on the Tennessee River. From New Orleans it is possible to continue via the Intracoastal Waterway to Galveston, Texax (see Practical Information, Cruises).

The American South

From New Orleans the boat sails upstream through the Old South, the region once dominated by the plantation economy, passing handsome old mansions and estates, and comes to Baton Rouge, capital of the state of Louisiana, and St Francisville, with the extravagantly beautiful Rosedown Plantation (1835), once the home of Martha and Daniel Turnbull. The next port of call is Natchez, with its magnificent antebellum (pre-Civil War) buildings. Further upstream is Vicksburg, the "Gibraltar of the Old South", which was the scene of bloody fighting in the Civil War. Then by way of the port of Helena to Memphis, the legendary cotton-growing centre, which has associations with W.C. Handy, father of the blues, and Elvis Presley.

The section of the river between Memphis and St Louis is known as the "crossroads of America". In this area the Mississippi is joined by its most important tributaries, the Missouri and the Ohio, major north–south and east–west roads and railroads intersect and the most important economic and cultural regions of the United States meet.

Crossroads of America

From Memphis in the south the boat continues upstream, negotiating the great New Madrid Bend, and comes to New Madrid, Missouri. Further north the Mississippi is joined by the Ohio River. For several miles arms of the two rivers, differing in the colour of their water, run parallel to one another. The boat passes the little towns of Cairo and Cape Girardeau, with the very interesting River Heritage Museum. Then come Chester, Illinois, with its buildings recalling the French colonial

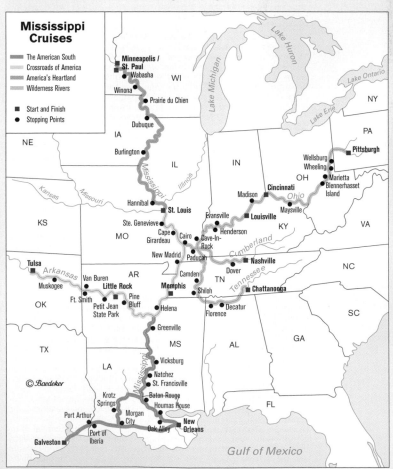

Mississippi Cruises

- The American South
- Crossroads of America
- America's Heartland
- Wilderness Rivers

■ Start and Finish
● Stopping Points

© Baedeker

141

period, and Ste Genevieve, the oldest French base in this area, founded in the mid 18th c., where the townscape is still dominated by French-style buildings. This section of the river ends at St Louis, Missouri, "Gateway of the West", with the world-famous Gateway Arch. A few miles above the city the Missouri, bringing an abundant flow of water from the prairies and the Rockies, flows into the Mississippi.

Going in the other direction, southwards from Memphis, the boat passes Helena before turning west into the Arkansas River and continuing upstream via Pine Bluff to Little Rock, state capital of Arkansas – familiar the world over at least since Bill Clinton became president. Beyond Little Rock the river winds its way along the foot of the Ozark Mountains to Tulsa, where the cruise ends.

America's Heartland

The region between St Louis in the south and Minneapolis/St Paul in the north is known as "America's Heartland". This section of the Mississippi, formerly difficult to navigate on account of its rapids and its wide meanders, has been tamed by the construction of more than two dozen lock systems and now offers a comfortable journey through "God's own country" with its carefully tended farmland, large orchards, great expanses of arable land and ancient riverine woodland.

From St Louis the journey continues past the junction with the Missouri to the small town of Hannibal, Missouri, where Samuel Clemens, who later, as Mark Twain, was to introduce the Mississippi into world literature, spent his early years. Further upstream is the picturesque little town of Burlington. The boat sails past a number of old ports from which the early settlers shipped minerals, timber and agricultural produce and comes to Dubuque, Iowa, a little town founded in 1788 where lead was formerly mined. Beyond this is Prairie du Chien, Wisconsin, an old fur-trading town where the Sioux, Winnebago and Fox Indians exchanged their furs for firearms, brandy and a variety of trinkets. Another interesting place is Winona, Wisconsin, settled in the 1860s by large numbers of immigrants from Germany, Poland and Ireland, which developed into the fourth largest grain market in the United States, with more than a dozen large mills. 35 mi. further upstream is Wabasha, Minnesota, a picturesque little town from which large quantities of timber were formerly shipped. The cruise on the Mississippi ends at Minneapolis/St Paul, a very busy double city with an active cultural life.

Wilderness rivers

The second finest river cruise in the United States runs down the Ohio River from Pittsburgh through country of great scenic beauty and historic interest. At the Pittsburgh Golden Triangle the Allegheny River and the Monongahela River join to form the Ohio. Here the first steamboat was launched in 1811. From Pittsburgh the boat sails south-west down the river to Wellsburg, West Virginia, a port over 200 years old that formerly shipped mainly grain and whiskey; it has preserved a number of handsome 19th c. buildings. At Parkersburg, also in West Virginia, is Blennerhasset Island, with a magnificent old mansion. After Marietta comes Portsmouth, Ohio, chief town of the Bonneyfiddle Country, which is famed as the home of the legendary cowboy Roy Rogers. The gateway to the Bluegrass Country is Maysville, Kentucky, where the old Natchez Trace crosses the Ohio River.

In the heyday of the steamboats Cincinnati, Ohio, was a boom town, in which over 1000 buildings were erected in the year 1846 alone. Now a very modern industrial city, in the past it was derisively called Porkopolis because it had for many years one of the largest stock markets (mainly pigs) in the United States; to Longfellow, on the other hand, it was "queen among the cities of the west". Soon after that comes Louisville, Kentucky, which claims to be the "horse-racing capital of the world". Here every year in spring is held the famous Kentucky Derby, preceded by a 14 mi. race on the river between two aged paddle steamers, the "Delta Queen" and the "Belle of Louisville". Further downstream is the little town of Henderson, Kentucky, founded in 1779, with a carefully tended park. A few miles beyond this is the Cave in Rock, a cavern scooped out by the river from which is the late 18th c. bandits and robbers lay in wait for passing ships. The notorious Samuel Mason invited the crews of ships into his House of Entertainment, where they were robbed of all their possessions. Just below the junction with the Tennessee River is Paducah, founded by white settlers in 1821 and named after an Indian chief, where during the Civil War 42,000 Union troops embarked on 173 steamboats and twelve gunboats and sailed for Shiloh on the Tennessee River (see below).

From Paducah, on the Ohio River, boats sail up the Tennessee River into Kentucky Lake (formed by a dam on the Tennessee) and Lake Barkley (on the Cumberland River). The first place of interest is Dover, Tennessee, where Union forces won their first considerable victory in the Civil War. The boat then continues up the Cumberland River to Nashville, Tennessee, world-famous as the home of country and western music. From Nashville it returns to Kentucky Lake and sails up the Tennessee River to Shiloh, scene of one of the fiercest battles of the American Civil War on April 6th 1862. The next place up river is Florence, Alabama, birthplace of W.C. Handy, "father of the blues". Near the point where the states of Alabama, Georgia and Tennessee meet the boat sails through Guntersville Lake and comes to that town on that railway, Chattanooga, Tennessee.

Sights from A to Z

Alabama (State)

P–T 37–41

Area: 51,610 sq. mi.
Population: 4.03 million
Capital: Montgomery
Popular names: Heart of Dixie,
Camellia State

The state of Alabama (from the Choctaw word alibamu, "clearing of the bush") lies in the south-eastern United States, extending into three great natural regions. In the north and east the landscape is patterned by the southern outliers of the Appalachians and part of the Cumberland and Piedmont Plateaux. The north-west of the state is occupied by the North-West Plateau in the central lowlands. The greater part of the state, to the south, takes in part of the Gulf Coast plain, descending in terraces from the Piedmont Plateau, with the fertile Black Belt. On both sides of the Alabama River estuary and Mobile Bay Alabama reaches down to the Gulf of Mexico. The climate is warm and humid, with high summer temperatures and mild winters. The coast is exposed to the danger of hurricanes. Much of the state is covered by forest (particularly oak, hickory and pine).

History The area was explored by the Spanish at the beginning of the 16th c. In 1702 French immigrants, disregarding British claims, settled the area round the Mobile River, but in 1763 France was compelled to cede the territory to Britain. Twenty years later the southern part of the area fell to Spain. In 1817 Alabama was incorporated as a United States territory and only two years later, in 1819, became the 22nd state of the Union. For many years cotton growing was a major element in the economy, supported by slavery. Alabama was one of the focal points of the civil rights movement.

Economy Alabama lies in the Cotton Belt, but in recent decades cotton growing has considerably declined, and maize, soya beans and peanuts are now important crops. Most of the abandoned cotton fields have now been given over to extensive cattle rearing. The forested southern part of the state supplies firewood and woodpulp for papermaking. The iron and coal mined in the southern Appalachians led to the development of Birmingham's iron and steel industry. Other important contributions to the state's economy are made by the chemical, textile and foodstuffs industries. Hydro-electric power stations have been established on the Tennessee and Alabama Rivers and some of their tributaries. There is lively inland shipping traffic on the dense network of rivers and waterways. Mobile has one of the largest and most important ports on the Gulf Coast. The beautiful bathing beaches on the Gulf of Mexico are attracting increasing numbers of holiday-makers.

Birmingham

The industrial city of Birmingham (pop. 266,000; iron and steel) was one of the centres of the civil rights movement and the Civil Rights District is one of the most interesting parts to visit. The history of the Civil Rights Movement is documented in the Civil Rights Institute. Also of interest are the Museum of Art (including Renaissance art), the Alabama Jazz Hall of Fame, Red Mountain with a statue of the god Vulcan (1904) and the Sloss Furnaces Industrial Museum, a former steelworks. South-west of the city is Tannehill Historic State Park, with a 19th c. village.

There is a detour by way of Talladega, a stock-car stronghold, to the **De Solo Caverns** lying to the south-west, a mythical site of the aboriginal Indians.

The main attraction in Huntsville (pop. 160,000), which has preserved some attractive old quarters, is the US Space and Rocket Center, where visitors can try out flight simulators and see the newest spacecraft. **Huntsville**

Mobile (pop. 197,000), one of the more important ports and industrial towns on the Gulf of Mexico, lies in a bay in south-western Alabama that reaches over 25 mi. inland. The town was founded by French immigrants at the beginning of the 18th c. Mardi Gras (Carnival) is still a lively annual event. A number of well preserved antebellum houses (e.g. Oakleigh Mansion, De Tonti Square) and beautiful gardens planted with azaleas give the town its special atmosphere. Other places of interest are the Fine Arts Museum of the South, the Museum of the City of Mobile, the Cathedral (1835) and an old French fort (rebuilt), Fort Condé. **Mobile**
  In Battleship Memorial Park are the destroyer "Alabama" and the submarine "Drum", which fought in the Second World War and the Korean War.

20 mi. south of Mobile on Mobile Bay lie the wonderful ★**Bellingrath Gardens** with thousands upon thousands of azaleas. At the south-west entrance to the bay lies the Dauphin Island bird sanctuary with Fort Gaines, which played a part in the Civil War. From there visitors can take a ferry to the western point of Pleasure Island with Fort Morgan. In the south-eastern corner of the bay are the fine bathing beaches of Gulf Shores and Orange Beach. **Mobile Bay**

Montgomery (pop. 187,000), capital of Alabama, lies in the centre of the state on the east bank of the Alabama River. It can be said to be the birthplace of the Civil Rights Movement, and in the Baptist church in Dexter Avenue the first activities gathered around Martin Luther King (see Baedeker Special, p. 146/7). Nearby is the Civil Rights Memorial in memory of a man who gave his life for the movement. Old Alabama Town with its 19th c. houses preserves something of the atmosphere of old Montgomery, once an important cotton market. Other places of interest are the Capitol and the White House, the oldest in the Confederate states. On the eastern outskirts of the town are the Museum of Fine Arts and the renowned Alabama Shakespeare Festival Theater. 43 mi. east of Montgomery is Tuskegee University, which originated as a college for the education of blacks founded by the former negro slave Booker T. Washington (see Famous People) in 1881. **Montgomery**

Selma, 48 mi. east of Montgomery, is also connected with the Civil Rights Movement. Here, in 1965, a protest march near Edmund Pettus Bridge was broken up by police wielding truncheons. The National Rights Museum documents the struggle for equal voting rights for black Americans. **Selma**

Tuscaloosa (pop. 78,000), former capital of Alabama and seat of the University of Alabama (founded 1831), lies on the Black Warrior River in the west of the state. It preserves a number of historic old houses. 16 mi. south of the town is the Mound State Monument, a prehistoric Indian cult centre or settlement site. **Tuscaloosa**

145

"I have a dream!"

When, on December 1st 1955, Rosa Parks refused to give up her seat on a bus to a white person, she had not planned to do so but simply acted spontaneously. At the same time what she did was no accident – it was the product of the self-awareness on the part of blacks that had steadily grown since the end of the Second World War and which, in the 1950s, had resulted in a few, albeit modest, successes in the political arena. Above all, however, Rosa Parks kindled the initial fire that ushered in a decade of spectacular campaigns arising not so much from any civil rights organisation as from the anger of those directly affected and which were viewed with some concern by the more moderate black leaders. The decisive years of the American civil rights movement between 1955 and 1965 also involved a turning away from the "legalistic" policies of the National Association for the Advancement of Colored People (NAACP), formed in 1909, which aimed at improving the lot of coloured people both in the courts and by political lobbying. Now, however, tactics changed "from below" – spontaneously, spectacularly and radically, but without the use of force.

Naturally this movement was not devoid of speakers and leaders, but they too did not spring from the existing organisations. The most prominent of them, Martin Luther King Jnr., came into the public eye a few days after the Rosa Parks affair. He was elected chairman of the Montgomery Improvement Association that organised the boycotting of public transport lasting almost a year. He above all it was who, following the example of both Christ and Ghandi, preached a gospel of nonviolence as the overriding principle to be followed. In 1957 he and his co-campaigners founded the Southern Christian Leadership Conference (SCLC), which was destined to become the country's major civil rights organisation. However, neither it nor the NAACP had any influence over the political action of the four college students who, on February 1st 1961, sat down at a counter in a Woolworths restaurant in Greensboro, NC that was reserved for white people and demanded to be served. Greensboro saw the "sit-in" form of political action spread like wildfire through over sixty towns in the more northerly of the southern States, and almost everywhere the locally organised civil-rights leaders strived in vain to control the students.

Moreover, in the next large campaign headed by the civil rights movement the organised sections found themselves acting as mere spectators. In the spring of 1961 the Congress of Racial Equality (CORE) sent thirteen so-called "freedom riders" on a bus ride through the south in order to protest against racial segregation on buses and at bus stations. When attacks by racist whites became more and more violent CORE called off their campaign, but others spontaneously decided to continue the protests. In Jackson, MS they were arrested but new "freedom riders" came to their support until finally throughout 1961 "freedom rides" regularly made the headlines.

The following three years, however, proved to be the heyday of the organised civil rights leaders, especially for King and the SCLC. Once again they resorted to the idea of sending activists to towns in the south to campaign among the poorer black workers and to urge them to demonstrate. The saddest element of this phase was signalled by the violent clashes between demonstrators and police in Birmingham, AL in the spring of 1963, while a more positive feature and the highlight of the whole civil rights movement was the march in August of that year on Washington, DC, where Martin Luther King made his famous "I have a dream!" speech before a crowd of 200,000. The Civil Rights Act passed by Congress in 1964 and the Voting Rights Act a year later meant the civil rights movement had attained its goal. On paper, at least, black Americans now had equal rights with the whites.

Attaining its goal, however, seemed to drain the strength out of the movement, and it found itself unable to convert formal equality into everyday reality and disunity threatened to split its ranks. Here would be practised King's peaceful approach, there the militant ideas of the Black Panthers, some still saw the southern states as their field of activity, while others wanted to concentrate their efforts on the wretched economic situation among the black urban communities

of the north. When King – the outstanding figure in the civil rights movement and perhaps the one most capable of bringing about true integration – was murdered in Memphis in 1968 there was nobody to take his place.

Without Rosa Parks, however, and the four from Greensboro, without the "freedom riders" and all those who died in the name of civil rights and whose memories are preserved in the Civil Rights Memorial in Montgomery, perhaps even King might have remained just one among many. They all struggled successfully to enable more and more African-Americans to make the great leap into parliament, to make themselves economically secure and, above all, to become self-confident and proud Americans.

However, it must be said that many African-Americans are still obliged to lead a life that gives them little to be proud or self-assured about, and that a normal, everyday coexistence of blacks and whites has not fully come about.

"The Beginning of a Dream": mural in Dexter Avenue King Memorial Baptist Church, Montgomery

★★Alaska (State)   Inset in map of USA

Area: 591 million sq. mi.
Population: 607,000
Capital: Juneau
Popular name: Last Frontier

Alaska, the largest and most northerly of the states of the Union, lies in the extreme north-west of the North American sub-continent, separated from the Asiatic land mass by the Bering Strait and Bering Sea. Its western and southern coasts are washed by the north-eastern Pacific and its north coast lies on the ice-cold Arctic Ocean. Just under 20 per cent of its population are Inuits (Eskimos), Aleuts and Indians. The name Alaska means "great land" in the language of the Aleuts.

Alaska is separated from the main United States by western Canada. The southern tip of the state, the Panhandle, reaches down to latitude 54°40′ north, with numerous fjords and islands. The most northerly point in the United States is Cape Barrow on the Arctic Ocean. Some two-thirds of the area of Alaska is under permafrost, with the soil frozen to depths of up to 1300 ft.

Geography Alaska is made up of three main regions: a narrow southern coastal strip, with the Panhandle to the south-east and the Aleutians to the south-west; the interior plains and tablelands; and the Arctic North.

The topography of south-eastern Alaska is dominated by the Coast Mountains, a range that suffered folding at a geologically recent period and is slashed by numerous tectonic faults. Rising to 8200 ft, it cuts off the Panhandle from Canada. Between Glacier Bay in the east and the Kenai Peninsula in the south numerous glaciers calve into the sea.

The Gulf of Alaska in enclosed by the Chugach Mountains (Mount Marcus Baker, 13,176 ft) and the Kenai Mountains, which extend into the Kodiak Peninsula. Other ranges of mountains striking further inland reach considerable heights: the St Elias Mountains (Mount Logan, 19,555 ft), the Wrangell Mountains (Mount Blackburn, 16,523 ft) and the mighty arc of the Alaska Range, with Mount McKinley (20,320 ft), the highest peak in the whole United States.

The whole of the south-west coast of Alaska forms part of the "Ring of Fire", the very active circum-Pacific volcanic and earthquake zone. This has been demonstrated by recent volcanic activity on Mount Redoubt and in the Katmai National Park.

The interior tablelands of Alaska, with their extensive plateaux and relatively low hills, are traversed by the 2000 mi. Yukon River, which rises in the Yukon Territory in Canada and flows into the Bering Sea in a wide delta.

The interior tablelands are bounded on the north by the 600 mi. Brooks Range, which rises from 4900 ft in the west to 9239 ft in Mount Michelson in the east.

Climate The coastal mountains have very high precipitations. The Yukon Basin, in the lee of the mountains, has a very cold and dry continental climate: an extreme temperature of 65°F has been recorded at Fort Yukon. The coasts on the Arctic Ocean are ice-bound almost all year round. The Bering Strait is ice free from June to October. Some two-fifths of Alaska is forest- covered, with hemlock, Sitka spruce, birch and willow most strongly represented. The Arctic tree-line is approximately on the 68th parallel. Beyond this and at higher altitudes the vegetation cover is that of the treeless tundra, characterised by dwarf pine, various shrubs, lichens and mosses.

History In 1741 Vitus Bering, a Dane in the Russian service, discovered the south coast of Alaska, then thinly peopled by Eskimos, Aleuts and Indians. Subsequently Spanish, British, Russian and American fur traders made their way into the territory, then administered by Russia. From 1799 the Russian-American Company had a monopoly of the fur trade in Alaska. In 1867 Russia sold the territory to the United States for 7.2 million dollars, and 17 years later, in 1884, it was given its own civil administration and a constitution modelled on that of Oregon. The discovery of gold on the Yukon River in 1897 led to an increase in population; and later the discovery of other raw materials, notably the deposits of oil found on the north coast in 1968, increased the economic importance of Alaska. In 1912 it became an independent territory. During the Second World War it was of strategic importance (construction of the Alaska Highway; United States military bases). In 1959 it became the 49th state of the Union.

Economy The economic wealth of Alaska lies in its enormous reserves of raw materials (timber, coal, copper, platinum, silver, oil). The extraction of oil and natural gas (since 1968) on the Arctic Ocean plays a major part in the economy of the state. Fishing and fish processing are also important sources of income. The timber industry is active mainly in the south-east of the territory. Agriculture, confined to small areas round Anchorage and Fairbanks, is in decline. Of interest to tourists is the magnificent landscape; there are also opportunities to observe animals, especially bears.

Alaska Highway

The 1510 mi. Alaska Highway runs from Dawson Creek in British Columbia (Canada) through the Yukon Territory to Fairbanks, in the centre of Alaska. It was built for military purposes in 1942, during the Second World War, in the record time of only eight months, and since the end of the war has been the most important means of access by land to the Yukon Territory and southern Alaska. For most of the way it is asphalted (with a gravel surface only in Canada), but at certain times of year is in only moderately good condition. There are motels, shops and gas stations at intervals of 30–50 mi.

From Dawson Creek the road runs north-west over the plain of the Peace River, passing Stone Mountain and Muncho Lake Provincial Park. Beyond Fort Nelson (about 310 mi.) it approaches the Rockies. The first place of any size in the Yukon Territory is Watson Lake, the "Gateway to the Yukon", with an information centre on the construction of the Highway and a famous collection of signposts. The route continues by way of Teslin, on the 800 mi. long lake of that name, to Whitehorse (930 mi.), capital of the Yukon Territory. Beyond Whitehorse the road heads for the St Elias Mountains. At the little township of Haines Junction is the entrance to Kluane National Park, a unique nature reserve with Canada's highest peak, Mount Logan (19,525 ft). At Soldiers Summit (1060 mi.) the Alaska Highway was officially opened on November 20th 1942. On the right of the road, some 37 mi. beyond Haines Junction, is the 46 mi. long Kluane Lake (campgrounds, good fishing). After 1240 mi. the Highway comes to the Canadian-United States frontier and moves from the Pacific into the Alaska time zone. On the final 310 mi. to Fairbanks it runs through the fertile Tana Valley. At Tok Junction (about 1320 mi.) the Glen Highway branches off, running by way of Glacier Park, with the Matanuska Glacier, to Anchorage (see below).

Alaska

Cruises

A cruise along the coast of Alaska is an unforgettable experience. Both the Inside Passage through the rocky reefs to the Panhandle (e.g. from Vancouver to Skagway) and cruises through the Gulf of Alaska (e.g. from Whittier to Seward) offer fantastic views. There are also land trips, of course.

Anchorage

The port of Anchorage (pop. 250,000) lies at the head of Cook Inlet, surrounded by the Chugach Mountains. It is Alaska's largest town, its commercial and economic centre and its most important traffic hub (intercontinental air services; the world's largest seaplane base). Among places of interest are the Anchorage Museum of History and Art and Earthquake Park, which commemorates the devastating 1964 earthquake. Anchorage appeals to visitors as a good base for excursions by air or boat and for the scenic attractions of its immediate surroundings. Within easy reach of the town are Mount Alyeska Ski Resort, which offers skiing throughout the year, the magnificent Portage Glacier (50 mi. south-east) and the Kenai Peninsula (see below). Chugach National Forest and Chugach State Park offer unspoiled natural landscapes.

★★Denali
National Park

In the northern part of the Alaska Range is the Denali National Park, the second largest National Park in the United States, with an area of 9375 sq. mi. – a region of depressions and wide river valleys, areas of tundra and high alpine ranges of mountains from which glaciers flow down. In the south-west of the park is majestic Mount McKinley (20,320 ft), the highest mountain in the United States. This is the home of grizzly bears, wolves, reindeer, elk and other animals, the reflection of which in Reflection Pond is popular with photographers. Visitors can try their hand at panning for gold in Moose River. Open mid-May to mid-Sep.

Fairbanks

Fairbanks, Alaska's second largest town and the terminus of the Alaska Highway, developed around 1900 from a gold-diggers' camp. The

Denali National Park

University of Alaska Museum has a collection illustrating the history of the territory. In the Alaskaland leisure park are reconstructions of a gold-diggers' village and Eskimo and Indian settlements. In the Large Animal Research Station wild animals can be seen living in natural conditions. There are paddle-steamer trips on the Chena and Tanana Rivers. The Midnight Sun is visible from September to April. Fairbanks is a good base for excursions (by air) to northern and eastern Alaska, for example to Fort Yukon, the largest Indian settlement in Alaska, or by road to Marley or Chena Hot Springs.

An impressive natural spectacle is to be seen at Glacier Bay, 60 mi. north-west of Juneau, an inlet between two promontories where 16 glaciers reach down to the sea. There are cruises to the bay (day trips and longer trips) in the course of which whales are sometimes seen.

★**Glacier Bay National Park**

Juneau, capital of Alaska, was originally a gold-diggers' settlement (founded in the 1880s) on Gold Creek. It lies in the most southerly part of the state on the Panhandle, a narrow tongue of land slashed by fjord-like inlets that is separated from the sea by a string of small islands. There is no road to Juneau, and it can be reached only by sea or air. Places of interest are the Alaska State Museum, the House of Judge Wickersham and the Russian Orthodox church (1894). Juneau is a good base from which to explore the scenic beauties of the Panhandle, either by sea or by air. Particularly worthwhile are the Admiralty Island National Monument, the Tongass National Forest and Glacier Bay National Park (see above).

Juneau

The Kenai Peninsula, south of Anchorage, is a popular excursion and holiday destination. The larger settlements on the peninsula – Homer, Seward and Kenai, the chief town, are easily accessible on Highway 1 or 9; and Seward, a fishing port, is also the terminus of the Alaska Railroad. Seward is an excellent base for excursions into Kenai Fjords National Park. With its glaciers and fjords, the scenery of this National Park, centred on the Harding Icefield, is reminiscent of the west coast of Norway; there is a motorable road to the Exit Glacier. Here birdwatchers will be able to observe many species of birds. Highway 1 ends in the fishing village of Homer, a popular resort for visitors with its comparatively mild climate and beautiful situation on Kachemak Bay (Pratt Museum, with exhibits illustrating the culture of the Eskimos, Aleuts and early Russian settlers; camping, fishing, boat trips).

★**Kenai Peninsula**

In the south of the Panhandle lies the fishing village of Ketchikan. In the Totem Bight State Historical Park, 10 mi. to the north, can be seen an imposing number of Indian totem poles all grouped together – a rare sight.

★**Totem Bight State Historical Park**

Most of this island off the south-west coast of Alaska (boats from Homer and Seward on Kenai Peninsula) is now the Kodiak National Wildlife Refuge, established to protect the Kodiak bear and other rare animals. The waters round Kodiak are among the richest fishing grounds in Alaska. The town of Kodiak at the north-eastern tip of the peninsula, now an important fishing port, was occupied for over 6000 years by the indigenous Aleuts, until Russian fur traders settled here in 1784 and made the town first capital of the Russian territory. Places of interest are the old Russian Orthodox church and a small museum on the history of the island.

Kodiak

The port of Nome, situated some 500 mi. west of Fairbanks on the Seward Peninsula (Bering Sea), can be reached only by air. Founded by gold-diggers about 1900, during the gold rush, it is the economic and commercial centre of north-western Alaska; gold panning is now only a show for tourists. Nome is the end point of the 1049 mi. Iditarod dog-

Nome

Sitka

sled race from Anchorage, lasting anything from two to four weeks, which is run annually in March. The Eskimo villages in the surrounding area can be visited either by air or by hired car.

The fishing port of Sitka on the west side of Baranoff Island in the Alexander Archipelago, founded by Alexander Baranoff in 1804, was once the chief town of Russian America. Places of interest are icons and vestments from the Orthodox church of St Michael (built 1844, burned down 1966) and the Sheldon Jackson Museum (artefacts, masks, craft products and clothing of Eskimos and Indians). In the Sitka National Historical Park are a display of material illustrating the culture of the original Indian tribes and the Russian settlers and the scene of the last battle (1804) between Russians and Tlingit Indians, commemorated by Indian totem poles.

Skagway

The old gold-diggers' town of Skagway lies in the Klondike Gold Rush National Historical Park. It is the start of the Ckikout Trail that led Jack London and thousands of others to the Klondike. It can be reached either by road or by way of the Inside Passage, the shipping route that links the towns and settlements on the Panhandle with one another.

★Wrangell-St Elias National Park

The Wrangell-St Elias National Park is the largest and most magnificent of the National Parks of Alaska, with nine of the 16 highest peaks in the United States. This grandiose mountain region on the frontier with Canada contains numerous glaciers, lakes and mountain streams and is home to a rich variety of wild life. It is superb country for climbers, walkers and water sports enthusiasts.

Albuquerque   O 19

State: New Mexico
Altitude: 5005 ft
Population: 385,000

The city of Albuquerque lies on the Rio Grande, surrounded by the Sandia Hills. The climate is dry, with hot summers and cold winters. Almost a third of the total population of New Mexico live in the city, on which Indians, Spaniards and Anglo-Americans have all left their mark. Albuquerque has long been an important commercial town and traffic hub and the old Route 66 runs through the centre of it. It is an important centre of research and development, with many institutes and laboratories (including nuclear research), as well as the University of New Mexico.

History The Spanish colonial settlement of Albuquerque, situated on the trade route between Santa Fe and Mexico City, was founded in 1706 and soon developed into a considerable town. The Stars and Stripes was hoisted over the town in 1846 by General Stephen Kearny when he established a military post here. A boost was given to the town when the railway reached it in 1880. A new town was established that soon outstripped and incorporated the old Spanish colonial settlement.

Sights

★Old Town

The Old Town of Albuquerque is the picturesque core of the old Spanish colonial settlement. Dominating the Spanish-style Plaza is the church of San Felipe de Neri, built in 1706. Round the square, on which various craftsmen (not only Indians) offer their products for sale, are a range of shops, galleries, cafés. Between April and October there are guided tours of the Old Town, starting from the Albuquerque Museum, which boasts the largest collection of Spanish colonial exhibits in the United States. For those who like that sort of thing there is the Rattlesnake Museum at 202 San Felipe Street, NW.

The New Mexico Museum of Natural History (1801 Mountain Rd.) offers a fascinating survey of the natural history of the American south-west from prehistory to the present day. Particularly impressive are a life-size model of a dinosaur, an artificial volcano, a reproduction of an Ice Age cave habitation. There is also a cinema in which spectacular nature films are shown.

★New Mexico Museum of Natural History

The Indian Pueblo Cultural Center (2401 12th St. NW) gives an informative picture of the history and culture of the Pueblo Indians. Visitors can watch as beautiful craft objects are produced by traditional techniques and can sample Indian cooking. At weekends there are performances of traditional Indian dances.

★Indian Pueblo Cultural Center

The University of New Mexico (Central Ave.) is built in the style of an Indian pueblo. It contains three fine museums – the Geology Museum, the Meteorite Museum and the Maxwell Museum of Anthropology.

University of New Mexico

The National Atomic Museum (Kirtland Air Force Base, Wyoming Blvd., Building 20358), including full-size models of the bombs dropped on Hiroshima and Nagasaki.

National Atomic Museum

Surroundings

7 mi. north-west of the city is the Indian Petroglyph State Park, with symbols and drawings scratched in the rock by prehistoric Indians, the significance of which has not been established.

★**Indian Petroglyph Park**

There are superb views from Sandia Peak (10,375 ft; cable railway) in the north-east of Albuquerque.

Sandia Park

By visiting a *pueblo* in the vicinity of Albiuquerque visitors can come very close to Indian culture. Always be courteous and be sure to ask for permission before taking photographs. Near Bernalillo, 15 mi. to the north, lies the large Pueblo Kuana. The Spanish *conquistador* Francisco Vasquez de Coronada is said to have camped here in 1540.

★**Pueblos**

On a 365 ft high mesa south-west of Albuquerque, **Acoma Pueblo** are the remains of what is thought to be the oldest continuously inhabited settlement in the United States, securely dated on archaeological evidence to 1150 but quite probably occupied since the beginning of the Christian era. Beside the pueblo Spanish Franciscans established the mission of San Esteban del Rey in 1629.

South-east of Albuquerque is the **Salinas Pueblo** National Monument, which contains within its extensive area remains left by the Spanish conquistadors as well as the native Indians: the San Benaventura Mission (begun 1659) and 21 pueblo mounds at Gran Quivira, the ruins of the mission church of San Gregorio de Abo, adjoining a large pueblo to the west of Mountainair and the ruins of the mission of the Purísima Concepcion to the north of Mountainair.

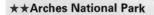

★★Arches National Park   L 16

State: Utah

Area: 120sq. mi.
Established: 1929

Arches National Park lies at altitudes between 3900 ft and 5600 ft in the desert-like south-eastern part of Utah, through which flows the Colorado River. It is world famous for its extraordinary rock formations – several hundred sandstone arches, some of them of gigantic size, mushroom-shaped rocks, high sandstone rock faces, pinnacles, battlements, buttresses and ridges – created mainly by the action of wind and weather.

With luck visitors to the Park may encounter desert hares, deer, coyotes, red foxes and porcupines.

Information The Park is open throughout the year. The best time to visit it is from April to September. The Visitor Centre lies at the south entrance on the US 191.

Within the Park there is only a small campground near the Devil's Garden. There are motels in Moab.

The 21 mi. **Scenic Drive** takes visitors round the most impressive features in the National Park (nature reserve). From Moab Canyon it runs to the LaSal Mountains View Point, from which mountains rising to almost 13,000 ft can be seen in the distance. Then follow the Courthouse Towers, a series of unusual rock formations (including the Three Gossips and the Tower of Babel). The road continues along the Great Wall and past the Petrified Dunes. At the Balanced Rock, which is almost 130 ft high, a road goes off on the right to the Windows Section with its rock arches (Cove Arch, Double Arch.) and rock windows (North Window, South Window.). Then down into Salt Valley, with a road branching off on the right to the Wolfe Ranch (once owned by a Civil War veteran) and the Delicate Arch View Point. From Salt Valley the road continues past

Natural architecture in the Arches National Park

Salt Valley Overlook, the Fiery Furnace Viewpoint and the Skyline Arch to end at the Devil's Garden car park.

Walking In view of the very fragile desert vegetation there are only a few hiking routes in the National Park. Among them are the Devil's Garden Trail (2 mi.), on which there are eight rock arches, including the Landscape Arch, one of the largest of its kind, and the Delicate Arch Trail (1½ mi.), which starts from the Wolfe Ranch. The rock labyrinth known as the Fiery Furnace, in which it is easy to lose your way, should be entered only on a guided walk conducted by a park ranger. There is an attractive walk from the car park at Klondike Bluffs to the Tower Arch area on the north-western edge of the National Park.

The little Mormon town of Moab has developed into a tourist centre. It **Moab** is the mecca of mountain bikers and a starting point for a visit to Castle Valley with its picturesque, castle-like rock formations and also for organised white-water rafting on the Colorado River. Here, too, is the original Moab to Monument Valley Film Commission Museum that illustrates which films were made against the splendid backdrop of south-east Utah, including "Rio Grande" with John Wayne, "Indiana Jones" and "The Last Crusade" or "Thelma and Louise".

Arizona (State)   N–S 12–16

Area: 114,000 sq. mi.
Population: 3.75 million
Capital: Phoenix
Popular name: Grand Canyon State

Arizona (from the Indian ari-zonac, "land of the little rivers") lies in the south-western United States, bounded on the south by Mexico. It consists of two differ-ent geological and morphological regions within the intermontane zone of the Cordilleras. Northern Arizona forms part of the Colorado Plateau, with the Grand Canyon, hewn from the rock to depths of up to 6600 ft. The plateau, traversed by innumerable faults and flexures, falls away to the south and west in a series of steep scarps. In this area are the high-est mountains in the state, rising to 12,668 ft in the San Francisco Peaks. In the south of Arizona is the Basin and Range Province, its north-east-ern part reaching into the highlands of Mexico, its south-western part ending in the Gila Desert. As a result of the hot and very dry climate steppeland and desert predominate, accounting for some two-thirds of the state's area. Giant cactuses and yuccas are characteristic of its drought-loving vegetation. At higher altitudes, with a more humid cli-mate, the hills are partly forest covered.

History Some areas in Arizona are among the longest-settled parts of North America. Archaeological evidence points to continuous human occupation for some 11,000 years. In the 16th c. Spaniards began to move into Arizona from Mexico. Under the peace of Guadalupe Hidalgo at the end of the Mexican War (1846–8) Arizona passed to the United States (the Gadsden Purchase), and in 1912 it was admitted to the Union as the 48th state. After Oklahoma and California, Arizona has the third highest pro-portion of Indians (mostly Apache, Navajo and Hopi) in its population.

Economy A major element in Arizona's economy is cattle-rearing, but in the valleys of the Gila and Salt Rivers arable farming is made possible

155

by irrigation. Huge artificial lakes formed by damming the rivers provide water throughout the year for lucrative crops of cotton, citrus fruits, winter vegetables and forage cereals. The mining of the state's large deposits of copper ore (roughly half total United States output) and its processing make an important contribution to the economy. Other important minerals are molybdenum, gold, silver, zinc, lead and oil. Important industries in the secondary sector are metalworking and electronics (aircraft, rockets), foodstuffs and textiles. Tourism has also developed rapidly and become an important element in the state's economy, thanks to Arizona's magnificent scenery (e.g. the Grand Canyon), its pleasant climate and the numerous remains of old Indian cultures. The climate has also helped to persuade a large number of senior citizens to retire here.

Flagstaff

The university town of Flagstaff (alt. 7028 ft; pop. 46,000), within the Coconino National Forest, is a good base from which to visit the Grand Canyon and the Navajo Indian Reservation (see entries). Places of interest in and around the town are the Pioneer Museum of the Arizona Historical Society, the Coconino Center for the Arts (art exhibition) and the Museum of Northern Arizona (3 mi. north-west of the town; crafts of the Navajo and Hopi Indians). On Mars Hill, to the west of the town, is the Lovell Observatory, from which the planet Pluto was discovered in 1930.

Walnut Canyon

16 mi. east of Flagstaff is the deep Walnut Canyon, with some 300 rock dwellings of the old Indian Sinagua culture (12th/13th c.; the name Sinagua in Spanish means "waterless"). Some 30 mi. further east is the best preserved meteorite crater on earth, which has been used for the training of astronauts.

★Sunset Crater

Sunset Crater, 14 mi. north of Flagstaff, Arizona, is the 1000 ft high crater of a volcano that erupted in 1065. Round the crater are interesting lava flow formations.

Wupatki National Monument

In Wupatki National Monument, 30 mi. north of Flagstaff, are extensive remains of 12th and 13th c. pueblos. The largest of them, the three-storey Wupatki Pueblo, had more than a hundred rooms with an ingenious heating system.

★Montezuma Castle

An hour's drive south of Flagstaff is Montezuma Castle, a dwelling of the Sinagua culture built into a recess in a sandstone cliff that rises to a height of 100 ft above Beaver Creek. The first whites who came here thought that this was an Aztec settlement. The dwelling, which is about 700 years old, has 20 rooms on five levels and could be entered only on ladders.

Lake Havasu City

In the far west of Arizona, on the border with California, is Lake Havasu, a popular resort with water sports enthusiasts. Lake Havasu City (alt. 600 ft; pop. 25,000) was founded only in 1964. Its main attraction is the 1831 London Bridge that was bought in 1968 and re-erected here (it is said that the owner actually thought he had bought Tower Bridge and was somewhat disappointed when it arrived.

★Organ Pipe National Monument

In south-western Arizona, on the frontier with Mexico, is Organ Pipe National Monument, in which are three distinct desertic vegetation zones with some 30 different species of cactus, in particular the characteristic organ pipe cactus, up to 23 ft high, which blooms from May to July but because of the great heat during the day opens up its flowers only after sunset. The area can be explored on various roads and hiking trails.

★Petrified Forest National Park

The Petrified Forest National Park lies in the arid north-east of Arizona in the Painted Desert (so called because of its brilliantly coloured sandstone in shades of red and blue).

Petrified trees in the Petrified Forest National Park

In the Mesozic era this was a plain traversed by numerous water-courses. with a vegetation of horsetails, ferns and coniferous trees in particularly well watered areas. When a tree fell it was covered by river-borne sediments and sealed off from the air, hindering the natural process of decay. In wet periods water containing silicon oxides filtered into the rotten wood, and when it became drier the water evaporated and the silicon oxides crystallised. The concentration gradually became so high that quartz (rock crystal, amethyst, agate, onyx, cornelian, jasper) was formed, preserving the internal cell structure and the external appearance of the trunk. Then in geologically recent times erosion by wind and weather freed the petrified plant remains from the overlying sandstone and brought to light not only fossilised plant remains (fern leaves, pine cones) but fossils of shellfish, snails, fish, amphibians and reptiles.

The 23 mi. **Park Road** runs through the finest parts of the National Park. After passing through a particularly impressive part of the Painted Desert it comes to the Puerco Indian Ruin, the remains of a settlement occupied by Pueblo Indians 600 years ago. To the south of this is the Newspaper Rock, a huge block of sandstone with Indian rock drawings. In the Blue Mesa area it can be seen how the petrified remains of trees have been exposed by erosion. Further south is a viewpoint overlooking the Jasper Forest, a valley filled with fossil remains of trees. Beyond this again is the Crystal Forest, so named for its wealth of semi-precious stones and fossil remains of plants. The road then runs through the Rainbow Forest, with the Long Logs.

Prescott (alt. 5368 ft; pop. 27,000), north-west of Phoenix (see entry) in the beautiful Prescott National Forest, has developed in recent years into a popular tourist centre. Its places of interest are Sharlot Hall (1864; historical museum), home of the first Governor of Arizona. In the shops **Prescott**

Daily showdown in Tombstone

along Whiskey Road, once the scene of many a "shoot out", one can buy Wild West outfits.

Arcosanti 38 mi. south-west is the settlement of Arcosanti, designed by the Soleri firm of architects with careful concern for ecological considerations.

★Tombstone In the south-eastern corner of Arizona is Tombstone (pop. 1200), the famous Wild West township of the silver boom. Many buildings of that period, including the printing office of the town's daily newspaper "Epitaph", the Bird Cage Theatre, the Crystal Palace Saloon, the Rose Tree Inn and the Court House, have been lovingly restored. The OK Corral, scene of the famous shoot-out in 1881 between the Earp and Clanton gangs, is also preserved.

Yuma The town of Yuma (pop. 45,000) lies in the extreme south-west of Arizona, in a region of great heat that has been made fertile by irrigation. It preserves a number of buildings, including an adobe prison and the US Army Quartermaster Depot, which recall its troubled history.

Other sights Canyon de Chelly (see Navajo Indian Reservation), Grand Canyon, Phoenix (see entries), Scottsdale (see Phoenix), Tucson (see entry).

Arkansas (State) N–Q 31–36

Area: 53,187 sq. mi.
Population: 2.38 million
Capital: Little Rock
Popular names: Land of Opportunity, Natural State

The state of Arkansas, in the southern United States, is divided into two by the Arkansas River, which flows from north-west to south-east to join the Mississippi. In the north of the state the Boston Mountains, part of the Ozark Plateau, rise to heights of up to 2900 ft; in the south are the Ouachita Mountains. To the south the flood plain of the Mississippi

merges almost imperceptibly into the Gulf Coast plain. Roughly half the state is forested. The climate is marked by mild winters, warm summers and precipitations that are distributed evenly over the year.

History The first European to pass through the region, then occupied by the indigenous Indian inhabitants, was the Spanish explorer Hernando de Soto, who was looking for the legendary Well of Eternal Youth (1541). In the 17th c. the territory was occupied by France and in 1731 became part of Louisiana. In 1763 it passed to Spain but was recovered by France in 1799. Under the Louisiana Purchase it was acquired by the United States for 15 million dollars. On June 15th 1836 it became the 25th state of the Union.

Economy Arkansas lies in the climatically favoured Sun Belt. Its agriculture is mainly devoted to the growing of soya beans, rice and fruit and to cattle rearing and poultry farming. Its industry is mainly concerned with the processing of local produce (e.g. attar of roses for use in the manufacture of perfume) and timber.

Arkansas also has substantial mineral resources, including oil, natural gas, coal, manganese and diamonds. It also produces some 95 per cent of the total American output of bauxite. Tourism is still relatively little developed.

In south-eastern Arkansas is the Arkansas Post National Memorial, commemorating the first permanent French settlement, established in 1686. | Arkansas Post

In northern Arkansas, round the Buffalo River, is a popular and very beautiful recreation area that in summer attracts large numbers of canoeists. | ★Buffalo National River

In south-western Arkansas, a short drive from Murfreesboro, is the Crater of Diamonds State Park, the only source of natural diamonds in the United States that is open to the public. | Crater of Diamonds

Within the area of Eureka Springs, a tourist resort in the extreme north-west of Arkansas, there are more than sixty springs. With its attractive old Victorian buildings, an artists' colony, two small museums, a varied programme of entertainments (including a Passion Play) and the old-time Eureka Springs and North Arkansas Railway, it draws visitors throughout the year. To the east of the town is the interesting Onyx Cave; to the west is the Blue Spring, one of the most abundant springs in the Ozark Mountains. | Eureka Springs

In the north-western corner of Arkansas is the town of Fayetteville (pop. 38,000), seat of the University of Arkansas. Places of interest include Headquarters house (1853), which served as headquarters for both the Unionists and the Confederation, and Prairie Grove Battle field State Park where a Civil War battle was fought on December 7th 1862. South of the town is the picturesque Devil's Den State Park. | Fayetteville

The town of Fort Smith, situated on a bend in the Arkansas River on the | Fort Smith border with Oklahoma, grew out of a fort established in 1817 to protect the westward trek of settlers. During the Californian gold rush it became the haunt of gun-happy bandits. The Belle Grove Historic District has been beautifully restored.

★Hot Springs

Hot Springs, 55 mi. south-west of Little Rock, is one of the most popular spa resorts in the United States. The heyday of this little town of rather European aspect was in the 1920s and 1930s, but it still attracts large numbers of visitors to Hot Springs National Park take the cure, practise various sports or walk in Hot Springs National Park, part of the Ouachita Mountains. The old Fordyce Bathhouse still gives some impression of spa life in earlier times.

Little Rock

Little Rock, political and economic centre of Arkansas, lies in the heart of the state, separated from its sister city of North Little Rock by the Arkansas River. The town, founded in 1812, took its name from the French "petite roche"; it became capital of the state in 1821. The Quapaw Historic District (named after a local Indian tribe) preserves some handsome remains of old Little Rock, including the classical Old State House and the Arkansas Museum of Science and History in MacArthur Park, housed in the only surviving building of Little Rock's Arsenal (1836), in which General Douglas MacArthur (1880–1964) was born. Fans of "Gone with the Wind" will want to visit the Old Mill (a watermill of 1828) in North Little Rock, where the early scenes of the film were shot.

★Ozark Mountains

Large areas of the beautiful Ozark Mountains are now protected as a National Forest. Their lakes, waterfalls, wild gorges and hills offering magnificent views, like Magazine Mountain, draw large numbers of visitors in summer. Also of interest is the Ozark Folk Center (folk art) at the little town of Mountain View.

Stuttgart

Stuttgart, founded around 1880 by a German from Swabia in southern Germany and named after the Swabian capital, is now a centre for rice growing and poultry farming. It has an interesting Agricultural Museum illustrating the development of farming in the prairies.

Atlanta   Q 41

State: Georgia
Altitude: 1050 ft
Population: 394,000

Atlanta, capital of the state of Georgia, is in almost all respects the principal centre of the American South. It lies in the foreland of the southern foothills of the Piedmont Plateau, on the watershed between the Gulf of Mexico and the Atlantic. The city was originally planned as a railway junction, and rapidly developed into an important commercial town. In recent years it has become a major economic and cultural centre in the American south-east and an important hub of air traffic. Internationally famed businesses (e.g. Coca-Cola and the CNN new network) have their headquarters here. A brief high point of this development was the staging of the 26th Summer Olympic Games in 1996 – although sadly these have gone down in history more as the olympiads of troubles and shameless commercialism. Those visiting Atlanta should not expect to find a romantic southern state, even though Margaret Mitchell wrote "Gone with the Wind" here, but rather a vibrant American city with southern charm, as exemplified in Atlanta Station – all as a result of Coco-Cola (see Baedeker Special, p. 164/5), perhaps the most American of all American things.

History A military outpost was established in 1814 in the Indian village of Standing Peachtrees on the east bank of the Chattahoochee River, and in 1837 this became the terminus of the Western and Atlantic Railroad. The settlement that grew up was at first known simply as Terminus; then in 1843 it was renamed Marthasville in honour of the daughter of the then governor. Only two years later, in 1845, it was given its present name of Atlanta. During the Civil War it was an important Confederate stronghold, supply base and hospital centre. In 1864 the Union General William Sherman, noted for his ruthless conduct of the war, captured the town and reduced it to rubble. These events were described by Margaret Mitchell in her best-selling novel "Gone with the Wind", which won her the Pulitzer Prize. In 1868 Atlanta became capital of the young state of Georgia. In 1886 the soft drink with the largest world sale was created in Atlanta. Large areas of the city were destroyed by a great fire in 1917. In 1929 Martin Luther King (see Famous People) was born in Atlanta. After the Second World War Atlanta enjoyed a huge economic upswing, and today it can almost bear comparison with New York and Chicago.

Sights

At the point where two covered shopping malls now meet (Alabama St., between Peachtree St. and Central Ave.) there once stood the terminus of the Western and Atlantic Railroad, the nucleus of the present city. During the Civil War there was an assembly point for wounded here. Since 1865 this area has lain below the present street level. For many years it was hidden and forgotten; then in the 1980s, when its possibilities were realised, it was restored in period (1880–1900) style and reopened in 1989. The underground passages, enlivened by musicians, entertainers and street traders, are now occupied by restaurants, bars and over a hundred shops and boutiques.

Underground Atlanta

In 1886 a chemist named Dr John Pemberton devised a syrup designed to relieve headaches. A friend of his mixed the glutinous liquid with water and carbonic acid, and the result of the mixture soon became the world's most popular soft drink. The World of Coca-Cola (55 Martin Luther King Jr Dr.) entertainingly illustrates the history and triumphal progress of the world-famous drink. Open Mon.–Sat. 10am–9.30pm, Sun. noon–6pm.

★★The World of Coca-Cola

On Capitol Square and Washington Street is the State Capitol of Georgia, completed in 1889, with a gilded dome 236 ft high.

Georgia State Capitol

The Peachtree Center, a futuristic complex of tower blocks designed by John Portman (between Baker St., Ellis St., Williams St. and Courtland St.), with the world's tallest hotel, rises to varying heights between 302 ft and 722 ft. With numerous offices and a wide variety of shopping, dining and entertainment facilities, it forms a second city centre. Westin Peachtree Plaza is the tallest hotel in the United States; the fantastic atrium of the Hyatt Regency should also be seen.

Peachtree Center

On Marietta Street and Techwood Drive is the CNN Center, the head-quarters of Cable Network News, where visitors can see something of the work (including the television studios) of the most famous and most up-to-date news broadcasting system in the world. Tours daily 9am–4pm.

CNN Center

Next to the CNN Center is the Olympic Centennial Park, the new heart of Downtown Atlanta, which was laid out at the time of the 1996 Olympics.

Olympic Centennial Park

Two blocks on Auburn Avenue are now protected as a National Historic Site. They include the birthplace of the civil rights campaigner Martin Luther King Jr at 501 Auburn Avenue, which dates from 1895, and the

★★Martin Luther King Jr National Historic Site

Atlanta

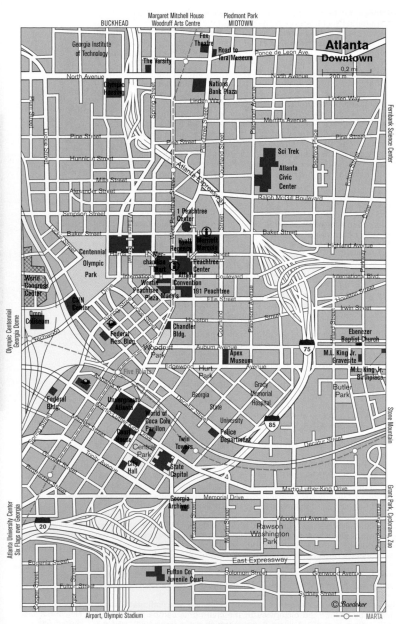

BUCKHEAD
Margaret Mitchell House
Woodruff Arts Centre
Piedmont Park
MIDTOWN

Georgia Institute of Technology

Fox Theatre

Road to Tara Museum

Ponce de Leon Ave.

Atlanta Downtown

0,2 mi
200 m

The Varsity

North Avenue

North Avenue

Linden Way

Olympic Housing

NationsBank Plaza

Merritts Avenue

Pine Street

Pine Street

Hunnicut Street

Mills Street

Sci Trek

Atlanta Civic Center

Ralph McGill Boulevard

Alexander Street

Simpson Street

Baker Street

1 Peachtree Center

Baker Street

Highland Avenue

Centennial Olympic Park

Hyatt Regency

Marriott Marquis

Merchandise Mart

Peachtree Center

Fernbank Science Center

World Congress Center

Westin Peachtree Plaza

Atlanta Convention

Macys

191 Peachtree

Boulevard

International Blvd.

Houston Street

Irwin Street

CNN Center

Ellis Street

Omni Coliseum

Federal Res. Bldg.

Chandler Bldg.

Houston

Ebenezer Baptist Church

Olympic Centennial Georgia Dome

Woodruff Park

Auburn Avenue

M.L. King Jr. Gravesite

Apex Museum

M.L. King Jr. Birthplace

Five Points

Hurt Park

Edgewood

Butler Park

Federal Bldg.

Underground Atlanta

Georgia

Grady Memorial Hospital

State

World of Coca Cola Pavillon

University

Police Department

Atlanta University Center
Six Flags over Georgia

Court House

Twin Towers

Central Park

Decatur Street

City Hall

State Capitol

Memorial Drive

Georgia Archives

Martin Luther King Drive

Stone Mountain

Grant Park Cyclorama Zoo

Woodward Avenue

Rawson Washington Park

East Expressway

Fulton Co. Juvenile Court

Solomon Street

Glenwood Avenue

Fulton Street

Sydney Street

©Baedeker

Airport, Olympic Stadium

MARTA

Birthplace of Martin Luther King Jr

Ebenezer Baptist Church (407–413 Auburn Ave.), in which he and his father were ministers. Immediately adjoining, in the Freedom Hall Complex, is his grave. The Martin Luther King Jr Center for Nonviolent Social Change (with an exhibition) is also in this area. Conducted tours are run by the Visitor Center at 522 Auburn Avenue.

In Grant Park (Georgia and Cherokee Aves.) is the Atlanta Cyclorama, with a large circular painting (by German artists, 1885–6) depicting the battle for Atlanta in 1864.

Atlanta Cyclorama

Atlanta, of course, is also the city of Margaret Mitchell, author of "Gone with the Wind". Burnt down in 1994, the house in which she was born (999 Peachtree St., NE) was burnt down again in 1996 after it had been rebuilt, and has now been rebuilt once more. The heroes of her novel can be found in the road to Tara Museum to the south of the house. Opposite it lies Fox Theatre, a 4600-seater cinema in 1930s and 1940s style (guided tours).

Margaret Mitchell House

The architecturally noteworthy High Museum of Art (architect: Richard Meier) possesses an extraordinary collection of art from the renaissance to the present day, with 19th c. French masters predominating. The museum forms part of the Robert W. Woodruff Arts Center (1280 Peachtree St., NE).

★High Museum of Art

Opened in 1992, this museum portrays the natural history of Georgia as well as technical and scientific phenomena with the aid of modern techniques (767 Clifton Rd.).

★Fernbank Museum of Natural History

On the northern outskirts of the city is the select residential district of Buckhead. In addition to the sumptuous houses it has fashionable boutiques, unusual galleries, upmarket restaurants and Lennox Square, the largest shopping mall in the south-east.
In a 32 acre park at 3101 Andrews Drive NW/West Paces Ferry Road are two handsome but very different buildings: Swan House, an elegant Renaissance-style mansion built in 1928 that now houses the Atlanta Historical Society and the Tullie Smith House, a plain Georgian farmhouse built in 1840. The McElreath Hall contains extensive collections on the Civil War and the history of Atlanta.

★Buckhead

Surroundings

Atlanta's international airport (Hartsfield Airport), 10 mi. south of the city centre, is the second busiest airport in the United States and in the world after Chicago O'Hare (over 63 million passengers in 1996).

★Atlanta International Airport

16 mi. east of the city centre, at 6867 Memorial Drive, is Stone Mountain Park (area 5 sq. mi.), commemorating the soldiers of the southern states who fell in the Civil War. In the centre of the park is Stone Mountain, an 863 ft high mass of exposed granite with a circumference of 5 mi. On the east flank of the hill is an equestrian relief, hewn from the rock between 1923 and 1970, depicting the three Confederate leaders, President Jefferson Davis and his two generals, Stonewall Jackson and Robert E.

★Stone Mountain Park

Let's take a break ...

Drink Coca-Cola! Who has not heard the advertising slogan for this fizzy drink from Atlanta, which, even if there is nothing else available, can almost always be found on sale even in the remotest corners of the Earth. Coca-Cola is the world's most successful proprietary article, and symbolises the American way of life more than anything else.

However, its beginnings were extremely modest. John Styth Pemberton (1833–88), a chemist by trade in Atlanta, earned a reasonable living selling hair dyes, tooth powder, photographic chemicals and various other items. Above all, however, he mixed up elixirs for all forms of gouty complaints. The entry for May 8th 1886 in his experiments diary shows when he "hit the jackpot"; he mixed extracts of cola nut and coca leaves with sugar and "some other plant extracts", diluted the whole with water and called it "French Wine of Coca". It was said to help to cure headaches, nervous attacks, neuralgia, hysterics and melancholy and had one great advantage over Pemberton's previous concoctions – it tasted good!

It tasted just as good when mixed with soda and sold well enough for a certain Asa Chandler to buy the recipe for just over $2000. But neither Pemberton nor Chandler invented the proprietary name or the characteristic script used. The credit for these goes to Mr Frank M. Robinson, the bookkeeper in the Pemberton drugstore. He had the idea of forming a name from the brew's two main ingredients. It was his refined handwriting, too, which made the name Coca-Cola into a trademark, and he it was who devised the slogan "Delicious and Refreshing". It was 1893, however, before the trade name was registered.

Asa Chandler granted marketing licences throughout the United States and bottling began. The first to do so was Joseph Biedenham in Vicksburg. Mississippi in 1894, but like the others he used the only type of bottle available at the time. About 1910 he had the idea of designing a bottle that "can be recognised even when picked up in the dark ... and can even be recognised if it's broken." This led to a competition between America's glass factories. The Root Glass Company in Terre Haute, Indiana,

Lee. The top of the hill can be reached by cable car, and round it runs an old steam railway. Nearby is an artificial lake on which there are paddle-steamer cruises. Other features are a museum devoted to the early days of industrialisation in the southern states, a Civil War Museum and an antebellum plantation (restored).

made the running; their Alex Samuelson was inspired by the shape of the cola nut, and in 1915 the designer Earl Dean created the bottle that now every child in the world can recognise – yes, he made more than just a bottle, he succeeded in designing the icon of the 20th c. Coca-Cola was sold in these bottles from 1916 onwards.

Back in 1919 Ernest Woodruff bought up Coca-Cola from Asa Chandler for several million dollars. His son Robert made it his ambition to make Coca-Cola a world-renowned drink, but in spite of a number of successes it remained confined mainly to America as late as the outbreak of the Second World War. (In this connection, it is interesting to note that after 1929 Coca-Cola was bottled and sold in Germany until the start of the war under the name of Fanta). One might well cynically regard it as just a blatant sales ploy, but by the time the United States entered the war the Coca-Cola managers introduced a brilliant marketing strategy; they promised that every GI, no matter in which theatre of war he might find himself, would be able to buy a bottle of Coca-Cola for just 25 cents. With logical precision, rumoured by many on occasion even to have surpassed that employed by the military, Coca-Cola kept its promise and the American forces carried the brown liquid with them all over the world.

However, that alone does not explain Coca-Cola's success. There are many cola drinks, and not everybody prefers Coca-Cola. The secret of its success lies in high-quality advertising. Actually Coca-Cola with its

characteristic written symbol and its unique bottle has established itself everywhere, namely, in 195 countries of the world. One would be hard put to name a prominent American figure who has not been photographed with a bottle of Coca-Cola in his hand, a town or city anywhere in the world without a Coca-Cola advertising sign, or a large sporting event not involving Coca-Cola in some form or other – the sponsoring of the Summer Olympics in Atlanta in 1996 was certainly only the first of many.

Only once in its history did the firm fail to come out on top. When it attempted to take by storm the Soviet Union, Pepsi-Cola actually got its nose in front and opened the first outlet in Moscow – however, this was not too serious for the patriotic southern states, because Coca-Cola's larger and somewhat sweeter competitor is in fact no "Yankee" – Pepsi is actually made in New Bern in North Carolina.

This amusement park (7561 Six Flags Rd., near I 20 W), named after the flags of the six countries that have ruled in Georgia since the age of discovery, has a varied range of over a hundred attractions, from a hair-raising roller coaster to the Batman Stunt Show.

Six Flags Over Georgia

Atlantic City   K 51

Federal state: New Jersey
Population: 38,000
Altitude: sea level

Where once the Vanderbilts and similarly wealthy Americans spent their holidays on the Atlantic coast, today around 37 million visitors a year feed the slot machines, lose and win at roulette and blackjack, and await the annual proclamation of Miss America. Atlantic City, on New Jersey's southern Atlantic coast, is now the most visited seaside resort on the eastern seaboard, though only a few visitors are drawn there by the coast itself. A glance at an American Monopoly board reveals the connection between the "Las Vegas of the east" and money: all the roads in the game can be found in Atlantic City.

History By the middle of the 19th c. Atlantic City was an upmarket seaside resort on Absecon Island where, thanks to the influence of the Gulf Stream, it was possible to holiday all year round. In 1870 the first wooden beach promenade of the United States was built in Atlantic City, the Boardwalk, some 5 mi. long and 19 yds wide. After the Second World War, however, Atlantic City declined as visitors preferred to go to Florida. Only after 1976, when a new law legalised gambling, did it make a revival – by 1996 gamblers were spending $8 million a day in Atlantic City.

Sights

Hotels and Casinos

Atlantic City does not quite achieve the standard of Las Vegas, but a dozen large casinos, innumerable theatres, and various bars and restau-

Atlantic City the "Las Vegas of the East"

rants leave little to be desired. The large casinos, all based in hotels, line the Boardwalk and offer an ambience not dissimilar to those of Las Vegas: the "Taj Mahal", for example, an Indian fairy-tale palace, is difficult to overlook as a landmark; "Caesar's" is an attempt to resurrect antiquity; "Trump Castle" takes you on a journey into the Middle Ages; the "Showboat" is a tribute to the Mardi Gras in New Orleans; and the "Sands" surprises with its sea-floor decoration in pink and green.

The original 19th c. Boardwalk can still be seen near the Central Pier that, like all the other piers, offers a mile-long mixture of shopping and entertainments. The Historic Museum, on the Garden Pier, explains the history of the resort with special emphasis on famous visitors and night-time celebrities.

Boardwalk

It is possible to swim at Atlantic City, but quieter and more family-friendly beaches can be found a short way to the south, in Ventnor City and Ocean City.

Beaches

Injured marine mammals are taken care of in this centre, while the museum documents the natural history of the whale. Boat trips for whale watchers are also on offer (2 mi. north, on the corner of Atlantic and Brigantine Blvd.).

Marine Mammal
Stranding Center
and Museum

A survivor of the early days in Atlantic City is Lucy, a six-storey wooden elephant that can be climbed. Lucy was erected in Margate, south of Atlantic City, in 1881.

Lucy, the Margate
Elephant

★Badlands National Park   F 23/24

State: South Dakota
Area: 422 sq. mi.
Established: 1939

Badlands National Park lies in the south-west of the state of South Dakota. It was originally scheduled as a National Monument in 1939 and became a National Park in 1978. In 1976 its area was almost doubled and the Pine Ridge Indian Reservation was incorporated in it. In 1991 it attained world fame as one of the settings of the Kevin Kostner film "Dancing with Wolves". The "bad lands" – a name originally given to the area by the Prairie Indians because of the rough nature of the terrain – are a prairie plateau up to 200 ft high that has been furrowed by erosion, with deeply indented dry valleys and bizarre rock formations (pinnacles, towers, ridges, small tabular hills) in multi-coloured strata (numerous fossils) consisting mainly of solidified clay, sand, slate and volcanic ash. The National Park includes the most rugged and fissured part of the bad lands.
    A road runs through the park from the north-western entrance (Pinnacles Entrance), lined with parking places and viewpoints that offer changing vistas of the rugged rock formations to the south and of the Buffalo Gap National Grassland, one of the last remaining intact prairie landscapes in North America.

Information The Badlands National Park is open throughout the year; there are Visitor Centers in Cedar Pass (open throughout the year) and White River (Jun.–Sep.). In summer it can be very hot and there may be violent storms. The best times of year to visit the park are spring and autumn.
    There is only limited accommodation for visitors in the National Park. The Cedar Pass Lodge is open only from May to the middle of October. There is only one campground open all year, with 110 places. Outside

the park there are motels at Wall and Kadoka. The nearest town of any size is Rapid City (see South Dakota).

Walks Throughout the park, particularly in the Cedar Pass area, there are waymarked hiking trails. Maps can be obtained from the park administration (see Practical Information, National Parks) or from visitor centres. There are guided walks on nature trails.

Fauna On either side of the unsurfaced Sage Creek Rim Road (10 mi.) in the north-west of the park grazes a herd of bison that has now increased to several hundred head. In this area too is a colony of prairie dogs (Robert Prairie Dog Town). Other animals to be seen in the park include mole and white-tailed deer, pronghorn antelopes and bighorn sheep.

Pine Ridge Indian Reservation

In the early days of white settlement the Indians living round the Badlands and Pine Ridge put up fierce resistance to the takeover of their land, and there were frequent bloody encounters with United States troops. On December 29th 1890 153 Indians were massacred by the United States Cavalry at Wounded Knee Creek – an inglorious operation that broke the resistance of the Indians. The massacre of Wounded Knee, however, is still not forgotten: in 1973 members of the American Indian Movement occupied the area around Wounded Knee, and in 1993 there was a further protest there against the United States government's Indian policy. The site is marked by a memorial stone just off the SD 18.

Baltimore   K 49

State: Maryland
Altitude: 0–446 ft
Population: 736,000

Baltimore, the largest city in Maryland (see entry) and an important seaport, lies north of Washington on the wide estuary of the Patapsco River, which forms a much ramified natural harbour, 14 mi. from Chesapeake Bay and 170 mi. from the Atlantic. Its industries include shipbuilding, aircraft construction, automobile manufacture, engineering, the production of electronic apparatus and oil processing. With several famous universities, in particular the Johns Hopkins University, museums and a renowned symphony orchestra, Baltimore is a major east coast cultural centre. It was the birthplace of Edgar Allan Poe (see Famous People).

History The settlement of Baltimore was established in 1729 and named after the Barons Baltimore, founders of the colony of Maryland. Commerce and shipping brought it prosperity, and in 1796 it was granted its municipal charter. Its place in American history was won in 1814, when British forces bombarded Fort Henry for 25 hours without bringing about its surrender. The sight of the American flag still flying over the fort on the morning after the bombardment inspired Francis Scott Key's poem "The Star Spangled Banner", which became the text of the national anthem. Over the last twenty years the old town centre and the inner harbour area have been thoroughly renovated.

Downtown Baltimore

Mount Vernon Place

In the northern part of the central area is park-like Mount Vernon Place, with the Washington Monument in the centre.

★Walters Art Gallery

In the south-west corner of the square, in Centre Street, is the Walters Art Gallery, with a collection, originally assembled by the Walters family, which has grown to become one of the finest in the United States. The high points of the collection include ancient art, European old masters, particularly from Italy (Pietro Lorenzetti, Carlo da Camerino, Giovanni Bellini, Raphael, Guido Reni) and Spain (El Greco), Fabergé Easter eggs from Russia and 19th c. European painting. Open Tue., Wed., Fri. 10am–4pm, Thu. to 8pm, Sat., Sun. 11am–5pm.

The Maryland Historical Society, a couple of blocks west, has a fine library and historical collections, including Francis Scott Key's original manuscript of "The Star Spangled Banner" and War of Independence uniforms.

Maryland Historical Society

South of the Walters Art Gallery, in Cathedral Street, is the Basilica of the Assumption, the oldest Roman Catholic cathedral in the United States, built in the time of Archbishop John Carroll. In the crypt are the tombs of Archbishop Carroll (1735–1815) others.

Basilica of the Assumption

To the south of the cathedral, on Charles Street and Lombard Street, is the busy Charles Center, a complex of office buildings and apartment blocks built from 1959 onwards. The building at One Charles Center was designed by Mies van der Rohe (1962). Further south, on Baltimore Street and Charles Street, is the Morris Mechanic Theatre, which puts on Broadway productions. Adjoining this is the Hopkins Plaza (concerts and theatrical shows). Also on Charles Street is the granite and steel façade of the Sun Life Building, with the 26-storey Charles Center South immediately south of it.

Charles Center

The grave of the writer Edgar Allan Poe (see Famous People) is in the churchyard of the Westminster Presbyterian Church. His house, at 203 North Amity Street, is now a museum. There are guided tours of the churchyard from the house.

Edgar Allan Poe's House

Further west is the Babe Ruth Birthplace and Boston Orioles Museum (216 Emory St.). The house in which the famous baseball player (see Famous People) was born is now a baseball museum.

Babe Ruth Birthplace

Pratt Street runs west to the Mount Clare Railroad Station of the Baltimore and Ohio Railroad, from which the first passenger train in the United States ran west to Ellicott's Mills in 1830.

The Baltimore and Ohio Railroad Museum takes in the Mount Clare Station (1851), the Print Shop (1884) and a roundhouse that now houses an excellent collection of historic locomotives. The centrepiece is the turntable, which connects with 22 lines containing locomotives and coaches. With only a few exceptions all the exhibits are originals and in working order. In front of the building is a large open area with more locomotives. There is also a miniature railway system. Open daily 10am–5pm.

★Baltimore and Ohio Railroad Museum

East of the Charles Center lie the Battle Monument (1815) and the old City Hall (1875). The Peale Museum in the block behind (Holiday St.) was opened in 1814 as the Baltimore Museum and is thus the oldest museum in the United States. Today it displays paintings by the Peale family.

Peale Museum

On East Fayette and Front Streets stands Shot Tower (1828), which until 1892 produced most of the American forces' ammunition requirements. Today it belongs to the Morton K. Blaustein Center (City Life Museums) that displays the history and everyday life of the city of Baltimore.

Morton K. Blaustein City Life Exhibition Center

★Inner Harbor

Harborplace, an attractive modern complex with two glass-enclosed

Harborplace

pavilions in historical style, is both a shopping centre and a market place, with a plethora of shops, restaurants and open spaces. Street artists display their skills in the Amphitheater on the Promenade.

Baltimore World Trade Center

The Inner Harbor area is dominated by the Baltimore World Trade Center (401 Pratt St.), a pentagonal tower designed by I.M. Pei. From the viewing platform on the 27th floor there are fine views of the harbour and the city.

Baltimore Maritime Museum

The Baltimore Maritime Museum on Piers 3 and 4 offers visitors the opportunity to explore some museum ships – the lightship "Chesapeake" and the submarine "Torsk", the last United States vessel to sink a Japanese submarine during the Second World War, and the coastguard cutter "Roger B. Taney".

★★National Aquarium

On Pier 3 is the modern National Aquarium, built in 1981. Features of particular interest are the five-storey Tropical Basin, the Open Ocean Exhibit (sharks) and the "Wings under Water" basin, with various species of ray. On Pier 4 is a separate Marine Mammals Pavilion. Open daily 10am–5pm, later in summer.

Columbus Center

In the Exploration Hall of the Columbus Center on Piers 5 and 6 visitors can experience marine biology at close hand, including diving for sharks.

Star Spangled Banner Flag House

The flag that F.S. Scott saw flying over Fort McHenry was woven in a house built in 1793 at 844 East Pratt Street on the far side of the canal; the house is still furnished in contemporary style.

Maryland Science Center

The south-west corner of the Inner Harbor is occupied by the modern Maryland Science Center, with a planetarium. On its three floors are

Baltimore Habor

scientific displays, particularly on space travel and physics, and experiments are laid on in which visitors can take part.

Further south-west, on Key Highway, is the Baltimore Museum of Industry, which is devoted to the industrial history of the city. Among the exhibits are reconstructions of an old workshop, a printing office and a canning factory. At the quay is moored the tug "Baltimore".

Museum of Industry

Other sights

The old harbour quarter of Fell's Point was once the shipbuilding district of Baltimore, with places of entertainment for the seamen. Behind the brick façades of this beautifully restored quarter are now mainly restaurants, cafés and bars.

★Fell's Point

3 mi. south-east of the city centre via Key Highway and Fort Avenue is Fort McHenry, built between 1798 and 1803 to command the harbour entrance. In 1814 it withstood a 24 hour bombardment by a British warship and thus saved Baltimore from occupation. In the fort's Visitor Center are displays and a film on the history of the fort, referring to the origins of the national anthem. However, the original of the famous flag now hangs in the Museum of American History in Washington, DC (see entry).

Fort McHenry

The Great Blacks in Wax Museum (1601 N Ave.) is devoted to African-American history. It contains wax figures of black personalities and tableaux on important historical themes such as slavery, the Civil War and the civil rights movement.

Wax Museum

In the north of the city (Museum Dr. and Charles and 31st Sts.) is the Baltimore Museum of Art, the largest art museum in Maryland. The high point of the museum is the Cone Collection, mainly of French art, with an excellent representation of works by Matisse – the result of the artist's friendship with Etta Cone. The new wing houses post-war art. Open Wed.–Fri. 11am–4pm, Sat., Sun. 11am–6pm.

★Baltimore Museum of Art

This park in the northern residential quarter of Guilford is at its most splendid in April and May when the tulips and azaleas are in bloom.

★Sherwood Gardens

★Big Bend National Park   U 22

State: Texas
Established: 1935
Area: 1250 sq. mi.

Big Bend National Park is in south-western Texas, on the frontier with Mexico, round the great bend in the Rio Grande from which it takes its name. Lying at altitudes of between 1870 ft and 7875 ft, it is made up of three different zones: the valley of the Rio Grande, the desolate landscape of the Chihuan Desert and the Chisos Mountains. Thanks to its great extent and to its range of altitudes it is home to over 400 species of birds, including the golden eagle and the roadrunner, and over 1100 species of plants – a paradise for nature lovers.

Information The park is open throughout the year. The best months for a visit are March and April. In summer it is often extremely hot. Visitors should fill up with gas before driving to Big Bend: there are only two filling stations in the park, both closing at 5pm. There are only 74 hotel rooms in the park and these are often fully booked a year in advance, so prior reservation is essential. Better accommodation is available in Terlingua, Alpine and Ford Stockton, and camp sites can be found in Chisos Basin and Rio Grande Village. The main car park is at Panther Junction (junction of the US 385 and TX 118).

Altogether the park has some 240 mi. of **hiking trails**. Among the shorter routes are the Lost Mine Trail, a 5 mi. nature trail affording beautiful views, the Window Trail and 17 mi. of other waymarked trails in the Chisos Mountains. There are a number of longer trails into the desert, allowing hikes of several days. On these trails it is essential to take enough drinking water – at least 7 pints per person per day.

Apart from the flora and fauna the great attractions of Big Bend National Park are the three **canyons** on the Rio Grande, the Mariscal, Boquillas and Santa Elena Canyons, with rock faces rising almost 1650 ft above the river, and the Chisos Mountains, with Emory Peak (7835 ft), once a refuge of the Comanche Indians, a region of wild gorges, precipitous rock faces and gentle valleys.

Boat trips through the breathtaking canyons on the Rio Grande can be booked in the Park headquarters.

★★Black Hills   E/F 22

States: South Dakota and Wyoming

The Black Hills, now mostly a National Forest, are a fairly isolated range of hills in the northern Great Plains and on the border between the states of South Dakota and Wyoming, some 125 mi. east of the Rockies as the crow flies.

The highest point is Harney Peak (7242 ft). The crystalline rock is rich in minerals, particularly gold and silver. The Black Hills are also of interest for their flora, lying as they do on the boundary between the western (Pacific) and eastern (Atlantic) plant worlds. By far the commonest conifer is the western yellow pine (Pinus ponderosa).

Indian country To the western Dakota Indians (Teton-Sioux or Lakota) the Black Hills are a sacred region, the place of origin of their people. In the past they were also very conscious of the material value of this region with its rich stores of gold, uranium and other ores. In 1868, in the treaty of Laramie, the American government guaranteed the Indians possession of the Black Hills. When gold was found in the area in 1874, however, they were anxious to get it back. Negotiations with the chiefs Red Cloud (see Famous People) and Spotted Tail broke down; but in 1876 the Americans compelled the Lakota Indians to hand the land back without compensation. The Indians are still fighting in the United States courts for appropriate reparation for the rich lands they have lost.

Rapid City

Rapid City, the chief town of a wide surrounding area, lies on the eastern edge of the Black Hills, near Mount Rushmore. It is a good centre from which to explore the Badlands National Park (see entry). The Museum of Geology, in the grounds of the South Dakota School of Mines and Technology, has large geological and mineralogical collections. The Sioux Indian Museum illustrates the history and everyday life of the Sioux Indians. Other popular attractions are the Dinosaur Park (with reproductions of prehistoric animals which once lived in this part of the world) and the Reptile Gardens (giant turtle). To the east of the town is the Air and Space Museum. The road to Mount Rushmore runs past Bear Country (a park through which visitors can drive in their own cars to see the bears).

Mount Rushmore, the "shrine of American democracy", attracts millions of visitors every year. In 1927 the American sculptor Gutzom Borglum (1867–1941), a great admirer of Abraham Lincoln, began the task of hewing heads of Presidents George Washington, Thomas Jefferson, Abraham Lincoln and Theodore Roosevelt, each over 60 ft high, out of the granite rock of Mount Rushmore (5725 ft). Work continued until 1941, involving the blasting away of no less than 400,000 tons of rock. After Gutzom Borglum's death in March 1941 his son Lincoln carried on the work. Shortage of money and the uncertainties of the Second World War led to the suspension of the project in October 1941; but 50 years later, in a ceremony on July 3rd 1991, President George Bush was able to formally to declare the huge work of sculpture completed. An avenue flanked by the flags of all the states of the Union now leads to the Visitor Center. From mid-May to mid-September the monument is illuminated. The lights are switched on every evening at 9pm in a ceremony accompanied by the playing of the national anthem, which many spectators join in singing. Visitor Center open mid-May to mid-Sep. daily 8am–10pm; rest of year 8am–5pm.

★★Mount
Rushmore

The little town of Hot Springs, in the south of the Black Hills, has long been a popular tourist resort thanks to the mineral springs, whose qualities were already known to the Sioux and Cheyenne Indians. The springs now supply Evans Plunge, the world's largest natural warm-water indoor pool.

Hot Springs

Hot Springs hit the international headlines in 1974, when during building operations on the outskirts of the town the remains of mammoths were found. Some 26,000 years ago it lay on the edge of a steep-sided sinkhole some 80 ft deep filled with water from a hot spring, whose luxuriant vegetation, even during the Ice Age, attracted the mammoths that lived in this region. Many of these heavy creatures, standing up to 13 ft

Mount Rushmore: a shrine of American democracy

high, tumbled over the edge of the hole or sank into the soft soil. Painstaking work on the site has brought to light the remains of some four dozen Columbus mammoths. These and other finds are on display.

★Wind Cave

10 mi. north of Hot Springs is the Wind Cave, part of one of the largest karstic cave systems so far found on earth. It was discovered in 1881 when a hunter noticed a strong current of air emerging from a narrow cleft in the rock. Differing air pressures inside and outside the cave produce air currents that can reach a speed of up to 50 mi. an hour. A local peculiarity is the occurrence of very delicate honeycomb structures of brown calcareous spar known as "boxwork". Part of the cave system can be visited.

On the beautiful park-like "roof" of the cave system, now a National Park, several hundred bison graze.

Custer State Park

North of Wind Cave National Park is Custer State Park, which is no less beautiful and is richly stocked with game. A drive on the Wildlife Loop Road, particularly in the early morning or late afternoon, is a rewarding experience. Harvey Peak is a towering feature of the park.

★Needles Highway

The Needles Highway is a magnificent scenic mountain road (SD 345/349, CR 87) through the imposing landscapes of the central Black Hills, with their bizarre rock pinnacles and the fairytale Sylvan Lake.

Custer

The little town of Custer is a popular tourist resort. Its particular attraction is Flintstone's Bedrock City, a theme park dedicated to dinosaurs and the Stone Age. The town also has the interesting National Museum of Woodcarving.

★Crazy Horse Memorial

A few miles north of Custer is the Crazy Horse Memorial – a kind of Indian counterpart to Mount Rushmore National Monument. The initiative for this other gigantic piece of rock sculpture (606 ft) came from a Lakota chief named Standing Bear, who sought thereby to remind the world that the Indians too had produced great heroes like Crazy Horse, the real victor in the battle on the Little Bighorn River. Work on the monument was begun in 1947 by Korczak Ziolkowski (1908–82), a sculptor of Polish origin, and continued after his death by members of his family. It is still not completed, but as the head and upper body are finished the memorial was officially dedicated in 1998. The Indian Museum of North America also stands on the site.

★Jewel Cave

13 mi. west of Custer is the Jewel Cave National Monument, a karstic cave in which crystals of calcareous spar sparkle like jewels. With a maze of passages over 75 mi. long, this is one of the largest cave systems in the United States.

Sturgis

In the north-eastern Black Hills is Sturgis, where some 200,000 Harley Davidson enthusiasts gather every summer for somewhat unbridled festivals. East of the town is the Fort Meade Cavalry Museum, recalling the days when this really was the Wild West.

★Lead

The little town of Lead is a centre of the Black Hills gold-mining industry. Homestake Surface Tours (weekdays only) show visitors round one of the largest operating goldmines in the western hemisphere. Also of interest is the Black Hills Mining Museum, which gives an excellent survey of the history of gold mining, going back more than 100 years.

Deadwood

A short drive north-east of Lead is Deadwood, with the Adams Memorial Museum (recalling the time of the Black Hills gold rush) and the old Broken Boot goldmine. During the main holiday season there are highly realistic performances of the Wild West play "The Trial of Jack McCall" every evening (except Sundays). Visitors can also enjoy a whisky in the saloon made famous by Calamity Jane and Wild Bill Hickock.

In the north of the Black Hills is Spearfish, where the Black Hills Passion Play is performed during the summer. From here a rewarding excursion can be made to the wild Spearfish Canyon, with two waterfalls, the Bridal Veil and the Rough Lock Falls, and two striking hills, Spearfish Peak and Little Crow Peak. A few miles north of Spearfish is the geographical centre of the United States.

27 mi. north-west of Sundance is the Devil's Tower, an extraordinary natural monument and a landmark visible from many miles away. This huge isolated crag (alt. 5118 ft) was declared a National Monument, the first in the United States, in 1906. This monadnock, 865 ft and 1000 ft in diameter at the base, is now a Mecca for rock climbers.

The crag, known to the local Indians as Mateo Tipi, was the subject of an old legend. A giant bear, it was said, was pursuing two children when suddenly the land on which the children were standing was thrust up into the air, out of the bear's reach; and the grooves in the crag were made by the bear's claws as it scrabbled at the rock to get at them. Under the south-east side of the Devil's Tower, which is

The legendary Devil's Tower

particularly impressive in the morning or evening sun, lives a large colony of prairie dogs.

★★Boston   G 65

State: Massachusetts
Altitude: 0–300 ft
Population: 574,000

Boston, capital of the state of Massachusetts and the largest city in New England, lies at the mouth of the Charles River in Massachusetts Bay, some 185 mi. north-east of New York City. The city centre occupies a peninsula between the Charles River and the arm of the sea known as Boston Harbor and is linked with the university town of Cambridge (Harvard University) by several bridges. During the War of Independence Boston, capital of the British colony, played a prominent role. It is now the leading economic, commercial and cultural metropolis of New England, with a variety of industry (including fish processing), renowned universities and research centres, many publishing houses

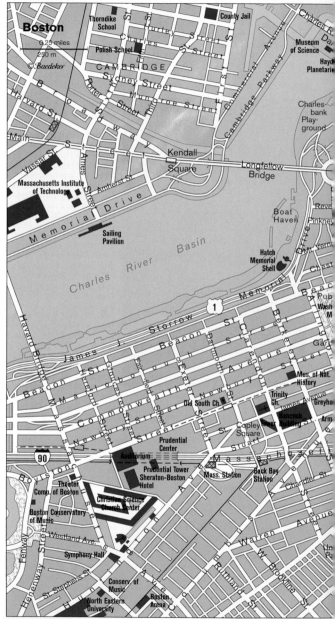

Boston

0.25 miles
250 m
© Baedeker

Thorndike School
County Jail
Museum of Science
Hayden Planetarium
Polish School
CAMBRIDGE
Sydney Street
Charles Street
Munroe Street
Charlesbank Play-ground
Harvard St.
Main
Vassar St.
Massachusetts Institute of Technology
Ames Street
Amherst St.
Kendall Square
Longfellow Bridge
Memorial Drive
Sailing Pavilion
Boat Haven
Pinkney
Revere
Hatch Memorial Shell
Charles River Basin
Memorial
Beacon
Pub
Wash
M
Havard Bridge
James J. Storrow
Memorial
Gar
Beacon
James
Beacon Street
Mus. of Nat. History
Commonwealth Avenue
Newbury Street
Trinity Ch.
James Avenue
Greyho
Old South Ch.
Hancock Tower Building
Arm
Copley Square
90
Prudential Center
Auditorium
Massachusetts
Prudential Tower
Sheraton-Boston Hotel
Mass. Station
Back Bay Station
Chandler St.
Boylston
Theater Comp. of Boston
Christian Science Church Center
Boston Conservatory of Music
Westland Ave.
Avenue
Warren
Fenway
Huntington
Symphony Hall
Conserv. of Music
North Eastern University
Boston Arena
Rutland
St. Stephens St.
W. Brookline
Un
P

Museum of Fine Arts

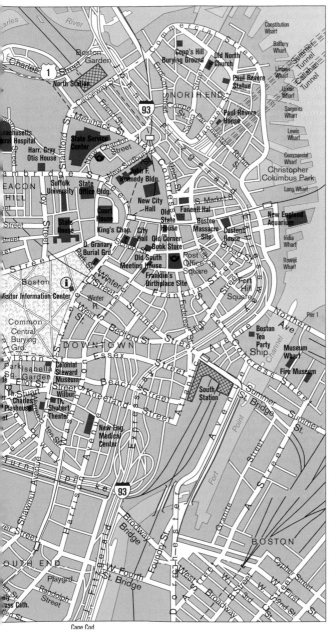

and numerous cultural institutions and events. Some of America's most influential families, such as the Kennedy's, originated in Boston.

History Boston was originally built on three hills, still commemorated in the names of the Beacon Hill, Copp's Hill and Fort Hill districts. The English settlers who came here in the mid-17th c. named their new home after the birthplace of one of their leaders, Boston in Lincolnshire. Governor John Winthrop made Boston capital of the new colony. The little town, governed by strict Puritan principles, grew rapidly. The inhabitants soon developed an overseas trade, and the town's first ship-yard was built in 1673. By the middle of the 18th c. Boston was the largest and most important town in North America, overshadowing New York and Philadelphia with its 25,000 inhabitants. The first American newspaper was printed here in 1704. The main centre of opposition to the mother country as early as the reign of Charles II (1660–85), Boston became the starting point of the War of Independence. It was the scene of the Boston Massacre on March 5th 1770 and of the Boston Tea Party on December 16th 1773, when a mob threw tea imported from Britain into the sea. During the War of Independence Boston was occupied by British troops, until on March 4th 1776 Washington's forces crossed the Charles River, took the Dorchester Heights and drove the British out. After the United States achieved independence Boston grew steadily, with only brief interruptions, and by 1900 its population had passed half a million. In 1872 a great fire caused much destruction in the central area, which has since then been more than doubled in size by the recla-mation of land from the sea.

Boston was the birthplace of a number of notable Americans, includ-ing Benjamin Franklin (see Famous People), Samuel Morse, inventor of morse telegraphy, and John F. Kennedy (see Famous People).

★★Freedom Trail

The 3 mi. Freedom Trail, which takes in the city's principal historic mon-uments and sites, starts from Boston Common. Some of the sights form part of Boston National Historical Park.

The Freedom Trail is marked by a line of red bricks in the sidewalk and by footprints at street crossings.

★Boston
Common

The starting point of the Freedom Trail is the Visitor Center on Boston Common, the large park that lies between downtown Boston and the Black Bay area. This is the oldest public park in the United States, municipal property since 1634, and throughout its history the home of free speech and free assembly. In the park are monuments commemo-rating the War of Independence and the Civil War. At the south end is the Central Burying Ground of 1756.

Public Garden

Adjoining Boston Common, on the west side of Charles Street, is the Public Garden (opened 1859), with a large artificial lake (boating; skating in winter). It contains Victorian-style monuments and statues, including an equestrian statue of George Washington (1869) near Arlington Street.

★State House

The trail cuts across Boston Common to Beacon Street, with the State House (1798) of Massachusetts, on Beacon Hill. The middle section, with a high gilded dome, was designed by Charles Bulfinch, who built the Capitol in Washington, DC. On the terrace in front of the buildings are statues of two New England statesmen, Daniel Webster (1782–1852) and Horace Mann (1796–1859). On the first floor are the Doric Hall, which is used for civic occasions, the Hall of Flags (with flags and historical paintings) and the Great Hall (1990). On the second floor are the Governor's offices, the Senate Chamber, the Senate Reception Room and the Chamber of the House of

Representatives. In the north wing is the State Library. Tours Mon.–Fri. 9am–5pm.

On the ground floor of State House is the **Archives Museum**, whose most precious possession is the "History of the Plimouth Plantation", a manuscript account by the governor of Plymouth Colony. Other items of particular interest are a number of treaties signed with the Indians and the Constitution of 1780, which is still in force. Tours Mon.–Fri. 10am–4pm.

From State House Park Street runs south-east to Park Street Church, built in 1810 on the site of an old granary. Here in 1829 William Lloyd Garrison made his first speech against slavery.

Park Street Church

Adjoining Park Street Church, in Tremont Street, is the Old Granary Burying Ground, which contains the graves of several governors of Massachusetts, Benjamin Franklin's parents, the victims of the Boston Massacre of 1770 and a number of notable Bostonians, including Samuel Adams, John Hancock and Robert Treat Paine, three signatories of the Declaration of Independence.

Old Granary Burying Ground

At the corner of Tremont Street and School Street is King's Chapel, on the site of Boston's first Anglican church of 1686. This modest place of worship, Episcopalian until 1787, now belongs to the Unitarians. In the churchyard, the oldest in Boston, is the grave of Governor John Winthrop (1588–1649).

King's Chapel

Further along School Street, set back from the street, is Old City Hall, now occupied by offices and a restaurant. In front of it are statues of Benjamin Franklin and Josiah Quincy (1772–1864), second mayor of Boston and founder of Quincy Market. Also in School Street is Boston's first public school, at which Benjamin Franklin and John Hancock were pupils.

Old City Hall

At the corner of School Street and Washington Street is the Old Corner Book Store, one of Boston's oldest buildings. Originally built in 1712 as a dwelling house and business house, in the mid-18th c. it was occupied by a publishing house. In the 19th c. it was a meeting place of writers and poets.

Old Corner Book Store

A little way south, at the corner of Washington Street and Milk Street, is the Old South Meeting House, built in 1729 as the Old South Church and Meeting Hall. A number of lively meetings were held here during the War of Independence, and it was from here that the people of Boston set out to throw a British ship's cargo of tea into the harbour (the Boston Tea Party). The Old South Meeting House is now occupied by a Historical Museum.

Old South Meeting House

Opposite the Old South Meeting House, at 7 Milk Street, is the site of the house in which Benjamin Franklin was born and spent his early years.

Franklin Birthplace Site

From here Devonshire Street runs north to Old State House. Built in 1713 and subsequently several times restored, this was the seat of the British colonial government. From the balcony on the east end John Adams read out the Declaration of Independence in 1776. John Hancock resided in the house from 1780 as first Governor of Massachusetts. Thoroughly restored in the early nineties, it now houses a museum of Boston history. Open daily 9.30am–5pm (later in summer).

★Old State House

A stone cross outside the east end of the building marks the site of the Boston Massacre of March 5th 1770, in which five people were shot down by British troops.

Old State House

★Faneuil Hall

The next section of the Freedom Trail runs along Congress Street, with the Government Center (see below) on the left-hand side. On Dock Square is Faneuil Hall, known as the "cradle of liberty". Originally built in 1740–2 by a Huguenot merchant, Peter Faneuil, as a market hall, it was presented to the city on condition that it should always be open to the public. The ground floor is still occupied by market stalls; on the upper floor is a council chamber that in the 18th and 19th centuries was the meeting place of revolutionaries and later of abolitionists. On the top floor the Ancient and Honorable Artillery Company of Massachusetts, founded in 1638 and thus the oldest militia in the United States, displays its weapons and uniforms.

Faneuil Hall Marketplace

East of Faneuil Hall is Faneuil Hall Marketplace, a not wholly successful example of 1970s urban renewal, which is nevertheless a popular meeting place.

★North End

The Freedom Trail continues by way of Marshal Street (Ebenezer Hancock House, 1767) and under a freeway to North End, the oldest and one of the most interesting parts of the town, now mainly occupied by Italians (good restaurants).

At 19 North Square is the shingle-clad **Paul Revere House** (now a museum), one of Boston's oldest buildings, dating from about 1680, which now seems incredibly tiny. From 1770 to 1800 it was the home of Paul Revere, famed for his ride to Lexington on April 18th 1775 to warn the patriots of an impending British attack.

The route continues along Prince Street to Hanover Street. At St Stephen's Church (1804) it turns north-west towards Paul Revere Mall, with an equestrian statue of Paul Revere. Adjoining, at 123 Salem Street, is the **Old North Church** or Christ Church, Boston's oldest church (1723). In 1775 lanterns were hung from the church tower to warn the citizens of the British advance.

The red line of the Freedom Trail now heads north-west over Charlestown Bridge into the district of Charlestown and beyond the bridge turns north-east. Alternatively there is a ferry from Long Wharf to Charlestown Navy Yard. The first point on the Freedom Trail is **Bunker Hill Pavilion**, with a multi-media show on the battle of Bunker Hill.

★Charlestown

Charlestown **Navy Yard**, part of Boston National Historical Park, occupies the site of an old naval dockyard. The only vessels to be seen here now are museum ships like USS "Constitution", a warship launched in 1797 (open daily 9.30am–3.50pm). There is a Visitor Center with displays on the Navy Yard. To the north-east is the USS Constitution Museum (ship models).

Further north-west the Freedom Trail ends in Monument Square, with the **Bunker Hill Monument**, a 220 ft high granite obelisk commemorating the battle of Bunker Hill on June 17th 1775; a spiral staircase leads up to the top. The battle, which was actually fought on Breed's Hill and not on Bunker Hill, ended in a British victory over the American militia.

Along Congress Street and Merrimack Street extends the Government Center, with the offices of the city and state authorities as well as some federal departments.

Government Center

In the south-east part of the area is New City Hall, on the south side of which is Government Square. To the north is the John F. Kennedy Federal Building.

Between New City Hall and State House on Pemberton Square is the Suffolk County Court House in Somerset Street, a granite building in German Renaissance style. A little way south-west of this, in Beacon Street (No. 10), is the Boston Athenaeum, which has a fine library and collections of art and antiquities.

Between Beacon Street and Cambridge Street, to the west of State House, is the picturesque Beacon Hill district, with many red brick houses belonging to old Boston families. There are a number of galleries, shops and cafés expressing the spirit of the times. Louisburg Square is particularly attractive.

★Beacon Hill

In the 19th c. Beacon Hill had many black residents. The **Black Heritage Trail** (guided walks) takes in many places that have featured in the history of the black population of Boston, including the African Meeting House (8 Smith Court), the first church of the African-American population (established 1806), the Museum of African-American History (46 Joy St., from where guided tours of the district start), the Smith Court Residences (typical 18th and 19th c. houses), the George Middleton House (Pinkney St.), the oldest surviving house (1797) of a black resident in Beacon Hill, and, at the corner of Beacon Street and Park Street, a monument to Robert Gould Shaw and the Massachusetts 54th Regiment, the first regiment recruited from blacks to serve in the Civil War.

The Lewis and Harriet Hayden House at 66 Phillips Street was once a "safe house" on the legendary "underground railroad" that enabled large numbers of blacks to flee to Canada.

1 mi. north of Beacon Hill, on an artificial island in the river linked with Boston by the Charles River Dam, is the Science Park, with the Museum of Science and the Hayden Planetarium. The Museum has a permanent collection and special exhibitions covering many branches of science and technology, including oceanography, astronomy, medicine and space travel.

Science Park

On the south side of the same building is the Hayden Planetarium, which puts on presentations on the planets and a 3-D laser show.

Back Bay and Brookline

South-west of Boston Common, between the Charles River and Huntington Avenue, is the Back Bay area, laid out on a regular grid, with numerous office and commercial tower blocks and cultural institutions. Newbury Street, with its internationally known strores and expensive cafés, is an exclusive shopping area; a stroll along the esplanade by the Charles River offers a considerably cheaper alternative. South of Boylston Street are many modern skyscrapers. On Berkeley Street (No. 200) is the 495 ft high John Hancock Building, with a pyramidal top, headquarters of the insurance corporation of that name.

★Hancock Tower

The 790 ft high Hancock Tower not only overtops its immediate neighbours but is in fact the highest building in the whole city. Its 60 floors are concealed behind a reflective glass façade.

★Copley Square

To the west of the Hancock Tower is Copley Square, the main square of the Back Bay area, surrounded by both old and modern buildings, department stores, hotels and shops. On the east side of the square is Trinity Church, a Neo-Romanesque red sandstone building with fine stained glass, some of it by Edward Burne-Jones and William Morris, one of the finest church buildings in America. On the west side is Boston Public Library (1895), in Italian Renaissance style. Further west is the modern Prudential Center, with the Prudential Skywalk on the 50th floor offering a fantastic panoramic view of Boston and the surrounding area.

★Museum of Fine Arts

Between Huntington Avenue and Back Bay Fens Park is the Museum of Fine Arts, with comprehensive collections from every major period. Of particular interest are the departments of European painting (with works by leading masters from El Greco to Monet and Max Beckmann) and Asian art and the representative collection of American art, which ranges from the 18th c. Boston painter John Singleton Copley to such modern masters as Edward Hopper and Jackson Pollock. There is also an interesting exhibition of American decorative arts. Open Mon.–Fri. 10am–5pm, Wed. to 10pm, Sat., Sun. 10am–6pm.

★Isabella Stewart Gardner Museum

Near the south-west end of the Back Bay Fens (280 The Fenway) is the Isabella Stewart Gardner Museum, with a small but distinguished collection of furniture, tapestries, sculpture, decorative art and European art. The charm of this museum lies in its character as a former private collection reflecting the personal preferences of the owners. Open Tue.–Sun. 11am–5pm.

John F. Kennedy Birthplace

To the south of Commonwealth Avenue is the suburb of Brookline (pop. 55,000). In Beals Street (No. 83) is the house in which John F. Kennedy was born, with mementoes of the 35th President of the United States. Open daily 10am–4.30pm.

Inner Harbor

To the east of Faneuil Hall Marketplace is the waterfront on the Inner Harbor. The Harbor Walk (indicated by blue markings) takes visitors round the main sights of Boston's former harbour.

★New England Aquarium

On Central Wharf is the very interesting New England Aquarium. Its main attraction is the four-storeys high Giant Ocean Tank, containing some 185,000 gallons of water, with tropical fish, sharks, giant turtles

Skyline of Boston harbor

and other marine creatures (which are fed by divers several times a day). The Aquarium runs boat trips to observe whales off the coast.

To the south of Central Wharf, at the point where Congress Street crosses Fort Point Channel, is moored the Boston Tea Party Ship, a replica of the brig "Beaver II". The scene is re-enacted for visitors several times daily. In the Museum are audio-visual shows and a model of old Boston.

Boston Tea Party Ship and Museum

On the far side of Fort Point Channel (300 Congress St./Sleeper St.), housed in an old warehouse, are two museums. The Children's Museum is laid out in the form of a 1930s house, with hands-on exhibits that encourage children to play and make discoveries. The Computer Museum has informative displays on the development of information and data-processing technology and allows visitors to play computer games and try their hand at programming and computer graphics. Other fascinating features are a walk-through computer and an exhibition on artificial intelligence.

★Computer/ Children's Museum

5 mi. south of the city, in the Columbia Point Campus of the University of Massachusetts on Dorchester Bay, is the John F. Kennedy Library and Museum, designed by I.M. Pei and opened in 1979. The Museum contains mementoes of President Kennedy (films, photographs, slides, letters).

John F. Kennedy Library and Museum

Cambridge

From Boston Massachusetts Avenue leads over the Charles River on Harvard Bridge into Cambridge, an independent town with a population of 95,000. The quickest way to reach it from downtown Boston is on the Red Line of the subway. Cambridge, named after its English counterpart, has an international reputation as a centre of teaching and research, with Harvard University and the Massachusetts Institute of Technology.

Massachusetts Institute of Technology

Immediately beyond Harvard Bridge, on both sides of Massachusetts Avenue, is the extensive campus of the Massachusetts Institute of Technology (MIT), one of the most important in the United States. Originally founded in 1861, it moved to its present site in 1916.

Information about guided tours can be obtained from MIT Information at 77 Massachusetts Avenue, Art and Science are displayed in the MIT Museum at 265 Massachusetts Avenue. The MIT Chapel and the Kresge Auditorium were designed by the Finnish-born architect Eero Saarinen.

Harvard University

From the MIT Massachusetts Avenue runs north to Harvard University, the oldest university in the United States (founded 1636), at which many prominent Americans have been students. It is named after the clergyman John Harvard, who left his private library and a half of his estate to the university. The Holyoke Center at 1350 Massachusetts Avenue houses considerable informative material.

University Museums To the east of the University campus are the Carpenter Center for the Visual Arts, designed by Le Corbusier, with displays on visual communication, and the Fogg Art Museum (32 Quincy St.), with old prints, drawings and paintings. Further north, beyond Broadway, is the Arthur M. Sackler Museum (opened 1985), with collections of Oriental and Islamic art. At 29 Kirkland Street is the Busch-Reisinger Museum, with an excellent collection of pictures of the German Modernist school and one of the largest Bauhaus collections outside Germany.

Also well worth visiting are the University Museums of Cultural and Natural History at 24 Oxford Street. In the south wing is the Peabody Museum (ethnology of the Indians of North, Central and South America), in the west wing Museums of Geology and Mineralogy and in the north wing the Museum of Comparative Zoology and the Botanical Museum.

★★Bryce Canyon National Park   M 13/14

State: Utah
Area: 56 sq. mi.
Established: 1928

The bizarre rock formations of Bryce Canyon National Park in southwestern Utah were created at a relatively late period in geological history. The park lies on the eastern edge of the Paunsaugunt Plateau, which was formed by marine deposits around 60 million years ago. The forces of erosion began to operate on the scarped rim of the limestone tableland, creating huge semicircular amphitheatres, a fairytale landscape of intricately patterned rock formations in brilliant shades of colour ranging from salmon pink to red. Bryce Canyon is one of the most magnificent scenic spectacles in the North American West, whose magical and quickly changing play of colour is seen at its finest at sunrise.

There is evidence of occupation in this area by Anasazi Indians from AD 700, and later by Paiute Indians. The latter gave the canyon the very appropriate name of the "red rocks that stand like men in the shell-shaped gorge". The first white settlers reached this area with the

Spring in Queen's Garden, Bryce Canyon ▶

Mormons about 1870. The canyon is named after Ebenezer Bryce, who tried for some years to rear cattle here.

Information The park is open throughout the year; the best time to visit it is from April to October. On account of its altitude (8000–9000 ft) the nights can be cool even in summer. The Visitor Centre lies near the entrance from the UT 63. Overnight accommodation is available at Ruby's Inn at the park entrance, in the park itself (Bryce Lodge) and in the vicinity; there are two camp sites in the park.

Fauna Squirrels and jays (Steller's jay) are frequent visitors to picnic and campgrounds. Other animals that may be spotted are mule deer, foxes, coyotes, skunks, marmots and prairie dogs.

★Scenic road The UT 63, a side road off the UT 12, is about 19 mi. long and ends at the high rock formation known as Rainbow and Youimpa Point (9015 ft) with viewpoints offering wide and ever-changing prospects. From the viewpoints there are hiking trails of varying length and strenuousness leading down into the canyon.

Hiking trails The Navajo Trail (2¼ mi.) and the Queen's Garden Trail (1½ mi.) are the best choice for visitors who want a quick look into the canyon; the highlights of this route are Thor's Hammer, Two Bridges and a view of the Silent City. The Rim Trail (5½ mi.) is a level route, also with magnificent views, running from Fairyland Point by way of Sunrise Point, Sunset Point and Inspiration Point to Bryce Point. The Peekaboo Loop Trail (5½ mi.) leads to the Cathedral, the Wall of Windows, the Alligator and the Fairy Castle. The Fairyland Loop Trail (8 mi.), which can be combined with a short side trip to the Tower Bridge, runs past the Chinese Wall and innumerable unnamed formations that may stimulate visitors' imagination to devise names of their own and affords views of Fairyland Canyon and the Boat Mesa. Those who want only to see the Tower Bridge can take the Tower Bridge Trail (3 mi.), which also runs past the Chinese Wall. The Bristlecone Loop (1 mile), a short level walk, is a good introduction to the park's vegetation, particularly its conifers. The Under the Rim Trail (22 mi.) runs below the rim of the canyon from Bryce Point to Rainbow Point.

The park rangers in the Visitor Center run guided walks and rides (see Practical Information, National Parks).

Cedar Breaks National Monument

A rewarding day trip (which can also be done by coach) is to the Cedar Breaks National Monument, 65 mi. west. This, like Bryce Canyon, is an amphitheatre that has been eroded out of a sedimentary tableland (the Markagund Plateau), with brilliantly coloured though less elaborately patterned rock formations than those of Bryce Canyon.

California (State)   H–R 1–11

Area: 158,704 sq. mi.
Population: 31.87 million
Capital: Sacramento
Popular name: Golden State

California, the third largest state of the Union (after Alaska and Texas), is the most southerly of the four Pacific mainland states. It has a very varied landscape pattern. The coastal strip along the Pacific, much of it of great beauty, is sheltered by the Coast Range, which reaches its highest point in Thompson Peak (9003 ft). East of this is the Central Valley, running along a geological fault zone that from time to time gives evidence of its existence in the form of violent earthquakes. The northern part of this wide and very fertile valley is watered by the Sacramento River, the southern part by the San Joaquin River, both flowing into San Francisco Bay. Further east again is the Sierra Nevada with its snow-capped peaks, rising to 14,495 ft in Mount Whitney, the highest point in the continental United States.

To the south-east California occupies part of the Great Basin, an enclosed basin with no outlet, with the hot and arid Death Valley, in which is the lowest point in the western hemisphere, 282 ft below sea level. In the extreme south California extends into the Mojave and Colorado Deserts. In the forests of the Coast Range grow the world's tallest trees, the sequoia and the redwood. The Central Valley, originally covered by scrub and grassland, now yields rich crops of wine grapes, fruit and vegetables.

The climate of California ranges between Mediterranean and subtropical, with dry, warm summers and heavy rain in winter. Only to the east of the Sierra Nevada, in the lee of the mountains, and in the far south is it dry throughout the year. Occasionally warm desert winds (the Santa Ana winds) reach even into the coastal regions and the Los Angeles area.

History Long before the arrival of pioneers and settlers from Europe California had a relatively dense Indian population, including the Na-Dene, Hoka, Penuti and Aztek-Tano tribes. In 1542 the Portuguese navigator Cabrilho sailed along the Pacific coast of California, the first European to reach this area. From 1769 onwards the Spaniards established themselves on the Californian coast, setting up no fewer than 21 mission stations. In 1821 California became a province of Mexico, now independent of Spain. In 1846, when war broke out between Mexico and the United States, California sought to achieve independence; but two years later, under the treaty of Guadalupe Hidalgo, it was assigned to the United States. On September 9th 1850 it became the 31st state of the Union. Between 1846 and 1848 some 250,000 new settlers streamed into California, almost all of them bitten by gold fever. Thereafter California soon developed into the economic leader of the West.

Economy California has considerable mineral resources (non-ferrous metals, oil, natural gas), but the economy of the "Golden State" is centred on "agro-business", largely dependent on irrigated agriculture. In addition to grain, fruit and vegetables the principal crops are cotton, citrus fruits, wine grapes and walnuts. Some 80 per cent of all American wine is produced in California. Industrial development took off in the 1940s, stimulated by arms production and aircraft construction, which promoted the development of a flourishing electronics and computer industry. "Silicon Valley", south-east of San Francisco, was later to enjoy an unprecedented boom. Other important branches of industry are automobile construction and foodstuffs.

Hollywood, a suburb of Los Angeles, is the centre of the American **film industry**, which dominates the international market. Since the end of the Second World War California has attracted increasing numbers of visitors, drawn not only by Hollywood but also by the state's many interesting cities, world-famous amusement parks (including Disneyland and Universal Studios) and great range of leisure and recreational facilities.

Lying in the Pacific north-west of Los Angeles are a series of islands that attract many divers and nature lovers – Santa Cruz, Santa Rosa and San Miguel, together with the small Anacapa group and the little islet of Santa Barbara, which together form the Channel Islands National Park

★**Channel Islands**

Living with San Andreas

On January 17th 1994, at 4.31am, the inhabitants of Los Angeles had a rude awakening, when an earthquake of medium strength (6.6 on the Richter scale) hit the city, causing billions of dollars worth of damage and killing over 40 people, many of the deaths being caused by the collapse of buildings and bridges. Five years before, in 1989, San Francisco Bay had been struck by one of the most violent earthquakes ever recorded in California, with the loss of 59 lives.

The cause of these movements in the earth's crust lay in the process of "continental drift" first postulated by the German scientist Alfred Wegener. California, with its many zones of tectonic weakness and lines of disturbance, is the American state most exposed to the threat of earthquakes. The best known of these stress lines, and the most spectacularly evident in the landscape, is the San Andreas Fault, which runs north-west from the north end of the Gulf of California through Imperial Valley and the Mojave Desert to the San Bernardino range. From there it turns west, and then at Santa Barbara resumes its

© Baedeker

north-westerly course. It then runs along the side of the Coastal Range, skirting the west side of the Central Valley, to Point Arena, which projects into the Pacific 110 mi. north-west of San Francisco, and from there continues under the sea. Along the San Andreas Fault the Pacific Plate, drifting north-west, and the North American Plate, advancing south-east, come up against one another. Over the past 140 million years the two continental plates have pushed over one another for a distance of some 350 mi., creating severe tensions in the earth's crust that have repeatedly produced strong earth tremors.

The city of San Francisco, which extends along the San Andreas Fault, has frequently suffered severe earthquakes – in 1857, 1865 and 1868, but particularly in 1906, 1940, 1986 and most recently in 1989. There are likely to be further earthquakes – perhaps in the not too distant future – but in spite of all warnings the construction of dams and canals and the development of towns has continued on land that is basically unstable.

Sealions on the Channel Islands

(see Practical Information, National Parks). Here visitors can see various species of seals (including sealions) and in winter whales.

The Golden Chain Highway (Route 49) runs along the west side of the Sierra Nevada from Oakhurst, north of Fresno, to the Yuba Pass north of Sacramento, giving access to the Gold Country, with the gold-diggers' towns of Columbia, Sutter Creek, Placerville, Coloma, Auburn, Grass Valley and Nevada City.

★Golden Chain Highway

Visitors should make a stop in **Coloma** at all costs, because it was here that in 1848 James Marshall's discovery of gold at Sutter's Mill started the gold rush, and information about this can be found in several museums, in Marshall Gold Discovery State Historic Park where there is a reconstruction of Sutter's Mill, in Columbia State Historic Park, where visitors can pan for gold and ride horses, and in the California State Mining and Mineral Museum. Grass Valley was the home of Lola Montez, the dancer who became the mistress of King Ludwig I of Bavaria. The present tourist town of Nevada was one of the great showplaces of the gold-rush, and a number of well-preserved buildings and sites bear witness to that splendid period, although more and more cafés and specialist shops are gaining a foothold.

Imperial Valley in southern California ranks along with Death Valley (see entry) as the hottest region in North America, with summer temperatures of up to 126°F. Thanks to irrigation with water brought from the Colorado River by the All-American Canal the valley has developed highly productive agriculture and stockbreeding and all-year horticulture, earning it the name of the "winter garden of the United States". On the eastern edge of Imperial Valley are the Imperial Sand Dunes, whose fragile ecosystem is now increasingly threatened by thoughtless sand buggy and jeep drivers.

Imperial Valley

California

★Lassen Volcanic National Park

Lassen Park (10,475 ft) in the extreme south of the Cascade Mountains, which takes its name from the Danish pioneer Peter Lassen, is the most southerly of a chain of mighty volcanoes which includes Mount St. Helens, which erupted in 1980. Lassen Peak is the remnant of Mount Tehama, which was active from 1914 to 1921. Its most violent eruption took place in 1915. There are many traces of volcanic activity to be found in the national park today: hot springs, simmering mud pots and fumaroles venting sulphurous vapours at the "Sulphur Works" or Bumpass Hell, cooled lava flows and volcanic ash in the Fantastic Lava Beds, or Hot Rock, a boulder weighing several tons which was hurled throug the air for many miles by a volcanic eruption.

Mojave Desert

The huge Mojave Desert extends to the south of the Sierra Nevada and is a land of extremes: dry salt lakes and luxuriantly green oases, sparse woodlands with dwarf trees and sand dunes, abandoned mine workings and closed military areas. This extremely sparsely populated region is one of the hottest places in the United States, with more than 3000 years of constant sunshine a year.

Information about the desert is available from the California Desert Information Center in Barstow. Popular places for excursions are the abandoned silver-mining settlement of Calico Ghost Town and the 20 Mule Team Museum in Boron, which recalls the days when the borax mined in this region was laboriously transported by mule trains.

In the south-west of the Mojave Desert, the area around Rogers Lake, a dried-out salt lake, has been used by the US Air Force (**Edwards Air Force Base**) as a test ground and by Nasa Space Shuttles as a landing site.

★Mendocino

In a beautiful coastal setting in northern California is Mendocino (pop. 1000), a picturesque little town founded in the mid-18th c., which has retained its village-like character in spite of the intrusion of galleries and boutiques.

★Mount Shasta

In northern central California Mount Shasta (14,162 ft), the south-western buttress of the Cascade Mountains, rears its twin peaks. From this extinct volcano with its deep crater five glaciers flow down. The Everett Memorial Highway affords magnificent views. Some miles east of the town of Mount Shasta is a large ski circus.

From Mount Shasta a road runs south, following the upper course of the Sacramento River, to **Lake Shasta**, a much ramified artificial lake that is now a popular recreation area (many houseboats). The lake was formed by the construction of the 600 ft high Shasta Dam. On the McCloud arm of the lake, to the north, are the Lake Shasta Caverns, with magnificent stalactites and stalagmites.

A good base from which to visit Lake Shasta and Mount Shasta is Redding, a station on the California and Oregon Railroad established in the late 19th c.

★Muir Woods National Monument

An hour's drive north of San Francisco (see entry) is the Muir Woods National Monument, a 500 acre forest area with giant redwoods (Sequoia sempervirens) over 230 ft high and 20 ft in diameter, some of which are over 2000 years old. The forest is named after John Muir, the 19th c. Scottish immigrant who promoted the conservation of the natural landscape and the establishment of National Parks.

★Point Reyes National Seashore

Point Reyes National Seashore is a very beautiful promontory reaching into the Pacific north-west of San Francisco that attracts holidaymakers all year round with its magnificent beaches, luxuriant vegetation and over 125 mi. of hiking trails.

Sacramento, capital of the state of California, lies at the junction of the American River with the Sacramento River and is now the commercial centre of a productive agricultural region, an industrial city (aerospace industries, foodstuffs) and an important traffic hub. The settlement grew up round a fort established here in 1839 by Swiss Captain J.A. Sutter. The original adobe building has been faithfully reconstructed and now houses a museum (L St. and 27th St.). ★Sacramento

In the city centre, with its regular layout of streets, the most prominent feature is the ★**State Capitol**, built between 1869 and 1874. Towards the Sacramento River lies the Old Town, rebuilt in the style of the 1850s, with the Central Pacific Passenger Station and Old Eagle Theatre.

On the edge of the Old Town stands the ★**California State Railroad Museum**, one of the largest museums of its kind in the world. The Discovery Museum next to it is particularly popular with children. Also of interest is the Towe Ford Museum with its collection of over 150 Ford cars old and new and the Crocker Art Museum (2160 St. and 3rd St.), which has a collection of 19th c. European and American painting and modern Californian art.

In the centre of the southern Californian desert is the Salton Sea, lying 235 ft below sea level, which was filled with water conveyed from the Colorado River in 1905. Round it there is now a flourishing oasis, with forests of date palms and plantations of wine grapes and citrus fruits. Salton Sea

1½ hours' drive from Los Angeles is the town of San Bernardino (pop. 130,000), which originally grew up round a Franciscan mission established in 1810. Later the Mormons also passed this way. The town is now a centre of citrus fruit growing. From San Bernardino a scenic highway, the Rim of the World Drive (CA 18) runs east into a magnificent mountain region, with Lake Arrowhead, Big Bear Lake and Baldwin Lake. San Bernardino

Founded in 1777, San Jose is today the world centre of the computer and microchio industry. Together with Silicon Valley to the north-west it has grown rapidly in recent years. Its major attraction is the new **Tech Museum of Innovation**, where visitors can sit at some 240 computer stations and bring onto the screen such things as heart operations or simulated weightlessness. Also worth seeing are the Rosicrucian Egyptian Museum and Winchester Mystery House (525 S Winchester Blvd.). Sarah Winchester, the heiress to the famous arms factory fortune, kept adding to the house from 1880 until 1922, because her stars said that she would not die while building work was going on. It was all in vain, of course, but the strange building now has 160 rooms with countless doors, windows and staircases leading nowhere. ★San Jose

17 mi. north-west of San Jose lies Palo Alto, the seat of Stanford University. The area bordered by Palo Alto, San Jose and Santa Clara Valley is known worldwide as Silicon Valley, the computer forge of the United States; however, there is little here to interest the tourist. Silicon Valley

The commercial and university town of San Luis Obispo (pop. 40,000), lying a few miles inland to the north-west of Los Angeles, was founded by Junípero Serra in 1772 as the Franciscan mission of San Luis Obispo de Tolosa. The church and museum of the mission are well worth a visit. Pismo State Beach south of the city is superb for bathing and surfing. San Luis Obispo

Santa Barbara (pop. 80,000), a bathing resort with a distinctly Spanish atmosphere in a beautiful setting, is also a university town and a centre of the electronics industry. The Franciscan mission founded by Junípero Serra in 1786 is surrounded by olive groves. On the university campus is an interesting art museum. On the seafront is Stearns Wharf, with a Santa Barbara variety of shops and restaurants. Every Sunday there is an arts and crafts show in Palm Park, displaying work by Californian artists. Round Santa Barbara are 30 mi. of sandy beaches with facilities for surfing, swimming, diving and sailing.

Solvang

A piece of Denmark in California, Solvang (Danish for "sunny meadow" lies 27 mi. north of Santa Barbara. It was founded in 1911 and boasts Danish-style houses, four windmills, smorgasbord and smoked salmon, together with a Danish Festival every September.

Other sights

Los Angeles, Monterey, Napa Valley, Sanoma Valley, Redwood National Park, San Diego, San Francisco, Sequoia and Kings Canyon National Park, Yosemite National Park (see entries).

★★Canyonlands National Park   L 16

State: Utah
Area: 527 sq. mi.
Established: 1964

The Canyonlands National Park lies in the dry, hot and relatively remote south-east of Utah. The Colorado River and its tributary the Green River have in the course of some 300 million years carved out of the sandstone of the Colorado Plateau a basin some 45 mi. across and 2000 ft deep with fantastic rock formations, narrow gorges and rugged cliffs.

Information The National Park is open throughout the year. It is best, however, to avoid the hot summer and visit it in spring or autumn. At the northern entrance to the park is the Island in the Sky Visitor Center. There is a campsite in each of the three park sections.

Island in the Sky

The National Park consists of three parts. The area between the Green River and the Colorado is known as the Island in the Sky. It is bounded by the White Rim (up to 4800 ft), which falls down almost 1000 ft to the valleys of the Green River (Stillwater Canyon) and the Colorado River. From the Visitor Center an asphalted road leads deep into the Island in the Sky to the Grand View Point Overlook (6100 ft), which offers the finest views in the whole park. A turn-off leads to Upheaval Dome, a 1180 ft deep meteor crater.

★Needles District

To the south of the junction of the Green and Colorado Rivers is the Needles District, with a profusion of rock pinnacles, buttresses and battlements. The remains of numerous old Indian settlements can also be found here.

The Maze

To the west of the Green and Colorado Rivers is the Maze, a landscape of rock faces banded red and yellow, gorges, fissures and spurs of rock.

★ Horsehoe Canyon

To the west outside the park itself lies Horsehoe Canyon, where, in the Great Gallery, some wonderful 2000 year-old rock drawings have been found. These drawings, discovered by show that this region was occupied by man some 3000 years before the Christian era.

Hiking There is a very attractive walk on the White Rim Trail, with fine views into the deep valleys of the Green and Colorado Rivers. From Grandview Point (6650 ft) there are spectacular panoramic views. Another trail runs from the Needles District to the Confluence Overlook at the junction of the Green and Colorado Rivers.

A **rafting** trip through the spectacular Cataract Canyon on the

The Colorado and its tributaries have shaped these stunning sandstone gorges in the Canyonlands National Park

Colorado River or the Stillwater Canyon on the Green River will provide a memorable experience. The tourist information offices in Moab (see Arches National Park) and Green River will help in organising the trip.

Surroundings

60 mi. west of Canyonlands National Park is the Capitol Reef, a reeflike wall of banded sandstone rising above the Fremont River. It is the most impressive section of the Waterpocket Fold, which strikes north-south for some 100 mi. This geological flexure (an S-shape fold of the strata) is the largest of its kind in the United States, with a variety of bizarre rock formations and chimneys carved out by erosion. Near the Visitor Center by the UT 24 can be seen the remains of the 19th c. Mormon settlement of Fruita. The most beautiful places in Capital Reef are Capital Dome and Cathedral Valley. The bandits Butch Cassidy and Sundance Kid had a hiding place at Cassidy Arch.

★Capitol Reef

80 mi. north-east of Canyonlands National Park is a popular rafting area in the Westwater Canyon on the Colorado River.

★Westwater Canyon

Just under 100 mi. south-east of Canyonlands National Park is the Natural Bridges National Monument. Other places of interest in this area are remains of the prehistoric Anasazi culture and the largest solar field in the world, with an area of 11½ sq. mi.

★Natural Bridges

Cape Canaveral   V 45

State: Florida

On the east coast of Florida is Cape Canaveral, a promontory studded with lagoons, mangrove swamps and marshland that is now world-famous as the site of the United States Air Force's largest rocket testing and launching area (23 sq. mi.) On its west side is Merritt Island, on which is the Kennedy Space Center (area 130 sq. mi.), with Spaceport USA, from which manned space flights are launched.

From 1963 to 1973 Cape Canaveral was known as Cape Kennedy in honour of the murdered President. The NASA (National Aeronautics and Space Administration) installations on the Atlantic coast of Florida are one of the most popular tourist sights in the United States. From this rocket-testing site, established in 1949, the first men were launched into orbit and sent to the moon, and from here, at irregular intervals, the United States space shuttle is launched. In the heyday of American space travel anything up to 25,000 people were employed.

Launches If they are lucky visitors can watch the launch of a space shut-tle. The Space Center itself and the southern part of Cape Canaveral National Seashore are closed to the public on launch days, but on such days great crowds of spectators gather on the west bank of the Indian River between Titusville and the Bennett Causeway or in Jetty Park on Highway A1A on Cape Canaveral, while others watch from boats. For information about forthcoming launches tel. 1 800 KSC INFO (Florida only) or in writing to Public Affairs Office, PA-PASS, Kennedy Space Center, Fl 32899.

History The rocket testing area was established in 1949, and in July 1950 a German V 2 was tested here. The first rockets developed by Wernher von Braun and his colleagues for space travel were launched from Cape Canaveral Air Force Station, where experiments with ballistic missiles had been carried out since 1953; but it was only with the establishment of NASA in 1958 that the development of civil space travel in the United States really got under way. On January 31st 1958 the first United States satellite, Explorer 1 (weighing only 30 pounds), was sent into orbit round the earth, and on May 5th 1961 Alan Shepard, in Mercury 1, became the first American to be sent into space. This first manned space flight was followed by other Mercury and Gemini flights. With the start of the Apollo moon programme the rocket-launching area, now known as the Kennedy Space Center, was extended on to neighbouring Merritt Island. Cape Canaveral continued to be used, however, for the launch of unmanned rockets carrying satellites. The high point of the Apollo pro-gramme was the Apollo 11 mission, which on July 20th 1969 landed the first men on the moon. In 1976 the Kennedy Space Center was enlarged to become Spaceport USA, from which the reusable space shuttles were launched, the first of them, "Colombia, on December 4th 1981.

★★Kennedy Space Center

The Space Center is normally open from 9am to 8pm, although seasonal variations are possible. It is closed at times of launchings and landings. There are bus tours every 15 min., commencing at 9.30am. The Blue Tour, which is concerned more with the earlier history of American space travel and the rockets and aircraft of the 1950s and 1960s, takes visitors to Cape Canaveral Air Force Station with its Atlantic Missile Range. The more contemporary and thus perhaps more interesting Red Tour runs through the Kennedy Space Center area to the most absorb-ing sites and attractions, a brief description of which follows:

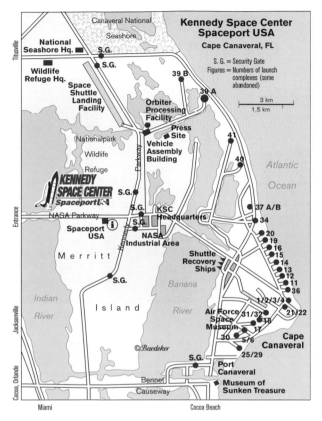

Kennedy Space Center Spaceport USA
Cape Canaveral, FL

S. G. = Security Gate
Figures = Numbers of launch
complexes (some
abandoned)

3 km
1,5 km

Canaveral National
Seashore

National
Seashore Hq. ■   S.G.
■   S.G.
Wildlife
Refuge Hq.
Space
Shuttle
Landing
Facility
Orbiter
Processing
Facility
Press
Site
Vehicle
Assembly
Building
Nationalpark
Wildlife
Refuge
**KENNEDY
SPACE CENTER** S.G.
Spaceport USA
NASA Parkway   S.G.
KSC
Headquarters
S.G.
S.G.
Spaceport
USA   ⓘ
NASA
Industrial Area
Shuttle
Recovery
Ships
S.G.
Merritt
Indian
River
Island
Banana
River
Air Force
Space
Museum
Cape
Canaveral
Atlantic
Ocean
39 B
39 A
41
40
37 A/B
34
20
19
16
15
14
13
12
11
36
1/2/3/4
31/32
18
17
21/22
30
5/6
25/29
Port
Canaveral
Bennet
Causeway
Museum of
Sunken Treasure
©Baedeker
S.G.

Titusville
Entrance
Jacksonville
Cocoa, Orlando
Miami
Cocoa Beach

This is the very core of the operations, and visitors can witness the actual way preparations are made for a launch.

Launch Status Center

Eight different space flight vehicles are displayed in the open, including a carrier rocket, a lunar module, a space shuttle and the prototype of a future orbiter. On occasions a "spaceman" in a space suit will pose for a souvenir photograph. The Astronauts Memorial is in honour of the American space travellers.

Rocket Garden

In the Galaxy Center visitors can view an exhibition covering the Space Shuttle programme together with a model of the International Space Station. In the giant IMAX Cinema three films are shown describing a flight in a Space Shuttle, a Russian MIR programme and the colonization of space.

Galaxy Center

Here there are displays of actual space flight equipmemt and utensils and space vehicles, including such veterans as the Mercury and Gemini capsules.

Gallery of Spaceflight

A true highlight of the tour is the exhibition relating to the Apollo moon landing programme. Original vehicles such as a lunar landing unit and a

Apollo/Saturn V Center

195

One small step ...

The second American on the moon: Edwin Aldrin

In 1919 a certain Robert Goddard from Massachusetts produced calculations that, he said, proved it was possible to make a moon rocket – an assertion that made him a figure of fun at the time. He retired and on March 16th 1926 started to make the first ever liquid-fuel propelled rocket on his aunt's farm. After that Germans led the field of development; Wernher von Braun and his colleagues constructed the V2 for Hitler's forces in Peenmünde and this was destined to become the nucleus of future space travel for both the superpowers. Even during the last few weeks of the war the military chiefs of the United States and the Soviet Union ordered their advancing troops to collect as much in the way of material, plans and personnel concerned with German rocket research as they could. The United States was the more successful in doing this – as well as manufactured and semi-manufactured V2 rockets and whole wagon loads of materials and plans, the US forces shipped some 1600 scientists and rocket builders across the Atlantic. Initially space research in the United States was limited to military ventures, with the aim of employing the new techniques for nuclear carrier systems, spy satellites and as vehicles for reconnaissance space stations. People were convinced that the first nation to launch an earth satellite would become "the leading economic and military power in the world".

To the dismay of the United States, the Soviet Union appeared to have attained this goal when, on October 7th 1957, their first satellite "Sputnik 1" entered the earth's orbit. "Sputnik 2" followed a mere two months later. The "sputnikshock" hit home because the United States were simultaneously busy equipping Redstone rockets to carry atomic weapons, while their satellite programme was still in the development stage. They quickly realised that rocket research under military leadership did not contribute much to genuine space research. These deliberations led to the establishment in 1958 of NASA, the civil space exploration authority, led by Wernher von Braun together with his whole Peenmünde team. In the same year the first American satellite, "Explorer", was launched from Cape Canaveral and orbited the earth.

The race between the two superpowers, the United States and the Soviet Union, had begun in earnest, and NASA did not get off to a very good start. While in 1959 the Soviets took the first pictures of the other side of the moon with their "Lunik 3" probe fired from Baikonur, the United States' newly developed "Vanguard" exploded at Cape Canaveral without even leaving its launch pad. In 1961 the Soviets launched the first manned space flight with Yuri Gagarin on board; the United States' counterpart "Mercury Redstone", with the eyes of the world upon it, failed to leave the ground.

"We live in an age of discovery; space is our vast new frontier". With these words John F. Kennedy made it clear what failure might mean for the United States. Feverishly they sought to develop a space programme that could better that of the Soviet Union. On May 25th 1961 Kennedy announced that an American would land on the moon before the end of the decade and return to earth. This dream was to cost Congress in Washington 25 billion dollars.

The American manned space programme had begun. Cape Canaveral was to be the launch centre, controlled by Houston in Texas. Wernher von Braun was to lead the project while Arthur Rudolph would be the development manager for the rocket programme. On May 5th 1961 Alan B. Shepard became the first American in space – but only for 15 minutes an a ballistic sub-orbital trajectory, as a result of which he was to be overshadowed for the rest of his life by John Glenn, who on February 20th 1962 became the first American to fly around the earth, which he did in a Mercury capsule (and in 1998, at the age of 77, went into space for the second time in a space shuttle). The Mercury programme was followed by the Gemini flights during which the two crew tested out steering and docking techniques necessary for the Apollo programme. In 1966 the United States successfully carried out the first docking manoeuvre in space, shortly afterwards the first American "space walked" outside a Gemini capsule – the Soviets had already done so on their Vostock flights.

Now, however, the times were past when the Soviets always won by a nose. In 1967 "Apollo 7" with a three-man crew was fired into orbit. A few months previously three Apollo astronauts had been burned alive in the nose of their rocket. In 1968 the aim of landing a man on the moon came a decisive step nearer. Fired into space

from a gigantic Saturn V, "Apollo 8" circled the moon. In the following year the goal was finally reached – the Apollo 11 mission landed the first men on the moon. Fired from the command module "Columbia" as it orbited the moon, the lunar module "Eagle" with the astronauts Neil Armstrong and Edwin Aldrin landed in the "Sea of Tranquillity" At 21.17 hours mid-European time on July 20th 1969 Neil Armstrong set foot on the moon. Almost the whole of the world's population sat glued to their televisions and radios as he stepped down onto the moon dust and uttered the immortal words "One small step for a man, one great step for mankind".

But his optimism was not to be realised. Admittedly there were six further moon landings, but after the near catastrophe of "Apollo 13", which was struck by a mini meteorite shower and almost lost all its crew, the last three planned Apollo missions 18 to 20 were cancelled. NASA's budget was slashed to one-third of the original sum, doubts were cast on the viability of manned space flights and more invested in unmanned travel. Probes such as Magellan, Pioneer, Mariner and Viking explored the planets and the solar system. In 1976 a Viking probe landed on Mars and sent pictures and soil analyses back to earth. In 1977 Voyager 1 set off for Jupiter and Saturn, Voyager 2 reached Uranus and Neptune in 1989 and then left our solar system in order to venture still further into interstellar space. During 1979 the Skylab space station plunged to earth over Australia and NASA was employed in designing reusable systems. As a result the first space shuttle, "Columbia" set off in 1981. On January 28th 1986 the spaceship "Challenger" exploded on take-off, killing its crew of seven. However, the programme is being continued, as these ships have been helping since June 1999 to convey building parts to the international space stations up in orbit. After the reconnaissance of Mars by the Sojourn mobile in July 1997 this has become a further spectacular phase in the history of American space travel.

moon buggy are grouped around a Saturn V that is as tall as a church tower. Rockets of this type transported the Apollo spaceships and Skylab stations into space.

LC 39 Observation Gantry

Space shuttles are launched from Launch Complex 39. From a recently built observation tower visitors have a superb panoramic view of the launch pad, the control centre, of one of the largest buildings in the world, the 525 ft high Vehicle Assembly Building (VAB) in which space vehicles are assembled, and of the gigantic "crawlers" that transport the assembled spacecraft to the launching ramps. A shuttle launch is simulated by means of an interactive film show.

International Space Station Center

In the KSC Industrial Area in this building there is an exhibition illustrating the international space station programme supported by life-size models.

Surroundings

Completely unconnected with anything technical are the Merritt Wildlife Refuge and Canaveral National Seashore, areas of marshland and dunes where, in spite of the noise of the rockets, alligators, turtles and numerous seabirds appear to feel perfectly at home. The unprotected beaches are also good for bathing and surfing.

Cape Cod H 57

State: Massachusetts

South-east of Boston (see entry) the Cape Cod (The Cape) peninsula reaches out into the Atlantic like a gigantic crab's claw. With its beautiful sandy beaches Cape Cod is now also a popular holiday area for the people of nearby Boston and New York. Bathing, cycling, eating lobster, strolling along the beaches, looking at cute houses and visiting a harbour bar in the evening are the favourite pursuits of those who visit Cape Cod. Some prominent and prosperous American citizens have holiday homes here – the Kennedys in particular.

But Cape Cod is not just a holiday resort, The National Seashore facing the Atlantic in the east is an area of great natural beauty, and local boat owners offer trips out to sea to watch the whales.

Popular bathing **beaches** on Cape Cod are Scusset Beach, at the north entrance to Cape Cod Canal; Old Silver Beach on the south-west coast (Buzzard's Bay); Craigville Beach and West Dennis Beach on the south coast; and Nauset Beach, Coast Guard Beach and Head of the Meadow Beach on the east coast. On Cape Cod Bay is the favourite Sandy Neck Beach.

Sandwich

Sandwich (pop. 16,000), an attractive little New England town at the west end of Cape Cod, was a considerable centre of the glass industry in the 19th c., as is illustrated in the local Glass Museum.

Brewster

In Brewster, on Cape Cod Bay, are the Cape Cod Aquarium and the Drummer Boy Museum (story of the American Revolution). Outside the town is the interesting Cape Cod Museum of Natural History, devoted to the natural history of the peninsula.

Hyannis

The ferry port of Hyannis, on the south coast of the peninsula, is the busy hub of Cape Cod life. On Lewis Bay, in which many yachts sway at anchor, is a monument commemorating the murdered President

Picturesque houses in Oak Bluffs on Martha's Vineyard

Kennedy. (The Kennedy family have a holiday retreat in the Hyannis Port district.)

Almost the whole of the east coast of Cape Cod is under protection as Cape Cod National Seashore. Its marvellous beaches, beautiful coniferous woodland (particularly Atlantic white cedar) and many attractive hiking trails draw thousands of visitors, particularly during the summer months. Information about the area can be obtained at the Salt Pond and Provincetown Visitor Centers.

★★Cape Cod National Seashore

The picturesque little tourist resort and artists' haunt of Provincetown (pop. 4000), at the northern tip of Cape Cod, was the landing place in 1620 of the first Pilgrim Fathers, but they decided to continue further because they could not find any land here suitable for building. Those pious men would probably also decide not to set foot here today, because Provincetown has now become the haunt of artists with a gay and lesbian community on the east coast, as can be witnessed by strolling down Commercial Street where heterosexual couples are a comparative rarity. Two thirds of the town is under a preservation order. On High Pole Hill (253 ft; views) is the Pilgrim Monument. Provincetown Heritage Museum is devoted to the history of the town.

★Provincetown

On December 21st 1620 the Pilgrim Fathers landed from the "Mayflower" in what is now Plymouth Bay, west of the northern tip of Cape Cod. At Plymouth's State Pier is moored "Mayflower II", an accurate replica of the original "Mayflower".

Plymouth

3 mi. south-east of the town of Plymouth is the **★Plimoth Plantation**, an open-air museum with a reconstruction of the first colony. It presents "living history", with actors in period costume reliving the everyday life

of the 17th c. Relics of the Pilgrim Fathers are also displayed in the Pilgrim Hall Museum.

Hobammock's Homesite Near Plimoth Plantation visitors can see replicas of the huts lived in by the Hobammock family of Indians. This family moved in with the settlers in the 1620s and helped them to find their feet in their new enviroment.

★Martha's
Vineyard

There are ferries from Hyannis to Martha's Vineyard, an island 20 mi. long and 10 mi. wide south of Cape Cod and an extremely popular holiday resort with superb beaches. Bill Clinton takes his holidays here. There are no individual attractions as such, the attraction is the island itself. There are a number of handsome Victorian houses in Vineyard Haven, Oak Bluffs and Edgartown Harbor. Instead of simply going to the Black Dog Tavern in Vineyard Harbour, like most people do, try Homestead in Meneshma – nowhere is the fish fresher than here.

The bridge from Martha's Vineyard to Chappaquiddick Island is where Edward Kennedy's political career ended when his car crashed into the sea in 1969 – he survived but his lady secretary drowned.

★Nantucket
Island

Also popular with holidaymakers is Nantucket Island (pop. 6000), 12 mi. long by 6 mi. across, off the south-west coast of Cape Cod. It too has beautiful beaches. The Whaling Museum recalls the great days of the Nantucket whalers in the 18th and 19th centuries.

★★Carlsbad Caverns National Park   R 21

State: New Mexico
Area: 73 sq. mi.
Established: 1930

The Carlsbad Caverns lie in south-eastern New Mexico, on the northern edge of the arid Chihuahua region, a desert area near the Guadalupe Mountains. The entrance to the park is about 20 mi. south-west of Carlsbad on the US 62/US 180.

Carlsbad Caverns are one of the largest and most impressive cave systems in the world – to date 80 caves have been discovered – notable for the variety of their stalactitic formations and spectacular chambers.

The caves are home to about a quarter of a million bats whose evening antics have long attracted fascinated audiences. The best place to view them is from the Natural Entrance.

The National Park is open throughout the year. It is particularly beautiful in spring, when the desert blossoms; in the hot summer the caves are pleasantly cool; and in autumn temperatures are perfectly tolerable even outside the caves. The temperature in the caves is 55°F all year round, while humidity is a constant 90 per cent. Suitable clothing is recommended.

Origins The cave system has been created over many millions of years, and the process is still continuing. Some 200–250 million years ago calcareous sediments were deposited by a warm sea, and thereafter upthrusts and subsidences of the earth's crust in this part of the world, advances and retreats of the sea and varying climatic conditions brought about chemical disintegration processes that were particularly active during the rise in the level of the land that took place some 40–20 million years ago. Groundwater and rainwater seeped into the limestone through fissures and crevices, creating cavities that grew steadily larger. In course of time the water filtering through the rock, with its high lime content, created the marvellous stalactites and stalagmites and the cascading limestone terraces to be seen today.

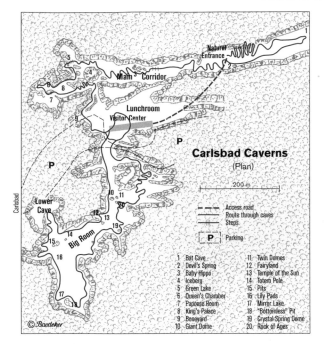

Carlsbad Caverns

(Plan)

|---- 200 m ----|

– – – Access road
――― Route through caves
|||||| Steps

[P] Parking

1 Bat Cave
2 Devil's Spring
3 Baby Hippo
4 Iceberg
5 Green Lake
6 Queen's Chamber
7 Papoose Room
8 King's Palace
9 Boneyard
10 Giant Dome
11 Twin Domes
12 Fairyland
13 Temple of the Sun
14 Totem Pole
15 Pits
16 Lily Pads
17 Mirror Lake
18 "Bottomless" Pit
19 Crystal Spring Dome
20 Rock of Ages

© Baedeker

★**Tours** There are different types of tours, starting from the Visitor Center. For visitors who are pressed for time there is the Red Tour, which takes them down by elevator to see the finest cave chambers, 750 ft below the surface. Much more interesting is the Blue Tour (1½ hours on foot; stout footwear essential), which leads down through the main passage to the fascinating Big Room. It first runs down into the first chamber, the Bat Cave, and then past the Devil's Spring (with stalactites and stalagmites still in course of formation) and the Natural Bridge to reach the main show caves, with the Veiled Statue, the Green Lake Room, the Queen's Chamber, the King's Palace and Iceberg Rock. The tour continues past the elevator to the striking stalactitic formations in the Hall of Giants, the Twin Domes and the Temple of the Sun; then on to the Lower Cave and the Big Room. Particularly fascinating is the Top of the Cross, a huge chamber 255 ft high. The route continues by way of Mirror Lake and the Bottomless Pit, a sinkhole over 130 ft deep, to the Crystal Spring Dome, with stalagmites still in process of formation, and the Painted Grotto, where water containing iron has coloured the rocks in tones of red.

56 mi. south-west of Carlsbad is the Guadalupe Mountains National Park, an area of 135 sq. mi. in the state of Texas that is still poorly provided with roads. Within the park are mountains of Permian age, with the Guadalupe Peak (8750 ft), the highest point in Texas, and the prominent mass of rock known as El Capitán (8078 ft). There is evidence of human occupation in this area 12,000 years ago.

★**Guadalupe Mountains National Park**

★Chaco Culture National Historical Park   O 18

Federal state: New Mexico
Founded: 1980

The Chaco Culture National Historical Park, in the very north-east of New Mexico, is a high point for everyone interested in pre-Columbian cultures and travelling through the south-west of the United States. Chaco Canyon was the intellectual and cultural centre of the Anasazi culture from 900 to 1200.

The park is open all year round, but the ruins themselves can only be visited between sunrise and sunset. The visitor centre is on the NM 57, no more than a dirt track in some areas. The entire park lacks any shopping facilities, and the camping facilities are fairly basic. The towns of Gallup and Farmington are good bases for exploration.

History Artefacts dating back to the 9th c. BC can be found in the entire area. From about 500 AD there is ample evidence of an ancient native American society of simple farmers who established the first cave dwellings here. From the 7th c. AD the first clay buildings appeared, and from the 9th c. the influence of Chaco culture began to spread. Altogether a total of twelve large town-like pueblos were built on the north side of the canyon, while about 400 villages with primitive one-storey buildings existed on the south side. By the 11th c. the Chaco Canyon, which housed up to 6,000 people, had developed into the political, cultural and economic centre of the Anasazi.

By the mid-13th c., following a period of drought, survival became almost impossible and the population began to drift away from the Canyon in the direction of the Rio Grande. During the 13th c. the Chaco Canyon was briefly inhabited by the Anasazi from the Mesa Verde region, before being permanently abandoned at the end of the century. In the late 16th c. the area was populated by the Navajo who also coined the name Anasazi, meaning something like "those who had once been".

In aerial photographs it is still possible today to make out the system of roads, hundreds of miles long and up to 30 ft wide, at the centre of which the Chaco Canyon can be found. Messages were exchanged using an advanced communication system of fire and smoke signals, and even astronomy was practised. For trade and exchange the Anasazi produced fine jewellery and ceramics. They erected impressive buildings made from sandstone slabs and blocks, with smaller stones or mud filling in the gaps. The ceiling timbers were made from Ponderosa pine, while willow and juniper branches were interwoven and filled with trampled soil to make the floor above. Metal tools were unknown to the Anasazi.

Tours A one-way excursion circuit leads past all the important sights (but you are advised to inquire about the state of the roads), and there are a further five tours through the park that can be taken by tourists on their own. Maps, available from the visitor centre, also indicate four trails for ramblers and a track for mountain bikers.

Pueblo Bonito

Without doubt Pueblo Bonito is the most impressive site in the Chaco Canyon. Surrounding a large square with three larger and several smaller *kivas* (the ceremonial houses of the tribes in the south-west) in a semicircle, Pueblo Bonito has become the epitome of an entire period of ancient native American architecture. From the 9th c. onwards, many generations of masons and builders were active in this place. Towards the final period, between 1020 and 1120, the total area occupied in the Pueblo measured 14,352 sq. yds. It is estimated that 1200 people were accommodated in between 600 and 800 rooms built on five levels. One theory is that the Pueblo Bonito was some sort of "hostel" for pilgrims.

The Pueblo Bonito might once have been a "pilgrim's hostel"

Towards the end the Pueblo only had one entrance – all the others had been bricked in, and many rooms had been closed off too, presumably for fear of attack from outside.

Built around 1100, the **Casa Rinconada**, 65 ft in diameter, is one of the largest kivas in the south-west. Inside, wall niches and holes for ceremonial and astronomical purposes can be seen.

Further interesting sights on the circuit are the D-shape Pueblo del Arroyo, the Pueblo Kin Kletso, and the ruins of Tsin Kletsin where it is still possible to recognise signalling posts of the communication system.

★★Charleston   R 46

State: South Carolina
Altitude: 10 ft
Population: 81,400

If you want to see a well preserved "Southern belle" and breathe the atmosphere of the old white South, you must go to Charleston. Built on a peninsula where the Cooper River and the Ashley River flow into the Atlantic, it retains, to a greater extent than any other town in the southern states, the luxurious, almost aristocratic, ambience of the great days of plantation society – dependent as it was on the sweat and the misery of the blacks. A walk or a drive in a horse-drawn carriage through the Historic District, with its Georgian mansions fronted by verandas and Classical columns and its slender church towers, makes it easy to see why the heroine of "Gone with the Wind" preferred to live in Charleston.

Tourism is now a major element in the **economy** of Charleston, but the armed forces also make a considerable contribution. Transport planes of the United States Air Force drone almost constantly over the town, and ships of the United States Navy set out from the port on exercises.

History The first British settlers landed on the marshy banks of the Kiawah (now the Ashley) River in April 1670, naming their settlement Charles Towne in honour of Charles II. A few years later, however, they moved to the more conveniently situated peninsula and began to develop a new town. Reinforced by new settlers, including French Huguenots, Charles Towne grew to become an important port that owed its prosperity to the trade in skins, rice and indigo. The planters living in the interior sought entertainment and relaxation in the town, and it acquired the first theatre, the first museum and the first college in North America. In 1773 Charleston was described as the wealthiest town in the American South. During the War of Independence the town was occupied in 1780 by British forces, who held it until December 1781. Eighty years later the bombardment of Fort Sumter, at the entrance to Charleston harbour, marked the beginning of the Civil War. The town suffered much damage during the war, but was rebuilt in the old style. It was similarly rebuilt in 1989 after being devastated by Hurricane Hugo.

★★Historic District

The best starting point for a walk through old Charleston is the intersection of Meeting and Market Streets, in the heart of the town. Here is the main building of the City Market (1841), now housing the Confederate Museum. Beyond this are the market halls, bustling with life and colour. Further down Meeting Street is Cumberland Street, with the Powder Magazine (1713). Beyond it, in Church Street, can be seen the tower of St Philip's Church (1835–8; Protestant), occupying the site of the first church founded in 1670. Back on Meeting Street is the circular Congregational Church (1891; originally founded 1681), the meeting house that gave its name to the street. At 135 Meeting Street is the Gibbes Museum of Art, with a very fine collection of paintings and graphic art, including old views of Charleston. At No. 134 is the house in which the secession of South Carolina was signed on December 20th 1860.

Four Corners Law   Beyond this is the intersection with Broad Street, known as the Four Corners of Law. On the north-east corner is Old City Hall (1801), originally built as a bank; it now houses a collection of pictures, including John Trumbull's fine portrait of Washington. At the north-west corner is the County Court House (1752), originally State House.

At the south-west corner is the Federal Court, built in 1886 on the site of the old Town Guardhouse; and at the south-east corner is St Michael's Church (1752–61; Protestant), which has the town's finest church tower.

Old Exchange   At the east end of Broad Street is the Old Exchange, the last building to be erected by the British in Charleston; originally a stock exchange and custom house, it was used during the War of Independence as a prison.

Returning to the intersection, call in at the Old Slave Mart, in Chalmers Street, where a Slavery Museum was opened in 1998.

Mansions Further down Meeting Street are the quieter residential districts of Charleston. Among the handsome mansions open to the public are the Heyward-Washington House (87 Church St.), built in 1752, with a particularly fine 18th c. bookcase; the Adam-style Nathaniel Russell House (51 Meeting St.), built in 1808, with a marvellously light staircase; and the sumptuous Edmonston-Alston House (21 E Battery), built in 1828 for a wealthy shipowner and remodelled in Greek Revival style in

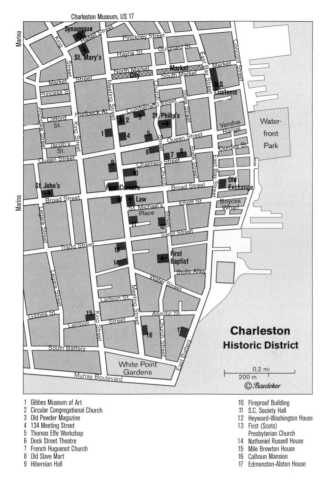

Charleston Museum, US 17

Charleston Historic District

0,2 mi
200 m
© Baedeker

1 Gibbes Museum of Art
2 Circular Congregational Church
3 Old Powder Magazine
4 134 Meeting Street
5 Thomas Elfe Workshop
6 Dock Street Theatre
7 French Huguenot Church
8 Old Slave Mart
9 Hibernian Hall
10 Fireproof Building
11 S.C. Society Hall
12 Heyward-Washington House
13 First (Scots)
   Presbyterian Church
14 Nathaniel Russell House
15 Mile Brewton House
16 Calhoun Mansion
17 Edmonston-Alston House

1838. We are now in the elegant Battery district, with other splendid mansions lining the seafront promenade.

The return to the City Market can be either along King Street, lined by antique dealers' shops, or on East Battery, with the beautiful Waterfront Park, from which there is a good view of the gigantic steel structure of the Grace Memorial Bridge, a double bridge spanning the Cooper River.

Waterfront Park

Other sights

The Charleston Museum (360 Meeting St., opposite the Visitor Center) is the oldest municipal museum in North America, founded in 1773. It is devoted to the history and natural history of the coastal region. In front of the building is a replica of the Confederate submarine "Hunley",

★Charleston
Museum

205

which carried out the first underwater attack in history. Nearby are two luxuriously furnished old mansions that are managed by the Museum: the Aiken-Rhett House (1817) at 48 Elizabeth Street and the Joseph Manigault House (1802) at 350 Meeting Street. Open Mon.–Sat. 9am–5pm, Sun. 1–5pm.

★Fort Sumter

From the Charleston Marina on Lockwood Drive there are boat trips to Fort Sumter, which guards the harbour entrance. From the boat there are fine views of the town and the handsome mansions on the Battery.

The bombardment of Fort Sumter, held by Union forces, from Fort Johnson on April 12th 1861 marked the beginning of the Civil War. After 34 hours of artillery bombardment the garrison surrendered, and thereafter Fort Sumter was held by the Confederates until February 1865. After withstanding incessant attacks from 1863 onwards the Confederate forces at last withdrew, leaving the fort a heap of rubble. The history of the fort is documented on the site.

Patriot's Point

On the east bank of the Cooper River, clearly visible from the town, lies the aircraft carrier USS "Yorktown", which recovered the crew of Apollo 8 in 1968. It is now part of the Maritime Museum on Patriot's Point, whose other major attraction is the nuclear-powered freighter USS "Savannah".

Surroundings

Charles Towne Landing

From Charleston US 17 and SR 171 lead to the site of the landing by the first settlers in 1670 (reconstructed timber fortifications).

★★Boone Hall Plantation

8 mi. north-east of Charleston on US 17 a signpost points to Boone Hall Plantation, one of the finest plantations in the southern states, orig-

A relaxing way to explore the streets of Charleston

Slave hut at Boone Hall

inally established by Major Boone in 1681. During the 18th and 19th centuries cotton was grown on the plantation, which then switched to pecan nuts. The mansion (restored), with its gardens and its magnificent half-mile avenue of oaks, has been a favourite setting for film and television producers. A reminder of the slaves who made this splendour possible is provided by nine 18th c. brick huts, among the few surviving examples of original slave huts in the United States.

Equally beautiful is Drayton Hall (9 mi. north-west of Charleston), one of the oldest plantations in the south to survive the Civil War unscathed. The fine Georgian mansion built in 1738 by the Draytons, who came here in 1679 and owned the estate for seven generations, can thus be seen in its original condition.

★★Drayton Hall

1 mi. beyond Drayton Hall on the same road is the Magnolia Plantation. The most impressive feature here is not so much the house as the gardens, lavishly laid out around 1680 – the oldest man-made gardens in North America. The bridges over the quiet ponds and arms of the river have a fairytale look. Also within the estate are the Swamp Gardens, which give some impression of the swamp country inhabited by alligators which the first settlers found here.

Magnolia Plantation

The last of the series of plantations on SR 61 is Middleton Place, once the home of Henry Middleton, first President of the Continental Congress. In 1941 he laid out the oldest surviving landscaped garden in North America, which falls away in grassy terraces to the Ashley River.

★Middleton Place

★★Chicago   H 38

State: Illinois
Altitude: 580 ft
Population: 3 million

Chicago extends, including its suburbs, for more than 60 mi. along the south-western shores of Lake Michigan. The city is at its most impressive when approached from the lake, for then it presents its fantastic skyline, second only to that of New York. That also constitutes Chicago's main problem – it is for ever the "second city", involved in a "love-hate" relationship with the city on the east coast. However, Chicago can always make the most of its opportunities; its enjoys a worldwide reputation as a focal point of 20th c. architecture and art, on which architects such as Louis Sullivan, Frank Lloyd Wright, Mies van der Rohe or Helmut Jahn and artists like Picasso, Mirō, Dubuffet and Chagall with their open-air sculptures have left their mark. As a centre of culture. too, Chicago is second only to New York. It is home to no fewer than nine universities and numerous internationally renowned research institutes; the Chicago Symphony Orchestra and the Art Institute of Chicago are synonymous with culture. On an even more popular level, Chicago is often claimed to be the true "home of the blues", a distinctive style of jazz that musicians from the Mississippi Delta developed here. In the clubs countless bands hope to follow in the footsteps of Muddy Waters, B.B. King, Charlie Parker or Dizzy Gillespie. That Chicago has much to offer in the sporting sphere, too, is demonstrated by the Chicago Bears in American football, the Chicago White Sox and Cubs in baseball and, above all, the Chicago Bulls in basketball. Last but not least; what other cities with populations in the milions can boast such beautiful beaches so close to the city centre?

Windy City The climate of the city is characterised by extremes, with winds – sometimes very violent winds – blowing throughout the year. In spite of its situation on Lake Michigan the city can become intolerably hot in summer. In winter influxes of cold air, accompanied by heavy snowfalls and very low temperatures, lead almost regularly to catastrophic conditions in the city.

Economy The metropolis of the American Midwest has the world's busiest airport and largest inland port and is one of the most important road and rail hubs in the United States. It is the world's leading commodity futures market, the most important financial centre in the United States after New York and a long-established major industrial centre. Originally the foodstuffs industries (meat processing, milling), with such

The skyline of Chicago

firms as Kraft and Libby, played a major part; later came mechanical engineering (including agricultural machinery) and motor vehicle construction (Pullman, International Harvesters) and the steel industry (particularly in the suburb of Gary); and in recent years high-tech industries have flourished. Some firms with their headquarters in Chicago are synonymous with the United States throughout the world – McDonald's, Nike, Wrigleys.

Chicago's rapidly growing **population** – from 20,000 in 1848 to 1.6 million at the turn of the 19th c. and 3.2 million in the 1940s – has recently shown a falling trend, resulting from a move to the suburbs, and now stands at around 3 million. The heterogeneous nature of the population is demonstrated by the growth of districts of particular ethnic or national origin, like Bronzeville, inhabited by the coloured population, Chinatown, a Polish quarter that is the third largest concentration of Poles in the world and other districts with predominantly Lithuanian, Swedish, German, Italian, Greek and Jewish populations.

History The first whites to come to this area, in 1673, were French prospectors and fur traders. The local Indians called the marshy region "Checagon", which loosely translates as "the place which stinks of onions". The first real settlement on the site of Chicago grew up round Fort Dearborn, which was established in 1803, and was incorporated as a town in 1837. Boosts were given to its growth by the development of the rail network and steam-powered shipping on the Great Lakes. After the Civil War Chicago became the country's leading centre of major industry, attracting a great influx of immigrants from all over the world. Temporary economic difficulties and the enormous pressure of population led to social and ethnic conflicts, reflected in such incidents as the Hay Market riot of 1886 and the Pullman strike in 1894. Gangster activity, too, developed on an unprecedented scale. In October 1871 large areas of the city were destroyed in a catastrophic fire; but recovery was swift, and only 22 years later, in 1893, Chicago hosted the World's Columbian Exposition. After the great fire, too, the Chicago school of architects, including such masters as L.H. Sullivan, D.H. Burnham and D. Adler, established their reputation. During the Prohibition era (1919–33) Chicago was tyrannised by gangs, often with the cooperation of bribed police and government officials. One of the leading gangsters of this period was Al Capone (see Famous People). In the 1920s, too, the city became the great centre of jazz, which although born in New Orleans (see entry) enjoyed a fresh flowering in Chicago. In 1933–4 another very successful world's fair was held in the city. During the economic difficulties of the 1930s a neo-liberal school of economists came to the fore in Chicago. In the 1940s the "second Chicago school" of architects, led by Mies van der Rohe, established their reputation. In 1959 the opening of the St Lawrence Seaway gave the city access to the oceans of the world. Right up to the present day Chicago has perpetuated its tradition as a flagship of international architecture with more and more new buildings.

The Loop

Chicago's financial and business district is known as the Loop: in the strict sense only the area enclosed by the "El" (elevated railway), but in practice taking in a dozen or so blocks on both sides of the Chicago River. The El follows Wabash Street, Lake Street, Wells Street and Van Buren Street, on which are many buildings designed by great architects. On the squares and in the public buildings of the Loop there are over 60 works by well-known artists, including Picasso, Chagall and Alexander Calder.

The ArchiCenter, in the Monadnock Building (330 S Dearborn St. and

Exploring the "Loop" by an excursion on the Chicago River

53 W Jackson Blvd. – see below) offers instructive guided tours and houses a large selection of architectural books.

★★State of Illinois Center

In the north-western part of the Loop, at 100 West Randolph Street, is the very handsome modern complex of the State of Illinois Center, regarded by many as the German architect Helmut Jahn's masterpiece. Its interior is strikingly impressive, with a huge atrium mall housing many excellent shops, cafés and restaurants. Here too is the State of Illinois Art Gallery. Outside stands a sculpture by Jean Dubuffet.

City Hall and County Building

The classical City Hall and County Building, in the northern part of the Loop, was completed in 1911.

Richard J. Daley Center

Adjoining, to the east, is the Richard J. Daley Center (1965), a 31-storey tower. In the plaza in front of the building is a 50 ft high piece of abstract sculpture by Picasso (1967) opposite which is Joan Miró's sculpture of "Chicago".

★State Street

Still further east is State Street Mall, a shoppers' paradise, with the 450 departments of Marshall Field's great store.

To the east of the First National Bank, at 1 South State Street, is the **Carson Pirie Scott Building**, a richly ornamented department store (turn of the 19th c.) designed by Louis Sullivan. One of the most recent buildings in State Street is the postmodern Harold Washington Library dating from 1991 (400 S State St.), the largest public library in the world.

Tiffany glass and marble distinguish the **Chicago Cultural Center** (a little to the north-east, at 78 E Washington St.) where the Museum of Broadcast Communication celebrates the golden age of radio.

The next block to the south, between Madison Street and Monroe Street, is occupied by the 60-storey First National Bank Building (1969, by Murphy, Perkins and Will). In its attractively laid out plaza is a mosaic of the "Four Seasons" by Marc Chagall (1974).

Along Dearborn Street, which extends southwards from the First National Bank, can be found some fine buildings both old and new. First, at 30 West Monroe Street, is the Inland Steel Building, supported by massive steel columns on the Dearborn Street front.

At the corner of Monroe Street and Dearborn Street is the eye-catching Xerox Building, its aluminium and glass façade reflecting the neighbouring buildings. The Marquette Building of 1894 (140 S Dearborn St.) boasts a fine terracotta façade and inside are mosaics portraying the city's history.

A short walk south, at 230 South Dearborn Street, is the ★**Federal Center**, with the low Central Post Office, the 45-storey Federal Office Building and the 30-storey Court House (by Mies van der Rohe, 1964). In the plaza is a 50 ft high stabile by Alexander Calder, "Flamingo".

Further south (330 S Dearborn St. and 53 West Jackson Blvd.) is the **Monadnock Building** of 1893, still the tallest masonry office block. It now houses the ArchiCenter. Further south, at 343 South Dearborn Street, is the Fisher Building (designed by Daniel H. Burnham), with a particularly handsome façade. Further south again, at 407 South Dearborn Street, is the Old Colony Building (by Holabird and Roche, 1894). Nearby, at 431 South Dearborn Street, is the Manhattan Building, the first steel-framed high-rise building (designed by William LeBaron Jenney, ca. 1890).

At 47 West Polk Street is ★**Dearborn Station**, the city's oldest railroad station, built in the 1880s. Now lovingly restored and protected as a national monument, it is a popular and photogenic meeting place, with a variety of attractive shops and restaurants.

LaSalle Street, which runs north-south to the west of the Federal Center, is known as Chicago's "financial heart".

A short walk north, at South LaSalle Street/141 West Jackson Boulevard, is the 44-storey ★**Chicago Board of Trade**, the largest grain exchange in the world. On the 5th floor is a Visitor Gallery (open Mon.–Fri. 9.30am–2pm). The building is topped by an aluminium statue of Ceres, goddess of fertility.

On Wacker Drive, which runs along the west side of the Loop, roughly parallel to the Chicago River, are some outstanding architectural achievements.

Dominating the skyline of Chicago is the 110-storey ★★**Sears Tower** (233 S Wacker Dr.), which rises to a height of 1450 ft in successively smaller stages. It was built in 1974 for the then powerful Sears, Roebuck company and became the highest office block in the world and is still the highest building in the United States. In the lobby is a mobile by Alexander Calder, "Universe". From the observatory on the 103rd floor there are spectacular views, particularly in the evening. Open Mar.–Sep. daily 9pm–11pm, Oct.–Feb. to 10pm. South-west of the Sears Tower, beyond the Chicago River, is the Main Post Office (433 W Van Buren St.), the largest post office in the world.

Further north, at 20 North Wacker Drive, is the imposing ★★**Civic Center for the Performing Arts** (1929), with the Civic Theatre and Civic Opera, home of the world-famed Chicago Lyric Opera.

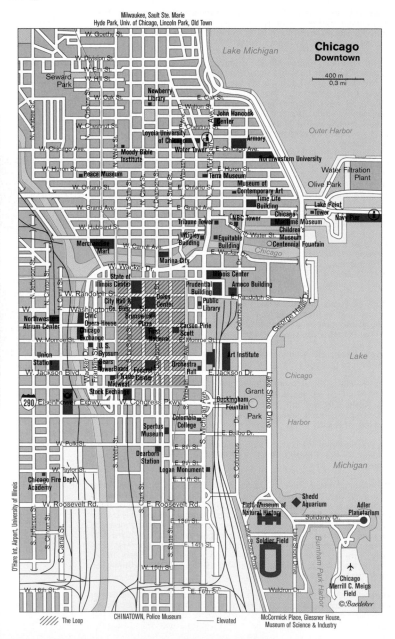

Milwaukee, Sault Ste. Marie
Hyde Park, Univ. of Chicago, Lincoln Park, Old Town

W. Goethe St.

Chicago
Downtown

Lake Michigan

400 m
0,3 mi

W. Division St.
W. Elm St.
W. Hill St.

Seward
Park

Newberry
Library

E. Oak St.

W. Oak St.

E. Walton St.

John Hancock
Center

W. Chestnut St.

E. Chestnut St.

Outer Harbor

Loyola University
of Chicago

Water Tower

Armory

W. Chicago Ave.

E. Chicago Ave.

Moody Bible
Institute

Northwestern University

W. Huron St.

Peace Museum

Terra Museum

E. Huron St.

Water Filtration
Plant

W. Ontario St.

E. Ontario St.

Museum of
Contemporary Art

Olive Park

W. Grand Ave.

E. Grand Ave.

Time Life
Building

NBC Tower

Chicago
Maritime Museum

Lake Point
Tower

Navy Pier

W. Hubbard St.

Tribune Tower

Wrigley
Building

Equitable
Building

Children's
Museum

Water St.

Centennial Fountain

Merchandise
Mart

W. Carroll Ave.

Marina City

Chicago

W. Wacker Dr.

State of
Illinois Center

Illinois Center

Ameco Building

W. Randolph St.

Prudential
Building

E. Randolph St.

City Hall &
Co. Bldg.

Daley
Center

Public
Library

W. Washington St.

Northwestern
Atrium Center

Civic
Opera House

Brunswick
Plaza

Chicago
Exchange

First
National

Carson Pirie
Scott

W. Monroe St.

E. Monroe St.

U. S.
Gypsum

Union
Station

Sears

Art Institute

Tower

Board

Federal

Orchestra
Hall

W. Jackson Blvd.

Trade Center

E. Jackson Dr.

Midwest
Stock Exchange

290

Eisenhower Expwy.

W. Congress Pkwy.

Grant
Park

Lake Michigan

Chicago

Buckingham
Fountain

Harbor

Columbia
College

Spertus
Museum

E. Balbo Dr.

Michigan

W. Polk St.

Dearborn
Station

E. 8th St.

E. 9th St.

W. Taylor St.

Logan Monument

E. 11th St.

Chicago Fire Dept.
Academy

Shedd
Aquarium

W. Roosevelt Rd.

E. Roosevelt Rd.

Field Museum of
Natural History

Adler
Planetarium

E. 13th St.

Solidarity Dr.

Burnham Park Harbor

E. 14th St.

Soldier Field

Chicago
Merrill C. Meigs
Field

W. 15th St.

W. 16th St.

E. 16th St.

Waldron Dr.

©Baedeker

O'Hare Int. Airport, University of Illinois

///// The Loop

CHINATOWN, Police Museum

—— Elevated

McCormick Place, Glessner House,
Museum of Science & Industry

At the bend into West Wacker Drive is the slightly curved ★**333 West Wacker Drive Building**, its gleaming steel and glass façade reflecting the Chicago River and neighbouring buildings. It is particularly eye-catching at sunset.

North Michigan Avenue runs along the east side of the Loop. Here too there are a number of notable buildings.

North Michigan Avenue

Magnificient Mile, Near North, River North

The section of Michigan Avenue north of the Chicago River, with its numerous galleries, boutiques and luxury shops, is known as the "Magnificent Mile". All the world's designer products can be found here and, for the sportsman, there is Niketown at 669 North Michigan Avenue.

★Magnificent Mile

The only buildings in this area to survive the devastating 1871 fire were the 205 ft high Water Tower (800 N Michigan Ave.) and the associated Pumping Station. Here now are housed the tourist information office and "Here's Chicago", a multi-media show about the city.

To the north-west, housed in the 74-storey **Water Tower Place** Building, is a shopping mall centred on a seven-storey atrium (over 120 shops, restaurants, seven movie houses).

The John Hancock Center, an 1125 ft high tower, tapering towards the top, was completed in 1970 to the design of the renowned SOM firm of architects. From the observatory on the 94th floor (1030 ft above ground level; open 9am–midnight) there are magnificent panoramic views. On the roof are two 345 ft high telecommunications aerials.

★John Hancock Center

Further south, at 666 North Michigan Avenue, is the Terra Museum of American Art, with one of the largest collections of American art, covering two centuries (many famous works by John Singer Sargent, W.M. Chase, Mary Cassat, Samuel F.B. Morse, Winslow Homer and E. Hopper). Open Tue. noon–8pm, Wed.–Sat. 10am–5pm, Sun. noon–5pm.

★Terra Museum of American Art

South-east of the Water Tower, at 237 Ontario Street, is the Museum of Contemporary Art one of the outstanding collections of contemporary art. It displays the work of both established and lesser artists of the Modernist and Avantgarde schools, and offers very informative guided tours. Open Tue.–Sat. 11am–6pm, Wed. to 9pm, Sun. 10am–5pm.

Museum of Contemporary Art

Another architectural landmark is the 32-storey Wrigley Building at 400 North Michigan Avenue, with a bell tower in French Renaissance style built for the chewing-gum firm in 1924.

Wrigley Building

This district is a very handsome part of the city, fronted by the gleaming façades of modern skyscrapers, behind which are two- and three-storey 19th c. houses, now much sought after. In this area there are excellent jazz spots, one or two night clubs, good restaurants, interesting boutiques, antique dealers and well-stocked bookshops.
    Practically in the middle of the city the Oak Street beach offers scope for relaxation.

Near North Side Gold Coast

Between East Division Street and East North Boulevard is the Astor Street district – six blocks with notable modern buildings by famous architects (Frank Lloyd Wright, David Adler, Bertrand Goldberg).

★Astor Street district

The **International Museum of Surgical Sciences** (1524 N Lake Shore Dr.) has one of the world's largest collections of material on the history of

View of the Michigan Avenue Bridge and the Loop from the Wrigley Building (right)

medicine, extending from the simple implements of primitive peoples to the most modern technical apparatus.

River North

The River North district caters for those interested in art, galleries and fashion. Here too there are a number of imposing buildings.

An architectural highlight of the area is ★**Marina City** (by Bertrand Goldberg, 1963–4), a 590 ft high twin-towered 61-storey office and apartment complex on the Chicago River with its own theatre, railway and marina.

Some 550 yds further west is the gigantic **Merchandise Mart**, which belongs to the Kennedy family. This furniture and building materials "supermarket", originally built in 1928 and since then repeatedly enlarged, now has no fewer than 1800 showrooms.

A little way south-west, at 430 West Erie Street, is the only **Peace Museum** in the United States.

New East Side/Cityfront Center

In the last few years the area round the mouth of the Chicago River has been refurbished and smartened up at great expense, and is now a popular leisure area.

★North Pier

The focal point of the refurbishment programme is the North Pier, now a multi-functional centre with marina, museums (including the Maritime Museum and the Children's Museum), luxury shops, good restaurants, sidewalk cafés and a variety of indoor entertainment facilities.

A little way south is the ★**Centennial Fountain**, which every ten minutes shoots an arch of water up to 100 ft high across the Chicago River, and when the sun is shining produces a marvellous spectrum of colour.

North-east of the mouth of the Chicago River is the Navy Pier, constructed in 1916, from which there is a breathtaking view of Chicago's skyline. This is the scene of all-year festivities, including the Chicago Festival in August and has now become a leisure park and fairground. There are boat trips across the lake.

Navy Pier

South-west of the NBC Building, beyond the Chicago River, is the 35-storey 333 North Michigan Avenue Building (1928), on the site of Fort Dearborn (see History). Regarded at the time of its erection as a state- of-the-art building, it is now protected as a historic monument.

333 North
Michigan Avenue

Further south is the 80-storey **Amoco Building** (1973), its white marble façade soaring up to a height of 1135 ft.

Grant Park/South Michigan Avenue

The Grant Park and South Michigan Avenue area attracts millions of visitors annually with its world-famous cultural institutions and its architecture by Louis Sullivan and Daniel Burnham. Grant Park, which is under a protection order, stretches eastwards from South Michigan Avenue to Lake Mitchigan and southwards to the Field Museum of Natural History some 2 mi. away. All together here are some of Chicago's most interesting museums. Buckingham Fountain is a favourite meeting place.

Lake Shore Drive runs along the shores of Lake Michigan, with some beautiful stretches of beach (crowded at weekends).

Lake Shore Drive

The Art Institute of Chicago (Michigan Ave. and Adams St.), one of the largest art collections in the world, is housed in a building in Italian Renaissance style erected by Shepley, Rutan and Coolidge for the World's Columbian Exposition of 1893. The collections cover every field of art from antiquity to the present day – paintings, graphic art, sculpture, photography, applied and decorative art and ethnographic material from Asia, Africa and America. The French Impressionists and Post-Impressionists are particularly well represented, with works by Monet, Renoir, Cézanne, Gauguin, Seurat, Degas and Van Gogh. On the lower floor are the Thorne Miniature Rooms, a kind of gigantic dolls' house with 68 different rooms (representing every type of dwelling from a peasant's hut to a palace) reproduced on the scale of 1:12. Open Mon., Wed., Thu., Fri. 10.30am–4.30pm, Tue. 10.30am–8pm, Sat. 10am–5pm, Sun., pub. hols. noon–5pm.

★★Art Institute of Chicago

A little way south of the Art Institute, at 220 South Michigan Avenue, is the home of the world-famous Chicago Symphony Orchestra, built in 1900 to the design of Daniel Burnham.

Chicago
Symphony
Orchestra Hall

To the west of the Buckingham Fountain are the Fine Arts Building (410 S Michigan Ave.), formerly the city's cultural centre, and the striking Auditorium Theater (by Dankmar Adler and Louis Sullivan), which is famed for its excellent acoustics.

★Fine Arts
Building

At 430 South Michigan Avenue is the Auditorium Building (by Adler and Sullivan, 1887–9), which now houses the private Roosevelt University (founded 1945), the O'Malley Theater and the Ganz Recital Hall. To the south are a number of large hotels, including the Conrad Hilton Hotel ("mother house" of the renowned Hilton chain).

Auditorium
Building

Chicago

Spertus Museum
At 618 South Michigan Avenue is the Spertus Museum, devoted to Jewish culture. It houses a large number of objets d'art from synagogues all over the world.

★★Field Museum of Natural History
At the south end of Grant Park is the Field Museum of Natural History (Roosevelt Rd. and Lake Shore Dr.), named after the department store proprietor and art patron Marshall Field. The collection, founded in 1893, covers geology, botany, zoology and anthropology. Most popular are the Egyptian mummies, the spectacular dinosaur presentation, the multi-media Africa department and the section devoted to the development of living organisms. Open daily 9am–5pm.

★John G. Shedd Aquarium
North-west of the Field Museum, at 1200 South Lake Shore Drive, is the John G. Shedd Aquarium, the largest of its kind in the world, with well over 6000 different marine creatures. On an artificial coral reef divers feed sharks, turtles and other denizens of the Caribbean (daily at 11am, 2 and 3pm). In the new Oceanarium live inhabitants of the north-western Pacific, including whales, dolphins and sea otters. Open Tue.–Fri. 9am–5pm, Sat., Sun. to 6pm; weekdays to 6pm Jun.–Aug.

★Adler Planetarium
Further south, on an area of land reclaimed from Lake Michigan, is the Adler Planetarium (1300 S Lakeshore Dr.), from which there is a particularly fine view of the skyline of Chicago. The Planetarium puts on regular presentations (with special sessions for children), accompanied by exhibitions on astronomy and space travel.

Soldier Field
South of the Field Museum is Soldier Field, a huge sports stadium built between 1922 and 1940, with seating for up to 200,000 spectators.

★Prairie Avenue Historic District
South-west of Soldier Field is the Prairie Avenue Historic District, centred on this exclusive 19th c. residential street (recently restored), once the home of such wealthy citizens of Chicago as the department store magnates Marshall Field and Joseph Sears. Of particular interest are the Neo-Romanesque Glessner House (1886) at 1800 South Prairie Avenue, now the headquarters of the Chicago Architecture Foundation, and Clarke House, in Greek Revival style, one of the oldest houses in Chicago.

McCormick Place-on-the-Lake
The McCormick Place-on-the-Lake, the largest trade fair ground in the United States, extends southward towards Lake Michigan.

West Loop/Near Northwest

Chicago Fire Academy
The Chicago Fire Academy at 558 West Dekoven Street stands on the precise spot where in October 1871 Mrs O'Leary's cow upset a lamp and started the fire that devastated Chicago.

★Jane Addams' Hull House
North-west of the Fire Academy, at 800 South Halsted Street, is Jane Addams' Hull House, a social work settlement modelled on London's Toynbee Hall that was founded in 1889 by the social reformer Jane Addams (1860–1935), later awarded the Nobel Peace Prize. It lies on the eastern edge of the campus of the University of Illinois (20,000 students).

★Mexican Fine Arts Center Museum
The Mexican Fine Arts Center Museum at 1852 West 19th Street, the largest establishment of the kind in the northern United States, displays the work of both well-known and lesser-known Mexican artists and also folk art.

United Center
The United Center at 1901 West Madison Street is the home of the Chicago Bulls baseball team, one of whose stars is Michael "Air" Jordan.

Burnham Park/Chinatown

The area round Burnham Park, formerly neglected, has recently been refurbished at great expense. Its excellent shops, restaurants, bars, cafés, entertainment facilities and various features of interest attract numbers of visitors as well as locals.

The Police Museum at 17025 South State Street has relics of the Haymarket Riot of 1886 and of the gangsters of the 1920s and 1930s (Al Capone, John Dillinger).

Police Museum

South of the Burnham Park area, round Cermark Road and Wentworth Avenue, is Chicago's lively Chinatown, with its own town hall and temple and the interesting Ling Long Museum. Most of the restaurants are, however, run by Vietnamese.

Chinatown

1 mi. south of Chinatown is the renowned Illinois Institute of Technology, built between 1942 and 1958 to the design of Mies van der Rohe.

Illinois Institute of Technology

Hyde Park/University of Chicago

To the south of the city is the large campus of the University of Chicago, one of the leading American universities, which was founded in 1890 by John D. Rockefeller and now has some 10,000 students. On the campus is Robie House, built by Frank Lloyd Wright in 1909 as a private residence, which is now occupied by the Institute of International Studies. There are also buildings designed by Mies van der Rohe and Eero Saarinen. The first controlled nuclear chain reaction was achieved by the University physicist Emrico Fermi.

The University has a number of interesting museums, the most famous of which is the Museum of the Oriental Institute (1155 E 58th St.), which has valuable collections illustrating the development of the civilisations of the Near and Middle East. Among the most notable exhibits are Egyptian mummies, a statue of Tutankhamun, gold from Iran and a massive animal relief from an Assyrian palace. It was reopened in 1998 after extensive renovation.

★Oriental Institute

At the north end of nearby Jackson Park (S Lakeshore Dr. and 57th St.) is the Museum of Science and Industry, founded in 1933, which is devoted to the application of natural laws in technological and industrial development. Among many notable exhibits are the Apollo 8 space module, a German submarine captured during the Second World War, a walk-through model of the human heart and a full-size model of a coal mine. Visitors can experience a flight in a space shuttle, and other items of interest include Coleen Moore's House, a dolls' house in the form of a fairytale castle, and a large model railway layout. Open daily 9.30am–5.30pm

Museum of Science and Industry

The DuSable Museum of African-American History (740 E 56th St.) boasts a very extensive collection of pictures and documents relating to the history of blacks in America.

★DuSable Museum

Lakefront/Old Town/Lincoln Park

A few miles north of the city centre is the Lakefront, with beautifully laid out parkland, beaches, marinas and a variety of sporting and leisure facilities (golf, tennis, jogging, cycle tracks, cross-country skiing).

★Lakefront

217

Chicago

★Chicago Academy of Science

The renowned Chicago Academy of Science (2001 N Clark St.) was founded in 1857 to promote the study of science. Its excellently presented and informative displays illustrate many aspects of the biosphere, concentrating particularly on the development of animal species in the different periods of the earth's history. There is a special "hands-on" section for children.

Lincoln Park

In Lincoln Park are one of the largest municipal zoos in the United States and the Lincoln Park Conservatory (designed by J.L. Silsbee), with a large collection of exotic plants.

Biograph Theater

North-west of Lincoln Park, at 2433 North Lincoln Street, is the Biograph Theater, in front of which the notorious gangster John Dillinger was shot down on July 22nd 1934.

Wrigley Field

Further north-west is Wrigley Field, one of the oldest baseball pitches in North America, home of the Chicago Cubs.

Scholl Museum of Folk Culture

Between Lincoln Avenue and the Chicago River, at 909 West Armitage Avenue, is the Scholl Museum of Folk Culture, with a large collection of musical instruments and music.

★Historical Society Museum

Chicago's oldest cultural institution is the Historical Society's museum on the history of the city (Clark St. and North Ave.), where visitors can see, among much else, Chicago's first locomotive, the bed in which Abraham Lincoln died and a film reconstruction of the great fire of 1871.

Old Town

The Old Town of Chicago, an area of just over 1 sq. mi. between North Wells Street and Eugene Street, has recently been cleaned up and refurbished on the model of New York's Greenwich Village. Many of the

When the "Cubs" are playing at home, the stadium is packed

houses built here after the 1871 fire are now occupied by boutiques, souvenir shops, restaurants and bars. In the past there was a considerable German element in the population, as is reflected in the streets named after German writers.

Surroundings

A visit to Oak Park, a suburb on the west side of Chicago, is a must for anyone interested in modern architecture. A major part in the development of this district was taken by Frank Lloyd Wright and the Prairie School of architects, including George C. Maher (1864–1926), Robert C. Spencer Jr (1864–1953) and Thomas Eddy Tallmadge (1876–1940). Particularly notable examples of their work are the Frank Lloyd Wright Home and Studio, the Unity Temple (1908; an early example of the use of concrete), the Fricke House and Heurtly House (both 1902), the Martin House (1903) and the Cheney House (1904). The best-known son of Oak Park is the writer and bullfight enthusiast Ernest Hemingway, who is remembered both in a museum at 200 North Oak Park Avenue and in the house in which he was born at 339 North Park Avenue. Both open Fri.–Sun.

★Oak Park

11 mi. west of Chicago is the popular Brookfield Zoo, in which more than 2000 species of animals can be seen in enclosures as close as possible to their natural conditions. There are a children's zoo, a safari train and dolphin shows.

★Brookfield Zoo

North of Chicago is the suburb of Evanston, with the Northwestern University. The Mary and Leigh Block Gallery has a notable art collection covering the period from the 15th to the 20th c. The sculpture garden has works by Henry Moore, Barbara Hepworth, Jacques Lipschitz, Joan Miró and other modern sculptors.

★Evanston

Further north, in Glencoe, is the 300 acre Botanic Garden, covering 20 different botanical fields. There are daily guided visits and tram tours.

Chicago Botanic Garden

West of Waukegan is the gigantic theme park Six Flags Great America, the largest in the Middle West (via I 94, Route 132, E Gurnee).

Six Flags Great America

George Pullman, the inventor of the luxury rail coach that bears his name, dreamed of a model village for his firm's workers. He had it laid out between 1880 and 1884 on a site 14 mi. south-east of the city. In the centre he built the Florence Hotel, named after his daughter, which today is a museum portraying the grandeur of the times. Following the great strike of 1894, however, Pullman lost interest in the project.

Pullman

Cincinnati   K 41

State: Ohio
Altitude: 540 ft
Population: 364,000

The city of Cincinnati lies in a wide basin on the north bank of the Ohio River, surrounded by hills. In the past its beautiful situation earned it the styles of the "Pearl of the West" and the "Queen City". It is now a busy industrial city, with the headquarters of several large firms, and the seat of a university. It has a wide range of cultural and recreational facilities.

History The first white settlers established themselves here in 1788, to be followed a few years later by the United States Army. The town was given its name by a group of revolutionary admirers of the Roman general Cincinnatus. Its excellent situation on the navigable Ohio River promoted its further development, and for many years it was the dominant centre of the Middle West. The coming of the railway reduced the importance of the river and of the town, but it soon recovered from this setback. By 1869 it could boast the first professional baseball team in the world, the Cincinnati Reds. Until the First World War the city's life showed the influence of its many German immigrants, and it still holds annually a large Oktoberfest on the Munich model. In the Second World War Cincinnati was one of the United States' largest manufacturer of arms. William Howard Taft (1858–1930), the 27th President of the United States, was born here.

Sights

★Fountain Square

The focal point of the city centre with its modern tower blocks is Fountain Square, in which is the Tylor Davidson Fountain (cast in Munich in 1871). The Contemporary Arts Center at 115 East 5th Street offers temporary exhibitions of contemporary art.

Carew Tower

From the roof of the 575 ft high Carew Tower (5th and Vine Sts.) there are superb views of the city and the valley of the Ohio River. From here there is access to the Skywalk, a network of arcades and flyovers spanning sixteen city blocks that offers abundant opportunities for shopping.

★Museum Center

The Cincinnati Union Terminal at 1301 Western Avenue, an art-deco railroad station built in 1933, has been occupied since 1990 by the Museum Center (natural history and history of the city; cinema shows including "Cincinnati Goes to War").

★Cincinnati Zoo & Botanical Gardens

The Cincinnati Zoo and Botanical Gardens (3400 Vine St.) are famed for their white Bengal tigers and gorillas. Here too there is one of the largest insectariums in the world.

Eden Park

Eden Park lies north-east of Downtown. Its Krohn Conservatory is one of the largest public greenhouses in the United States.

In Eden Park is the **Cincinnati Art Museum**, with works of art (sculpture, ceramics, pictures) from the great civilisations of five millennia.

Mount Adams

To the south of Eden Park is the picturesque Mount Adams quarter with its popular bars and cafés.

William Howard Taft National Historic Site

The venerable old house in which William Howard Taft (1857–1930), 27th President of the United States, was born is open to visitors. There is also a museum in his honour at 316 Pike Street.

★Arnoff Center for Design & Art

The campus of the University of Cincinnati is a mecca for those interested in architecture. In the Arnoff Center for Design & Art Peter Eisenman was able to exercise freely his portrayal of deconstructivist building methods.

Surroundings

Covington

In Covington (Kentucky) on the far side of the Ohio River is the district of Main Strasse, showing the influence of German immigrants. A carillon in the bell tower plays the "Pied Piper of Hamelin" tune. Access to Covington is by way of the Roebling Suspension Bridge, built by the constructors of the Brooklyn Bridge in New York.

Like California, Ohio can also produce good wine, as a visit to Meiers Wine Cellars, the oldest in Ohio, at 6955 Plainfield Pike, will show.

Meiers Wine Cellars

Some 23 mi. north-east of Cincinnati (I 71, exit 25A) lies the large amusement park known as Paramount's Kings Island with Hanna Barbara Land (Yogi Bear & co.) for the little ones and the big dipper "The Beast" or the James Bond action show "Licensed to Kill" for the adults.

Paramount's Kings Island

54 mi. north of Cincinnati is the industrial town of Dayton, the home of the air pioneers the Wright brothers. On Old Wright Field (enter by Gate 28B) is the US Air Force Museum, the oldest and largest museum of military aviation, with over 200 aircraft and missiles including a Wright Flyer and the Apollo 15 spacecraft. Near here is a monument to the Wright brothers. In Carillon Historic Park (2001 S Patterson Blvd.) are reproductions of the Wright brothers' bicycle factory, one of their aircraft and the covered wagons and log cabins of the early settlers. In the Old Courthouse (3rd and Main Sts.) are numerous relics and documents on the Wright brothers.

Dayton

Cleveland   H 44

State: Ohio
Altitude: 575–865 ft
Population: 506,000

Cleveland, the second largest city in the state of Ohio, lies at the outflow of the Cuyahoga River into Lake Erie. Immediately south begins the long Appalachian Plateau; to the west are the Central Lowlands. The city has a strong economic base, with steel and metal processing and the manufacture of machine tools and automobile parts. This means it is not a particularly attractive city, but much is being done to improve matters, as witnessed by the successful redevelopment of Lakefront and The Flats. In the cultural field, the Cleveland Orchestra has a high reputation.

History The newly acquired territory of New Connecticut, an area of 770 sq. mi., was mapped by Moses Cleveland in 1796 for the Connecticut Land Company, but the settlement that he founded (on the site of the present city centre) was soon abandoned. Three years later Lorenzo Carter established a permanent community, in whose harbour the first cargoes were discharged in 1813. With the completion of the system of canals between the Ohio River and Lake Erie and the coming of the railroad the town developed into one of the most important ports in the eastern United States and an industrial centre in which some of the biggest American entrepreneurs made their fortunes – demonstrating their wealth in luxury residences on Euclid Avenue, known as Millionaires' Row. Among those who lived here around the turn of the 19th c. were John D. Rockefeller, founder of the Standard Oil Company, and Samuel Mather, who made his fortune in steel production and transport – though almost nothing is left to show for it. After the Second World War Cleveland suffered an economic decline, which even the efforts of Carl B. Stokes, the first black to be elected mayor of a major American city, were unable to stem. In the 1980s, however, a restructuring of the economy produced positive results, and in recent years the city has been largely modernised.

Sights

The central feature of Cleveland is Public Square, which in 1879 became the first public square in the United States to be lit by electricity. Round

Public Square

The Rock and Roll Hall of Fame in Cleveland, by the renowned architect I.M. Pei

it are the Tower City Center, a shopping centre converted from an old railroad station, with the 52-storey Terminal Tower (viewing platform on 42nd floor), and the 46-storey BP America Building. North-east of Public Square is the Mall, the largest square in the city centre, which is decorated with fountains and sculpture and dominated by the Society Center, Cleveland's tallest building (890 ft).

★Rock'n Roll Hall of Fame

North Coast Harbor, at the north end of East 9th Street, has been redeveloped as a promenade and a setting for festivals; also situated here is Cleveland's latest attraction, the Rock'n Roll Hall of Fame. Designed by I.M. Pei, it is more an experience than a museum. The history of popular music is spread over six floors in an atmosphere of multimedia exuberance, with such rarities as the manuscript of "Purple Haze" written by Jimi Hendrix or "The Psychedilic Porsche", as sung by Janis Joplin. The CD shop can meet every need. Open summer Mon., Tue. 10am–5pm, Wed.–Sun. 10am–9pm; winter Tue.–Sun. shorter hours.

Moored at the quay is the "William G. Mather", an ore and coal carrier built in 1925. Some distance away, at Burke Lakefront Airport, is USS "Cod", a United States navy submarine.

Flats

The Flats, the low-lying area of old industrial buildings round the outflow of the Cuyahoga River into Lake Erie that was the original nucleus of Cleveland, is now a favourite haunt of nightbirds, attracted by its numerous restaurants, cafés and bars. On the west bank of the river is the Powerhouse of 1892, which until 1954 supplied the city's streetcars with electricity.

Playhouse Square Center

Playhouse Square Center (1501 Euclid Ave.) is a Mecca for theatregoers and lovers of variety; four theatres – the Ohio, the State, the Allen and the Palace – built in the 1920s and now restored, put on everything from musicals to avant-garde theatre.

Round University Circle, 5 mi. east of the city centre on Wade Park, are a number of interesting museums. In Severance Hall the Cleveland Orchestra performs in a series of concerts from September to June.

University Circle

The Museum of Art at 11150 East Boulevard is particularly strong on medieval art from Europe and Asia and American art. Among notable American artists represented are John Singleton Copley ("Portrait of Anna Dummer Powell", 1764), Frederic Edwin Church ("Twilight in the Wilderness", 1860) and Thomas Eakins ("The Biglin Brothers Turning the Stake", 1873). Medieval European art is represented by nine items from Brunswick Cathedral, modern art by the French Impressionists and Picasso.

★Cleveland
Museum of Art

Surroundings

5 mi. south of the city centre, to the east of Brookside Metropolitan Park, is the Cleveland Metroparks Zoo, one of the oldest in the United States.

Cleveland
Metroparks Zoo

South of Cleveland is the popular Cuyahoga Valley National Recreation Area, a 22 mi. stretch of country along the Cuyahoga River that has been restored to its original state. Through the northern part of the park runs the old Ohio and Erie Canal. To the south is Hale Farm, an open-air museum with restored early 19th c. houses in which old crafts are demonstrated.

Cuyahoga Valley
National
Recreation Area

Akron, 35 mi. south of Cleveland, is the "rubber capital of the world" – Goodyear, Bridgestone and Uniroyal have their headquarters here. Those interested in the way tyres are made should join the guided tour of the factory provided by Goodyear and visit the firm's museum. Those keen to find out more about American inventors should visit the National Inventor's Hall of Fame at 221 South Broadway.

Akron

Colorado (State)   J–M 16–23

Area: 104,332 sq. mi.
Population: 3,295,000
Capital: Denver
Popular name: Centennial State

The state of Colorado (from Spanish colorado, "coloured") lies in the western United States. The smaller eastern part of the state belongs to the Great Plains, lying at altitudes between 3300 ft and 5900 ft. The soils of this region, originally grass steppe, yield abundant crops with the help of irrigation. The larger western part of Colorado lies in the Rocky Mountains, which are made up mainly of two parallel ranges striking north–south and separate two widely different climatic zones. The Front Range, rising in places to over 13,000 ft, forms the imposing eastern boundary of the Rockies. The Sawatch Range in western Colorado is the watershed between the Pacific and the Atlantic (Gulf of Mexico), rising to 14,433 ft in Mount Ebert, the highest peak in Colorado. In the mountains coniferous forests predominate, giving place above the 11,500 ft mark to a vegetation of alpine type dominated by mountain pines.

History From the 11th to the 13th c. the farming culture of the Anasazi Indians, now well documented, flourished in south-western Colorado.

Their heirs are believed to have been the Ute Indians and the bison-hunting Cheyenne and Arapaho tribes. In the 17th c. Spanish conquistadors explored at least the southern part of the territory and gave it its name (the "coloured" country, after the rocks in light and dark reddish tones which outcrop here). Soon afterwards French prospectors pushed into eastern Colorado from Louisiana. Thereafter the French and Spanish fought for predominance until 1763, when the territory passed to the Spanish crown. In the first half of the 19th c. the United States gained control of the area; then in 1861 it was incorporated as a United States territory, and fifteen years later became the 38th state of the Union. In 1913 a Norwegian introduced skiing to the Rockies and thus sparked off the development of the tourist trade.

Economy Agriculture is well developed in the Great Plains. In the south and east irrigated arable farming predominates; the north-west is given up to cattle ranching. In the eastern foreland of the Rockies (particularly in north-western Colorado) considerable quantities of oil and natural gas are extracted, and there are rich mineral resources in the mountainous west of the state – coal, silver, gold, zinc, vanadium, uranium and, in the Sawatch Range, molybdenum. Steel manufacture and metalworking, as well as arms production, are old-established industries; also of importance are the foodstuffs industries. Younger, but highly successful, is the electronics industry, with its dynamic centre round Colorado Springs. Tourism also makes a major contribution to the economy: the Rockies are increasingly popular with summer vacationists, and they also have a number of world-famous winter-sports centres, notably Aspen, Vail, Keystone and Steamboat Springs.

★Aspen

The internationally renowned resort of Aspen lies in the valley of the Roaring Fork River, some 156 mi. south-west of Denver (see entry). Originally an important mining town, Aspen is now an exclusive winter sports resort and a rather less expensive summer holiday resort. In the surrounding area are the beautiful Maroon Lake, set against the backdrop of three mountains over 13,000 ft (Maroon Peak, North Maroon Peak and Pyramid Peak). Among the finest skiing areas round Aspen are Aspen Mountain, the Aspen Highlands, Snowmass and Buttermilk Mountain.

From Aspen CO 82 runs up via Independence Ghost Town into the grandiose mountain world of ★**Independence Pass** (12,095 ft and Mount Elbert (14,433 ft), the highest peak in the state of Colorado.

★Colorado
Springs

The city of Colorado Springs, a popular resort both in summer and in winter, lies on the eastern slope of the Front Range, here dominated by Pikes Peak (14,110 ft). The lovingly restored old town of Colorado City still retains something of the atmosphere of the Wild West. In the Fine Arts Center (30 W Dale St.) notable exhibits include Indian sand paintings and works of art of the Spanish colonial period (e.g. the carved figures known as "santos"). There are other interesting exhibitions in the Pioneers Museum at 215 South Tejon Street and the Pro Rodeo Hall of Fame (history of the rodeo) on the northern outskirts of the city, I 25, exit 147.

6 mi. north-west of the city is the ★**Garden of the Gods**, a nature reserve with bizarrely shaped red sandstone formations (the Kissing Camels, the Balanced Rock) and ancient cypresses. It is at its most impressive in the early morning light or at twilight.

★★**Pikes Peak** (14,110 ft), 3 mi. north-west of Manitou Springs, site of the Cave of the Winds, is best accessed by means of the Pikes Peak Cog Railway. From the summit there are breathtaking views, extending on clear days as far as Denver (see entry) and into New Mexico, which

"The Garden of the Gods"

attract large numbers of visitors throughout the year. Katherine Lee Bates was inspired by Pikes Peak to write the words of the song "America the Beautiful".

12 mi. north of Colorado Springs, at the foot of the Front Range, is the **US Air Force Academy**, where over 4000 Air Force cadets are trained. The "Moon Meal Parade" is held daily at noon, and there is also a large parade on Saturdays at 11am.

Near the Academy is the North American Aerospace Command (NORAD).

44 mi. west of Colorado Springs, at a height of 10,000 ft, is the old gold-diggers' town of Cripple Creek (which can be reached by all-terrain vehicles from the Gold Camp Rd.). In the 1890s there was a swarming population of over 10,000 gold prospectors; nowadays Cripple Creek – in which gaming is now legal – has no more than 600 inhabitants. Visitors can take an interesting excursion through the area on a steam train of the Cripple Creek and Victor Narrow Gauge Railroad.

Cripple Greek

Dinosaur National Monument, famed for its fossils, lies in north-western Colorado, with a tip reaching into Utah. The area round the Yampa and Green Rivers became world-famous when the fossilised remains of saurians (dinosaurs), crocodiles and tortoises were found there. In the Jurassic period giant creatures, including Allosaurus, Apatosaurus, Brontosaurus and Stegosaurus, roamed over this part of America. 7 mi. north of Jensen (Utah) is the very informative Dinosaur Quarry Visitor Center.

From the Park offices in Dinosaur (Colorado) a 31 mi. road runs round the finest sites in Canyon Country.

★Dinosaur National Monument

There are facilities for adventurous ★★**rafting** trips on the Yampa River

Colorado

(from Deerlodge Park) and the Green River (from Gates of Lodore). Finest of all is a trip through the Split Mountain Gorge.

Durango

Also in south-western Colorado is the old mining town of Durango Concert on the squnare, Aspen (pop. 13,000), which flourished during the gold and silver boom of the 19th c. It is a good base for excursions into the San Juan Mountains. From here the "Million Dollar Highway" (US 550) runs north through magnificent scenery. Another expensive attraction is the Durango and Silverton Narrow Gauge Railroad, on which old-time trains run up the narrow valley of the Animas River into the San Juan National Forest and to Silvertom, where Wild-West shows are given.

Fort Collins

An hour's drive north of Denver, in the oil-rich eastern foreland of the Front Range, is Fort Collins (pop. 68,000), a town founded in 1864 which is now the seat of Colorado State University. Features of interest are the lovingly restored old town centre with its attractive shops and restaurants, the Fort Collins Museum and the large Anheuser-Busch brewery on the north-eastern outskirts of the town.

Grand Junction

The town of Grand Junction (pop. 28,000) lies in the far west of Colorado at the junction of the Gunnison River with the Colorado. It is a starting point for mountain-bike, climbing or rafting trips into the wild country-side. The town is also a winemaking centre. Its attractions are the Museum of Western Colorado (natural and cultural history of the region), Dinosaur Valley (fossils) and the Cross Orchards Historical Site (history of agricultural development in the region).

A few miles west of Grand Junction is ★**Colorado National Monument**, a nature reserve with bizarre rock formations and canyons.

★Black Canyon of the Gunnison

130 mi. south-east of Grand Junction is the spectacular Black Canyon of the Gunnison, a narrow gorge, over 2600 ft deep in places, cut through dark rocks of the Palaeozoic era.

★Great Sand Dunes National Monument

In southern Colorado are the impressive Great Sand Dunes (now protected as a national monument). Over a period of 15,000 years the wind has carried great masses of sand from the semi-arid San Luis Valley to the foot of the Sangre de Cristo Mountains. Some of the dunes are over 650 ft.

Hovenweep

In Hovenweep National Monument, 40 mi. west of Cortez, Colorado, are the ruins of Indian pueblos and defensive towers dating from the 12th–14th c.

★Leadville

High up in the Rockies is Leadville (alt. 10,190 ft; pop. 2500), once an important silver-mining centre. Gold and silver are still worked in the area.

The National Mining Hall of Fame and Museum has a large collection of material on the history of mining. Leadville is now also an important winter sports centre which, thanks to its high altitude, has a very long season. Features of interest are the restored Healy House and the Matchless Mine Cabin, reminders of the great days of the gold and silver boom. From Leadville you can take a rail trip through the mining country on the Leadville, Colorado and Southern Railroad. The upper reaches of the Arkansas River are popular with white-water rafters.

★Steamboat Springs

In the mountains of northern Colorado is the beautiful Yampa Valley, the chief town in which is Steamboat Springs, with more than 150 hot mineral springs. In 1914 Carl Howelsen, a Norwegian, made this a centre of Nordic (langlauf) skiing, and it is now one of the leading winter sports resorts in the United States. Notable sights in the area are the

Thunderhead (aerial cableway), the Fish Creek Falls and Routt National Forest. The best skiing region is the Mount Werner Ski Area.

In the mountains of south-western Colorado is Telluride (alt. 8745 ft; pop. 1400), where gold and silver were found in the 19th c. The town then acquired a luxury hotel, the Sheridan, and even an opera house. In 1889 the notorious bank robber Butch Cassidy made a haul of 30,000 dollars here. Telluride is now a popular winter sports centre. Outside the town are the beautiful Bridal Veil and Bear Creek Falls.

Telluride

Vail, like Aspen, is a world-famous winter sports resort. It lies in the Rockies 100 mi. west of Denver on I 90. The town's lightning development began after the Second World War, and it is now an important centre on the international skiing circuit. Features of interest are the Ski Museum, with the Ski Hall of Fame, and the charming Betty Ford Alpine Garden, named in honour of President Ford's wife.

Vail

In White River National Forest is the world's largest skiing area on a single mountain, with 53 cableways and lifts. The season is from the end of November to the middle of April and the sun shines on 300 days of the year.

The only building in the centre of Vail that has remained unchanged since it was founded in 1962 is Pepi Grashammer's tyrolean restaurant.

Denver, Mesa Verde National Park, Rocky Mountain National Park (see entries).

Other places of interest

Connecticut (State)   H 14/15

Area: 5018 sq. mi.
Population: 3.3 million
Capital: Hartford
Popular names: Constitution State, Nutmeg State

The relatively small state of Connecticut (from the Indian quinnehtukqut, "on the long tidal river") in the north-eastern United States lies between Long Island Sound on the Atlantic and the foothills of the northern Appalachians. The hilly western part of the state, rising to a height of 2380 ft in Mount Frissell, is separated from the gently rolling country, up to 1000 ft high, of the eastern part by the wide valley (up to 20 mi. across) of the Connecticut River. The temperate climate, with warm summers and abundant snow in winter, makes possible a wide variety of outdoor activities throughout the year, with bathing in the Atlantic in summer and skiing in the Mohawk Mountains in winter. The forests of deciduous trees (mainly oak, chestnut, hickory and poplar) make the state's "Indian summer" in autumn a memorable experience.

History The land on the Connecticut River was settled by Indians long before the coming of the Europeans. In 1614 a Dutchman, Adrian Block, explored the course of the river, and twenty years later English Puritans founded Windsor, the first permanent white settlement. The local Pequot Indians put up a stubborn resistance, which was not overcome until 1637. In 1662 the British colony was granted a considerable degree of self-government, with its own constitution. In 1776 the independent state of Connecticut was proclaimed, and on January 9th 1788 it became the fifth state of the Union.

Economy Soon after the Declaration of Independence the state's economy began to develop rapidly. One of the factors in this development was Connecticut's abundant supply of water power, which made possible a remarkably early process of industrialisation. The timber industry, shipbuilding, arms production and engineering are still major pillars of the economy; but the proximity of markets in neighbouring cities has also provided a powerful stimulus to the development of agriculture (particularly dairy farming, poultry and fruit and vegetable growing). Tobacco growing enjoys a fine tradition in the valley of the Connecticut River – the best Havana wrappers come from Connecticut.

Bridgeport

Bridgeport (pop. 142,000) has a museum devoted to the celebrated showman and circus proprietor Phineas T. Barnum but has little else to recommend it, Greenwich to the south-west, on the other hand, is an attractive holiday resort with some fine restaurants.

Hartford

Hartford (pop. 140,000), capital of the state of Connecticut, is also the "insurance capital of the United States" and has a large plant manufacturing aircraft engines. In the town are houses once occupied by Mark Twain, who wrote "Tom Sawyer" here, and Harriet Beecher Stowe, author of "Uncle Tom's Cabin". Other features of interest are the Wadsworth Atheneum, one of finest American collections (works of the Hudson River school), and the State Library, with the large Colt Collection of hand guns.

★Mystic

The old boatbuilding and whaling town of Mystic is now a popular tourist resort, with the Marinelife Aquarium and the Mystic Seaport as its principal attractions; the latter is the largest open-air martime museum in the United States with some wonderful old ships.

New Canaan

New Canaan is a very typical New England colonial town, with the renowned Silvermine Guild Arts Center.

★New Haven

The port of New Haven (pop. 131,000), at the mouth of the Quinnipiac River, was founded by English Puritans in 1638, and has been famed since 1716 as the seat of Yale University. On the university campus are the Peabody Museum (natural history; Dinosaur Hall), the Art Gallery (with important finds from Mesopotamia), the Reinecke Rare Book and Manuscript Library (whose principal treasure is a Gutenberg Bible), the Sterling Memorial Library (4 million volumes; archives of the University) and the Center for British Art (particularly art of the 16th–19th c.). Popular with children (and with adults) are the Children's Museum and the Shoreline Trolley Museum (old streetcars).

New London

The old whaling port of New London (pop. 29,000), now the seat of the US Coast Guard Academy, has preserved a number of handsome old 17th, 18th and 19th c. buildings. Other features of interest are Monte Cristo Cottage (home of the playwright Eugene O'Neill), the Lyman Art Museum (dolls' houses) and the Arboretum, on the campus of Connecticut College. Ocean Beach Park is a popular recreation area. From New London there are ferries to Block Island, Fisher Island and Long Island, which attract many visitors. The town of Groton is an important American submarine base. In the Submarine Museum the nuclear submarine "USS Nautilus", the first to pass under the Arctic, lies at anchor.

★Crater Lake National Park G 3

State: Oregon
Area: 251 sq. mi.
Established: 1902

Crater Lake National Park lies in the Cascade Mountains in south-western Oregon. The striking feature of Crater Lake is the intense blue colour of its water. This unusually deep lake (1935 ft) is almost exactly circular, with a diameter ranging between 4½ mi. and 6½ mi. and a circumference of 26 mi., and is surrounded by lava cliffs rising to heights of between 500 ft and 2000 ft. Crater Lake is the water-filled caldera of Mount Mazama, an extinct volcano that was once 11,970 ft high. Continuing eruptions hollowed out the summit of the mountain, which collapsed some 6850 years ago, leaving the present circular cavity. Later eruptions within the crater gave rise to a volcanic cone that now emerges from the lake as Wizard Island. When volcanic activity ceased some 4000 years ago the crater began to fill up with melt water and rainwater. It has no other sources of water.

Information The National Park and Steel Visitor Center are open throughout the year; the Rim Drive, however, is negotiable only between July and mid-October, and the facilities in Rim Village operate only from June to September. Even in summer it is advisable to take warm clothing. There are two campsites in the park and motels in nearby Klamath Falls.

There is an informative display on the geology and formation of the lake on the Sinnott Memorial viewing terrace on the southern rim of the crater.

Sinnott Memorial

Rim Drive runs round the lake in a clockwise direction a short distance from the edge of the crater, beginning at Rim Village; its total length is 33 mi.

★Rim Drive

The first spectacular viewpoint is the **Watchman**, to the west of Wizard Island; a path (1400yd) leads up to the top, from which there are mag-

Wizard Island in Crater Lake

nificent views extending, in good weather, as far as Mount Shasta (14,162 ft) in northern California. To the north of the Watchman is Hillman Peak (8189 ft), the highest point on the rim of the crater. Then to the east of North Junction, on the north side of a lake, is Llao Rock (8045 ft), a former glacier valley filled up with obsidian. Further on the Cleetwood Trail (1 mi.) runs down from the Rim.

Drive to Cleetwood Cove, from which there are hourly cruises on the lake, landing on **Wizard Island**. Thereafter the road turns south, opening up a view of Mount Scott, to the east of the crater rim – the highest point (8928 ft) in the National Park. The Mount Scott Trail (2½ mi.) leads up to the top of the hill, while a side road runs up to the Cloudcamp viewpoint, the highest point on the Rim Drive (8061 ft).

From Kerr Notch there are good views of the curious Pinnacles, carved from the pumice rock by erosion, and the **Phantom Ship**, a bizarrely shaped rocky island near the steep shore of the lake (also seen from the Sun Notch viewpoint). The Rim Drive then continues over the Tututni Pass (6600 ft) and the Vidae Ridge to the park offices, where it meets the road coming from the west and south entrances to the National Park. From here it is another 3 mi. to Rim Village.

Hiking trails In addition to those already mentioned there are a number of other hiking trails in the National Park, including the Garfield Peak Trail (1¾ mi.), which runs up to the top of Garfield Peak; the Discovery Point Trail (2¼ mi.), running along the crater rim from Crater Lake Lodge; the Godfrey Glen Trail (2¼ mi.) to the Duwee Falls on Munson Creek; and the Annie Creek Canyon Trail (1¼ mi.) along Annie Creek with its basalt columns. The Pacific Crest Trail (here called the Oregon Skyline Trail) also cuts through the western part of the National Park. This long-distance trail follows the crest ridges of the Cascade Mountains and the Sierra Nevada for a total distance of 2350 mi. from the Canadian to the Mexican frontier.

Dallas   R 29

State: Texas
Altitude: 465 ft
Population: 1 million

Dallas, now the largest city in Texas after Houston (see entry), owes its origin to John Neely Bryan, who in 1841 built himself a hut on the banks of the Trinity River in north-eastern Texas. Until after the Civil War Dallas was overshadowed by its sister city Fort Worth, but after the coming of the railroad in 1873 Dallas grew rapidly. While until the Second World War the city's economy depended on the grain and cotton grown in the surrounding area and later on oil, it has now become, with its numerous insurance corporations and banks, the business and financial centre not only of Texas but of the whole of the south-west. It was natural, therefore, that the famous soap opera of power, money and intrigue should have Dallas as its setting. The city's main industrial products are electronic apparatus, oil drilling equipment, chemicals and, since the Second World War, aircraft, rockets and electronics. Important contributions to the economy are also made by textiles and publishing.

Sights

Dallas County
Historical Plaza

On Dallas County Historical Plaza (Main and Record Sts.) is the log cabin (restored) in which John Neely Bryan is said to have lived.

Immediately adjoining, on Kennedy Plaza, is the John F. Kennedy Memorial, a monumental open granite cube commemorating the murder of President Kennedy here on November 22nd 1963.

JFK Memorial

The presumed murderer of President Kennedy, Lee Harvey Oswald, is believed to have fired the fatal shots from the sixth floor of the Texas School Book Depository at the intersection of Houston and Elm Streets. Here now is the Kennedy museum known as the Sixth Floor, devoted to John F. Kennedy's life, work and death. Open daily 9am–6pm.

★The Sixth Floor

Many of Dallas's older districts and buildings have been restored in recent years, for example the West End Historic District between Elm, Record and Lamar Streets, a rebuilt warehouse district now occupied by clubs, movie houses and restaurants. Here too (Main and Houston Sts.) is the Old Courthouse of 1892. In the Old City Park (1717 Gano St.) are a number of restored buildings dating between 1840 and 1910 – some of them originally situated here, some brought here from other sites – which form an interesting open-air museum.

Historic districts

Deep Ellum, a 20 min. walk from Downtown, is home to Dallas' artists and "alternative society" cafés and galleries abound.

Among important examples of modern architecture in Dallas are City Hall (by I.M. Pei), a huge pyramid lying on edge; the First Interstate Bank Tower; and the Crescent Court Center (by Philip Johnson) to the north of the city centre, a complex occupied by restaurants, clubs, antique shops and art galleries. Thanksgiving Square, between Pacific Avenue, Bryan Street and Ervay Street, was also designed by Philip Johnson.

Modern architecture

Dallas's great landmark is the Reunion Tower in Reunion Park (viewing platform). In the same complex is the restored Union Station (400 S

★Reunion Tower

The futuristic skyline of Dallas

Houston St.), now housing the tourist information office. The First Republic Bank Plaza, 70 storeys high, is another landmark visible from afar.

Pioneer Plaza

On Pioneer Plaza near the City Hall stands what is said to be the world's largest bronze sculpture. The work of Robert Summer in 1995, it depicts 70 Texas longhorn cattle and three cowboys.

State Fair Park

State Fair Park (on 2nd Ave., to the south of US 67/I 30), Dallas's Civic Center and scene of the annual State Fair, is dominated by the Big Tex Towers. Originally laid out for the Texas Centennial Exposition of 1936, the park contains a number of museums: the Age of Steam Museum, the Museum of Natural History, Science Place I and II, and the Museum of African-American Life and Culture. Also in the park are the art-deco Hall of State (commemorating great Texans), the Sports Stadium of the Southern Methodist University, the Cotton Bowl, the Music Hall (opera and ballet; Dallas Summer Festival) and the Dallas Aquarium. The art-deco Exhibition Hall is also a sight in itself.

Dallas Museum of Fine Art

North of Main Street and Thanksgiving Square, at 1717 North Harwood Street, is the Dallas Museum of Fine Art, notable particularly for its col-

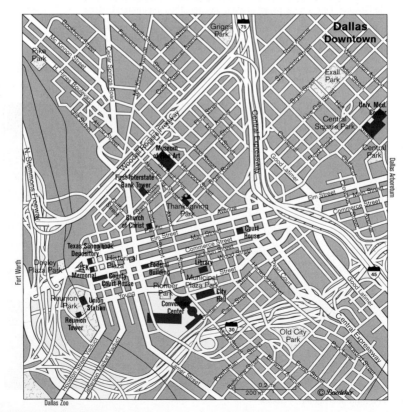

lection of pre-Columbian sculpture. Open Tue.–Fri. 11am–4pm, Thu. to 9pm, Sat., Sun. 11am–5pm.

To the north-east of the city, at 8617 Garland Road, is the Dallas Arboretum and Botanical Garden, on the shores of White Rock Lake.

Dallas Arboretum and Botanical Garden

To the north of the city, on Hillcrest Avenue, between Dallas North Tollway and US 75, is the extensive campus of the Southern Methodist University, with the Meadows Museum (Spanish painting of the 15th–20th c.) and the Meadows Sculpture Garden (modern sculpture). Further north, near Hillcrest Memorial Park, is the Biblical Arts Center, with a collection of religious works of art – pictures, icons, liturgical utensils, a reproduction of the Holy Sepulchre and an outside painting of the Resurrection, with son et lumiére effects.

Northern districts

Southfork Ranch, home of the Ewing family in the television soap opera "Dallas", has been reopened as a tourist attraction. It lies in Plano, 6 mi. east of US 75 by way of Parker and Hogge Roads. Open daily 9am–5pm.

Southfork Ranch

Fort Worth

The city of Fort Worth (pop. 450,000), which has now almost joined up with Dallas, grew out of a military post established in 1849 and rapidly developed into a leading cattle-ranching centre, where cattle were collected for transport to the slaughterhouses of the south – earning it the nickname of "Cowtown". Fort Worth itself prefers to be known as "the city where the Wild West begins".

The Stockyards Historic Area (123 E Exchange St.) takes visitors back to the great days of the cattle round-ups.

★Stockyards Historic Area

Fort Worth has three interesting museums: the Amon Carter Museum of Western Art (Camp Bowie Blvd.), in a building designed by Philip Johnson; the Kimbell Art Museum (3333 Camp Bowie Blvd.; designed by Louis Kahn, with a fine collection of European masters and of art of the Aztecs and Mayas). In contrast, there is the Will Rogers Center, named after the singing cowboy, with Western shows and agricultural exhibitions.

Museums

Log Cabin Village, a restored settlement of log cabins in Forest Park, to the south-west of the city, gives some impression of life in Texas in the time of the cattle barons.

Log Cabin Village

Water Gardens Park (15th and Commerce Sts.), designed by the top architect Philip Johnson, shows a modern city layout.

Water Gardens Park

In Arlington, between Dallas and Fort Worth, is the Six Flags Over Texas entertainment park, with a variety of typically American rides, shows and attractions, including a cable railway, an old-time steam railway, boat trips and a number of hair-raising roller coasters, including one with three loops (taken both forwards and backwards) and a track that rises to the height of a 14-storey building.

Six Flags Over Texas

★★Death Valley National Park   M–P 8/9

State: California
Altitude: up to 282 ft below sea level
Established: 1994

Death Valley National Park

Death Valley, declared a National Park in 1994, today comprises an area of 3860 sq. mi., centred on a depression 140 mi. long and between 4 mi. and 16 mi. across which is bounded on the west by the Panamint Range and on the east by the Amargosa Range. Something like a fifth of the area lies at or below sea level.

At Badwater is the lowest point on the North American continent (282 ft below sea level).

A drive through Death Valley in summer can be hazardous, and on no account should drivers disregard any restriction or ban on driving. Check the cooling system and take plenty of water. It should be borne in mind, too, that accommodation in the area is limited: advance reservation is essential; note that campsite reservations are possible only in Texas Springs and Furnace Creek.

Information The best time to visit Death Valley is from October to May, when temperatures range between 68°F and 91°F. From June to September it can be intolerably hot, with average maximum temperatures above 104°F; a July temperature of 134.1°F has been recorded. The average annual rainfall is about ¼ in. There are in all nine campsites and two (expensive) motels – Furnace Creek and Stove Pipe Wells Village.

Furnace Creek Visitor Center, Hwy 190; open daily 8am–5pm, winter to 8pm.

History Death Valley was given its name in 1849, when a party of gold prospectors, seeking a short cut to the Californian goldfields, lost their way here and some of them died in the inhospitable terrain. Other prospectors and adventurers were attracted to the area by the hope of finding gold. Apart from some unproductive ore deposits they found only borax, a salt used in the manufacture of soap, detergents and cosmetics and in the industrial production of glass and enamel. In 1881 the Harmony Borax Works were opened at Furnace Creek, and thereafter there was a regular borax boom. This "white gold" was transported by mule train to the railroad station of Mojave, 164 mi. away.

Flora and fauna In spite of the extreme natural conditions Death Valley has, thanks to a number of hidden springs, a relatively varied flora (mainly succulents) and fauna (lizards, rattlesnakes and even coyotes). This varied desert landscape appeals to many visitors with its rugged rocks, salt lakes and sand dunes.

★**Dante's View**

From Death Valley Junction the CA 190 climbs to the Amargosa Range in the north-west. Before reaching the Furnace Creek Visitor Center roads branch off to Dante's View, from where there is a magnificent prospect of the salt lakes and barren hills.

★**Zabriskie Point**

Then continue further to Zabriskie Point (which cinemagoers will remember from Michelangelo Antonio's film), the bizarrely eroded badlands that are at their most magical at sunrise and sunset. From the Visitor Center the CA 178 leads into the south of Death Valley. Turning off by way of Artist's Drive some multicoloured rock formations can be seen then, after passing the Devil's Golf Course, a rock-hard salt flat with thousands of small salt pinnacles.

★**Badwater**

Badwater, the lowest point in America (282 ft below sea level), lies on the edge of a salt lake that never completely dries out even in summer and is occupied by waterweeds and myriads of tiny flies.

On the CA 190 north of the Visitor Center lie the Harmony Borax Works. In the northern section of the park will be found Mosaic Canyon, the sand dunes of Stove Pipe Wells and Ubehebe Crater, which is 875yds in diameter and 500 ft deep.

In Grapevine Canyon, a few miles east of the crater, stands **Scotty's**

Badwater, the lowest point in the United States

Castle, a desert villa in Spanish colonial style built by Albert W. Johnson and Walter E. Scott ("Death Valley Scotty"); today it houses a Death Valley exhibition.

Delaware (State) K/I 51

Area: 2045 sq. mi.
Population: 725,000
Capital: Dover
Popular names: First State,
Diamond State

Delaware (named after Baron De La Warr, governor of Virginia), the first of the thirteen founding states of the Union and its second smallest, lies in the eastern United States on a well watered peninsula reaching out into the Atlantic between Delaware Bay and Chesapeake Bay. In the north it extends on to the Piedmont Plateau. It has a temperate maritime climate.

History The first European to explore this section of the North American coast, then inhabited by Indians, seems to have been John Cabot (1498), who was followed in the early 17th c. by Dutch navigators. The first permanent settlement, however, was established by Swedes in 1638. In 1655 Ny Sverige (New Sweden) passed to Holland and nine years later to Britain. In 1682 Delaware was incorporated in the colony of Pennsylvania, but in 1775 recovered its independence and in 1787 was the first state to sign the new Constitution of the Union.

Economy Delaware is highly industrialised, and benefits from its proximity to Philadelphia (see entry). In addition to its dominant chemical and petrochemical industries (Wilmington area) it has a number of major metalworking firms (including automobile construction and steelworks), textiles and foodstuffs industries. Agriculture also makes an important contribution to the state's economy, and the holiday and tourist trade is of importance in the coastal areas.

Delaware Bay
Delaware Bay, over 50 mi. long and up to 30 mi. across, is the estuary of the 280 mi. long Delaware River, which flows down from the Catskill Mountains.

Lewes
For bathers there is the somewhat overcrowded Rehoboth Beach at Lewes or the quieter beaches to the south. Lewes itself is a pretty little town, founded by Dutch settlers from Hoorn in 1631 – the Zwaanendael Museum (local history) looks very much like the town hall of Hoorn.

Dover
The state capital, Dover (pop. 25,000), was founded by William Penn in 1717, and has preserved something of its colonial-period charm. Features of interest include the Old State House (1787), the Delaware State Museum (history of the state), the Delaware Agricultural Museum and Village. There is a well-stocked Aircraft Museum at Dover airbase.

Wilmington
31 mi. south-west of Philadelphia (see entry) is the port and industrial city of Wilmington, founded by Swedish immigrants in 1638. It is an important centre of the chemical industry (DuPont).

Henry Francis Du Pont's collection of American art and crafts from 1640 to 1860 can be seen in the ★**Winterthur Museum** north of the town. The restored mill in the Hagley open-air museum between Wilmington and Winterthur shows where his wealth came from. Nearby lies the Museum of Natural History.

Denver   K 21

State: Colorado. Altitude: 5280 ft
Population: 470,000

The "mile-high city", as Denver, capital of the state of Colorado, is known, lies at the junction of Cherry Creek with the South Platte River, at the foot of the Front Range (Rocky Mountains). It is the dynamically developing economic and cultural centre of a wide hinterland extending widely over the Great Plains and into the Rockies. It has an agreeable continental climate, with plenty of sunshine and low rainfall.
  Denver is the see of a Roman Catholic archbishop and the seat of the University of Denver and the renowned University of Colorado Medical Center. It is also an important industrial centre, with over 180 large firms (power production, electrical apparatus, petrochemicals, foodstuffs, publishing), a major destination for business travel and a good base for vacation trips into the Rockies. Development has been aided further by the opening of the new aiport in 1995.

History In 1858 gold was discovered on Cherry Creek, and the three gold-diggers' settlements of Aurora, Highland and Denver that grew up there amalgamated in 1860–1 to form the town of Denver. In 1868, when it had a population of over 4000, it became capital of the territory of Colorado. After the coming of the railroad in 1870 Denver was a boom town, and in 1876 became capital of the 38th state of the Union. In the late 1980s it became involved in the silver and gold rush, when increasing numbers of people passed through Denver on their way to the Rockies or settled in the town. By the turn of the 19th c. it had a population of 134,000. Thereafter it developed into an important traffic hub and industrial centre. It has also been popular for many years as a good base from which to explore the beauties of the Front Range. The importance of the business and tourist trade was recognised by the opening of a large new airport in 1994.

Civic Center/Capitol Hill

In the heart of Denver is the green and in summer agreeably shady Civic Center Park, laid out in Classical style, with numerous monuments.

Civic Center Park

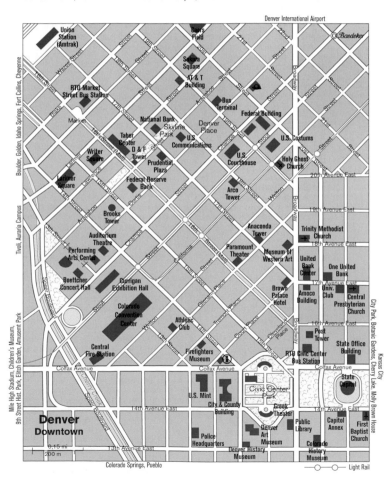

Round the park are the principal administrative buildings of the state of Colorado, and along its north side runs Colfax Avenue, the city's principal traffic artery.

★Colorado State Capitol

On a low hill on the east side of the park is the classical State Capitol, crowned by a gilded dome 250 ft high. From the viewing platform on the drum of the dome there are magnificent views of the city's imposing skyline and the Front Range. The 13th step on the west side of the Capitol is exactly 1 mi. above sea level (the "mile-high city").

★US Mint

Immediately beyond the City and County Building is the US Mint, one of the United States' three mints (the others being in Philadelphia and San Francisco). Part of the country's gold reserves is also stored here. There is a small museum on the history of coining. Open Mon.–Fri. 8am–2.45pm.

★Denver Art Museum

To the south-west is the massive, fortress-like Denver Art Museum, with a collection that includes the art of the Indians as well as outstanding works from Europe and the Far East. Of particular interest are the "santos", figures of saints carved by Indian craftsmen following models brought in by Spanish missionaries in the 17th c. Open Tue.–Sat. 10am–5pm, Sun. noon–5pm.

★Colarado History Museum

To the south-east of Civic Center Park is the Colarado History Museum (prehistoric Indian cultures, including the Anasazi; relics of pioneering days; gold mining). Open Mon.–Sat. 10am–4.30pm, Sun. noon–4.30pm.

Molly Brown House

A short walk south-east of the State Capitol, at 1340 Pennsylvania Street, is the Molly Brown House, which belonged to a survivor of the "Titanic" disaster (celebrated in the musical "Unsinkable Molly Brown") who was famed for her lavish parties.

Lower downtown

16th Street Mall

In an effort to bring a little more life into downtown Denver amid the skyscrapers 16th Street, which runs through the city centre, has been made a European-style pedestrian precinct, with shady trees, flowerbeds and park benches, in which the only traffic is a free shuttle bus. The street is lined with department stores, boutiques, souvenir shops, restaurants and the stalls of street traders (mostly "Indios" from Latin America).

Particularly round the south end of the street there are numerous modern and postmodern skyscrapers. Among the tallest are the 56-storey Republic Plaza, the 690 ft high United Bank Center, the Denver Post Tower, the Amoco Building, the Anaconda Tower and the Denver Club Building.

D. and F. Tower

On north-western 16th Street (corner of Arapahoe St.) is the D. and F. Tower, which was modelled on the Campanile in St Mark's Square in Venice. Adjoining is the modern Tabor Shopping Center.

★Larimer Square

Larimer Street is the oldest part of the town. Another successful example of urban refurbishment is nearby Larimer Square, where Buffalo Bill (see Famous People) lived at one time, with well restored buildings of the Civil War period, art galleries, gift shops, cheerful restaurants and gas lamps.

Denver Center for the Performing Arts

On the south side of Larimer Square is the Denver Center for the Performing Arts, a gigantic cultural centre with the Boettcher Concert Hall, the Auditorium Theatre and the DOPA Theatre.

The dominating business skyline of Denver

To the west of the Performing Arts Center is the extensive Auraria Campus, with the modern buildings of the University of Colorado, the Learning Resources Center, the Metropolitan State College.

    Nearby, beyond Cherry Creek, is the Tivoli shopping and entertainment centre, housed in a former brewery.

Auraria Campus

At 1727 Tremont Place is the Museum of Western Art, with a collection that includes important pictures by Albert Bierstadt, Frederick Remington and Georgia O'Keeffe, three artists who found their inspiration in the American West.

    Immediately south is the Brown Palace Hotel (1892), with a fine art-deco interior. It is known as the "White House of the West" because President Eisenhower often operated from here.

Museum of
Western Art

City Park

To the east of the city centre is City Park, with a variety of facilities for entertainment and relaxation.

The Denver Zoo is beautifully laid out, with enclosures adapted to different species (polar bears' den, monkeys' island, "stroke the animals" zoo).

★Denver Zoo

In the south-east of City Park is the Natural History Museum. Among the most notable exhibits are imposing dinosaur skeletons, remains of Ice Age animals, the collection of minerals presented by the Coors brewing family, one of the largest nuggets of gold found in Colorado and artifacts of prehistoric Indian peoples. Open daily 9am–5pm.

★Natural History
Museum

Attached to the Museum are the C.H. Gates Planetarium and an IMAX cinema with a giant screen. Open daily 9am–5pm.

Botanic Gardens

1 mi. further south are the Botanic Gardens, laid out in the 1950s, with large glasshouses.

Surroundings

★Denver
International
Airport

23 mi. north-east of downtown Denver is the huge new Denver International Airport, which came into operation only at the beginning of 1995, 53 sq. mi. in area, Denver International is the largest airport in the world. Critics however are sceptical as to whether a city like Denver needs such as massive airport. The very imposing tent roof over the vast terminal building symbolises the snow-capped peaks of the Rocky Mountains.

Golden

14 mi. west of Denver is the town of Golden (pop. 13,000), which from 1862 to 1867 was capital of Colorado. Features of interest are the 12th Street Historic District; the Colorado Railroad Museum; the geological and mineralogical collections and earthquake observatory of the Colorado School of Mines (founded 1874); and the large Coors Brewery, established by a German immigrant of that name. Open Mon.–Sat. 10am–5pm.

★Lookout
Mountain Park

From Lookout Mountain Park there are superb views of the city of Denver and the eastern foreland of the Rockies. High up in the hills is Buffalo Bill's grave, with a small museum devoted to his memory. In a nearby enclosure a herd of buffaloes (bison) graze.

Idaho Springs

In a narrow valley 37 mi. east of Denver is the old gold-diggers' town of Idaho Springs (alt. 7550 ft). At many places in the surrounding area various ores (including gold) are still mined. Some mines (among them the Phoenix Gold Mine) can be visited.

★★Mount Evans

From Idaho Springs the highest mountain road in the United States runs steeply up past the beautifully situated Echo Lake to the alpine pastures on Mount Evans (14,266 ft), from the summit of which there are breath-taking panoramic views.

★Black Hawk

In a deep V-shape valley north-west of Golden, still frequented by numerous hopeful gold prospectors, is the old Western settlement of Black Hawk, nostalgically refurbished, with various gaming houses and saloons to tempt the tourist. There are similar establishments in Central City nearby.

Boulder

North-west of Denver is Boulder, a good centre from which to explore the Arapahoe National Forest and the Rocky Mountain National Park (see entry). Visitors can also take a stroll through the historic district of the town between 11th and 15th Streets and enjoy a coffee on the campus of the University of Colorado after visiting the Art Gallery.

Detroit G 42

State: Michigan
Altitude: 597 ft
Population: 1,028,000

Detroit, by far the largest city in the state of Michigan, lies on the north-west bank of the Detroit River and on Lake St Clair, between Lakes Huron and Erie. The "metropolis of the automobile", Detroit ranks with New York and Chicago as one of the largest industrial cities in the United States. It is the country's busiest inland port after Chicago and Duluth – accessible, since the construction of the St Lawrence Seaway, to ocean-going vessels of up to 25,000 tons.

History The city's name is derived from the French dÇtroit (strait), refer-ring to the narrow waterway between Lakes Huron and Erie. In 1701 Antoine de la Mothe Cadillac established a fort on the site of the present-day city. In 1760 this passed into British hands, and in 1796, after the American victory in the battle of Fallen Timber, was incorporated in the United States. After being incorporated as a town in 1802 and suffering great devastation in a fire in 1805, Detroit was from 1807 to 1847 capital of the state of Michigan. Its economic rise began in earnest with the opening of the Erie Canal in 1825 and the development of steamship traffic and was accompanied by a rapid increase in population. The auto-mobile industry, founded by Henry Ford around the turn of the 19th c., soon took the city's population above the million mark (and by 1930 to 1.5 million); and in spite of its considerable chemical, electrical and elec-tronics industries, its shipyards and its oil refineries, there can be few cities more heavily dependent on automobile production than Detroit. In the late 1960s Detroit hit the headlines as a result of the serious racial disturbances among its large coloured population.

Sights

Along the Detroit River are huge skyscraper complexes. Dominating them all is the Renaissance Center, with the 73-storey Westin Hotel and five other 39-storey towers containing hotels, shops, theatres, restau-rants and public institutions.

★Renaissance Center

Mariners' Church (1849), the oldest in the city, was moved to make room for the Civic Center with its extensive congress and conference facilities and exhibition halls. Among them are the Convention Arena which, with the Cobo Hall, forms one of the largest exhibition halls in the United States, with numerous conference rooms of all sizes. Immediately west of the Cobo Hall is the Joe Louis Arena; in front of it is a bronze statue of the Detroit-born boxer whose name it bears. Between the Renaissance Center and the Civic Center is Hart Plaza, designed by the Japanese sculptor Isamu Noguchi, which is a popular meeting place in spring and summer (concerts and other performances, including part of the Montreux-Detroit Jazz Festival in May).

Civic Center

East of the Renaissance Center, the storage sheds and quays dating from the 1880s have been given a new lease of life with conversion to bars, restaurants and shops.

Rivertown

There are many interesting high-rise blocks to the north of the Civic and Renaissance Centers, on Griswold Street and Woodward Avenue, Detroit's main north–south axis. Particulary imposing is the 47-storey Penobscot Building (550 ft; built 1928), the city's tallest office block.
    Beyond John F. Kennedy Square, between Griswold Street and Woodward Avenue, are the 23-storey First Federal Savings Building (427 ft), one of the world's largest department stores, the J.L. Hudson Store, on the front of which the largest Stars and Stripes in the country (236 ft long) is hung on Flag Day. Further north, on the semicircular Grand Circus Park (with the Edison Fountain), is the 34-storey David Broderick Tower.

Griswold Street/Woodward Avenue

3 mi. north-west of the city centre along Woodward Avenue is the modern Cultural Center, where a number of fine museums lie close to one another.

Cultural Center

241

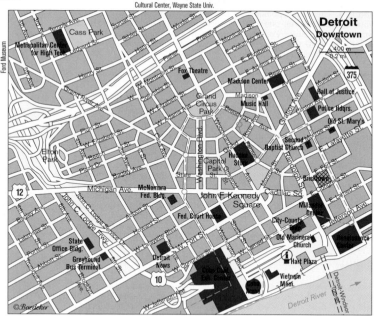

Cultural Center, Wayne State Univ.

— ◦ — People Mover

The Detroit ★**Institute of Arts** (5200 Woodward Ave.) displays a representative cross-section of man's artistic creation from the earliest cultures to the present day. Its strong points are the art of China; the art and culture of the Near East and classical antiquity; works of art, arms and armour of medieval Europe; and American art and culture (including 18th c. domestic interiors in Whiteby Hall, a mansion of 1754). The collection includes many masterpieces of European painting, including works by Rembrandt, Van Gogh (self-portrait), Matisse and Picasso. Open Wed.–Fri. 11am–4pm, Sat., Sun 11am–5pm.

A little way east, at 301 Frederick Douglas Street, is the ★**Museum of African-American History**, which illustrates the role of blacks in the history of the United States and their position in the city of Detroit. An interesting feature is the "underground railway" that enabled slaves to flee from Michigan into Canada.

Opposite the Institute of Arts is Detroit Historical Museum (5401 Woodward Ave.), with reconstructions of old Detroit streets, model railways, dioramas and periodic special exhibitions on the history of the city.

General Motor Building

At the intersection of Second Bvld. and Grand Bvld. is the New Center Area, with the General Motors Building, which is made up of several parallel wings.

Motown Museum

At 2648 West Grand Boulevard is the Motown Museum, the small shingle-clad building that was occupied from 1957 to 1972 by the studio where records of the "Motown sound" were produced. Visitors can see the actual recording studio where Marvin Gaye and others produced hit songs.

Grand Boulevard and the General MacArthur Bridge over an arm of the
Detroit River lead on to Belle Isle, an island in the river (3 mi. long and
up to 1 mi. wide) laid out with beautiful parkland, hiking trails, sports
facilities and other attractions, including an Aquarium (freshwater
fishes), a Safari Zoo, a Botanical Museum and the Dossin Great Lakes
Museum (numerous ship models and other exhibits illustrating the history of shipping on the Great Lakes).

★Belle Isle

Henry Ford Museum and Greenfield Village

11 mi. west of the city centre is the suburb of Dearborn, in which the
automobile manufacturer Henry Ford (see Famous People) was born
(20900 Oakwood Bvld.). Here in 1929 he established two exhibition complexes as memorials to himself: the Henry Ford Museum (area 12 acres)
and an open-air museum, Greenfield Village (reached from Kennedy
Square by way of Michigan Ave., going west; bus 200 or 250).

The Henry Ford Museum offers a general survey of the development of
American life and technological advances from pioneering days to the
present time. These include the Decorative Arts Galleries, a series of
rooms decorated in appropriate period style showing the development of
American decorative and applied art, a reconstruction of an early 19th c.
street, with different shops and workshops, and the Main Exhibition Hall.

**Henry Ford
Museum**

Main Exhibition Hall is devoted to the history of technology in the
United States. Among the most notable exhibits are George
Stephenson's first steam locomotive (1829); some 200 automobiles,
including the first Ford and the car in which John F. Kennedy was assas-
inated; the Fokker in which Admiral Byrd made the first flight over the
North Pole in 1926; and the Junkers W 33 in which Hermann Köhl,

Ford's T Type: 17 million were built

Freiherr von HÅnefeld and James Fitzmaurice made the first east-west crossing of the Atlantic in 1928. Open daily 9am–5pm.

Greenfield Village A little way north of the Henry Ford Museum is the entrance to Greenfield Village, an open-air museum with some 100 historic buildings of the 18th and 19th centuries from all over the United States. Among them, in addition to different types of houses, are a school, a railroad station and other public buildings, the house in which Henry Ford was born, Edison's laboratory and the Wright brothers' bicycle factory. The numerous shops in the Village Craft Center sell the products of the various workshops in the village.

Legendary cars from all over the world are displayed here, to the delight of all enthusiasts. Open Jun.–Oct. daily 10am–7pm; Nov.–May daily 10am–5pm.

★★Everglades National Park Y 44/45

State Florida
Area: 2186 sq. mi.
Established: 1947

The National Park occupies the whole of the southern tip of Florida. Known to the Indians as Pa-hay-okee ("River of Grass"), this great expanse of subtropical swamplands, famed for its alligators (plus a small number of crocodiles) and its innumerable species of birds, is the surviving southern part of an area of swamp and marshland that originally covered fully a third of the Florida peninsula. To the north and east the Everglades have largely been drained and converted into fertile farming country. Down to the northern boundary of the National Park

A trip through the Everglades by canoe is not for the faint-hearted

the land is now under cultivation (producing mainly winter vegetables for the northern states). Before being drained the Everglades were often under water for anything up to nine months in the year. The great attractions of this exotic landscape are the extraordinarily rich subtropical and sometimes tropical flora and fauna, without parallel anywhere else in the world, and the largely unspoiled and inaccessible wilderness. This is not country for the motorised tourist in a hurry: it requires plenty of time. Visitors during the summer months are often disappointed to see only a few alligators or birds. This is because during the rainy season much of the National Park is under water and the animals and birds have no difficulty in finding food: it is only during the dry winter season that they gather at the few water points. At this time of year, too, millions of migrant birds arrive in the National Park. Nowadays the sensitive ecosystem of this unique wilderness region is under threat from agricultural development and the uncontrolled building developments on the east and west coasts.

The National Park is open throughout the year. The best time for a visit is in winter, preferably towards the end of the dry season (Mar.–Apr.). In summer (May–Nov.), when the climate is predominantly hot and humid, an insect repellent is a must.

When walking away from the surfaced roads or when camping or picnicking visitors should watch out for possible encounters with **dangerous animals**. Among the snakes that live in the Everglades are the venomous coral snake, the black water mocassin snake, which may be anything up to 10 ft long, the diamondback snake and a dwarf rattlesnake. Caution is also required in approaching too close to alligators; and even raccoons, which like to forage or to beg for remains of food, are best kept at a distance. It is strictly forbidden to feed animals in the National Park.

There are also a number of **poisonous plants** in the Everglades, including poison ivy (Rhus radicans) and poisonwood (Metopium toxiferum), which is related to the sumach. Contact with these plants, particularly with the sap, can have unpleasant consequences.

Florida (State)   T–Z 38–45

Area: 58,560 sq. mi.
Population: 13 million
Capital: Tallahassee
Popular name: Sunshine State

The state of Florida (from the Spanish *Pascua Florida*, Palm Sunday, the day on which it was discovered in 1513) occupies the peninsula of that name in the south-eastern United States, which separates the Atlantic Ocean from the Gulf of Mexico, together with the "Panhandle", a narrow strip of land on the north-eastern Gulf Coast.

The Florida peninsula is a region of sedimentary rocks with great expanses of sand, limestone tableland much dissected by karstic action and wide areas of swamp. The landscape is patterned by numerous lakes (often formed in dolines or poljes), coastal lagoons and spits of land, mangrove swamps in the south and south-east, wide estuaries and offshore coral reefs. Seen from the air, it is clear that not so long ago the northern part of the peninsula was mainly covered with pine forests, the south with marshy grassland, cypress swamps and "hammocks" (patches of primeval forest).

Florida

History Between about 10,000 and 8000 BC hunter-gatherers began to move into the Florida peninsula. There is evidence of a first cultural flowering in the 6th and 5th centuries BC Palm Sunday (Pascua Florida) in 1513 Ponce de León landed in the estuary of the St John's River. Soon afterwards Spaniards and Frenchmen were fighting for predominance in the newly discovered territory. In 1665 the first European settlement in the United States was established at St Augustine. In the 18th and 19th centuries Florida was a bone of contention between Spain and Britain; then in 1819 it passed to the United States. After the Seminole War (1835–42) most of the Indians were deported to Oklahoma. During the American Civil War (1861–5) Florida sided with the Confederates. Towards the end of the 19th c. the railroad magnates Flagler and Plant began to open up the south-eastern United States for tourism. In 1958 the first American space satellite was launched from Cape Canaveral, followed three years later by the first manned space flights. In the 1980s more than 140,000 Cuban refugees poured into southern Florida.

Economy The most important branch of Florida's economy is the holi-day and tourist trade. Broad beaches of white sand and primeval swamps, the lair of alligators and panthers, crystal-clear rivers and springs, coral reef with their multi-coloured marine life, giant theme parks and the space station at Cape Canaveral all make a visit to Florida an unforgettable experience. It is also becoming an increasingly import-ant financial centre, with over 170 international financial institutions based in Miami alone. In the industrial sector the most important elements are the processing of agricultural produce and aircraft and space technology. The main agricultural crops are citrus fruits, sugar cane and vegetables. Other sources of income are phosphates (one-third of world output), titanium and zircon from dune sands, lime and cement production and offshore oil and natural gas.

★**Apalachicola**
The little town of Apalachicola (pop. 3000) in the Panhandle of Florida has a charming old Historic District. It is now the centre of Florida's oyster fisheries (Apalachicola Bay). Within easy reach of the town are the offshore St George Island with its beautiful beaches; St Vincent Island, a nature reserve (turtles, various species of birds); and the St Joseph Peninsula, an unspoiled region with magnificent beaches. On the southern edge of the Apalachicola Forest is Fort Gadsden (1814).

Daytona Beach
Daytona Beach, famed for the 20 mi. stretch of firm sand on which Malcolm Campbell five times broke the world land speed record, now also has an international racing circuit, the Daytona International Speedway. A recent tradition has been the "spring break" during the university vacation (beginning of March to Easter), when hundreds of thousands of young people converge on Daytona, the scene is domi-nated by brilliantly chrome-plated motorcycles, convertibles, beach bug-gies, jeeps and pickups and there are almost daily concerts of deafening rock music.

★**Florida Keys**
To the south of Miami (see entry) are the Florida Keys (from the Spanish cayo, "islet, reef"), a chain of coral islands of varying size that extends for more than 110 mi. between the Atlantic and the Gulf of Mexico. Until a devastating hurricane in 1935 they were linked by a rail line extending to Key West, from which there were boats to Havana (Cuba). The boldly engineered Overseas Highway (US 1) now runs over 38 bridges and numerous artificial causeways to the south-eastern tip of the United States. The little islands of Sands Key, Elliot Key, Cotton Key and Old Rhodes Key, lying off Biscayne Bay, are now part of the Biscayne National Underwater Park, established in 1980. Off Key Largo (pop. 11,000) are the John Pennekamp Coral Reef State Park and the Key Largo National Marine Sanctuary, the only living coral reef in the conti-nental United States. The rich underwater life and a number of wrecks

attract large numbers of snorkellers and scuba divers. Islamorada claims to be the "sport fishing capital of the world". On Grassy Key is the Dolphin Research Center, where the TV series "Flipper" was filmed. Marathon (pop. 10,000) is the second largest town on the Keys. The new Seven Miles Bridge (1982) leads to the Bahia Honda State Recreational Area, with a beautiful bathing beach. On Big Pine Key is the National Key Deer Refuge, home to the last few hundred of the shy, miniature (only 2 ft high) roe-deer of the Keys.

The military and trading post of Fort Lauderdale, established in 1837, has now developed into the "Venice of the United States". Its 160 mi. of palm-fringed artificial waterways, tens of thousands of moorings for pleasure craft, elegant holiday apartments and beautiful 6 mi. long beach draw visitors from all over the world throughout the year. Particular attractions are Ocean World (trained dolphins and seals), the International Swimming Hall of Fame (with mementoes of Johnny Weissmuller, famous as a swimmer and as Tarzan, the record-breaking swimmer Mark Spitz and many others), the beautiful Flamingo Groves (planted with various species of citrus fruits) and Butterfly World on Coconut Creek. From the offshore Port Everglades, the second largest cruising port in the United States, there are daily departures of musical and gambling cruises to the Bahamas and the Caribbean.

★Fort Lauderdale

Fort Myers, a town in process of dynamic development, lies on the Gulf of Mexico at the mouth of the Caloosahatchee River. Abundant traces of human settlement going back 7000 years have been found in the surrounding area. The town became widely known in the 1880s, when Thomas Alva Edison (see Famous People) began to establish his home and his laboratory here during the winter. His example was followed in 1916 by his friend Henry Ford (see Famous People), who also built him-

★Fort Myers

Fort Lauderdale, often called the "Venice of the USA"

self a winter home opposite Edison's. The two "Winter Homes" are open to visitors. From Fort Myers the select Palm Alley (planted with royal palms from Cuba) runs down to the Gulf Coast, with the beautiful bathing resorts of Fort Myers Beach and Estero Island.

To the west of Fort Myers (see above) are the islands of ★**Sanibel and Captiva**, famed for their magically beautiful beaches, strewn with a great variety of seashells. On the shores facing the mainland are areas of marshland and mangroves, home to a wide variety of animal life. On the north-east coast of Sanibel is the "Ding" Darling National Wildlife Refuge.

Fort Walton Beach

The family resort of Fort Walton Beach lies on the north-western Gulf Coast. The Temple Mound Museum illustrates the history of Indian settlement and culture over 10,000 years. Off Fort Walton Beach is the narrow coral island of Santa Rosa, part of the Gulf Islands National Seashore. Inland from Fort Walton Beach is the Eglin Air Force Base, the largest in the United States; there is an Air Force Museum.

Naples

The town of Naples (pop. 20,000) on the Gulf coast of south-western Florida was founded in 1877 at a time of much speculation in land. It is now a popular holiday resort with elegant shopping streets and a famous wooden pier. Round Naples are a number of beautiful bathing beaches (Vanderbilt Beach, Wiggins Pass, Marco Island).

Ocala

Ocala (pop. 43,000), a country town in "Cracker Country" (northern central Florida), is a horse-breeding centre. Within easy reach of the town are Silver Springs, setting of the James Bond film "Never Say Never Again"; Orange Lake, an anglers' paradise; and Ocala National Forest.

Pensacola

The port of Pensacola (pop. 60,000), situated on the best and largest natural harbour in Florida, is the economic centre of the western edge of the Panhandle, the "Miracle Strip". Its history goes back more than 400 years, and the carefully restored Historic Village contains buildings of the Spanish, French and British colonial periods.

Features of interest in the surrounding area are the US Naval Aviation Museum; Fort Pickens (1834), at the west end of Santa Rosa Island; and Pensacola Beach with its expanses of brilliantly white sand.

★Sarasota

In a bay on the south-western Gulf coast of Florida is Sarasota (pop. 52,000), founded in 1842, now a rather exclusive retreat for the wealthy known as a centre of the arts. It owes this reputation mainly to the millionaire circus owner John Ringling and his wife, who established here not only a circus museum but an important art museum and a theatre. The Ringling Museum of Art possesses major works by Cranach, Rubens, Van Dyck and many other European artists. The Theatre, a faithful reproduction of the Baroque theatre in the Italian town of Asolo, is the home of a successful drama company. The Ringlings' winter residence (1926) is in the form of a Venetian Renaissance palazzo. Other sights in Sarasota are Belim's Cars and Music of Yesterday Museum (veteran and vintage cars, old musical boxes, mechanical musical instruments, gambling machines), the Sarasota Jungle Gardens (with flamingoes), the Mary Selby Botanical Gardens (orchids) and the Mote Science Aquarium (marine flora and fauna). There are beautiful bathing beaches on the narrow little offshore islets of St Amands, Lido, Longboat and Siesta Keys.

Sebring

In the hilly country of central Florida is Sebring, a town well known to motor-racing enthusiasts for the races held at the end of March and in October on the old military airfield.

Tallahassee (founded 1824), capital of the state of Florida, is a quiet town of some 127,000 inhabitants at the east end of the Panhandle. Its main features of interest are the Old Capitol (1839), the New Capitol (1978) and the richly stocked Museum of Florida History. Outside the town are the Lake Jackson Indian Mounds (an Indian cult site), the Lafayette Vineyards, the Natural Bridge Battlefield (on which the defenders of Tallahassee defeated the Union forces), the Spanish fort of San Marcos de Apalache (1679) and Wakulla Springs, with one of the biggest karstic springs in Florida.

Tallahassee

The main attraction of Winter Haven is Cypress Gardens, opened in 1936, where glamorously costumed "Southern belles" pose for photographers and a famous water-skiing show is presented.

★Winter Haven

Amelia Island (see Jacksonville); Cape Canaveral, Everglades National Park, Jacksonville, Key West, Miami, Orlando, Palm Beach, St Augustine, St Petersburg, Tampa (see entries); Walt Disney World (see Orlando).

Other places of interest

Georgia (State)   P–T 40–44

Area: 58,910 sq. mi.
Population: 6.63 million
Capital: Atlanta
Popular names: Empire State of the South, Peach State

The state of Georgia (named after King George II) lies in the south-eastern United States, bounded on the south by Florida. Most of the state lies in the Atlantic coastal plain. Offshore are numerous islands, on which there are beautiful bathing beaches. Inland there are extensive areas of marshland. To the north-east the land rises gradually to the Appalachians and the Cumberland Plateau. The highest point in the state is the hill of Brasstown Bold (4784 ft). The warm temperate and humid climate fosters a lush growth of vegetation. Some two-thirds of the state is covered by forest, with oak, hickory, fir and pine predominating in the hills. In the coastal plain and the marshland areas there are cypresses, various species of palms and arbor vitae.

History The territory of Georgia, discovered by Europeans in 1540, had long been settled by Indians. During the 16th, 17th and 18th centuries Britain, Spain and France fought for predominance in the south-east of the North American continent. In 1733 the British established a settlement, and in 1754 the territory became a Crown Colony. In 1776 the colony ratified the Declaration of Independence, and twelve years later signed the Constitution of the United States as the fourth of the founding states. Cotton growing on plantations worked by slave labour soon became the basis of the state's economy. During the Civil War Georgia set out to play a leading role, but was devastated by Sherman's march through the state. It was re-admitted to the Union only in 1870. The abolition of slavery and competition from other parts of the world brought Georgia's plantation economy into crisis. In more recent times the banning of racial segregation and the granting of full civil rights to blacks led to serious social conflicts. During this period Martin Luther King (see Famous People) became a symbol of the awakening African-American consciousness.

Economy Agriculture is still one of the main pillars of Georgia's economy. In addition to cotton, dominant for 150 years, the main crops are soya beans, maize and peanuts. Stock farming (cattle, pigs) and above all poultry farming have gained greatly in importance. The great forests of pines provide raw material for papermaking and the manufacture of turpentine. Considerable quantities of granite, marble and kaolin are also worked in Georgia. Alongside the highly developed cotton and textile industries chemical and foodstuffs industries have also been established in recent decades. Georgia lies in the Sun Belt, a region remarkable for its dynamic economic development. This is particularly true of the Atlanta region.

Athens

Athens (pop. 48,000), seat of the University of Georgia, is noted for its Greek Revival architecture. There are a number of particularly fine classical buildings on Prince Avenue The Georgia Museum of Art has a notable collection of pictures.

Augusta

On the eastern borders of Georgia, on the Savannah River, is Augusta, founded by James Oglethorpe in 1735, long the centre of a large cotton- and tobacco-growing area. The atmosphere of days gone by can still be felt along Riverwalk and at the Old Cotton Exchange. Today Augusta is famous maily for its golf.

Chickamauga and Chattanooga National Military Park

In north-western Georgia are the Civil War battlefields of Chickamauga and Chattanooga, where 34,000 Union and Confederate troops fell.

Columbus

In the far west of Georgia, on the Chattahoochee River, is the town of Columbus (pop. 170,000), with its well restored and refurbished Historic District. During the Civil War it was an important supply base. Features of interest are the Confederate Naval Museum; the Columbus Museum; and the National Infantry Museum in Fort Benning, outside the town.

★Callaway Gardens

North of Columbus, on Pine Mountain, is a popular leisure centre established by the industrialist Cason Callaway, with artificial lakes, gardens of magnolias and azaleas and a butterfly house.

Georgia Mountains

The mountainous region of north-west Georgia is just the place for nature lovers. Interesting towns include Dahlonega, where gold was discovered in 1828, leading to the United States' first gold rush here and in the surrounding area (with the ghost towns of Aurania, Clarksville, Cleveland and Helen), Helen is a curiosity in itself; the town fathers decided to rebuild it in the "Bavarian" style, and it is now known as Alpine Helen.

★Macon

Macon (pop. 120,000), formerly an important inland port on the Ocmulgee River, is now the cultural and economic centre of a large surrounding area. It has a number of well preserved old buildings, including City Hall, the Grand Opera House, Hay House, in Italian Renaissance style, and the birthplace of the poet Sydney Clayton Lanier.

To the east of the town is the Ocmulgee National Monument. Originally (10,000 years ago) an Indian settlement of the prehistoric Mound Builder culture, the site was still occupied in the 19th c.

Golden Isles

The Golden Isles lie off the coast of Savannah (see entry) and stretch as far as the Florida border. They offer leisure and holidaying facilities that can be expensive but may be worth considering. The best known are St Simon's Island, Jekyll Island, the former "millionaires' island", and Cumberland Island with its unspoilt natural beauty.

★Okefenokee Swamp

The Okefenokee Swamp, known to the Indians as the "Land of the Quaking Earth", is an area of swampland in southern Georgia, over 770 sq. mi. – a maze of watercourses, cypress swamps and swamp grassland. Interesting features are the "floating islands", which quake under foot but nevertheless support whole forests and in the past provided protection for Indian settlements. The swamp is home to many endangered species and has no fewer that 10,000 alligators. From the little town of Waycross there are boat trips into the swamp.

Atlanta, Savannah (see entries)

Other places of interest

★★Grand Canyon National Park   N 12–14

State: Arizona
Area: 1905 sq. mi.
Established: 1919

The Grand Canyon National Park lies in north-western Arizona, bounded on the west by Lake Mead National Recreation Area, where the Colorado River is dammed by the Hoover Dam, and on the north-east (following the course of the Colorado River) by Canyonlands National Park and the Glen Canyon. The South Rim can be reached from Williams or Flagstaff on AZ 64 and US 180, the North Rim from Jacob Lake on AZ 67. Although the North and South rims are only 10 mi. apart as the crow flies, the distance by road is 215 mi. During the main summer holiday season there are bus services between the two.

The Grand Canyon Railway operates from the town of Williams (on I 140) daily in high season, weekends during the rest of the year.

Information The National Park is open throughout the year. The best times for a visit are from April to June and September to mid-November. In summer it can be intolerably hot. During the main holiday season, too, the National Park's facilities tend to be overstrained. In winter the North Rim is under heavy snow, and most of the roads and tracks are closed from November to mid-May.

Since the South Rim in particular is at times overrun by tourists it is advisable to book accommodation or a camping site and to apply for a "backcountry permit" (required for hiking in the National Park) in plenty of time – during the main holiday season months in advance. The North Rim, which has equally fine views, gets less busy but access is difficult.

The Visitor Center on the South Rim, which is much more heavily visited than the North Rim, is on South Rim Drive, 1¼ mi. east of Grand Canyon Village (open Sep.–May daily 8am–5pm, Jun.–Aug. 7.30am–8.30pm). On the North Rim information can be obtained in Grand Canyon Lodge or the Ranger Station. There are daily lectures and guided walks by park rangers.

Sightseeing There are sightseeing flights by helicopter and light aircraft from several airfields along the South Rim of the Grand Canyon.

On the South Rim there are bus trips (with commentary) along the Rim Drive, starting from Grand Canyon Village. On the North Rim there are buses between Grand Canyon Lodge and the Cape Royal viewpoint.

On both the North and South rims there are half-day and whole-day trips into the Canyon on muleback; early reservation advisable.

For the adventurous there are rafting trips in rubber dinghies (from 2 to 18 days) down the Colorado River. There are operators in Flagstaff, Page and Peach Springs (Arizona) and in Kanab, Orem and Salt Lake City (Utah).

For hikers a descent into the Grand Canyon, where there are more than three dozen maintained paths totalling 400 mi. in length, is an exceptionally strenuous undertaking, requiring both fitness and stamina. Essential items of equipment are stout footwear, protection against the sun and plenty of drinking water. Before setting out you must inform a park ranger of your intention. Bear in mind, too, that the Grand

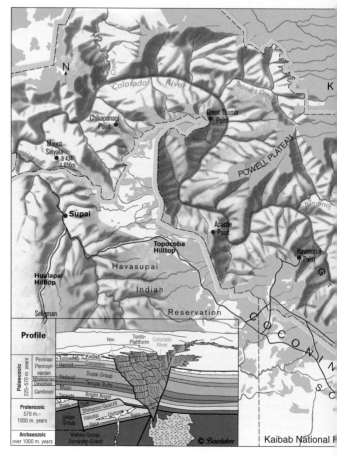

Canyon National Park is rattlesnake country, and keep a watchful eye for these venomous reptiles.

Grand Canyon

The Grand Canyon created by the Colorado River was described by the Scottish-born pioneer of conservation John Muir as the grandest place on God's earth. The breathtaking width and depth of this canyon, its beauty, its forms and colours, leave even the most travelled visitor lost in admiration.

Here the river winds its way for a distance of 277 mi. through the Kaibab plateau, into which it has cut a deep yawning gorge ranging in width between 4 mi. and 18 mi. On the south side the rock face falls down 5000 ft to the river below (alt. 2400 ft), on the north side no less than 6000 ft.

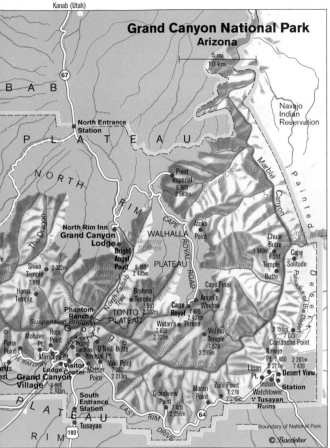

Grand Canyon National Park
Arizona

5 mi
10 km

Kanab (Utah)

Navajo
Indian
Reservation

B A B

67

North Entrance
Station

P L A T E A U

N O R T H

R I M

The Dragon

CAPE

ROYAL

Point
Imperial
8 803
2 683m

Nankoweap Creek

Marble Canyon

Painted

Atoko
Point

WALHALLA

ROAD

Roaring
Springs

North Rim Inn
Grand Canyon
Lodge

Bright
Angel
Point 8 153
2 485m

Shiva 2 322m
Temple
7 618

Horus
Temple

PLATEAU

North Kaibab Trail

Chuar Creek

Chuar
Butte
1 949m 8 394

Temple
Butte

Cape
Solitude

Little Colorado R.

Cape Final
7 529

Ribbon Falls

Bright Angel Creek

Brahma
Temple
7 553
2 302m

Cape
Royal 7 976
2 401m

Angel's
Window

Phantom
Ranch
Suspension Bridge

TONTO
PLATEAU

G o r g e

Wotan's
Throne
7 633
2 327m

Vishnu
Temple
7 073
2 295m

Palisades of the Desert

2 156m

D e s e r t

Mohave
Point

Hopi
Point

Pima
Point

Maricopa Pt.

Lodge

Visitor
Center

Garden
Creek

Indian
Gardens

O'Neill Butte

Yavapai Pt.

Yaki Point

Mather
Point 7 260
2 213m

Colorado River

Comanche Point

Navajo
Pt. 7 450 2 267m
2 271m 7 438

Desert View

Grand Canyon
Village

8 085
2 100m

South
Entrance
Station

P L A T E A U

Grandview
Point
7 400
2 256m

EAST

RIM DRIVE

Moran
Point

Zuni Point
7 278

Lipan
Pt.

Indian
Watchtower

Tusayan
Ruins

Station

2 216m

R I M

180

Tusayan

64

Boundary of National Park

© Baedeker

Williams, Flagstaff

Flagstaff, Cameron

The **history** of the formation of the Grand Canyon has not been certainly established, but the general view is that the reduction in the height of the Colorado river bed has been brought about mainly over the past 9 million years. The lowest level of erosional activity now runs through a narrow gorge cut out of Palaeozoic rocks up to 1700 million years old. The canyon becomes wider towards the top, where younger, horizontally bedded sedimentary rocks of varying degrees of resistance have been eroded away. These layers of sandstone and limestone, in brilliant red, blue-grey and yellow tones, depending on light conditions, were laid down during the Cambrian, Devonian, Carboniferous and Permian periods, and the steep rock faces descending in steps to the bottom of the canyon display a complete stratigraphical sequence. Going down into the canyon, you pass 1700 million years of the earth's history.

Much evidence has been found of Indian settlement in the Grand Canyon dating back more than 4000 years. The most impressive remains are the 1000 year old rock dwellings of the Anasazi Indians. When a member of Francisco Vásquez de Coronado's expedition questing for

The Grand Canyon: the mightiest and most famous of all gorges

gold became the first European to discover the Grand Canyon in 1540 these had probably long been abandoned. In 1869 Major John Wesley Powell, later director of the US Geological Survey, travelled by boat through the inhospitable gorges of the Colorado and Green Rivers, starting from Wyoming. In the 1880s the tourist potential of the Grand Canyon began to be realised; the first hotel was built on Grand View Point in 1892, and ten years later visitors were able to visit the Grand Canyon by rail. Thereafter the numbers of visitors grew steadily, particularly after the establishment of the Grand Canyon National Park in 1919. In 1965 the number of visitors was over 1.6 million, and by 1997 the figure had risen to 4 million.

South Rim

From Grand Canyon Village the Rim Drive runs east and west along the edge of the canyon, affording magnificent views into the canyon.

East Rim Drive

The East Rim Drive (25 mi.) runs east from the Visitor Center, passing Yavapai Point and the Yavapai Museum, which has interesting displays illustrating the origins and geology of the Grand Canyon. Then on to Desert View and pass the east exit of the National Park, towards Cameron. Halts can be made at a number of viewpoints – Yaki Point, Grandview Point, Moran Point, Lipan Point and finally Navajo Point with the Indian watchtower, built in 1932. 3 mi. west of Desert View on the East Rim Drive is the Tusayan Ruin, one of over 2000 remains of Indian settlements in the Grand Canyon region. In the late 12th c. the Tusayan pueblo was home to some three dozen Anasazi Indians, but – like most of the pueblos in this region – it was abandoned in the 13th c. The Tusayan Museum surveys the history of the Anasazi culture.

West Rim Drive

The West Rim Drive (8 mi.) also offers spectacular views into the canyon, with viewpoints at Trailview Overlook, Maricopa Point, Hopi Point, Mohave Point, the Abyss, Pima Point and Hermits Rest. The West Rim Drive is barred to private automobiles from May to September; instead there is a free shuttle bus.

Hiking trails The South Rim Nature Trail (3 mi.) is an easy walk from the Yavapai Museum along the rim of the canyon to Maricopa Point. Part of this scenic route is signposted as a nature trail.

The Bright Angel Trail (8 mi.) starts from Bright Angel Lodge (6861 ft) and runs down by way of the Indian Gardens (3806 ft; campground) either to Plateau Point (3780 ft), or right down to the Colorado River (2395 ft).

The South Kaibab Trail (6 mi.) runs steeply down from Yaki Point to the Colorado River, 4865 ft below.

North Rim

Since the North Rim of the Grand Canyon is between 1000 and 1250 ft (300 and 380m) higher than the South Rim, it offers a whole range of new and spectacular prospects. The most popular viewpoints are Bright Angel Point, Point Imperial and Cape Royal.

★Bright Angel
Point

Bright Angel Point, at the end of SR 67 near Grand Canyon Lodge, lies high above the gorge of Bright Angel Creek and opens up a grandiose prospect of the Grand Canyon landscape.

★Point
Imperial/Cape
Royal

A few miles north of Bright Angel Point a 22 mi. road branches off. This then forks, one road running north-east to Point Imperial, the other south-east over the Walhalla Plateau to Cape Royal. Point Imperial, the highest point in the National Park (8803 ft), affords views into the Marble Canyon to the east and of the Painted Desert on the south side of the Grand Canyon. From Cape Royal there are views of the Painted Desert and of the striking rock towers known as Wotan's Throne and the Vishnu Temple.

Hiking trails From Grand Canyon Lodge the Transept Canyon Trail (2 mi.) runs to the North Rim Inn. There is also a short trail to Bright Angel Point.
    The North Kaibab Trail (14 mi.) starts at a parking area (8242 ft) at the head of Roaring Springs Canyon, 2½ mi. before Grand Canyon Lodge, and runs through Bright Angel Canyon, passing the Cottonwood Campground (4003 ft), the Phantom Ranch (see above) and Bright Angel Campground, to the Colorado River (2395 ft).

Surroundings

In the canyon of Havasu Creek, a tributary of the Colorado River, some 450 Havasupai Indians (the "people of the blue-green water") live a secluded life, subsisting on their modest farming activities but now mainly dependent on the tourist trade. In this paradisiac valley the Havasu has created a number of waterfalls and carved out basins in the travertine rock that form attractive bathing pools. The Indian village of Supai can be reached only by helicopter from Grand Canyon Airport or on foot or horseback on an arduous 8 mi. long trail from Hualapai Hilltop (70 mi. north-east of Peach Springs). Accommodation, camping sites and horses must be booked in advance. Information from Havasupai Tourist Enterprise, Supai, AZ 86435, tel. (602) 448 2121.

★Havasupai Indian Reservation

The romantic Grand Canyon Caverns lie 12 mi. east of Peach Springs on the legendary Route 66. An elevator takes visitors down into the caves with their beautiful mineral formations and a constant temperature of 55°F.

Grand Canyon Caverns

★★Grand Teton National Park   F 15/map p. 529

State: Wyoming
Area: 485 sq. mi.
Established: 1929

Grand Teton National Park, established in 1929 and enlarged in 1950 by the inclusion of Jackson Hole, lies in north-western Wyoming a few miles south of Yellowstone National Park (see entry), with which it is linked by the John D. Rockefeller Jr Memorial Parkway. It consists of Jackson Hole, a mountain valley 50 mi. long and up to 14 mi. wide lying at a height of almost 6500 ft, and the jagged Teton Range, whose highest peaks rise to around 13,000 ft (Grand Teton, 13,770 ft; Middle Teton, 12,804 ft; South Teton, 12,514 ft; Mount Owen, 12,927 ft). The range was named Grand Teton by French fur trappers (*grands tétons*, big breasts). The landscape of the National Park is of extraordinary beauty. Jackson Hole is surrounded by lakes, some of them of considerable size, and traversed by the beautiful Snake River. Popular leisure activities here are hiking, fishing and canoeing, and for experienced climbers there are a variety of challenging routes.

Information The Grand Teton National Park is open throughout the year. The best time for a visit is between June and September. In winter all the facilities except the Moose Visitor Center are closed, but there is ample scope for winter sports (downhill and langlauf skiing, skating; trips in dog sleds, horse or motor sleighs; ice fishing). As well as in Moose there are further Visitor Centers in Colter Bay and on the banks of Jenny Lake. There are hotels in Colter Bay, and camping facilities at five sizeable and many smaller sites, the latter catering for a maximum of six people and one car.

Fauna This well watered mountain valley is the home of elk, wapiti and mule deer; on the lakes and rivers there are beavers, trumpeter swans, white pelicans, wild ducks, wild geese and ospreys; and a herd of bison is usually to be seen grazing to the east of the Oxbow Bend on the Snake River (near the Buffalo Entrance at Moran). Black bears are now rare. On the south side of the National Park is the National Elk Refuge, where the largest herd of wapiti in the United States regularly winters. In the winter tourist season horse-drawn sleighs from Jackson offer trips out to observe the wild life.

Two **scenic roads** offer magnificent views of the mountains: the Rockefeller Parkway, which runs north–south, following the east side of Jackson Lake and the Snake River, and the Teton Park Road, which runs south–east from Jackson Lake and along Cottonwood Creek.

The National Park has more than 200 mi. of **hiking trails** and footpaths running through the forests, to the various lakes and into the mountains. Among the easiest are the path from the east side of Jenny Lake to Inspiration Point (2½ mi.) and the Colter Bay Nature Trail (2 mi.). A whole-day hike is from Jackson Lake Lodge to Emma Matilda Lake and Two Ocean Lake.

A longer trail, taking several days but offering magnificent views, starts from the upper cableway station at Teton Village (outside the park to the south) and runs north along the west side of the Grand Teton

Grand Teton: view from Signal Hill

range, returning to the valley by way of Death Canyon, Cascade Canyon or Paintbrush Canyon.

In the Visitor Center in Colter Bay on the east side of Jackson Lake is the Indian Arts Museum (Indian arts and crafts, implements, clothing).

Indian Arts Museum

The little town of Jackson lies on the southern edge of Jackson Hole and is an excellent base from which to explore the Grand Teton National Park and Yellowstone Park. Jackson is still redolent of the atmosphere of the Wild West, particularly on the Town Square with its dozens of saloons, bars, galleries and souvenir stands. The Jackson Hole Museum (105 N Glenwood St.) traces the history of settlement in the valley, the Teton County Historical Center (105 Mercell Ave.) is devoted to the fur trade and the cultural history of the Indians, and the Wildlife of the American West Art Museum (110 N Center St.) has an extensive collection of pictures and sculptures on the wildlife of the west, including works by Albert Bierstadt and Karl Bodmer, Charles M Russell and Ernest Thompson.

Jackson

Snow King Mountain (7750 ft) is a popular skiing area, with breathtaking view of the Teton Range and the 10,926 ft high Rendezvous Peak. For the more adventurous there are also rafting trips on the Snake River

★Great Smoky Mountains National Park   O 42

States: North Carolina, Tennessee
Area: 814 sq. mi.
Established: 1934

The Great Smoky Mountains, a central range of the Appalachians running roughly east–west, are one of the finest forest regions in the United States. The name of the National Park, through which runs the border between the states of North Carolina and Tennessee, comes from the clouds and mist that frequently rise out of the lonely mountain valleys like smoke signals and swathe the mountains rising above the valleys to heights of over 6500 ft. The "Great Smokies" are hillbilly country.

Information The Great Smoky Mountains National Park, the most visited National Park in the United States, is open throughout the year – though in winter some roads may be impassable. There are Visitor Centers in Sugarlands near Gatinburg (TN) and in Ocanoluftee near Cherokee (NC). There are ten camping sites in the park and many hotels and motels in the surrounding towns.

Flora and fauna With its abundant rainfall, mainly in the summer months, and fertile soils, the National Park has a wide variety of flora and fauna (including bears). At lower levels dense deciduous forests predominate; higher up there are conifers. Well over 1400 species of flowering plants can be found here, including mountain magnolias, wild azaleas, mountain laurels and orchids; from the Rhododendron blossom beginning of June to the middle of July there are splendid shows of rhododendrons.

The full beauty of the National Park can best be appreciated by exploring it on foot. There are a total of some 900 mi. of **hiking trails**: information from Visitor Centers and the Park administration (see Practical Information, National Parks).

The National Park can be approached from the east on the Blue Ridge Skyway (see Virginia), which ends at the Oconaluftee Visitor Center. Here, in the extreme west of North Carolina, is the largest Indian reser-

Cherokee Indian Reservation

vation east of the Mississippi, the Qualla Reservation, occupied by the descendants of the Cherokees who refused in 1838 to follow the "Trail of Tears" to Oklahoma. In the little town of Cherokee there is an informative museum, and the Oconaluftee Indian Village above the town seeks to re-create the old life of the tribe.

Newfound Gap

To the west, reached by way of Gatlinburg, a little town now given over to the tourist trade, and the Sugarlands Visitor Center, is Newfound Gap (5050 ft), on the crest line of the mountains, which offers a magnificent view of the mountain forests.

Clingmans Dome

Still finer is the prospect from the viewpoint (closed in winter) on Clingmans Dome (6642 ft), the highest hill in Tennessee, which can be climbed from Newfound Gap either by road or on a 6 mi. section of the Appalachian Trail (see Practical Information, National Parks).

Cades Cove

Round Cades Cove, in the western part of the National Park, runs an 11 mi. road, passing the fields, houses, wooden churches and mills of the pioneers who settled here in the 19th c.

Dollywood

In Pigeon Forge, north of Gatinburg, lies Dollywood, the garishly modern leisure park owned by Dolly Parton, the country and western singer.

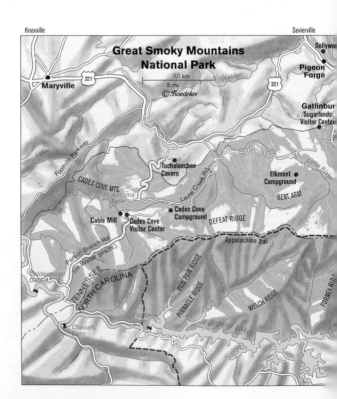

★★Hawaiian Islands (State)

Area: 6385 sq. mi.
Population: 1.1 million
Capital: Honolulu. Popular name: Aloha State

The Hawaiian Islands lie in the northern Pacific some 2400 mi. south-west of San Francisco (see entry). The archipelago consists of eight larger islands – from east to west Hawaii, Maui, Kahoolawe, Lanai, Molokai, Oahu, Kauai and Niihau – and over a hundred small islands and coral atolls, the north-western Hawaiian Islands. The eight large islands lie in the tropics and have lush tropical vegetation, while most of the north-western islands are north of the Tropic of Cancer. The mild climate, beautiful scenery and good bathing and surfing beaches attract large numbers of visitors from the United States, Europe and Japan. In spite of heavy
   Americanisation the islands have preserved much of their native culture and unspoiled natural beauty.

Origins The Hawaiian archipelago consists of the tips of volcanoes of the type known as Hawaiian (i.e. open craters with expulsion of lava but no explosive activity). Only two volcanoes on the island of Hawaii, Mauna Loa and Kilauea, are still active. The formation of Hawaii, in a seismically

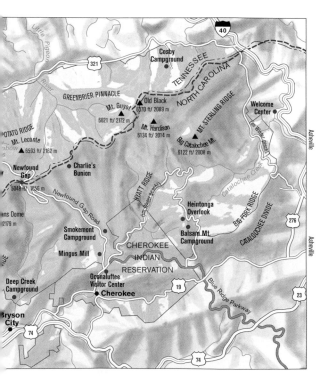

unstable zone of the Pacific, began in the Middle Tertiary era and continued over a period of 70 million years. This activity is explained by the theory of "hot spots": at certain points on the earth's mantle magna accumulates and is then released through faults and crevices in the crust in the form of volcanic eruptions and cools to form new land. Since the Hawaiian Islands lie on the Pacific Plate, which is drifting from southeast to north-west, the islands are also moving north-west at the rate of 3–4 in. a year. As a result of this movement the "hot spot" under Hawaii has given rise not merely to one volcano but to a whole chain of volcanoes, with the oldest on the Kure atoll to the north-west and the youngest on Hawaii to the south-east.

History The Hawaiian Islands were settled by Polynesians between AD 300 and 600. In 1778 Captain James Cook landed on the islands, but thereafter they remained an independent kingdom, though during the 19th c. they became increasingly dependent on the United States both economically and politically. A coup d'état against Queen Liliuokalani in 1893 put an end to the monarchy, and in 1894 a republic was proclaimed. Soon after the outbreak of the war with Mexico in 1898 the United States annexed the islands, which in 1900 were incorporated as a United States territory. In 1959 Hawaii became the 50th state of the Union. The Japanese attack on the American naval base of Pearl Harbor in the Hawaiian archipelago on December 7th 1941 brought the United States into the Second World War.

The most important element in the **economy** of Hawaii by a long way is tourism, followed by agriculture (sugar, canned pineapples) and fishing. The United States Navy continues to be a major employer.

★★Hawaii

This section is deliberately abridged, since there is a special AA/Baedeker guide "Hawaii".

Hawaiian Volcanoes National Park

On Hawaii, the largest and most south-easterly island in the archipelago, are the two active volcanoes of Mauna Loa (13,672 ft) and Mauna Kea (13,797 ft). Kilauea, a subsidiary of Mauna Loa, is the world's most active volcano. Both of these volcanoes are included within the Hawaiian Volcanoes National Park, which offers unique opportunities to see an active volcano, for example from the Crater Rim Road round the caldera of Kilauea or on branches off this such as the Devastation Trail or the trail to the Thurston Lava Tube.

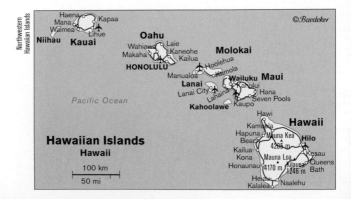

Maui

West of the island of Hawaii, separated from it by the Alenuihaha **Haleakala**
Channel, is Maui. Here too, in the Haleakala National Park, can be seen **National Park**
the results of vulcanism, not in its active form but after the end of
activity: the last eruption of Haleakala was in 1790. Large numbers of
endemic plants flourish on the volcanic soil of Haleakala's crater, on a
scale no longer seen anywhere else in the islands. To the original
Polynesian inhabitants the crater was a sacred place where they buried
their dead and built their temples.

Oahu

Oahu, the third largest island in the archipelago, is the political, economic and cultural centre of the Hawaiian Islands.

The main place of interest on the island is Honolulu, capital of the state **Honolulu**
of Hawaii, which consists of the three districts of Downtown, Pearl
Harbor and Waikiki. In the centre of downtown Honolulu is the modern
State Capitol, the architecture of which is designed to reflect the two
main elements determining the character of the islands, water and volcanic activity. The Iolani Palace, built by King David Kalakaua in 1879,
has the distinction of being the only royal palace in the United States.
There are three interesting museums: the Bishop Museum, one of the
finest ethnographic museums in the United States; the Hawaii Maritime
Museum on Honolulu Harbor; and the Honolulu Academy of Arts (old
Hawaiian art). The luxuriant plant world of the Hawaiian Islands can be
seen in the Foster Botanic Gardens, to the south of which is Honolulu's
Chinatown. In Pearl Harbor is the USS "Arizona" Memorial, erected over
the wreck of the battleship "Arizona", sunk by the Japanese on
December 7th 1941. The 2 mi. long Waikiki Beach is one of the most
beautiful town beaches in the world, with Diamonds Head, an extinct
volcano that is Honolulu's principal landmark, looming over it.

Also on Oahu is the Polynesian Cultural Center, with a reconstruction of **Polynesian**
a Polynesian village and displays of traditional handicrafts and dances. **Cultural Center**

Houston   U 30

State: Texas. Altitude: 55 ft
Population: 1.75 million

Houston, the fourth largest city in the United States and the greatest
metropolis of the south, situated only a few miles inland from the Gulf
of Mexico near the border with Louisiana, is a centre for the processing
of oil from the Texan oilfields and the offshore drilling rigs; since 1962 it
has been the seat of the Mission Control Center of the United States'
space programme; and, with the third largest port in the country (the
sixth largest in the world), it is a commercial centre of major importance.
The port is linked with the Gulf of Mexico by the 50 mi. Houston Ship
Canal, which can take ocean-going vessels. The economic importance of
Houston, which is also a great banking centre, is reflected in the
impressive skyline of its skyscrapers and the plans for further development that are under way. The fact that things were once very different is
shown by the Houston Livestock and Rodeo Show held each year in
February, the largest event of its kind in the United States.
  Houston is "mighty proud" of the fact that its name was the first word
to be spoken on the moon. "Houston. Tranquility base here. The Eagle
has landed," announced Neil Armstrong when the successful landing

took place on 20 July 1969. One of many superlatives applied to Houston is "Air Condition Captial of the World". There is scarcely a building without air conditioning – which adds a horrendous billion dollars to the annual electricity bill.

History Houston was founded in 1836 by two brothers, John and August Allen, and named after Sam Houston, a hero of the Texan war of liberation and first President of the independent Republic of Texas, of which it was the capital from 1837 to 1839 and from 1842 to 1845, when Austin (see Texas) finally took over that function. During the second half of the 19th c. Houston was overshadowed by the coastal town of Galveston, but became increasingly important following the construction of a ship channel to the Gulf of Mexico between 1873 and 1914. When Galveston was almost completely destroyed by a hurricane in 1900 Houston succeeded it as the leading port in Texas.

Sights

The skyscrapers of downtown Houston offer within a relatively small area a cross-section of modern architecture – the 75-storey pentagonal column of the Texas Commerce Bank Tower (by I.M. Pei; viewing hall on 60th floor), the green glass façade of the Allied Bank Plaza (by Edward Basset; 71 storeys), the Pennzoil Place high-rise complex with its prismatic trihedral forms (by Philip Johnson) and the postmodern Republic Bank Center (also by Philip Johnson). The towering lobby of the Hyatt Regency is not to be missed. The "ravines" between the tower blocks are not too crowded as people prefer to take refuge from the heat in the air-conditioned, 6 mi. underground tunnel system that connects all the important downtown buildings.

Skyscrapers in downtown Houston

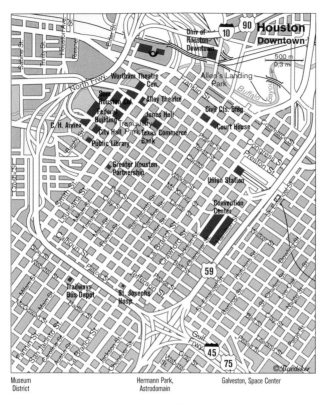

| Museum District | Hermann Park, Astrodomain | Galveston, Space Center |

The focal point of the city's cultural life is the huge complex of the Houston Civic Center (Capitol St., between Milam and Bagby Sts.), with the Jones Hall for the Performing Arts (home of the Houston Symphony Orchestra), the George R. Brown Convention Center (conventions, exhibitions, concerts), the Nina Vance Alley Theater, the Music Hall, the Sam Houston Coliseum (sporting events, concerts) and the Wortham Center (opera, ballet). On the same site is City Hall.

Houston Civic Center

The attractive Tranquility Park commemorates the Apollo moon landing programme, with bronze plaques giving information in 15 different languages.

South of the Sam Houston Coliseum, at 1100 Bagby Street, is the Sam Houston Historical Park, with the Museum of Texas History, an open-air museum with houses in early 19th c. style, old shops and a Victorian church.

Sam Houston Historical Park

The Boyou Bend Collection of 17th–19th c. furniture and art is housed in the home of millionairess Ima Hogg (Memorial Park, 1 Westcott St.)

Boyou Bend

In the south-western part of the city, between downtown Houston and the Rice University, are three fine art museums: the Contemporary Arts Museum (Montrose Bvld. and Bissonet St.), with periodic special exhibitions of modern art and films; the Museum of Fine Arts (1001 Bissonet St.), largely designed by Mies van der Rohe, with works of art from

Museum District

many countries, including the Kress Collection of Renaissance art and Indian art of the south-west; and the Menil Museum (1515 Sul Ross St.), housed in a building designed by Renzo Piano, which has an excellent collection of art of all periods and styles.

Rothko Chapel — East of the Menil Museum, at 3900 Yupon Street, is the Rothko Chapel, designed by Philip Johnson, with tapestries by the Russian-American artist Mark Rothko.

Galleria Area — Still further east is the Galleria Area, dominated by Philip Johnson's 64-storey Transco Tower, with the luxury Galleria shopping centre.

Hermann Park — To the south of the Museum of Fine Arts, round the Grand Basin, is Hermann Park, in which are the large Houston Museum of Natural Science, with the excellently equipped Burke Baker Planetarium, the Miller Outdoor Theater, the Houston Zoological Gardens and the Kipp Aquarium. Open Mon.–Sat. 9am–6pm, Sun. 11am–6pm.

★Astrodomain — To the south of the city is the Astrodomain, an extensive leisure complex. Its central feature is the massive Astrodome (Harris County Domed Stadium), the world's first roofed stadium. This immense hall, fully air-conditioned, is 645 ft across and 205 ft high and can accommodate between 55,000 and 65,000 spectators according to requirements.

On the south side of the stadium is the lower Astrohall, which is used for exhibitions and rodeos. Still further south, beyond I 610, is the 460 ft high Astroneedle, in Astroworld, a large amusement park, next door to which is Waterworld, an aquatic recreation park.

Port of Houston — To the east of the city is the Port of Houston. There are free sightseeing cruises on the "Sam Houston". A good general view can be had from the platform on Pier 8.

Surroundings

★★Space Center Houston — 25 mi. south-east of Houston, on the west side of Clear Lake, is the Lyndon B. Johnson Space Center, with the world-famous Mission Control, the monitoring centre for all NASA manned space flights. In the Visitor Orientation Center is a space exhibition, with film shows, models of space capsules, astronauts' rations, samples of moon rock and a variety of objects from the Mercury, Gemini and Apollo manned space programmes. Visitors can try on astronauts' helmets, steer a spacecraft in the simulator and, in the extensive grounds of the Space Center, wonder at huge space rockets and perhaps meet a real astronaut on his way to the Mission Simulation and Training Facility, where in the course of training he may be hurled around in a centrifuge measuring 100 ft across. Open daily 9am–7pm; summer Mon.–Fri. 9am–5pm.

San Jacinto Battleground State Historic Park — On April 21st 1836 General Sam Houston inflicted a decisive defeat on the Mexican army at San Jacinto and thus brought the Texan fight for independence to a successful conclusion. The scene of the battle, 20 mi. east of Houston, is marked by the San Jacinto Monument, a 570 ft column. From the platform at the top there are magnificent views. The Museum of Texas History on the ground floor of the monument traces the development of Texas from the early Indian cultures by way of the Spanish and Mexican periods to the present time. Also to be found in the State Park is the battleship "USS Texas", built before the First World War and flagship of the Normandy invasion fleet of 1944.

Galveston — South-east of Houston, on a narrow island in the Gulf of Mexico that is linked with the mainland by a highway, is Galveston, which in 1836 was briefly capital of the Republic of Texas. During the 19th c. Galveston was the largest and wealthiest town in Texas, and its earlier splendour is still Historic buildings recalled by a number of handsome mansions. Examples of such Victorian buildings are Ashton Villa (24th St. and Broadway), Bishop's Palace (1402 Broadway) and the Grand Opera House of 1894 (2020 Post Office). The well restored warehouse district known as the Strand (between Strand and Mechanic Sts.) still preserves the original faáades, now concealing restaurants and shops. One of Galveston's finest parks is Moody Gardens, whose particular attraction is a large glass pyramid for tropical plants. The 32 mi. long beach on Galveston Island has made the city a favourite holiday resort.

Idaho (State)   B–G 9–14

Area: 83,557 sq. mi.
Population: 1,039,000
Capital: Boise
Popular name: Gem State

The mountain state of Idaho (a name that probably comes from an Indian word meaning "mountain precious stone") lies in the north-western United States. The northern two-thirds of the state, the most mountainous part, are on the western slope of the northern Rockies, whose highest peaks here rise above 10,000 ft and offer excellent conditions for winter sports. Central Idaho, which includes the plateaux of the Clearwater Mountains and Salmon River Mountains, merges in the south and south-west into the arid, steppe-like Snake River plain, along the edge of which flows the Snake River, in a valley which at some points is deeply indented. The climate is dry in summer. More than 40per cent of Idaho, particularly in the north and centre, is covered with coniferous forests.

History In 1805 Meriwether Lewis and William Clark travelled through the territory that is now Idaho and opened it up to white settlement. Originally part of the neutral territory of Oregon, it passed in 1846 into the possession of the United States. Large numbers of settlers heading for the north-west coast passed through the area, in which regular settlement began only in 1860. An independent territory from 1863, it was the scene in 1877 and 1879 of fierce fighting between whites and Indians, culminating in the flight of the Nez Perce Indians led by Chief Joseph. On July 3rd 1890 Idaho joined the Union as the 43rd state.

The main element in the **economy** of Idaho is agriculture. In the mountainous parts of the state sheep and cattle are reared and on the irrigated Snake River Plains fodder plants, grain, vegetables, fruit and potatoes – Idaho is the largest potato producer in the United States, a fact proudly proclaimed on every numberplate ("Land of Famous Potatoes"). Agriculture and the huge areas of forest provide the raw materials for the foodstuffs and woodworking industries. The mining district of Cöur d'Alene in northern Idaho has the United States' richest reserves of silver, zinc and lead ores. Tourism also makes a major contribution to Idaho's economy, thanks to its beautiful forests and lakes and the winter sports centres of which Sun Valley and Schweitzer are the largest.

The little town of Blackfoot in the south east, one of the main centres in the potato-growing area, hosts the World Potato Exhibition.   **Blackfoot**

In the centre of the state's capital Boise, originally a French foundation,   **Boise** is the State Capitol. Other features of interest are the Ann Morrison Memorial Park, the romantic Platt Gardens and above all the Julia Davis Park, in which are the Zoo, the State Historical Museum and the Boise Art Museum.

Of particular interest is the Basque Museum and Cultural Center – Boise has the largest Basque community in the United States. Outside the town to the south is the World Center for Birds of Prey.

Cöur d'Alene

The holiday resort and timber-working town of Cöur d'Alene lies amid magnificent forest scenery on the lake of the same name, one of the most beautiful in the United States, with ample facilities for boating and fishing.

Silver Valley

To the east of the town, Silver Valley extends along I 90. The Museum in Wallace provides information about this, the world's largest silver-mining area.

★Craters of the Moon

South of Arco in south-eastern Idaho is a lunar landscape created by volcanic eruptions between 15,000 and 2000 years ago. This region of lava flows can be explored on well signposted circular routes.

Lewiston

Lewiston is picturesquely situated at the junction of the Clearwater River with the Snake River, on the border with Washington state. Originally dependent mainly on the timber-working industry, it still has one of the largest woodworking factories in the world, but is now also a popular tourist centre, a good base from which to explore the surrounding area.

★Hell's Canyon

From Lewiston there are boat trips through Hell's Canyon, the deepest on the American continent (6500 ft), carved out by the Snake River for a distance of 95 mi. along the border with Washington and Oregon.

Nez Perce National Historical Park

In the Nez Perce National Historical Park are 24 signposted sites illustrating the history and culture of the Nez Perce Indians. The chief place in the park is Spalding, 11 mi. east of Lewiston.

Sun Valley

Sun Valley in southern Idaho attracts skiing enthusiasts throughout the year with its magnificent facilities for winter sports and its excellent tourist infrastructure.

Ketchum is the birthplace of Ernest Hemingway. The great Sawtooth National Recreation Area begins to the north.

★Twin Falls

The main sight in the little town of Twin Falls is the Shoshone Falls, over which the Snake River plunges down 200 ft – 50 ft more than the Niagara Falls (see entry). The falls are best seen in spring and autumn, for during the summer most of the water is diverted for irrigating farmland.

Mesa Falls Scenic Byway

In the extreme north-west, Idaho borders the Yellowstone National Park in Wyoming. The Mesa Falls Scenic Byway (ID 47) offers fantastic views towards the park.

Illinois (State)   G–M 34–38

Area: 56,400 sq. mi.
Population: 11,430,000
Capital: Springfield
Popular name: Prairie State

Illinois (from the Indian word illini, "men"), one of the northerly states of the Middle West, extends from Lake Michigan in the north to the Mississippi in the west and south-west and the Ohio River in the south.

Most of its territory lies in the Central Lowlands, with small upland regions only in the south and north-west; its highest point, in the north-west, is Charles Mound (1240 ft). The climate is continental, with extreme temperatures both in summer and in winter, the latter being characterised by sharp inflows of cold air, with heavy

snowstorms. In summer cyclones moving north, frequently accompanied by violent storms and heavy rain, can cause great destruction. Most of the land is given up to arable farming and stock rearing. Only a small part of the state is forested.

History The first whites to reach the territory that is now Illinois in the mid-17th c. encountered the Indian tribe from which the state takes its name. In 1680 the Sieur de la Salle built the first French fort on the site of present-day Peoria. In 1763 Illinois passed to Britain. In 1778, during the War of Independence, it was captured by the Americans. On December 3rd 1818 it joined the Union as the 21st state. Indian resistance was broken in the Black Hawk War of 1832.

Economy Thanks to its highly fertile soil over four-fifths of the state's area is in agricultural use. The main crops are soya beans, maize, grain, potatoes, fruit and vegetables; livestock farming (cattle, pigs) is also important. Illinois also has considerable mineral resources (oil, coal, lead, zinc, fluorspar). Most of its industry is concentrated in the Chicago area (iron and steel, meat processing, mechanical and electrical engineering, chemicals). Tourism is of relatively little importance except in the skiing areas in the north and on the shores of Lake Michigan.

Arcola, in eastern Illinois, has one of the state's largest Amish communities (see Baedeker Special, p. 44/5). Their way of life can be observed in Rocksome Gardens, 5 mi. west of the town. — **Arcola**

The Cahokia Mounds, to the east of St Louis (Missouri), are the remains of an Indian settlement of the 8th c. AD that comprised more than a hundred buildings. The most prominent feature is the Monks' Mound, on which French Trappist monks established themselves in the early 19th c. Finds from the site are displayed in a small museum. — **★Cahokia Mounds State Historic Site**

See entry — Chicago

The little town of Galena at the extreme north-western tip of Illinois was originally a French outpost, a base for the exploration of the north-west. In the 19th c. lead mining in the surrounding area made it the wealthiest town in the state. Galena has largely preserved its 19th c. aspect, with many handsome antebellum houses bearing witness to its former prosperity. Particularly fine is the Old Market House, once occupied by General (later President) Ulysses S. Grant. — **★Galena**

Nauvoo, situated on the Mississippi, on the border with Iowa, played a prominent part in the history of the Mormons. After their prophet Joseph Smith (see Famous People) was driven out of Missouri they followed him to this area and established a kind of independent state. Conflicts with opponents and within the Mormon church culminated in the lynching and murder of Smith and his brother in the local prison. Brigham Young then led the Mormons to Utah. The Mormon period in Nauvoo is recalled by the Joseph Smith Historic Center and the Brigham Young Home in the Nauvoo Restoration Visitor Center. — **Nauvoo**

269

Peoria

Peoria, south-west of Chicago on the Illinois River, is the oldest town in the state. Features of interest, in addition to a number of historic old houses, are the Wildlife Prairie Park (native animals of Illinois, houses of the pioneers) and the Wheels o' Time Museum (old automobiles, agricultural machinery, domestic equipment, tools and implements).

Springfield

The capital of Illinois, Springfield, located roughly in the centre of the state, is a national place of pilgrimage. Here, in Oak Ridge Cemetery, are buried Abraham Lincoln (see Famous People), his wife and three of his four children. Lincoln worked in the town as a lawyer from 1837 to 1861, when he was elected President. Places in Springfield associated with Lincoln –

Touching the nose of Lincoln's bust in Springfield may bring good luck

his house, lawyer's office, the Old State Capitol and New Salem, where he spent his youth (20 mi. to the north-west) are open to the public. Other features of interest are the Illinois State Museum, the Governor's Mansion (the third oldest in the United States) and the Dana Thomas House, designed by Frank Lloyd Wright (see Famous People).

Starved Rock State Park

This nature park south-west of Chicago on the Illinois River, noted for its sandstone formations, is named after a group of Illini Indians who were left by their enemies to starve to death on one of the rocks.

Indiana (State) H–M 38–41

Area: 36,185 sq. mi.
Population: 5,544,000
Capital: Indianapolis
Popular name: Hoosier State

The Middle Western state of Indiana extends from Lake Michigan in the north to the valley of the Ohio River in the south. The wide gently undulating lowlands and plateaux of the Central Lowlands here reach heights of between 300 ft and 1260 ft. The landscape, formed during the Ice Age, is dotted in the north-east with numerous small lakes. The climate is temperate continental.

History The fertile plains of Indiana were settled as early as the 10th c.

by Indians, who have left traces of their occupation in numerous mounds. The first European to explore this area, in 1679, was a Frenchman, the Sieur de la Salle. The territory passed to Britain in 1763, but twenty years later became part of the United States. At first part of the Northwest Territory, it became a separate territory in 1809, with approximately its present boundaries. After the defeat of the Shawnee Indians at Tippecanoe in 1811 it became the 19th state of the Union on December 11th 1816.

Economy Indiana's location in the Corn Belt makes it one of the leading agricultural states of the Union. The main crops are maize, soya beans and grain, providing the basis for intensive pig farming and a large dairy farming industry. The state's main industries, principally concentrated in the cities on Lake Michigan, are iron and steel, automobile construction, chemicals, oil refineries and foodstuffs. Its mineral resources include oil, limestone and coal (from opencast mines in the south-west of the state).

In the late 1930s the city fathers of Columbus, situated to the south of Indianapolis (see entry), commissioned the Finnish architect Eliel Saarinen to redevelop part of the city. Saarinen brought in other leading architects, and as a result Columbus is now a museum of modern architecture, with buildings designed by Saarinen, I.M. Pei, J.C. Warnke, Kevin Roche and other distinguished names.

Columbus

Fort Wayne, in north-eastern Indiana, owes its name to General "Mad Anthony" Wayne, who in 1791 defeated the Miami Indians and their chief Little Turtle at the strategically important junction of the St Mary and St Joseph Rivers. This event and the later history of the region are illustrated in the Allen County-Fort Wayne Museum.

Fort Wayne

The Indiana Dunes State Park extends for 3 mi. along the southern shore of Lake Michigan. Its sandy beaches, backed by beautiful white dunes, of-fer magnificent bathing.

Indiana Dunes State Park

See entry

Indianapolis

North-west of Indianapolis on the Wabash River is Lafayette, scene of a decisive battle in 1811 between government troops and Shawnee Indians led by the "Prophet", Tecumseh's brother. The event is commemorated on the Tippecanoe Battlefield and in the Tippecanoe County Historical Museum.

Lafayette

Between 1814 and 1824 New Harmony, in south-western Indiana, was the scene of a social experiment. Here a deeply religious German named Georg Rapp and his followers, among whom absolute equality prevailed, settled down to cultivate the land in the expectation that the Last Judgment was near. When this failed to materialise the community returned to Pennsylvania, from which they had come. Their village can be seen on a signposted tour.

New Harmony

South Bend, in the extreme north of Indiana, is the seat of the University of Notre Dame, founded in 1842. Features of interest on the campus are the Art Museum and the Church of the Sacred Heart, which has the oldest carillon in North America.
  To the south-east of South Bend, Indian's Amish Country extends as far as Fort Wayne.

South Bend

Vincennes, in south-western Indiana on the border with Illinois, is the state's oldest town, founded in 1732. The main sights are the George Rogers National Historical Park, which commemorates the revolutionary battles against the British, and Grouseland, the home of William Henry Harrison, 9th President of the United States.

Vincennes

Indianapolis   K 39

State: Indiana
Altitude: 650–915 ft
Population: 731,000

Indianapolis, a typical Midwest city and capital of Indiana, lies south-east
of Lake Michigan on the White River – almost exactly in the centre of
Indiana, on a site selected by ten government commissioners in 1820 for
the new capital of the state. Indianapolis is now a university town
(Indiana State University/Purdue University and University of
Indianapolis) and an important commercial centre. The agricultural
products of the fertile surrounding area – cattle and grain – are traded
and processed in Indianapolis, and among its main industrial products
are medicines (insulin products), automobile parts and electrical apparatus. The city's world fame, however, comes from the "Indianapolis
500", the car race held annually on the Sunday before Memorial Day on
the Indianapolis Motor Speedway. This is the world's biggest single-day
sporting event, drawing hundreds of thousands of motor sport fans.

Sights

Monument Circle

In Monument Circle, an oasis in the city centre, is the Soldiers' and
Sailors' Memorial, erected in 1902 to commemorate the dead of the Civil
War. To the north of the Monument whole rows of houses were demol-
ished to make room for the Mausoleum and Memorial Hall. Three blocks
to the south have recently disappeared, replaced by the large Circle
Center Mall.

Indiana State
Museum

In the former City Hall (202 N Alabama St.) is the Indiana State Museum
(natural history, art and history of Indiana).

★Eiteljorg
Museum of
American Indian
and Western Art

To the east of Monument Circle, beyond the State Capitol (1888), is the
Eiteljorg Museum of American Indian and Western Art, situated at the
entrance to the White River State Park (500 Washington St.). Here is displayed the remarkable collection assembled by the Indianapolis businessman Harrison Eiteljorg: painting and sculpture of the west from the

Indianapolis International Airport

Full house for the legendary Indy 500 (p. 274)

early 19th c. onwards, including works by the landscapists Albert Bierstadt and Thomas Moran and pictures and sculpture by the leading Western artists Frederick S. Remington and Charles M. Russell; an extensive collection of works of the Taos Society of Artists; and Indian arts and crafts from all over North America. Open Tue.–Sat. 10am–5pm, Sun. noon–5pm.

The construction of the huge RCA Dome (100 S Capitol Ave.) in 1984 signalled the beginning of a comprehensive redevelopment of the city centre. This is the home of the local football team, the Indianapolis Colts. The flag-decked Pan American Plaza in the immediate neighbourhood of the Hoosier Dome, the Convention Center and Union Station was laid out to commemorate the Pan American Games of 1987.

RCA Dome

Benjamin Harrison, Senator of Indiana (1880), who was re-elected President of the United States in 1888, died in Indianapolis in 1901. His house at 1239 North Delaware Street, with its original Victorian furniture, can be visited.

Benjamin Harrison Home

The Indianapolis Museum of Art (1200 W 38th St.) lies to the north of the city centre in a spacious park. The Museum is housed in four pavilions: the Krannert Pavilion, which is devoted to American art from pre-Columbian times to the present day (including Edward Hopper's "Hotel Lobby") and Asian art; the Hulman Pavilion (painting from Baroque to Neo-Impressionism and the Eiteljorg Gallery of African and South Pacific Art); the Clowes Pavilion (medieval and Renaissance art, 18th c. British painting, watercolours by Turner); and the Lilly Pavilion (British and American furniture and silver, German porcelain). Open Tue.–Sat. 10am–5pm, Sun. noon–5pm.

★Indianapolis Museum of Art

Iowa

★Indianapolis
Motor Speedway

The United States' most celebrated car race, the legendary Indianapolis 500, is run on the Indianapolis Motor Speedway, 7 mi. north-west of downtown Indianapolis, which is used only for this one race. The circuit, a 2½ mi. oval, was originally designed as an automobile test track, but the first 500 mi. race in 1911 was so successful that it became a regular fixture. In the course of time the track, which was originally paved with bricks (still used to mark the finishing line), was adapted to cope with ever-increasing speeds and the accommodation for spectators increased: there is now room for 250,000 in the stands and another 150,000 in the ground.

When the track is not in use for practising and training (one month before the race) visitors are taken round it in minibuses. The **Speedway Hall of Fame Museum** traces the history of the race and displays numerous old racing cars, including 30 winners of the 500. Open daily 9am–5pm.

Iowa (State)   F–J 29–35

Area: 56,290 sq. mi.
Population: 2,795,000
Capital: Des Moines
Popular name: Hawkeye State

Iowa (the name of a Sioux tribe) lies in the Midwest, in the Central Lowlands of North America, bounded on the west by the Missouri and on the east by the Mississippi. It is a gently undulating region that falls gradually from the north-west (maximum height 1675 ft) to the south-east (515 ft). Iowa has the best soils (for much of its area loess) in the United States, and is accordingly a region of farmland and prairies. The climate is continental, with very hot summers and winters of extreme cold.

History The territory that is now Iowa was a favoured Indian hunting ground. Like the neighbouring state of Illinois to the east, it was first discovered by the French, but organised settlement began only in 1788. As part of the French territory of Louisiana it passed to the United States under the Louisiana Purchase of 1803. After the local Indians – now living in a small reservation – had been driven back and replaced by European settlers Iowa was incorporated as an independent territory, and on December 28th 1846 was admitted to the Union as the 29th state.

Economy Iowa's agriculture is the most productive in the United States. The main crops are maize, soya beans and oats, mainly used for feeding cattle and pigs: Iowa is by a wide margin America's leading pig-farming state, with some 14 million pigs. As a result the state's industries are largely related to agriculture (agricultural machinery, foodstuffs). Also of great importance to the economy is the largest aluminium rolling mill in the United States. Tourism is of secondary importance, though the state has some attractions that draw visitors – the skiing areas in the north and the charming little towns and river scenery on the Mississippi.

Amana Colonies

The settlement of Amana was founded in 1850 by "Inspirationists" of German origin – the first of seven villages in eastern Iowa in which they led a God-fearing life and tilled their communally owned land. A local museum traces the history of the sect, which adopted 20th c. ways of life only in 1932.

Iowa's capital, Des Moines, lies approximately in the centre of the state. Features of interest are the State Capitol with its gilded roof (1871), the Iowa State Historical Museum, the Botanical Center and the Des Moines Art Center. Outside the city, to the north-west lies the Heritage Village, with four "living history farms" in which country life in the 18th and 19th c. is re-created. In Indianola, 12 mi. to the south, is the National Balloon Museum. A major hot-air balloon event is held here at the end of July.

Des Moines

Although it is another 50 mi. further south-west to Winterset, no true fan of John Wayne will be put off by this distance, as the tiny house where the "Duke" was born can be visited here.

Winterset

The town of Dubuque, situated on the Mississippi on the border with Illinois, was founded in 1788, the first European settlement in what is now Iowa. Its attractions are its numerous historic old buildings, a beautiful botanical garden and above all paddlewheeler cruises on the Mississippi.

Dubuque

Iowa City, in the east of the state, was its first capital. It is the seat of the University of Iowa, founded in 1847. Its other feature of interest is the birthplace of Herbert Hoover (1874–1964), 31st President of the United States.

Iowa City

Sioux City lies on the border with Nebraska, in the heart of Indian country. Here was buried Sergeant Charles Floyd, the only casualty of Lewis and Clark's expedition from the Mississippi to the Pacific in 1804–5. Woodbury Country Courthouse, a long, low brick structure, is the largest building so far erected by Chicago's "Prairie school" of architecture.

Sioux City

Jacksonville   T 44

State: Florida
Altitude: 0–23 ft
Population: 690,000

The city of Jacksonville, situated in the extreme north-west of Florida on the navigable St John's River, only 20 mi. from the Atlantic coast, is a major port and industrial centre as well as an important military base. The largest city in the United States in terms of area, it developed considerably in the 1980s and is now a major business and financial centre.

History In pre-Columbian times there was a settlement of the Timucua Indians here. The present town, named after the famous General Jackson, first Governor of Florida, was founded in 1822. It soon developed into an important port, one of the main centres for the export of the produce of the south (cotton, timber, cattle). Around 1884 the Jacksonville area, thanks to its spacious bathing beaches, enjoyed a brief period of prosperity as a holiday resort. During the two world wars Jacksonville was a boom town with a flourishing shipbuilding industry and military training areas.

Sights

In recent years downtown Jacksonville has undergone a thorough transformation. Dreary industrial areas and residential quarters have given way to gleaming skyscrapers, including Helmut Jahn's 40-floor Barnett Bank Tower on Bay Street. On the north bank of Street John's River is Jacksonville Landing, a modern architectural complex that had become a popular meeting place. Riverwalk, on the South Bank, is an attractive area for walking. Built on the site of an old shipyard, it has hotels, restaurants, shops and a mile-long boardwalk.

★Museum of Science and History

The Museum of Science and History (1025 Gulf Life Dr./S Main St.) offers an introduction to the world of science and technology. Its main attractions are the "Dinosaurs Alive" show (a dinosaur garden) and the Living World (marine aquarium, songbird aviary, insects, reptiles). Open daily 10am–5pm.

★Avondale-Riverside Historic District

The old residential district of Avondale and Riverside offers a survey of the architectural styles fashionable in the first three decades of the 20th c. An impressive example is Riverside Baptist Church (by Addison Mizner, 1925). The Avondale Shopping Village is a friendly and attractive neighbourhood, with shops, restaurants and public gardens.

Surroundings

★Fort Caroline

10 mi. east of the city centre is a reconstruction of the historic old Fort Caroline. In the 16th c. French Huguenots attempted to establish a settlement in this area. Here too, in 1565, took place the first clash between France and Spain on the American continent.

Jacksonville Beach

15 mi. east of the city centre is Jacksonville Beach (pop. 20,000), a resort well equipped to cater for the tourist trade. Immediately on the Atlantic is the Seawalk, an attractive seafront promenade. To the south of Mayport Naval Station is Seminole Beach, the most beautiful bathing beach in the area.

★Amelia Island

32 mi. north-east of Jacksonville is Amelia Island (pop. 15,000), an exclusive holiday island of coral limestone that has become a frequent venue of major tennis tournaments. In the north-west of the island is the very attractive bathing resort of Fernandina Beach. At its northern tip is Fort Clinch, built in 1847. Perhaps the most beautiful holiday resort on the island is the Amelia Island Plantation, with an enchanting 12 mi. long beach, a golf course and a variety of facilities for water sports.

Kansas (State)   K–M 23–31

Area: 82,277 sq. mi.
Population: 2,477,000
Capital: Topeka
Popular name: Sunflower State

The state of Kansas (from an Indian term, "people of the south winds") lies in the geographical centre of the United States, in the extensive stepped tableland of the Great Plains, which rises from around 650 ft in the east to 3900 ft in the west. In the eastern part of the state the rock formations strike north–south, traversed by valleys up to 330 ft deep cut by the Kansas River and its tributaries. Except in the hilly and forested north-east the predominant vegetation pattern before the land was brought into cultivation was short-grass steppe, familiar to moviegoers as Hollywood's version of the Wild West. The climate is continental, with periods of drought, hot dust storms and tornadoes.

History The first European to travel over the wide prairies of Kansas was the Spanish conquistador Francisco Coronado in 1541. In 1762 the area, then part of Louisiana, passed to Spain. In 1803 it was acquired by the United States, and in 1817 was declared Indian territory. As a result of the Kansas-Nebraska Act of 1854, which separated the two states, Kansas was drawn into the conflict between North and South over slavery and became known as "bleeding Kansas". On January 29th 1861 it became the 34th state of the Union and threw in its lot with the south.

Economy Although processing industries (foodstuffs, aircraft construction, helium production, printing) make a larger contribution to the economy than agricultural produce, Kansas is a typically agricultural region: predominantly cattle and pig rearing, together with the growing of wheat, millet and maize. The principal minerals worked in Kansas are oil, natural gas, lead and zinc. Tourism is concentrated mainly on the State Parks in the east and the lakes in the centre and south.

The little town of Abilene lies in the north-east of the state. Its wild days as the "cowtown" of Kansas are past, but Abilene Old Town still preserves something of the atmosphere of the Wild West. Apart from this the town is known to fame as the boyhood home of General Dwight D. Eisenhower (1890–1969), 34th President of the United States, who is commemorated by a museum, the Presidential Library and his tomb in the Eisenhower Center.

Abilene

In its heyday this famous Wild West town saw a whole posse of sheriffs – Batt Masterson, Bill Tilghman and above all the notorious Wyatt Earp (see Famous People) – plus a host of buffalo hunters who within a few years slaughtered millions of buffaloes at 100 dollars a time. The town's wild past can be relived in Historic Front Street with its reconstructions of the celebrated Long Branch Saloon, the barber's shop, the general store and many other establishments familiar from Western films. In the Boot Hill Museum, on the hill of that name (the cemetery), are other relics of a bloodstained past. Your nose will tell you how Dodge City gets its livelihood nowadays: with 50,000 cattle passing through on the meadows to the east, this is the United State's largest cattle-trading centre.

Dodge City

America's newest National Park extends from Nebraska through Kansas to Oklahoma, and still gives an impression of the enormous grasslands of bygone days. The gently rolling Flint Hills, about halfway between Topeka and Wichita, are especially delightful, and the little town of Cottonwood Falls with its Grand Central Hotel dating from 1886 is a true Wild West town, unspoilt by tourism.

Flint Hills National Prairie

See entry

Kansas City

North-east of Dodge City is Fort Larned, an important military post on the Santa Fe Trail. Here William T. Sherman, Philip Sheridan, George A. Custer, Kit Carson, Wild Bill Hickock guarded the railroad to the west. Nine of the original buildings are still preserved.

Larned

In 1854 anti-slavery campaigners founded this town 40 mi. west of Kansas City, only for it to be burned down by supporters of

Lawrence

A denizen of the prairie

277

slavery, including Jesse James, in 1863. Lawrence was rebuilt and is now the seat of the University of Kansas. Its Nature Museum holds one of the few "white" survivors of the Battle of Little Bighorn, the horse "Comanche" that has been preserved.

Topeka

The capital, Topeka, has the State Capitol and the Kansas State Historical Socity and Kansas Museum of History, where the history of the state can be studied. The Combat Air Museum exhibits 75 military aircraft from 1917 to 1980; something less warlike would be a visit to the beautiful zoo with its reconstruction of a rainforest.

Wichita

Wichita, now the largest city in Kansas, had humble beginnings in 1865, when Jesse Chisholm began the driving of cattle from here along the famous Chisholm Trail to the Union Pacific railroad station in Abilene. Pioneering days are recalled in the Wichita Historical Museum and the Historic Old Cowtown Museum, a museum village with 40 old buildings. The Mid-America All Indian Center and Museum is dedicated to the Indians. Today Wichita is the main aircraft construction centre, even though only small craft, such as Beech, Lear and Cessna, are produced here.

Kansas City   K 31

States: Kansas and Missouri
Altitude: 775 ft
Population: 685,000

This double city in the Midwest, straddling the border between Kansas and Missouri, lies at the junction of the Kansas River with the Missouri, extending along the high banks of both rivers (the Bluffs). World-famous for its steaks and its jazz, Kansas City is now the centre of an extensive agricultural region. The great stockyards and packing stations of the 19th c. have given place to highly efficient foodstuffs industries and other processing industries (automobile construction, engineering, chemicals, paper). A glance at the skyline of Kansas City, Missouri is enough to show that it remains the more important of the two sister cities. Not for nothing does it enjoy national renown as the "Barbecue Capital" and jazz metropolis – this is where Charlie "Bird" Parker created "bebop".

History Kansas City, Kansas (pop. 186,000) developed in the mid-19th c. out of a small town established by white settlers. For a time it was the eastern terminus of the first transcontinental railroad and thus gained importance as a commercial centre. Kansas City, Missouri (pop. 450,000), grew out of a settlement of French fur traders and a Jesuit mission and during the 19th c. rapidly developed into a lively economic and cultural centre.

Kansas City (KS)

Shawnee Indian
Mission

The most interesting feature in Kansas City, Kansas, is the Old Shawnee Town, with an Indian mission school founded in 1839, an old Wells Fargo mail station and other historic buildings.

Bonner Springs

A few miles up the Kansas River is Bonner Springs, with the Wyandotte Historical Museum (regional history) and the Agricultural Hall of Fame (displays on agricultural themes).

Sights Kansas City (MO)

In the centre of the city, the Country Club Plaza, the oldest shopping mall in the United States, which opened in 1922, extends along several blocks. It has many inviting shops, restaurants and theatres, and its fountains and statues give it something of an Andalusian air.

Downtown

The Nelson Atkins Museum of Art, three blocks to the east, has a very large collection of East Asian art and a large sculpture garden. North-west of the Plaza the Kemper Museum is devoted to contemporary art and design.

★Nelson Atkins Museum of Art

The old district of Westport has been lovingly restored. Visit Kelly's Tavern for a drink in the city's oldest building.

Westport

The Crown Center, the city's second centre was built in the 1970s, north of downtown. It includes many striking buildings by Helmut Jahn and other leading contemporary architects.
    To the north-west, the 215 ft high Liberty Memorial honours the fallen of the First World War.

Crown Center

This quarter, north-east of the Crown Center, was a hotbed of jazz in the 1930s and 40s, as commemorated by the new Jazz Museum. The same building also houses the Negro Leagues Baseball Museum, dedicated to the black heroes of America's national sport.

18th & Vine Historic District

The Save a Corrie Museum at Downtown Airport on the northern edge of the city is guaranteed to make any flight enthusiast's heart beat faster. Here you can relive the days when people still flew with propeller machines over the Atlantic and Kansas City was the TWA headquarters. Flight veterans will be only too happy to tell their stories, and take a turn in a DC or a Super Constellation.

★Save a Corrie Museum

This 1772 acre park is the recreation centre for the whole of the Kansas City conurbation, with a variety of leisure facilities, an interesting Zoo and a brand-new IMAX cinema.

Swope Park

These two theme parks offer a wide variety of entertainments for families.

Worlds of Fun, Oceans of Fun

Kentucky (State)   K–N 36–43

Area: 40,395 sq. mi.
Population: 3,714,000
Capital: Frankfort
Popular name: Bluegrass State

The state of Kentucky (from the Indian *ken-tah-keh*, "land of tomorrow") is bounded on the north by the Ohio River. The western end of the state extends into the Mississippi lowlands, while in the south-east is the Cumberland Plateau. From the fertile Bluegrass region in the north-east that gives the state its popular name the land rises to the Cumberland Plateau. Central Kentucky is a region of karstic limestone, with numerous dolines, bizarre rock formations and the magnificent Mammoth Cave. Almost half of the state is covered by mixed deciduous forests. The climate is temperate continental.

Kentucky

History The first whites to reach the region, from 1670 onwards, were French and British. Permanent settlement began around 1770. During the War of Independence Kentucky suffered severely from raids by Indians allied with the British. On June 1st 1792 it became the 15th state of the Union.

Economy Kentucky is also world-famous for its stud farms, which produce excellent thoroughbreds. The fertile soils of the Bluegrass region yield high-quality tobacco, making Kentucky the largest tobacco producer in the United States after North Carolina. Other important crops are soya beans, maize, grain, vegetables and potatoes. Livestock farming (dairy and beef cattle, pigs, sheep) thrives on the great expanses of pastureland. The state's principal mineral resources are coal, oil and natural gas. The most important branches of industry are engineering, the manufacture of electrical appliances, textiles, foodstuffs (including Bourbon whiskey) and tobacco.

Bowling Green

Many a dream of youth will come true when you enter the National Corvette Museum in Bowling Green, south-west Kentucky. There are more than 50 of these cult sports cars to admire.

★Cumberland Gap National Historical Park

South-eastern Kentucky extends into the Cumberland Mountains. The most important passage through the hills is the Cumberland Gap (1663 ft), an 760 ft deep cut through the range that was used as a traffic route in Indian times and was discovered by pioneers moving west in the mid-18th c. After the legendary Daniel Boone had driven his Wilderness Trail into Kentucky in 1775 over 200,000 white settlers made their way through the Cumberland Mountains to the west. The Visitor Center is situated in Middleboro, KY. From Pinnacle Overview (2460 ft) there are magnificent views of the hills and the Gap. A popular hike is to the Hensley Settlement, a well preserved old country township.

Natural bridge in the Daniel Boone National Forest

In the Daniel Boone National Forest south-east of Lexington (see entry) is the Natural Bridge (65 ft high, 75 ft wide), created by the erosive forces of wind and water. In the surrounding area, now a State Park, are other bizzare rock formations. A few miles north the Red River, surges through a wild and romantic gorge.

★**Daniel Boone National Forest**

Frankfort, capital of the state of Kentucky, grew out of a fort established by a pioneer named Frank. It is the chief place in a productive grain- and tobacco-growing region on the Kentucky River. The Museum of the Kentucky Historical Society is housed in the old State Capitol of 1836. Daniel Boone and his wife Rebecca are buried in the town cemetery.

Frankfort

See entry

Lexington

The largest city in Kentucky, Louisville, was founded on the Ohio River in 1778 and named in honour of the French King Louis XVI. It is the head-quarters of famous companies such as Philip Morris Tobacco, American Tobacco, Kentucky Fried Chicken, United Parcel and the Seagram Whiskey distillery. Downtown Kentucky has the largest collection of cast-iron buildings outside New York. The J.B. Speed Museum has pictures by Rembrandt, Rubens, Picasso and Monet, whilst the Harlan Sanders Museum, dedicated to the founder of Kentucky Fried Chicken, and the Louisville Slugger Museum, devoted entirely to baseball, are thoroughly American. River trips on the Ohio can be taken on the venerable old sternwheeler "Belle de Louisville".

★**Louisville**

The **Kentucky Derby** has been held annually since 1875 on the first Sunday in May, in the exclusive suburb of Churchill Downs. This horse race, one of the most famous and remunerative in the world, is the subject of the Kentucky Derby Museum.

To the south of Louisville begins **Bourbon Country**, where whiskey is distilled. Visitors can find out all about this in the Jim Beam American Outpost Museum in Clermont, or in the Maker's Mark Distillery south of Bardstown.

Bardstown itself, made famous by the song "My Old Kentucky Home" by Stephen Foster (1826–64) has the Oskar Getz Museum of Whiskey History and the Old Bardstown Village & Civil War Museum, a reconstruction of a settlement at the front, in the days of the civil war.

Bardstown

A further 25 mi. south-west of Bardstown lies Hodgenville, and the simple log cabin where Abraham Lincoln first saw the light of day on 12 February 1809.

Hodgenville

Some 30 mi. south-west of Louisville is Fort Knox, where most of the United States' gold reserves are stored. There is an interesting Cavalry Museum.

Fort Knox

The Mammoth Cave lies in the "Land of 10,000 Sinks" (Caveland Corridor), an area in south-western Kentucky approximately 80 mi. south of Louisville, strongly marked by karstic features of all kinds. With over 300 mi. of passages so far surveyed, the Mammoth Cave is one of the world's largest known cave systems, and was already known to the original Indian inhabitants of the region in the 1st millennium BC. A variety of tours are available: the Historic Tour (which must be booked in advance in the summer) takes in the underground Booth's Amphitheater and the old saltpetre quarry. The high points of the tour are the Mammoth Dome (almost 200 ft high) and the Ruins of Karnak. The Half Day Tour runs past the Snowball Dining Room with the extraordinary rock formations (originally snow white) on its roof, the imposing Frozen Niagara with its magnificent stalactites and stalagmites and the beauti-

★**Mammoth Cave National Park**

ful Crystal Lake. The Echo River Tour (Jun.–Sep.) follows the Echo and Styx Rivers through a series of chambers and passages. The strenuous Wild Cave Tour is for experienced and properly equipped cave explorers only.

★★Key West   Z 44

State: Florida
Altitude: 0–10 ft
Population: 25,000

The town of Key West, on an island of coral limestone at the south-west end of the Florida Keys (the natives of which call themselves Conchs), is the most southerly point in the continental United States. In earlier days it was a notorious pirates' lair and later a flourishing port. In 1822 the southern tip of Florida began to be developed as a naval base, and by 1870 Key West was the largest and wealthiest town in Florida. A number of handsome Conch houses still bear witness to the prosperity of the old wreckers and sea captains. During the 19th c. immigrants from Cuba introduced cigar production to Key West.

The carefree Caribbean way of life attracted many artists and writers to the town. Among those who lived and worked here during the 1930s and 40s were Ernest Hemingway and Tennessee Williams.

Sights

★Old Town

The Old Town at the south-west end of the island, with its many pastel-coloured 19th c. houses, is particularly attractive. Duval Street and its

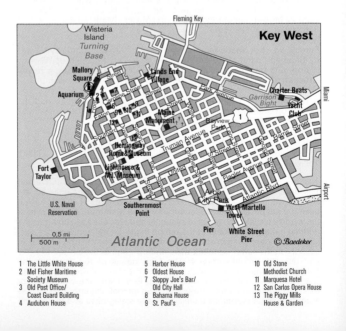

1 The Little White House	5 Harbor House	10 Old Stone
2 Mel Fisher Maritime	6 Oldest House	Methodist Church
Society Museum	7 Sloppy Joe's Bar/	11 Marquesa Hotel
3 Old Post Office/	Old City Hall	12 San Carlos Opera House
Coast Guard Building	8 Bahama House	13 The Piggy Mills
4 Audubon House	9 St. Paul's	House & Garden

charming side streets are lined with boutiques, art galleries, sidewalk cafés, restaurants and bars.

A particular attraction is the Aquarium (Whitehead St.), with giant turtles, barracudas, Florida lobsters, sharks and other spectacular denizens of the sea.

Key West Aquarium

Mel Fisher's Treasury Exhibit (200 Green St./Front St.) displays Spanish gold jewellery, silver coins and other valuable objects recovered in recent years by Mel Gibson from the Spanish galleons "Nuestra Señora de Atocha" and "Santa Margarita", which sank off the Marquesas during a hurricane in 1622. There is also an interesting exhibition on underwater archaeology.

★Mel Fisher's Treasury Exhibit

The famous American bird painter John James Audubon (1785–1851) stayed in Key West in 1832 in a typical Conch house (Whitehead and Greene Sts.) that contains some of his original engravings.

Audubon House

Captain Tony's Saloon in Greene Street was known from 1933 to 1937 as Sloppy Joe's Bar and was a favourite haunt of Ernest Hemingway, who often ended the day on the stool that was reserved for him.

Captain Tony's Saloon

The new Sloppy Joe's Bar, just round the corner at 201 Duval Street, is decorated with photographs of Hemingway.

Key West's main attraction is the Ernest Hemingway Home and Museum (938 Whitehead St.) This charming house in Spanish colonial style (built 1851) was bought in 1931 by Hemingway, who wrote many of his works here, including "For Whom the Bell Tolls" and " The Old Man and The Sea". Open daily 9am–5pm.

★★Ernest Hemingway Home and Museum

The luxuriant tropical garden is occupied by numerous descendants of Hemingway's pet cats.

At the end of Whitehead Street is a large concrete buoy marking the southernmost point in the continental United States. From here it is only 90 mi. to Cuba.

★Southernmost Point

Surroundings

From the landing stage at the north end of Duval Street there are trips in glass-bottomed boats to the coral reefs round Key West, still largely undamaged, with their marvellous underwater world.

The south-western outliers of the Florida Keys are the home of a wide variety of birds, including rare terns, cormorants and frigate birds with a wingspan of more that 6 ft.

From Key West there are boat trips westward to the mangrove-fringed Marquesas Keys, the centrepiece of the extensive Key West National Wildlife Refuge.

Marquesas Keys

See Florida

Other Keys

★★Lake Tahoe K/L 5/6

States: California, Nevada
Altitude: 6235 ft

Among the most beautiful holiday destinations in the American West is Lake Tahoe, which lies on a plateau between the Sierra Nevada and the Carson Range. This lake, high in the mountains, is equally popular in summer and in winter. It is just under 22 mi. long, up to 12 mi. across and up to 1600 ft deep, with a surface area of 200 sq. mi.: about the same size as Lake Constance. Described by Mark Twain as the most beautiful landscape in the world, Lake Tahoe is a holiday paradise all year round. Thanks to plentiful quantities of snow, all kinds of winter sports are possible from November until the end of April, and in summer the lake and its shores have facilities for bathing, sailing, windsurfing and many other leisure activities. Unfortunately, as there are numerous hotels, motels and holiday homes along the shores, few places are accessible to the general public.

There are excellent roads around Lake Tahoe, which at many points offer spectacular views of the lake and the majestic snow-capped mountain peaks beyond.

South Lake Tahoe The best starting point is South Lake Tahoe on the southern shore, through which runs the boundary between California and Nevada. The two sides of the street are therefore very different: on the Californian side there are numerous small motels and shops, whilst on the opposite side, across the State Line in Nevada, where gambling is permitted, the street is lined with luxurious hotels and casinos.

Heavenly Aerial Tram The aerial tram runs from the Top of Ski Run Boulevard in Stateline, NV,

Lake Tahoe in winter

into the Heavenly Ski Area. From the Top of the Tram, at a height of 8250 ft, there is a fantastic view of Lake Tahoe and the Sierra Nevada.

Past Zephyr Cove, from where trips can be taken on the paddle steamer "Dixie II" in the summer, and past Lake Tahoe Nevada State Park, with its comprehensive watersports facilities, at the north-eastern end of the lake, only a few miles from the Californian boundary, lies the tourist centre of Incline Village – which means nature, casinos and wedding chapels.

Incline Village

However for many visitors to Incline Village, the real goal is **★Ponderosa Ranch Western Theme Park**, where Ben Cartwright's Ranch, from the television series "Bonanza" has been reconstructed.

To the east and north-east of Incline Village are three excellent ski areas (diamond Peak Ski Area, Mount Rose Ski Area, Slide Mountain).

On the Californian side, the road returns to South Lake Tahoe through a series of tourist resorts.

After Tahoe City on the north-west shore, is the beautiful Squaw Valley, venue of the Winter Olympics in 1960. It now boasts the style of "USA Ski Area" and is well equipped for winter sports. Other winter sports areas at this corner of the lake are Alpine Meadows, Homewood, North Star at Tahoe, and slightly further away, the Tahoe Donner Ski Bowl and the Boreal Ski Area.

★Squaw Valley

Surroundings

South of Lake Tahoe is the imposing Desolation Wilderness Area, with Emerald Bay State Park, a magnificent recreation area dotted with numerous lakes.

Desolation Wilderness Area

The Donner Memorial State Park (Donner Lake) commemorates a group heading for the goldfields under the leadership of one Donner, most of whom perished in a violent snowstorm here in October 1846.

Donner Memorial State Park

★Lancaster County   J 49/50

State: Pennsylvania

In south-eastern Pennsylvania, west of Philadelphia, is the intensely cultivated and densely populated Lancaster County, also known, mistakenly, there being little evidence of any Dutch presence, as **Pennsylvania Dutch Country**. In fact the name derives from the area's settlement, from the 18th c. onwards, by the Amish Mennonites and Moravian Brothers (see Baedeker Special p. 44) who, fleeing from persecution in Germany (Deutschland), were called "Dutch" rather than "Deutsch" by the people already living there. These religious communities still maintain their traditional way of life, rejecting the modern aids to living others take for granted. They are aware nevertheless of their potential as a tourist attraction, with the result that in summer the approach roads to Lancaster County are often quite congested.

Sights

In Bird-in-Hand, 7 mi. east of Lancaster, is a well-known Farmers' Market (summer Wed.–Sat.), at which the Amish People and Mennonites offer their produce for sale.

Bird-in-Hand

Amish Country: an old world idyll

★Ephrata	Between Reading and Lancaster (12 mi. from the latter town) is Ephrata, where German Pietists established a community of monastic type in 1732. Eleven buildings of the Ephrata Cloister (632 W Main St.), erected between 1735 and 1749, have been preserved, and some of them are open to the public.
Hopewell Furnace National Historic Site	South-east of Reading on the Schuylkill River, reached by way of Birdsboro (6 mi.) and SR 345, is Hopewell, with a historic ironworks that operated from 1771 to 1883. On the extensive site (Visitor Center) are coal-fired smelting furnaces, a smithy and a variety of other equipment. In summer there are demonstrations of old crafts.
★Intercourse	10 mi. east of Lancaster on SR 340 is Intercourse, oldest of the Amish settlements and hub of the community. In People's Place, on Main Street, visitors are introduced to the history and the crafts of the Amish, Mennonites and Hutterites (films, well prepared background information). Local craft products, cakes and pastries, can be bought in the Country Market and Old Country Store. In Kitchen Kettle Village are 30 shops selling craft goods and local culinary specialities. The Quilt Museum displays beautiful examples of the traditional patchwork quilts.
★Lancaster	Lancaster, founded in 1721, is the heart of the Pennsylvania Dutch Country. Features of interest are the Heritage Center Museum in Penn Square; the Central Market, housed in the historic market halls beside the Heritage Center; and the Farmers' Market (Tue., Fri. and Sat.), which has been held without interruption since 1730 – the oldest public farmers' market in the country.
	The **Amish Homestead** (2 mi. east of Lancaster on SR 462) and the Amish Farm and House (5 mi. east on US 30) are two typical Amish

farms that are open to visitors (guided tours). 5 mi. south of Lancaster is the oldest building in Lancaster County, the Hans Herr House (1719).

Less to do with religion is Bube's Brewery (about 10 mi. west of Lancaster in Mount Joy). It is the only brewery dating from before the Civil War to survive in the United States.

Lebanon

The industrial and market town of Lebanon; 27 mi. north of Lancaster) has two old churches, the Tabor United Church of Christ (10th St./Walnut St.) and the Salem Lutheran Church (8th St./Willow St.), both dating from 1760. A sight of a different kind is the sausage factory of the Weaver's-Baum's Lebanon Bologna Company.

Cornwall Iron Furnace

4 mi. south of Lebanon on SR 419 (north of I 76) is the Cornwall Iron Furnace, which operated from 1742 to 1883, producing everyday domestic requisites, weapons. A number of old buildings and coal-fired smelting furnaces have been preserved.

Lititz

In Lititz, 8 mi. north of Lancaster, are the Candy Americana Museum and Candy Outlet (48 N Broad St.) and the Sturgis Pretzel House (219 E Main St.), the oldest pretzel bakery in the United States (1784).

Reading

Reading (32 mi. north-west of Lancaster), founded in 1748, is the industrial centre of the Pennsylvania Dutch Country, with historic old quarters and fine 18th and 19th c. buildings. In the surrounding area are various factory shops and shopping centres selling branded goods at reasonable prices. At 940 Centre Avenue is the Berks County Historical Society Museum (local history).

★Strasburg

Strasburg, 10 mi. south-east of Lancaster, the centre of German immigration in the Pennsylvania Dutch Country, is famed for its railroad museums, in particular the Railroad Museum of Pennsylvania, with a reconstructed station, old locomotives and wagons and an exhibition on railroad history in Pennsylvania. The Strasburg Rail Road Company runs 45 min. trips round Lancaster County in an old steam train. The Toy Train Museum in Paradise Lane displays historic model railways. 2 mi. north of the town on SR 896 is the Amish Village, an open-air museum illustrating the houses and way of life of the Amish People.

★★Las Vegas   N 10

State: Nevada
Altitude: 2020 ft
Population: 260,000

Las Vegas, the world-famous gambling metropolis, lies in a pale brown desert landscape surrounded by barren hills, in south Nevada. It had approximately 32 million visitors in 1998. At present 125,000 rooms are available to visitors, but with an occupation rate of over 90 per cent, new hotels are always being built, or existing ones extended. Income from tourism in 1998 amounted to more than 24 billion dollars, with guests being relieved of almost 6 billion in the casinos alone. The Las Vegas "pleasure machine" operates around the clock, and many of its facilities are so far unrivalled anywhere in the world.

Las Vegas really only comes to life in the evening, when its neon signs light up, especially along the Strip that is lined with architecturally remarkable hotels and luxurious entertainment palaces, set in beautiful gardens. As hotel and casino operators are under strong pressure from competition, the townscape is constantly changing. The outmoded is ripped down and replaced by the new and ultramodern. The latest pro-

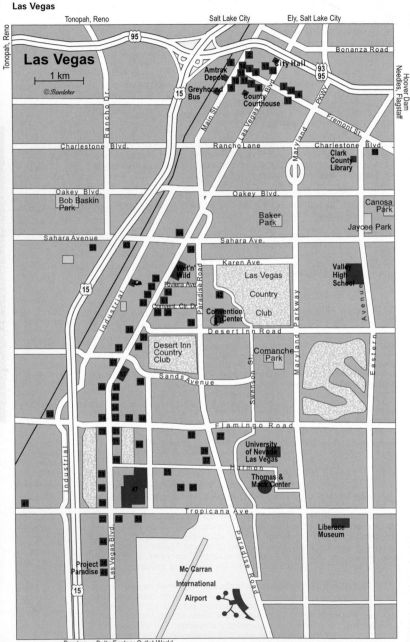

Las Vegas

ject is the "Venetian" with 6000 rooms and gondola trips on an artificial Canal Grande.

History In Spanish colonial times, the oasis of Las Vegas (Spanish for "watered land") was already an important resting place on the trade route from Santa Fe to California. However Las Vegas remained essentially only a large ranch, until a small railway settlement grew up here in 1905. Las Vegas' great boom started with the legalisation of gambling in Nevada and the arrival of thousands of workers to build the Hoover Dam. In 1940 investors from Los Angeles – backed by a few gentlemen with Sicilian connections and not entirely honest money – built Las Vegas' first hotel with an amusement arcade: El Rancho, the nucleus of what is now the Strip.

Accommodation There is an enormous number of hotel beds, ranging from the sinfully expensive luxury suite to the simple motel room. Weekend stays are particularly expensive, but special offers are available from Sunday to Thursday. As the hotels' main attractions are their casinos and other leisure facilities, the cost of accommodation for "normal" visitors does not reach giddy heights. The same is true of the catering. In the dining rooms of the large casino-hotels guests can still serve themselves from sumptuous buffets on an "all you can eat" basis – although the trend is now towards highly priced luxury accommodation, with bow ties and dinner jackets being preferred to T-shirts.

Entertainments In the large casino-hotels there are two **shows** every evening: the "Dinner Show", which starts at 8 or 9pm, and the same programme repeated at 11pm or midnight – the less expensive "Cocktail Show" or "Late Night Show". In the huge amusement arcades, (almost) all games of chance can be tried. The ranks of one-armed bandits, or slot machines, promise fast money; at the adjacent gaming tables you can play blackjack, roulette, and baccarat, or, for larger amounts, poker. Keno and bingo are also popular. But beware: the arrangement of gaming possibilities has been worked out by sales psychologists to ensure that every visitor plays for as long as possible.

The laws of the state of Nevada allow for quick, uncomplicated divorce, which is why Las Vegas has a **wedding chapel** in every large casino-hotel and at (almost) every corner, where thousands of couples get married every year. The latest is a "drive-through": getting married in the wedding car.

Downtown Casino Center

Over the last few decades, Las Vegas Downtown, the gambling city's nucleus, has lost in importance to the Strip, in spite of expensive modernisation. In Downtown, everything is still cheaper than on the Strip. Its best venue is the "Golden Nugget", with the "Fremont" opposite providing a favourably priced alternative.

★Fremont Street Experience

Only in the area around Union Pacific Station and Fremont Street, where Vegas Vic, the world-famous neon cowboy has been greeting visitors since 1951, has it been possible to provide the scene with more glamour, thanks not least to 2 million light bulbs in the multimedia high-tech star-studded sky stretching over Fremont Street

★★The Strip (Las Vegas Bvld.)

Las Vegas Boulevard extends south from Las Vegas Downtown. The 2½ mi. stretch between Stratosphere Tower and "Luxor" contains all the famous megahotels and casinos.

★Stratosphere Tower

From the 1010 ft Stratosphere Tower there is a breathtaking view over the Strip and the Downtown Casino Center. The switchback ride will impress even the most hardened cynic.

Wet 'n Wild Guinness World of Records

The leisure park, "Wet 'n Wild", with its giant flumes and wave pools, and the Guinness World of Records are situated to the south.

★Circus Circus

The popular, and good-value "Circus Circus" (2880 Las Vegas Blvd. S; tel. (702) 7340410; 3800 r.) puts on breathtaking circus performances.

★Las Vegas Hilton

The "Las Vegas Hilton" (3000 Paradise Rd., tel. 7325111; 3174 r.) is one of the town's most luxurious hotels. Its theme park "Star Trek: The Experience" is a must for any fan of Captain Kirk and Mr Spock.

Debbie Reynolds Museum

The Debbie Reynolds Hollywood Film Museum is situated to the south, on Convention Center Drive.

★Desert Inn

The newly built "Desert Inn Hotel & Casino (3145 Las Vegas Blvd. S, tel. 7334524) is modelled on a European spa and golf course.

★★Treasure Island

The 36-storey "Treasure Island" hotel (3300 Las Vegas Blvd.; tel. 8947111; 2900 r.) takes its theme from the adventure story by Robert L. Stevenson. Every day from 6pm onwards at 90 min. intervals it stages a raging sea battle in the "Buccaneer Bay" in front of the hotel.

★Venetian

The "Venetian", opened in 1999 (3355 Las Vegas Blvd.; tel. 18882-VENICE; 3036 r.), is modelled on the Doges Palace in Venice and when completed will have more than 6000 rooms.

★★The Mirage

An artificial volcano erupts every 15 min. in front of the "Mirage" (3400 Las Vegas Blvd.; tel. 7917111; 2700 r.). Inside Siegfried & Roy present their white tigers during the day in the White Tiger Habitat. The Mirage has acquired a select art collection.

Imperial Palace

The "Imperial Palace's" (3535 Las Vegas Blvd.; tel. 7313311; 2275 r.) Auto Collection contains some 200 veteran cars.

★Caesar's Palace

"Caesar's Palace" (3570 Las Vegas Blvd.; tel. 7317110, 1500 r. and a further 1200 r. in the new tower) is based on a Roman palace. The Forum has a choice of 70 boutiques selling fashions by internationally renowned manufacturers, whilst diners in the "Planet Hollywood" restaurant can admire objects of devotion from the dream factory.

The "Bellagio" (3650 Las Vegas Blvd.; tel. 6938771; 3000 r.) was opened in 1998, and besides offering Italian flair it also has an art gallery, a luxurious shopping passage, a botanical garden and the best show in town: the Cirque du Soleil, which is famous in Europe. ★Bellagio

Diagonally opposite, the "Paris" opened at the end of 1999. Needless to say, it has an Eiffel Tower, even if it is "only" 50 storeys high. Paris

The largest hotel and casino complex in Las Vegas is the "MGM Grand" (3799 Las Vegas Blvd.; tel. 8917777; 5005 r.), guarded by a golden lion. In addition to a gigantic casino, it offers a 15,000-seat Garden Arena and the "MGM Adventure Complex" theme park. ★★MGM Grand

The "New York, New York" (3790 Las Vegas Blvd. S; tel. 7406969, 2035 r.), opened in 1997, is a tribute to the skyline of New York. ★New York, New York

The world-famous illusionist Lance Burton appears at the Monte Carlo (3770 Las Vegas Blvd. S; tel. 7307000; 3000 r.). ★Monte Carlo

Opposite the MGM Grand, to the south, lies the "Tropicana" (3801 Las Vegas Blvd. S; tel. 739222; 1900 r.) with an artificial tropical paradise and the "Folies Bergère" casino show. Tropicana

The "Excalibur" (3850 Las Vegas Blvd. S; tel. 5977700, 4000 r.) is an illuminated fairy-tale castle. Twice daily a knightly spectacle is performed. Excalibur

Reminiscent of the New York stock exchange, this is a play hall in the "New York, New York" casino

★Luxor | A sphinx guards the entrance to the "Luxor" (3900 Las Vegas Blvd. S; tel. 2624000; 4400 r.), a 30-floor, dark pyramid. Take a boat trip on the "Nile" and journey in time through Ancient Egypt in the Amusement Park.

Mandalay Bay | Guests of the "Mandalay Bay" (Las Vegas Blvd./Russell Rd.; tel. 6327000; 3200 r.) can go surfing on the artificial lake with its 6 ft waves.

Little Church of the West | The Little Church of the West (4617 Las Vegas Blvd. S) is where many celebrities have been married.

Other sights

Liberace Museum | Any illusions that wealth and good taste necessarily go hand in hand are dispelled by this museum (1775 E Tropicana Ave.) dedicated to showbiz pianist Liberace. Exhibits include a Rolls Royce with snakeskin trim.

Las Vegas Natural History Museum | The Las Vegas Natural History Museum (900 Las Vegas Blvd.) has fossils of primeval creatures, including dinosaur skeletons.

Nevada State Museum | The Nevada State Museum, in the west of the town, beyond I 95 to the north, is dedicated to the social and cultural history of south Nevada.

Surroundings

★Hoover Dam | 40 mi. east of Las Vegas is the Hoover Dam, built between 1931 and 1936. This gigantic structure (1247 ft wide, 725 ft high), which dams the Colorado River to form Lake Mead, is a must for all visitors to the American south-west. Lake Mead itself (115 mi. long, 590 ft deep) offers excellent opportunities for recreation and bathing in the midst of the desert can be enjoyed on Boulder Beach, at the south end of the lake, and Overton Beach at the north end.

★Valley of Fire State Park | The Valley of Fire stretches along the west bank of Lake Mead, only an hour's drive (52 mi.) north-east of Las Vegas. The valley gets its name from its red sandstone rocks, which glow in the sunlight. A short trail leads from the Visitor Center into the sandstone labyrinth, past rock pictures drawn by pre-Columbian Indians. A scenic drive, which is several miles longer, also starts at the Visitor Centre.

Spring Mountain Range | The Spring Mountain Range rises to the west of Las Vegas; its highest peak is Mount Charleston (11,920 ft). Visitors can recover from the bustle of Las Vegas, perhaps in the wildly romantic Red Rock Canyon or in Old Nevada, a reconstructed town of the Wild West.

Lexington   L 41

State: Kentucky
Altitude: 955 ft
Population: 225,000

The city of Lexington, seat of the University of Kentucky and an important economic and cultural centre, lies in the heart of the Bluegrass Country, a fertile rolling plateau on which tobacco is grown. The region is famed for its horse breeding, and Lexington claims the title of "horse capital of the world". The horse paddocks enclosed by white fences are characteristic features of the landscape.

History The town was officially founded in 1781, but the place had already been given its name by a group of patriots some years earlier, after the battle of Lexington in Massachusetts. It is now an important centre of the tobacco trade and an industrial town.

Sights

Many plantation owners from the southern states built magnificent villas in Kentucky, with its milder climate, to escape the sultriness of the south. Several of these very beautiful houses are to be found in the Gratz Park Area, north-east of Downtown. They include Waveland (225 Highbee Mill Rd.) built by the great nephew of Daniel Boone in 1847, a fine example of Greek Revival architecture, the magnificent mansion of Ashland (Richmond & Sycamore Rd.) built by Henry Clay inn 1806, and finally Hunt Morgan House (201 N Mill St.) built for John Wesley Hunt, the first millionaire west of the Alleghenies. This is where Thomas Hunt Morgan, later to win the Nobel Prize for Medicine, was born.

Gratz Park

Surroundings

The world-famous Kentucky Horse Park (4089 Iron Works Park) lies 10 mi. north of Lexington (I 75, exit 120). Here, in Bluegrass country, everything centres on the horse. There is a Visitor Center that shows films on the park and supplies information on particular activities and events.

★★Kentucky
Horse Park

The International Museum of the Horse, with the Calumet Trophy Collection, and the American Saddle Horse Museum give a comprehensive view of the history and importance of the horse, while great race horses are honoured in the Hall of Champions. There is an interesting walk through the park (the Walking Farm Tour) that includes demonstrations of the crafts of blacksmiths, wagoners, harness makers, and a

In Kentucky Horse Park

parade of thoroughbreds (Parade of Breeds Show). Visitors can also enjoy horse trekking and rides in horse-drawn carriages.

Kentucky Horse Center

The Kentucky Horse Center (3380 Paris Pike; tours Apr.–Oct.) is a training centre for thoroughbreds.

Racecourses

There are race meetings for thoroughbred horses several times annually at the Keeneland Racecourse (4201 Versailles Rd.) and Red Mile Harness Track (South Broadway and Red Mile Rd.).

Stud farms

There are several hundred privately owned stud farms of varying size and importance within a radius of some 30 mi. of Lexington. The most famous are Calumet, Manchester Farm, Whitney, Normandy, Spendthrift and Three Chimneys Farm. Only the last two are open to visitors.

Harrodsburg

The small country town of Harrodsburg, 32 mi. to the south-west, is the oldest settlement of European immigrants west of the Alleghenies, founded in 1774. Old Fort Harrod State Park has a Living History Museum and open-air theatre where the life story of Daniel Boone is presented on stage.

★Shaker Village

Shaker Village, an open-air museum with more than thirty buildings, illustrating the way of life the celibate sect of Shakers, can be visited to the north of Harrodsburg.

★★Los Angeles   P/Q 7/8

State: California
Altitude: 0–285 ft
Population: 3.6 million

Los Angeles, on the Pacific Ocean in south-west California, is the centre of the largest conurbation in the United States after New York. Since the First World War it has spread in all directions and now measures more than 75 mi. across. Its original nucleus lies some 15 mi. inland from the Pacific coast.

The modern medium, film, has set its stamp on "L.A." but this is not all that makes it a thoroughly 20th c. city. Apart from the usual sky-scraper architecture, modernity finds expression in inescapable motor mania. To be in Los Angeles without a car is to be practically lost; firstly because the sights are situated so far away from one another, and also because public transport remains woefully inadequate. The city planners of Los Angeles believed that the only way to deal with traffic problems was to build the most expensive network of motorways and freeways, and as a result almost half the built-up area of the city is now taken up by the requirements of traffic. The two largest works of traffic engineering are the world-famous Stack (where the Santa Ana, Hollywood, Pasadena and Harbor Freeways, Temple Street and Sunset Bvld. intersect on four levels) and the seven-level intersection of the San Diego and Century Freeways, with eleven ramps and eleven bridges. With well over four million cars, not to mention the air traffic using the four large airports, the world-famous Los Angeles smog has become an almost daily phenomenon.

History In 1781 a party of Spanish missionaries, among them Junípero Serra, founded the San Gabriel mission on a site 8 mi. north-east of the present city centre. The settlement that grew up round it took the name of El Pueblo de Nuestra Señora la Reina de los Angeles de Porciuncula, of which the city's present name is a shortened version. The first inhabitants ("Angelenos") were Spaniards, Mexicans, Indians and blacks.

Thereafter the town grew rapidly, and for a time was capital of the Mexican province of Alta California. During the war with Mexico in 1846 the town was occupied by American forces, and under the treaty of Guadalupe Hidalgo passed to the United States. The finding of gold in the Sierra Nevada (1848) gave a boost to its development, and by 1860 it had a population of 5000. With the completion of the first transcontinental railroad, the South Pacific, the first great wave of immigrants began to arrive in 1883, and within a decade the population had risen to over 50,000. Further impetus was given to the town's development by the discovery of oil in the region in 1892 and the construction of artificial harbours at San Pedro and Long Beach between 1899 and 1914. By the early 20th c. the population had risen to 250,000.

Economy A further economic impulse was given by the development of the film industry, and by 1910 most American films were being made in Los Angeles. The districts of Hollywood and Beverly Hills now came into being, and in 1927 the Academy of Motion Picture Arts and Sciences awarded the first Oscar. The first sound film was produced in 1930. Thereafter Los Angeles developed into the most important industrial and services centre west of the Mississippi. New industries were established – petrochemicals, automobile manufacture, aircraft and spacecraft construction, engineering, electronics. Numerous major banks and insurance corporations established themselves in the city, and tourism increased steadily in importance, given additional impetus by the siting of the Summer Olympics of 1932 and 1984 in Los Angeles. In recent years, however, the Los Angeles region has been in a state of crisis, mainly as a result of changes in economic structures (e.g. the reduction in the armaments industry). The resulting social tensions between dif-

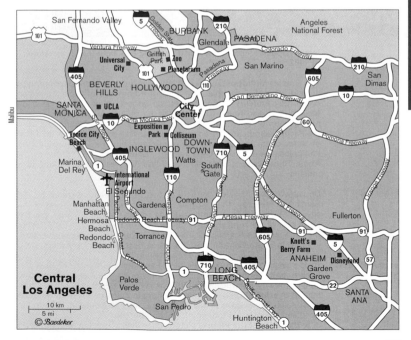

Central Los Angeles

10 km
5 mi
© Baedeker

Hollywood   Dodger Stadium, Echo Park

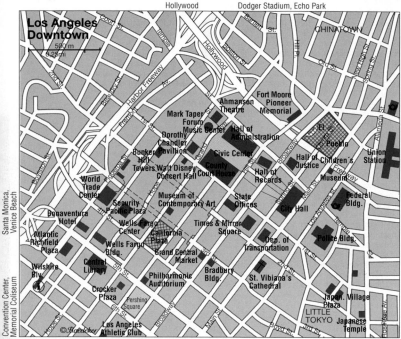

ferent population groups reached a violent climax in the "hot summer" of 1992.

The Greater Metropolitan Area of Los Angeles now has a **population** of around 16 million people, one-third of whom are of Latin American origin. Los Angeles is regarded as the largest "Mexican city" outside Mexico. It is also home to more than 1.2 million African-Americans, a high proportion of whom are unemployed. Asians and immigrants from the Pacific Islands are a dramatically increasing population group. Most of them come from Japan, Korea, China, Vietnam, Thailand and the Philippines, and live in "Little Tokyo", "Chinatown" and "Koreatown". About 10 per cent of the residents of Los Angeles are native American Indians.

Downtown

Downtown Los Angeles consists of two main areas separated by the Santa Ana Freeway: the Plaza lies in the centre of the older part of the city, while the modern centre extends round the Civic Center. On the north side of the central area is Chinatown, on the east side Little Tokyo, the Japanese Los Angeles quarter. To the south, beyond extensive parking lots, is South Central, a problem area best avoided by visitors.

★El Pueblo de los Angeles

To the west of the imposing Union Passenger Terminal (1939) is the Pueblo de los Angeles (protected as a historic monument), the historic core of the city, established in 1781. Its central feature is the Plaza, with the old mission church of Nuestra Señora la Reina de los Angeles, built by Spanish Franciscans in 1822. Nearby is the Fire House of 1884. In the Sepulveda House is a tourist information bureau.

    To the north of the Plaza is picturesque Olvera Street, a Mexican-style market street with attractive boutiques and restaurants and many stalls ("puestos") selling craft products. Of particular interest is the Avila Adobe House (1818; now a museum), one of the oldest buildings in the city.

A few steps to the north of Pueblo lies the Chinatown of Los Angeles, where the Street of the Golden Palace and Gin Ling Way are bustling.

Chinatown

South of the Pueblo, beyond the Santa Ana Freeway, is the Civic Center with its modern office blocks – the largest concentration of offices and government buildings outside Washington.

Civic Center

The central feature of the Civic Center is the 28-storey ★City Hall, built in 1928. From the top of City Hall Tower there are – in clear weather – breathtaking panoramic views, extending in the north-east to Mount Wilson with its Observatory, in the east to San Antonio Peak and in the south to the port area of Los Angeles. A short distance away to the south-east is the striking architecture of the Police Building.
    South-west of City Hall, on Broadway, is the massive Los Angeles Times Building, with its main lobby decorated by a gigantic globe.

From the City Hall the park-like Paseo de los Popladores leads up to the Music Center, home of the world-famous Los Angeles Philharmonic Orchestra. Every year in spring, celebrities from the world of film gather for the presentation of Oscars in the Dorothy Chandler Pavilion, whilst the Mark Taper Forum and Ahmanson Theatre put on performances of straight and experimental theatre.

★Music Center

A short walk south from the Music Center, on Grand Avenue is the important Museum of Contemporary Art, housed in a red sandstone building designed by the leading Japanese architect Arata Isozaki.

★MOCA

The permanent collection includes spectacular works by Warhol, Lichtenstein, Oldenburg and other contemporary artists. Open Tue.–Sun. 11am–6pm, Thu. to 8pm.

A short walk south-east is the Grand Central Market, surrounded by the bustling life of a Chicano quarter. Here a variety of tasty delicatessen and international specialities can be bought.

Grand Central Market

To the east is the **Bradbury Building** (1893), with a well preserved Victorian interior. This imposing building will be familiar to film enthusiasts from Orson Welles' first film, "Citizen Kane", which was inspired by the career of newspaper tycoon Randolph Hearst.

The City Hall was LA's first skyscraper

Further to the south-west is Pershing Square with its

★Pershing Square

rich tropical vegetation, the busy and attractive central feature of the Financial District, with the elegant Biltmore Hotel, whose magnificent lobby has been used in numerous feature films and television new reports.

Central Library

On the other side of Grand Avenue, between 5th and 6th Street, stands Central Library, an imposing building, strongly influenced by Egyptian and Classical Roman architecture.

★Bunker Hill

Behind Central Library is Bunker Hill, with its eye-catching complex of high-rise buildings occupied by banks and insurance companies. If you prefer not to walk up, take the "Angels Flight" funicular, which first opened in 1901 and has recently reopened following restoration. Particularly striking on Bunker Hill are the Security Pacific Plaza, the Arco Plaza with two 52-storey skyscrapers, a large shopping centre and a fountain by the Bauhaus sculptor Herbert Bayer, and the Westin Bonaventure Hotel (1973) by the architect John Portman, with 1500 rooms, a huge atrium and a revolving cocktail lounge with views of the city. Wells Fargo Court, laid out in gardens, is enclosed by the glass façades of the Wells Fargo Bank and the IBM Building, with California Plaza presenting a pleasant prospect across Grand Avenue.

However the dominant feature in the landscape is the **First Interstate World Center**, the tallest building in the American West (1015 ft). From here an elaborate staircase resembling the Spanish Steps in Rome leads down to 5th Street.

Little Tokyo

South-east of the Civic Center and to the east of Broadway is the Japanese quarter, with its shops, tearooms and restaurants. Particularly striking is Noguchi Plaza, designed by the Japanese architect Isamo Noguchi. On the square are the American Cultural and Community Center and the Japan American Theatre. Round the Japanese Village Plaza, to the north, are a number of attractive shops and restaurants. To the north-east is the Japanese American National Museum.

Wilshire Boulevard

Wilshire Boulevard runs west from downtown Los Angeles, towards Beverly Hills and Santa Monica.

★Miracle Mile

Between Highland Avenue and Fairfax Avenue is the famous Miracle Mile, with fashionable shops and impressive art-deco buildings. At 6060 Wiltshire Boulevard is the Petersen Automotive Museum, exhibiting the expensive limousines of Hollywood greats.

Hancock Park

Just before Fairfax Avenue is Hancock Park, with the Rancho La Brea Tar Pits, famous for the fossils found here – several hundred skeletons of animals who lived between 40,000 and 5000 years ago.

At the west end of the park is the **★County Museum of Art**, with a wealth of art treasures, including works by Rembrandt, Holbein, Canaletto, Cézanne, Toulouse-Lautrec, Kandinsky and Chagall.

Farmers Market

To the north of Hancock Park is the lively Farmers Market (Fairfax Ave. and 3rd St.), overflowing with fruit and delights of all kinds.

Hollywood

North of Farmers Market is Hollywood, impossible to miss because of the massive white letters spelling out its name up on the hillside. Originally a little farming settlement, founded at the turn of the 19th c., it was incorporated into Los Angeles in 1910. The first film studio in California – the

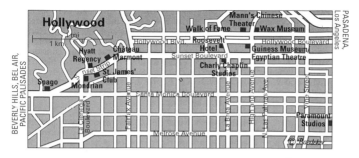

nucleus of the world-famous film metropolis – was established here in 1911. Today Hollywood is a shadow of its former self, having lost its glamorous image. Only a few large film companies (including Columbia and Paramount) still operate here, along with numerous smaller firms mainly engaged in making television films and commercials.

The main street, running from west to east, is Hollywood Boulevard Unfortunately little remains of its former splendour and many tourists would turn away disappointed, were it not for ★**Mann's Chinese Theatre**, guarded by a dragon and built in the style of a Chinese pagoda, the most famous film premier theatre in the world. In the forecourt are the footprints and handprints of over 150 stars, set in concrete, the first having been made by Mary Pickford and Douglas Fairbanks in 1929.

Hollywood
Boulevard

Mary Pickford and Douglas Fairbanks started it – many have followed their footsteps: Meryl Streep's contribution to the Walk of Fame

At the Chinese Theater begins the most photographed section of Hollywood Boulevard, the ★**Walk of Fame**. Set into the black terrazzo paving of the sidewalk are a series of brass plates and pink marble stars bearing the names of famous film stars. There are now 1800 of them, commemorating the greats of the film world, and those who consider themselves to be such. Taking advantage of proximity to Mann's Chinese Theater are a number of museums and exhibitions: the Hollywood Wax Museum with wax figures of famous film actors and politicians, the Guinness World of Records and Ripley's "Believe it or not!"; the Egyptian Theater is also popular.

Further west is the **Roosevelt Hotel** (7000 Hollywood Blvd.), which opened in 1927 as the "Home of the Stars" and was lovingly renovated a few years ago. The first Oscar award ceremony was held here in 1929. Later, Marilyn Monroe and other stars saw to it that the building would not be forgotten.

★Sunset
Boulevard

To the south of the Roosevelt Hotel, Sunset Boulevard runs east – west. **Sunset Strip** is well known as an entertainments centre, with the famous "Château Marmont" and the no less well-known "Hyatt on Sunset" Hotel. Anyone who wants to dine particularly well, and if possible in the company of a few Hollywood starlets or even stars, should book a table at the "Spago"; tel. (310) 6524025 – having first established his credit-worthiness!

Studios

Near Farmers Market visitors can see round the studios of the CBS television company (Columbia Broadcasting Systems; Fairfax Ave. and Beverly Blvd.). Paramount Pictures (5555 Melrose Ave.) also offer guided tours, with a look behind the scenes of television and film productions (Mon.–Fri. 9am–2pm; bookings and information tel. (213) 9561777).

Hollywood
Memorial
Cemetery

Next to Paramount Studios is the cemetery where numerous Hollywood celebrities, including Rudolf Valentino and Douglas Fairbanks, are buried. A plan is available from the entrance (6000 Santa Monica Blvd.), showing where to find the last (often highly individual) resting places of the stars.

Westside

West Hollywood

Further west Sunset Boulevard runs through West Hollywood, the first of a whose series of famous residential suburbs between Los Angeles and Malibu on the Pacific coast.

★Beverly Hills

West Hollywood is followed by Beverly Hills, where the stars of film and show business have their luxury – and sometimes quite extraordinary – residences. A plan showing where these are can be bought from bookshops and newspaper stands.

A must for any visitor to Beverly Hills is **Rodeo Drive**, a very upstage mile of sinfully expensive shops, with names such as Gucci, Hayman and Tiffany to be found in the exclusive triangle enclosed by Santa Monica Boulevard and Wilshire Boulevard.

Century City

On the south-western edge of Beverly Hills is Century City, a neighbourhood of modern offices, shops and apartment blocks built on the site of the old 20th Century Fox studios. In Century City Shopping Center is the "Dive", built by Steven Spielberg.

In the Simon Wiesenthal Center in Century City (9760 W Pico Blvd.) is the ★**Museum of the Holocaust**, which commemorates the Nazis' extermination of the Jews during the Second World War.

Sunset Boulevard continues west through the very select residential district of Bel Air. To the south is the scarcely less exclusive district of Westwood.

In the Brentwood hills, above the San Diego Freeway, the Getty Center, which opened in 1997, is the largest and most beautiful building on Westside. The travertine-clad citadel is a spectacular creation by the New York architect Richard Meier. The heart of this luxurious complex, the Getty Museum (entrance on Sepulveda Blvd.) houses most of the art treasures collected by the oil millionaire J. Paul Getty (1872–1976) or acquired by the $4 billion Foundation that he established. Its principal treasures include French Rococo furniture and above all an important collection of old master paintings, amongst them Rembrandt's "Old Man in Armour", a "Descent from the Cross" of the school of Rogier van der Weyden, and Van Gogh's famous "Irises". Decorative art and photography also have their place, with pictures by Man Ray and Cunningham. Open Tue.–Fri. 11am–7pm, Thu., Fri. until 9pm, Sat. and Sun. 10am–6pm.

The Getty Museum in Malibu (see below) is currently being renovated and will not reopen until 2001.

Between Westwood and Bel Air is the campus of the University of California at Los Angeles. It has an impressive Botanic Garden and the Franklin Murphy Sculpture Garden with works by Auguste Rodin, Henry Moore and other famous artists. Westwood Village is dominated by student life, and it is still possible to walk here, to some extent at least.

On Sunset Boulevard opposite the San Diego Freeway, the estate of the "singing cowboy" Will Rogers (1879–1935), complete with stables, corral and riding track, is preserved as an historic monument.

On the Pacific Coast Highway, near Santa Monica Bay with its broad sandy beach, is Pacific Palisades, another residential district for the wealthy. During the Nazi period in Germany a number of German Émigrés, including Thomas Mann and Bertolt Brecht, lived here.

The beautiful bathing resort of Malibu, celebrated in the songs of the Beach Boys, and highly popular with surfers, is also a residential area favoured by stars of show business (among them Bob Dylan). The original houses on stilts, along the beach, will be familiar from films and television series.

On a hill overlooking the Pacific Ocean stands J. Paul Getty's villa, a reconstruction of the Villa dei Papiri in Herculaneum, below Vesuvius, which until 1997 housed the Getty Museum. The villa is currently being renovated and will not reopen until 2001. Most of the art collections are now on display in the Getty Center in Westside (see above).

To the south of Pacific Palisades, Santa Monica is a favourite bathing resort. This is where the Santa Monica and Wiltshire Boulevards, and also the legendary Route 66 end. Santa Monica Pier, with its old-fashioned merry-go-round, was used in the film "The Sting".

At the corner of Washington and 22nd Streets. is the **Frank Gehry House** (1977–8), the rebuilding of an old house with corrugated iron, which caused much controversy at the time. It now ranks as a masterpiece of Deconstructivism.

Beyond Santa Monica is the densely built-up town of Venice, modelled on its Italian prototype, with the resort of Venice Beach, much favoured by roller skating and skateboarding enthusiasts and the fitness conscious.

On the southern edge of Venice, the **Marina del Rey** is one of the largest yacht stations on the Pacific coast, with some of the largest, most expensive yachts in the world.

North Hollywood

★Griffith Park

On the north-east side of Los Angeles, above the Hollywood Freeway, is Griffith Park, the largest municipal park in the United States (4000 acres), with a variety of sport and leisure facilities. Its main attractions include "Travel Town" with a transport and fire service museum, the Los Angeles Zoo, the Greek Theater (open air), the Ferndell Nature Center and the Griffith Observatory, Planetarium & Hall of Science with its fascinating exhibition on space travel. From here there is a superb view of Los Angeles on clear days.

Muscle men on Muscle Beach in Venice

Hollyhock House

Below Griffith Park, at the east end of Hollywood Boulevard, Hollyhock House (4800 Hollywood Blvd.) was designed by the great architect Frank Lloyd Wright for heiress Aline Barnsdall. The house is open to the public.

★★Universal Studios

The main attraction in North Hollywood is Universal Studios, an extensive film city with studios, Wild West sets, waterfalls, artificial lakes and the wardrobes of famous film stars. Visitors are shown the sets for such films as "Back to the Future", "Psycho" and the television series "Columbo" and can experience an attack by the great white shark of "Jaws", Wild West stunt shows and scenes from various thrillers with wild motorboat chases. This is a theme park as much as a studio tour that attracts many thousands of visitors. Open daily 8am–5pm.

★Santa Monica Mountains

Between North Hollywood and Beverly Hills, the Santa Monica Mountains have many expensive villas, as well as deep canyons. Mulholland Drive offers excellent views down over the well-tended parks and gardens of the villas of Beverly Hills and Bel Air.

Excursions north of Los Angeles

San Fernando

From North Hollywood, the Hollywood Freeway leads northwards to San Fernando, which grew out of the mission station founded by Spanish monks in 1797. A few parts of the original monastery still remain. The exceptionally interesting museum, housed in old workshops, has amongst other things a collection of Indian art. The cemetery, with its range of exotic plants, contains a great number of graves of Spanish Franciscan monks and Shoshone Indians.

A short drive north-west of San Fernando on the I 5 near Valencia, the **Six Flags Magic Mountain** is not for the faint-hearted. Its switchback rides – "Batman's Ride," "Revolution", and "Shock Wave" – are really quite something.

In the suburb of Burbank, south-east of San Fernando are the Lockheed Aircraft Company's factory (guided tours) and the headquarters of the National Broadcasting Corporation (NBC; studio tours).

Burbank

On Olive Avenue or Hollywood Way, the **★Warner Brothers Studios** are open to the public. Tours take two hours, and with luck you might see Clint Eastwood or Sharon Stone at work. Guided tours Mon.–Fri. 9am–4pm, in summer also Sat. 10am–2pm.

North-east of Los Angeles is Pasadena, seat of the California Institute of Technology.

★Pasadena

The **Norton Simon Museum of Art** (411 W Colorado Blvd.) has works by Paul Klee, Lionel Feininger, Wassily Kandinsky, Alexey Jawlensky and many other artists.

A short drive south-east of Pasadena is the **Huntington Library and Art Gallery**, a magnificent collection of rare books (including a Gutenberg Bible) and pictures (including Gainsborough's "Blue Boy"). It is set in very beautiful gardens.

From Pasadena, Highway CA 2 winds up into the beautiful San Gabriel Mountians, whose woods are part of the Angeles National Forest. Until well into April, skiing is possible here.

★San Gabriel Mountians

To the south is the suburb of San Gabriel (pop. 35,000), with the fortress-like mission of San Gabriel Arcángel, founded in 1771. Its church is one of the finest in California.

★San Gabriel

Excursions south of Los Angeles

3 mi. south-east of the Civic Center are the campus of the University of Southern California and the beautifully laid out Exposition Park, with a large rose garden.

Exposition Park

The central feature of the park is the **Memorial Coliseum** (1928), which has seating for 100,000 spectators. Some of the events in the 1932 and 1984 Summer Olympics were held here.

The California **Museum of Science and Industry** is devoted to the scientific and technological achievements of the "seventh greatest economic power in the world", as California likes to call itself. Included in the museum are a Hall of Health and a Hall of Economics and Finance. Open daily 10am–5pm.

Nearby is the California **Afro–American Museum**, that illustrates the contribution made by African–Americans to the development of California.

The richly stocked **County Museum of Natural History** illuminates the natural history of California with its geological and mineralogical collections.

In the district of Watts, much troubled in recent years by race riots, are the Simon Rodia Towers (1765 East 107th St.), four towers built by an Italian immigrant of that name from fragments of concrete, glass,

Simon Rodia Towers

pottery and mirrors. Begun in 1921, the task took 33 years. The towers are now protected as a monument of folk art.

Long Beach

Some 19 mi. south of Downtown, the city of Long Beach on San Pedro Bay remains independent in spite of its having merged with Los Angeles many years ago. The world's largest artificial habour has been steadily enlarged and developed here since the beginning of the 20th c.

The main attraction of Long Beach is the ★**"Queen Mary"**, which is moored at Pier J. The world's largest passenger liner (over 80,000 tons), it was launched in Britain in 1934 and was until the 1960s the flagship of the Cunard line. Today it is used as a floating hotel and museum.

One astonishing exhibit of the museum is the **"Spruce Goose"**, the huge wooden aircraft that was built by the eccentric millionaire Howard Hughes in the 1940s, and which even flew at least once.

★**Worldport L.A.**, the largest harbour on the Pacific Ocean, stretches out to the west of Long Beach. This enormous area is best discovered by taking a boat trip around the harbour. The boats set out daily at 11am, 1pm and 4pm, from Pier J where the Queen Mary is moored.

Marineland of the Pacific

10 min. drive west of San Pedro Bay is Marineland of the Pacific, one of the largest ocean parks in the world (trained dolphins and whales).

Buena Park Movieland Wax Museum

19 mi. south-east of downtown Los Angeles is the suburb of Buena Park (pop. 70,000), with the Movieland Wax Museum (famous film and television stars depicted in scenes from their best known films).

Knott's Berry Farm

To the south, on Beach Boulevard, is Knott's Berry Farm. In the 1920s a farm selling blackberries, it is now a large theme park (gold-diggers' town, Snoopyland). In the more modern part of the park are spectacular roundabouts and roller coasters.

★★Disneyland

A few miles south-east of Knott's Berry Farm lies Anaheim, originally a settlement established by German immigrants in 1857. Anaheim's main attraction today is Disneyland, the huge and now world-famous theme park first opened in 1955 by animator/film producer Walt Disney. A visit to Disneyland is not cheap. An adult ticket for one day, including all rides costs $34, whilst children under 12 pay $26. Opening times are constantly changing, but the core times are between 9am and 10pm (for more detailed information tel. (714) 7814560).

Disneyland comprises several different areas, each with its own special theme:

Main Street USA

The entrance leads into a turn of the 19th c. Main Street USA, with horse-drawn street cars and old-time automobiles.

Tomorrowland

Next along, "Tomorrowland" has been completely redesigned. Here visitors can experience the future – or at least the Walt Disney idea of it – with the "Astro-Orbiter".

Fantasyland

In Fantasyland you can meet Snow White with her Seven Dwarfs and visit the Sleeping Beauty's Castle, or fly with Peter Pan and Dumbo.

Mickey's Toontown

Mickey's Toontown is the home of Mickey Mouse, Goofy and Donald and Daisy Duck.

Frontierland

In Frontierland visitors are taken back to the days of the Wild West and

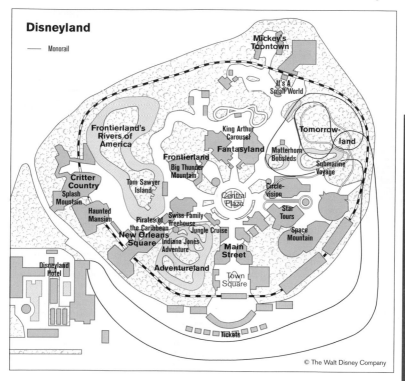

Disneyland

—— Monorail

Mickey's Toontown

It's A Small World

King Arthur Carousel

Tomorrow-land

Frontierland's Rivers of America

Fantasyland

Matterhorn Bobsleds

Submarine Voyage

Frontierland

Big Thunder Mountain

Critter Country

Tom Sawyer Island

Circle-vision

Splash Mountain

Central Plaza

Star Tours

Haunted Mansion

Pirates of the Caribbean

Swiss Family Treehouse

Jungle Cruise

Space Mountain

New Orleans Square

Indiana Jones Adventure

Main Street

Disneyland Hotel

Adventureland

Town Square

Tickets

the gold-diggers. A mining railroad runs through deserts, canyons and mountains, and the sternwheeler "Mark Twain" sails on the Rivers of America.

In Critter Country you will encounter a dancing bear and see Davy Crockett's canoes, and can take an adventurous trip down the rapids.

Critter Country

New Orleans Square re-creates the atmosphere of the city in the Mississippi delta, with 18th c. pirates and 19th c. street scenes.

New Orleans Square

Here visitors sail on an expedition through the jungle, menaced by wild animals, and can visit the Tiki Room with its tropical plants and birds. The latest of Disneyland's many thrills is here, the "Temple of the Forbidden Eye", where visitors follow in the footsteps of Indiana Jones.

Adventureland

Surroundings

3 mi. south of Disneyland is the Crystal Cathedral (by Philip Johnson, 1980), a futuristic structure of tubular steel clad with mirror glass.

Crystal Cathedral

25 mi. south of San Pedro Bay, in the Pacific, is Santa Catalina Island. Once a pirates' lair, this rocky islet was developed in 1919 by Wrigley, the chewing-gum king, as a holiday centre, a "second Capri" (diving, swim-

Santa Catalina Island

ming, tennis, golf, riding). At the south-east end of the island is a large colony of seals.

Louisiana (State)   R–V 31–36

Area: 47,752 sq. mi.
Population: 4,351,000
Capital: Baton Rouge
Popular name: Pelican State

The southern state of Louisiana (named after King Louis XIV of France) occupies the western part of the Gulf Coast plain and the riverine meadowland and delta of the Mississippi (which alone accounts for a third of the state's area). Much of the land, lying at an average height of only 100 ft above sea level, has to be protected by levees from flooding; only in the north-west does it rise to around 525 ft. The climate is subtropical, with hot and sultry summers, mild winters and occasional devastating hurricanes.

History The Mississippi delta region, first discovered in 1530 by two Spaniards, Cabeza de Vaca and Panfilo de Narváez, was occupied in the name of France by the Sieur de la Salle in 1682. After the French failure to prevent the westward extension of the British colonies, in 1762, the territory west of the Mississippi as far north as the Canadian frontier fell to Spain and the territory east of the river to Britain, passing in 1783 to the United States. In 1801 France recovered the Spanish part of the territory and in 1803 sold it to the United States (the "Louisiana Purchase"). On April 30th 1812 Louisiana was admitted to the Union as the 18th state. During the Civil War, in 1862, the Northern states captured much of Louisiana, which supported the Confederates. After the war it remained a state with sharp social and racial tensions.

Economy The main crops grown on the productive soils of the Mississippi delta and along the Red River are cotton, sugarcane, soya beans and rice. Cattle rearing and fishing in the well stocked coastal waters are increasing in importance. The basis of the state's industry is provided by its rich resources of oil, natural gas, sulphur and rock salt, which supply the petrochemical and aluminium smelting plants along the Mississippi between New Orleans and Baton Rouge. New Orleans, Louisiana's largest city and the second most important seaport in the United States, is the tourist centre of the state, whose particular charm lies in its Creole and French heritage.

Baton Rouge

The state capital of Baton Rouge, north-west of New Orleans (see entry), owes its name to two Indian tribes who marked the boundaries of their territory with red posts. Its main features of interest are its handsome old mansions, including Mount Hope Plantation (19th c.) and Magnolia Plantation (1791), one of the oldest in the town. Any visit to the town should include a stroll along the river front.

★Cajun country

The land of the Cajuns stretches west from New Orleans up to the Texan border. These were people of French descent, who created their own particular culture in the bayous of the Mississippi Delta. The word "Cajun" is an Americanized form of the French "Acadiens", the name given to French settlers deported from Canada by the British from 1755 onwards.

Houma, south-west of New Orleans, is a very good base from which to explore the adventurous, romantic landscape of the Mississippi Delta, either on the "Bayou Drive" (LA 56 and 57) or by boat. Various companies offer "swamp tours", including Annie Miller whose restaurant also serves delicious Cajun food.

Houma

Lafayette, the capital of Cajun country, has the Jean Lafitte National Park, where visitors can discover Cajun culture in the Vermilionville museum village and the open-air museum Acadian Village.

Lafayette

In New Iberia you can visit the magnificent pre-war villa "Shadows on the Teche", and then continue to Avery Island, where the famous Tabasco sauce is mixed (guided tours) and the Rip van Winkle Gardens with their superabundance of tropical plants.

New Iberia

See entry

New Orleans

Between New Orleans and Baton Rouge, both sides of the Mississippi are lined with magnificent pre-war estates, the most beautiful of which are Destrehan, San Francisco, Oak Alley, Nottoway, Myrtles Plantation, Greenwood and Oakley, on which the painter John James Audubon (1785–1851) lived. Here he painted 32 of the finest pictures in his "Birds of America".

★★**Plantation Country**

A sneeky spectator on a Swamp-Tour in the Bayous of Houma

Maine (State)   B–F 54–58

Area: 33,215 sq. mi.
Population: 1,243,000
Capital: Augusta
Popular name: Pine Tree State

Maine, the largest and most thinly populated of the New England states, lies in the extreme north-east of the United States, on the frontier with Canada. It consists of three main geographical regions. The much indented Atlantic coast with its innumerable offshore islands runs from south to north-east for a distance of more than 300 mi. To the west of this coastal strip, some 60 mi. across, the ground rises gradually into a hilly upland region. Northern Maine is a region of lakes and morainic hills; to the west the White Mountains rise to 5270 ft. More than four-fifths of the state is covered with forests (mainly pine and spruce). In the coastal regions the climate is cool temperate, under strong maritime influence; further west the maritime influence declines.

History The territory that is now Maine was occupied by Indians of the Algonkian language family when the first Europeans arrived in 1498–9. In the 17th c. French settlers established themselves in the area, later followed by British settlers. In 1691 Maine became part of Massachusetts. Thereafter the fur trade, logging, shipbuilding and fishing brought it prosperity. On March 15th 1820 Maine was separated from Massachusetts and became the 23th state of the Union.

★Acadia National Park

Bass Harbour Lighthouse in Acadia National Park

Economy Thanks to the state's wealth of forests the woodworking and papermaking industries are major elements in its economy. The most important product of the fisheries, now in decline, is lobsters. The predominant agricultural crop is potatoes, followed by other vegetables and poultry feed; dairy farming is also important. Other industries are leather goods, textiles and foodstuffs. Tourism is making a steadily increasing contribution to the economy.

The Acadia National Park (area 60 sq. mi.), one of the most visited nature reserves in the United States (open throughout the year; particularly fine in the fall), lies on the coast of Maine near the

Canadian peninsula of Nova Scotia. It is a region of rocky coasts, forests with clear rivers, streams and lakes, and rolling hills, offering ideal conditions for a variety of sports and leisure activities both in summer and in winter.

The core of the National Park is the hilly Mount Desert Island, on the east coast of which is the chief town, Bar Harbor. Particularly attractive are the Otter Cliffs and Otter Point, where a varied Arctic flora can be studied and numbers of birds (cormorants, seagulls) can be observed. There is a beautiful drive round the National Park on the Park Loop (28 mi.).

Augusta, the state capital, lies some 40 mi. inland. Founded by English settlers in 1628, it is now predominantly an industrial town. Features of interest are the massive State House (by Charles Bulfinch, 1832), with the Maine State Museum (natural history, economic and social history of Maine); Blaine House, the Governor's residence; and Old Fort Western (1754), with "living history" presentations.	**Augusta**
This large nature park lies in the north of the state round Mount Katahdin, Maine's highest peak.	**Baster State Park**
North-east of the inlets and islands of Casco Bay is Brunswick, a commercial and educational centre. Features of interest are the house in which Harriet Beecher Stowe wrote "Uncle Tom's Cabin", the Museum of Art and the Peary-MacMillan Arctic Museum (Arctic exploration).	**Brunswick**
Thanks to its spectacular situation on the south side of Penobscot Bay, framed by high hills, the little town of Camden is a popular holiday resort, with excellent sport and leisure facilities.	**Camden**
On Casco Bay is Portland (pop. 65,000), the largest town in Maine, best visited in summer (boat trips round the bay). For adults there is the Portland Museum of Art, for children the Children's Museum of Maine. There are numbers of fine old houses in the town, including particularly the home of the Portland-born poet Henry Wadsworth Longfellow (1807–82). The Old Port Exhange has excellent shops and restaurants.	**Portland**
The little coastal town of Kennebunkport, 12½ mi. south of Portland, is very popular in summer. Features of interest are the Seashore Trolley Museum and the local history collection in Town House School.	**Kennebunkport**
The picturesque little port of Wiscasset is the haunt of artists and writers. Features of interest are the Maine Art Gallery and the Lincoln County Museum. The Musical Wonder House has a collection of old mechanical musical instruments.	**Wiscasset**

Maryland (State)   K/L 47–50

Area: 10,460 sq. mi.
Population: 4,860,000
Capital: Annapolis
Popular names: Old Line State, Free State

The state of Maryland (named after Queen Henrietta Maria, wife of Charles I) lies on both sides of Chesapeake Bay in the eastern United States, extending inland from the Atlantic to the Allegheny Mountains. The coastal region has numerous inlets and offshore sandbanks. In the west a narrow strip of land reaches into the Appalachians, reaching a height of 3360 ft in Backbone Mountain. The eastern part of the state has a humid subtropical climate, the western part a climate of continental type. In the hills hardwood forests predominate; elsewhere the landscape is patterned by meadows and arable land.

History The area was first explored by Captain John Smith in 1608, and in 1632 a colony was founded by Leonard Calvert, a brother of Lord Baltimore. After the arrival of 200 Catholic refugees from persecution in 1634 the inhabitants of Maryland were guaranteed religious freedom by law in 1649. The Calvert family lost their rights over the colony only in 1776, with the signing of the state's constitution and the Declaration of Independence. Maryland entered the Union as the 7th of the founding states in 1788.

Economy The agricultural produce of the state – maize, soya beans, tobacco, fruit, potatoes and other vegetables – goes largely to supply the two cities of Baltimore and Washington. Livestock farming and oyster culture also make important contributions to the state's economy. The principal industries are steel production, engineering, foodstuffs and shipbuilding. Maryland also has substantial tourist attractions in its towns and cities, its bathing beaches and its skiing facilities.

Annapolis

The state capital, Annapolis, is the seat of the US Naval Academy, with the Academy Naval Museum. Other features of interest are the Old Senate Chamber in State House, the Governor's Mansion, the William Paca House and Gardens and the Chase-Lloyd House.

Baltimore

See entry

Cambridge

The finest of this old port town's historic houses are on the High Street. Other features of interest are the Brannock Maritime Museum, the Meredith House (1760) and the Neild Museum. The 17th c. Old Trinity Church in Church Creek is one of the oldest churches in the United States.

Ellicott City

The first terminus of the United States railroad system was in Ellicott City. The original station is now in the B and O Railroad Station Museum.

Great Falls of Potomac

The old Chesapeake and Ohio Canal is now a National Historic Park. Its history is documented in Great Falls Tavern and Museum in Potomac.

Historic St Mary's City

Right on the southern tip of the west side of Chesapeake Bay, St Mary's was founded by English settlers in 1634. Today an open-air museum brings the past to life.

Ocean City

Maryland's only bathing resort on the Atlantic coast, Ocean City is busy and bustling. But visitors should not be put off by all the hotels and snack bars crowding the sea front; the beach is truly magnificent.

Assateaque Islands National Seashore

A complete contrast to Ocean City, the Assateaque Islands National Seashore nature reserve to the south is a haven for rare sea birds, as well as wild ponies, presumably descended from those released here in the 17th c.

St Michaels

This small town on the east of Chesapeake Bay once had a flourishing shipbuilding industry, as shown by the large collection in the Chesapeake Bay Maritime Museum.

Massachusetts (State)   G/H 52–55

Area: 8257 sq. mi.
Population: 6,092,000
Capital: Boston
Popular names: Bay State, Old Colony

Massachusetts (from an Indian term, "big hill in the east"), one of the New England states in the north-eastern United States, is divided into two parts by the Connecticut River, flowing from north to south through the state. To the west of the river the Berkshire Hills (3491 ft) and the Taconic Mountains rise above the rump plateaux of the Appalachians; to the east the central plateau slopes down gradually to the coast. Off the much indented coast, with sandy beaches towards the south end, lie numerous islands and peninsulas. In the east the climate is temperate, in the west more continental in character. Two-thirds of the area of the state is covered by mixed forests, mainly oak, Weymouth pine, spruce and hemlock.

History The Pilgrim Fathers who arrived in the "Mayflower" in 1620 settled in Plymouth, where in 1629 they established a community governed by strict Puritan principles. Their conflicts with the Indian population culminated in 1675–76 in King Philip's War, in which the colonists were victorious. Resistance to British rule and the movement for American independence began in Massachusetts (see Boston), and the first battle in the War of Independence was fought at Lexington in 1775. In 1780 the state adopted the constitution that is still in force. It entered the Union as the 6th state on February 6th 1788.

Economy In economic terms Massachusetts is the most important of the New England states. Its highly specialised agriculture achieves high yields in the cultivation of tobacco, vegetables and fruit (particularly cranberries) and in dairy farming and poultry rearing. The state's fisheries, including lobster and shellfish culture, are also important. A major element in the economy, in addition to the commercial and services sectors, is industry, particularly engineering, foodstuffs, metalworking, printing, electrical engineering and electronics. In Harvard Massachusetts has one of the most renowned universities in the United States. The varied beauties of the landscape and the cultural attractions of the cities draw large numbers of visitors every year, making tourism an important factor in the economy.

★**Berkshires**

The Berkshires in north-west Massachusetts with their green hills, little white churches, picturesque villages and narrow country lanes, epitomise picture-book New England. A drive along the Mohawk Trail (ME 2) offers all these features as it winds from Millers Falls in the east to Williamstown in the west. From there the US 7 to the south is scarcely less romantic. The Hancock Shaker Village beyond is another attraction.

Gloucester

The inhabitants of this little town on Cape Ann have been since time immemorial fishermen and seamen. This old tradition is commemorated in the bronze statue of the Gloucester Fisherman in the harbour and the museum of the Cape Ann Historical Association. Gloucester is also noted for the artists' colony of Rocks Neck.

Rockport

The picturesque little fishing town of Rockport, north of Gloucester, has also been the home of many artists.

Lexington

The first two battles of the American War of Independence took place north-west of Boston. The battlefields are now part of the Minuteman National Historical Park and can be visited on the Battle Road Trail. The first battle took place at Lexington on April 19th 1775. Features of historic interest are the Minuteman Monument, the Monroe and Buckman Taverns, the Hancock-Clarke House and the Museum of Our National Heritage.

Concord

Shortly afterwards Concord was the scene of the second battle. Later, a number of notable writers, such as Ralph Waldo Emerson, Nathaniel Hawthorne and Henry David Thoreau lived here; their houses can be visited. They are buried in Sleepy House Cemetery.

Lowell

Lowell lies on the Merrimack River in northern Massachusetts. The heyday of the textile industry is recalled in two open-air museums, the Lowell National Historic Park and the Lowell Heritage State Park. Also in the town is the birthplace of the artist James MacNeill Whistler, which contains some of his pictures.

★Salem

Salem, north-east of Boston on Massachusetts Bay, has one of the best historical museums in America, the Essex Institute. It preserves a number of handsome mansions of the 17th–19th centuries with their original interiors, notably the Stephen Philips Memorial Trust House. The House of Seven Gables (1668; guided visits) was the birthplace of the writer Nathaniel Hawthorne (1804–64).

The Salem Witch Museum is devoted to the witchcraft trials of 1692.

Springfield

In Springfield, in the interior of the state on the border with Connecticut, is the oldest American arms factory. This is also where the national sport, basketball, was invented, witness the Basketball Hall of Fame. And if one Harley Davidson is not enough, visit the motorcycle museum, and pay homage to the legendary "Indian".

Worcester

Worcester lies between Boston and Springfield. Features of interest are the Art Museum (Dutch and Italian paintings) and the Higgins Armory (medieval and Renaissance weapons).

Other places of interest

Boston (see entry), Cambridge (see Boston), Cape Cod (see entry)

★Memphis   O 35

State: Tennessee
Altitude: 260 ft
Population: 610,000

If Nashville (see entry) is the capital of country music, Memphis is the home of Gospel, blues and rhythm and blues. The clubs in Beale Street were for decades the objective of all the singers, mainly black, who hoped for the big chance that would lead to their "discovery". One of them was Elvis Presley, whose grave on his Graceland estate is now the chief tourist attraction of Memphis.

The city, situated at the junction of the Wolf River with the Mississippi, ranks as the greatest market for cotton and hardwoods in the world. These and other products of the surrounding area (alfalfa, soya, rice) are shipped from the second largest inland port in the United States. Industry, with over 1100 firms, also plays an important part in the city's economy.

History Andrew Jackson, later seventh President of the United States, along with two partners established a settlement here on a site suitable for a harbour, and is therefore regarded as the founder of Memphis. The town was named Memphis because of the similarity of its situation on the high river bank to that of the Egyptian city of Memphis on the Nile. Capital of the Confederation in the early days of the Civil War, the town was taken by Union troops in 1862. In the 1920s, thanks mainly to W.C. Handy ("father of the blues"), Memphis became the great centre of black music. It gained an unhappy place in history when Martin Luther King Jr (see Famous People) was shot here on April 4th 1968.

Downtown Memphis

One of the most recent additions to the skyline of Memphis is the Great American Pyramid at 1 Auction Avenue, on the banks of the river. The steel and glass façade of this 32-storey structure, modelled on the Pyramid of Cheops, encloses an auditorium with seating for 22,000 spectators.

Great American Pyramid

On Mud Island (also known as Festival Island), in the Mississippi, is a ¾ mi. long model of the course of the river from Cairo, Illinois, to the Gulf of Mexico. The model is part of the Mississippi River Museum, the central feature of this family park on the island where the B-17 Bomber "Memphis Belle" can also be viewed.

Mud Island

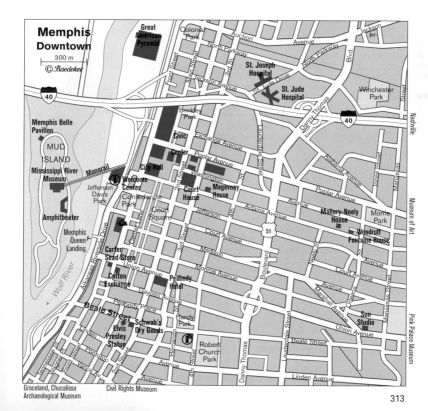

★Beale Street

To the east of Riverside Drive is Beale Street Little remains of its charm in the days when the blues resounded from the many bars along the street. Almost all the old buildings have been pulled down and replaced by replicas, and the music heard in the present-day establishments is often a mere shadow of the real thing. Even so, it is worth paying a visit to W.C. Handy's house (325 Beale St.), Handy Park and especially A. Schwab's Dry Goods Store at No. 163, founded in 1876 with the motto "If you can't find it a Schwab's you don't need it!"

Peabody Hotel

Some of the residents of the time-honoured Peabody Hotel (149 Union Ave.) are ducks. Every day at 11am they are brought down in the lift from their apartment on the top floor, taken to their pond in the lobby, with musical accompaniment, and taken back at 5pm.

Cotton Row

The crossing of Union Avenue and Front Street was where the cotton dealers formerly had their offices. The Cotton Exchange still exists today, but the electronic revolution means that only a few traders are to be found in the old exchange building.

★National Civil
Rights Museum

A short distance south of Beale Street, at 406 Mulberry Street, is the Lorraine Motel, where Martin Luther King Jr (see Famous People) was shot in 1968. The building is now occupied by the National Civil Rights Museum, which traces the history of civil rights movements in the United States. Its centrepiece is the hotel room with the balcony on which Martin Luther King was killed.

★★Graceland

Even though not everyone shares the cult for Elvis Presley (see Famous People), Graceland, the palatial house at 3734 Elvis Presley Boulevard that he acquired in 1957 is a national place of pilgrimage.

Here fans of the "King" can walk through his home, lay flowers on his tomb, see his two private jets and his automobiles and stock up in the museum shop with mementoes of their idol, who lived here in his days of glory and in the last unhappy years of alcohol and drugs – though there is no reference to these years on the guided tours of the house. Open Mar.–Oct. daily; Nov.–Feb. daily excursions Tue.

Outer districts

On Adams Avenue, which runs east from Mud Island, there are a number of handsome 19th c. mansions (restored). The finest are the Magevney House (No. 198) of 1836, the Mallory-Neely House (No. 652) of 1855 and the Woodruff-Fontaine House (No. 680) of 1870, which contains a costume collection.

Overton Park

To the east of downtown Memphis, between Poplar Avenue and East Parkway, are Overton Park and Overton Square, the centre of midtown Memphis's night life. In addition to numerous restaurants and bars there is the Memphis Brooks Museum of Art, the oldest and largest art museum in Tennessee, with a collection that ranges from pictures by way of printed graphic art to textiles. In the north-west corner of the park are Memphis Zoo and Aquarium.

South-east of Overton Park, at 3050 Central Avenue, is the Pink Palace Museum (geology, flora and fauna and history of the Middle South). It is housed in a villa that belonged to Clarence Saunders, who in 1916 founded the Piggly Wiggly supermarket chain (still flourishing).

Pink Palace Museum and Planetarium

In the south-west of the city is the T.O. Fuller State Park, in which are the excavated and partly restored remains of an Indian village discovered by archaeologists from Memphis State University. The village is believed to have been inhabited from about AD 900 to 1500. There is an interesting site museum.

Chucalissa Indian Village

★Mesa Verde National Park   M 17

State: Colorado
Area: 80 sq. mi.
Established: 1906

The Mesa Verde ("Green Table") is a tabular hill covered with coniferous forest, rising abruptly to 2000 ft above the semi-desert foreland of the Rockies in the extreme south-west of Colorado. It is of interest not so much for the natural landscape as for the relics of a past Indian culture.

Information The park, museum and Spruce Tree House are open all year; other facilities are closed in winter. The Far Views Center lies on the main drive through the park, 20 mi. from the main entrance. Inside the park there are several motels, a lodge and a campsite.

A permit must be obtained from the National Park administration (see Practical Information, National Parks) for **hiking** on the Spruce Canyon Trail (2 mi.) and the Pictograph Point Trail, in the area of the Chapin Mesa Museum; no permit is required for the Prater Ridge Trail (7¾ mi.) or the Knife Edge Trail (1½ mi.), in the Morfield Village area.

History Around the beginning of the Christian era the river valleys in this region were occupied by nomadic Indians who later took to a settled life. In the 6th c., for reasons that are not understood, they moved back to the densely forested plateau and its gorges, where they found fertile soils and a sufficiency of water. Here considerable remains of rock habitations (pit houses on the plateau, cliff dwellings on the sides of the canyons), multi-storey houses of adobe or stone built round a central square (pueblos) and cult sites (kivas) of the Anasazi Indians have been preserved. Then in the 14th c. the inhabitants left their settlements for some unknown reason and moved south-west.

There are an estimated 4000 statutorily protected **archaeological sites** in the National Park. Admission to the park is restricted and strictly controlled, and some areas can be visited only in the company of a park ranger.
    From the entrance on the north side of the park a winding road leads to Morfield Village (campground, services). It then continues past Montezuma Valley Overlook and Park Point, the highest point in the park (8572 ft; access road), to the Far View Visitor Center. From there a 13 mi. long road runs to Wetherill Mesa (summer only, 8am–4.30pm), with the Step House, which shows remains of two periods of settlement (c. 7th and 13th centuries), and the Long House (only under the guidance of a park ranger), the second largest ruin in the park, with a large open space in which dances and ceremonies were performed.
    The other road leads from the Visitor Center to Chapin Mesa, passing the Far View Ruins (access road), which were occupied from the

10th–14th c., and Cedar Tree Tower (access road), from which it is a short walk to the terraced fields once cultivated by the Indians.

Chapin Mesa
Museum

In 25 mi. the road comes to the Park Headquarters Area, with the Chapin Mesa Museum (archaeological remains, Indian arts and crafts).

Spruce Tree
House

To the south-east, on the edge of Spruce Canyon, is Spruce Tree House, the best preserved settlement in the park and one of the largest, with 114 rooms and 8 kivas.

★Ruins Road
Drive

The Museum is the starting point of Ruins Road Drive, which takes in the main features of the Mesa Verde in two long loops, with a total length of 12 mi. The high spots in the western part of the park are the Square Tower House, a four-storey structure built against the rock wall of the Navajo Canyon; the Sun Point Pueblo, the remains of a village that was pulled down by its inhabitants in the 13th c. to provide material for new dwellings in a cave in nearby Cliff Canyon; and the unfinished **Sun Temple**, a large D-shape cult building.

On the eastern loop of the road are the 299-room **Cliff Palace**, in a large cave on the east side of Cliff Canyon – the largest cave settlement in the park and the first to be discovered in 1888 – and the **Balcony House**, built into a wide, low recess on the wall of Soda Canyon.

Miami/Miami Beach   Y 45

State: Florida
Altitude: 0–25 ft
Population: 386,000

The city of Miami lies on the south-east side of the Florida peninsula, separated from the Atlantic Ocean by the Biscayne Bay lagoon and Miami Beach with its huge hotels and apartment blocks. Miami's pleasant winter climate has led to its mushroom growth into a vastly popular holiday resort that draws more than 8 million visitors every year. It has the world's biggest passenger seaport, a port of call for numerous cruise ships, and a large international airport. It has more than 600 large and medium-size hotels, numerous motels, several thousand restaurants and cafés and some 50 foreign consulates – reflecting the city's importance as a centre for business as well as holiday travellers. Following changes in banking law and the resultant inflow of capital from Latin America and Saudi Arabia Miami has developed into a leading financial centre. There is also considerable industry in the Miami region, notably the aircraft and space and foodstuffs industries. Miami has the largest Cuban community outside Cuba.

History The first European to sail into Biscayne Bay was the Spanish navigator Ponce de León in 1513. In 1567 Spanish Jesuits established the mission station of Tequesta, on the site of Miami, and the settlement that grew up round it became a base for the Spanish silver fleet on its voyage to Europe. After the Spanish withdrawal in 1821 the first American settlers came here to grow cotton and tropical crops. In 1871 William Brickell established a trading post on the estuary of the Miami River (the Indian name Mayami means "Great Water"). Five years later Julia Tuttle, an incomer from the North, acquired a considerable area of land to the north of the river, and on her initiative Henry M. Flagler extended his East Coast Railroad to Miami in 1895–96. The Royal Palm Hotel was then built at the rail terminus. The Spanish–American War of 1898 brought great profits to Miami. The development of the offshore island of Miami Beach now began. During the Second World War Miami

Miami

3 km

2 mi

© Baedeker

was a hospital and recreation centre. After the war began the building boom that is still continuing.

Fidel Castro's revolution on Cuba led many Cubans to leave home and settle in the Miami area, and Cuban refugees played a considerable part in the development of the Miami conurbation. In the early 1980s there was a further great wave of refugees from Cuba. This period also saw an influx of refugees from Haiti, who for the most part live the life of underdogs in the Miami area. In August 1992 Hurricane Andrew devastated much of southern Florida. In 1993 Miami acquired an unsavoury reputation for attacks on tourists but extensive security measures, including a stronger police presence, have done much to calm fears.

Miami

Biscayne
Boulevard

Miami's main traffic artery is the southern section of palm-lined Biscayne Boulevard, which is flanked by imposing tower blocks.

★Bayfront Park

Bayfront Park, on the east side of Biscayne Boulevard, has recently been completely replanned. An attractive feature is the electronically controlled Pepper Fountain. Also in the park are an amphitheatre that is used for musical performances of all kinds and a tower for laser illuminations, as well as three important monuments: the Torch of Friendship, symbolising Miami's relationships with the countries of Central and South America; the World War II Memorial; and the Challenger Memorial, commemorating the crew of the Challenger spacecraft that exploded in 1986.

★Bayside
Marketplace

Just north of Bayfront Park are Bayside Marketplace and the Miamarina (formerly Pier 5, which features in the television series "Miami Vice"), with good shops and restaurants that attract many visitors. The American Police Hall of Fame (3801 Biscayne Blvd.) has many astounding exhibits relating to the history of the United States police.

Downtown

From Biscayne Boulevard the busy Flagler Street runs west to the Guzman Cultural Center (1926; formerly the Olympia Theatre, renovated in 1972 for its present function), Dade County Court House (1926), the modern Federal Building (Government Center) and the attractive Mediterranean-style Metro Dade Cultural Center, with the Center of Fine Arts (periodic special exhibitions), the Main Library and the Historical Museum of Southern Florida (history of southern Florida, early Indian tribes, pirates, pioneers; 3 D film on Miami).

A more recent landmark of downtown Miami is the 52-storey ★**Centrust Bank Tower** (1987), which is brilliantly floodlit in many colours at night. It was designed by I.M. Pei, America's best known contemporary architect, in association with Spillis Candela and Partners. The floodlighting scheme, with several hundred lamps and different colours for different occasions (for example green on St Patrick's Day and red on St Valentine's Day) was devised by Douglas Leigh. The Centrust Bank is overtopped by the modern Southeast Financial Center with its 55 storeys.

★Calle Ocho

From Bayfront Park (Brickell Ave.) 8th Street runs west over the Miami River. Outside the city centre with its skyscrapers it is known as Calle Ocho, and continues into the Tamiami Trail, which runs through the Everglades (see entry). The district on the west side of downtown Miami through which it runs is known as Little Havana because of the many Latinos, particularly Cuban exiles, who live here: hence also the Spanish name Calle Ocho ("St. 8"). Between SW 12th Avenue and SW 27th Avenue is an area of shops, small markets and cheerful cafés and restaurants with a friendly and relaxed atmosphere. The everyday language of

Little Havana is Spanish. Planning controls seek to maintain the "Cuban" character of 8th Street

A particular attraction in this area is the Orange Bowl, a football stadium that is also used for the Orange Bowl Musical Festival.   Orange Bowl

The Port of Miami, on two artificial islands (Dodge Island and Lummus Island), is now the world's leading passenger seaport, which can accommodate over a dozen cruise liners at the same time. It handles some 3 million cruise passengers a year, most of them heading for the Bahamas or the Caribbean.   Port of Miami

The MacArthur Causeway, a "road on stilts", crosses Biscayne Bay to Watson Park, with the Japanese Garden (pagoda, teahouse, waterfall), and a Tivoli-style amusement park. Nearby are a helicopter pad (sightseeing flights) and a seaplane landing stage (excursions to the Bahamas).   Watson Park

Brickell Avenue, a residential street for upmarket old Miami families, is now lined by modern high-rise office blocks and condominiums. It is famed as the "Wall Street of Miami".   Brickell Avenue

At the southern tip of Virginia Key is Miami Seaquarium the largest seawater aquarium in southern Florida.   ★Seaquarium

The Rickenbacker Causeway leads to the island of Key Biscayne, famed as the venue of major golf and tennis tournaments with sports facilities to match.   ★Key Biscayne

In the 1840s dark-skinned incomers from the Bahamas, known as Conchs, began to settle to the south of Miami. Later the Caribbean atmosphere appealed to artists and intellectuals from New England, who came to spend the winter here. There are now numbers of exclusive shops and restaurants on Grand Avenue, in the Mayfair Shopping Center and on Cocowalk. Yachts can be moored in the Dinner Key Marina, the largest in Miami. With its tiled walkways and little coral-built houses, the old centre of Coconut Grove has a charming appearance.   ★Coconut Grove

To the south of the Rickenbacker Causeway, set in classical gardens with fountains, is the beautiful Villa Vizcaya (3251 South Miami Ave.). The mansion, in Italian Renaissance style, was built in 1912–16 as the winter residence of the wealthy harvester manufacturer James Deering. Its opulently appointed rooms now house the Dade County Art Museum, a collection of French, Spanish and Italian art, as well as a variety of furniture, tapestries and sculpture and a collection of old Baedekers. Open daily 9.30am–4.30pm.   ★Villa Vizcaya

South of Coconut Grove, on a lagoon, is the select Cable Estate, a district of luxury villas set in beautiful gardens with their own yacht moorings.   ★Cable Estate

South-west of the city centre is the suburb – now not quite so select as it originally was – of Coral Gables (pop. 47,000), laid out in Mediterranean style by George Merrick from 1926 onwards to the design of his father, with extensive parks and sports grounds.   Coral Gables
  Notable features are City Hall, the Miracle Mile, the Colonnade Building, the Venetian Pool (a swimming pool in a quarry of coral limestone) and Coral Way, with Coral Gables House (1907). A striking architectural feature is the former Biltmore Hotel, designed by George Merrick in the 1920s. The Lowe Art Museum of the University of Miami has collections of the arts and crafts of the Pueblo and Navajo Indians, American painting and old masters of the Renaissance and baroque (the Kress Collection).

South Miami

The main attractions of South Miami are the Parrot Jungle (parrots, flamingos), the Metro Zoo and the Moorish-style district of Opa Locka, built in the 1920s.

Miami Beach

From Miami five causeways and bridges cross Biscayne Bay to a narrow strip of land 10 mi. long. The small beach settlement that grew up here developed within a few decades into the largest holiday, entertainment and bathing resort in the United States.

History In 1912 this was merely a small sandy island in Biscayne Bay; then John Collins, founder of the settlement, and Carl Fisher, a millionaire who had already built the Indianapolis motor-racing track, set about developing it. In the 1920s, 30s and 40s there was a great flowering of art deco here. Nowadays Miami Beach is the playground of the rich and famous, many of them homosexual. One such was the fashion designer Gianni Versace, who was killed in front of his villa on Ocean Drive in July 1997.

★★Art Deco
District

The Art-Deco District extends from 5th Street in the south to Indian Creek in the north and between Ocean Drive/Collins Avenue and Lennox Avenue It contains several hundred buildings dating from the 1930s, in typical pastel colours. Many of the old hotels and apartment buildings have been given a new lease of life, and there are numerous inviting cafés and restaurants with coloured neon signs.

Ocean Drive is lined with handsome art-deco buildings, including "Waldorf Towers" (860 Ocean Dr.; by Albert Anis, 1937), a corner building with ornamental turrets, and the "Cardozo" (1300 Ocean Dr.; by Henry Hohauser, 1939), whose bar is never short of guests, day or night.

Bird's eye view of Miami Beach

Below Ocean Drive is a broad beach of firm white sand that is busy throughout the year.

The main traffic artery of Miami Beach is **Collins Avenue**, also known as "The Strip", which is also flanked by handsome art-deco buildings. Of special interest are the "Fairmont" (1000 Collins Ave.; by L. Murray Dixon, 1939) with its famous terrace café, and "Essex House" (1001 Collins Ave.; 1938), one of Henry Hohauser's most interesting buildings, in "nautical modern" style. Three of the largest art-deco hotels can also be seen on Collins Avenue: the "National", "Delano", and "Ritz Plaza". The streamlined structures and architectural detail are designed to recall the 20th century's revolutionary forms of transport – rockets, submarines and aircraft.

Miami Beach's principal business and shopping street is **Washington Avenue** The "George Washington Hotel" (534 Washington Ave.; by William P. Browns, 1924) was one of the first seafront hotels in Miami Beach. Also of interest are the Main Post Office (1300 Washington Ave.; by Howard L. Cheney, 1939) in federal-deco style, with a decorative rotunda, and Old City Hall (1130 Washington Ave.; by Martin Luther Hampton, 1927). Washington Avenue also has Miami Beach's most fashionable dance club, the "Bash" (No. 655).

Of all the buildings on Spanish-style **Española Way**, the "Cameo Theater" (by Robert Collins, 1938) is the most striking, whilst 21st Street is also lined with art-deco buildings, including the former luxury hotel "Plymouth" (No. 266; by Anton Skislewicz, 1940), and the adjacent Adam's Hotel (by L. Murray Dixon, 1938).

The **Bass Museum of Art** (Collins Park), built of coral limestone in 1930, is reminiscent of Maya architecture. The museum exhibits paintings by both old and modern masters, including works by Dürer and Rubens, and some Impressionists.

The Municipal Park lies almost exactly in the centre of Miami Beach, with the City Hall, the Miami Beach Garden Center & Conservatory (rare tropical plants, flower shows) and the gigantic Convention Center.

Municipal Park

Behind the Convention Center is the Holocaust Memorial, commemorating the 6 million Jews who died a violent death before and during the Second World War.

Holocaust Memorial

The dominant building complex in the northern part of Collins Avenue (No. 4441) is the Fontainbleau Hilton ("Big Blue") Hotel. Its swimming pool was featured in the James Bond film "Goldfinger".

Fontainebleau Hilton

Along the beach from 21st Street to 46th Street, a distance of some 2 mi., runs a boardwalk that is frequented from early morning until late at night by promenaders and joggers.

Beachfront Promenade

Indian Creek – frequently the setting for dramatic film chases by land and water – separates northern Miami Beach with its hotels and apartment blocks from the exclusive residential district of Alton Road.

Indian Creek

In northern Miami Beach are the Cloisters of the Monastery of Street Bernard, built in Segovia, Spain, in 1141, which were transported to America and re-erected here at the expense of the publishing magnate William Randolph Hearst (1863–1951).

The Cloisters

Michigan (State)   B–H 38–43

Area: 58,525 sq. mi.
Population: 9,594,000
Capital: Lansing
Popular names: Great Lakes
State, Wolverine State

Michigan (from the Chippewa *mica gama*, great water, a region of many lakes in the Midwest, on the frontier with Canada, is divided into an upper and a lower part by the Straits of Mackinac. Upper Michigan, between Lake Superior in the north and Lake Michigan in the south, consists of an eastern region with a good deal of marshland and a western section that is hillier and more rugged, while Lower Michigan, between Lake Michigan in the west and Lakes Huron and Erie in the east, is a gently undulating tableland. In Upper Michigan, with a moderately continental climate, temperatures in winter, with continuing north-west winds, can fall as low as 47°F. Fully half the area of the state is forested, with mixed deciduous and, in the north, coniferous forests.

History From the early 17th c. French missionaries and fur traders began to move into the territory of Michigan, then inhabited by Algonquin Indians, and in 1686 founded the first European settlement at Sault Ste Marie. The French with their Indian allies were defeated by the British in 1763, and twenty years later, under the Peace of Paris in 1783, the area passed to the United States. In 1794, after repeated bloody clashes, the Indian tribes were finally defeated. Michigan was incorporated as an independent territory in 1805, was occupied by British forces in 1812–13 and was admitted to the Union as the 26th state on January 26th 1837.

Economy Michigan's agriculture produces mainly grain, root crops and soya beans, together with considerable quantities of cattle feed and even wine. The most important element in its economy is industry, lying as it does in the "manufacturing belt" of the United States. Thanks to its convenient situation the dominant automobile industry developed in Detroit, together with various associated supply industries. The state's tourist and holiday trade is increasing in importance, thanks to its facilities for winter sports, hiking and other leisure activities. Lakes Michigan and Superior have some of the most beautiful freshwater beaches in North America.

Ann Arbor

Ann Arbor, to the west of Detroit (see entry), is the seat of the University of Michigan, founded in 1837. Features of interest on the campus are the Neo-Gothic Law Quadrangle, several museums (science, art, archaeology) and a botanic garden.

Detroit

See entry

Grand Rapids

Grand Rapids, in western Lower Michigan, was the boyhood home of Gerald Ford, 38th President of the United States. Among the exhibits in the Museum that bears his name is a model of the President's Oval Office in the White House. The Meyer May House was designed by Frank Lloyd Wright.

The little town of **Holland** sout-west of Grand Rapids, is a microcosm of the country of the same name, complete with tulip festival.

★Isle Royale National Park

The Isle Royale (area 432 sq. mi.) lies in north-western Lake Superior near the Canadian frontier. Its varied topography, shaped by Ice Age glaciers (with many lakes, streams and fjords), its dense deciduous and coniferous forests and its rich wild life (elks, wolves, foxes, otters, ospreys, herring gulls, falcons, trout) attract many visitors to this relatively unspoiled tract of country, which can be explored on waymarked hiking trails and boat trips.

The eastern shore of Lake Michigan is a holiday paradise par excellence – with bathing in summer, and a snow-covered landscape in winter. Grand Haven, in the south, has a magnificent sandy beach, Sleeping Bear Dunes are quiet and unspoilt, whilst all kinds of water sports are catered for around Grand Traverse Bay. Half of all the cherries harvested in the United States come from the area around Traverse City.

Lake Michigan Shore

The northern shore also provides plenty of opportunities for holidays by the water, in the Charlevoix region or on the Keewenaw peninsula, which projects into the lake.

However the main attraction is the narrow strip of land between Lake Huron and Lake Michigan, the Mackinac Strait, whose name is derived from the Algonquin word for "big turtle". Traffic crossing the large bridge and river traffic can best be observed from the west side of Mackinac Island. It was once of great strategic importance, and Fort Michilimackinac, a British fort built in the late 18th c., was the scene of fierce fighting between British and French forces. Fourteen buildings have been restored, and private cars are banned on the island. Ferry services operate from Street Ignace and Mackinaw City.

★Mackinac Strait

The Pictured Rocks National Seashore on the south shore of Lake Superior gets its name from the colours of copper, iron and manganese oxide. As every American child knows, this picturesque coast is the set-

★Pictured Rocks National Seashore

The Soo Locks in Sault Ste. Marie connect Lake Huron to Lake Michigan. They are among the world's largest locks and can be used by seagoing vessels

ting for the story of the young Hiawatha. Grand Island, off this shore, once provided a peaceful refuge, but has now been discovered by tourists.

★Sault Ste Marie   The main importance of the American–Canadian double town of Sault Ste Marie (known locally as the Soo) lies in the 1¼ mile long canals on the St Mary River (navigable from mid April to mid December) linking Lakes Huron and Superior – the world's most important waterway, on which 100 million tons of goods are transported annually. The ships pass through two mighty locks (the Soo Locks), one on the Canadian and the other on the American side, which can be seen on boat trips. Histroric vessels are on display in the Maritime Museum on the waterfront.

Milwaukee   F 37

State: Wisconsin
Altitude: 580 ft
Population: 610,000

The city of Milwaukee lies some 90 mi. north of Chicago (see entry) on the west side of Lake Michigan at the inflow of the Milwaukee River, which is joined within the city area by two tributaries, the Menomenee and the Kinickinnic. The town grew out of a trading post established in the 18th c. near the Indian village of Melleoki. Much of the population is of German origin, and the city has been called the German Athens of America.

German influence is still apparent in many features of the city. It was German immigrants who brought brewing to Milwaukee, which is still the beer capital of the United States. However its greatest claim to fame is as the home of Harley Davidson, the legendary motorcycle. Milwaukee has an important port, accessible all year round on the Street Lawrence Seaway.

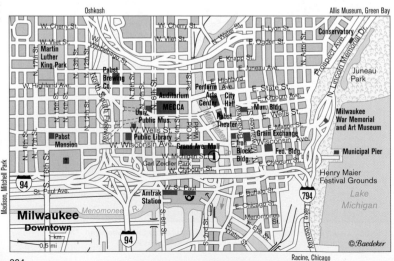

Racine, Chicago

Sights

A must for any visitor to Milwaukee is a tour round a brewery – a large one such as Miller (4251 W State St.; Mon.–Sat. 10am–3.30pm, twice hourly), or a smaller one such as the Lakefront Brewery (818 E Chambers St.) or Sprecher Brewing (701 W Glendale; open Mon.–Fri. 4pm, Sat. 1pm, 2pm and 3pm).

Breweries

The main sight on the Lakefront is the **War Memorial Center** (1957), commemorating the dead of the Second World War and the Korean War. It was designed by the celebrated architect Eero Saarinen. In the same complex is the Milwaukee Milwaukee Art Museum Art Museum (750 North Lincoln Memorial Dr.), another striking building, with collections that include American and European works from the 19th and 20th centuries.

★Lakefront

To the south of the War Memorial Center are the Municipal Pier and the **Henry Maier Festival Grounds**, where the famous SummerFest is held annually in June/July.

To the north of the War Memorial, the **Charles Allis Art Museum** (1801 N Prospect Ave.) has more American and European art from the 19th and 20th centuries, exhibited in the rooms of a Tudor-style villa built in 1911, with windows by Louis C. Tiffany.

To the west of the Lakefront is the First Wisconsin Center, the city's tallest building, erected in 1974 to the design of the famous architectural firm SOM. From the observatory on the 41st floor there are magnificent panoramic views.
  A short distance west is the Federal Court, in a venerable granite building dating from 1892.
  To the north-west is the Milwaukee Grain Exchange (Milwaukee and Madison Sts.), and the Iron Block Building, constructed from iron castings during the Civil War.

Downtown East

Further north-west, on the east bank of the Milwaukee River, is the old heart of the city, with the late 19th c. ★**City Hall** (by Armand Koch), for many years the great landmark of Milwaukee. Beyond it is another fine late 19th c. building, the ★**Pabst Theater**, built at the expense of the brewing magnate F. Pabst.

On the west bank of the Milwaukee River is the Päre Marquette Park, commemorating the French Jesuit who was the first European to reach this part of America (1674). Here too is the Milwaukee County Historical Museum.
  Beyond this, running north-south, is Old-World 3rd Street, on which the city's German immigrants left their stamp (restaurants, shops).

Downtown West

The heart of Downtown West is the **Civic Center** with the Milwaukee Exposition and Convention Center and Arena (MECCA), built in 1974, linked by covered walkways to the multi-storey Grand Avenue Mall.

To the west of the Civic Center is the ★**Public Museum**, with fascinating natural history displays of life-size dinosaurs and a reconstruction of a tropical rainforest, as well as a presentation of Milwaukee's past in the "Sts of Old Milwaukee".

Westside

Beyond I 43 is the campus of the private **Marquette University**, founded in 1864, with two notable sacred buildings, the 15th c. St Joan of Arc Chapel, transferred here from its original site in eastern France, and the Gothic-style Gesú Church, modelled on the original Gesú in Rome.

North-east of the university campus is the ★**Pabst Mansion** built in 1893 for the brewing magnate F. Pabst, a steamer captain whose interest in beer resulted from his marriage to Maria Best, a brewer's daughter. The Pabst Brewery was unfortunately forced to shut down at the end of 1996, in the face of fierce competition.

At 9400 West Congress Street is the ★**Greek Orthodox Church** of the Annunciation (1961), by Frank Lloyd Wright.

★Harley Davidson

The world-famous Harley Davidson motorcycle came into being at the corner of Highland Boulevard and 38th Street. Here in 1901 William S. Harley, Arthur and Walter Davidson and a German engineer produced the first Harley Davidson. They went into mass production in 1903, and thereafter the fame of the Harley Davidson spread round the world. The present very modern factory (Harley Davidson Engine Plant, 11700 W Capitol Dr.) on I 45 can be visited. Guided tours Mon.–Fri. 8am, 9.30am, 11am, 1pm.

★Mitchell Park Conservatory

The Mitchell Park Conservatory (524 S Layton Blvd.) in the western part of town has three gigantic glass domes containing plants from the tropics and from desert areas. To the north-west, on the outskirts of the city is Milwaukee County Zoo.

Surroundings

Old World Wisconsin

At Eagle, south-east of Milwaukee is the Old World Wisconsin open-air museum, where 65 historic buildings have been constructed, many of them showing where their inhabitants came from: Germany, Denmark, Norway and Finland.

Minneapolis/St Paul   E 32/33

State: Minnesota
Altitude: 690–98 ft
Population: Minneapolis 368,000, St Paul 272,000

Minneapolis and St Paul, the Twin Cities on the upper course of the Mississippi, together form the largest city in Minnesota, but yet are very different from one another. While the larger city of Minneapolis is the quintessence of the glistening modern American city, the more spaciously laid out St Paul, built on terraces above the Mississippi, has preserved something of the character of an old frontier town (e.g. in Summit Ave.). Features common to both cities, however, are their extensive parks and their economic importance as centres of the electronics, printing and publishing industries. Minneapolis is also the commercial centre of one of the largest farming areas in the United States and has one of the largest grain exchanges in the world.

History St Paul, the older of the two cities, originated as a military post established at the junction of the Minnesota River with the Mississippi in 1807 that later became Fort Snelling. From 1823 it became a port of call for river boats. In 1840 fur traders and trappers established a settlement nearby, originally called Pig's Eye after the leader of the group, a Frenchman, but renamed St Paul in the following year. When Minnesota was incorporated as a town St Paul was declared state capital.

A quiet spot within the hectic city, on the Milwaukee River ▶

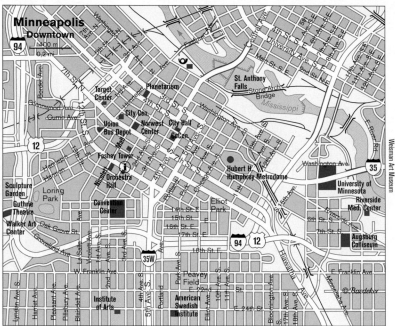

Minneapolis Downtown

Mall of America   St. Paul, Minnehaha Park

Minneapolis grew out of two mills built at the St Anthony Falls in 1847. Although this was Indian country, other settlements soon followed, and these displaced the Indians, whose reservation was moved elsewhere. The city's name comes from the Indian word minne (water) and the Greek polis (city).

Minneapolis

★Nicollet Mall

The main shopping centre in downtown Minneapolis is Nicollet Mall, a beautifully laid out precinct with a large concentration of shops, restaurants, galleries and other attractions like the Minneapolis Planetarium. The central feature of the complex, over which looms the 775 ft tower of the IDS Center, is the Crystal Court, from which a network of glazed skyways lead to other buildings. Further skyscrapers tower all around: the 57-storey Norwest Center by I.M. Pei, and next to it the new Gaviidae Common shopping mall, the 42-storey Piper Jaffray Tower (222 S 9th St.) and the Foshay Tower (821 Marquette Ave.), the oldest tower block in the city.

City Hall

To the east of Nicollet Mall is City Hall (1891). The statue in the Rotunda, "Father of the Waters", is carved from a single block of Carrara marble.

★Institute of Arts

The Institute of Arts (2300 3rd Ave. S) has a large collection of works from many countries and in many styles, including pictures by European masters (Rubens, Rembrandt).

American Swedish Institute

The American Swedish Institute on the east side of I 35 West has many different exhibits that demonstrate the importance of the surrounding region's Swedish heritage.

The Walker Art Center (Vineland Place, south-west of the city centre) is devoted to 20th c. art. Opposite it is the Sculpture Garden, the finest work in which is Claes Oldenburg's "Spoonbridge and Cherry".

Walker Art Center

There is an excellent view of the Mississippi and the 49 ft high St Anthony Falls from the walkway of the Stone Arch Bridge, a 19th c. railway bridge. Beyond the waterfalls begins the navigable stretch of the Mississippi to the Gulf of Mexico. There are also good views from the locks at Portland Avenue and Westriver Parkway.

The Mississippi

To the south-east of the city, extending along the banks of the Mississippi at the 55 ft high Minnehaha ("Laughing Water") Falls, is **Minnehaha Park**, with statues of Hiawatha and Minnehaha, the chief characters in Longfellow's "Song of Hiawatha".

The campus of the University of Minnesota lies on both banks of the Mississippi. On the east bank are the Bell Museum of Natural History and the Frederick R. Weisman Art Museum, designed by Frank Gehry, which is worth a visit for its eccentric architecture alone.

University of Minnesota

To the south of the city, near the airport, is the Mall of America, the world's largest shopping centre, opened in 1992. In addition to 400 shops, 50 restaurants and bars it includes a film centre and Camp Snoopy, the largest roofed theme park in the United States.

★Mall of America

St Paul

Among the finest of the more than 90 parks in the city of St Paul are Rice Park (W 5th and Washington Sts.) dating from 1849, the glass-roofed Town Square Park (7th and Minnesota Sts.); Como Park, with the Zoo (Midway and Lexington Parkway); and Indian Mounds Park (in the Dayton's Bluff district), in which are six pre-Columbian mounds.

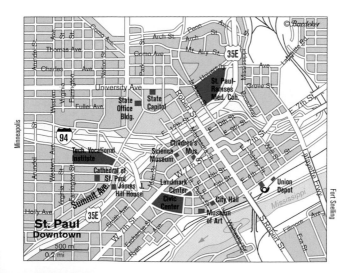

Minnesota

State Capitol

The marble dome of the State Capitol (1905) is a prominent feature of the district north-west of Downtown Minneapolis. The Minnesota History Center and Museum, a short distance to the south, are concerned with the history of the state.

★Summit Avenue

The Cathedral of St Paul, a scale version of St Peter's in Rome, dominates the eastern part of Downtown. Here Summit Avenue begins, the largest and longest collection of Victorian buildings in the United States. Close to the cathedral stands James J. Hill House, built by the founder of the Great Northern Railroad. Summit Avenue runs 3¾ mi. down to the Mississippi; from that end of the street there is an impressive view of the river valley ravine.

City Hall

In the lobby of City Hall (1932; 4th and Washaba Sts.) is a 36 ft high piece of sculpture by Carl Milles, weighing 60 tons, representing the Indian God of Peace.

Landmark Center

The Landmark Center (75 W 5th St.) is housed in the finely restored old Federal Courts Building of 1902, which now contains restaurants, galleries, function rooms and the department of contemporary American art of the Minnesota Museum of Art.

Fort Snelling

Near the airport is Fort Snelling, which recalls the frontier days of around 1820.

Minnesota (State)   A–F 29–34

Area: 84,070 sq. mi.
Population: 4,432,000
Capital: St Paul
Popular names: North Star
State, Gopher State

Minnesota (from the Sioux name, "sky-coloured water"), halfway along the northern frontier of the United States, is bounded on the north by Canada, on the north-east by Lake Superior and on the west by the Red River of the North. The Ice Age left behind in this area a gently undulating morainic landscape with more than 11,000 lakes, so that Minnesota is often compared with Finland. The highest point in the state (2228 ft) is in the Misquah Hills in the north-west; the south-west of the state is occupied by natural grass prairie. Roughly a third of its total area is occupied by forest (maples and limes in the centre, firs and spruces in the north). The state has a markedly continental climate, with winters that can be extremely severe (an annual average of 60 days of snow cover in the south and 120 days in the north).

History From the middle of the 17th c. French fur traders began to operate in the territory of present day Minnesota, which in 1763 passed into British hands. A military post was established in 1820 on the site of Fort Snelling, and this became the nucleus of the city of Minneapolis. Incorporated as an independent territory in 1849, Minnesota joined the Union as the 32nd state on May 11th 1858. Four years later the Sioux rose in arms, in protest against the American failure to observe treaties made with them, but were defeated by the superior strength of government forces.

Economy Minnesota is an important farming state. Its principal crops are oats, maize, flax, peas, soya beans and sugar beet, and dairy farming, poultry and cattle rearing also flourish. Mining is mainly for iron: roughly half the United States output of iron ore comes from Minnesota, though its reserves are gradually being exhausted. The most important branch of industry is foodstuffs, followed by engineering and tool production, electronics and papermaking. The tourist attractions of Minnesota lie in its vast forests and numerous lakes, which appeal particularly to sportsmen and walkers.

The life of Duluth, at the western tip of Lake Superior, centres on the world's largest inland port, which ocean-going vessels can reach via the St Lawrence Seaway, with the help of a lift bridge that can be raised within a minute from 155 ft to 225 ft. At the bridge is a museum on the history of shipping on Lake Superior. The old Union Railroad depot now houses a museum, with old steam locomotives and a street of shops in the style of 1910.

Duluth

From Duluth North Shore Drive (wide views) runs to **Grand Portage**, in the extreme north-eastern tip of the state, from which missionaries, fur traders and trappers used to travel on old Indian trails into the forests of Canada. The old trading post has been partly reconstructed. From Grand Portage there is a ferry to the Isle Royale National Park in Michigan.

Chippewa National Forest, central North Minnesota, is an area with many lakes, the largest being Lake Leech, which has more than 4,500 members of the Minnesota Chippewa tribe living along its shores.

Chippewa National Forest

Itasca State Park, 30 mi. west of Chippewa National Forest, has a small stream that is believed to be the origin of the Mississippi.

Itasca State Park

Between Chippewa and Superior National Forest lies Hibbing, the centre of the Iron Range mining district. It has three claims to fame: it has the world's largest opencast iron-ore workings, the Hull Rust Mahoning Mine, which is open to the public; its local bus company gave rise to the Greyhound bus system; and it was the birthplace of Bob Dylan. The neighbouring town of Chisholm has the Ironworld theme park.

Hibbing

The "thousand lakes" were once the heartland of the Dakota Indians. Their history is related in the Mille Lacs Indian Museum.

Mille Lacs

See entry

Minneapolis-St Paul

The Pipestone National Monument owes its name to the soft reddish stone from which the Indians make their ceremonial pipes. Each tribe has access to this sacred site, where peace must prevail; and even today only Indians are allowed to quarry the stone (an aluminium silicate, known as catlinite after the pioneer and painter of Indian life George Catlin). Examples of Indian pipes can be seen in the Upper Midwest Indian Cultural Center.

Pipestone National Monument

Rochester is the seat of the celebrated Mayo Clinic, famed particularly for its heart operations. There are guided visits on weekdays.

Rochester

Superior National Forest covers large areas of north-east Minnesota. The town of Ely, where the International Wolf Center tells all there is to know about this grey predator, is an excellent base from which to explore the unspoilt lake landscape. The Bounded Waters Canoe Area Wilderness provides the best facilities for canoeing.

Superior National Forest

The Voyageurs National Park Visitor Center is also situated in Ely. The park, in the far north-west of Minnesota on the Canadian frontier, is a beautiful forest region with more than 30 lakes dotted with over 900 little

★Voyageurs National Park

islands, offering magnificent opportunities for canoeing and fishing. It takes its name from the French voyageurs who explored the area in their canoes in the 18th c.

Mississippi (State)   P–T 34–37

Area: 47,690 sq. mi.
Population: 2,600,000
Capital: Jackson
Popular name: Magnolia State

The southern state of Mississippi (from the Indian maesi, "broad", and sipu, "river") is bounded on the west by the riverine meadowland of the Mississippi, which here fol-
lows a winding course, and on the south by the Gulf of Mexico. From the terraced Gulf Coast plain to the gently undulating uplands in the interior the land rises only to 820 ft. The humid subtropical climate, with occasional extreme temperature fluctuations, fosters a long growing period that produces pine forests in the south-east and mixed deciduous forests (oak, hickory, cypress) in the north-east and west.

History The first journey of exploration along the Mississippi was carried out in 1540 by a Spaniard, Hernando de Soto. After the Sieur de la Salle had mapped the river from Illinois to its mouth in 1682 and claimed the area for France the first settlers established themselves near present-day Biloxi in 1699. Thereafter the territory was divided between Spain and Britain, until in 1795 it was taken over by the United States. At first combined with Alabama in a single territory, Mississippi was made an independent territory and on December 10th 1817 was admitted to the Union as the 20th state. Thanks to the use of slave labour in the cotton fields the state prospered. At the beginning of the Civil War Mississippi joined the Confederation, and a number of bloody battles were fought on its soil, in particularly the siege of Vicksburg. In the present century Mississippi stood out against equal rights for all races well into the 1960s.

Economy Cotton is still the characteristic crop of this state, situated as it is in the Cotton Belt. It is no longer a monoculture, however, and other crops such as maize, soya, wheat and rice are grown alongside cotton. The coastal waters are well stocked with fish and yield rich catches. Mississippi's mineral resources include particularly natural gas round Jackson and oil in the south of the state. The principal industries are foodstuffs, textiles, papermaking and furniture manufacture.

★Biloxi

Biloxi, the chief place on the Gulf coast of Mississippi, is the state's oldest town, founded by the French in 1699. Features of interest are the Lighthouse (1849), the harbour (prawn fishing, pleasure craft) and, 5 mi. west, Beauvoir Mansion, where Jefferson Davis, President of the Confederation, spent the last twelve years of his life.
   The coast and offshore islands and sandbanks are nature reserves with a rich diversity of flora and fauna. They also have excellent bathing beaches, for example, Ocean Springs. There are boat trips from Biloxi to some of the islands.

Clarksdale

Clarksdale, home of the Delta blues, produced musicians such as John Lee Hooker, Robert Johnson and Howlin Wolf, mementoes of whom, and of many others, can be seen in the Delta Blues Museum.

Jackson (named after Andrew Jackson, 1767–1845, seventh President of the United States), capital of Mississippi, is the economic centre and transport hub of the surrounding area with its oilfields. Here in 1861 the Southern states resolved on secession from the Union. Features of interest are the State Historical Museum in the old Capitol.

The little town of Natchez in south-western Mississippi, founded in 1716, was the most important port on the Mississippi in the heyday of the cotton trade, and many handsome mansions and estates, mostly in Greek Revival style, bear witness to the wealth of those days. Among them are the House on Ellicot Hills (1798); Rosalie (1820–3), beautifully situated on high ground above the Mississippi; Stanton Hall (1851–7), with a large ballroom; Magnolia Hall, now housing a museum of fashion and costume; and Longwood, a very large house that was never fully completed.

Natchez Trace Parkway is a tourist road following the line of the Natchez Trace, an old route from Natchez to Nashville, Tennessee (see entry), which is first mentioned in 1733. It was at its busiest between 1800 and 1820, when the crews of boats that had sailed down the Mississippi to Natchez returned home on foot or horseback. The Parkway runs past Emerald Mound (12 mi. north of Natchez), the second largest pre-Columbian site in the United States, which was occupied between 1250 and 1600 by the Mississippi people, ancestors of the Natchez and Choctaws.

Springfield Plantation (1786–90), north of Natchez, believed to have been the first in Mississippi, has been preserved almost unchanged. Andrew Jackson was married in the house.

Tupelo's most famous son was Elvis Presley (see Famous People), and

A room with a view on the Mississippi is what you can expect in the "Rosalie" in Natchez

333

his birthplace is its great tourist attraction. 23 mi. from the little town is Brice's Crossroads, where a Confederate army defeated a larger Union force in 1864.

Vicksburg

During the Civil War Vicksburg, part of which lies just above the Mississippi, was a thorn in the flesh of the Union forces, since from there the Confederates controlled shipping on the river. After several unsuccessful attempts to take the town Union troops commanded by General Grant finally captured it in 1863 after a 47-day siege; its fall was one of the bitterest defeats of the Confederates. These events are commemorated in the Vicksburg National Military Park and Cemetery, with the Union gunboat "Cairo" which sank in 1862, and in a museum in the Old Court House. Other features of interest in the town are a number of handsome antebellum houses and the Biedenham Candy Company and Museum of Coca Cola Memorabilia, a restored candy shop where the famous brew was first bottled in 1894.

Port Gibson

28 mi. south of Vicksburg in Port Gibson, thought by General Grant to be almost as beautiful as Natchez, which explains why it has remained relatively unspoilt and still has some lovely pre-war houses. "Windsor", south of the town, was not so lucky – all that remains of that mansion are some impressive ruins.

Missouri (State)   J–N 30–36

Area: 69,695 sq. mi.
Population: 5,158,000
Capital: Jackson City
Popular name: Show Me State

The state of Missouri (from the Indian name "place of the big canoes"), in the central Midwest, is divided by the Missouri River into a northern and a larger southern part. Southern Missouri is occupied by the rolling Ozark Plateau, which is broken up by deep, narrow gorges. The northern part of the state lies in the Central Lowlands, a fertile morainic region covered with loess; the state is bounded on the east by the Mississippi plain, while in the west grass prairie predominates. The climate is warm in summer; there are frequent tornadoes, particularly in the summer months.

History The territory was occupied by Osage Indians when French settlers arrived in the 18th c., founding Ste Genevieve in 1735 and St Louis in 1764. Originally part of the French colony of Louisiana and from 1763 Spanish, the area passed to the United States in 1803 (the Louisiana Purchase). After separating from Arkansas in 1819 Missouri was admitted to the Union on August 10th 1821 as the 24th state. In subsequent decades the state was an area of passage for settlers travelling to the West, and St Louis became the "Gateway to the West". The Civil War threatened to split the state; but although Missouri was a slave-owning state it did not join the Confederates.

Economy The main crops grown on the productive loess and clay soils of the plains are maize, rice, cotton and soya beans. Cattle rearing and, particularly in the Ozark Mountains, sheep farming play an important part in the economy. Missouri is the largest producer of lead in the United States. In the two industrial centres of Kansas City and St Louis the principal activities are the aircraft and space industries, automobile construction, engineering and metalworking.

Branson, in south-west Missouri, with no false modesty, calls itself "Live country music capital of the universe". The "Strip" is crowded with music palaces, where country music greats perform, souvenir booths selling all imaginable kinds of kitsch, motels and restaurants. However, there is not a gambling den to be found, and the cinemas run sterile family films and pithy westerns. Every year six million Americans, most of them pensioners in buses, descend on this town of only 4,000 souls. Branson is the epitome of squeaky-clean American culture, even though its most popular entertainer comes from Japan.

Branson

However Branson is also a good base for excursions into the wild and romantic ★**lake district** in south-western Missouri, on the border with Arkansas. Features of particular interest are the dam that has formed Table Rock Lake and the Silver Dollar theme park.

Before visiting Hannibal, a small town on the Mississippi, you should read "Tom Sawyer", for it was here that Mark Twain (see Famous People) grew up. Here you will find his boyhood home (now a museum), Becky Thatcher's house, Mark Twain's father's law office and many other places that feature in the novel.

Hannibal

This park south-east of Kansas City (see entry) is a popular recreation area. One of the chief places in the park is Osage Beach.

★**Ozarks State Park**

Liberty, north of Kansas City, was the scene of the first bank robbery by Jesse James (see Famous People), who was born in nearby Kearney; the bank is now the Jesse James Museum.

Liberty

Jesse James's life came to an end in St Joseph in north-western Missouri, and in his house (12th and Penn Sts.) it is still possible to see the hole in the wall made by his killer's bullet. The town also has another claim to fame; it was from here that the first Pony Express rider set out in April 1860 to carry mail to Sacramento, almost 2000 mi. away in California. The invention of telegraphy put an end to the Pony Express only a year later. Its story is related in the Pony Express Museum and in the Patee House Museum, its old headquarters.

St Joseph

Kansas City, St Louis (see entries)

Other places of interest

Montana (State)   A–E 8–21

Area: 139,415 sq. mi.
Population: 808,000
Capital: Helena
Popular name: Treasure State

Montana (in Spanish "mountainous") lies in the north-western United States, bounded on the north by Canada. The western third of the state is traversed by the Rocky Mountains, which here reach heights of up to 12,800 ft. The eastern part, in the Great Plains, is a gently undulating plateau rising to a height of 5000 ft, deeply slashed by the upper Missouri and the Yellowstone River. Montana lies in a region of dry continental climate and is particularly arid to the east of the Rockies. The Rocky Mountains are covered by forests that are home to elk, mule deer, grizzlies and brown bears, while in the short grassland of the Great Plains herds of pronghorn antelopes and occasionally bison can still be seen.

Montana

History Around the middle of the 18th c. the first trappers and fur traders came into this area, until then inhabited exclusively by Indians, including Gros Ventre and Blackfeet. Lewis and Clark passed through this inhospitable upland world in 1805. Permanent settlements were established only in 1862, after the discovery of gold, and two years later the United States territory of Montana was formed. After the discovery of other minerals (silver, copper) there was a further wave of settlement from 1875 onwards, but the taking of Indian land by the incomers led to bitter fighting with the Sioux and Cheyennes. In the battle of the Little Bighorn the United States army commanded by Custer suffered its worst defeat. On November 8th 1889 Montana joined the Union as the 41st state.

The **economy** of Montana is centred on agriculture: cattle and sheep in the Rockies, arable farming on the prairies. The principal crops are lucerne, sugar beet, maize, beans and vegetables. The main minerals worked in the state are copper, zinc, silver, gold, nickel, platinum, phosphates and oil. The predominant industries are ore smelting, foodstuffs and woodworking. The tourist and holiday trade is of great economic importance, for the excellent conditions that Montana can offer for winter sports, fishing, hiking, cycling, bathing in warm springs and canoeing attract large numbers of visitors to this "Big Sky Country".

Nez Perce National Historical Park

South of Chinook, near the Canadian frontier, the flight of the Nez Perce Indians, led from Idaho by Chief Joseph, ended in 1877. After a six-day battle with government forces the Indians surrendered – marking the end of Indian resistance in Montana.

Billings

Montana's largest town, Billings, lies in the south, and is a good base for visits to the ★**Little Bighorn** battle field and the Crow Indian Reservation, where the five-day Crow Fair is held every year in August.

Here, in the Crow Reservation, the United States Army suffered its greatest defeat at the hands of the Sioux and Cheyennes. On June 25th 1876 a detachment of the 7th United States Cavalry commanded by George Armstrong Custer attacked a larger Indian force led by Crazy Horse and was annihilated. On the battlefied are a museum, a military cemetery and a monument commemorating Custer's last stand, erected on the spot where he fell.

Bozeman

The town of Bozeman, in the south of the state, owes its name to John M. Bozeman, who established a trail from Wyoming to here through Indian country and thus incurred the continuing hostility of the Oglala Indians under their chief Red Cloud (see Famous People). The main attraction of Bozeman is the Museum of the Rockies, with its unique dinosaur remains, including the largest skeleton ever found of a Tyrannosaurus Rex.

Butte

100 years ago Butte, south-west of Helena, was known as the "richest hill in the world", for the town lay in the centre of an immensely productive silver, copper and gold-mining area. The great days of the gold-diggers of Butte are recalled by the Mineral Museum and the World Museum of Mining, whilst the Towe Ford Museum has more than 100 Ford motor cars.

Glacier National Park

See Waterton-Glacier National Park

Great Falls

The famous painter of the Wild West, Charles M. Russell, lived and worked in Great Falls, north-east of Helena. His works, displayed in a museum devoted to him, are classics of their kind. The museum also displays his collection of Indian art and everyday objects.

Helena

Montana's capital, Helena, situated in the centre of the western half of the state, was originally known as Last Chance, for a party of disheartened gold-diggers decided to have one final dig here and struck gold – a seam that produced 20 million dollars' worth. In the State Capitol is one of Charles M. Russell's major works, a large mural showing Lewis and Clarke meeting the Flathead Indians. The Montana Historical Society Museums exhibits Indian artefacts and objects relating to the Wild West.

Bisons, antelopes, elks and other animals can be observed from signposted roads in this reserve, north of Missoula in the Flathead Reservation. As a complete contrast, the Miracle of America Museum in Polson, further to the north, has an astonishing collection of pure American kitsch.

★National Bison Range

West Yellowstone at the south-western tip of Montana is the westernmost entrance to Yellowstone National Park (see entry) that is mostly situated in Wyoming.

Yellowstone National Park

Monterey   N 4

State: California
Altitude: sea level
Population: 32,000

The town of Monterey lies at the south end of Monterey Bay, 125 mi. south of San Francisco (see entry). It was founded in 1770, when there was a Spanish military post here. From 1775 to 1822 Monterey was the chief town of the southern part, then in the Spanish sphere of influence, of what is now California, and for a further 24 years it was capital of the Mexican province of Alta California. In 1846 it was occupied by American forces. During the 1930s, when the sardine fishers were bringing in large catches and the fish-canning industry was flourishing, the town enjoyed a considerable economic boom. This period was described by John Steinbeck in his novel "Cannery Row".

The town's main source of income is now the tourist trade in and around Cannery Row.

Sights

Monterey's main sight is Cannery Row (made famous by the work of John Steinbeck), on which until the 1940s was the greatest concentration of fish canning factories in the world. Some of the canneries have been carefully restored and now house boutiques, souvenir shops, craft shops, galleries and a variety of restaurants and cafés.

Cannery Row

At 886 Cannery Row is the very interesting Monterey Bay Aquarium, with tanks showing the marine flora and fauna of Monterey Bay and excellent explanatory displays. The biggest aquarium window in the world provides an unimpeded view into a gigantic tank – and an underwater world inhabited by shark, ray and turtles. Open daily 10am–6pm.

★★Monterey Bay Aquarium

The Monterey State Historic Park contains a number of well restored historic buildings, including the Custom House Plaza, California's oldest theatre.

Monterey State Historic Park

Fishermen's Wharf is now a great tourist attraction, with numerous fish restaurants and souvenir shops. You may be lucky enough to see sea otters or even sealions gambolling in the bay.

Fishermen's Wharf

A rich man's world: Hearst Castle

Surroundings

★17 Mile Drive

A beautifully engineered tollroad opens up the magnificent scenery of the Monterey peninsula, between Pacific Grove and Carmel. It runs through the Del Monte Forest, passes Pacific Grove (pop. 20,000; Natural History Museum), the Seal Rocks and Cypress Point with its ancient cypresses and finally skirts the world-famous golf course on the equally famous Pebble Beach. Cyclists do not pay the toll, and have more fun.

Carmel

A short distance further on is the beautifully situated former mission station of Carmel, founded by Junípero Serra (whose tomb is in the basilica). Carmel is now an exclusive residential resort. However Carmel is chiefly famous for having had Hollywood star Clint Eastwood as its mayor.

★Big Sur

From Carmel to 15 mi. before San Simeon extends Big Sur, a rugged stretch of the Pacific coast that is of breathtaking beauty. Highway 1 follows a winding course through the hilly coastal scenery, affording magnificent views. There are three inviting State Parks along the route (Andrew Molera SP, Julia Pfeiffer Burns SP, Pfeiffer-Big Sur SP).

The town of Big Sur lies 33 mi. south of Monterey on the river of the same name. In the past it was a sleepy hamlet but since the end of the Second World War it has grown at a tremendous rate, thanks to its beautiful setting and to the prominent figures (including Henry Miller) who have made it their home.

Hearst Castle

About two hours' drive (100 mi. on the CA 1) to the south of Carmel, at San Simeon, is Hearst Castle, the former residence of newspaper publisher William Randolph Hearst (1863–1951) and the largest mansion ever to have been built by a private individual. A tour of the 100-room castle will explain how Hearst managed to spend an estimated $30 million on a hotchpotch of European architectural styles and a collection of genuine antiques that say more about his immense wealth than his personal taste.

★★Monument Valley   M/N 15/16

States: Arizona, Utah
Area: 46 sq. mi.

Monument Valley, in the north of the Navajo Indian Reservation (see Navajo Inidian Reservation), is one of the most remarkable landscapes in the United States. Since 1960 it has been statutorily protected as the Navajo Tribal Park and is managed by Indians. Out of a great expanse of steppe and desert extraordinary sandstone formations rear up to heights of 1100–2000 ft huge monoliths, pinnacles, sculptured buttes, high mesas, rock arches. The play of colour, ranging from salmon pink to purple, is at its finest in the early morning and at sunset.

Numerous Westerns have been filmed in Monument Valley, including "Stagecoach" (with John Wayne), "Fort Apache" and "The Black Falcon". It was also the setting of the Walt Disney nature film "The Living Desert".

Information Monument Valley is accessible throughout the year, but the best times for a visit are spring and autumn, since the summers are very hot and subject to thunderstorms in the afternoon. The Visitor Center lies bejond the US 163 south-west of Mexican Hat (UT)or north-east of Kayenta (AZ). Overnight accommodation is available there and on the campsite at the Visitor Center.

Monument Valley

The **origins** of Monument Valley go back some 70 million years to a time when the area was covered by a Mesozoic extension of the Gulf of Mexico. Following a gradual rise in the level of the land the water receded, leaving an extensive plain with numerous faults and clefts that were then subject to erosion.

Sightseeing Visitors can drive round the park in their own cars on Valley Drive, a 17 mi. long unsurfaced road, starting from the Visitor Center. Alternatively there are guided tours starting from Gouldings Trading Post, Kayenta (in all-terrain vehicles on the more rugged roads, also sightseeing flights) and from the Visitor Center. Recently introduced tours also take in the Navajo settlements.

Navajo National Monument

The Navajo National Monument (150 mi. north-east of Flagstaff, Arizona) consists of three separate 13th c. cliff dwellings, some of them accessible only on foot or horseback: Betatakin, constructed around 1200; Keet Seel, the largest and best preserved, built between 1274 and 1286 under a rock overhang; and Inscription House, the smallest of the three.

★Mount Rainier National Park   C 4

State: Washington
Area: 368 sq. mi.
Established: 1899

Mount Rainier (14,410 ft), also known as Mount Tacoma, in the south-west of Washington state, is one of a geologically recent chain of volcanoes in the Cascade Mountains that in the last few years have made news with spectacular eruptions. The volcano grew in size from the late Tertiary period onwards, the crater becoming ever larger. Over the last 2000 years it has been highly active. Its last major eruption was in the 19th c., but the clouds of vapour that still rise from the crater are a reminder that the volcano is not yet quiescent. From the fields of Névé in the summit region over two dozen glacier tongues reach down on all sides. On Mount Rainier is the largest mass of ice on any mountain in the United States outside Alaska. This is ideal territory for mountaineers and ice climbers.

Information The park is accessible throughout the year, but many roads and tracks are closed in winter. The best time for a visit is summer, when the rich mountain flora is in flower.

The park facilities, four Visitor Centers and fine campsites, tend to be overcrowded on summer weekends; it is quieter midweek. The volcanic massif is often shrouded in cloud for days on end, but on clear days is a landmark visible from many miles away (see Practical Information, National Parks).

Flora and fauna Mount Rainier has a wide variety of flora, ranging from Douglas firs, hemlocks, Sitka spruces and ancient arbor vitae to modest anemones and heath plants. Red deer and roe-deer, marmots and mountain goats are frequently to be seen, and occasionally even bears and cougars.

★The road to Paradise

The busiest road in the National Park is the winding mountain road from the Nisqually entrance (2000 ft), which runs through beautiful forest country by way of Kautz Creek to Longmire (2765 ft; mineral springs; National Park administration) and up to Paradise (5400 ft; winter sports facilities). From here there is a choice of memorable hikes (e.g. to the foot of the Nisqually Glacier).

Mount Rainier rising out of the mist

The eastern part of the National Park can be explored on the WA 123 that runs through magnificent scenery from the south-east entrance to the park to the Ohanapecosh Visitor Center (1915 ft) and on to Stevens Canyon, a typical glaciated valley with spectacular waterfalls. From there a short side trip (on foot) can be made to the Grove of the Patriarchs with its giant trees hundreds of years old. From Stevens Canyon the road climbs northward to the Cayuse Pass (4695 ft), where the WA 123 runs into the Mather Memorial Parkway (WA 410). From here the Parkway continues north to Tacoma and Seattle (see entry).

Eastern part

From the White River entrance (3470 ft), on the Parkway, a road affording wide views runs up to Sunrise (6400 ft), from which in good weather sunrises of breathtaking beauty can be observed.

★Sunrise

The 95 mi. long Wonderland Trail runs round Mount Rainier through magnificent scenery with numerous fine viewpoints. As the trail is very demanding, walkers must first obtain permission from the park administration (see Practical Information, National Parks).

★Wonderland Trail

★Napa Valley/Sonoma Valley   L 3

State: California

An hour's drive north of San Francisco (see entry) is the Napa Valley, California's most famous wine-growing valley, and Sonoma Valley, which produces the best wine in the United States.

Viniculture The first wine grapes in this climatically favoured valley were grown by George Yount in 1836. In course of time other wine makers came to the area, mainly from Germany and Italy, and laid out ever increasing areas of vineyards. However it was not until the early 1970s that wine became economically important, and when a vintage Stag's Leap beat a Château Lafitte-Rothschild at a blind tasting in Paris in 1976, Californian wine was literally on everyone's lips.

Napa Valley

The most important places in the 31 mi. Napa River valley are Napa, in the south and St Helena and Calistoga in the north. Here there are more than 250 wine producers, most of them situated along the CA 29, which attract millions of tourists every year with their programmes of guided visits and wine tastings. The most famous vineyards include Beringer Vineyards (2000 Maine St.) in St Helena, the Robert Mondavi Vineyards (7801 Rte. 29) in Oakville, the Domaine Chandon (1 California Dr.) in Yountville and the Stag's Leap Wine Cellars (5766 Silverado Trail) in Napa.

St Helena

Features of interest in St Helena are the Napa Valley Wine Museum and the Silverado Museum, which is devoted to Robert Louis Stevenson (author of "The Silverado Squatters" as well as other better known books).

Old Faithful of California

At Calistoga is the "Old Faithful of California", a geyser that shoots a column of hot water into the air at regular intervals. Nearby are a number of mineral springs and remains of a petrified forest.

Marine World Africa USA

This theme park south of Napa in Vallejo may have nothing to do with wine, but it attracts masses of visitors.

Sonoma Valley

To the west of the Napa Valley is the Sonoma Valley, that is also famed for its wine. The chief place in the valley is the little town of Sonoma, founded in the 19th c. as the last Franciscan mission station in California. Viticulture was introduced by a variety of winemakers from Germany, France, Hungary and Italy, and the wines produced here are perhaps the best in the United States. The best-known wineries, which are open to the public, include the Sebastiani Winery (389 E 4th St.) and the Buena Vista Winery (18000 Old Winery Rd.), which was established in 1832.

Jack London State Park

North-west of Sonoma, at Glen Ellen, is a ranch that belonged to the writer Jack London (1876–1916; "The Call of the Wild", "The Sea Wolf"), who lived here from 1904 until his death. The ranch is now a museum.

★Nashville   N 39

State: Tennessee
Altitude: 440 ft
Population: 488,400

Nashville, capital of Tennessee, is situated almost in the centre of the state on the Cumberland River. With its 16 universities and colleges and its reproduction of the Parthenon, it is known as the "Athens of the South". Founded in 1779, Nashville is one of the most important banking and insurance centres in the southern United States, but it is perhaps better known as the capital of country music, which is heard nationwide in the Grand Ole Opry, a long-running radio programme, as well as in countless bars in the city (many of them no more than tourist traps).

Sights

In the centre of the city is the **State Capitol** (1845–59). Its architect, William Strickland, did not live to see its completion; his tomb is in the building. Facing the Capitol on the south is the Tennessee State Museum (history and natural history of Tennessee). The Museum of Tobacco Art and History (800 Harrison St.) is both informative and entertaining. In addition to tracing the history of this ancient American product it displays a large collection of pipes, tobacco tins, advertising material.

Downtown

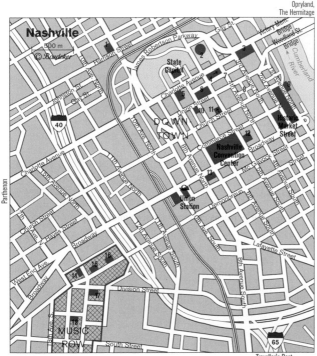

DOWNTOWN

1 Museum of Tobacco Art & History
2 Municipal Auditorium
3 Davidson Country Courthouse
4 St Mary's Church
5 War Memorial Building
6 Tennessee State Museum
7 Men's Quarter
8 Printers Alley
9 Fort Nashboro
10 Hermitage Hotel

11 Downtown
Presbyterian Church
12 Ryman Auditorium
13 Customs House

MUSIC ROW

14 Country Music Wax Museum
15 Car Collectors Hall of Fame
16 Hank Williams Jr. Museum
17 Country Music Hall of Fame
18 RCA Records Studio B

343

On the banks of the Cumberland River is a reconstruction of **Fort Nashborough**, the original nucleus of the city, established by pioneers in 1779.

At 116 5th Avenue N is the ★**Ryman Auditorium**, in which the Grand Ole Opry show was performed from 1943 to 1974, which is now a museum.

The area round ★**Music Square**, in southwestern downtown Nashville, is the heart of the music industry. Apart from souvenir shops and museums devoted to musicians of greater or **Country Music Hall of Fame** lesser fame the main sight is the Country Music Hall of Fame, which commemorates the greats of the music business and displays memorabilia of famous singers. There are also guided tours of the historic RCA Studio B in which many a hit first made its mark. The limousines of the great ones, including Elvis Presley's Cadillac, can be seen in the nearby Car Collectors Hall of Fame (1534 Demonbreun St.), whilst the Hank Williams Jr. Museum is dedicated to one of the greatest performers of country music.

★Opryland

North-east of the city (I 40 and Briley Pkwy.) a gigantic new leisure centre, known as Opry Mill, is under construction and is expected to open in 2000. Opry Mill is presented as comprising a theme park, an enormous hotel, more than 200 shops and restaurants and the Cumberland Landing Area. However, its heart remains the Grand Ole Opry. Anyone who loves country music should come here on Friday or Saturday evening (even during the construction work), when the Grand Old Opry radio programme, which has been running since 1925, is transmitted from the park's 4500-seat theatre; for ticket reservations: tel. (615) 8893060.

Parthenon

In the Centennial Park, southwest of the city centre (West End Ave. and 25th Ave. N), is the famous reproduction of the Parthenon, originally

A concert in the Grand Ole Opry is every country music lover's dream

built in wood in 1897 to commemorate the centenary of the state of
Tennessee and later rebuilt in cement on the same site.

To the south of the park is the Belmont Mansion (1900 Belmont Blvd.),
built in the 1850s. One of the finest houses of its kind in the United
States, it has thirteen rooms preserving much of their original decoration and furnishings.

Belmont Mansion

The Belle Meade Plantation (southwest of the city centre at Harding Rd.),
built in 1853, is another handsome old Southern mansion, set in one of
the finest plantations in Tennessee.

★ Belle Meade
Plantation

To the east of Nashville by way of I 40 and Old Hickory Boulevard is
Hermitage, the home of Andrew Jackson (1767–1845), seventh
President of the United States. In the park surrounding the house (originally built 1819, rebuilt in 1834 after a fire) are the graves of Jackson
and his wife.

Hermitage

Surroundings

15 mi. north of Nashville on I 65 is Millersville, with the Museum of
Beverage Containers and Advertising, which claims to have the largest
collection of drink cans (36,000 items, mainly beer), together with a large
collection of advertising material.

Millersville

★★Navajo Indian Reservation   N/O 14–16

States: Arizona, New Mexico, Utah
Area: 24,980 sq. mi.

The Navajo Indian Reservation (Navajo Country), established in 1868, is
the largest Indian reservation in the United States. Lying for the most
part in Arizona, it is bounded on the west by the Colorado River (see
Grand Canyon) and on the north by Lake Powell, a long artificial lake
formed in a canyon, and the San Juan River; the boundaries on the east
and south are ruler straight. Much of the central part of the territory,
roughly half of which is barren and infertile, is a desertic tableland
slashed by canyons. To the east, striking north–south, are the Chuska
Mountains, with Pastora Peak (9413 ft to the north-east is the Ute
Mountain Indian Reservation in Colorado; and to the south-west is the
Hopi Indian Reservation, which has an area of some 560 sq. mi.. The
most interesting parts of Navajo Country, both scenically and culturally,
are organised and protected as Tribal Parks or National Monuments.
The largest settlements in the reservation are Window Rock (Navajo),
the Indian-run administrative centre of the reservation, and Hotevilla
(Hopi).

Conduct A visit to the reservation leads into a different world, fascinating and anything but backward, not withstanding the need to
observe a few rules. It is forbidden to take photographs of people or
places without permission, and cameras, video recorders and tape
recorders must not be used at religious ceremonies. On all Indian
reserves there is an absolute ban on alcohol that is enforced by the
tribal police. The reason for the ban is that the Indians lack a particular enzyme that breaks down alcohol and facilitates its absorp-
tion in the body, and in consequence alcohol has a much more
powerful effect on them. Visitors must of course themselves observe
the ban.

Navajo nation

History The Navajo or Navaho, who call themselves the Diné ("people of the earth"), are the largest of the Indian tribes of the United States, with some 200,000 members. Around the middle of the 16th c. the Navajo, then semi-nomadic, ranged over North America from northwestern Canada to the south-western United States, where they came in contact with the local Pueblo Indians. From them the Navajo learned weaving and, on a modest scale, farming (maize, pulses). The Spaniards introduced them to the use of tools and firearms and to horses, cattle, sheep and goats, and they then took to livestock rearing (mostly sheep). They put up a fierce resistance to the advance of the whites into their territory, but in 1864, under their chief Manuelito, were compelled to acknowledge defeat after Kit Carson and his forces, avoiding open battle, burned their pastureland, crops and dwellings. The survivors were then forced to undertake a 300 mile trek to Bosque Redondo, by Fort Sumner in New Mexico, on which many died. There the Navajo, now reduced to only 8000, were held prisoner for four years in appalling conditions, after which they were allowed to return to the area of the present reservation on condition that they gave up all resistance to the presence of the whites.

Present day The Navajo now live mainly by cattle rearing and the sale of craft objects. The mineral resources of the reservation (coal, uranium) are still mainly worked by whites, the Indians having been bought off with derisory sums. There is little in the way of industry, and the unemployment rate is high. Many of the Navajo, who are reserved but not unfriendly, live in "hogans" – windowless huts of wood, brushwood and clay – and stick to their traditional social structure and beliefs. The reservation is run by a 74 member tribal council based in Window Rock. It has some schools, and in Many Farms is the Navajo Community College, established in 1969.

Navajo **art** of the early period is represented mainly by pottery vessels and pipe bowls. The Navajo learned their craft skills from the Spaniards and the Pueblo Indians, achieving a great cultural flowering in the 19th c. The weaving techniques of the Pueblo Indians, which were practised by men, were imitated by Navajo women. Their favourite products were the patterned blankets that were used for clothing, bed covers, hogan doors or wall decoration. The abstract geometric patterns, rarely repeated, which gave expression in allegorical form to themes from tribal history or the conflict with the whites, consisted originally of plain horizontal stripes (the "chief" pattern), later supplemented by squares, lozenges and zigzag lines (the "eye-dazzler" pattern). The colours (predominantly shades of brown) were obtained by dyes made from plants. When European yarns and synthetic dyes were introduced in the later 19th c. the traditional artistic elements were increasingly abandoned, the weave became looser, the colours brighter, the patterns more standardised, abstract patterns being replaced by representational designs. Textiles imitating the Indian blankets were now manufactured commercially by whites and sold widely throughout the United States. In addition to weaving the Navajo produce attractive silver jewellery inlaid with precious and semi-precious stones (mainly turquoise). Like the Hopi, they practise the ritual art of sand painting.

Customs Apart from rock drawings no written material survives from the early days of the Navajo, but over a thousand Indian legends and hundreds of prescriptions for ceremonies have been handed down orally and in more recent times recorded in writing or on tape. Among traditional rituals is the sacred sun dance, which was prohibited for many years by the United States authorities.

In Window Rock, the main town in the Reservation, the Navajo Tribal Museum relates the history of the tribe.

Window Rock

At Ganado, 50 mi. west of Window Rock, is the Hubbell Trading Post, established by John Lorenzo Hubbell in the late 1870s. The present establishment, which dates from 1885, has an interesting interior and displays an ethnological collection; Indian souvenirs are also sold here.

Hubbell Trading Post

The Canyon de Chelly (pronounced de Shay) National Monument, 100 mi. north-west of Gallup, New Mexico, is notable for its series of steep canyons up to 1000 ft deep. In the main canyon are Spider Rock, the most striking rock foundation, and the White House (constructed ca. 1050, discovered in 1849), the best known of over a hundred cliff dwellings, mostly in inaccessible situations, which were occupied from around AD 350 to 1300. Other cliff dwellings are the Antelope House and Mummy Cave (in which mummies were found) in the Canyon del Muerto. In 1864 the Navajo entrenched themselves in the canyons, and the tall cliff known as the Navajo Fortress, the last stronghold against the attacks of Kit Carson's men, in which more than 300 Navajo were besieged and starved out, is a sacred place that may not be entered by whites. There is an informative archaeological museum in the Visitor Center, and there are various guided tours and walks. The only trail open to visitors without a guide is the 2½ mile long White House Trail. The most beautiful viewing points can be reached by car on the North Rim Drive or the South Rim Drive.

★Canyon de Chelly

Hopi Reservation

The Hopi (the Indian term is Moki, the "peaceable people"), numbering only about 6000, belong to the group of sedentary Pueblo Indians (Shoshones) and are totally different from the Navajo, within whose territory their small reservation lies. As village dwelling tillers of the soil and cattle rearers the Hopi inevitably came into conflict with the Navajo, ever looking for new pasturages for their herds. Living in seclusion for more than a thousand years in pueblos on three large tabular hills (the First Mesa, Second and Third Mesas – the village of Orabi on the Third Mesa is probably the oldest continuously occupied settlement in the United States) – the Hopi Indians have a common tribal council, but the individual villages are largely self-governing under a hereditary or elected chief. The Hopi are very reserved in their dealings with outsiders and try to keep "palefaces" away from their traditional religious ceremonies (the fire dance, the eagle dance, the masked dances of the kachina spirits). Before visiting a village the permission of the chief must be obtained, and this is not readily granted; and taking photographs and making sketches are frowned upon.

The Hopi practise various **crafts** (basketwork, jewellery, pottery), but their speciality is carving figures of kachinas – spirits representing various life forces that form a link between men and their Creator – usually from the roots of poplar trees. The sand painting that is still practised – a ritual in which the medicine man scatters coloured sand in magical symbols, which are wiped away after the ceremony – also has an artistic aspect.

In the Hopi Cultural Center on the Second Mesa (on US 264) are an interesting museum and shops selling Indian crafts, as well as a motel.

Hopi Cultural Center

The village of Oraibi on the Third Mesa dates

Oraibi

from the 12th c. and has probably been continuously inhabited longer than anywhere else in the United States.

Nebraska (State)   G–J 21–30

Area: 77,225 sq. mi.
Population: 1,652,000
Capital: Lincoln
Popular name: Cornhusker

Nebraska (from the Omaha Indian name for the Platte River), in the west central part of the United States, lies on the plateau of the Great Plains. It rises from the Missouri in the east to a height of 5425 ft at the foot of the Rocky Mountains in the west. The south and east of the state have very fertile loess soils, but to the north-west is a great expanse of sand hills and valleys, the characteristic Hills of Nebraska. The climate is continental, with hot summers and cold winters. The original vegetation (grassland in the east, short-grass and wormwood steppe in the west) now survives only in patches, and the huge herds of bison that once roamed here are now represented by small numbers in the National Parks.

History The territory of Nebraska was originally occupied by Dakota, Omaha, Cheyenne, Pawnee and many other tribes. In 1682 it became part of the French colony of Louisiana, which was acquired by the United States in 1803. For many years it was only sparsely settled; then from the mid 19th c. onwards it became an area of transit for pioneers making their way to the west. It was declared a territory of the United States in 1854, and on March 1st 1867 it became the 37th state of the Union.

Economy Nebraska is one of the leading agricultural states of the United States, and large areas of its territory are occupied by livestock farming, mainly cattle (about 6.5 million head). The principal crops on arable farms are maize, wheat, millet, soya beans and sugar beet. The state also has oil and natural gas. The most important industry is the processing of agricultural produce, in particular meat canning. Other industries include metalworking and electrical engineering. Tourism is of increasing economic importance, since the varied landscapes of Nebraska with their 3000 lakes offer scope for a wide range of leisure and recreational activities (shooting, canoeing, fishing, swimming, riding, skiing).

In the south-east of the state is its capital, Lincoln. Features of interest are the State Capitol, the State University with a Natural History Museum, Planetarium and the Sheldon Art Gallery of modern American art, designed by top architect Philip Johnson. Its most original museum however is the National Museum of Roller Skating tells the history of roller skating from 1700 to the present day.

Lincoln

Ogallala, in south-western Nebraska, takes visitors back to the days of cattle droving, with its saloon, general store, Cowboy Museum (Front St.) and Boot Hill Cemetery.

Ogallala

◀ *Spider Rock in the Canyon de Chelly*

Nevada

Lake McConaughy

To the north of Ogallala, the white sandy beaches of Lake McConaughy are ideal for relaxing, bathing, camping and fishing.

Omaha

Omaha, on the west bank of the Missouri, is the largest city in Nebraska. In the winter of 1846/47 the Mormons set up their winter quarters here on their way to the Salt Lake valley in Utah, and several hundreds of them died in the extreme cold. Omaha is the birthplace of one-time president Gerald Ford and black leader Malcolm X. The city has some interesting museums and cafés on the Old Market Place where it is pleasant to relax.

The ★**Joslyn Art Museum** (2200 Dodge St.) has a find collection, including works by Indian artists and craftsmen, and sketches recording Prince Maximilian zu Wied's journey to the Missouri in 1832–4.

The ★**Western Heritage Museum**, housed in the station building erected by Union Pacific in 1932, illustrates the building of the railroad over the Great Plains, and brings the great age of rail travel back to life.

10 mi. west of the city centre is **Boys Town**, an institution for the care of young people founded by Father Edward Joseph Flanagan in 1917, and made famous by the film starring Spencer Tracy.

12 mi. south of the city centre at Mahoney State Park is the gigantic **Strategic Air Command Museum**, displaying aircraft, intercontinental rockets and much more from the arsenal of the SAC, which was (and in principle still is) responsible for the conduct of atomic war from the air during the cold war.

★Scotts Bluff National Monument

Within easy reach of Scottsbluff, in the far west of the state, are several places of interest. Scotts Bluff, just south of the town was an important landmark for settlers and Pony Express riders on their journey to the west. A circular road takes visitors round the most notable features (including the tracks of wagon wheels) and to the interesting Oregon Trail Museum.

★Chimney Rock

This 500 ft pinnacle of rock 24 mi. south-east on the North Platte River was a landmark on the Oregon Trail, telling the settlers travelling on it that after crossing the Great Plains they had the much more arduous passage of the Rockies ahead of them.

Agate Fossil Beds

56 mi. north of the town is Agate Fossil Beds National Monument, where fossils of primeval mammals dating back 20 million years were found. The museum displays some of these finds, as well as items belonging to Ogallala Chief Red Cloud.

Fort Robinson

Further to the north, in the extreme north-west of Nebraska, Fort Robinson was built in 1874. With its palisades and watchtowers it gives an excellent impression of conditions in the time of the Indian wars. Here in 1877 the Indian chief Crazy Horse, who had come to the fort for peace negotiations, was murdered.

Nevada (State)   H–O 6–11

Area: 110,560 sq. mi.
Population: 1,603,000
Capital: Carson City
Popular name: Silver State

The predominant features of the landscape of Nevada (Spanish "snow-covered") are two great deserts, the Mojave and the Great Basin. The northern two-thirds of the state is occupied by the Great Basin, a region of cold, dry climate that is traversed by numerous ranges of hills striking north–south and rising to over 1000 ft. The southern third consists of the hot, dry Mojave Desert, in which the vegetation

is mainly of cacti; only on the eastern slopes of the Sierra Nevada are there forests of conifers.

History The earliest inhabitants of Nevada, who settled in the Moapa Valley around AD 100 and belonged to the Pueblo culture, were Anasazi Indians. In 1776 the area was explored by Spaniards, and thereafter became part of the Spanish viceroyalty of New Spain. In 1848 it was ceded by Mexico to the United States. Until 1861 it was joined with Utah in a United States territory; then on October 31st 1864 it became the 36th state of the Union. After the Second World War numerous tests of atom bombs were carried out in the Nevada desert.

Economy Nevada and the cities of Las Vegas and Reno in particular are famed as centres of legal gambling: not surprisingly, therefore, tourism is the state's principal source of income, to which the holiday areas on Lake Tahoe and Lake Mead also make contributions. Mining (particularly gold, silver, copper and iron) is also an important element in the economy. Nevada's processing industries are mainly iron smelting, the chemical industry and woodworking. Agriculture is almost entirely confined to pastoral farming.

The state capital, Carson City, which lies south of Reno, takes its name from the Wild West hero Kit Carson. Features of interest are the State Capitol, with a silver dome, and the Nevada State Museum, which includes a reproduction of a silver mine. Also of interest are the Nevada State Railroad Museum and the Stewart Indian Cultural Center.

Carson City

Round Ely, in the east of the state, are a number of ghost towns that grew up during the 19th c. silver boom and were then abandoned. From Ely, where visitors can find out about mining in this region at the White Pine Museum, and admire old locomotives in the Railroad Museum, it is 80 mi. south-east to Pioche, one of the wildest towns in the Wild West.

Ely

The Great Basin National Park, in the desert region on the border with Utah, is centred on Wheeler Peak (13,062 ft). The major attraction is the Lehman Caves, with fantastic rock formations.

★Great Basin National Park

165 mi. north of Las Vegas (see entry) Highway 375 branches off from the US 93, past the gigantic Nellis Air Force Base and the Air Force test site. This is the place for anyone who believes in UFOs, as more flying saucers have allegedly been sighted here than anywhere else on earth, which explains why this stretch of road has now been officially designated "Extraterrestrial Highway". Confirmed UFO enthusiasts will be interested to know that the American government keeps extraterrestrials on the top-secret test site around Groom Lake, the mysterious Area 51, where it tries out aircraft. The local information exchange is the bar "Little Ale-Inn" in Rachel (population 300), where with a bit of luck, guests can have a drink with a guaranteed genuine alien.

Extraterrestrial Highway

90 mi. south of Las Vegas, where Nevada, Arizona and California meet, Don Laughlin opened his gambling den on the Colorado River in 1969.

Laughlin

The place has now grown into a "boomtown" of casinos and hotels. Its trademark, and the centre of its gambling industry is the casino ship "Colorado Belle", floating on the Colorado River.

Reno

Reno, the "biggest little city in the world", lies in western Nevada. A rather smaller edition of Las Vegas (see entry), it allows visitors to get married or divorced and to lose their money just as expeditiously as in the larger city. The establishments "Circus Circus", "Eldorado" and "Peppermill" have proved highly successful.

★Pyramid Lake

For something different, visit the National Automobile Museum with its 220 veteran cars or relax on the beautiful desert lake, Pyramid Lake, 36 mi. to the north.

Other places of interest

Lake Tahoe, Las Vegas (see entries)

New Hampshire (State)   D–G 53–55

Area: 9280 sq. mi.
Population: 1,162,000
Capital: Concord
Popular name: Granite State

New Hampshire (named after the English county) lies in the north-eastern United States between Maine and Vermont. The northern part of the state is dominated by the granite massif of the White Mountains, part of the Appalachian range, with Mount Washington (6290 ft), the highest peak in the New England states. To the south of the hills is a wooded upland region with innumerable lakes formed during the Ice Age; the largest of them is Lake Winnepesaukee. In the south-east the state reaches the Atlantic coast in a strip only 20 mi. wide. Roughly 80 per cent of the state is covered with mixed deciduous and coniferous forests, in the latter of which Weymouth pines predominate. Lying as it does between high ranges of hills and the coast, there are considerable differences in climate in different parts of the state.

History After exploratory voyages in the early 16th c. the first Puritan settlers from England landed on the coast in 1623. In 1775 New Hampshire deposed its British Governor and thus became the first colony to break away from the mother country. On June 21st 1788 it became the ninth of the founding states to adopt the United States Constitution.

Economy New Hampshire's agriculture, now declining, specialises mainly in milk production and poultry rearing. In the south-east of the state is a dense industrial zone in which the most important branches of industry are electrical and mechanical engineering, papermaking and textiles. Tourism is of great economic importance; the hills in the north in particular offer ideal conditions for nature and sporting holidays (excellent skiing).

Concord

Concord, on the Merrimack River in southern New Hampshire, has been capital of the state since 1808. Features of interest include State House (1819) and the Historical Society Museum (with an example of the old coaches made in Concord, which had a reputation for indestructibility).

Hanover

It is worth making a trip to Hanover in the far west of the state on the

Vermont border, just to see the Hood Museum of Art with works from all over the world.

In the centre of the lake district to the south of the White Mountains is Lake Winnipesaukee, which attracts large numbers of visitors, particularly in summer. Weirs Beach, on the west side of the lake, has the widest range of leisure and recreational facilities (two water parks, bathing beaches, steamer trips) but is also the most crowded resort. Quieter places are the old bathing resort of Wolfsboro on the east side of the lake, and also Center Sandwich, Tamworth and Ossippee, with their numerous pretty antique shops. A peaceful, if somewhat antiquated way of life can be led in Canterbury Shaker Village. Laconia is the largest village in the region.

Until 1808, the port town of Portsmouth, founded in 1630 at the mouth of the Piscataqua, was the state capital. A walk round the district of Strawberry Bank with its handsome old houses will introduce visitors to the town's past.

Though not spectacular, the Museum of American Independence in Exeter, south of Portsmouth, is a gem – it has one of the 25 original copies of the Declaration of Independence and the Constitution.

Nature lovers, hikers and winter sports enthusiasts will all find what they are looking for in this mountain region. The I 93, the US 302 and the NH 16 run through or past the most important places and natural features in the western part of the National Forest.

One of the most visited holiday areas in the White Mountains is the **Franconia Notch (Gorge) State Park**. A striking feature is the "Old Man of the Mountains", a 1200 ft high crag that suggests the profile of an old man.

The easiest way to reach the top of Mount Washington is on the steep cog railway that was opened in 1869. By contrast, the 6¼ mile long Mount Washington Auto Road is by no means straightforward. The highest peak in the White Mountains is notorious for its rough and stormy weather: in 1934 the record wind speed of 240 mi. an hour was recorded here!

North Conway basically consists of one single street, but one lined with massive factory outlets selling well-known brands of textiles (fabric sales), and outdoor and winter-sports equipment shops with incredible bargains – New Hampshire has no sales tax.

New Jersey (State)   J/K 50/51

Area: 7835 sq. mi.
Population: 7,988,000
Capital: Trenton
Popular name: Garden State

New Jersey (named after Jersey in the Channel Islands) is one of the smaller states on the north Atlantic coast. It is bounded on the west by the Delaware River, on the north-east by the Hudson River, on the east by the Atlantic and on the south by Delaware Bay. The north-western part of the state extends into the foothills of the

Appalachians and the hilly Piedmont Plateau. Along the edge of the coastal plain are extensive lagoons and spits of land. There are considerable variations in temperature between the dry, cold north and the subtropically humid south. The hardwood forests that originally covered the whole state except the areas of marshland have now largely disappeared, giving place to low coniferous and oak scrub forest and large areas devoted to the growing of bilberries and cranberries.

History The territory of New Jersey, originally occupied by Lenni-Lenape Indians, was settled in the 17th c. by Dutch immigrants. Until 1664 it was part of the colony of Nieuw Holland; thereafter, under pressure from Britain, it became a Quaker colony. In 1701 Britain gained control of New Jersey. During the War of Independence its strategic situation made it the scene of major battles between American and British forces. On December 18th 1787 it signed the United States Constitution as the third of the founding states.

Economy New Jersey's highly developed agriculture is primarily directed towards supplying the large cities with basic foodstuffs (vegetables, fruit, dairy products). It is also one of the leading industrial states of the United States, the most important branches of industry being steel production, engineering and automobile construction. Its long and varied coastline is the main tourist attraction.

The Atlantic **coast** of New Jersey extends 127 mi. from Sandy Hook in the north to Cape May in the south and is ideal for holidaymakers, with its unspoilt natural areas, small harbour towns, quiet old and noisy new resorts and with Atlantic City, the "Las Vegas of the East".

Atlantic City	See entry
Hoboken	Frank Sinatra fans should take a trip from New York City (see entry) to Hoboken, opposite Manhattan, the town where "Ol' Blue Eyes" was born, at 415 Monroe Street. Today he would have enjoyed visiting the shops, bars and restaurants of Washington Street.
★Island Beach State Park	For idyllic natural surroundings, with hardly any people, there is Island Beach State Park, approximately halfway along the coastline and only a few miles from the busy holiday complexes of Seaside Heights and Seaside Park.
★Cape May	The attractions of Cape May, at the southernmost tip of New Jersey, on Delaware Bay, were discovered by the more prosperous citizens of Philadelphia in the 18th c., and in the 19th c. it enjoyed a heyday as a fashionable bathing resort. Six Presidents of the United States had houses here. Today the attractions of the town are its fine beaches, Cape May Point Lighthouse, built in 1859 and its handsome Victorian-style holiday homes. There are also boat trips to see whales and dolphins.
Newark	The only real reason for visiting Newark, the largest city in the state, and the third most important airport serving nearby New York, is to see the laboratory of Thomas Alva Edison in the suburb of New Orange.
Morristown National Historical Park	In this National Historical Park in northern New Jersey, Washington's forces camped during the winter of 1779/80. Features of interest are the Historical Museum, Ford Mansion and Fort Nonsense.
★Princeton	A few miles north-east of Trenton lies the small town of Princeton, which owes its international reputation to its university and associated research institutes, including the Institute for Advanced Study, where Albert Einstein carried out his final work. The university, founded in 1946 as the College of New Jersey in Elizabeth, moved to Princeton in 1756.

With Harvard and Yale it belongs to the "Ivy League" of prestigious universities in the north-east United States. Features of particular interest include the building of the Woodrow Wilson School for political science, built in 1965 to plans by Minoru Yamasaki, the Nassau Hall, the Marquand Chapel and the H.S. Firestone library.

★Valley Forge

During the most difficult period of the American War of Independence, the patriots' army, badly equipped and provisioned, waited in Valley Forge from December 1777 to June 1778. Of between 12,000 and 20,000 men, 2,000 died of disease or starvation. "Living History" performances are staged daily in summer and at weekends in winter.

Trenton

In the centre of the state, on the Delaware River, is the state capital, Trenton, which preserves a number of historic buildings and sites. This is where Washington inflicted a decisive defeat on the Hessian soldiers stationed in the Old Barracks.

Before doing so he had to cross the Delaware, which he did at Christmas 1776 in icy cold conditions, north-west of Trenton in what is now **Washington Crossing State Park** – a name that recalls the famous painting "Washington Crosses the Delaware", an icon of American art.

New Mexico (State)   N–S 16–22

Area: 121,595 sq. mi.
Population: 1,713,000
Capital: Santa Fe
Popular name: Land of Enchantment

The state of New Mexico in the south-western United States is divided between three geographical regions. The western part of the state is occupied by a plateau traversed by ranges of hills and slashed by numerous canyons; in the centre are the southern foothills of the Rocky Mountains (highest point Wheeler Peak, 13,161 ft), through which flows the Rio Grande; and in the east the hills fall down to the wide expanses of the Great Plains, with the Llano Estacado. The climate is extremely dry – New Mexico has an annual rainfall of only 14in., the lowest in the United States – and as a result the country ranges between steppe and desert. Typical trees in the mountain regions are spruce, fir, nut pine and juniper. Yuccas and mesquites grow in the desert regions.

History In New Mexico – known as Indian Land – impressive cliff dwellings and ruins bear witness to the cultures of the Pueblo, Apache, Navajo and Anasazi Indians. The first European to reach the area round the Rio Grande was Francisco Marcos de Niza, who came here in 1539 in the quest for gold.

The territory was colonised in the 17th c. by Spaniards, who encountered fierce resistance from the local Indian tribes. In 1821 it was occupied by Mexico; then in 1846, after the outbreak of the Mexican–American War, it was annexed by the United States. In 1850 (combined with Arizona until 1863) it was incorporated as a United States territory, and on January 6th 1912 it was admitted to the Union as the 47th state. The first atom bomb was exploded on July 16th 1945 at the Alamogordo test site.

Economy New Mexico's agriculture is predominantly extensive pastoral farming; arable crops include vegetables, cotton, fruit, wheat and hay.

The state has the largest deposits of uranium in the United States, as well as potassium salts, copper, oil and natural gas. Its principal industries are chemicals, foodstuffs, electronics and engineering. The main assets of the tourist trade are natural beauties such as the Carlsbad Caverns, the remains of early Indian cultures, and former wild west towns such as Santa Fe.

★Aztec Ruins National Monument

In the far north-west of New Mexico, on the border with Colorado, settlers who reached this area around 1800 found a settlement of the Pueblo Indians and thought it was an Aztec town. The settlement, which was occupied between 1100 and 1300, consists 450 rooms; the most famous being the Great Kiva, the only completely restored ceremonial building of this type in the United States. An Aztec museum gives a vivid account of this extinct culture.

Gallup

In the extreme north-west of New Mexico, on Route 66, is Gallup, the south-eastern corner of the Navajo Indian Reservation (see entry). This was where the Navajo, Hopi and Zuni always used to meet, hence the fact that the town is known today as the "Gateway to Indian Country". Gallup may have little to offer in the way of interesting buildings, but it is the best place to buy Indian souvenirs.

Red Rock State Park

Red Rock State Park, north of Gallup in western New Mexico, is the venue, annually in August, of the Intertribal Indian Ceremonial, which is attended by members of 50 different tribes from all over the United States, Canada and Mexico.

Zuni Pueblo

Zuni Pueblo, 39 mi. south-east of Gallup, is one of the legendary "Seven Cities of Cibola". The Zuni are masters in the production of silver and

The Great Kiva in the Aztec Ruins National Monument is the only completely renovated ceremonial room of the Pueblo Indians

turquoise jewellery and ceramics, and the town has many workshops selling these artefacts.

To the west of Albuquerque (see entry) is the El Morro National Monument, a sandstone cliff over 200 ft high topped by a pueblo with pre-Columbian rock drawings. There are also later inscriptions by Spanish conquistadors, including Don Juan de Oñate in 1605.

El Morro National Monument

North of the old mining town of Silver City are the Gila cliff dwellings: 42 rooms in six caves in the cliff face constructed by the Mogollon Indians around 1300.

Gila Cliff Dwellings

Roswell, in the south-eastern part of the state on the Pecos River is the second place of pilgrimage for UFO aficionados after the Extraterrestrial Highway in Nevada (see p. 351). It is all said to have begun in July 1947 when a UFO crashed and was concealed by the military. The town takes full advantage of UFO-mania, with two UFO museums and an annual UFO festival, whilst the Roswell Museum & Art Center is dedicated to more earthly objects such as Indian art.

Roswell

No Wild West fan should miss Lincoln, for it still has visible traces of the famous outlaw Billy the Kid. The fact that the town has a population of less than one hundred may well account for the fact that the town, 57 mi. west of Roswell, has hardly changed since the days of the Lincoln County War. Billy was sentenced to death in the Old Courthouse, but shot his way to freedom – a bullet from his revolver is still lodged in his cell. The Old Lincoln Days are brought back to life every year during the first weekend in August.

★Lincoln

Albuquerque, Carlsbad Caverns, Santa Fe, White Sands National Monument (see entries)

Other places of interest

★★New Orleans   U 35

State: Louisiana
Altitude: 0–13 ft
Population: 497,000

New Orleans, the largest city in the state of Louisiana and one of the largest inland ports (also handling seagoing vessels) in the United States, lies on the Mississippi, 105 mi. from where it enters the Gulf of Mexico. New Orleans is a true melting pot of cultures. In addition to the French speaking Cajuns (Acadians: descendants of the French settlers who were expelled from Nova Scotia in the 18th c.), its population includes Creoles, Italian, Irish and German immigrants and descendants of black slaves. The city's cultural diversity is reflected particularly in its music, its food and of course in its calendar of festivals. Its individuality also finds expression in its popular names "Queen of the South", or even better, "The Big Easy". At the end of the 19th, and beginning of the 20th c., this was the birthplace of jazz, which is still actively practised at various places. This metropolis of the Old South draws hosts of visitors, especially at the time of the Carnival (Mardi Gras). It should be mentioned that New Orleans has one of the highest crime rates in the United States, so it is best to keep to the Vieux Carré, the Central Business District and Garden District that are relatively safe.

The city lies in an area of marshland, formerly malaria infested but now drained, between the Mississippi, here up to half a mile wide, and Lake Pontchartrain, which is drained by a series of bayous (ditches, sluggish waterways). Much of the crescent-plan city centre lies below the high-tide mark and is protected by a levee 6 mi. long and over 13 ft high.

Originally dependent mainly on shipping and shipbuilding, the town's **economy** later centred on the produce of its rich hinterland (particularly cotton, sugar, rice and timber) and on fishing. More recently there has been a major restructuring of the economy as a result of the working of natural gas and, even more importantly, offshore oil. The New Orleans region is now one of the leading world centres of the petrochemical industry. Tourism is an increasingly important source of revenue: with over 7 million visitors annually, New Orleans is now one of the most important tourist centres in the United States.

New Orleans is the home of **jazz**. The chief protagonists of this new musical style were "King" Oliver, J.R. Morton and above all Louis Armstrong (see Famous People). The jazz of New Orleans continues to attract fans from all over the world to the New Orleans Jazz and Heritage Festival in spring and to the many clubs. Black music, i.e. blues and Dixieland, ragtime and swing, Cajun and Zydeco, Creole jazz and the more recent funky jazz, can be heard in Preservation Hall (726 St Peter St.), the legendary Lulu White's Mahogany Hall (309 Bourbon St.), the Palm Court Jazz Café (1204 Decatur St.) and countless other night spots. Other places that are at present "in" are "Dragon's Den (435 Esplanade Ave.; Modern Jazz), "Tipitina's" (501 Napoleon Ave.; all kinds of music), "Muddy Waters" (8301 Oak St.; Blues), "Mulate's" (201 Julia St.; Cajun, Zydeco), "Jimmy's" (8200 Willow St.; Rock, Reggae) and the "Maple Leaf Bar" (8316 Oak St.; Cajun, Zydeco, Rhythm & Blues). The "Old Absinthe House" (400 Bourbon St.) is one of the oldest clubs in the city.

The high spot in the city's programme of festivals is the Carnival (**Mardi Gras**), which was introduced by French settlers and flourished particularly at the end of the 19th c. During the Carnival, particularly on the Monday before Ash Wednesday, and Shrove Tuesday, the town is taken over by the revellers with a series of lively parades and masked balls.

History New Orleans was founded in 1718 by the French governor Jean-Baptiste Lemoine de Bienville and named after the Duc d'Orléans, then Regent of France. In 1721 it became capital of Louisiana. Soon afterwards a large party of German immigrants arrived, and by 1732 the population had risen to 5000. In 1762 France was compelled to cede the

town to Spain, though for several years the population successfully resisted the takeover. New Orleans was again in French hands from 1800 to 1803, when under the Louisiana Purchase it passed to the United States. In 1815 General Andrew Jackson inflicted a decisive defeat on British forces near the town. During the Civil War New Orleans surrendered to Union forces in 1862.

★★Vieux Carré (French Quarter)

The Vieux Carré or French Quarter of New Orleans, the old town centre, extends along a crescent shaped bend on the Mississippi. French influence is particularly marked in the

Jazz was born in New Orleans

buildings, some of them between 100 and 270 years old, with their arcades, wrought iron balconies, red-tiled roofs and picturesque fountain decked courtyards. The blacks who settled in the town, together with the old established Creole inhabitants, created jazz around the turn of the 19th c. in the entertainment quarter, which was demarcated by municipal ordinance in 1897 and marked out with red lamps, and in nearby Bourbon Street. Nowadays the district contains a profusion of jazz spots and places of entertainment of very varying quality, well-known restaurants, cheerful cafés, souvenir shops, galleries and old hotels, all refurbished and titivated for the tourist trade.

The main square of the old town is tree-planted Jackson Square (Place d'Armes), with an equestrian statue (1856) of General Andrew Jackson. Very attractively laid out is the area along the banks of the Mississippi, with the Riverboat Docks, the promenade known as the Moon Walk, the Millhouse and the former Jackson Brewery, as well as a variety of boutiques and fast food outlets. ★Jackson Square

On the north side of the square is the **St Louis Cathedral** (RC), built in 1794 on the site of two earlier churches.

The ★**Cabildo**, to the left of the cathedral, was built in 1795 as the residence of the Spanish governor. The Louisiana Purchase was agreed here in 1803. This building now houses the Louisiana State Museum with its large collections of material on the history of the town and the region.

To the north-east is the **Presbytère** (1817), originally the presbytery, which later housed the Supreme Court of Louisiana and is now occupied by a section of the Louisiana State Museum.

The **Pontalba buildings** (mid-19th c.), the first apartment blocks in America, extend along two sides of Jackson Square. In the block on the eastern side, known as 1850 House, the Louisiana State Museum has a display of valuable furniture.

At the north-west corner of the square is the **Petit Théâtre** (1797). Adjoining is the attractive Petit salon

A picturesque and lively little street (many street artists), particularly in spring, is the Ruelle d'Orléans (Pirates' Alley), also known as Pirates' Alley after the freebooters who used to haunt this area. ★Ruelle d'Orleans

To the north-west behind the cathedral is the Anthony Garden, in which duels were once fought. Nearby is La Branche House (1835) with beautiful wrought iron balconies. Anthony Gardens

Leading from the east corner of Jackson Square, Moon Wall contains the long-established Café du Monde, with its tempting café au lait and beignets. Next along are the long market halls of the picturesque French market with an abundance of culinary delights and a busy flea market. ★French Market

At the north-east end of the French Market is the Old US Mint (1835), in which American coins were minted until 1910. It now houses the ★**Mardi Gras and Jazz Museum**. To the south-west, on Decatur Street, is the original "streetcar named Desire".

In Chartres Street is the Ursuline Convent, built about 1735. Adjoining is St Mary's Church (1780) and opposite, the Beauregard-Keyes House, built in 1826. Old Ursuline Convent

Back along Chartres Street, Dumain Street on the right has one of the Dumaine Street

St. Augustine Church

New Orleans Downtown

300 m
0,15 mi

Louis
Theatre of the Performing Arts

Armstrong Park

Cultural Center

Beauregard Square

St. Augustine Church

Canal St

St. Philip St
St. Ann St
N. Villere St
Lafitte Ave
N. Robertson St
Marais St
St. Louis St
Orleans

Roman St
N. Derbigny St

St. Louis Cemetery No. 2

Municipal Auditorium

St. Louis Cemetery No. 1

Municipal Court Bldg.

Boucvalt House

St. Anthony's Church

Audubon's Little House

Our Lady of Guadalupe Church

S. Robertson St
N. Villere St
Iberville St
Marais St
Treme St
Crozat St
Basin St

Musée Conti-Wax Museum

Grima House

Jazz Museum

S. Villere St
LSU Med. Center

Charity Hosp.

Simon Bolivar Mon.

Joy Theatre

Saenger Theatre

Athletic Club

Audubon Bldg.

Old Absinthe House

Home of Si de Blenvi

Tulane Medical Center

Public Library

Loew's State Theatre

Orpheum Theatre

Jesuit Church

Boston Club

Supreme Court Bldg.

Duncan Plaza

Common St
Gravier St

Louisiana State Bldg.

City Hall

Civic Center

Public Service Bldg.

Cotton Exchange

Gateway Building

U.S. Custom House

Civil Courts Bldg.

Perdido St

Hibernia Bank (Tower)

International House

Chamber of Commerce

Union St
Western Union

Masonic Temple

Federal Reserve Bank

Medallion Towers

Board of Trade

Monu

River Exhibi Cer

Federal Building

Lafayette St

Scottish Rite Temple

Gallier Hall

Lafayette Square

U.S. Federal Courts

Poydras

Julia
Union Station

Plaza Towers

St. Patrick's Church

Greyhound, Internat. Airport

Superdome

Pontchartrain Expressway
Garden City

Lee Circle, Confederate Museum,
Contemporary Arts Center, Children's Museum

oldest houses in the city, the trim building known as "Madame John's
Legacy", built in 1726 and elegantly furnished.

The **Voodoo Museum** illustrates the mingling of Christian elements and
pagan African rites in the mysterious voodoo cult, which still has its followers in the Caribbean today. The lady in charge of the museum is also
keen to show visitors all kinds of charms and potions.

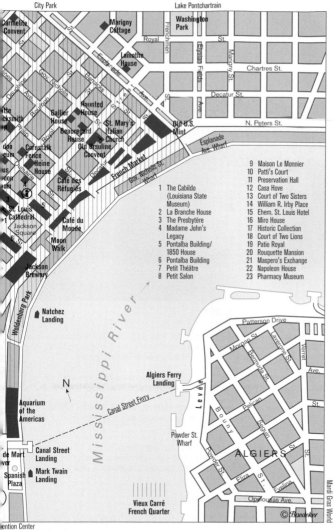

City Park — Lake Pontchartrain

Carmelite Convent

Marigny Cottage

Washington Park

Royal   St.

Lamothe House

Frenchmen St.

Elysian Fields Ave.

Chartres St.

Decatur St.

Marigny St.

N. Peters St.

Haunted House

Gallier House

St. Mary's Italian Church

Beauregard House

Old Ursuline Convent

Old U.S. Mint

Esplanade Ave. Wharf

Cornstalk Fence

Heine House

The Blacksmith Shop

Voodoo Museum

Café des Réfugiés

French Market

Gov. Nicholas St. Wharf

St. Louis Cathedral

Café du Monde

Jackson Square

Moon Walk

Jackson Brewery

Woldenberg Park

1 The Cabildo (Louisiana State Museum)
2 La Branche House
3 The Presbytère
4 Madame John's Legacy
5 Pontalba Building/1850 House
6 Pontalba Building
7 Petit Théâtre
8 Petit Salon

9 Maison Le Monnier
10 Patti's Court
11 Preservation Hall
12 Casa Hove
13 Court of Two Sisters
14 William R. Irby Place
15 Ehem. St. Louis Hotel
16 Miro House
17 Historic Collection
18 Court of Two Lions
19 Patio Royal
20 Rouquette Mansion
21 Maspero's Exchange
22 Napoleon House
23 Pharmacy Museum

Natchez Landing

Mississippi River

N

Algiers Ferry Landing

Patterson Drive

Morgan St.

Bermuda St.

Lavergne St.

Verret St.

Ave.

Aquarium of the Americas

Canal Street Ferry

Levée

Bouny

Pelican   St.

Seguin St.

Canal Street Landing

Powder St. Wharf

Powder St.

ALGIERS St.

de Mart

ver

Spanish Plaza

Mark Twain Landing

Eliza St.

Evelina St.

Opelousas Ave.

Vieux Carré French Quarter

ention Center
walk, Cruise Ship Terminal

© Baedeker

Mardi Gras World

There are a number of fine buildings on Royal Street, including the old Bank of Louisiana, the old established Antoine's Restaurant, the Spanish Governor's House (1784), the Court of Two Sisters (1832), Patti's Court (1860; once occupied by the famous singer Adelina Patti), the Historic New Orleans Collection and finally Dr Le Monnier's House (1811).

★Royal Street

The best known street in New Orleans is Bourbon Street, with famous

★★Bourbon Street

Bourbon Street, the heart of the French Quarter

jazz spots, the famous Preservation Hall and the Old Absinthe House (1807), in which Andrew Jackson and the guerrilla leaders Jean and Pierre Lafitte planned the decisive battle with British forces.

Hermann Grima House

This interesting house with stables (820 St Louis St.) was built in 1831 for a successful businessman named Hermann Grima.

Musée Conti

A short walk north, at 917 Conti Street, is the Musée Conti (Wax Museum), with tableaux of wax figures depicting scenes from the turbulent history of the city.

Napoleon House

Back to Chartres Street, and east to Napoleon House; this is where French patriots wanted Napoleon to stay after his planned release from St. Helena. The adjacent pharmacy museum is worth a visit.

North-west of Vieux Carré

Garden of the Americas

Between Rampart Street and Basin Street, which marks the north-western boundary of the Vieux Carré, is the Garden of the Americas, with monuments commemorating the freedom fighters Benito Juárez Gracia, Simón Bolívar and Francisco Morazán. Close by are the church of Our Lady of Guadeloupe and the Old St Louis Cemetery, with numbers of handsome monuments, including that of the Voodoo Queen Marie Laveau. The cemetery should only be visited as part of a guided tour as this is not the safest of districts.

Louis Armstrong Park

On the north-west edge of the Vieux Carré is Louis Armstrong Park, with a bronze statue of the legendary musician and entertainer (see Famous People). The area was originally known as Congo Square (Beauregard

Square), for Negro slaves were allowed to gather here on Sundays. Here now are the Municipal Auditorium, the Theatre of Performing Arts and the Treme Community Center.

★Riverfront

Ideally, a riverfront tour should start at the French Market: go along Moon Walk past the Café du Monde and the Jackson Brewery to Natchez landing, where the paddle steamer Natchez, which plies on the Mississippi, is moored.

Natchez Landing

Through Woldenberg Park is the Aquarium of the Americas, which attracts great numbers of visitors. Here can be seen more than 7000 different representatives of the freshwater and saltwater fauna of the Mississippi, the Amazon and the Caribbean (Gulf of Mexico). Open Sun.–Wed. 9.30–6pm, Thu. to 9pm, Fri., Sat, to 7pm.

★Aquarium of the Americas

At the end of Canal Street is the attractive Spanish Plaza, on which a lively masked ball takes place on the Monday before Ash Wednesday.

Spanish Plaza

The **Canal Street Ferry** crosses the Mississippi, here 700 yds wide, to the eastern suburb of Algiers. At 233 Newton Street is Blaine Kern's Mardi Gras World, where the floats for Mardi Gras are prepared.

Riverwalk, with more than 200 boutiques, restaurants and cafés, joins the square at its northern edge. Further south is the modern New Orleans Convention Center.

Riverwalk

Central Business District (CBD)

To the west of the Riverfront is the Central Business District, with various bank buildings (including the Hibernia Tower), the Cotton Exchange and a number of hotels. Canal Street, the busy main shopping street of the city, separates the Vieux Carré from the CBD.

The CBD is dominated by the 33-storey World Trade Center, from the viewing platform of which there is a breathtaking view over the city.

World Trade Center

In the centre of the district is Lafayette Square, with three monuments, including one to Benjamin Franklin. On the west side of the square is the Gallier Hall, formerly the City Hall.

Lafayette Square

Near the Pontchartrain Expressway is the beautifully laid out Lee Circle, with a bronze statue of the southern General Robert Lee on a tall column. Close by is the Confederate Museum (929 Camp St.), which is devoted to the Civil War.

Lee Circle

This museum claims to be the oldest in New Orleans, having been founded in 1891. Exhibits include old bloodstained uniforms, sabres and guns.

Confederate Museum

To the west of the Central Business District is the 272 ft high Louisiana Superdrome, one of the largest stadiums in the United States, with seating for 90,000 spectators. To the south are the Union Passenger Terminal and the Head Post Office.

★Louisiana Superdrome

To the west of the Pontchartrain Expressway is the 51-storey skyscraper One Shell Plaza, one of the city's tallest buildings.

One Shell Plaza

Outlying districts

★Garden District

The Garden District, a prosperous residential area, lies south-west of the Pontchartrain Expressway. It is best to travel here on the St Charles Streetcar, a survivor of New Orleans' tram system, getting out at Charles Street/First Avenue (Stop 14). On First Street, Camp Street and Prytania Street there are many large elegant, 19th c. houses with extensive gardens.

Audubon Park

In the south-west of the Garden District is Audubon Park, laid out in 1915, with fine stands of oaks, a zoo, hothouses, a golf course and a number of small lakes. North of the park are the Tudor-style buildings of the Roman Catholic Loyola University, founded in 1912. Beyond it is the campus of Tulane University.

New Orleans Museum of Art

The beautifully laid out City Park is in the north of the city near Lake Pontchartrain. This park, the oldest and largest in the city, was won from the swampland. In the south part of the park the New Orleans Museum of art has an excellent collection of European classical modern art as well as treasures of Indian and black African art.

Surroundings

Lake Pontchartrain

To the north of the City Park is Lake Pontchartrain (40 mi. long, 25 mi. across and only 20 ft deep), round the shores of which are many speciality restaurants (particularly fish and game). There are also marinas and bathing beaches, and an amusement park that appeals particularly to families with children. The 25 mi. long Lake Pontchartrain Causeway runs across the lake.

Chalmette National Historical Park

6 mi. east is Chalmette National Historical Park, where General Jackson defeated the British forces in 1815. In the National Cemetery are the graves of 12,000 Union soldiers who fell in the Civil War.

New York (State)   F–J 46–52

Area: 48,420 sq. mi.
Population: 18,185,000
Capital: Albany
Popular name: Empire State

New York State lies in the north-eastern United States on the Canadian frontier, extending northward from New York City to Lake Ontario and north-westward to Lake Erie. The landscape of the state shows great diversity, with high mountain ranges in the north-east, expanses of plain in the centre and a coast fringed with spits of land in the south. It has a cool temperate climate, with inflows of cold air from the north in winter. The plateau and mountain regions are mostly forest covered and rich in game. The plains are predominantly arable land.

History In 1609 Henry Hudson, then in the Dutch service, sailed up the river that bears his name as far as the site of present-day Albany. In 1623 the Dutch colony of Nieuw Holland was founded here, and settlers were brought in from the Netherlands. In 1664 the colony was ceded to Britain and in 1665 became a Crown Colony. The town of New York was occupied by British forces during the whole of the War of Independence. On July 26th 1788 New York became the eleventh of the founding states to adopt the Constitution.

Economy The produce of the state's highly specialised agriculture (poultry rearing, dairy farming; fruit and vegetables, including potatoes) is mainly devoted to supplying the great city conurbations. It also has the highest industrial output in the United States after the state of California, with roughly half of its total industrial production coming from New York City. The main tourist areas in the state are the Adirondacks and the Great Lakes, with Niagara Falls and New York City as the principal highlights.

The Adirondacks, a range of hills of medium height, forest covered and with numerous lakes, lie in the far north of New York State; geologically they form part of the Canadian Shield. The highest peak is Mount Marcy (5345 ft). The Adirondacks have long been a favourite holiday and recreation area, offering excellent fishing, shooting and walking. The area can be explored by canoe on the 125 mi. long waterway from the Old Forge in the west to Saranacs in the north-west of the Adirondack Park.

★Adirondacks

The world-famous winter-sports resort of Lake Placid, at the foot of Whiteface Mountain, has twice hosted the Winter Olympics (1932, 1980).

★Lake Placid

The state capital, Albany (pop. 110,000) lies 150 mi. north of New York in the valley of the Hudson River. It was given a great boost as an industrial and commercial centre by the opening of the Erie Canal in 1825. There is a fine view of the town and the Hudson River from the Corning Tower of the modern Empire State Plaza. Albany has many fine old 18th and 19th c. buildings that have been carefully restored in recent years. The Albany Institute of History and Art has one of the oldest collections in the United States (including pictures of the 19th c. Hudson River school).

Albany

At the east end of Lake Erie is Buffalo, the state's second largest city, and one of the leading ports on the Great Lakes. Besides an architectural monument – the Guaranty Building in Church Street designed by Bankmar Adler and Louis Sullivan in 1896 – the city also has the Albrecht Knox Art Gallery, with a fine collection of European and American art of the 18th–20th centuries, the Museum of the Buffalo & Erie County Historical Society, and the Naval and Military Park on the harbour, with some warships. In the old Allentown district are many finely restored Victorian buildings now housing art galleries, boutiques and small restaurants. From Buffalo it is not far to Niagara Falls (see entry).

Buffalo

On the Canadian side, across the Niagara from Buffalo, where the river leaves Lake Erie, is the town of Fort Erie, founded by British loyalists in 1748. About a mile south of the bridge stands Fort Erie itself, constructed in 1764 and captured by the Americans in 1814.

Fort Erie

When New Yorkers want to get back to nature, they drive into the Catskill mountains, to go hiking and skiing. One of the many pretty villages, Woodstock, shot to fame in August 1969, when it was the scene of the legendary, three-day music festival. The "three days of peace and music" have left their mark, and tourists still flock here in considerable numbers. Phoenicia is a good base, and also has the Empire State Railway Museum, commemorating the age of steam.

Woodstock

To the west of Albany, in central New York State, is Cooperstown, made famous by James Fenimore Cooper, author of the Leatherstocking tales. Its other tourist feature, for devotees of the American national game, is the Baseball Hall of Fame, for this is where the national sport was invented.

Cooperstown

★Finger Lakes

According to Iroquois legend, the long, narrow lakes in the landscape west of Syracuse were formed by the impression of the fingers of the Great Spirit. This is a wine-producing area, which can be discovered on the Cayuga Trail, the Seneca Lake Trail and the Keuka Trail. Tastings are also available. In Ithaca is the youngest of the "Ivy League" universities, Cornell University with is Art Museum and Planetarium, and in Seneca Falls the American feminist movement came into being in 1848, as documented by the National Women's Hall of Fame. Rochester, home of Kodak, has an excellent Museum of Photography and in Corning the Museum of Glass has an outstanding glass collection. For recreation there is the Watkins Glen State Park, where the peace is not even disturbed by the sound of engines on the famous race trace.

★Hudson River Valley

One of North America's loveliest landscapes begins immediately behind the northern city boundary of New York City. On the west side are Bear Mountain State Park, and the famous West Point Military Academy (guided tours). On the east side, near Kingston, President Franklin Delano Roosevelt's (see Famous People) birthplace and residence can be visited. Further towards Albany is Olana, a Moorish-style palace, built by Frederic Church, a protagonist of the Hudson River School.

★Saratoga Springs

With its handsome 19th c. spa facilities (in Saratogo State Park) and other amenities Saratoga Springs, north of Albany on I 87, is a very fashionable resort. During the high season (June to August) there are race meetings, and leading dramatic companies from New York and Philadelphia put on shows in the Saratogo Performing Arts Center.

Other places of interest

New York City, Niagara Falls (see entries)

★★New York City   H–J 51/52

State: New York
Altitude: 0–410 ft
Population: 7.32 million

The description of New York in this guide is abridged, since there is a detailed account of the city in the Baedeker guide "New York".

New York City, the largest city in the United States – the "Big Apple", the "world capital of excitement" – lies in the south-east of New York State, at the point where the Hudson River and East River flow into Long Island Bay. New York is the world centre of finance and capital, the seat of the United Nations, a cultural Mecca without equal, a mosaic of nations and a city of stark social contrasts in which extravagant luxury and the bitterest poverty are often only a street apart. Greater New York – officially so designated since 1898 – consists of five boroughs, each of which has a population of over a million: Manhattan, the real economic and cultural centre, together with the Bronx, Brooklyn, Queens and Staten Island. The city is headed by the Mayor, who controls a great army of municipal officials and police. Since 1993 this post has been held by Rudolph Giuliani, a conservative Republican, who faced a host of problems when he took office: a volume of traffic almost out of control and the resultant environmental pollution, a desperate financial situation, the degeneration of whole quarters of the city into disaster areas, with housing shortages and homelessness, and a frighteningly high crime rate. Giuliani was re-elected for a second term in 1997, having achieved considerable success in checking the crime rate by means of rigid prison sentences, even for minor offences, and an increased police presence – a strategy not without its critics. Whatever one's point of view, New York has shed its crime-ridden image and is now again regarded as safe.

Population The waves of immigrants from all over the world have given New York an unusual diversity of ethnic groups that is reflected in an extraordinary cultural range and also in racial and social tensions. It is not quite accurate to talk of a melting pot of races, for many population groups live in their own special quarter: African–Americans in Harlem, Chinese in Chinatown, Italians in Little Italy, Poles and Ukrainians in East Village, Hungarians, Czechs and Germans on East Side, Hispanos in the Barrio, and so on.

Economy New York City occupies a predominant position in the economy of the United States and is the largest capital market and banking centre in the world. Seven of the ten largest American investment banks have their headquarters on the Hudson River, along with a third of all retail businesses in the United States, almost a fifth of all wholesale firms, three commercial exchanges and innumerable service establishments, including 17,000 restaurants, famous department stores like Macy's and Bloomingdale's and a host of advertising and media people and lawyers. Industry is also strongly represented, a leading position being occupied by the traditional textile industry, followed by foodstuff processing and printing and publishing. New York is also the media capital of the United States, with the headquarters of all the major television and radio companies and publishing houses and an immense range of newspapers and periodicals. The big film companies also have their offices in New York, although the films themselves are mostly produced in California. Tourism is also an important element in the economy: the city attracts 32 million visitors annually, including 5.8 million from overseas.

Culture New York is also the cultural centre of the United States, with 35 Broadway theatres and perhaps 200 little theatres, two opera houses, including the world-famous Metropolitan Opera, several orchestras of outstanding quality, including the New York Philharmonic (founded 1842), and over a dozen ballet and dance companies. It is also a world art centre, with some of the world's greatest museums, headed by the Metropolitan Museum, and several hundred galleries. Science and education are represented by over 50 universities and colleges, the best known of which is Columbia University. And this is by no means the whole story, for what would New York be without its restaurants, bars, jazz clubs and noisy discotheques and its nightbirds, who would agree with Frank Sinatra's song "I wanna wake up in a city that never sleeps!"?

History The first European to sail into the bay and see the Manhattan peninsula (though without setting foot on it) was Giovanni da Verrazano, an Italian in the French service, who came here in 1524. The first to land here, in 1609, was Henry Hudson, who was looking for the North-West Passage on behalf of the Dutch East India Company, and he was followed four years later by the first Dutch settlers. The foundation of the town that was to become New York is dated to 1626, when Governor Peter Minnewit or Minuit bought the peninsula from the Manna-Hatta Indians and founded the settlement of Nieuw Amsterdam. Under his successor Peter Stuyvesant, who proved something of a dictator, the town grew, but was increasingly threatened by the British, who captured it in 1664 and consolidated their hold in 1674, when the town was renamed New York.

At the beginning of the War of Independence the Americans were defeated in a battle on Long Island and were compelled to abandon the town, recovering it only in 1783. In 1789 George Washington took the oath as first President of the United States in Federal Hall, and New York briefly became the country's first capital. By 1820 it was the largest city in the United States with a population of 150,000. With the opening of the Erie Canal in 1825 it consolidated its position as the leading port on the eastern seaboard. During the 19th c. the city's population was multiplied many times by the influx of immigrants from Europe and, after the Civil War, of former slaves from the south. By 1898 the population had risen to 3.5 million, and by 1913 it had passed the 5 million mark. That year also saw the beginning of the skyscraper era with the completion of the Woolworth Building: a development that reached its first peak in 1931 with the Empire State Building, the Chrysler Building and the RCA Building. Two years earlier, however, a different note had been struck on "Black Friday", the stock market crash that marked the beginning of the world economic crisis.

After the Second World War New York became the headquarters of the United Nations. Important postwar dates were 1965, when the city was paralysed by a total power blackout; 1970, when the World Trade Center was completed; 1975, when New York was threatened with bankruptcy; the early 1980s, when large numbers of new skyscrapers were built; 1987, when the Stock Exchange suffered a worse crash than in 1929 on "Black Monday"; 1990, when the city elected its first black Mayor, David Dinkins and 1993, when Muslim fundamentalists bombed the World Trade Center, and Rudolph Giuliani was elected Mayor for the first time.

Sights

A first general view of the city can be had from the observation platform of the World Trade Center or the Empire State Building, which both afford breathtaking panoramic prospects. The city's unique skyline is best appreciated from the sea, either on one of the sightseeing cruises that are offered to visitors or, no less strikingly but much more cheaply (50 cents) by taking the Staten Island Ferry from the southern tip of Manhattan to Staten Island and back again. There are many firms offering coach tours, and there are also sightseeing flights by helicopter.

The Statue of Liberty against the skyline of Lower Manhattan

Information about all these various possibilities can be obtained from the New York Convention and Visitors Bureau, 2 Columbus Circle, ground floor; Mon.–Sat. 9am–6pm, Sun. 10am–3pm. The best way of getting around New York is by the subway, which has an extensive network covering all the places you will want to see; all the same, for safety's sake it should not be used for visits to the outer districts and carriages with few or no passengers should be avoided; it is better to take the middle carriages with the conductor, and to use the "off-peak waiting area" that is surveyed by station officials or video cameras. Late in the evening it may be better to take a taxi.

Lower Manhattan

Lower Manhattan (Downtown) is the area on the Manhattan peninsula to the south of 14th Street.

On a rocky island 2½ mi. south-west of the southern tip of Manhattan is the world-famous Statue of Liberty holding her torch aloft – for millions of immigrants the first they saw of America and the symbol of their hopes. The 305 ft high figure by the Alsatian sculptor Frédéric Auguste Bartholdi was a gift from France to commemorate the 100th anniversary of the United States. From the observation platforms in the head and in the torch – which are usually crowded – there are marvellous views of the city's skyline and, in the opposite direction, of the Verrazano-Narrows Bridge (one of the world's longest suspension bridges (4567 yds), which links Staten Island with Brooklyn. In the base of the statue is a small museum recording the creation of the statue and its effect on immigrants.

★Statue of Liberty
Ferry: daily from 9am, every half-hour from Battery Park

Before entering their new home all immigrants were required to pass through admission procedures on Ellis Island. By the beginning of the First World War some 17 million people had been processed here: their fate was often decided in a few minutes, so that Ellis Island became known as the "island of tears". Since 1990 the immigration buildings have been a museum, in which – more directly than in the Statue of Liberty – visitors can follow the history of immigration. There is also a computerised data base from which they can discover the date of entry of their ancestors or relatives.

Ellis Island
Ferry: see above

The southern tip of Manhattan – the Battery, with the South Ferry Plaza – is dominated by the skyscrapers of New York Plaza.

Battery

Crouching in their shadow is **Fraunces' Tavern**, originally the oldest building on Manhattan (1719) but later twice burned down and rebuilt. In this famous tavern (the present version of which is not an exact reproduction of the original) Washington spent his last days as commander-in-chief of the revolutionary forces before retiring to his country house, Mount Vernon (see Washington, DC).

North-west of the tavern is the square known as the Bowling Green, with the old Customs House, now housing the ★**Museum of the American Indian** with its exceptionally fine and rare collections. It stands at the beginning of Broadway, New York's best known street, which runs north from the southern tip of Manhattan for over 12 mi.

The western half of the southern tip of Manhattan is occupied by Battery Park, with the **Castle Clinton** National Monument. The castle was completed in 1811, and from 1824 to 1855 housed entertainments and concerts; it was then used as an immigration station, and later, until 1941, was occupied by an Aquarium. It has now been restored to its original state.

New York City

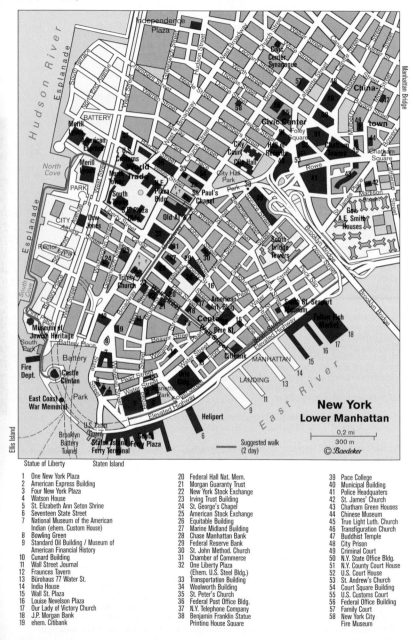

1 One New York Plaza
2 American Express Building
3 Four New York Plaza
4 Watson House
5 St. Elizabeth Ann Seton Shrine
6 Seventeen State Street
7 National Museum of the American
  Indian (ehem. Custom House)
8 Bowling Green
9 Standard Oil Building / Museum of
  American Financial History
10 Cunard Building
11 Wall Street Journal
12 Fraunces Tavern
13 Bürohaus 77 Water St.
14 India House
15 Wall St. Plaza
16 Louise Nevelson Plaza
17 Our Lady of Victory Church
18 J.P. Morgan Bank
19 ehem. Citibank

20 Federal Hall Nat. Mem.
21 Morgan Guaranty Trust
22 New York Stock Exchange
23 Irving Trust Building
24 St. George's Chapel
25 American Stock Exchange
26 Equitable Building
27 Marine Midland Building
28 Chase Manhattan Bank
29 Federal Reserve Bank
30 St. John Method. Church
31 Chamber of Commerce
32 One Liberty Plaza
   (Ehem. U.S. Steel Bldg.)
33 Transportation Building
34 Woolworth Building
35 St. Peter's Church
36 Federal Post Office Bldg.
37 N.Y. Telephone Company
38 Benjamin Franklin Statue
   Printing House Square

39 Pace College
40 Municipal Building
41 Police Headquaters
42 St. James' Church
43 Chatham Green Houses
44 Chinese Museum
45 True Light Luth. Church
46 Transfiguration Church
47 Buddhist Temple
48 City Prison
49 Criminal Court
50 N.Y. State Office Bldg.
51 N.Y. County Court House
52 U.S. Court House
53 St. Andrew's Church
54 Court Square Building
55 U.S. Customs Court
56 Federal Office Building
57 Family Court
58 New York City
   Fire Museum

370

To the north is ★**Battery Park City**, an ambitious scheme carried out in the 1980s to rehabilitate and redevelop the south-western shore of Manhattan, which had come sadly down in the world. The dominant architectural features are now the buildings (designed by Cesar Pelli) of the World Financial Center, with the headquarters of Dow Jones, American Express and Merrill Lynch; particularly notable is the spacious and airy Winter Garden.

This newest of New York's museums is concerned with Jewish life and culture from the 19th c. until the present day, focusing especially on the Holocaust.

Museum of Jewish Heritage

To the east of the World Financial Center are the 1380 ft high twin towers of the World Trade Center, designed by Minuro Yamasaki and opened in 1973. The two main towers and six other buildings, including the Commodity Futures Exchange, accommodate a total staff of 50,000, who find their way to their offices with the help of 104 elevators. Visitors are taken up to the observation deck in the south tower, from which there are spectacular views. On the 107th floor is the exclusive Windows on the World restaurant. Open daily 9.30am–9.30pm.

★★World Trade Center

From the World Trade Center we go east to return to Broadway and, turning south, pass a number of skyscrapers, including the Old AT & T Building and One Liberty Plaza (742 ft high), and come to Trinity Church (originally built in 1698; present building 1846). Its churchyard, the oldest in the city, contains the graves of Alexander Hamilton (1755–1804), the first US secretary of the treasury, and Robert Fulton (1765–1815), constructor of the first successful steamship.

Trinity Church

Opposite the church, running east, is Wall Street, heart of the American financial world, which takes its name from a wall built by the Dutch as a

★Wall Street

The Federal Hall stands, where George Washington once was sworn in as a president

371

defence against British attacks. On the corner is the 640 ft high tower of the Irving Trust, and beyond this the **New York Stock Exchange**, housed in a building of 1903 resembling a Roman temple. Activity on the floor of the Exchange (illustration, p. 54) can be watched from the visitors' gallery, and there are also guided tours (open Mon.–Fri. 9am–4pm). Adjoining the Exchange, at the corner of Broad Street, are the fortress-like headquarters of the J.P. Morgan Bank.

At the intersection with Nassau Street is the **Federal Hall National Memorial**, the city's finest neoclassical building, built in 1842 as the Custom House. It occupies the site of Federal Hall, in which Washington was sworn in as President in 1789 and Congress met for a time. To the north, on Nassau Street, is the 810 ft high tower of the Chase Manhattan Bank; the building at 60 Wall Street is only 65 ft lower. Wall Street continues east – to the north, at 80 Pine Street, is a 950 ft high skyscraper – and finally runs into South Street, on the East River.

★South Street Seaport

On South Street, below the Brooklyn Bridge, is South Street Seaport, once the heart of the Port of New York and now a museum area. Here can be seen a number of historic ships, including one of the legendary "flying P Liners", the four-master "Peking" (1911). There are also harbour cruises in the schooner "Pioneer". Between Water and Front Streets are a number of shops and restaurants. For early risers a visit to the noisy and colourful Fulton Fish Market.

★Brooklyn Bridge

From the South Street Seaport there is a good view of the Brooklyn Bridge (1150 yd long), the oldest bridge over the East River (1867–83) and the first to be suspended on steel cables.

City Hall

City Hall, half way down Lower Manhattan, was built in 1803–12 in French Renaissance style. In the Governor's Room are the chair on which Washington sat during his inauguration and the seats used in the first Congress.

Woolworth Building

South-west of City Hall, on Broadway, is the neo-Gothic Woolworth Building (by Cass Gilbert, 1913). Until the completion of the Chrysler Building (see below) in 1931 this 790 ft high skyscraper was the tallest building in the world.

Civic Center

The area north of City Hall and east of Broadway is occupied by the Civic Center, with the 580 ft high Municipal Building, the Federal Building, the Police Headquarters, the United States Courthouse, the New York County Courthouse and the old Tombs Prison.

★Chinatown

To the east of the Civic Center is Chinatown, whose population is estimated at 150,000, making it the largest Chinese inhabited city outside China. In its narrow lanes, so different from everywhere else in New York, in addition to great numbers of shops selling Chinese wares and numerous Chinese restaurants, visitors will come across Buddhist temples and the Chinese Museum in Mott Street. There are lively celebrations of the Chinese New Year, with colourful parades, between the end of January and mid February.

Little Italy

To the north of Chinatown is Little Italy, a land of pasta and grappa – though it is steadily losing ground to the ever expanding Chinatown.

Lower East Side

Lower East side – the blocks to the east of Chinatown and Little Italy, extending to the East River – is still a slum area occupied by the poorer classes of the population. Here, particularly in Orchard Street, there are many Jewish shops selling good quality fashion goods, shoes and furs at low prices.

The name of this district has nothing to do with London's Soho, but merely indicates its situation, South of Houston Street (pronounced "House-ton"). This old factory and warehouse quarter was "discovered" in the 1970s by artists, who brought after them galleries, shops, bars and restaurants. There are many interesting old cast-iron buildings in this area. The brick Guggenheim SoHo building at 575 Broadway houses a branch of the Guggenheim Museum of Modern Art, opened in 1992.

★SoHo

Nowadays the "Village", between 14th Street and Broadway, is a hand-some (and therefore expensive) residential district. Until the 1960s it was the haunt of writers and artists, and something of this reputation still lingers.

★Greenwich Village

Its central feature is the lively **Washington Square**. Round the square are the buildings of New York City University, and in the centre is a tri-umphal arch commemorating the centenary of Washington's inaugura-tion as President. Other interesting streets and squares are Bleecker Street (antique shops, restaurants, movie houses, bars, theatres), Commerce Street, Christopher Street (centre of the New York gay scene) and Union Square, once the city's entertainment district.

To the east, beyond Broadway, is East Village, formerly occupied exclus-ively by Ukrainians and Poles but discovered in the 1960s by the "flower children" and now the refuge of all those who can no longer afford a flat in Greenwich Village and have made East Village a fashionable address. Round St Mark's Place are numerous second-hand shops offering an extraordinary variety of wares. St Mark's in the Bowerie, on the corner of Second Avenue and 10th Street is the second oldest church in the city, dating from 1799.

East Village

Midtown Manhattan

Midtown Manhattan lies between 14th Street in the south and 57th Street in the north. It is laid out on a regular grid plan, with avenues run-ning north–south, beginning with First Avenue in the east, and streets running east–west, and with Broadway cutting diagonally across it.

Its main axis is Fifth Avenue, which begins at Washington Square and runs north for several miles, skirting the east side of Central Park. It divides Manhattan into an eastern and a western half, with streets named accordingly (E 14th St., W 14th St.). The Midtown section of Fifth Avenue is the real heart of the city, the scene of the various parades that take place throughout the year. Here, between 34th and 57th Streets, is a great concentration of skyscrapers, on Broadway itself and in the side streets; here too are the city's most exclusive shops, the jewellers Tiffany, Van Cleef and Cartier, the Bergdorf Goodman fashion house, and numbers of luxury hotels.

★★Fifth Avenue

At the corner of Fifth Avenue and 34th Street is the Empire State Building, New York's most celebrated skyscraper, its fame enhanced by its role in the film "King Kong". It is particularly striking when floodlit at night. Built of limestone and granite in 1932, this 1250 ft high tower (1475 ft including the aerial) was for many years the world's tallest build-ing. From the observation platforms on the 86th and 102nd floors there are incomparable views of New York. Open daily 9.30am–midnight.

★★Empire State Building

Two blocks north-east of the Empire State Building, at 29 East 36th Street, is the Pierpont Morgan Library, which houses the collection of rare books and works of art assembled by the banker John Pierpont Morgan (1837–1913). In the East Room are displayed incunabula, manu-scripts and autographs; in the West Room are works of art, including the

Pierpont Morgan Library

New York City

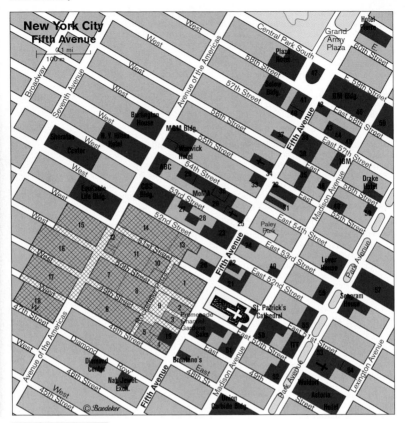

© Baedeker

▓▓▓ **ROCKEFELLER CENTER**

1 International Building
2 British Empire Building
3 Maison Française
4 Sinclair Oil Building
5 One Rockefeller Center
6 U.S. Rubber Company
7 General Electric Bldg. West
8 General Electric Bldg. (RCA Bldg.)
9 Rockefeller Plaza/ Prometheus
10 Associated Press Building
11 Radio City Music Hall
12 Amer. Metal Climax Building
13 15 W. 51st St. Building
14 Sperry Rand Building
15 Time & Life Building
16 Exxon Building
17 McGraw Hill Building
18 Celanese Building

19 Swiss Center
20 640 Fifth Avenue Building
21 Olympic Tower
22 Cartier (Juwelier)
23 Tishman (666 5th Ave.) Building
24 Rolex Building
25 St. Thomas Episcopal Church
26 Museum of Modern Art
27 American Craft Museum
28 Museum of Television & Radio
29 Hotel Dorset
30 A.A. Rockefeller Garden
31 Elizabeth Arden (Beauty)
32 St. Regis Sheraton Hotel
33 Hotel Gotham
34 Fifth Ave. Presbyterian Church
35 Corning Glass Building
36 Sony Building (ehem. AT & T)
37 Doubleday (Buchhandlung)
38 Tiffany's (Juwelier)
39 Trump Tower

40 Van Cleef (Juwelier)
41 Bergdorf Goodman (Mode)
42 Bergdorf Goodman (Mode)
43 Galeries Lafayette
44 Escada (Mode)
45 Hermès (Mode)
46 F.A.O. Schwarz (Spielwaren)
47 Pulitzer Memorial Fountain
48 Hotel Winslow
49 Hotel Inter-Continental
50 Palace Hotel
51 Newsweek Building
52 Colgate Palmolive Building
53 St. Bartholomew's Church
54 General Electric Building
55 Manuf. Hanover
     Bank Building
56 Racquet & Tennis Club
57 Citibank Building
58 Mercedes-Benz
59 Standard Brands Building

marriage portraits of Martin Luther and Katharina Bora by Lucas Cranach the Elder.

To the west of the Empire State Building, beyond Herald Square, is Macy's, the world's largest department store.

Macy's

Still further west, between Sixth Avenue (Avenue of the Americas) and Eighth Avenue, is the famous Madison Square Garden Center, its position marked by the 765 ft high tower of One Penn Plaza. Underground is the large Pennsylvania Station.

Madison Square
Garden Center

From Macy's Broadway runs north–west to Times Square, the heart of the Theater District round Broadway. With many of its theatres closing down to give place to porno movie houses and night spots, the square had lost its former splendour, becoming not altogether safe, the haunt of drug dealers. However, at the beginning of the 1990s a group of investors from Manhattan took steps to clean up the streets, providing support for drug dependants and the homeless, whilst of course introducing ambitious building programmes. A gold-rush atmosphere now pervades Times Square, and former red-light establishments have been replaced by Disney, Virgin, Marriott Marquis, Bertelsmann, palatial cinemas and the elephant department store Gap.

★Times Square

Six blocks east of Times Square along 42nd Street, which runs past New York Public Library (the largest library in the United States after the Library of Congress in Washington, DC), is the Chrysler Building. The World Trade Center may be the tallest skyscraper in New York and the Empire State Building the most famous; but in the eyes of New Yorkers the 1045 ft high Chrysler Building (1931) is the hand-

★★Chrysler
Building

No longer the tallest, but certainly the world's most famous skyscraper: the Empire State Building in Midtown Manhattan

somest, with its fine art-deco exterior and its fantastic art-deco entrance lobby.

★United Nations Headquarters

At the end of 42nd Street, on the East River, is the United Nations Headquarters, occupying a site acquired through the munificence of John D. Rockefeller. It is dominated by the 440 ft high Secretariat Building (by Le Corbusier and Niemeyer, 1949–53), with the offices of the Secretary General on the 38th floor. In the Conference Room is a remarkable world clock. Adjoining is the low General Assembly Building, with the chamber in which the General Assembly meets; here too are a souvenir shop and the United Nations post office, whose stamps and special postmarks are much sought after. To sit in on meetings of the General Assembly (at 10.30am and 3.30pm) you must apply in the lobby an hour in advance. Guided tours Mar.–Dec. daily 9.15am–4.45pm, Jan., Feb. only Mon.–Fri.

PanAm Building

Back along 42nd Street, at the intersection with Park Avenue, is the 807 ft high PanAm Building (by Emery Roth, Pietro Belluschi and Walter Gropius, 1963), now occupied by an insurance corporation. At its foot is the huge **Grand Central Station**.

Park Avenue

On three parallel avenues, Park Avenue in the centre, with Lexington Avenue to the east and Madison Avenue to the west, are a series of notable skyscrapers and other buildings. On Park Avenue: Union Carbide Building (No. 270; 705 ft high), Chemical Bank (No. 277; 690 ft), American Brands (No. 245; 650 ft), Seagram Building (No. 375; 525 ft; by Mies van der Rohe and Philip Johnson, 1958), Citibank (No. 399; 742 ft), Lever House (1952; first glass façade on Park Ave.), the long-established Waldorf Astoria Hotel (No. 301) and the neighbouring St Bartholomew's Church (1919).

Lexington Avenue

★**Citicorp Center** (No. 575; 915 ft; by Hugh Stubbins, 1978, with sloping roof), General Electric Building (No. 570; 640 ft) and No. 599 (653 ft).

Madison Avenue

IBM Tower (No. 590; 600 ft; by E.L. Barnes, 1984), with a marvellous roofed plaza and the IBM Gallery of Science and Art, and the ★**AT & T Building** (No. 550; 646 ft), the controversial icon of the postmodern movement (by Philip Johnson, 1983), with a spectacular roof.

★St Patrick's Cathedral

In the block bounded by Madison and Fifth Avenues and East 50th and 51st Streets is St Patrick's Cathedral (RC), whose 330 ft high tower is dwarfed by the surrounding skyscrapers. The cathedral, seat of the Archbishop, was built between 1858 and 1888. In its spacious interior is a figure of Elizabeth Ann Seton (1774–1821), foundress of the Sisters of Charity and the first American saint.

★Rockefeller Center

Between Fifth and Sixth Avenues and 47th and 52nd Streets is the Rockefeller Center (named after John D. Rockefeller Jr), the world's largest commercial and entertainment complex, decorated with numerous works of art. Its lively centrepiece is the Rockefeller Plaza with its Sunken Plaza (gilded figure of Prometheus), in summer a favourite meeting place and in winter converted into an ice rink dominated by a huge and splendidly decorated Christmas tree. Towering above the whole complex is the 850 ft high General Electric Building, formerly known as the TCA Building, with the studios of the NBC television company.

Beyond West 50th Street is the art-deco **Radio City Music Hall** (1930), with the world's largest auditorium (6200 seats).

Other striking **skyscrapers** in and around the Rockefeller Center are the Exon Building (1251 Sixth Ave.; 750 ft), the McGraw Hill Building (1221

Sixth Ave.; 673 ft), the Equitable Center Tower West (787 Seventh Ave.; 750 ft), the Olympic Tower (645 Fifth Ave.; 620 ft; by Skidmore, Owings and Merrill, 1976) and, rather further north, the Trump Tower (725 Fifth Ave.; 663 ft; by Der Scott), with a terraced exterior and a lavishly decorated atrium.

This museum at 25 West 52nd Street offers an impressive survey of the world of film, television and radio in the United States.

Museum of TV and Radio

North of the Rockefeller Center are the Museum Tower Apartments, a 650 ft high apartment block that marks the site of the Museum of Modern Art (MOMA). This, the world's finest collection of late 19th and 20th c. art, has been housed since 1984 in a building by Cesar Pelli at 11 West 53rd Street. Only a brief summary of the artists represented can be given here: Abby Aldrich Rockefeller Sculpture Garden: modern sculpture by Max Ernst, Alexander Calder, Picasso ("The Goat"), Henry Moore and many others. First floor: Post Impressionists (Degas, Gauguin, Munch, Toulouse-Lautrec, Modigliani), Cubists (Braque, Chagall), Expressionists, Futurists, the Blauer Reiter group (Kokoschka, Schmidt-Rotluff, Nolde, Macke, Heckel), Mondrian, Matisse (the largest collection of his work anywhere), Picasso ("Demoiselles d'Avignon", "Harlequin"), Dada (Max Ernst, Schwitters), Joan Miró, Surrealists. Second floor: mainly American artists (Hopper, O'Keefe, Prendergast), Pop Art (Oldenburg, Lichtenstein, Rauschenberg). Third floor: architecture and design, with original designs by leading architects. Open Sat.–Tue. 11am–6pm, Thu., Fri. noon–8.30pm.

★★Museum of Modern Art

Adjoining MOMA is the **American Craft Museum** (40 W 53rd St.), mainly devoted to craft products of the 20th c.

North of this, at 157 West 57th Street, is the venerable old Carnegie Hall, the venue of many celebrated concerts.

Carnegie Hall

Uptown Manhattan/Central Park

Uptown Manhattan extends from 57th Street all the way north to the Henry Hudson Bridge, taking in Central Park, the green lung of New York, the Museum Mile on the east side of the park, with the Metropolitan and Guggenheim Museum, and the black district of Harlem.

Central Park, New York's recreation area, lies between 59th Street in the south and 110th Street in the north and between Fifth and Eighth Avenues in east and west, with a total area of 840 acres. Here you can sunbathe, roller skate, row on the lake or drive round the park in a horse-drawn carriage. Among features of particular interest in the park are the Zoo at the south-east corner, opened in 1989; the old house known as the Dairy, dating from the park's 19th c. origins, with an exhibition on the history of the park; the Mall, a wide avenue lined with statues of writers and composers that leads to the Bethesda Fountain and to the lake with Loeb's Boathouse (boat hire); to the north of this Belvedere Castle, the highest point in the park, and Cleopatra's Needle (counterpart of the one in London), an Egyptian obelisk of about 1500 BC from Heliopolis; to the west of the Bethesda Fountain the Strawberry Fields, named after the Beatles' song, which lie opposite the Dakota Building on 72nd Street in front of which John Lennon was murdered in 1980. The northern section of the park is better avoided even during the day.

★★Central Park

New York City

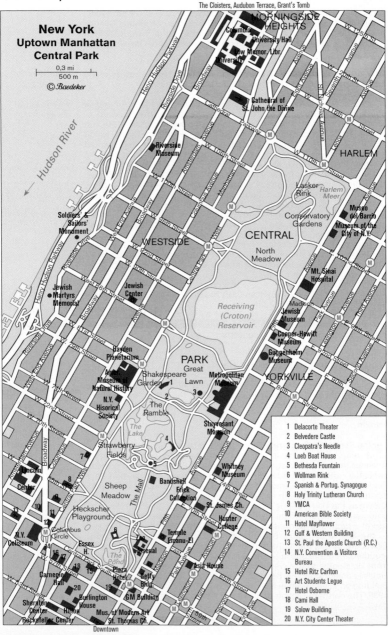

The Cloisters, Audubon Terrace, Grant's Tomb

**New York
Uptown Manhattan
Central Park**

0,3 mi
500 m
© Baedeker

1 Delacorte Theater
2 Belvedere Castle
3 Cleopatra's Needle
4 Loeb Boat House
5 Bethesda Fountain
6 Wollman Rink
7 Spanish & Portug. Synagogue
8 Holy Trinity Lutheran Church
9 YMCA
10 American Bible Society
11 Hotel Mayflower
12 Gulf & Western Building
13 St. Paul the Apostle Church (R.C.)
14 N.Y. Convention & Visitors
   Bureau
15 Hotel Ritz Carlton
16 Art Students Legue
17 Hotel Osborne
18 Cami Hall
19 Solow Building
20 N.Y. City Center Theater

378

East of Central Park

On the eastern edge of Central Park, at 1000 Fifth Avenue, is the extensive range of buildings occupied by the Metropolitan Museum of Art. The main building was erected between 1879 and 1898; the middle section was designed by Richard M. Hunt, the side wings by McKim, Meade and White. The Metropolitan Museum of Art, the largest art museum in the world after the British Museum in London and the Hermitage in St Petersburg, was founded in 1870 by a group of New Yorkers, and now contains over 3 million works of art, some 100,000 of which are on permanent display. When visiting the museum you should select on the printed plan the particular sections that interest you most; here only the briefest summary of the museum's contents can be given:

★★Metropolitan Museum of Art

In the **basement**, the Antionia Ratti Textile Center displays men's and women's clothing and costumes from the 17th to 20th centuries, whilst the Uris Center for Education seeks to make the world of museums and art accessible to young people.

Ground floor Ancient Egyptian art (including the temple from Dendur, taken down during the construction of the Aswan High Dam, presented to the United States and re-erected here, fourteen statues of Queen Hatshepsut and a princess's gold jewellery dating from about 1900 BC); Greek and Roman art (including finds from the palace of Knossos and Roman copies of Hellenistic sculpture); medieval and Byzantine art (sculpture, large tapestry gallery); European sculpture, period rooms (including a marble patio from the Spanish castle of Vélez Blanco, a study from a palace in Gubbio, Sävres and Meissen porcelain); arms and armour (Viking swords, parade and jousting armour); Robert Lehman Collection (paintings and drawings, with works by Dürer, Memling, Cranach the Elder, El Greco, Goya); American Wing (American art and

In Central Park, a green oasis surrounded by skyscrapers

applied art; continued on second floor); Michael C. Rockefeller Wing (art of the Pacific area); Lila Acheson Wallace Wing (20th c. art, including Picasso's portrait of Gertrude Stein, Paul Klee collection, Edward Hopper, sculpture garden; continued on second floor).

Second floor European painting (Raphael, Titian, Veronese, Frans Hals, Vermeer, van Eyck, van der Weyden, Memling, van der Goes, Cranach the Elder, Holbein the Younger, Dürer, Rembrandt, Rubens, van Dyck, Poussin, Hogarth, Reynolds, Turner); André Meyer Galleries (19th c. European art, including Symbolists, Romantics, Impressionists); Islamic art (woodcarving, ceramics, carpets); ancient Oriental art (Persia, Anatolia, Babylon); art of the Far East (including Chinese and Japanese lacquerwork, jade and bronzes); drawings and printed graphic art (including Leonardo da Vinci, Michelangelo and Dürer; woodcuts by Goya); musical instruments (including three Stradivariuses). Open Tue.–Thu., Sun. 9.30am–5.15pm, Fri., Sat. to 8.45pm.

★Frick Collection

South of the Metropolitan Museum, at 1 East 70th Street, is the Frick Collection, presented in the very different setting of a sumptuously appointed Empire-style mansion. This very fine private collection assembled by the Pittsburgh steel magnate Henry Clay Frick (1849–1919) concentrates particularly on painting of the 14th–18th centuries (Titian, Bellini, El Greco, Ingres, Vermeer, van Eyck), Italian Renaissance bronzes and enamelwork. Open Tue.–Sat. 10am–6pm, Sun. 1–6pm.

★Whitney Museum of American Art

The excellent Whitney Museum of American Art (945 Madison Ave.) is devoted to modern American art, including Pop Art and works left by Edward Hopper. Open Wed., Fri.–Sun. 11am–6pm, Thu. 1–8pm.

★Solomon R. Guggenheim Museum

The Guggenheim Museum, north of the Metropolitan Museum at 1071 Fifth Avenue, is impressive not only for the collection assembled by the industrialist Solomon R. Guggenheim (1861–1949) but also for the building itself. Designed by Frank Lloyd Wright (see Famous People), this is circular in form, each storey larger than the one below. Visitors walk up or down in a spiral as they go round the collection, which includes works by Kandinsky (largest collection in the world), Henri Rousseau, Braque, Picasso, Léger, Cézanne, van Gogh, Chagall and many other artists. Open Sun.–Wed. 10am–6pm, Fri., Sat. 10am–8pm.

Cooper-Hewitt Museum

A short distance north of the Guggenheim Museum, at 2 East 91st Street, is the Cooper-Hewitt Museum, a branch of the Smithsonian Institution (see Washington, DC) devoted to American design.

Jewish Museum

A little further north again (Fifth Ave. and 92nd St.) is the Jewish Museum, with one of the world's largest collection of Judaica.

Museum of the City of New York

Still further north (Fifth Ave. and 103rd St.) is the Museum of the City of New York, which is devoted to the history of the city.

West of Central Park

Columbus Circle

At the south-west corner of Central Park Broadway crosses the Columbus Circle, a busy roundabout in the centre of which is a column bearing a statue of Columbus, set up here in 1892. Here is the New York Convention and Visitors Bureau, housed in a Moorish-style building opposite the 680 ft high Gulf and Western Building.

★Lincoln Center for the Performing Arts

North-west of the Columbus Circle is the Lincoln Center for the Performing Arts, the city's cultural heart. The most important buildings in the complex are the Avery Fisher Hall, home of the New York Philharmonic Orchestra; the New York State Theater, home of the New

York City Opera and New York City Ballet; and the **Metropolitan Opera House**, the legendary "Met", one of the world's great opera houses. In the lobby is an Information Center (programmes of performances; guided tours).

On the west side of Central Park (79th St.) is the American Museum of Natural History, New York's largest museum after the Metropolitan Museum of Art. It illustrates the natural history of the United States with a great variety of displays and dioramas, with such outstanding items as the model of a whale in the Hall of Ocean Life and the "Brazilian Princess", the world's largest cut precious stone, a 21,327 carat topaz. Children will particularly enjoy the Discovery Room, where they can touch and experiment with the exhibits. Attached to the museum is the Hayden Planetarium, which puts on a series of special shows on the general theme of exploring the universe. Open daily 10am–5.45pm, Fri., Sat. to 8.45pm.

★★American Museum of Natural History

North of Central Park

Immediately north of Central Park is Harlem, home of New York's African–American population and still a neglected and dilapidated part of the city, although here too there is now a spirit of optimism, with an unprecedented amount of building and renovation in progress. It is better not to explore Harlem on foot, even by day: the best way of seeing its main features of interest – the Abyssinian Baptist Church, All Saints Church, Strivers' Row, the Schomberg Center for Research in Black Culture – is on a coach tour. In the evening, if you want to visit one of the excellent jazz clubs in the area you should take a taxi.

Harlem

Near the north-west corner of Central Park is the Cathedral Church of St John the Divine, begun in 1891 but still unfinished, although with room for 10,000 seated and 8,000 standing, it is already one of the largest churches in the world.

★St John the Divine

Much further north (Broadway and 115th St.), on Audubon Terrace that was named after the United States naturalist and illustrator John James Audubon, are the Washington Heights Museums, including the Museums of the Hispanic Society and Numismatic Society.

Washington Heights Museums

Picturesquely situated above the Hudson River at the northern tip of Manhattan, in Fort Tryon Park, are the Cloisters, which house the Metropolitan Museum's collection of religious art and architecture, including whole cloisters, chapterhouses and chapels, all harmoniously brought together in a new building fashioned from fragments of mainly 12th–15th c. French, Spanish and German monastic houses to create the atmosphere of a medieval monastery. Open Mar.–Oct. Tue.–Sun. 9.30am–5.15pm; Nov.–Feb. to 4.45pm.

★★The Cloisters

Brooklyn/Queens/Bronx/Staten Island

Brooklyn, the largest of New York's boroughs, lies on Long Island, to the east of Manhattan beyond the East River. North of Brooklyn, also on Long Island, is Queens, and north of this again, beyond the East River and separated from Manhattan by the Harlem River, is the Bronx. To the south of Manhattan, bordering on New Jersey, is Staten Island.

Brooklyn is linked with Manhattan by the Brooklyn-Battery Tunnel, Brooklyn Bridge, Manhattan Bridge and Queensboro Bridge.

Brooklyn

The delightful quarter of **Brooklyn Heights** stretches between Brooklyn

Bridge and Atlantic Avenue From Brooklyn Promenade on the East River there is a fantastic and much photographed view across to Manhattan.

The principal feature of interest is the ★**Brooklyn Museum** (200 Eastern Parkway), which has one of the finest collections anywhere of Egyptian, Near Eastern and Oriental art, together with American and European painting, costumes and applied and decorative art. Beside the Museum is Brooklyn Botanic Garden, with 12,000 different plants, including 900 varieties of roses.

At 145 Brooklyn Avenue is the **Brooklyn Children's Museum**, the first children's museum in the world, founded in 1899. It seeks to promote practical experience of technology and nature, allowing children to touch everything and carry out their own experiments.

On Gowanus Heights (main entrance 5th Ave. and 25th St.) is **Greenwood Cemetery**, laid out in 1840. Among those buried here are Samuel Morse (1792–1872), inventor of the telegraph, Elias P. Howe (1819–67) who invented the first functioning sewing machine, and Lola Montez (1818–61), the dancer who became the mistress of King Ludwig I of Bavaria.

At the southern tip of Brooklyn is ★**Coney Island**, which before the Second World War was a famous amusement park and bathing beach on the Atlantic but has now rather come down in the world. Nevertheless it is still very attractive and the beach is clean. Here too is the New York Aquarium, with marine fauna from all over the world.

Queens

Flushing Meadows Park, where the World's Fairs of 1939–40 and 1964–5 were held, is known to tennis fans all over the world as the place where

The amusement park beside Coney Island beach

the US Open Championship is staged – though most of the stars feel that the noise of the traffic and the aircraft using LaGuardia Airport disturbs their concentration. The Shea Stadium is the home ground of the New York Jets football team.

The **American Museum of the Moving Image** (34–12 36th St.) is devoted to the history of American film.

Bronx

The Bronx has gained the reputation of a run-down area with a high crime rate; and it is certainly advisable to drive quickly through the broken-down landscape of South Bronx, without getting out, to visit the New York Zoological Park (the **Bronx Zoo**) in the centre of the Bronx, in which almost all the animals live in open-air enclosures.

Immediately north of the Zoo is the New York **Botanical Garden** (area 290 acres), laid out in 1891 on the model of London's Kew Gardens. Immediately to the east of the Harlem River lies the Yankee Stadium, home to the famous baseball team, the New York Yankees.

Staten Island

It is well worth while to take the ferry to Staten Island, not only for the sake of the marvellous view of Manhattan but also to visit **Historic Richmond Town**, a museum village with 39 houses of the 17th–19th centuries that seeks to re-create the life of the early colonists. Here too is the Mausoleum of the Vanderbilt family.

The **Gateway National Recreation Area** on the coast of Staten Island, to the south of Coney Island across the Verrazano Narrows, offers tired New Yorkers the relaxation of quiet natural surroundings.

Surroundings

Long Island

This 110 mi. long island in the Atlantic is the most popular area of relaxation in the New York region, with beautiful bathing beaches (e.g. on Jones Beach or in Robert Moses State Park). Further east are the quiet and elegant settlements known as the Hamptons, where there are more fashionable beaches and the rural retreats of the city's intelligentsia, as well as attractive old streets like East Hampton's Main Street, which ends at a fish restaurant. The northern part of the island, round Oyster Bay, is also a favourite getaway for the wealthy.

New Jersey

For those wishing to make an excursion into the adjacent state of New Jersey (see entry), places of interest include Frank Sinatra's birthplace Hoboken, Sandy Hook at the northern tip of the Jersey Shore and New Orange, with Thomas Alva Edison's laboratory.

★★Niagara Falls   F 46/47

New York State – Canadian province of Ontario

The Niagara Falls – among the largest, most impressive and best known falls in the world – lie in the extreme north-west of New York State. Here masses of water from Lake Erie plunge over an almost 200 ft drop to flow into Lake Ontario. First described and sketched by a missionary, Louis Hennepin in 1678, they attract over 12 million visitors a year.

The masses of water are used to produce energy. The present hydro-electric power stations have a total output of 3 million kW. Before the falls were harnessed to produce electricity, water poured down at the rate of almost 1,300,000 gallons per second. A Canadian–American agreement of 1951 on the joint use of the water guarantees a daytime flow of just under half that amount during the summer and just under a quarter at night and in the winter.

Formation The origins of the Niagara Falls go back to the Ice Age, when the river, flowing at a higher level than today over a limestone plateau on the Niagara escarpment, dropped down to the level of Lake Ontario near the present-day town of Lewiston. Then, as a result of retrograde erosion, the falls rapidly moved upstream. Over the last 3000 years they have moved back from the Rainbow Bridge to their present position. The pace of erosion depends on the volume of water going over the falls; but at present rates it can be expected that within a few hundred thousand years the Niagara Falls will be close to the American city of Buffalo.

Geography The masses of water from Lake Erie thunder over a horseshoe-shape rock wall 700 yds long at the Horseshoe Falls, which are in Canada, and, a short distance north-east, over the straight American Falls, 360 yds long. The frontier between the United States and Canada runs along the middle of the river.

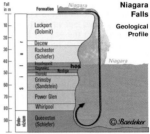

Below the falls the Niagara River flows through a deep gorge varying in width between 90 yds and 330 yds. To the north-west the gorge narrows and forms a series of rapids (the Whirlpool Rapids).

The "Maid of the Mist" on the whirlpool of the Horseshoe Falls

Daredevils of Niagara

Le Petit Journal

DEUX ENFANTS EMPORTÉS PAR LES CHUTES DU NIAGARA

Niagara makes headlines in Europe; "Le Petit Journal", July 1913

The Niagara Falls have exerted a fascination on daredevils and publicity seekers anxious to hit the headlines. A small selection:

1825: Three men die in an attempt to go over the falls in boats.

1829: Sam Patch twice jumps a distance of 120 ft from a ladder at the Cave of the Winds (near Goat Island) and survives.

1859: M. Blondin, a French rope-dancer, crosses the gorge on a tightrope several times, once carrying his impressario on his back and on another occasion with a stove on which he makes an omlette.

1873: An Italian named Belleni crosses the falls on a tightrope.

1876: An Italian woman, Maria Spetterini or Spelterina, becomes the first woman to cross the gorge on a tightrope.

1882: Steve Peer crosses the river on a tightrope several times by day and then falls to his death in attempting to cross by night.

1883: The Channel-swimmer Matthew Webb is drowned in an attempt to swim through the Whirlpool Rapids.

1886: Carlisle D. Graham traverses the Whirlpool Rapids four times in a barrel contructed by himself; Maud Willard is drowned attempting a similar feat; W.K. Kendall swims through the rapids.

1888: Robert W. Flack is drowned trying to sail down the rapids in a specially contructed boat.

1889: Steve Brodi goes over the Horseshoe Falls in a wooden barrel and survives.

1901: Martha Wagenführer traverses the Whirlpool Rapids in a barrel; a teacher named Annie Edson Taylor goes over the Horseshoe Falls in a wooden barrel weighted with an anvil and suffers only slight injuries; Lincoln Beach flies under the Upper Steel Arch Bridge in a light aircraft.

1910: Claus Larsen negotiates the rapids in a motorboat.

1911: An Englishman, Bobby Leach, goes over the Horseshoe Falls in a barrel but is severely injured.

1920: An English hairdresser named Charles Stephens dies in a plunge over the Horseshoe Falls in a wooden barrel.

1928: Jean Lussier launches himself over the Horseshoe Falls in a large rubber ball and survives.

1930: George L. Stathika survives a plunge over the falls in a steel and timber barrel but dies of suffocation as a result of delay in recovering the barrel.

1951: William "Red" Hill Jr, who along with his father had saved many lives at the falls, dies in a plunge over the Falls in a container made from automobile tyres.

1960: A seven-year-old boy name Roger Woodward survives a plunge over the falls after a boating accident.

1995: Robert Overacker from California races down the Falls on a jet ski wearing a parachute – it did not open.

385

3 mi. below the American Falls the river changes course again, forming the ★**Whirlpool** in a great cauldron originally created by tectonic movements and turning north-east over the Lower Rapids towards Lake Ontario.

The best views of the falls (which are illuminated at night) are to be had from terraces and observation towers on the Canadian side (see below).

Even more impressive is a rather damp boat trip in the **"Maid of the Mist"** (waterproof coats and hats provided). The boat sails past the American Falls into the clouds of spray under the Horseshoe Falls.

A cableway on the Canadian side, the **Spanish Aerocar**, crosses the surging waters of the Whirlpool.

Sightseeing **helicopter flights** are available both on the American side (Goat Island) and on the Canadian side.

Niagara Falls (New York, United States)

Prospect Park

Prospect Park flanks the Falls on the American side, from which there is a fine view. Here the Observation Tower rises above the bottom of the gorge, offering magnificent panoramic prospects. Elevators run down to the landing stage from which the "Maid of the Mist" departs. From the foot of the tower wooden gangways run below Prospect Point to the American Falls. On the upper rim of the gorge, across the road, is the New York State Parks Visitor Center.

North-east of the Rainbow Bridge is the **Schoellkopf Geological Museum**, which traces 500 million years of geological history in the Niagara area. From the museum the Upper Gorge Nature Trail leads to Whirlpool Rapids State Park.

On Rainbow Boulevard is the Native American Center for the Living Arts (25 Rainbow Blvd.), known as **The "Turtle"**, with displays illustrating the culture of the North American Indians. In summer there are performances of Iroquois dances here.

Goat Island

From Prospect Point a path crosses a bridge on to little Green Island, in the middle of the rapids just above the American Falls, and then over another bridge on to Goat Island, between the American and the Horseshoe Falls. From the northern tip of this wooded island a gangway leads on to little Luna Island, beyond the narrow Bridal Veil Falls, which are separated from the American Falls by Luna Island.

On Goat Island, at the foot of the American Falls, is the entrance to the Cave of the Winds (elevators and tunnel), from which boardwalks lead to just under the falls (open late May to early Sep. daily 10am–7pm; shorter hours at other times of year). From the end of the tunnel under the American Falls the Horseshoe Falls Lower Gorge Walkway leads to the foot of the Horseshoe Falls.

Aquarium

Near the museum (Whirlpool St./Pine Ave.) is the Niagara Falls Aquarium, with a variety of marine animals, including sealions, penguins and otters; natural world of the Great Lakes and North Atlantic.

Niagara Falls (Ontario, Canada)

It is best to go over to the Canadian side on foot, as there are often traffic jams on Rainbow Bridge. It is usually necessary to go through customs and passport controls.

Prospect Park's Canadian counterpart is Queen Victoria Park, which provides the best views of the Horseshoe Falls.

From Table Rock there is an overwhelming view of the Horseshoe Falls.
From Table Rock House elevators and three tunnels lead to the foot of
the falls from where a slippery, breathtaking path leads behind the
watery curtains of the Horseshoe Falls. Nearby is the lower station of the
Niagara Incline Railway, a funicular running up to the rim of the gorge.

From the observation platform of the **Minolta Tower** there are overwhelming views of the Niagara gorge and the falls.

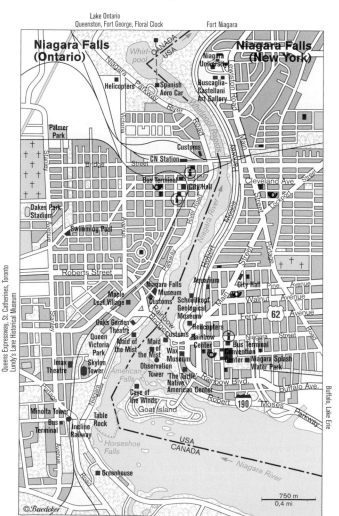

© Baedeker

Niagara Falls

Skylon Tower

On the west side of Queen Victoria Park is the 520 ft high Skylon Tower, from which also there are magnificent panoramic views. In the base of the tower is the Niagara International Center.

Maple Leaf Village

Maple Leaf Village, on the Canadian side of the Niagara River, is a lively shopping and entertainment centre. From the Maple Leaf Tower there are magnificent panoramic views. Here too is the Niagara Daredevil Museum, devoted to the many daring and often fatal attempts to master the falls and the rapids (see Baedeker Special, p. 385).

Other features of interest

Close by is the Niagara IMAX Theatre (6170 Buchanan Ave.), which presents impressions of Niagara on a screen six storeys high. At 4960 Clifton Hill is Ripley's "Believe it or not" Museum. Nearby, at 4915 Clifton Hill, is Louis Tussaud's Waxworks, and at 4943 Clifton Hill is the Guinness World of Records. In Marineland there are switch-back rides and dolphin shows.

Surroundings American side

The Robert Moses Parkway runs downstream through Whirlpool State Park and then along the Lower Rapids to Devil's Hole State Park. Ahead is a view of the massive Robert Moses hydroelectric station. Then comes the campus of the old Niagara University, with the Castellani Art Museum (art of the 18th–20th centuries). The road continues to the Robert Moses State Power Plant then on through the Niagara Escarpment, a fertile wine and fruit growing area, to where the Niagra River flows into Lake Ontario north of Youngstown.

Old Fort Niagara

To the north of Youngstown, at the point where the Niagara River flows into Lake Ontario, is Old Fort Niagara (State Park). The fort was built in 1726 on the site of an earlier French post established in 1679. There are presentations of historic events in authentic uniforms throughout the year.

Surroundings Canadian side

On the Canadian side the Niagara Parkway runs downstream, passing the Whirlpool (see above) and Niagara Glen, to the Sir Adam Beck Generating Plant, Canadian counterpart of the Robert Moses Plant on opposite bank.

★Niagara School of Horticulture

The beautiful gardens of the Niagara Parks Commission School of Horticulture are well worth a visit. Much photographed are the rose garden (in June) and the floral clock.

Fort George

Beyond this are McFarland House (1800; museum) and Fort George, built at the end of the 18th c. as a defence against attacks by the rebellious Americans. During the 1812–13 war the fort fell into the hands of the Americans. After 1820 it was abandoned. Recently restored, it is now protected as a National Historic Park. During the main tourist season soldiers put on a show depicting life in the fort in the early 19th c.

★Niagara-on-the-Lake

The little picture postcard town of Niagara-on-the-Lake (pop. 13,000) on Lake Ontario was the first capital of Upper Canada. Its trim little Victorian houses are set in beautiful gardens, Its main street, Queen Street, is lined with shops, restaurants and cafés. In the climatically favoured area round Niagara-on-the-Lake are a number of large vineyards.

North Carolina (State)   N–P 41–51

Area: 52,670 sq. mi.
Population: 7,323,000
Capital: Raleigh
Popular names: Tar Heel State,
Old North State

North Carolina (named in honour of King Charles I), on the middle Atlantic coast, was one of the thirteen founding states. Some two-fifths of its area is occupied by the swampy coastal plain, off which are the long, narrow Outer Banks; another two-fifths is accounted for by the gently undulating Piedmont Plateau to the west; and beyond this are the Blue Ridge Mountains and Great Smoky Mountains, with Mount Mitchell (6684 ft), the highest peak in the eastern United States. The climate, particularly in the south-east, is subtropical, with hot summers and mild winters; to the west the summers are cooler.

History In 1585 Sir Walter Raleigh founded the first English settlement on American soil on Roanoke Island, but this was later abandoned. Planned settlement began around 1660, with settlers moving in from Virginia. In 1689 the colony, hitherto known as the Carolinas, was divided into a northern and a southern part. On May 12th 1776 North Carolina became the first British colony in North America to resolve on independence, and on November 21st 1789 it joined the Union as the twelfth state. In 1834 the Cherokees living in the forests of the Appalachians were deported to reservations in Oklahoma on the "Trail of Tears". In April 1861, after the bombardment of Fort Sumter, the state joined the Confederation. On December 17th 1903 the brothers Wilbur and Orville Wright made the first powered flight in history at Kitty Hawk on the Outer Banks.

Economy North Carolina is the largest producer of tobacco in the United States, and the tobacco industry, centred on Winston-Salem, is a major contributor to the economy, followed by textiles, furniture manufacture, papermaking and the electrical industry. The principal crops apart from tobacco are maize and soya beans. Tourism is an important source of revenue on the coast.

Asheville, in the far west of the state, was the birthplace of the writer Thomas Wolfe (1900–38). It is an ideal centre for excursions on the Blue Ridge Parkway and into the Great Smoky Mountains National Park (see entry). The town's main attraction is Biltmore Estate, home of the Vanderbilts. Chimney Rock, south-east of Asheville, has magnificent views of the mountains.   **Asheville**

Charlotte (pop. 400,000), North Carolina's largest city, lies in the south-west of the state. It is named after Charlotte of Mecklenburg, wife of King George II: hence also the name of Mecklenburg County, in which it is situated. Charlotte/Douglas Airport is one of the most important inland airports in the eastern United States. Features of interest in Charlotte are the Mint Museum of Art (European, African and American art), housed in the former Mint; the Discovery Place, a science museum with the largest planetarium in the United States; and the Charlotte Museum of History, in the Hezekiah Alexander House (1774), the oldest house in Mecklenburg County. For motor sports enthusiasts there is the Charlotte Motor Speedway, for those in quest of entertainment the Carolwinds theme park (10 mi. south on I 77), which has no fewer than five roller coasters.   **Charlotte**

New Bern

To be transported back to colonial times, visit Tryon Palace in the coastal town of New Bern, which also has some beautiful pre-war buildings.

Research Triangle

One of America's largest think tanks is the "Research Triangle" in the Raleigh-Durham-Chapel Hill area, where famous universities and research institutes abound.

Raleigh

Raleigh, the state's capital and seat of the North Carolina State University is the least "scientific" of the towns in the research triangle. Sights include the State Capitol (1840), the Museum of History, the State Museum of Natural Sciences and the North Carolina Museum of Art.

Durham

In contrast, Durham owes its whole existence to the Duke University, which has a botanical garden and a museum of art on its campus.

The USS "North Carolina", Wilmington

Chapel Hill

Finally, the venerable University of North Carolina, the oldest state university in America, has its seat in Chapel Hill.

Wilmington

The port of Wilmington has a small and very attractive historic district. Its main tourist attraction is the Second World War battleship "North Carolina", now a museum.

★Winston-Salem

In the double town of Winston-Salem is the world's largest cigarette factory (R.J. Reynolds Tobacco Company, 1100 Reynolds Blvd.). The historic district of Salem, founded by the Moravian Brethren in 1766, has been handsomely restored. This is also where you will find the Museum of Early Southern Decorative Arts, which displays art and funiture of the period from 1690 to 1820, set out in 21 exhibition rooms. The Museum of American Art is housed in the mansion of the Reynolds tobacco family.

Other places of interest

Blue Ridge Parkway (see Virginia), Great Smoky Mountains National Park, Outer Banks (see entries)

North Dakota (State)   A–C 21–29

Area: 70,700 sq. mi.
Population: 644,000
Capital: Bismarck
Popular name: Peace Garden State

North Dakota (named after the Dakota tribe) lies in the Midwest on the frontier with Canada, in the centre of the North American continent. The landscape of the Great Plains in the west, traversed by the Missouri, changes towards the east from gently undulating ground moraines to steep hills and continues to rise fairly sharply in the Coteau du Missouri. Along the west of the state, on the border with Montana, are the barren Badlands, robbed of their topsoil by erosion. The climate is continental, with extremely cold winters (average January temperatures around 14°F) and short summers. The natural vegetation consists only of grassland and gallery forests along the rivers.

History The first European, a French fur trader named La Verendrye, reached the territory of North Dakota, then occupied by Dakota Indians, in 1738. It was part of the French colony of Louisiana until 1803, when it passed to the United States under the Louisiana Purchase. After the division of the territory into a northern and a southern half and the repression of Indian rebellions North Dakota entered the Union as the 39th state on November 2nd 1889.

On the prairie soils of the wheat belt the growing of grain makes the principal contribution to the **economy**. Other crops are sunflowers, sugar beet and flax. The working of minerals is of some importance (brown coal in the west of the state; oil and natural gas). In the industrial sector only the processing industries are of any consequence.
    The tourist trade centres mainly on the Theodore Roosevelt National Park, Lake Sakakawea and a number of historic sites.

The Badlands, a barren landscape formed by wind and weather, are situated in western North Dakota, and bison still live here. A visit to the ★**Theodore Roosevelt National Park** will provide a lasting impression of this landscape, described as a "hell without fire". It consists of three parts: North Unit, South Unit and Little Missouri National Grasslands. For a brief visit, Scenic Drive will take you to Painted Canyon Overlook, from where there is a good view. Both can be reached via Medora.
    Near Williston in the west of the state, on the border with Montana, is **Fort Buford** (restored), where Sitting Bull (see Famous People) gave himself up in 1881 after returning to the United States from Canada. A short distance away is the earlier **Fort Union** (also restored), once an important trading post and fur trappers' base, where George Catlin and John James Audubon studied and painted the landscape and its inhabitants.

Badlands

In the hope of attracting German capital the terminus of the Northern Pacific Railroad was named after the German Chancellor. Having grown into a town, Bismarck became capital of the territory of Dakota in 1883. Features of interest are the art-deco State Capitol (1933–4) and, to the south of the twin town of Mandan, **Fort Lincoln**, from which Custer set out with units of the 7th US Cavalry to encounter defeat at the hands of Cheyenne and Dakota Indians in the battle of the Little Bighorn; there is a museum in the fort.

Bismarck

Bottineau, in the far north of the state on the Canadian frontier, is the chief place in an extensive nature reserve and recreation area made up of the J. Clark Salyer National Wildlife Refuge (fishing, observation of wild life), Lake Metigoshe State Park (bathing, boating), the Bottineau Winter Park Ski Area and the **International Peace Gardens**, a landscaped

Bottineau

Return of the Bison

Before white settlers overran the grassy plains between Missouri and the Rocky Mountains, the American bison, or buffalo, was the main source of food and supplier of raw materials to the hunting tribes of the plains. From its hide they produced clothing, shields, packaging material, snow shoes and tents, its horns were made into spoons and drinking vessels and its sinews were stretched into bows or, with bone needles, used for sewing. Buffalo hair was used for various decorative purposes, and finally buffalo dung was the main fuel on these tree-less grassy plains. The buffalo's value in the culture of these people is demonstrated not least by the fact that many of their ceremonies revolved around this, to them, sacred animal and the maintenance of their herds as life-giving. The advance of white settlers into the area brought about the decline of this culture.

By purchasing the Louisiana territories in 1803, President Jefferson intended to cover American citizens' requirements for land for hundreds of years. Anyone interested was to be given 26 acres of land, which he was obliged to cultivate – enough land to support a family adequately, regardless of the condition of

the ground and the nature of the climate. 50 years later, these 26 acres of land were used as a lure to encourage European immigrants. By allocating free land in this way it was intended to transform the prairies into arable land. The "Homestead Act" of 1862 sealed the fate of the bison and Indians in the prairies. Although for years there had been a flourishing trade in bison hides and bison tongues between whites and Indians, hunting and processing had remained the preserve of the Indians, and since one Indian would be responsible for about a hundred animals, the stocks of these enormous herds were scarcely affected – so there was no risk to the bison. However the construction of the transcontinental railway brought about a dramatic change. Suddenly unprocessed products could also be supplied to the towns. Demand rocketed, with the recognition that buffalo leather made excellent drive belts for machinery. Thousands went buffalo hunting, shooting bison until the barrels of their guns glowed red-hot. Buffalo Bill Cody alone killed 4000 in just one year, whilst another famous hunter put paid to 2000 in a single month. The herds dwindled, and the Indian's livelihood was inexorably destroyed. During the Indian campaigns

park symbolising the friendship between Canada and the United States that extends into the Canadian province of Manitoba.

Lake Sakakawea

North-west of Bismarck the Missouri widens to form Lake Sakakawea, a long lake well stocked with fish which is harnessed to supply power by the Garrison Dam at the south end. The State Park round the lake offers scope for a variety of leisure activities. To the south of the lake, on an old camping ground of the Mandan and Hidatsa Indians, is the ★**Knife River Historic Site**, where a number of villages of the Prairie Indians have been rebuilt in an attempt to preserve their culture.

★Bison Monument at Jamestown

The world's largest – albeit concrete – bison, can be seen from afar, raising its head at the I 94, by Jamestown between Bismarck and Fargo.

the military soon recognised the strategic significance of exterminating the buffalo. Bison hunters became useful allies. General Phil Sheridan summed it up by saying "Carry on killing, skinning and selling until the bison have been wiped out. Only then can your prairies be settled with cows and cowboys."

Selling and skinning soon came to be regarded as inferior, which left killing. In the end, out of 50 million bison, only a handful were left. In 1872 a small herd of 50 animals that had survived the slaughter remained in Yellowstone Park. Tribes such as the Sioux, Cheyenne, Blackfoot and Crow were deprived of their livelihood and forced to live in reservations, dependant on the whites' charity. Investors from the United States, England and France advanced into the vast prairies, now completely cleared, to rear cattle on the grassland that had supported the bison. A few hard winters were enough; the beef barons retreated. The harsh climate had decimated their herds and they were forced to admit that cattle farming was not profitable in the region.

The small farmer also had little luck with the prairie. Working the land exposed the soil so that no root system could hold it. In dry years the whining wind blew the dried-out soil hundreds of miles, leaving infertile land behind. Today the cultivation of the prairie belt has been made possible by the tapping of ground water, and huge farms have replaced the countless small ones. However if the extrac-tion of water continues at its present rate, supplies will be exhausted in less than 30 years. Then the prairies will return to their original grassland condition, and be just as they were before the settlement.

Since the 1970s successful trials have been carried out on an alternative use of the grass belt: the return of bison as a meat supplier. Bison meat, lean and low in cholesterol, is enjoying increasing popularity, and as it brings in $1.30 per pound, and normal beef only 60 cents, bison farming is really gathering momentum. There are now about 250,000 bison living in the United States and Canada, either in nature reserves or in farmed herds. The North American Bison Cooperative in New Rockford, ND, has been marketing its products throughout the United States with increasing success. It has 210 companies in twelve American states and three Canadian provinces, which prefer bison farming because, unlike cattle, they do not require costly winter protection or veterinary assistance when the calves are born. Provided the bison have enough room to travel some 7½ miles every day in search of food, there is no need for additional fodder and staff to supervise the herds are not required. It would appear that in Dakota, Montana, Nebraska and Oklahoma, the bison is making a comeback. A group of Lakota-Sioux Indians have already laid claim to the whole of western South Dakota, where the reintroduction of an economy built exclusively on exploitation of the bison is scheduled for the year 2016.

Its living contemporaries graze at its feet, amongst them the albino "White Cloud", regarded by many Indians as a sacred animal. The National Buffalo Museum can be found nearby (see Baedeker Special above).

Ohio (State)

H–L 41–45

Area: 41,330 sq. mi.
Population: 11,173,000
Capital: Columbus
Popular name: Buckeye State

Ohio

Ohio (named after the river) lies in the northern part of the Central Lowlands between Lake Erie in the north and the Ohio River in the south. In the landscape of ground moraines formed during the ice ages that occupies much of the state's area are innumerable lakes, some of which have degenerated into bogs; the eastern half

of the state is part of the Allegheny Plateau. The climate is humid continental. Some 20 per cent of Ohio is covered with mixed forest (maple, oak, ash, hickory, walnut, and conifers).

History Ohio preserves much evidence of early human settlement in the form of numerous mounds formed by prehistoric men. The first Europeans to reach the territory, then occupied by the Iroquois, were Frenchmen coming from Canada. After the French and Indian War the area passed to the British Crown in 1763. At the end of the War of Independence, in 1783, it was incorporated in the United States. After bitter fighting with the Indians the white population rapidly increased from 1787 onwards. On March 1st 1803 Ohio was admitted to the Union as the 17th state.

Economy Ohio's highly developed agriculture produces maize, wheat, oats, soya beans and vegetables; dairy farming and meat production are also important. The principal minerals are coal, oil and natural gas. Thanks to its convenient situation and proximity to sources of raw materials Ohio developed a large iron and steel industry, which in terms of output takes fourth place in the United States. The most important branches of industry are automobile and aircraft construction, engineering, foodstuffs, porcelain, rubber and electrical engineering. The state's remains of prehistoric Indian culture, interesting cities, skiing areas, lakes, rivers and forests attract large numbers of visitors throughout the year.

Columbus

The state capital, Columbus, situated almost exactly in the geographical centre of the state, was founded in 1812 and named after Christopher Columbus. Features of interest are the State Capitol (1861), in the grounds of which is a monument commemorating the murdered President William McKinley (1843–1901), and the Ohio Historical Center, with two "history malls" illustrating the archaeology and history of the state with the most modern methods of presentation. The German Village, south of downtown Columbus, is a refurbished old quarter of the town well equipped with shops and bars.

Coshocton

Coshocton, north-east of Columbus on the Ohio-Erie Canal, preserves something of the atmosphere of the 1830s with its restored houses and lock-keeper's house.

Holmes County

In Holmes County, 87 mi. to the south of Cleveland (see entry) live 40,000 Amish, the largest community of this sect in the world, still speaking a Swabian dialect of German. The Amish do not have cars, radio, television, refrigerators or private telephones, and still use horse-drawn ploughs. The Amish Farm at Berlin is designed specifically to give tourists an insight into the world of the Amish.

Sandusky

Sandusky extends for some 6 mi. along the shores of Lake Erie, with a wide range of leisure facilities on its Kelleys Island beaches. Offshore is Kelleys Island, on which the Kelley family grew wine and reared fish in the early 19th c. On Inscription Rock are old Indian rock drawings.

Another vacation centre on the Sandy Lake Erie Beaches is **Port Clinton**, further west.

Toledo, at the south-west corner of Lake Erie, has a well stocked art museum ranging from ancient Egyptian art to the modern American school.

Toledo

Some of the most interesting of the prehistoric Indian mounds can be seen on a round trip from Columbus, starting on US 23, going south. Among them are the 23 mounds (200 BC–AD 500) of the Mound City Group National Monument at Chillicothe; the single large mound (250 ft long, 30 ft high) in the Seip National Monument (17 mi. west of Chillicothe); the Serpent Mound State Memorial on SR 73 (total distance 90 mi.), a quarter-mile long mound in the form of a snake (800 BC to AD100), the largest of its kind; and the Fort Ancient State Memorial at Lebanon (total distance 138 mi.), a cult site constructed about 500 AD by Indians of the Hopewell Culture.

★**Prehistoric Indian mounds**

Cincinnati, Cleveland (see entries)

Other places of interest

Oklahoma (State)

N–Q 23–31

Area: 69,920 sq. mi.
Population: 3,301,000
Capital: Oklahoma City
Popular name: Sooner State

The state of Oklahoma (from the Indian term "red people"), in the west central United States, lies mostly in the Inner Plains region. To the west these merge into the flat treeless grassland of the Great Plains, and on the south-west are bounded by the Wichita Mountains and tabular volcanic hills. The eastern part of the state is occupied by the forest-covered (mainly maple and oak) Ouachita and Ozark Mountains, between which runs the valley of the Arkansas River. Climatically Oklahoma lies in a zone of transition between the humid subtropical climate of the south and the dry continental climate of the north. Oklahoma has the largest Indian population of all the states in the United States.

History Spanish conquistadors passed through the territory of Oklahoma in 1541. In 1682 it was incorporated in the French colony of Louisiana, and in 1803 it was sold to the United States under the Louisiana Purchase. Regarded as worthless land, it was declared Indian territory in 1830. Between 1830 and 1840 the "five civilised tribes" (the Choctaw, Creek, Cherokee, Chickasaw and Seminole Indians) were driven out of their territory in the east and resettled here, and the 50,000 incomers had to share the land with the Comanche, Osage and other Prairie Indians who were already living in the area. From 1889 onwards the American government opened up parts of the territory to white settlement, and thereafter a number of towns with populations of 10,000 or so, like Oklahoma City, sprang up almost overnight. After the adoption of a constitution accepted by both Indians and white settlers in 1907 Oklahoma joined the Union as the 46th state on November 16th in that year.

Economy Oklahoma has a very varied farming pattern, ranging from highly developed cattle rearing to the growing of wheat, cotton and peanuts. The chief minerals are oil and, on a smaller scale, natural gas and brown coal, which are processed in the state's principal industry, petrochemicals. In the wide range of Oklahoma's tourist attractions the Indian Pow Wows take a leading place.

Anadarko

57 mi. south-west of Oklahoma City is the township of Anadarko. Here, in the Indian City USA, are reconstructions of the villages of seven different Indian tribes, which give an excellent impression of the daily life of the original inhabitants of North America. The Southern Plains Indian Museum has a collection of historic and contemporary Indian art and the National Hall of Fame for Famous American Indians has bronze busts of famous indians.

Bartlesville

In Bartlesville, in north-eastern Oklahoma, are the headquarters of a number of oil firms. It can also boast the only high-rise building designed by Frank Lloyd Wright, the 225 ft high Price Tower. Another example of modern architecture is Shin'en Kan, a house designed by Bruce Goff. The days of the oil boom are recalled by Nellie Johnstone's Oil Well, the first derrick in the state, still preserved in its original form. The Tom Mix Museum is devoted to the king of movie cowboys.

★Woolaroc

Bison, longhorn and many other animals roam the Woolroc Wildlife Preserve, south-east of Barlesville, which can be crossed by car. The museum is concerned with the Wild West.

The legendary country singer, Will Rogers, was born on the Dog Iron Ranch south-east of Woolaroc.

Lawton

The farming town of Lawton in south-western Oklahoma is one of the towns that grew up over night. In Fort Sill the Apache Geronimo spent the last years of his life as a prisoner; he is buried in the adjoining cemetery. The Museum of the Great Plains has a varied collection of material on life in frontier days.

The **Wichita Mountains Wildlife Refuge**, a protected area north of Lawton, has everything that hikers, climbers and animal watchers could possibly wish for (bison, longhorn and much more).

Oklahoma City

The capital of the state of Oklahoma lies on the southern Great Plains on the North Canadian River. It sadly became famous in April 1995, when a bomb attack by right wing radicals claimed 168 lives. The scene of the attack, the Murrah Federal Building, is still enclosed behind a fence.

The neoclassical **State Capitol** (without the usual dome) at the intersection of North-East 23rd Street and Lincoln Boulevard was completed in 1917. Oil is still worked in the immediate vicinity of the Capitol. The State Museum of History south-east of the Capitol has a very large collection of Indian artefacts.

In the **★Myriad Gardens** in the Central Business District to the south of the Capitol tropical and desert plant worlds have been created in the multi-storey glass tubes of the Crystal Bridge Tropical Conservatory.

2 mi. west of the Myriad Gardens are the **★Oklahoma National Stockyards**, the largest stock markets in the world. The noisy auctions (Mon. and Tue. from 8am) can be attended by non-dealers.

The **★Kirkpatrick Center** (2100 NE 52st St.) houses several museums, including the Oklahoma Air & Space Museum, the Center of the American Indian, the International Photography Hall of Fame & Museum, and the Omniplex Science Museum, a "hands-on" science museum with a two-storey high dinosaur.

3 mi. north-east of the Capitol, (1700 NE 63rd St.) is the ★**National Cowboy Hall of Fame** and Western Heritage Center, with a large collection of material on the history of the Wild West: pictures and sculptures, the Rodeo Hall of Fame and the John Wayne Collection recall the days of the pioneers and cowboys. Children can try out their skills as cowboys in the Children's Corral.

The **Spiro Indians** lived nearby, south of the I 40 a short distance before the Arkansas border, from the 7th to the 15th c. Eleven of their "mounds" can still be seen.

The oil capital of Tulsa, the second largest city in Oklahoma, lies in the east of the state. Thanks to the wealth brought by oil, it has a number of excellent museums: the Gilcrease Museum, which is devoted to the move to the west (Indian artifacts, pictures of the Wild West by Remington, Russell and other artists); the Philbrook Museum of Art (art of many periods and styles, including the Italian Renaissance, 19th c. English painting and Indian arts and crafts); and the Fenster Museum of Jewish Art.   ★Tulsa

South of Downtown Tulsa, the gold façade of the Christian fundamentalist Oral Roberts University gleams in the sun – this is a top-class architectural showpiece, with "praying hands" more than 76 ft high.

In the town of Muskogee in eastern Oklahoma is the very interesting Five Civilised Tribes Museum, which illustrates the cultures of the Cherokee, Chickasaw, Chocktaw, Creek and Seminole Indians.   ★**Muskogee**

Many of the Indian nations had their own "capitals", which now have interesting museums devoted to the cultures of the various tribes: Okmulgee for the Creek Indians, Pawhuska for the Osages, Ponca City for the Poncas, Tahlequah for the Cherokees, Wewoka for the Seminoles.

The US 62 and the OK 16 closely follow the historic trail (**Trail of Tears**) from Tahlequah, which the Indians were forced to take when they were driven out, having to suffer the most severe privations.

★★Olympic National Park   B 1/2

State: Washington
Area: 1420 sq. mi.
Established: 1938

The Olympic National Park lies on the Olympic Peninsula in the north-west of Washington State, which is bounded on the west by the Pacific, on the north by the Strait of Juan de Fuca (the Canadian frontier) and on the east by Puget Sound. On the peninsula is the largest and finest expanse of temperate rain forest in the western hemisphere, declared a National Monument in 1909. The Olympic National Park is one of most visited National Parks in the United States, drawing over 3-½ million visitors a year. Within a relatively small area, between sea level and the summit of Mount Olympus (7965 ft), it contains a wide range of different landscapes, the main types of which are covered in the sites described below.

The Olympic Mountains, lying in the centre of an area shaped by the encounter of two plates in the process of continental drift, are a geologically young and much folded range. The mountains are deeply fissured, with a complex system of steep valleys. The rocks are mainly marine sediments, with some volcanic intrusions (e.g. cushion lava). There are some 60 glaciers and numerous snowfields. Moraines, travelled granite blocks from Canada, corries, corrie lakes and U-shape valleys give evidence of strong local glaciation and of the advance of glaciers from the north during the Ice Age. There are still about 60 glaciers and numerous snowfields. Above the tree line is a region of alpine meadows with colourful mountain flowers.

Information The National Park is open all year round; the Visitor Center for the Olympics is in Port Angeles, and the Hoh Rain Forest Visitor Center is at Forks. There is also a hotel on the US 101; otherwise there are campsites scattered over the region, some of which can be used free of charge.

It is strictly forbidden to walk on the Alpine meadows. The ascent of the highest mountains is recommended only for the most experienced climbers with proper equipment. Rainwear and good boots are also essential for hikers.

Olympic Peninsula Scenic Drive

A good starting point for a motor tour of the park is the little harbour town of Port Angeles. The park is divided up into a narrow coastal strip 50 mi. long on the Pacific, and the main central area. The latter, with the adjoining National Forests to the west, north and east, is encircled by the 330 mi. long Olympic Peninsula Scenic Drive (US 101), from which side roads, partly asphalted, lead off into the central area, or towards the coast. The US 101 passes by ★**Lake Crescent**, a delightful mountain lake, 20 mi. west of Port Angeles. A road runs along the south side of the lake to the Marymere Falls, which plunge down from a height of 90 ft. 2 mi. further on, a 12 mi. long side road branches off to **Sol Duc Hot Springs**, where visitors can bathe in the hot springs.

Hurricane Ridge

A 20 mi. long scenic road runs up to Hurricane Ridge Lodge (alt. 5200 ft; no overnight accommodation), from which there are magnificent views of the glacier-covered mountains of the Olympic range and over the Strait of Juan de Fuca to Vancouver Island in Canada.

Impenetrable rain forest in Olympic National Park

The great attraction of the National Park is the magnificent expanse of rain forest one of the last surviving areas of rain forest in the temperate zone in the west-facing valleys of the Quinault, Queens and Hoh Rivers. The Hoh Rain Forest, 90 mi. from Port Angeles, caters for visitors with its three nature trails, including the very impressive Hall of Mosses Trail. The road up the Hoh valley and then over the Blue Glacier is the most favoured route for the ascent of Mount Olympus.

★★Hoh Rain Forest

The annual cycle of rain coming in from the Pacific and the heavy snowfalls on Mount Olympus in winter, melt water from which flows down the valleys, have fostered the lush green growth of the forest. While the coastal region lying in the rain shadow of the hills is extremely dry, Mount Olympus has the highest annual precipitations (200 in.) in the United States outside Alaska, which fall mostly during the winter. Rainproof clothing and stout footwear are a must for all visitors.

Flora The four main species of conifer found here Sitka spruce, hemlock, red cedar and Douglas fir and the Oregon maple and vine maple grow here to gigantic heights of up to 330 ft, with diameters of up to 13 ft. The trees and fallen trunks are covered with ferns of unusual size (including liquorice and sword ferns), lichens and moss, on which other trees take root. A fallen trunk that has rotted away will nourish whole colonnades of trees. Particularly striking is Selaginella, a species of moss related to club moss that hangs down from trees (mostly maples) in long garlands and curtains.

Fauna Visitors will rarely see any Roosevelt elk (wapiti) in summer, but the signs of their presence are everywhere: they graze on the rapidly growing vegetation and prevent it from flourishing too luxuriantly. Other animals that may be encountered are black bears, cougars and coyotes, whose tracks can sometimes be seen in the soft soil of the forest. The rivers are well stocked with fish.

Various **hiking trails** start from the US 101. One of the best is the 14 mi. Queets River Trail; more strenuous is the 44 mi. trail that crosses the whole park North Fork to Whiskey Bend.

The **coastal strip** is a region of sandy beaches, cliffs rising sheer out of the sea, rock arches, accumulations of driftwood and forests reaching right down to the shore. The northern part of the area is accessible only on side roads branching off US 101; the southern third is traversed by the Scenic Drive between Ruby Beach and Queets. The sea is not particularly inviting for bathers, since the cold current flowing here keeps the water temperature low. When walking on the numerous promontories visitors must keep a watchful eye on the tides. Among the many species of birds to be seen here is the white-headed sea eagle. Seals are common; and sometimes grey whales can be seen swimming past in spring and autumn.

Oregon (State)   D–G 1–9

Area: 97,073 sq. mi.
Population: 3,203,000
Capital: Salem
Popular name: Beaver State

Oregon (probably from the Indian river name ouragon) lies on the Pacific coast, bounded on the south by California and on the north by Washington, from which it is separated by the Columbia River. In the western third of the state the Coast Ranges run parallel to the coast; further east the state is traversed by the Cascade Mountains, rising to heights of up to 11,237 ft; and between the two ranges is the tectonic depression of the Willamette River. The eastern two-thirds of Oregon are on the steppe-like Columbia Plateau (4900 ft), with the Great Sandy Desert. The Cascade Mountains form a climatic boundary: to the east the climate is dry, with wide fluctuations in temperature, while the land to the west is in the cool temperate zone, with high precipitations on the west side of the hills. As a result the characteristic elements in the vegetation are spruce, Douglas fir and yellow pine, while in the east, on the Columbia Plateau, short grassland and a steppe vegetation of dwarf shrubs predominate.

History The Indian population of Oregon belonged to two different cultures: the coastal tribes like the Nootka and Kwakiutl, who lived by fishing, and the hunters and gatherers to the east of the Cascade Mountains, like the Shuswap and Nez Perce. After the first journeys of exploration by James Cook (1778) and George Vancouver (1792) and Lewis and Clark's expedition (1805) the territory, which from 1818 was held by Britain, was first settled by whites in the coastal areas. The main wave of settlement began around 1840, when thousands of settlers streamed into the region, then still relatively unspoiled, most of them travelling on the Oregon Trail. After a frontier dispute between Britain and the United States that was settled by negotiation the United States territory of Oregon, taking in broadly the present states of Oregon, Washington and Idaho, was established in 1849. In 1853 the territory was reduced to its present size, and on February 14th 1859 it joined the Union as the 33rd state.

Economy The forests that cover almost half the area of Oregon provide the basis for the state's most important industry, woodworking, in which 45 per cent of the employed population are engaged. Arable farming (wheat, fodder plants, potatoes and other vegetables, fruit) is possible in much of the state only with the help of irrigation, and accordingly the predominant element in the state's agriculture is meat production. As a result the second most important industry in Oregon is foodstuffs. Other industries include oil refineries, textiles, rubber, synthetic fibres, engineering and electronics. The third element in the economy is tourism; and Oregon offers many attractions to visitors, from the snow-capped mountains with their winter sports facilities to the Pacific coast with its wide range of water sports.

Ashland

Every year Shakespeare enthusiasts from all over the world flock to Ashland, in south-west Oregon near the California border. During the Shakespeare Festival, which lasts from February to October, the Bard's plays are performed by international stars.

★Bend

Bend lies roughly in the centre of Oregon, in a beautiful setting of lakes and forest. The High Desert Museum has informative displays on the arid regions to the north-west. Among the town's tourist attractions are rafting trips on the Deschutes River and excursions to the volcanic landscapes of Lava Butte (12 mi. south) and Newberry National Volcanic Monument (39 mi. south). 22 mi. south-west of the town is Oregon's largest skiing area, the Mount Bachelor Ski Area (11 ski lifts).

Eugene

Eugene, which is separated from its neighbour town of Springfield by the Willamette River, is the seat of the University of Oregon, which has a Museum of Art with an excellent collection of Asian art.

★Hell's Canyon National Recreation Area

In the extreme north-east of the state, the deepest canyon in the United States, Hell's Canyon, marks the Idaho border. A protected area, whose inaccessibility makes it all the more beautiful, extends along the Oregon side. For the adventurous, the Hell's Canyon National Scenic Loop Drive begins and ends in Baker City.

East of Portland (see entry) along the Columbia River is Hood River, the chief place in the vacation and winter sports area round Mount Hood (11,235 ft), Oregon's highest peak. From the viewpoint half a mile south of the town on SR 35 there are fine views of the mountain and the beautiful valley of the Hood River.

Hood River

To the west of Hood River is the ★**Bonneville Dam** (salmon ladder) on the Columbia River.

The US 101 runs along Oregon's Pacific Coast, a holiday paradise par excellence. At the northernmost point is Astoria, beautifully situated at the mouth of the Columbia River, which can be viewed from Coxcombe Hill. The river has a special museum devoted to it, the Columbia River Maritime Museum. 6 mi. south-west of the town is Fort Clatsop, now restored, where Lewis and Clark's expedition ended.

★Astoria

30 mi. south of Astoria begins Canyon Beach, a long, sandy beach, which is one of the most popular coastal bathing resorts. Further along is Tillamook Bay and Oregon's dairy centre.

★Canyon Beach

Formerly a fishing village, now an attractive bathing resort, Newport has preserved something of its Victorian atmosphere. Its attractions include the Oregon Coast Aquarium.

Newport

To the south of Newport is a quieter piece of the coast with the **Sea Lion Caves**, where sea lions can be observed romping all year round.

Behind Florence begins the magnificent dune landscape of Oregon Dunes National Recreation Area. Then it suddenly becomes noisy again, as the area around Coos Bay has the largest settlement on the coast. Leaving this behind, we soon see the Cape Blanco lighthouse, built in 1878, and then drive along what is probably the most beautiful section of the coast road, to Gold Beach.

★Oregon Dunes

The state capital, Salem, lies on the Willamette River to the south of Portland. Features of interest are the State Capitol, a number of museums (Weaving Museum, Museum of Agricultural Machinery) and Oregon's oldest winery, the Honeywood Winery (wine tasting). There are more than 40 vineyards in the hills between Salem and Portland.

Salem

Crater Lake National Park (see entry), Portland (see entry)

Other places of interest

★★Orlando   V 44

State: Florida
Altitude: 105 ft
Population: 164,000

The city of Orlando is at the centre of one of the world's most visited tourist regions, which draws some 10 million visitors every year. Its principal attraction is the Disney World giant theme park, closely followed by other complexes such as Sea World and Universal Studios, almost as large and no less attractive, which have become established in its vicinity. In addition the US Space Station at Cape Canaveral (see entry) is within easy reach of Orlando. There are now more than 70,000 hotel and motel beds, over 2000 restaurants, four dozen golf courses and numerous attractions large and small, in the Orlando area, making it a gigantic leisure machine, providing the complete family holiday, so far as American taste is concerned.

★★ Walt Disney World Resort

Walt Disney World lies just 20 mi. south-west of Orlando on Lake Buena Vista. Here in 1963 Walt Disney found a site on which he could realise his conception of a clean and perfect holiday landscape: a great expanse of open country not too far from the holiday centres on the coast of Florida, good communications and a climate that made all-year operation possible. On October 1st 1971 the Magic Kingdom of Disney World opened its gates. What began as a large, but still reasonably compact, amusement park, has now grown to cover an area of 43 sq. mi., is now known as Walt Disney World Resort, and offers four theme parks, three water parks, a tropical park, 26 hotels, six golf courses, a huge sports complex and a shopping, restaurant and nightlife mall that is almost as large. The resort is best reached via the I 4 or the US 192 (Irlo Bronson Hwy.).

Information The four theme parks are open from to 8pm daily. During the high season and for special events, these times may be extended to midnight.

A visit to Walt Disney World is not cheap. Admission to each of the theme parks costs more than $42 for adults and almost $34 for children. Add to this the cost of travelling on the various transport connecting the parks. If you think one day will not be anywhere near long enough, you

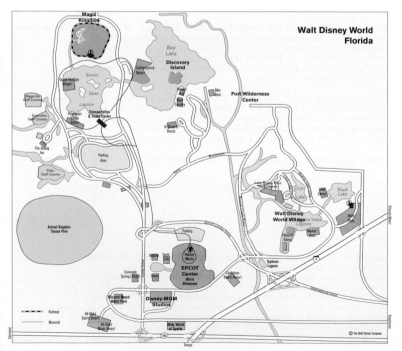

should buy an "All-in-One-Hopper-Pass" for four (Adults: $145), five ($189) or six days ($249), to cover all transport and unlimited admission to the parks. Disney Hotel guests are also given additional reductions. It is best to make bookings through a travel agent before leaving home. Information on the web: www.disney.com.MagicKingdom.

Magic Kingdom

The centrepiece of the Magic Kingdom is the fantastically towered and turreted Cinderella Castle, around which are seven different sections with 42 shows and rides and innumerable small souvenir shops and restaurants. Particular attractions are "Main Street USA", in late 19th/early 20th c. style, with the Penny Arcade; "Adventureland", with the Pirates of the Caribbean and the Jungle Cruise; and "Frontierland", with the "Big Thunder Mountain Railroad" and "Splash Mountain", providing somewhat damp entertainment. "Liberty Square" brings back colonial days, and the Hall of Presidents has all the United States Presidents, up to the present day. There is also a horrifying "Haunted Mansion". In "Fantasyland" visitors encounter characters from Walt Disney's famous films Snow White, Peter Pan and Captain Nemo. In "Mickey's Toontown Fair" everything is scaled down for children, and in "Tomorrowland" a roller coaster, "Space Mountain" clatters through the world of tomorrow. Every day at 3pm Micky Mouse and Co. take part in the great Disney Parade along Main Street into Frontierland. A live show is then held in front of Cinderella's Castle.

EPCOT Center

EPCOT Experimental Prototype Community Of Tomorrow is the high-tech counterpart of the Magic Kingdom, an area of 260 acres devoted to the past achievements and the future of technology. At its centre is the large globe "Spaceship Earth", which looks into the 21st c. Along the World Showcase Lagoon, eleven countries are represented, as envisaged by the designers of Disney World.

Disney MGM
Studios

The Disney MGM Studios combine operation as a television and film studio with a theme park. The Backstage Studio Tour provides a look behind the scenes, and the "Twilight Zone Tower of Terror" provides the stomach-churning experience of plummeting thirteen storeys in a run-away lift. The "Indiana Jones Epic Stunt Spectacular" presents the experience of exciting stunt scenes, whilst the Muppets Show provides less wild entertainment.

Animal Kingdom

The latest attraction, opened in spring 1998, is Animal Kingdom, where Disney seeks to enhance awareness of nature conservation through the vehicle of fun and adventure. The result is a mixture of the artificial Disney world, and the world of real plants and animals – and it is by no means clear where the boundaries between them lie. Animal Kingdom is divided into various themed areas: the "Oasis" with exotic plants and animals, "Safari Village", with shows, discovery trails, restaurants and the "Tree of Life", the "Minney–Mickey" Camp, with the ubiquitous Disney cartoon figures, "Dinoland", a kind of Jurassic Park, "Africa" where visitors can meet elephants, giraffes and lions on safari, and "Asia", opened in 1999.

Further attractions

As if these four huge parks were not enough, Disney World has more to offer: the "Discovery Island" nature park, with a large colony of scarlet ibis, the "River Country" water park (pure nostalgia), "Typhoon Lagoon" (a giant experience pool under palm trees), and "Blizzard Beach" where you can ski on artificial snow straight into the fun pool; as well as "Disney Village Marketplace" for shopping and "Pleasure Island" where a New Year's party is held every evening.

◀ *Cinderella's Castle, Walt Disney World*

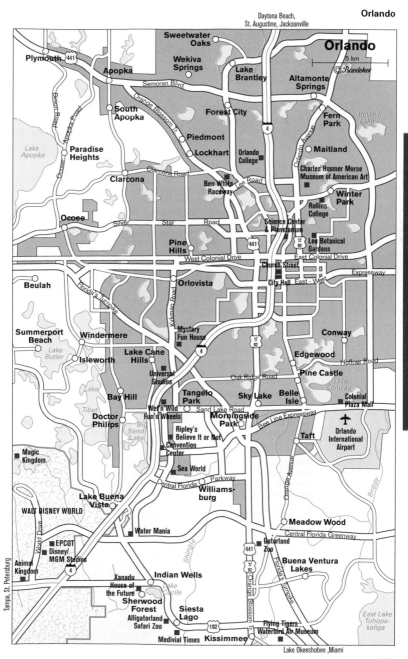

Daytona Beach,
St. Augustine, Jacksonville

Orlando

5 km

©Baedeker

Plymouth 441

Apopka

Semoran Blvd

Orange Blossom Tr.

South
Apopka

Piedmont

Lockhart

Clarcona

Clarcona Road

Ocoee

Silver   Star   Road

Pine
Hills

West Colonial Drive

Beulah

Orlovista

Florida's Turnpike

Kirkman Road

Summerport
Beach

Windermere

Lake
Butler

Isleworth

Lake Cane
Hills

Universal
Studios

Bay Hill

Lake
Tiber

Tangelo
Park

Wet'n Wild
Fun'n Wheels

Doctor
Philips

Big
Sand
Lake

Ripley's
Believe It or Not

Convention
Center

Magic
Kingdom

Sea World

Lake Buena
Vista

WALT DISNEY WORLD

World Drive

EPCOT
Disney/
MGM Studios

Animal
Kingdom

Xanadu
House of
the Future

Sherwood
Forest

Lake
Cecile

Indian Wells

Alligatorland
Safari Zoo

Medivial Times

Siesta
Lago

192

Kissimmee

Lake Okeechobee ,Miami

Tampa, St. Petersburg

Water Mania

Central Florida   Parkway

Williams-
burg

Shingle

Meadow Wood

Central Florida Greenway

Gatorland
Zoo

441

17
92

Buena Ventura
Lakes

Orange Blossom Tr.

Florida's Turnpike

East Lake
Tohope-
kaliga

Flying Tigers
Waterbird Air Museum

Sweetwater
Oaks

Wekiva
Springs

Lake
Brantley

Altamonte
Springs

Forest City

4

Fern
Park

Howell
Lake

Orlando
College

Ben White
Raceway

Lee Road

Orlando Avenue

Maitland

Charles Hosmer Morse
Museum of American Art

Rollins
College

Winter
Park

Science Center
& Planetarium

441

17
92

Leu Botanical
Gardens

East Colonial Drive

Church Street

City Hall   East - West

Expressway

Conway

Edgewood

Hoffner Road

Pine Castle

Oak Ridge Road

Sky Lake

Belle
Isle

Lake
Conway

Colonial
Plaza Mall

Morningside
Park

Sand Lake Road

Bee Line Expressway

Taft

Orange Avenue

Orlando
International
Airport

Boggy

Paradise
Heights

Lake
Apopka

Apopka Road

Lake
Apopka

Clinton Road

405

★★Sea World

Sea World of Florida (Sea Harbor Dr.; I 4, Exit 28) claims to be one of the largest aquatic zoos in the world, with various aquariums, an artificial coral reef, a pool for sharks and stingrays, a large enclosure for walruses, sealions, seals, otters and penguins, a flamingo garden, a manatee pool and numerous other attractions. The great draws, however, are the Dolphin Stadium, in which highly trained dolphins perform acrobatics, and the Shamu Stadium, in which trained killer whales are put through their paces. The latest attraction is a voyage to Atlantis. And anyone who can't actually make it to the real Key West (see entry) can make do with Sea World's replica.

★★Universal Studios

Another major attraction is Universal Studios (1000 Universal Studios Plaza; I 4, Exit 29), which opened in 1990. Here, in "the largest film and television studios outside Hollywood", filming started in October 1988. Visitors can take a tour giving an insight into production, and taking in more than three dozen film sets, including Norman Bates' Motel from Hitchcock's "Psycho". All this, together with re-enacted scenes, stunts, multi-media shows and exciting rides such as "Kongfrontation" – with King Kong in the same tram.

Other sights

The city of Orlando has of course benefited considerably from the tourist trade. This is evident from the old station at "Church Street Station" entertainments and shopping complex, and from International Drive, a 3¾ mi. long avenue that gives rapid access to the huge theme parks. Along the road are numerous hotels and restaurants, as well as a modern office complex with a congress and trade fair centre.

★Wet 'n' Wild

Wet 'n' Wild (6200 International Dr.) offers swimming pools with waves, water flumes and white-water trips.

★Orlando Museum of Art

The Orlando Museum of Art (2416 N Mills Ave.) is famed for its excellent collection of pre-Columbian art. The museum also puts on temporary exhibitions of American and African art of the 19th and 20th centuries and travelling exhibitions with loans from international museums.

★Charles Hosmer Morse Museum

This museum, in the suburb of Winter Park, is something quite special, displaying works of art made from glass, and jewellery ranging from medieval church windows to Tiffany windows and lamps, to pieces by Lalique and Fabergé.

★Cypress Gardens

This exotic garden to the south of Disney World at Winter Haven opened as long ago as 1936 and was central Florida's very first tourist attraction. Apart from its luxuriant vegetation, it is famous for its water-skiing events.

Kissimee

19 mi. south of Orlando is Kissimee, which has grown from a quiet little farming town into a popular holiday resort. Its principal tourist attractions are strung along the Irlo Bronson Memorial Highway. They include various alligator and snake farms, the "Water Mania" aquatic playground, and "Xanadu", the house of the future, depicting what life will be like in the coming century.

Splendid China is also in the parish of Kissimee, even though it lies beyond Disney World, to the west. This park is a microcosm of China, with the Great Wall of China (3000 Splendid China Blvd.) of course!

★Outer Banks   N/O 49/50

States: Virginia, North Carolina

Off the coasts of Virginia and (for most of the distance) North Carolina lies in a 175 mi. chain of long narrow islands extending from Back Bay, Virginia, in the north to Cape Lookout, North Carolina, in the south. These Outer Banks offer, at any rate in the southern two-thirds, an expanse of almost completely unspoiled natural scenery with interesting plants and bird life; the northern third, however, has been ravaged by the development of the holiday trade and is now a hotchpotch of hotels, motels, holiday homes, restaurants and shopping centres. The Outer Banks can be reached from the north on US 158 or in the south by ferry from Cedar Island or Swan Quarter to Ocracoke (advance reservation necessary during the season).

In the dunes of Kill Devil Hills on Bodie Island (mileposts 7 and 8 on US 158) the brothers Wilbur and Orville Wright made the first powered flight in history on December 17th 1903. Their aircraft, piloted by Orville, rose into the air for 12 seconds, covering the short distance marked by the memorial stones. Close by are the brothers' two shed workshops, and in the Visitor Center is a documentary exhibition. The tall Memorial stands on the hill from which the Wrights launched experimental gliders.

★Wright Brothers National Memorial

Sir Walter Raleigh landed on Roanoke Island (reached on US 158) in 1584. The following year the first English settlement in America was founded on the island by John White, and here on August 18th 1587 White's granddaughter Virginia Dare was born – the first child of English parents to be born in North America. Thereafter the settlement mysteriously disappeared. Returning from Europe some years later White found

Fort Raleigh National Historic Site

Kitty Hawk: scene of the Wright brothers' first flight

only the enigmatic word "Croatoan" carved on a tree, indicating perhaps an attack by a local tribe of Indians of that name. The Visitor Center tells the story of this "lost colony".

★Cape
Hatteras/Cape
Lookout National
Seashore

The southern two-thirds of the Outer Banks are now included in the nature reserve formed by the Cape Hatteras National Seashore and Cape Lookout National Seashore. Since these long, thin coastal islands lying between Pamlico Sound to the west and the open Atlantic to the east have been spared the invasion of mass tourism they form an undisturbed habitat for rare plants and for numbers of seabirds and migrants. Beside Bodie Island lighthouse is an observation platform.

Palm Beach   X 46

State: Florida
Altitude: 0–15 ft
Population: Palm Beach 10,000, West Palm Beach 68,000

The fashionable bathing resort of Palm Beach lies on a long sand island on the Gold Coast, 75 mi. north of Miami (see entry). West Palm Beach was originally established to house the large staffs of the hotels and their families. It is now the administrative and business centre of a considerable surrounding area.

History Palm Beach owes its name to a Spanish ship carrying wine and coconuts that ran aground here in 1878. The few inhabitants of what was then an inhospitable stretch of coast planted the coconuts, and in course of time a grove of palms grew up. The real fathers of Palm Beach were the financier Henry Morrison Flagler and the architect Addison Mizner. From 1874 onwards Flagler spent the winter in Florida and got to know the palm-fringed beach; then in 1894 he extended his Florida East Coast Railroad to Lake Worth and built the legendary Royal Poinciana Hotel in Palm Beach. Thereafter this became a popular resort with the great ones of the world, and a tremendous land and building boom developed. In 1895 Flagler built the less formal Palm Beach Inn (in 1901 renamed the Breakers) directly on the Atlantic, hoping to appeal to a younger public. Among patrons of the hotel were the millionaire industrialist John D. Rockefeller and the newspaper magnate William Randolph Hearst. In 1918 the architect Addison Mizner came to Palm Beach and introduced the Spanish Mediterranean style that was to become characteristic of the resort. His best known buildings are the Boca Raton Hotel and Club and the Everglades Club.

Sights

Here, particularly between Christmas and Easter, the "best people" meet on the wide beach, on the polo ground or on one of the excellent golf courses and tennis courts, and the life of the resort centres on the elegant Worth Avenue (Rodeo Dr.) and the many luxury hotels and gourmet restaurants. The long-established and internationally renowned hotels are directly on the beach, and many wealthy families from the worlds of business, politics, culture and fashionable society (the Kennedys, Estée Lauder, Burt Reynolds) have their holiday homes on Ocean Boulevard. Here too is the headquarters of the Professional Golfers' Association (PGA).

★Worth Avenue

Worth Avenue is Palm Beach's principal shopping street. In the select shopping centre known as the Esplanade are the establishments of such famous firms as Cartier, Yves Saint-Laurent and Gucci.

The palatial 73-room mansion, Whitehall, built by the railway magnate Henry Morrison Flagler on the shores of Lake Worth in 1901 is now a museum. In the grounds is Flagler's private railway coach.

The great landmark of Palm Beach, situated directly on the sea, is The Breakers (now protected as a national monument), the famous hotel designed by Leonard Schultze, architect of New York's Waldorf Astoria Hotel.

★The Breakers

West Palm Beach

The central feature of the old part of West Palm Beach is the Raymond F. Kravis Center for the Performing Arts at 701 Okeechobee Boulevard, opened in 1992, with a large theatre and concert hall (concerts by the Philharmonic Orchestra of Florida and the Palm Beach Symphony Orchestra). This attractive modern building was designed by the German-Canadian architect Eberhard Zeidler.

Raymond F. Kravis Center

The Norton Gallery of Art at 1451 South Olive Avenue (US 1) ranks as one of the best regional art museums in the United States. The collection includes French Impressionists, 20th c. American art and Chinese art; there is also a sculpture garden. Open Tue.–Sat. 10am–5pm, Sun. 1–5pm.

★Norton Gallery of Art

Surroundings

The sewing machine manufacturer Singer planned a large holiday complex here, but the project never materialised. The beach is one of the finest in the region. Other beautiful bathing beaches are Juni Beach and Boynton Beach.

★Singer Island

17 mi. west of Palm Beach is the Lion Country Safari Park (Southern Blvd. W/SR 80). Visitors drive their own cars (windows and doors must be kept closed) through the park, in which lions roam freely.

Lion Country Safari Park

10 mi. west of Boynton Beach is the Arthur R. Marshall Loxahatchee National Wildlife Refuge, which occupies the north-eastern tip of the Everglades, a region of freshwater wetland biotopes that gives an excellent impression of the sensitive ecosystem of the Everglades.

★**Arthur R. Marshall Loxahatchee National Wildlife Refuge**

The fashionable resort of Boca Raton ("rat's mouth") lies at the southern end of Palm Beach County, half way between Palm Beach and Fort Lauderdale in a sheltered bay, entrenched behind rocks, on the Atlantic coast. Its 6 mi. of coast and agreeably mild climate have made it a popular winter resort. It is famed for the professional tennis and polo tournaments held here. The Boca Raton Hotel and Club is a huge complex built by Addison Mizner in 1926. There is an interesting Museum of Art at 801 West Palmetto Park Road.

★**Boca Raton**

Palm Springs   Q 9

State: California
Altitude: 465 ft
Population: 42,000

The thermal resort of Palm Springs, the "oasis of the rich", lies in a wide valley between the San Jacinto Mountains in the west and the San Bernardino Mountains in the east, only two hours' drive from Los

Angeles (see entry). It was originally a group of seven small settlements that have now developed into one of the most celebrated holiday resorts in California. During the main season (December to March) the temperature here is very agreeable and the hotels are usually fully booked. Formerly this was a resort for the very old and the very wealthy: nowadays it appeals to successful younger people. In recent decades extensive irrigation systems have been installed and over 50,000 palms have been planted in order to improve the town's amenities. Palm Springs is now the golf metropolis of California, and it is also a Mecca for tennis fans. To the north of the town is a forest of wind-power installations that provide the town with electricity.

History The hot springs here were discovered by the Spaniards in the 18th c., but Palm Springs became a fashionable resort only in the 1930s, when Hollywood celebrities began to patronise it.

★Palm Springs Areal Tramway	This cable railway ascends to a breathtaking viewpoint almost 6500 ft up in the San Jacinto Mountains.
Desert Museum	The Desert Museum (101 Museum Dr.) has excellently presented displays illustrating the life of the desert. The museum also includes an art gallery, a display of Indian crafts and a sculpture garden.
Fabulous Palm Spring Follies	This not-to-be-missed show at the Plaza Theatre (128 S Palm Canyon Dr.) features retired vaudeville stars, often generating more atmosphere than the younger ones.
Palm Canyon	6 mi. south of Palm Springs, in Indian territory, is Palm Canyon, with some 3000 fan palms.

Palm Springs: an oasis in the desert

The Living Desert or Palm Desert (47–900 Potola Ave.) is an expanse of open country in which visitors can study various desert plants and desert animals (in enclosures).

Living Desert

95 per cent of the world's date crop comes from around Palm Springs, Shields Date Gardens, in Indio, south-east of Palm Springs, offer an insight into date cultivation, harvesting and use.

Shields Date Gardens

The Joshua Tree National Park east of Palm Springs is partly in the low-lying Colorado Desert to the south-east, and partly in the Mojave Desert in the north, which is up to 3300 ft higher. The part gets its name from the Joshua Trees (Yucca Brevifolia) growing there, whose branches, stretching upwards, reminded the passing Mormons of the upraised arms of the prophet Joshua. Well signposted roads through the park lead to interesting viewing points, and there are also clearly marked trails, such as the Willow Trail (7 mi.) that takes half a day.

★Joshua Tree National Park

Pennsylvania (State)   G–K 45–50

Area: 45,308 sq. mi.
Population: 12,056,000
Capital: Harrisburg
Popular name: Keystone State

The state of Pennsylvania (named after its founder, William Penn) lies in the north-eastern United States, reaching from Lake Erie to the Delaware River, on the border with New Jersey. In the east it extends on to the Piedmont Plateau and into the Appalachians and their longitudinal valley; the main part of the state lies on the Allegheny Plateau, which reaches its highest point in Mount Davius (3212 ft). In the humid continental climate, with warm summers and cool winters, deciduous forest predominates in fully half the area of the state, with conifers at higher levels.

Pennsylvania is called the Keystone State because some of the key events in the history of the United States took place here, in particular the signing of the Declaration of Independence at Philadelphia in 1776.

History The first white settlement in the territory of Pennsylvania, then occupied by the Iroquois, was established by Swedes in 1643. Thereafter it became a Dutch colony, and in 1664 passed to Britain. In 1681 Charles II granted the territory to the Quaker William Penn, charging him to speed up the process of settlement. In addition to English Quakers and Scottish and Irish groups the early settlers were mainly Germans, who left an enduring imprint on the state. On December 12th 1787 Pennsylvania became the second state to adopt the Constitution of the United States of America.

Economy Thanks to the deposits of anthracite in the Appalachians Pennsylvania is the leading coal-mining state in the United States. This has led to the development of an important iron and steel industry and a high degree of industrialisation in the state. Agriculture is concentrated mainly on supplying the needs of the industrial areas. The Appalachians and the Pocono Mountains with their excellent winter sports facilities and scope for other outdoor activities are popular tourist and holiday areas.

Accessible all year round, the Allegheny National Forest in the north-west of the state is a paradise for walkers, campers, anglers and skiers.

Allegheny National Forest

Pennsylvania

★Altoona

This town in the Alleghenies was founded in 1849 by the Pennsylvania Railroad Company, and the town still attracts railway buffs with the Railroader's Memorial Museum and the **Horseshoe Curve**, where trains turn through a 220° curve 795 yds long to overcome a height difference of 227 ft per mi.

★Bethlehem

The town of Bethlehem, north of Philadelphia (see entry), was founded by Moravian Brethren from Germany, who have left their mark on the town with the Christmas Festival, when choirs and orchestras join in a celebration that is well known throughout the United States, and in the Gemein Haus of 1741 (now a museum), the Brethren's House of 1748 and the Old Chapel of 1751. In the Moravian Cemetery on Market Street there are graves ranging in date from 1742 to 1910. The Bach Festival held on the campus of Lehigh University is world-famous.

★Delaware Water Gap

At this point in north-east Pennsylvania the Delaware River cuts through the Kittatinny Mountains. With its wild and beautiful landscape it is a popular recreation area and was so in earlier times, as witness the small Victorian resort of Jim Thorpe.

★★Gettysburg

The decisive battle in the Civil War was fought in southern Pennsylvania, near Gettysburg. It took place over a wide area on July 1st–3rd 1863, when Confederate forces commanded by General Lee that had advanced far into the north were defeated by General Meade's Union army. Altogether 51,000 men on both sides were killed or wounded. Here, four months later, President Abraham Lincoln pronounced his famous Gettysburg Address, in which he set out his ideas on the future of the Union.

The battlefield is now a **National Military Park**, traversed by more than

30 mi. of roads and tracks, with numerous monuments and memorial stones. Visitors can either find their own way to the main features on the battlefield or take part in a guided tour (2 hours). The course of the battle can be followed in detail on an electric map in the Visitor Center, which also displays a large collection of uniforms and weapons.

The town On the outskirts of the National Park is a farmhouse that was occupied by President Eisenhower and his wife. In the quiet little college town of Gettysburg are a number of museums and memorial sites commemorating the battle. The most notable features are General Lee's headquarters and Wills House, in which Lincoln spent the night.

Harrisburg

The National Soldiers Monument at Gettysburg

Until Chernobyl Harrisburg, the state capital,

situated in south-eastern Pennsylvania, had the dubious honour of being the scene of the world's worst nuclear accident, at the Three Mile Island power station on the Susquehanna River. Features of interest in the town are the State Capitol and the informative State Museum.

Hershey, to the east of Harrisburg, is known to Americans as the place where the country's favourite chocolate was first made in 1903 by M.S. Hershey – an event and a product that are celebrated in Hershey's Chocolate World.

Hershey

This State Park in south-west Pennsylvania is of interest to art lovers as well as nature lovers. The rapids on the Youghiogheny River attract white-water rafting. Fallingwater, a private house to the north of Ohiopyle, is an architectural masterpiece by Frank Lloyd Wright.

Ohiopyle State Park

York, to the south of Harrisburg, was for 90 days capital of the thirteen colonies when Congress was compelled to flee from Philadelphia (see entry). In the Colonial Court House (now a reconstruction) the Articles of Confederation, the founding document of the Union, were adopted in 1777. There are a number of other historic spots in the town. For visitors interested in more modern achievements there is the Harley Davidson motorcycle factory with its museum.

York

Lancaster County/Pennsylvania Dutch Country, Philadelphia, Pittsburgh (see entries)

Other places of interest

★★Philadelphia   K 50

State: Pennsylvania
Altitude: 0–482 ft
Population: 1.6 million

Philadelphia, the "cradle of the nation", lies in the urbanised Atlantic region between Boston and Washington, DC (see entries), in the extreme south-east of Pennsylvania, extending along the Delaware River, which is joined here by the Schuylkill River. The city is an important industrial and commercial centre as well as a major port. The most productive branch of industry is oil processing; other industries include the electrical industry, chemicals and printing and publishing. Philadelphia's theatres, concert halls, libraries and museums, together with the University of Pennsylvania, Temple University, Drexel University and the famed Philadelphia Orchestra, make it one of the leading cultural centres of the United States.

History The first settlers on the site of Philadelphia, in 1640, were Swedes and Finns, later followed by Dutch and British settlers. In 1681 Charles II granted possession of this territory to William Penn (1644–1718), leader of a Quaker colony, who then founded Philadelphia in 1682 as a place of religious freedom. This freedom attracted German Mennonites to settle in the town. In 1683 Penn made a treaty with the Delaware Indians that preserved the town from Indian attacks. In 1701 he granted Philadelphia, which then had a population of 4500, its charter as a town. A fresh impulse was given to the development of the town by Benjamin Franklin, who came to live here in 1723, published a newspaper and was instrumental in founding the University of Pennsylvania. In the liberal climate of Philadelphia the idea of separation from the mother country was first formulated, and on September 5th 1774 the Continental Congress met in Carpenters' Hall. During its second session in Independence Hall the Declaration of Independence was adopted on July 4th 1776. In 1787 the Constitutional Congress met in Philadelphia.

Until 1799 it was capital of Pennsylvania, and from 1790 to 1800 was also capital of the United States. In 1848, following the revolutions in Europe, large numbers of Germans settled in the town. The North's rejection of slavery also brought many blacks from the south.

Independence National Historical Park

The Independence National Historical Park contains a number of buildings that have played a great part in the history of the United States. The Visitor Center, beside which is the tower containing the Bicentennial Bell, a gift from the British government on the bicentenary of the United States, is at the corner of 3rd and Chestnut Streets.

★★Liberty Bell
Pavilion

To the west of the Visitor Center, opposite Independence Hall, is the famous Liberty Bell, cast in England, which was rung for the first time in 1776, on the occasion of the first public reading of the Declaration of Independence. The bell, previously in Independence Hall, was installed in the present pavilion in 1976. In 2000 the bell is to be moved to a new home, where there will be a small museum.

★★Independence
Hall

The central feature of the historic district is the Georgian-style Independence Hall, the "birthplace of the United States". Here the Declaration of Independence was signed in 1776 and the Constitution of the United States was written in 1787. In the restored chamber are a number of historic relics, including Washington's chair and the table on which the Declaration of Independence was signed. Guided visits Mon.–Thu. 9am–5pm, Fri.–Sun. to 8pm.

Independence Hall is flanked by Congress Hall, in which the first Congress of the United States met from 1790 to 1800 and George

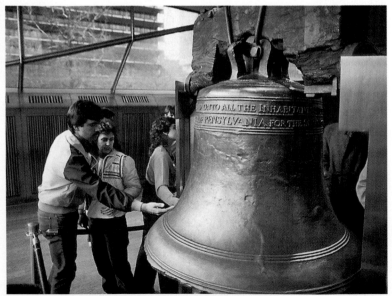

The Liberty Bell, Philadelphia

Independence Hall, birthplace of the United States of America

Washington and John Adams were elected President, and Old City Hall, which was never in fact the town hall but was the seat of the Supreme Court from 1791 to 1800.

On the section of Chestnut Street to the east of Independence Hall are a number of other historic buildings: the Second Bank of the United States (1824–41), now containing a collection of portraits of leading figures in the fight for independence; New Hall, with the Marine Corps Memorial Museum (recalling the role of the Marine Corps in the fight for independence); on the opposite side of the street the Philadelphia Marine Museum (history of shipping on the Delaware River and in Delaware Bay); beyond this Pemberton House, a reproduction of the home of the Quaker Joseph Pemberton, now occupied by the Army–Navy Museum; and beyond this again

Carpenters' Hall (No. 320), in which the First Continental Congress met in 1774, now a museum of the carpenter's craft.

From Chestnut Street 3rd Street runs south, passing the First Bank of the United States (1797–1811), the country's oldest bank, into Walnut Street. At the corner of 3rd Street is the Merchants' Exchange, originally the seat of the Stock Exchange (founded 1790), the oldest in the United States. At 325 Walnut Street are the headquarters of the Pennsylvania Horticultural Society, the oldest horticultural society in the United States. Further east, at the corner of 2nd Street, is the City Tavern, in which delegates to the First and Second Continental Congresses used to relax after their labours.

Concealed between Chestnut and Market Streets is Franklin Court, in which Benjamin Franklin once lived. In one of the reconstructed houses

Chestnut Street

Walnut Street

Franklin Court

415

Philadelphia

is a museum devoted to the life and work of the great statesman, inventor and journalist.

Washington Square

South-east of Independence Hall, in Washington Square, once the burial place of those who died in the fight for independence, is the Tomb of the Unknown Soldier of the Revolution, with an eternal flame.

★Society Hill

The area of higher ground to the south of Walnut Street and east of Washington Square, extending almost to Penn's Landing, is called Society Hill after the Free Society of Traders founded by William Penn. Many politicians of the revolutionary period lived in this area, and some of their houses are preserved.

At 252 South 4th Street is **Old St Mary's Church**, with the grave of Commodore John Barry, founder of the United States Navy, in the churchyard.

The Georgian-style **Powel House** at 244 South 3rd Street was built in 1765 by Samuel Powel, a popular mayor of Philadelphia. South-east of this is the Man Full of Trouble Tavern (1759).

On 2nd Street, between Pine and South Streets, is **Head House Square**, in which a street market has been held since 1745. It is pleasant to wander through its open sales halls and to relax in one of the cafés. The Mario Lanza Museum to the south commemorates the famous tenor (416 Queen St.).

Independence Mall

To the north of Independence Hall extends the park-like Independence Mall, laid out in 1948. On its east side, at 55 North 5th Street, is the

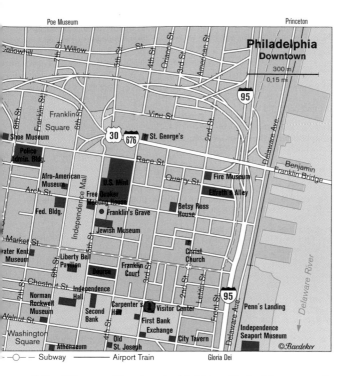

Poe Museum · Princeton

Philadelphia Downtown

300 m
0,15 mi

Subway ———— Airport Train

National Museum of American Jewish History. North of the museum, in Arch Street, is **Christ Church Burial Ground**, with the graves of Benjamin Franklin and his wife Deborah.

Further north again is the **US Mint**, established here in 1792, which is now the largest Mint in the world. Opposite the Burial Ground, in the Mall, is the Free Quaker Meeting House, in which the first Free Quaker meeting was held in 1874. South-east of the US Mint, in Arch Street, is the Friends' Meeting House, the city's oldest Quaker meeting house, built in 1804 though on a site acquired by the Quakers in 1693.

At the north-west corner of the Mall (7th and Arch Sts.) is the **Afro–American Historical and Cultural Museum**.

Spread over six storeys, the collection of the Shoe Museum in Race Street includes some fascinating items of footwear.

Shoe Museum

East of the Mint in Arch Street stands Betsy Ross House, where Betsy Ross sewed the original "Stars and Stripes". A short distance north-east lies Elfreth's Alley, the oldest residential street in the United States.

Betsy Ross House

To the north, below the Benjamin Franklin Bridge, which crosses the Delaware from Franklin Square, are Old St Augustine's Church (R.C.) and St George's Methodist Church (235 N 4th St.), the oldest Methodist church in the United States, built in 1769.

St George's
Methodist Church

417

Philadelphia

Edgar Allan Poe
Museum

Half a mile north of Franklin Square, at 532 North 7th Street, is the Edgar Allan Poe Historic Site, with the house in which Poe lived in 1843–4.

Delaware River

Penn's Landing

At Penn's Landing, where William Penn landed in 1682, there are now a wide range of leisure facilities, including a marina, sports and recreation grounds and old ships.

Maritime Museum

At Pier 11, south of the Benjamin Franklin Bridge, are USS "Olympia", Commodore Dewey's flagship in the battle of Manila Bay during the Spanish–American War (1898), the Second World War submarine USS "Becuna", and the "Gazela", a Portuguese rig built in 1883. The Maritime Museum embraces the whole field of navigation.

★New Jersey
State Aquarium

From Penn's Landing river buses cross the Delaware to Camden, with the New Jersey State Aquarium, whose principal attractions are an ocean pool (sharks) and a seal pool.

Gloria Dei Church

At the corner of Christian Street and Delaware Avenue (I 95) is the Gloria Dei Church (1700), also known as the Old Swedes, the oldest church in Pennsylvania.

City center

★City Hall

From Independence Mall Market Street, lined with shops and department stores, runs west to City Hall (1874–94), at the busy intersection of Market and Broad Streets. The building, in French Renaissance style, was designed by McArthur; it is crowned by a bronze statue of William Penn. Facing City Hall is the Temple of the Grand Lodge of Pennsylvania. Philadelphia is the heartland of Freemasonry in the United States.

★Academy of
Fine Arts

North of City Hall, at 118 North Broad Street, is the Pennsylvania Academy of Fine Arts, the oldest art school in the United States. It displays a large collection of American art of the last three centuries, including pictures by Peale, West, Sully and Eakins. Open Mon.–Sat. 10am–5pm, Sun. 11am–5pm.

Penn Center

North-west of City Hall is the Penn Center, a complex of hotels and high-rise office blocks, including the Central Penn National Bank and the IBM Building. Previously there was a tacit agreement that no buildings in this area should be higher than the statue of William Penn (550 ft), but in recent years a whole series of skyscrapers have been built. Among them are One Liberty Place, at 1650 Market Street, the city's tallest building (945 ft), Two Liberty Place (1601 Chestnut St.; 845 ft) and the Mellon Bank Center (1735 Market St.; 880 ft).

Rosenbach
Museum

South of Rittenhouse Square, south-west of City Hall, is the Rosenbach Museum, with a collection of paintings, valuable prints, manuscripts and first editions (2010 Delancey St.).

Logan Circle/Benjamin Parkway

From the Kennedy Plaza, adjoining City Hall, the Benjamin Franklin Parkway, spaciously laid out in the 1920s, runs north-west to Logan Circle and then on to Fairmont Park. Along it are situated some of the city's best museums.

Academy of
Natural Sciences

On the south side of the square is the Academy of Natural Sciences, the oldest scientific society in the United States. Its extensive collections include dioramas of groups of animals and dinosaur skeletons.

The west side of Logan Circle is occupied by the Franklin Institute Science Museum, which is in fact several museums under one roof, and among other things displays many of Franklin's own experiments. It is particularly concerned with the physical bases of technology, and the Science Center offers visitors the opportunity of trying their own experiments, in many fields – computers, information technology, space travel, astronomy, oceanography. Among the exhibits is a large walk-in model of the heart. On the ground floor is an over life-size statue of Benjamin Franklin. The Mandell Futures Center is concerned with the connections between technology and the natural sciences, and forecasts what life will be like in the 21st c. The Tuttleman Omniverse Theatre shows scientific films. There are also exhibitions on electricity and the biological sciences. On the second floor, among much else, is a section on shipbuilding, and on the third is an Observatory. In the basement is a Planetarium. Open daily 9.30am–5pm.

★Franklin Institute Science Museum

This library on the south side of the square is one of the largest in the country, with many rare books on display.

Free Library of Philadelphia

The Rodin Museum (22nd St. and Benjamin Franklin Parkway), opened in 1929, contains the largest collection of Rodin's work outside France, with 124 pieces of sculpture. The collection was assembled in the 1920s by the Philadelphia cinema magnate Jules E. Mastbaum. Open Tue.–Sun. 10am–5pm.

★Rodin Museum

At the south end of Fairmount Park is the prominently situated Philadelphia Museum of Art, approached by a broad flight of steps, which has one of the largest art collections in the United States, with some 300,000 exhibits, many of them presented by various foundations. Among the finest sections of the museum are the medieval galleries, which include pictures by Rogier van der Weyden and the van Eyck brothers and complete structures such as a Romanesque cloister and a Gothic chapel. In other rooms are Renaissance and baroque works and art of the 18th and 19th centuries, including pictures by Van Gogh, Renoir, Toulouse-Lautrec, Manet, Cézanne, Monet and Degas. 20th c. European art is represented by Picasso, Chagall, Matisse, Miró, Paul Klee and other artists, American art by the Philadelphia artists Thomas Eakins, Charles Wilson Peale ("The Staircase Group", 1795) and many others. There are also fine collections of Asian art, including a Buddhist and a Chinese temple, porcelain, jade and Oriental carpets. Open Tue.–Sun.10am–5pm, Wed. to 8.45pm.

★Philadelphia Museum of Art

Other sights

The Museum of Art is situated within Fairmount Park. Some 550 yds north-west of the museum, along the Schuylkill River and Kelly Drive, is Boathouse Row, with a series of old boathouses belonging to various rowing clubs. Between the Museum and Boathouse Row are the Fairmount Waterworks, with old turbines.

1 mi. south-east of the Zoo is Drexel University, and to the south of this is the campus of the University of Pennsylvania, of which Benjamin Franklin was co-founder. On the campus (33rd and Spruce Sts.) is the University Museum of Archaeology and Anthropology, with a rich collection of material from Egypt and the Middle East, South and Central America, Greece and Africa.

University of Pennsylvania

Near the junction of the Schuylkill and Delaware Rivers is Fort Mifflin,

★Fort Mifflin

419

built by the British in 1772. During the War of Independence it fell into the hands of the American patriots and defended Philadelphia against British attacks.

★Barnes Foundation

Though some distance away at 300 North Latches Lane (8 mi. west of Downtown Philadelphia), anyone with an interest in Impressionist and post-Impressionist painting should be sure to visit the Barnes Foundation. Opened in 1995, it boasts one of the world's finest collections of such paintings.

★Germantown

From City Hall Broad Street runs north into Germantown Avenue, which continues north-east to Germantown (7 mi.). Once an independent town occupied by German craftsmen and now a district of Philadelphia with a predominantly black population, it grew up on land that William Penn granted in 1683 to a German Quaker called Daniel Pastorius. The first protests against the import of slaves came from here in 1688. The first German school in North America was established in 1702, and in 1739 the first German newspaper, the "Germantowner Zeitung", was founded by Christoph Sauer.

The Germantown Historical Society in Market Square is a fund of information about Germantown. Other features of interest are the Georgian mansion of Cliveden (6401 Germantown Ave.), built for Judge Benjamin Chew in 1767, Stenton House (1730 18th St.), the Deshler-Morris House of 1773 (5442 Germantown Ave.), Germantown Mennonite Church (6117 Germantown Ave.) and Concord Schoolhouse (6309 Germantown Ave.).

Princeton

See New Jersey

Phoenix   Q 13

State: Arizona
Altitude: 1080 ft
Population: 1.1 million

Phoenix, capital of the state of Arizona, lies in the valley of the Salt River (which is frequently dry), in a basin known as the Valley of the Sun. The warm, dry climate attracts many sun lovers, particularly in winter. It is no accident then that the suburb of Scottsdale has evolved into an exclusive holiday resort and that Sun City, a town for senior citizens, should be located on the outskirts of Phoenix. Irrigation, with water pounded by dams, has made Phoenix and the surrounding area a green oasis in the middle of the desert. Agriculture (cotton, wine grapes, citrus and tropical fruit, vegetables) makes an important contribution to the economy. In recent years many research and development laboratories and firms engaged in the communications technology, aerospace and electronics industries have been established in and around the city. Tourism is showing a sharp increase. The city acquires a special character from the juxtaposition of high-rise modern buildings with architecture showing Indian and Spanish colonial influences, together with a touch of the Wild West. In recent years the entire Valley of the Sune has been extensively exploited for recreational purposes – there are 140 golf courses and more than 1000 tennis courts alone. The nearby countryside offers white-water rafting, sailing and hot air ballooning, as well as Wild West-style trekking and even gold panning. The Phoenix Suns are a top team in the US basketball league. But the image chiefly projected by Phoenix today is of an economically flourishing city in the Sun Belt.

History Around 200 BC the Phoenix region was occupied by Hohokam Indians, who already knew how to make the desert fertile by irrigation.

Amid the remains of settlements and irrigation channels left by the Hohokams, who mysteriously disappeared in the 13th or 14th c., a white settler established himself in 1864 to supply the needs of an army post. In the 1870s a new settlement grew up on the remains of the lost Indian culture and was named after the mythological phoenix that rose from its own ashes. In 1889 Phoenix became capital of Arizona, and after the completion of the Roosevelt Dam in 1911 developed into a regular boom town, which was given an additional boost by the coming of the railroad in 1926. Further stimulus came to the economy after the Second World War and from the "Sun Belt" migration that began in the late 1960s. Since the end of the war the population of Phoenix has multiplied more than tenfold.

Sights

In Heritage Square (in the heart of the city, between 6th and 7th Sts.) are several lovingly restored houses dating from the city's early days. Stevens House contains a collection of dolls and toys. At the corner of 6th and Monroe Streets is Rosson House, an elegant Victorian mansion (1895/96). The city's history is documented in the Phoenix Museum of History.

★Heritage Square

The huge Arizona Center further north contains a plethora of shops, cafés and restaurants.

Arizona Center

The Arizona Mining and Mineral Museum (1502 W Washington St.) is devoted to Arizona's mineral wealth. Its fascinating display of precious

Arizona Mining and Mineral Museum

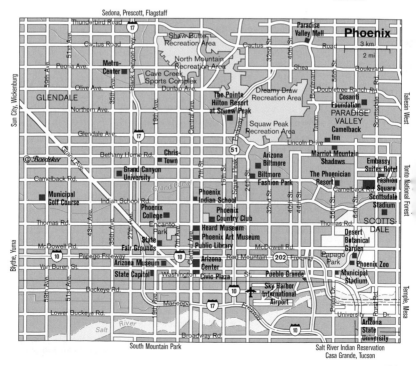

stones, many coloured minerals and various ores bears witness to the state's rich resources of minerals.

Arizona State Capitol Museum

Set in beautiful gardens is the old State Capitol (Washington St. and 17th Ave.), built in 1900, which was the seat of government until 1974. The imposing state apartments are now a museum on the history of Arizona. Here too can be seen the anchor of USS "Arizona", which was sunk in Pearl Harbor in 1941.

★Phoenix Art Museum

The Phoenix Art Museum (1625 N Central Ave.) has a collection covering the art of the European Renaissance and baroque, the Far East and the American West. Open Tue.–Sat. 10am–5pm, Wed. to 9pm, Sun. noon–5pm.

★Heard Museum

The renowned Heard Museum (22 E Monte Vista Rd.) is devoted to the art and culture of the Indian peoples of the south-west (basketwork, pottery, jewellery, textiles; large collection of kachina dolls). Open Mon.–Sat. 9.30am–5pm, Wed. to 9pm, Sun. noon–5pm.

★Pueblo Grande Museum

In the Pueblo Grande Museum (4619 E Washington St.) are the ruins of a 12th c. Hohokam settlement and remains of old irrigation channels.

★Hall of Flame

The Hall of Flame (6101 E Van Buren St.) illustrates the history of firefighting with exhibits dating back to 1725, including old fire engines and some very curious types of fire extinguisher.

Papago Park

In Papago Park are the Phoenix Zoo (455 N Galvin Parkway), which is famed for its Sumatra tigers and orangutans, and the Desert Botanical Garden (1201 N Galvin Parkway), with examples of vegetation from deserts in different parts of the world and a cactus garden. The flowers are particularly beautiful in spring.

Surroundings

Tempe

The suburb of Tempe is home to Arizona State University on whose campus the Nelson Fine Art Center was opened in 1989. Quite apart from its art collection, the Center is an architectural masterpiece in its own right.

Mesa

In Mesa, the suburb to the east of Tempe, the Mesa Southwest Museum (53 N MacDonald St.) focuses on the days of the Indians and pioneers.

The Champlin Fighter Museum (4643 Fighter Aces Dr, Falcon Field) has a collection of fighter planes of the two world wars, the Korean War, the Vietnam War and the Gulf War.

Sun City

The retirement town of Sun City, 11 mi. north-west of Phoenix, came into being in the 1960s, and now has a population of 70,000 mainly comfortably off senior citizens. Offering the attractions of leisure, a pleasant life style, an agreeable climate and beautiful scenery, it is almost entirely residential, with no schools or kindergartens, still less any industry. Another settlement of the same kind, Sun City West, has grown up in the immediate vicinity.

Scottsdale

To the east of Phoenix is the vacation resort of Scottsdale, with luxury hotels and excellent leisure facilities and shops. The Old Town has some well restored buildings dating from the beginning of the century. Other features of interest are the Center for the Arts (art exhibitions) and to the south of Scottsdale the McCromick Railroad Park (museum).

The **Cosanti Foundation**, situated about 5 mi. north of the Old Town at 6433 Doubletree Ranch Road, is the base from which the contemporary architect Paolo Soleri works, best known for his futuristic, eco-friendly settlement Arcosanti (Prescott).

Taliesin West, north-east of Scottsdale (108th St., near Shea Blvd.), was the desert hideaway of the celebrated architect Frank Lloyd Wright. Guided tours.

★Taliesin West

Another popular attraction is Rawhide (23023 Scottsdale Rd.), a reconstruction of a Western town of around 1880, with a saloon, a steakhouse and wild shoot-outs by professional stuntmen.

★Rawhide

In the hilly region north-east and east of Phoenix (Tonto National Forest, Mazatzal Mountains, Sierra Ancha Mountains) a series of dams have been built in recent decades, forming **artificial lakes** to ensure an adequate water supply for the rapidly growing population of the Phoenix Metropolitan Area. The oldest of these lakes is Theodore Roosevelt Lake, to the east of Scottsdale, which was formed by the construction of a dam in 1911. Various water sports (swimming, waterskiing, boating) are permitted in specially signposted areas.

To the south of Theodore Roosevelt Lake, near SR 88, is the Tonto National Monument, a pueblo constructed by Salago Indians in the 14th c.

Pittsburgh   J 45

State: Pennsylvania
Altitude: 680–1400 ft
Population: 370,000

On the north-western Allegheny Plateau, at the point where the Allegheny and Monongahela Rivers join to form the Ohio, lies the city of Pittsburgh, surrounded by the wooded hills of the western Appalachians. The wealth of the city came from these hills: the coal mined here was the basis of a great steel industry that at one time produced half the total requirements of the United States. This branch of industry is still a major element in the city's economy, but since the crisis of the antiquated American steel industry in the 1970s a process of restructuring has been under way, and Pittsburgh now has a range of other industries as well, in particular service industries, high tech industry and light industry. The city's good communications – it is an important inland port and has a large new airport opened in 1992 – have led major firms like Westinghouse Electric to establish their headquarters here. Pittsburgh is thus no longer the soot-encrusted coal and steel town of the past, but rather a metropolis with fine parks and gardens flanking the rivers and a modern city centre. According to a survey it is one of the pleasantest cities to live in the whole of the United States, with the "Steelers" ice hockey and "Pirates" baseball teams being part of the attraction.

History The first Europeans to reach the "Golden Triangle" between the rivers were Frenchmen, who built Fort Duquesne. The French fort was destroyed by the British in 1758 and replaced by Fort Pitt (named after William Pitt the Elder). The settlement that grew up round the fort was named Pittsburgh; the local coalfields began to be worked and blast furnaces were built. The demand for iron and steel for the Civil War brought prosperity to heavy industry, and thereafter industrialists like Andrew Carnegie and Henry Clay Frick built up their empires. Pittsburgh enjoyed further booms during the two world wars, but thereafter the crisis in the steel industry made a process of readjustment necessary.

Pittsburgh was one of the birthplaces of the American trade union movement: the American Federation of Labor was founded here in 1881, and the city was frequently the scene of bitter conflicts between workers and employers.

★Golden Triangle
Point State Park

The heart of Pittsburgh is the "Golden Triangle" at the junction of the Allegheny and Monongahela Rivers. At the tip of the triangle is Point State Park, with a large fountain symbolising the birth of the Ohio. This was the site of Fort Pitt, of which there now remains only a blockhouse. The fort's original appearance is shown in dioramas in the Fort Pitt Museum.

Market Square

With its gardens, its old buildings and its attractive restaurants and shops, picturesque Market Square is a pleasant relief from the rather overpowering skyscrapers that surround it.

The 31-storey skyscraper Fifth Avenue Place (Stanwix St.) contains a shopping mall, the Avenue of Shops, lavishly decorated with marble, glass and brass. Between 6th and 7th Streets is the granite CNG Tower, a major landmark on the city's skyline. In Grant Street, side by side, are the two tallest buildings in Pittsburgh, One Mellon Bank Center (715 ft) and the USX Tower (840 ft), the façade of which, constructed of steel, is quietly rusting. The postmodern complex PPG Place was designed by Philip Johnson. The Alcoa Building (425 5th Ave.) was a pioneering feat of building technology, the aluminium cladding having been applied without any internal scaffolding.

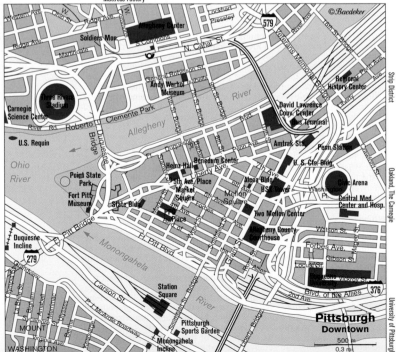

Pittburgh in all its beauty, seen from Mount Washington: view of the Golden Triangle and Downtown

Dating from Pittsburg's days as a steel boomtown are Union Station, the Flemish-Gothic style Two Mellon Bank Center (formerly the Union Trust Building; 5th Ave./Grant St.) and the neighbouring Allegheny County Courthouse (1184).

This new museum complex named after Senator John Heinz and located at the north end of Downtown offers a graphic insight into the history of West Pennsylvania.

Pittsburg Regional History Center

The Strip District, on the Allegheny River at the north-east corner of the Golden Triangle, formerly occupied by warehouses and railroad installations, is now the city's wholesale market centre, a scene of lively activity in the early morning and forenoon. There are guided tours of the complex, including the Wholesale Produce Terminal, the largest wholesale vegetable market in western Pennsylvania.

Strip District

In the Mount Washington district on the south bank (South Side) of the Monongahela River, between Smithfield Street Bridge and Fort Pitt Bridge, is Station Square, once occupied by railway yards but now an elegant shopping centre.

Mount Washington

From South Side two funiculars run steeply up Mount Washington – the last of the cable railways that used to carry coal from the mines in the hill down to the river for shipment. The Monongahela Incline starts from West Carson Street, opposite Station Square, the Duquesne Incline Railway further along the street, north-west of Fort Pitt Bridge. From the top of the hill there are fine views of downtown Pittsburgh.

North Side

★Carnegie
Science Center

In North Side (the north bank of the Allegheny River) is the huge Carnegie Science Center (1 Allegheny Ave.), a museum of science and technology. Among the subjects dealt with are industrial processing methods, the use of energy and sociocultural aspects of nutrition. The Pacific Coral Reef Aquarium displays a wide range of tropical fishes. In the Rangos Omnimax Theater visitors can make imaginary journeys through the human body; in the Henry Buhl Jr Planetarium and Observatory they can fly into space.

★Andy Warhol
Museum

The Andy Warhol Museum, opened in 1994, is devoted to the life and work of the Pop Art artist, who was born in North Side. Housed in a restored warehouse, it displays paintings, drawings, prints, films and videos by Warhol.

Mattress Factory

The Mattress Factory, far from being a factory, is an highly intriguing and imaginative museum of modern art, made even more exciting by its "live" performances and use of technology (5000 Sampsonia Way).

Less highbrow visitors may prefer to take their offspring to the large children's museum in the Allegheny Center.

East of the Golden Triangle

University of
Pittsburgh

To the east of the city centre is the campus of the University of Pittsburgh, dominated by the 535 ft high "Cathedral of Learning" (1935) containing lecture rooms, including 22 so-called nationality classrooms for different ethnic groups, including Jews and Armenians. South-east of the building is the Stephen Foster Memorial, commemorating the Pittsburgh-born composer of that name (1826–64), author of the popular song "Oh, Susannah".

The Carnegie

To the east of the University, at 4400 Forbes Avenue, are the Museum of Natural History, the Museum of Art and the Music Hall, in the complex known simply as "The Carnegie" after its founder Andrew Carnegie. The most interesting is the Museum of Natural History, famed for its large dinosaur collection, the Hillman Hall of Minerals and Gems and its displays of material on the cultures of the North American Indians and the life of the Inuit in the Arctic.

Frick Art Museum

Still further east is Frick Park, with the Frick Art Museum. This displays the art collection of Helen Clay Frick, with pictures ranging in date from the early Renaissance to the end of the 18th c. Further north is the country house that belonged to the Pittsburgh industrialist Henry Clay Frick.

Portland   D 3

State: Oregon
Altitude: 75 ft
Population: 437,000

Straddling the Willamette River, Portland is not only the largest town in Oregon but also the wettest in the United States. Perhaps by way of compensating for the damp winters, the city is culturally very alive, with bars, music and theatre. There are more (and the best) small breweries here than anywhere else in the States, which may help to explain why, despite the weather, statistics show Portland to be one of the most desirable places to live in the United States.

History Portland was founded in 1844 as a little port town on the west bank of the Willamette River. Much of the town was destroyed by a great fire in 1873, but after its rebuilding it developed into a thriving city. When new ports were built on Puget Sound in the early 20th c., however, Portland lost its leading role.

Sights

The places to go shopping or just have a look round are the Pearl District north of Burnside Street, the fine Northwest 23rd Avenue, the Nob Hill district or, for a more local, multi-cultural atmosphere, Southeast Hawthorne Boulevard on the East Side.

Pioneer Courthouse Square, between Southwest Broadway and Southwest Morrison Street, is a rendezvous for Portlanders at any time of day. It is also a good starting point for exploring the town.

Pioneer Courthouse Square

The Portland Art Museum in Park Avenue has a collection of high quality in a variety of fields, including Indian art and Renaissance pictures in the Kress Collection.

Portland Art Museum

Opposite the Art Museum is the Oregon Historical Museum, with a rich collection of material on the history of the state.

Oregon Historical Museum

At the corner of Madison Street and 5th Avenue is the Portland Building, with a glass and concrete façade with features borrowed from historic buildings that make it one of the forerunners of postmodern architecture.

Portland Building

From the Portland Building continue in the direction of the river to Waterfront Park. The park, through which runs Front Street, extends along the Yamhill Historic District. The converted premises now housing shops and restaurants were originally used for harbour business. To the north the park stretches as far as the Skidmore Fountain, where a colourful Saturday market is held. En route are the Maritime Center and Museum (113 Front Ave.) and the Jeff Morris Memorial Fire Museum (111 Front Ave.). North of Burnside Street, at 9 NW 2nd Avenue is the American Advertising Museum.

Waterfront Park

This large park to the west of the city centre contains a number of features of interest. The best known is the International Rose Test Garden, where new varieties of roses are grown; in the city's mild climate they continue to flower into autumn. An annual event for rose lovers is the Rose Festival in June. Other attractions are the Japanese Garden, one of the largest outside Japan, the zoo, the Oregon Museum of Science and Industry and a second museum of science and technology on the banks of the river in the city centre), and the Hoyt Arboretum.

★Washington Park

★★Redwood National Park   H 1/2

State: California
Area: 177 sq. mi.
Established: 1968

The Redwood National Park, which is formed from three smaller nature reserves (Del Norte Coast Redwoods State Park, Jedediah Smith State Park, Prairie Creek Redwoods State Park), lies on the Pacific coast between Orick and Crescent City, 330 mi. north of San Francisco (see entry). 50 mi. long and up to 7 mi. across, it contains some 37,500 acres of redwoods.

The park has some 150 mi. of waymarked roads and trails, four camp-grounds and some primitive overnight accommodation. There are facilities for swimming, fishing and boating on the Smith River in the Jedediah Smith State Park. Bathing is not recommended on the rugged but beautiful Pacific coast because of its high waves, strong currents and extremely cold water.

Information The National Park is open throughout the year. The best times for a visit are in spring, when the rhododendrons are in flower, and in autumn for the colouring of the foliage. During the summer the park tends to be crowded with visitors. The park headquarters is in Crescent City. In addition to several camp sites, there is overnight accommodation at the Redwood Youth Hostel and Marigold Cabin Lodge.

The coast **redwoods** (*Sequoia sempervirens*) grow only in a narrow belt of land along the coast from Oregon, down to the south of San Francisco. They are closely related to the mammoth trees (Sequoia gigantea), which grows only on some of the western slopes of the Sierra Nevada. The coast redwoods, which provide much sought after building timber and veneers, are the tallest trees on earth, reaching heights of over 330 ft. Trunks with a diameter of 20 ft are not uncommon. The average age of these giants is between 500 and 700 years, and some are over 2000 years old. They are almost immune to disease or attack by pests, and their thick bark, up to a foot thick, gives then protection against forest fires, but they have a relatively shallow root system that makes them vulnerable in a storm. Redwoods can be grown from seed, from a cone or from shoots.

Among the **highlights** of the park are: Tall Trees Grove, with the tallest tree on earth – 368 ft high and 46 ft in circumference (access only with the permission of the Redwood Information Center); Patrick's Point, offering a splendid view of the coast; the James Irvine Trail through the Fern Canyon to Gold Bluffs Beach; Klamath Overlook (whale watching); and the Coastal Drive in the Klamath area, a delightful stretch of coastline.

Rhode Island (State)   H 54

Area: 1214 sq. mi.
Population: 1,003,000
Capital: Providence
Popular names: Little Rhody,
Ocean State

Rhode Island, the smallest state in the Union, is one of the New England states in the north-east of the United States It was christened Rhode Island either by the explorer Giovanni di Verrazano, who was reminded of Rhodes, or by the Dutchman Adriaen Block who called it "Roode Eylandt" on account of its red clover. The eastern half of the state is occupied by Narragansett Bay, which reaches far inland, and to the west of this are the New England Uplands, the highest point in which is 900 ft above sea level. Rhode Island has a maritime climate, with mild winters and wet summers. Over 60 per cent of the state is forest covered, and its mixed forests of oak,

◀ *Giant redwoods in the Redwood National Park*

beech, maple, birch, pine, provide a valuable recreation area for the inhabitants of the neighbouring great cities.

Bathers should drive to the south coast where there are several attractive beaches, e.g. at Narragansett, South Kingstown and Charlestown.

History Refugees from Massachusetts established the first settlements in Rhode Island, where for the first time in a British colony there was a clear line of separation between state and church. Thereafter many refugees from religious persecution found a new home in Rhode Island. In 1675, in the "Great Swamp Fight", the settlers ended the previous predominance of the Narragansett Indians. Rhode Island joined the Union on May 29th 1790, the last of the thirteen founding states to do so.

Economy The economy of Rhode Island depends mainly on industry. A leading place is taken by the state's traditional textile industry (first cotton spinning mill, 1793), followed by engineering, tool manufacture and jewellery. The rubber and artificial fibre industries are also of some consequence. The state's agriculture (dairy farming, poultry rearing, fruit and vegetables) is geared only to meeting local needs. The fisheries are mainly concerned with mussel culture. Thanks to the state's 375 mi. long coast and its great expanses of forest the tourist and holiday trade makes a major contribution to the economy.

Block Island

This island 10 mi. offshore has been virtually abandoned to nature. There are ferries from Newport or from Galilee/Point Judith on the south coast. You can cycle, climb down the Mohegan Bluffs to the Atlantic or stop at the Old Harbor.

★★Newport

Newport, in Narragansett Bay, also made its name as a shipbuilding town, and it is still an important yachting port. Its main role, however,

In Newport harbour the New York Society lies at anchor

has been as an exclusive summer resort patronised by New York society which has preserved much evidence of its past.

The main tourist attractions of Newport are its sumptuous holiday residences of the 18th and 19th centuries, ranging from English-style country houses to neo-baroque palaces. The most splendid of them all is The Breakers, a 70-room mansion in the style of an Italian palazzo built for Cornelius Vanderbilt in 1895, still with its original decoration and furnishings. Others worth visiting are the Marble House, The Elms, Rosecliff Hunter House, Belcourt Castle. the Victorian-style Chateau-sur-Mer and the Samuel Whitehorne House with its exquisite 18th c. interior. John F. and Jacqueline Kennedy spent their honeymoon in Hammersmith Farm. From the 3 mi. long Cliff Walk, there are superb views of Rhode Island Bay and the houses of Newport.

Two features of unique interest in Newport are the oldest Synagogue in the United States (1763), with a number of treasures, including the oldest Torah in North America, and the Redwood Library and Athenaeum (1750), the earliest library in the United States that is still in use. For tennis fans there are the International Tennis Hall of Fame and the Tennis Museum.

★Providence

The state capital, Providence, situated at the northern tip of Narragansett Bay, was founded in 1636 and soon developed into a flourishing commercial port. It has a rich stock of restored buildings of the 17th–19th centuries, notably the John Brown House (1786), with a richly appointed interior, and the residence of Governor Stephen Hopkins (1707). Providence also has an unusual number of old churches, including the first Baptist church in America (1775). The shopping arcade, opened in 1828, was the first indoor arcade in America. The imposing domed State House (1901) was designed by the well-known firm of architects McKim, Mead and White. Below it are the Riverwalk and Waterplace Park, opened in 1997. The Rhode Island School of Design has a small but high-quality art collection. Pawtucket, to the north of Providence, was the cradle of American industry. In 1793 the fledgling United State's first "factory" opened here when Slater Mill set up its textile operation.

Richmond   M 48

State: Virginia
Altitude: 150 ft
Population: 203,000

Richmond, capital of Virginia, lies on the James River in the heart of the state. The townscape of Richmond – a banking centre, an industrial town (tobacco, papermaking, printing, chemicals) and the seat of two universities – is dominated by high-rise office blocks, but amid the skyscrapers there are still some reminders (the State Capitol and many old houses) of the town's great past as a centre of the American independence movement and one-time capital of the Confederation.

History When, during the revolutionary war, the patriots feared that the capital of Virginia, Williamsburg (Virginia), might be taken they made Richmond, which had been founded in 1737, the new capital. Here in 1775 Patrick Henry made the famous speech in which he called for separation from Britain with the slogan "Liberty or death!". From 1861 Richmond was capital of the Confederation until its capture in April 1865. At the end of the war the retreating Southern troops set their storehouses on fire, a fire that spread to the town.

Sights

★State Capitol

In Capitol Square is the imposing State Capitol, built in 1785–8 to the design of Thomas Jefferson, who took as his model the Roman temple known as the Maison Carrée in Nîmes. The Capitol was the scene of major events in American history, including the ratification of Virginia's secession and Robert E. Lee's appointment as commander of the Southern army. The statue of George Washington in the lobby was the work of Jean-Antoine Houdon (1741–1828).

Canal Walk

South of the State Capitol is the start of Canal Walk, which runs along the James River-Kanawha Canal, built at the suggestion of George Washington.

Court End District

In Clay Street in the Court End district two blocks north of Capitol Square, is the Valentine Museum (1015 E Clay St.), which is devoted to the social and industrial history of Richmond. The Museum of the Confederacy (1201 E Clay St.) traces the history of the Secession and the subsequent war. The White House of the Confederacy (12th and E Clay Sts.) was the seat of Jefferson Davis, President of the southern states (see Famous People).

Church Hill
Historic Area

To the east of the State Capitol, beyond I 95, is the Church Hill Historic Area, with some 70 antebellum houses that give some impression of what Richmond was like before the Civil War.

The district is named after St John's Episcopal Church (1741; 25th and Broad Sts.), in which Patrick Henry made his famous speech.

The Old Stone House (1737) at 1914 East Main Street, the oldest building in Richmond, now houses the Edgar Allan Poe Museum. Poe lived in the town for several years and worked on a local newspaper.

The principal treasure of the Victoria Museum of Fine Arts is a collection of Fabergé eggs. South of the Museum is Monument Avenue, which is lined with statues of Confederate heroes.

Philip Morris
Manufacturing
Center

To the south of the city centre (I 95, exit 69) is the Philip Morris Manufacturing Center, where visitors can see round the factory on a guided tour (no charge).

★★Rocky Mountain National Park   J 20

State: Colorado
Area: 414 sq. mi.
Established: 1915

The Rocky Mountain National Park, 2½ hour drive north-west of Denver (see entry), includes within its confines the Continental Divide (Watershed), formed by the main ridge of the Rocky Mountains, which on the east side fall abruptly down to the Great Plains in the Front Range. The highest point is Longs Peak (14,256 ft), in the south-east of the National Park. The deep U-shape valleys were scooped out by glaciers. The icefields and snowfields in the summit zone, the alpine meadows, the quiet lakes and rushing mountain streams and the varied flora and fauna (including wapiti) draw well over 2 million visitors every year.

Information The National Park is open throughout the year; Trail Ridge Road is open from the end of May to October. The park is particularly beautiful in spring (June), although most visitors come in July and August. The country is at its most colourful in early autumn (September). There are excellent winter sports facilities. Visitor Centers are located in the park headquarters in Estes Park, at the west entrance

The grandeur of the Rocky Mountains

by Grand Lake (Kawunchee), at Bear Lake Road (Moraine Park) and at Fall River Pass on Trail Ridge Road. There are hotels in Estes Park and Grand Lake. There are also plenty of camping sites.

A particularly rewarding trip is a drive along the 50 mi. Trail Ridge Road, which runs through the park from east to west, following an old Indian trail. The starting point is the Beaver Meadows entrance, above the little resort of Estes Park. From there the road runs by way of Deer Ridge to the Many Parks Curve and on to Forest Canyon Overlook, a viewpoint on a wooded gorge carved out by the Big Thompson River.

    From the Rock Cut, some miles further north-west, there is a magnificent view of the Mummy Range, which strikes in a north-easterly direction, with Ypsilon Mountain (13,514 ft). The High Point (12,182 ft) is, as its name indicates, the highest point on the road. At Fall River Pass is a Visitor Center that provides full information about the alpine zone of the Rocky Mountains. Here the Old Fall River Road comes in. Beyond the pass the Trail Ridge Road turns south-west to cross the Continental Divide at Milner Pass (10,758 ft) and then twists down into Phantom Valley, through which flows a source stream of the Colorado River. Further downstream is the Kawuneeche Valley, with the Never Summer Ranch (open-air museum). The road ends at the Grand Lake.

    ★Trail Ridge Road

The unsurfaced Old Fall River Road (one-way) runs up from Fall River Entrance Station in a north-westerly direction to the Visitor Center at Fall River Pass (see above), passing Horseshoe Park, the Sheep Lakes and the wild Chasm Falls.

Old Fall River Road

From the Beaver Meadow entrance the Bear Lake Road, a 10 mi. long branch road, runs past Moraine Park (Visitor Center) and Glacier Basin to Bear Lake, picturesquely situated among high peaks, from which a

★Bear Lake Road

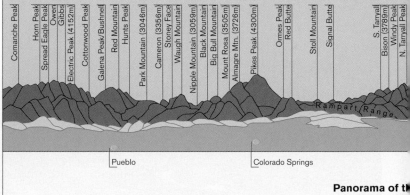

Comanche Peak · Horn Peak · Spread Eagle Peak · Owen · Gibbs · Electric Peak (4152m) · Cottonwood Peak · Galena Peak/Bushnell · Red Mountain · Hunts Peak · Park Mountain (3046m) · Cameron (3356m) · Stoney Face · Waugh Mountain · Nipple Mountain (3059m) · Black Mountain · Big Bull Mountain · Mount Rosa (3505m) · Almagre Mtn. (3726m) · Pikes Peak (4300m) · Ormes Peak · Red Butte · Stoll Mountain · Signal Butte · S. Tarryall · Bison (3789m) · Windy Peak · N. Tarryall Peak

Rampart Range

Pueblo

Colorado Springs

Panorama of the
(from the prai

variety of magnificent mountain hikes can be undertaken. There is a nature trail round the lake. Above Bear Lake is Dream Lake, sheltering between Flattop Mountain and Hallett Peak.

★Longs Peak/Chasm Lake

From SR 7, which runs along the south-eastern edge of the National Park, there is a strenuous mountain hike (a full-day climb) to picturesque Chasm Lake and from there up Longs Peak (14,256 ft the highest point in the National Park. This hike is really only for the experienced and even then they should seek advice at the Longs Peak Ranger Station before starting out.

Estes Park

On the north-eastern edge of the National Park, in the high valley of the Big Thompson River, is the mountain resort of Estes Park (alt. 7523 ft), named after a pioneer who settled here around 1860. Ten years later a British peer, the Earl of Dunraven, built a hunting lodge in this area, which was famed for its abundance of game and of fish, and soon afterwards the painter Albert Bierstadt came here and was enchanted by the beauty of the scenery. Estes Park is now busy with visitors all year round, offering them a wide range of activities – hiking, riding, fishing, mountain biking, rafting and even golf. There is a cableway up Prospect Mountain (8895 ft).

★Big Thompson River Canyon

The Big Thompson River below Estes Park is a famous trout river that attracts hundreds of anglers. Further downstream the river turns east towards the Great Plains in a narrow valley shaped by tectonic movement.

Arapaho National Recreation Area

To the south-west, outside the National Park, is the Arapaho National Recreation Area, in the centre of which are the "Great Lakes of Colorado" – Grand Lake, Shadow Mountain Lake, Willow Creek Reservoir, Monarch Lake and Lake Granby, all good fishing lakes.

St Augustine   U 44

State: Florida
Altitude: 0–10 ft
Population: 13,000

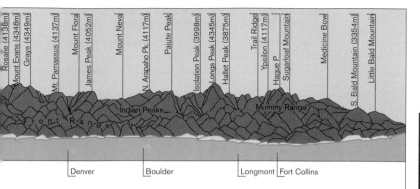

cky Mountains
ing west)

©Baedeker

St Augustine, the oldest town in North America founded by Europeans and continuously inhabited since then, lies on the Atlantic coast of north-eastern Florida. Its great tourist attraction is its Spanish heritage, which has been deliberately cultivated in recent years. The atmosphere of old Spanish is created by its narrow lanes and colonial-style houses with their characteristic patios, balconies and wrought-iron grilles.

History After Ponce de León's discovery of Florida in 1513 the Spaniards sought to populate the new territory. The first settlers, in 1565, were French Huguenots, who built Fort Caroline (see Jacksonville). In the same year the Spanish authorities established their base of San Agustín, on a site that was difficult of access, and this soon developed into the most important military post and mission station in Florida. During the 16th and 17th centuries the young settlement was frequently raided by pirates. When Britain began to promote its interests in the area in the 17th c. the Spaniards built the Castillo de San Marcos. In 1763 Florida, and with it St Augustine, passed to Britain. During the War of American Independence the town became a refuge for British loyalists until 1783, when Florida reverted to Spain. In 1821, when the United States acquired Florida, St Augustine was much impoverished. Then at the end of the 19th c., when Henry Flagler built his East Coast Railroad, St Augustine took on a new lease of life as a fashionable bathing resort.

Sights

The Old Town of St Augustine has been beautifully refurbished and is kept largely free of cars. The Casa Gonzáles-Alvarez is believed to be the oldest house in the town. The central Plaza de la Constitución is laid out in typically Spanish colonial style. The Wooden Schoolhouse (now a museum) is over 200 years old. In the fascinating Spanish Quarter Museum (San Agustin Antiguo) a number of old colonial houses form a "living history" museum; craftsmen in historical costume can be seen at work.

★★Old Town

On the north-east side of the Old Town is the Castillo de San Marcos, built in the last quarter of the 17th c. to protect the sea route from Cuba to Spain and provide defence against British attacks.

★Castillo de San Marcos

The "Golden Age" collection (Tiffany glass) of the publisher Otto C. Lightner is housed in a former grand hotel.

★Lightner Museum

435

Flagler College	The former luxury hotel, the Ponce de León (1888), built by the railway magnate Henry Flagler, is now occupied by an arts college.
Oldest Store Museum	This museum south of Flagler College contains a miscellany of everyday items from the 18th and 19th centuries.
Mission of Nombre de Dios	Situated north of the Old Town, the Mission of Nombre de Dios marks the place where the Spanish landed in 1565. It was probably here that the first Catholic mass on North American soil was celebrated. The little chapel of Our Lady of La Leche is the oldest shrine of the Virgin in the United States.
Foundation of Youth	Northwards again extends a park in which is commemorated Ponce de León and his fruitless search for the fountain of youth.

Surroundings

★Fort Matanzas National Monument	14 mi. south of St Augustine is the little Spanish fort of Matanzas (the name means "slaughter"), in an area that was the scene of bloody clashes in 1565 between the French Huguenot settlers and Spanish troops. The fort also played a key role in the conflicts between Spanish and British forces.
★Marineland of Florida	20 mi. south of St Augustine is Marineland of Florida, with spectacular performances by trained dolphins and sealions and numbers of sharks, barracudas and giant turtles. Open daily 9am–5pm.

St Louis   L 35

State: Missouri
Altitude: 515 ft
Population: 397,000

St Louis, the largest city in Missouri, lies just below the junction of the Missouri with the Mississippi, which here forms the boundary between the states of Missouri and Illinois. An industrial city (metalworking, foodstuffs, textiles, furniture), it is also the seat of the St Louis University (founded 1818), the oldest university west of the Mississippi. St Louis is still known as the "Gateway to the West", on account of its being from here that the Europeans set out to conquer the Wild West. Its connection with Scott Joplin, the "father" of ragtime, ensures its fame as a music city, third only to Memphis and Nashville, Tennessee (see entries).

History In 1764 a French fur trader named Pierre Laclede established a trading post here, named St Louis after the French King Louis IX (St Louis). In 1803 the town, which then had a population of only 1000, passed to the United States along with the rest of Louisiana under the Louisiana Purchase, and soon developed into an important staging post for settlers on their way to the west. In 1849 most of the town was destroyed in a great fire. During the Civil War St Louis was an important Union base.

Downtown

★Jefferson National Expansion Memorial	The tourist centre of St Louis is the Jefferson National Expansion Memorial Park, laid out on a site previously occupied by an old part of the town. It bears the name of President Thomas Jefferson (see Famous People), during whose Presidency the Louisiana Purchase opened up the west to settlement.

In the centre of the park is the **Gateway Arch**, symbol of the city's role as the "Gateway to the West". This parabolic arch of stainless steel, 625 ft high, was erected in 1959–65 to the design of Eero Saarinen, based on an unexecuted project by Adalberto Libera for the entrance to the Esposizione Universale di Roma of 1942. Eight elevators run up to the observation platform on the highest point of the arch. Under the arch are the Visitor Center and the Museum of Westward Expansion, and beyond it the boarding place for the Mississippi excursion boats. Moored in the river are a number of floating restaurants and casinos.

Along the river to the north, between the Martin Luther King Memorial Bridge and the arched steel Eads Bridge (1869–74), is Laclede's Landing, an old port district with a number of old buildings that have been renovated and are now occupied by shops, offices and restaurants.

Laclede's Landing

South-west of the Gateway Arch is the Old Cathedral, the Catholic Basilica of St Louis of France. Built in 1831–4 on the site of the first church of St Louis (1770) it survived the 1849 fire unscathed. In the basement is a museum on the history of the city.

Old Cathedral

Across the I 70, abreast the Gateway Arch, is the start of Market Street. The city's main street, it is lined by important buildings and, half way along, opens out into St Louis Memorial Plaza.

Market Street

St. Louis Downtown

Gateway Arch

On the right-hand side is a massive domed building, the **Old Courthouse** (1839–64), where an exhibition on local history can be seen.

On the left-hand side is the gigantic rotunda of the **Busch Stadium**, which has seating for 50,000 spectators. The stadium is home to the St Louis Cardinals, the city's baseball team, whose history is documented in the St Louis Cardinal's Hall of Fame. The neighbouring National Bowling Hall of Fame does the same for bowling. The city's second large sports arena, the Trans World Dome, home of the Rams football team, is situated further north.

Farther along Market Street, on the left, is **City Hall**, which was modelled on the Hôtel de Ville in Paris. There are some interesting buildings in the streets running north from Market Street. In 14th Street (corner of

Chestnut St.) is the Soldiers Memorial Building, commemorating all fallen American soldiers. At the corner of 14th Street and Market Street is the Kiel Auditorium, which is used for congresses, trade fairs, exhibitions, opera performances and concerts.

Market Street ends at the fortress-like Union Station, once the largest railway station in the United States and now a shopping centre. In Aloe Plaza, in front of the station, is a fountain by the Swedish sculptor Carl Milles (1875–1955), "Wedding of the Waters", with 14 bronze figures symbolising the union of the Mississippi and the Missouri.

Union Station

Scott Joplin, the "father" of ragtime, lived at 2658 Delmar Street, St Louis (north-west of Union St.) from 1901 to 1903. The house is chock-a-block with memorabilia.

Scott Joplin House

Other sights

On display at 1575 Woodson Road are more than 150 vintage cars and limousines.

St Louis Car Museum

2 mi. west (4431 Lindell Blvd. and Newstead Ave.) is St Louis Cathedral, an imposing Byzantine-style building (1907) with a gigantic mosaic in the dome.

St Louis Cathedral

¾ mi. west of St Louis Cathedral is Forest Park, an area of open space 2 mi. long by 1 mi. across. This was the site of the 1904 World's Fair (Louisiana Purchase Exhibition) marking the centenary of the Louisiana Purchase.

Forest Park

On the north side of the park, on Lindell Boulevard, is the **Jefferson Memorial** (1904), home of the Missouri Historical Society, with rich collections of material on the history of Missouri and St Louis and the Lindbergh Room, commemorating Charles Lindbergh's solo flight over the Atlantic in the "Spirit of St Louis".

At the south-west corner of the park is the ★**City Art Museum** (1904), which has a fine collection of works of art of many different cultures from prehistoric times to the present day, including Meissen porcelain, European and American sculpture and pictures and Chinese bronzes.

The **Science Center** in the south-east corner of the park offers a hands-on exploration of science and technology, particularly absorbing for children. They will also enjoy the zoo.

2 mi. south-east of Forest Park is the large Tower Grove Park. On its north side, along Tower Grove Avenue, is the beautiful Missouri Botanical Garden, also known as the Shaw Garden after the businessman and botanist Henry Shaw (1800–89) who laid it out in 1859. In the south-east part of the gardens are the richly appointed Tower Grove House, Henry Shaw's "garden house". The gardens themselves comprise a lovely rose garden, the rather unusual Climatron (erected 1960) for tropical plants, a Japanese Garden, an "aqua-tunnel" under a water-lily pool and a herbarium.

★Missouri Botanical Garden

Further out of town still, at 10501 Gravois Road, is Grant's Farm, which belonged to President Ulysses S. Grant. The farm makes a popular outing, especially on account of its large children's zoo.

Grant's Farm

In the south of the town (1127 Pestalozzi St.; bus 40 from Downtown) is the Anheuser-Busch Brewery, the world's largest (guided visits). Its "Budweiser" is sold all over the United States.

Anheuser-Busch Brewery

439

Surroundings

National Museum of Transport

South-west of St Louis, near the suburb of Kirkwood, is the interesting National Museum of Transport (3015 Barrett Station Rd.), which presents a wide-ranging survey of American transport from mule-drawn street-cars to modern air transport (steam, electric and diesel locomotives).

Six Flags over Mid-America

The Six Flags over Mid-America pleasure park (I 44 Exit 261) boasts nearly 100 amusement rides, most of them of the more exciting variety.

★St Petersburg   W 43

State: Florida
Altitude: sea level
Population: 240,000

The city of St Petersburg lies on the Pinellas peninsula on the central Gulf Coast of Florida, between Tampa Bay and Boca Ciega Bay. Off the peninsula is a chain of long, narrow islands. There are wide beaches and numerous marinas along this stretch of coast.

St Petersburg, famed for its perpetual sunshine, appeared in the Guinness Book of Records when the sun shone on every single day from 1967 to 1969. From 1910 to 1986 the local paper, the "Evening Independent", was given away free on any day on which the sun did not shine – in practice a mere 295 times. Sunsets are spectacular and sunset watching has become a sort of public "event" each evening (almost) on Pier 60.

History The town was founded in 1876 and named after the home town of a Russian businessman who was much involved in the enterprise. In the 1880s the Pinellas Sunshine Coast was already renowned for its healthy climate and attracted a steady increase in population, mainly older people.

Sights

★★Beaches

The obvious thing to do first on arrival in St Petersburg is head straight for the water – at Pass-Grille Beach perhaps, or the Municipal Beach on Treasure Island, Clearwater Beach, where there is also an aquarium, or Palm Pavilion.

St Petersburg has a wide beach of white sand extending along the Gulf Coast. Its most notable landmark is the luxury Don Cesar Hotel, built in 1928, which combines Moorish and Mediterranean features in its architecture.

★★Salvador Dalí Museum

The Salvador Dalí Museum (Poynter Park, Bayboro Harbor) has what is probably the largest collection anywhere of works by the Catalan Surrealist, who died in 1989 (collection built up by the Reynolds). Open Mon.–Sat. 9.30am–5.30pm, Sun. noon–5.30pm.

Great Explorations

Great Explorations (1120 4th St. S) is a hands-on museum that appeals particularly to children.

★The Pier

St Petersburg Pier is one of the longest of the kind, extending for over a quarter of a mile into Tampa Bay. At the end of the pier is an inverted pyramid containing shops, restaurants and an observation platform.

At the head of the pier is the **Historical Museum** (history of St Petersburg and surrounding area).

St Petersburg Pier

The Museum of Fine Arts (225 Beach Dr. NE), housed in a classical villa, possesses masterpieces of European and American painting of the 17th–20th centuries. Particularly notable is its collection of French Impressionists (Monet, Renoir, Cézanne). It also has interesting collections of Far Eastern and pre-Columbian art.

Museum of Fine Arts

North of the city centre are Florida's Sunken Gardens (botanical garden; parrot shows).

Florida's Sunken Gardens

This 1000 acre park, named after the Spanish conquistador Hernando de Soto, who landed here in 1539, extends over five islands in Tampa Bay. With its miles of sandy beaches, two piers for anglers, nature trails, cycle tracks, picnic areas and campgrounds it attracts large numbers of visitors throughout the year. At the south-western tip of Mullet Key is the historic Fort de Soto, built during the Spanish–American War of 1898.

★Fort de Soto Park

A must for all visitors is a drive along the Sunshine Skyway (I 275/US 19; toll), a masterpiece of engineering. This multi-lane "highway on stilts", 12 mi. long, curves gracefully across the entrance to Tampa Bay. Its central feature is a 4¼ mi. long high-level bridge, the middle section of which is suspended from two gigantic pylons, allowing the passage of large ocean-going vessels. The old bridge was rammed by a cargo ship in 1980 and partly collapsed; several vehicles were hurled into the sea, and more than 30 people lost their lives.

★★Sunshine Skyway

Surroundings

Pinellas Suncoast is the name given to a 28 mi. long stretch of coast on the Gulf of Mexico. Mile-long beaches of almost snow-white sand and

★Pinellas Suncoast

441

the warm, crystal-clear waters of the Gulf of Mexico with its gentle surf, combined with excellent tourist facilities, create ideal conditions for all kinds of water sports. The season here lasts all year round. A great variety of water sports can be practised here: sailing, windsurfing, deep-sea angling, diving, water-skiing The gently sloping beaches are ideal for families. Among favourite bathing resorts and port towns on the coast are Tarpon Springs, originally founded by Greek fishermen; Indian Rocks Beach; the Victorian-style Hamlin's Landing, with wooden quays and pleasant fish restaurants; Madeira Beach; John's Pass Village, a fishing and boating port in turn of the 19th c. style; and Treasure Island with its broad sandy beach, once a favourite pirate anchorage.

★Salt Lake City   J 14

State: Utah
Altitude: 4328 ft
Population: 160,000

Salt Lake City, the religious centre of the Mormons (Latter Day Saints) and capital of the state of Utah, lies in a high valley of the Jordan River, once an inhospitable tract of country between the rocky summits, rising to over 10,000 ft, of the Wasatch Range in the east, the Great Salt Lake

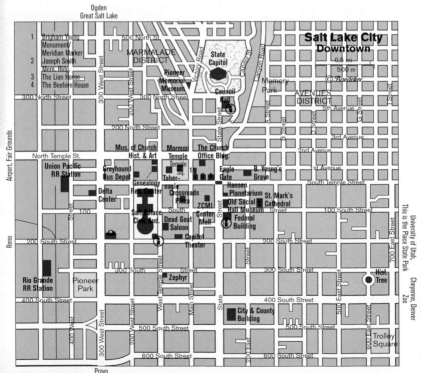

to the north-west and the Great Salt Lake Desert to the west. The Mormon leader Brigham Young certainly took his courage in his hands in proclaiming "This is the place!". But today Salt Lake City is a prosperous commercial and banking centre in the American West, attracting more and more high-tech firms. A thriving wintersports area, Salt Lake City is also to host the 2002 Winter Olympic Games.

History Salt Lake City was founded on July 24th 1847 by Mormons led by Brigham Young who had reached this desert valley after an 18-month trek from Illinois. The settlers soon began to irrigate the land and build up a town, which they called Great Salt Lake City after the large salt lake not far to the north. The area, then under Mexican sovereignty, was ceded to the United States under the treaty of Guadalupe Hidalgo in 1848. The Mormons took advantage of this change to establish a state of their own based on their religious ideas. The capital of this state of Deseret ("honey-bee") was Salt Lake City. The young city claimed a similar status for the territory of Utah (named after the Ute Indians), established in 1850, whose first Governor was Brigham Young. The gold rush in the west and the completion of the transcontinental railroad brought increasing numbers of people to the city, which now achieved a modest degree of prosperity. After the Mormons officially renounced polygamy Utah was admitted to the Union as the 45th state. During the 20th c. the city developed at a great pace, tripling its population between 1900 and 1930, and thereafter it grew rapidly into a large modern city.

★Temple Square

Temple Square is the holy place of the Mormons. On this large square (10 acres) with its trees and flowerbeds are the Temple, the Tabernacle, the Temple Annex, the Assembly Hall, several monuments and two Information Centers that supply information on the doctrines and the history of the Mormon faith. Guided tours start every 10 min. from the flag pole (summer daily 8am–10pm, winter 9am–9pm).

The Mormon Temple, in the so-called "Mormon style", was built between 1853 and 1893. At each end of this huge granite structure are three towers, the highest of which, at the east end, bears a 13 ft high gilded figure of the angel Moroni. The temple may be entered only by Mormons.

Mormon Temple

The Tabernacle is a massive oval building with a dome borne on 44 sandstone piers. The sober interior, with seating for over 6500 people, is noted for its fine acoustics. At the west end is the gallery for the celebrated Tabernacle Choir, and above it is the great 11,623-pipe organ (choir rehearsals Thu. 8pm; concerts Sun. 9.15am; organ recitals Mon.–Sat. noon, Sun. 2pm).

Tabernacle

The Seagull Monument in Temple Square commemorates the seagulls that saved the Mormons by destroying a plague of locusts that threatened their crops in 1848.

Seagull Monument

The Museum of Church History and Art (45 N West Temple St.) traces the history of the Mormon church and displays religious art of the 19th and 20th centuries.

Museum of Church History and Art

The high-rise block containing the offices of the Mormon church (50 E South Temple St.) is the city's tallest building (420 ft). From the observation platforms on the 26th floor there are magnificent views of the city, the valley of the Jordan River and the surrounding mountains.

LDS Church Office Building

At the intersection of South Temple Street and Main Street are a bronze

Brigham Young Monument

Non-Mormons are only allowed a look from the outside: the Mormon Temple in Salt Lake City centre

statue of Brigham Young and the Meridian Marker, which gives the exact geographical coordinates of the city. This was the point at which the original settlement was founded; the numbering of the streets starts from here.

Joseph Smith Memorial Building

Among the things to see in this Mormon community centre is a film about the Mormon's trek. The building also contains two restaurants.

★Beehive House

The Beehive House was Brigham Young's official residence as Governor of Utah and leader of the Mormons and the home of his large family of 19 wives and 56 children. On the turret of the house is a beehive, the symbol of the industriousness of the Mormons, which also appears in the state's coat of arms.

The **Lion House** (63 E South Temple St.) was built in 1855 to provide additional accommodation for Brigham Young's family. It is now occupied by a restaurant.

Eagle Gate

The Eagle Gate (State St. and E South Temple St.) was built in 1859 as the entrance to Brigham Young's farm. Originally 22 ft wide, it was several times enlarged to allow for increasing traffic and is now 75 ft wide. The gate is crowned by a massive eagle with a wingspan of over 20 ft.

Other sights

One of the main attractions of Salt Lake City is the Hansen Planetarium near Eagle Gate, with its popular presentations of astronomy (multi-vision and laser shows).

★Hansen Planetarium

In a small family cemetery on First Avenue, between State Street and A Street, are the graves of Brigham Young (d. 1877) and members of his family.

Brigham Young's Grave

The Governor's Mansion (603 E South Temple St.), built by Thomas Kearns, director of mining, in 1901, bears witness to the early prosperity brought by Utah's rich mineral resources. The house, with its period interior, is now the Governor's official residence.

Governor's Mansion

At the north end of State Street, on Capitol Hill, which rises to a height of 295 ft above the city, is the Utah State Capitol (1916), a neoclassical domed building 285 ft high that houses the House of Representatives, Senate and Supreme Court of Utah. It has a particularly fine interior, with its marble rotunda, the Golden Room (the Governor's reception room) and a small exhibition on the history and economy of Utah.

★State Capitol

The Pioneer Memorial Museum (300 N Main St.) traces the history of the settlement and the cultivation of the originally inhospitable valley to which the Mormons came in 1847, with numerous wagons, agricultural implements and other objects recalling the days of the pioneers.

Pioneer Memorial Museum

Marmalade District west of the Capitol got its name from the many trees whose fruit goes to making marmalade. Numerous houses survive here from the pioneering days.

Marmalade District

2 mi. east of the city centre is the University of Utah, which was founded in 1850. On the extensive campus are the Utah Museum of Fine Arts (with pictures by Rubens) and the Museum of Natural History, with a large collection of fossils (including dinosaur skeletons) and interesting departments of geology, palaeontology, biology and anthropology.

University of Utah

Immediately east of the campus, on Wasatch Drive, is the historic Fort Douglas (military museum).

Fort Douglas

When, after the Mormons' 1300 mi. trek, Brigham Young emerged from Emigration Canyon and saw the valley of his visions he exclaimed "This is the place!". The spot is now marked by an imposing monument (2601 E Sunnyside Ave.). Here too there is a reconstructed 19th c. pioneers' village, the Old Desert Village ("living history" presentations).

★This is the Place State Park

Surroundings

The Great Salt Lake, half an hour's drive north-west of Salt Lake City, is the largest inland lake west of the Mississippi, 72 mi. long, 34 mi. wide and up to 50 ft deep. It is a remnant of a much larger freshwater lake, Lake Bonneville. Following a fall in the water table this was left with no outlet and shrank as a result of evaporation, leaving the Great Salt Lake Desert. The combination of evaporation with the inflow of surface waters rich in minerals led the salt content of the lake to rise steadily, and at one stage it reached 27 per cent (eight times as high as the world's oceans). In the last few years the water level of the lake has risen

★Great Salt Lake

as a result of heavy rainfall in the surrounding mountains. At the south end of the lake are bathing beaches and a recreation park (boat hire).

★Timpanogos Cave National Monument

25 mi. south of Salt Lake City, on the northern slopes of Mount Timpanogos (11,750 ft), are three limestone caves linked by underground passages, with marvellous crystal and stalactitic formations.

★★Bingham Canyon Copper Mine

In Bingham Canyon, 25 mi. south-west of Salt Lake City near the township of Copperton, is the world's largest opencast copper mine, which is also the largest man-made hole in the earth's surface, almost 2½ mi. in diameter and over 2950 ft deep. From the Visitor Center (informative displays and video shows on copper mining) there is a good view into the terraced interior of the mine.

★Ski resorts

The Wasatch Mountains east of Salt Lake City offer fantastic downhill skiing on the famous "Champagne Powder", the exceptionally fine, light powdery snow for which the area is known. It is here that the alpine ski events are to be held in the 2002 Winter Olympics.

Alta

The drive on the SR 210 to Snowbird, and on to the winter sports resort of Alta with its top-class, reasonably priced pistes, takes barely half an hour. The SR 190 follows the deeply incised Big Cottonwood Canyon (well worth a visit in summer too), to the ski resort of Brighton.

Brighton

From Brighton a chair lift ascends Mount Millicent, the summit of which commands a breathtaking panorama of the mountains.

Park City

The I 80 connects Salt Lake City with Park City, 36 mi. to the east. This is where the alpine events will take place in the 2002 Winter Games.

San Antonio   U 27

State: Texas
Altitude: 700 ft
Population: 936,000

San Antonio lies on the San Antonio River and the narrow San Pedro Creek, on the south-eastern edge of the Texan tableland. It is the centre of a prosperous agricultural area (livestock farming), with important industries (engineering, aircraft servicing for the US Air Force, oil). San Antonio, originally a Spanish foundation, reflects more clearly than any other Texan city the influence of different cultures on the history of Texas. The western and southern districts in particular have a distinctly Mexican character, but there are traces of a once large German community. All come together in the annual San Antonio Fiesta in April, when celebrations take place in every corner of the city, the strains of Mexican conjunto music blending with the German polka and aroma of enchilada with that of roast potatoes.

History The Spanish military post of Presidio de Bexar and the Franciscan mission of San Antonio de Valero were established here in 1718, and soon afterwards San Antonio de Bexar became capital of the Spanish province of Texas. After the expulsion of the Spaniards (1821–36) the town was under Mexican sovereignty, until Texas broke away from Mexico in 1835. The famous battle of the Alamo was fought in the following year. In April 1836 Texas achieved its independence from Mexico, and until the incorporation of Texas in the United

States in 1845 San Antonio belonged to the independent republic of Texas.

Sights

On the east side of the city, on Alamo Plaza, is the most-famous building in the whole of Texas, the Alamo (from the Spanish word for "cotton-wood"), part of the mission station established in 1718. The Alamo church was built by Franciscans in 1744 and made into a fort in 1836. In that year, during the Texan war of independence, a small Texan force entrenched themselves in the Alamo against a Mexican army of 3000 men, and all the 187 defenders (among them Davy Crockett and James Bowie) were killed. Thereafter the Alamo became the "cradle of Texan independence", and "Remember the Alamo!" became the Texan battle-cry. The former mission is now a National Monument, visited annually by 2.5 million people. The mission buildings (restored) now house a museum of Texan history. In front of the Alamo is a cenotaph (by Pompeo Coppini) commemorating the fallen Texans. Open Mon.–Sat. 9am–6.30pm, Sun., pub. hols. 10am–6.30pm, Sep.–May to 5.30pm.

★★The Alamo

This is also the start of the Texas Star Trail taking in all the places of interest in the city. On the square too stands the **Menger Hotel** (1859), at the bar of which the Chisholm Trail cowboys used to wet their parched throats and Teddy Roosevelt recruited his "Rough Riders".

To the south of the Alamo is the Paseo del Rio or River Walk, which follows the windings of the San Antonio River, running below street level. The walk is lined by hotels, restaurants and shops, set amid lush subtropical vegetation; there are a number of departure points for cruises on the river.

★Paseo del Rio

The Alamo, the cradle of independence

447

San Antonio

La Villita
South of the Arneson Theater is La Villita, the Mexican quarter (mid-18th c.; restored), with many shops selling folk art, art galleries and restaurants in adobe houses.

HemisFair Park
South-east of the Alamo is HemisFair Park, scene of the World's Fair of 1968. It is dominated by the 750 ft high Tower of the Americas, with an observation platform and revolving restaurant. Beyond this are the Institute of Texan Cultures and the Mexican Cultural Institute (contemporary Mexican art).

Spanish Governor's Palace
To the west of the San Antonio River, reached by way of the Main Plaza and the archiepiscopal San Fernando Cathedral (originally built by settlers from the Canaries in 1738–58), is the Military Plaza/Plaza de Armas, with the low whitewashed palace of the Spanish governor, built in 1749 with materials imported from Spain. Open Mon.–Sat. 9am–5pm, Sun. 10am–5pm.

King William Historic District
To the south of these two plazas is the King William Historic District, built by prosperous German settlers in the 19th c. and named after King William of Prussia. The Steves Homestead (509 King William St.) a German house built in 1876, and Guenther House (205 Guenther St.), built in 1860, are open to the public.

Market Square
Further west, beyond San Pedro Creek, is the city's Mexican quarter, with the picturesque Market Square (El Mercado) on West Commerce Street.

Lone Star Brewery
South of the King Williams District on Lone Star Avenue is situated the Lone Star Brewery. Here, following a guided tour, visitors can enjoy a drink in a real saloon, the Buckhorn Bar, and inspect a whole menagerie of stuffed animals in the Star Buckhorn Museum.

Brackenridge Park
North of downtown San Antonio is the spacious Breckenridge Park, with a miniature railway and cableway for children, the Chinese Sunken Gardens and the Japanese Tea Garden. To the east, beyond Funston Place, are the beautiful Botanical Gardens.

McNay Art Museum
In northern San Antonio are two fine art museums. At 6000 North New Braunfels Street (to the north of US 81) is the McNay Art Museum, which specialises in modern art, including contemporary Indian art.

San Antonio Museum of Art
The San Antonio Museum of Art at 200 West Jones Avenue (2 mi. north-east of the city centre on US 81), housed in a finely restored brewery of 1883, displays North and South American art.

★Missions National Historical Park
South of the city centre, but still within the boundaries of San Antonio, are four other Spanish mission stations founded between 1718 and 1740. They now form part of the San Antonio Missions National Historical Park and can be visited by following the sign-posted Mission Trail. They are the Mission San Juan Capistrano (1731), the Mission San Concepción (1731–52), the best preserved Franciscan mission in Texas, the Mission San Francisco de la Espada (1731–40) and the "queen of missions", the Mission San José y San Miguel de Aguayo (1720–31), with a beautiful church doorway and carved sacristy window ("Rosa's Window"), Indian huts and corn stores.

Surroundings

Sea World of Texas
The large marine entertainment showplace, Sea World of Texas, lies 16 mi. north-west of San Antonio on Loop 1604 (10500 Sea World Dr.). It has over 25 shows, attractions and exhibitions, including the killer

whales, Cypress Gardens West Botanical Gardens, a large white-water run and, for children, Capt'n Kid's World.

17 mi. north-east of San Antonio on I 35 are the Natural Bridge Caverns, the largest stalactitic caves in Texas, with over 10,000 different stalactitic formations in chambers bearing such romantic names as Sherwood Forest. One of the finest features is the 40 ft high King's Throne in the Castle of the White Giants.

★Natural Bridge Caverns

30 mi. north-east of San Antonio on I 35 is New Braunfels, founded by German settlers in 1845. At the beginning of November each year it is the scene of the ten-day Wurstfest (Sausage Festival). Even more popular as a spectacle is the unusual sight of people floating down a 2½ mi. stretch of the Comal River squeezed into an inflated innertube. Further diversions of a similar kind will be found at the vast "Schlitterbahn" water park.

New Braunfels

In the hill country north-west of San Antonio there is still much evidence of German settlement, a prime example being the pretty down of Fredericksburg with its "Hauptstrasse". Fredericksburg's most famous son is Admiral Chester W. Nimitz, to whom a museum is dedicated. Luckenbach too was founded by Germans. Today it has 25 inhabitants, not much different from 1850.

★Fredericksburg

San Diego   R 8

State: California
Altitude: 45 ft
Population: 1.1 million

The southern boundary of San Diego, 124 mi. south of Los Angeles (see entry) in sunny California, lies along the frontier with Mexico. Thanks to the sheltered situation of its natural harbour with its rocky inlets and miles of sandy beaches the town developed into one of the leading ports on the west coast of the United States, and has been the headquarters of the US Pacific fleet since Pearl Harbor. The next most important elements in the city's economy after the Navy are the aircraft and hi-tech industries. The agreeable climate and scenic beauty of the surrounding area have made San Diego a favourite residential city, now the sixth largest conglomeration in the United States.

History In 1542 a Spanish expedition led by Juan Rodriguez Cabrillo landed in San Diego Bay and discovered the territory now known as California: this was "the place where California began". Sixty years later Sebastian Vizcaino named the bay after his flagship "San Diego de Alcalá". The foundation of the town, however, dates only from 1769, when the Franciscan friar Junípero Serra built the first of 21 mission stations. (The present mission of San Diego de Alcalá is 6 mi. inland from its original site.) In 1822 San Diego came under the control of the new Mexican government, but after the battle of San Pasqual in 1846 it passed into American hands. The admission of California to the Union in 1850 was followed by the establishment of San Diego County. The city's rise to prosperity began, however, after the coming of the Santa Fe Railroad (1885), the development of the port and the moving of the naval base from Hawaii to San Diego following the Japanese attack on Pearl Harbor in December 1941.

Downtown San Diego

Balboa Park (area 1400 acres), laid out in Spanish/Mexican style for the

★★Balboa Park

Mission Bay Park (Sea World), Old Town

San Diego
Downtown

----- Trolley   Marina Park, Coronado Bridge   Tijuana (Mexico)

1 Old Globe Theatre	7 Hall of Champions	14 Palisades Building
2 Museum of Arts	8 House of Hospitality	15 Conference Building
3 Botanical Building	9 Space Theatre	16 Federal Building
4 Natural History Museum	10 House of Pacific Relations	17 Municipal Gym
5 Timken Art Gallery	11 Organ Pavilion	18 Balboa Park Bowl
6 Museum of Man	12 Federal Building	19 Aerospace Historical Center
	13 Balboa Park Club	

Panama-California Exhibition of 1915–16, is now the cultural heart of the city, with a series of museums, theatres, restaurants and various leisure facilities.

Museums The Botanical Building, originally designed as a station on the Santa Fe Railroad, contains more than 500 species of tropical and sub-tropical plants. The House of Pacific Relations has displays on various Latin American countries. The Museum of Man contains material from the Indian pueblos of the south-western United States. The Museum of Photographic Arts in the arcades of the Casa de Balboa presents the work of modern photographers. The San Diego Aerospace Museum has a collection of over 70 original veteran aircraft and reconstructions. The collections of the San Diego Museum of Art include works by European masters from the early Renaissance to the 20th c. and a large depart-ment of American and Asian art; in the adjoining Sculpture Garden are works by Alexander Calder, Barbara Hepworth and Henry Moore. The Natural History Museum, founded more than 100 years ago, is devoted to the flora and fauna of southern California. The Timken Art Gallery has a large collection of Russian icons of the 16th–19th centuries and works by European and American artists. An imposing feature of the park, standing in the open, is the massive Spreckels Organ, with 4000 pipes, which was presented to the city in 1915 by Adolph Spreckels, a millionaire of German origin. In the Spanish Village Arts and Crafts Center visitors can watch various craftsmen at work.

More than a quarter of Balboa Park is occupied by the famous San Diego Zoo, in which the animals (elephants, bears, giraffes, big cats, reptiles, gorillas, flamingoes) live in their natural surroundings.

★★San Diego Zoo

In the historic Gaslamp Quarter between Broadway and K Street are 16 blocks of Victorian buildings dating from 1880–1910, with fashionable shops, restaurants and theatres and bars that are favourite haunts of night birds.

Gaslamp Quarter

Adjoining the Gaslamp Quarter, between 1st and 4th Avenues, is the modern shopping and entertainment centre of Horton Plaza, named after Alonzo Horton, who in 1867 bought for 265 dollars some 1000 acres of land in what was then a village and now amounts to practically the whole of downtown San Diego.

Horton Plaza

To the south-west, also on Harbor Drive, is Seaport Village, which attracts visitors with more than 75 speciality shops and restaurants.

Seaport Village

To the north-west, on Harbor Drive, is the San Diego Maritime Museum, with a fine three-master, the "Star of India" (1863), the ferryboat "Berkeley" (1898) and the motor yacht "Medea" (1904).

★San Diego Maritime Museum

Other sights

The Old Town San Diego State Historic Park, north of downtown San Diego on Presidio Hill, which rises above the San Diego River, takes visitors back to the early days of the city in Mexican and American times with its restored adobe houses and traditional craft workshops. The central feature of the Old Town is the colourful arcading round the Bazaar del Mundo, the lively scene of concerts and folk dancing.

Old Town

From downtown San Diego a bridge high above San Diego Bay leads to the beautiful garden city of Coronado, named after the Coronado Islands that lie off the coast of Baja California (Mexico).

★★Coronado

The most striking feature is the luxury **Hotel del Coronado** (1500 Orange Ave.), a four-storey wooden building in Spanish/Mexican style erected in 1888; the installation of the hotel's electricity is said to have been supervised by Thomas Alva Edison (see Famous People). Among illustrious guests have been crowned heads, show business personalities and American Presidents, including Bill Clinton, and the hotel has been the setting of a number of films, including the famous "Some Like It Hot", with Marilyn Monroe, Jack Lemmon and Tony Curtis.

At the south end of the Point Loma peninsula, to the west of Coronado, is the Cabrillo National Monument, commemorating the discovery of California by the Portuguese navigator Juan Rodríguez Cabrillo in September 1542. The monument, from which in clear weather there are fine views of the city, draws large numbers of people between mid December and mid February to watch grey whales on their long journey southward from the Bering Sea to the warm bays of Baja California. There are rewarding walks to the old lighthouse on the Bayside Trail and Sylvester Road, with a bizarre mixture of desert and coastal vegetation.
    Also on Point Loma are a naval exercise base and the Rosecrans National Cemetery, one of the largest naval cemeteries in the United States.

Point Loma
Cabrillo National
Monument

Hotel Del Coronado is a hotel legend: "Some like it hot" by Billy Wilder was filmed here

Ocean Beach
Further north, Ocean Beach draws California's surfers. Anglers can try their luck from the longest fishing pier in the United States and afterwards enjoy a meal in one of the many, reasonably priced fish restaurants.

★Mission Bay
Mission Bay (area 4500 acres), north-west of downtown San Diego, with its numerous inlets and 25 mi. of sandy beaches, is a water sports paradise, with joggers and roller skaters representing the fitness culture of California and elegant yacht clubs and luxury hotels for a more fashionable public.

★★Sea World
The highlight of the Mission Bay recreation complex is Sea World of California (1720 S Shore Rd.), with impressive shows by performing dolphins, sea lions, otters and whales.

★★La Jolla

The idyllic suburb of La Jolla (pronounced "La Haw-ya") extends along a 7 mi. stretch of coast north of downtown San Diego. Here visitors will find designer boutiques, inviting restaurants and good art galleries in and around Girard Avenue and Prospect Street. The University of California and various research institutes have made this almost village-like suburb a favourite residence of academics, artists and writers. The sandy beach of La Jolla Cove is frequented throughout the year by sun worshippers and also by seals and numbers of seabirds.

University of California
On the campus of the University of California (founded 1912) are a number of buildings of architectural interest. The Institute of

Oceanography (established 1903), which has a fine specialised library, is the oldest and largest oceanographic institute in the United States. Associated with it is the Scripps Aquarium, which is devoted to the underwater world of the Californian coast. Another major attraction on campus is the Museum of Contemporary Art.

Surroundings

The Mexican frontier town of Tijuana, 16 mi. south of San Diego, owed its rise mainly to the Prohibition period in the United States in the 1920s, when thirsty Californians could enjoy the pleasure of drinking alcohol legally only in Mexico. Nowadays it is the duty-free shopping facilities and the night life that stimulate the busy activity round the town's main square, the Parque Municipal Guerrero, the Avenida de la Revolución and the Bulevar Aqua Caliente. In the Centro Cultural is an exhibition on the history and culture of Mexico.

Tijuana

85 mi. north-east of San Diego, on the edge of the Colorado Desert, is the Anza-Borrego Desert State Park (area 600,000 acres), named after the 18th c. Spanish missionary Juan Bautista de Anza. The best time to visit the park is in the spring, when the cacti in the canyons of this fantastic desert region are in flower.

Anza-Borrego
Desert State Park

★★San Francisco   M 3

State: California
Altitude: 0–910 ft
Population: 744,000

The description of San Francisco in this guide is abridged, since there is a detailed account of the city in the Baedeker guide "San Francisco".

San Francisco, situated at the "Golden Gate" to the Pacific, is only the fourth largest city in California, but it is by a long way the most popular with both Americans and visitors from other countries. It is built on more than forty hills on a 7½ mi. wide peninsula between the open sea and San Francisco Bay. Augmenting its many attractions, of which the Golden Gate Bridge and the Cable Car are chief, is the special charm of a large city that won't admit to being one, insisting instead on seeing itself as a collection of neighbourhoods. And indeed each district has an identity all its own. Furthermore, nowhere apart from possibly New York can match San Francisco's engaging, multi-cultural atmosphere. This is the city that gave rise to the Beat Generation and Flower Power, and which today is the undisputed capital of the world's gay community. Just as distinctive is the fog that rolls in from the sea on summer afternoons, often completely enveloping the Golden Gate Bridge and caused by warm continental air interacting with cooler air generated by a cold Pacific current.

Society The gold rush of 1848 drew people to San Francisco from all over the world. They were followed by Chinese immigrants brought in to provide cheap labour. After World War II there was another large influx, mainly of African–Americans and Latinos. San Francisco now has a larger Asian population than any other American city, with sizeable groups of Chinese, Philippinos, Japanese, Koreans and Vietnamese. Put another way: more than 40 per cent of the city's inhabitants have a language other than English as their mother tongue. For this reason as much as any, San Francisco has become the very model of a multi-cultural society, adapting not just to incomers from other countries but also other lifestyles.

Originating in the 1950s, the Beatnik Movement was a revolt against the dollar-chasing consumer mentality. Many of its followers congregated in the North Beach area, meeting in bars and book shops and philosophising. Leading literary exponents of the movement were Allen Ginsberg, William Burroughs and Jack Kerouac. Later the Beatniks moved to Haight Ashbury, their numbers being swelled in the mid 1960s by the Civil Rights Movements and opponents of the Vietnam War. At this point the Hippies arrived on the scene: long hair, beards, drugs, communal living, free love, "Love not War". Some 6000 full-time hippies were joined at weekends in the "Summer of Love" of 1967 by a further 20,000 drawn by rock concerts and other such events. But the hippy environment also attracted criminals and drug dealers; violence became commonplace and the peaceable hippies moved away to set up communes in the country, enter the student scene at Berkeley or simply return to their homes.

Homosexuals of both genders have likewise made San Francisco their home. The rainbow flag of the gay community, which today represents about one sixth of the city's population, flies chiefly over the Castro quarter. The spread of AIDS having put an end to their once carefree existence, the emphasis is now on political demands for more resources to combat the disease and against discrimination against AIDS sufferers. It is estimated that every other homosexual male in San Francisco is HIV positive. A network of organisations are now concerning themselves with all aspects of the disease, from health education and preventive measures to research and the care of AIDS victims.

History San Francisco Bay was first discovered only in 1769 by a group of Spaniards led by Francisco de Ortega, and in 1776 a Spanish fort (presidio) was built at the Golden Gate as a centre of military administration and the mission of San Francisco de Asis, soon afterwards renamed the

Panorama of Downtown San Francisco

Mission Dolores, was established 4 mi. inland. Round the mission grew up the village of Yerba Buena, which at first was a place of no particular importance. It was only when the Mexican authorities developed the little harbour into a commercial port that it began to grow. From 1841 onwards the numbers of pioneers moving to the west increased steadily, and soon the population of the area was predominantly American. After the failure of American attempts to buy the territory from Mexico war broke out, and American settlers fought under the "bear banner" for an independent California (the Bear Banner Rebellion). On July 9th 1846 the American flag was hoisted, and a year later Yerba Buena was renamed San Francisco.

The 1848 gold rush brought a dramatic increase in population. At the beginning of 1848 the town's population was 2000: a year later it had risen to 35,000. By the 1860s San Francisco had established its position as the economic centre of the American West. In October 1865 an earthquake caused heavy damage in the town. In 1869 the Central Pacific Railroad reached San Francisco Bay, opening up a rapid transport link with the eastern United States. Economic problems led in July 1877 to serious rioting against the Chinese who had provided a cheap form of labour, mainly employed in railroad construction. On the early morning of April 18th 1906 the town was hit by a severe earthquake with an estimated strength of 8.3 points on the Richter scale. Even more devastating than the earthquake itself were the fires that broke out a few hours later and raged for three days. The bursting of the water mains made it impossible to combat the blazes effectively: much of the town was reduced to ashes, and 674 people were killed. Rebuilding proceeded rapidly, however, with financial aid from all over the United States.

A boost was given to the city's economy by the completion of the Golden Gate Bridge and the Oakland Bay Bridge in 1936–7, improving communications with the Bay Area. During the Second World War San Francisco was an important harbour for the US Pacific Fleet. The shipyards worked at high pressure, and within three years the number of jobs had tripled. In the spring of 1945 representatives of 52 states met in the War Memorial Opera House to discuss the final details on the foundation of the United Nations and finally signed the UN Charter.

On October 17th 1989 the city was visited by the worst earthquake (6.9 points on the Richter scale) since the catastrophe of 1906. The Loma Prieta Quake (named after its epicentre) caused most damage in the Marina district, and the partial collapse of the Bay Bridge between San Francisco and Oakland led to the loss of 59 lives.

Downtown San Francisco

The central feature of the south-western part of downtown San Francisco is the Civic Center Plaza, with City Hall (302 ft high dome) and the Civic Auditorium. To the north of City Hall are the State Building, with the Pioneers Museum, and the Federal Office Building. On the east side of the square is the Main Public Library. West of City Hall is the Veterans Memorial Building and, to the south of it, the **War Memorial Opera House**. Built in 1932, it was on the stage of the Opera House that the United Nations Charter was signed in 1945. Farther south is the Louise M. Davis **Symphony Hall**, one of the largest concert halls in the United States, opened in 1980. It is the home of the world-famous San Francisco Symphony Orchestra.

Civic Center Plaza

From the Civic Center Market Street (San Francisco's "main street") runs south-west in the direction of Twin Peaks and north-east towards Embarcadero Plaza and the Ferry Building on San Francisco Bay. Beyond the intersection with Powell Street (cable-car turntable) are two striking buildings: the 39-storey **Standard Oil Building** and the older Standard Oil of California Building.

Market Street

San Francisco

Union Square

The main square of San Francisco's downtown shopping area is palm-shaded Union Square, surrounded by the city's largest department stores and crowded throughout the day by tourists, office workers, street musicians and beggars. In the centre of the square is the Naval Monument, a 100 ft high column commemorating George Dewey, commander of the American fleet during the Spanish–American War of 1898, who won the Philippines for the United States. On the east side of the square is Maiden Lane, with a number of buildings designed by Frank Lloyd Wright, including the Circle Gallery (No. 140). Just round the corner are San Francisco's principal theatres.

Financial District

The very busy Montgomery Street runs through the Financial District, with the 52-storey marble-clad headquarters of the Bank of America (778 ft high; built 1969); on the top floor is an observation platform. Diagonally opposite is the 43-storey Wells Fargo Bank, with a History Room containing an excellent exhibition on the Californian gold rush and the hazards of transporting money in the mail-coach period.

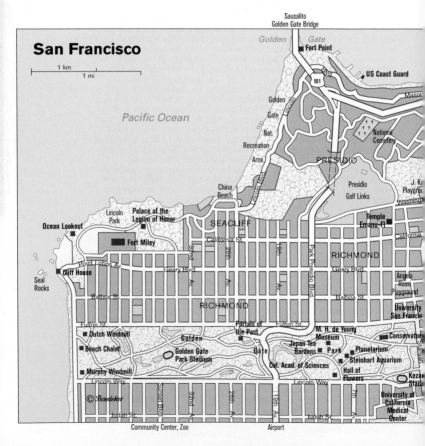

In the basement of the **Bank of California** (400 California St.), the oldest bank on the west coast, is the interesting Museum of Money of the American West, with nuggets of gold and silver and 19th c. gold coins and banknotes. Among other temples of Mammon are the Pacific Stock Exchange (Sansome & Pine Sts.) and the Stock Exchange Tower (155 Sansome St.).

The architectural highlight of the Financial District is the 850 ft high ★**Transamerica Pyramid**, built in 1972 to the design of William L. Pereira. Particularly striking is the (internally illuminated) top section of this steel-framed aluminium-clad structure. There is an observation platform on the 27th floor.

To the north of the Transamerica Pyramid is **Jackson Square** with its handsome turn of the 19th c. buildings (restored) housing a variety of shops.

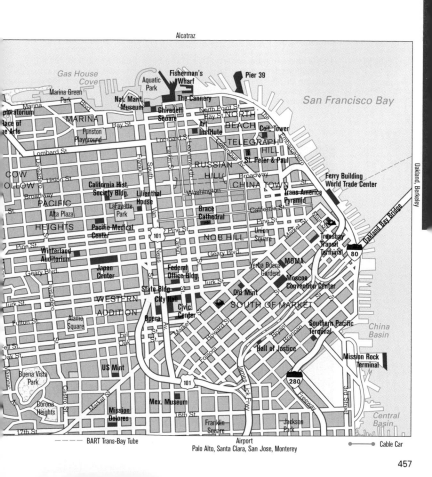

BART Trans-Bay Tube   Airport   Cable Car
Palo Alto, Santa Clara, San Jose, Monterey

South of Market

★San Francisco Museum of Modern Art

The San Francisco Museum of Modern Art (SFMOMA; 151 Third St.) has become an architectural showpiece in its own right. Designed by Swiss architect Mario Botta for this site south of Market Street, the building, dominated by a huge truncated cylinder, provides an appropriate setting for a collection of modern art of comparable merit by artists from the United States and Europe, a collection that sets the tone for many of the galleries in the surrounding streets.

Ansel Adams Center

On display at the Ansel Adams Center (250 4th St.) is a permanent collection of work by this master of photography.

Embarcadero

★Embarcadero Center

To the south-east of Jackson Square, beyond the Golden Gateway Center and Maritime Plaza, is the Embarcadero Center, with a number of imposing high-rise buildings, including the 42-storey Security Pacific Bank Building, the 31-storey Levi Strauss Building and the unconventional 17-storey Hyatt Regency Hotel with its 187 ft high atrium lobby. In Embarcadero Plaza is a striking fountain by Armand Vaillantcourt (1971).

Ferry Building

To the east of Embarcadero Plaza is the Ferry Building, built in 1903 as the headquarters of the ferry company that operated before the construction of the Oakland Bay Bridge. The 235 ft high tower is modelled on the tower of Seville Cathedral. The building now houses the Port Authority and an exhibition of minerals and rocks.

In Chinatown

Chinatown

To the west of Montgomery Street, bounded by Kearny Street, Bush Street, Stockton Street and on the north by Broadway, is San Francisco's Chinatown, after New York's the second largest Chinese urban community outside Asia, with a population of 120,000, making it the most densely populated part of the city. There are a multitude of shops and restaurants.

The main street of Chinatown is Grant Avenue, which is entered, when coming from the south, through the picturesque Chinatown Gate, decorated with dragons and other animals. Beyond this is St Mary's Square, with a monument to Sun Yat-sen (1866–1925), founder of the Chinese Republic, who had previously lived in San Francisco. On the north side of the square is Old St Mary's Church (1854).

Grant Avenue

Ross Alley is one of the oldest streets in the quarter. At the Golden Gate Cookie Company (No. 56). Chinese good-luck biscuit's can be seen being made, Stockton Street is also extremely attractive. In central Chinatown is Portsmouth Square, with a monument to the Scottish writer Robert Louis Stevenson (1850–94). On the north side of the square is the largest Buddhist temple in the United States (1960). From Portsmouth Square a footbridge leads to the Chinese Cultural Center (750 Kearny St.; in the Holiday Inn). At the north end of Chinatown is the Chinese Historical Society of America Museum (650 Commercial St.), which traces the history of a hundred years of Chinese immigration.

Ross Alley

A particularly interesting time to visit Chinatown is during the celebrations of the Chinese New Year.

★Chinese New Year

Nob Hill

To the west of Chinatown is Nob Hill (338 ft), where wealthy families whose money had come from railroad construction and gold mining – the "nobs" – lived at the turn of the 19th c. On Huntington Park is the famous 29-storey Fairmont Hotel, and opposite this is the 305 ft high Mark Hopkins Hotel, with a restaurant offering fine views. On the west side of the park is the large **Grace Cathedral** (1928), clearly influenced architecturally by Notre Dame in Paris, though its portals are copied from the Baptistry in Florence. Facing it, to the south, is the California Masonic Memorial Temple.

San Francisco's cable cars are one of the city's principal attractions. The system was devised by the English engineer Andrew S. Hallidie, who was concerned to relieve horses of the task of hauling streetcars up San Francisco's steep streets. The first section was opened in 1873. Nowadays only three lines still operate – No. 1, the California Street line, No. 2 the Powell Mason line and No. 3 the Powell Hyde line. To avoid long waits at the terminus points the cars can be boarded at any intermediate stop. From the gallery of the Cable Car Barn (Mason and Washington Sts.), built in 1887, the operation of the cable winches can be observed. There is a museum, whose exhibits include the first cable car, the cable-gripping and braking mechanisms and samples of cables.

★★Cable cars

Japantown

North-west of Cathedral Hill is Japantown (in Japanese Nihomachi), the cultural and economic centre of San Francisco's 14,000 Japanese citizens, with theatres, temples, shrines, restaurants and tearooms. The Peace Plaza, with beautifully laid out Japanese gardens and a five-tier

Nihomachi

Down Hyde Street with the Cable Car. In the distance: Alcatraz

Peace Pagoda, is entered through the Ronom, a gate designed by Yoshiro Taniguchi. In spring this is the scene of the Cherry Blossom Festival.

St Mary's
Cathedral

North-west of the Civic Centre is Cathedral Hill (340 ft), named after St Mary's Cathedral (RC), a very striking modern church with a 200 ft high dome, built in 1970 on the site of an earlier church destroyed by fire in 1962.

Russian Hill

North-west of Nob Hill is Russian Hill (295 ft), a pleasant residential district with well-kept gardens and outlook terraces.

Lombard Street

Winding its way up Russian Hill is Lombard Street, narrowing as it approaches the crest of the east side to a steep one-way street, its 40 per cent gradient negotiated by ten tight hairpin bends. Paved in red brick, the "crookedest street in the world" is beautifully laid out with beds of hydrangeas. Equally well-kept houses line both sides of the street.

Art Institute

To the north-east, at 800 Chestnut Street, is the San Francisco Art Institute, with an interesting collection of American and European painting and sculpture.

Cow Hollow

From Russian Hill Union Street runs west into the old district of Cow Hollow, where cows once grazed. There are numerous Victorian-style buildings, now occupied by elegant shops, art galleries and exclusive restaurants.

Telegraph Hill/North Beach

On the north side of downtown San Francisco, at the east end of Lombard Street, is Telegraph Hill (295 ft), on the slopes of which are artists' studios and handsome old houses. On top of the hill is the Coit Memorial Tower (210 ft high), built in 1934 in honour of the firefighting service. The interior walls are decorated with some notable murals by the Mexican artist Diego Rivera and others. Open Jun.–Sep. daily 10am–7pm; Oct.–May daily 9am–4pm.

Coit Memorial Tower

South-west of Telegraph Hill is the North Beach district, which in the 1960s became internationally known as the home of the hippies (flower children). The psychedelic movement originated here. Around Washington Square live over 50,000 Americans of Italian descent, whose shops and restaurants give this district its particular stamp. In the south-eastern part of this district, particularly round Broadway and Columbus Avenue, is the pulsating heart of San Francisco's entertainment quarter, with numerous bars, night clubs, jazz spots, cabarets, theatres and restaurants. The Tattoo Art Museum (841 Columbus Ave.) covers everything to do with tattooing.

★North Beach

North waterfront

To the north of Telegraph Hill the Embarcadero, a broad seafront avenue, runs along the northern exit from San Francisco Bay, lined by numerous piers. There's always something happening at Pier 39, with its myriad shops and places of entertainment, including an underwater gallery. Piers 39 and 41 are the departure points for ferries and excursion boats (the ferry to Alcatraz leaves from Pier 41).

Piers

The Embarcadero ends at Fisherman's Wharf, a Mediterranean-style harbour, which has been titivated and developed for the benefit of tourists,

★Fisherman's Wharf

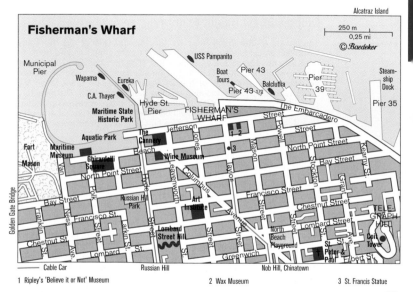

Fisherman's Wharf

1 Ripley's 'Believe it or Not' Museum 2 Wax Museum 3 St. Francis Statue

461

with a variety of colourful shops, restaurants, bars and fast food stands. Visitors may even encounter a few fishermen.

On the south-west side of Fisherman's Wharf is the **Cannery**, an old Del Monte fruit-canning plant that was restored in the 1960s and now houses galleries, boutiques, speciality shops, cafés, restaurants and various entertainment facilities.

On the west side of Fisherman's Wharf is the ★**Maritime State Historic Park**, with a number of restored vessels of earlier days, including the paddle steamer "Eureka" of 1890, the ferry "Alma" of 1891 and the three-masted schooner "Balchutha" launched in Glasgow in 1886. Nearby is the Maritime Museum, housed in a grandiose former casino, which charts the history of American shipping in the Pacific.

★Ghirardelli Square

To the south of the Maritime Museum is Ghirardelli Square. Here, housed in the restored brick buildings once occupied by Domenico Ghirardelli's chocolate factory, are a variety of shops, restaurants, art galleries and entertainments.

Alcatraz

The former prison island of Alcatraz in San Francisco Bay is now a tourist sight. From 1933 to 1963 it was perhaps the most notorious jail in the United States, one of its best known inmates being Al Capone. Six years after it was closed the island was occupied by Indians, who remained in possession for several years. There are ferries to the island from Pier 41 (summer daily 9.15am–4.15pm; autumn–spring daily 9.45am–2.45pm).

Other sights

To the west of Aquatic Park is Fort Mason, from which there is an attractive path leading to the Golden Gate Bridge. Farther west are Marina Park, the Yacht Harbor, Marina Green and the Palace of Fine Arts (1915), housing the ★**Exploratorium**, an innovative "hands-on" science museum. Other museums in the area are the African–American Museum, the Museo Italo Americano and the Mexican Museum.

Dolores Street/Height Ashbury

★Mission Dolores

South-west of the Civic Center is the Mission District. As the many "murales" in evidence proclaim, this is the Latino quarter, and here, on Dolores and 16th Streets, stands the Mission Dolores. This adobe mission station, built in 1776 and originally dedicated to San Francisco de Assisi, was the sixth of the 21 Spanish mission stations on the Californian coast. The adjoining basilica dates from 1918. The cemetery contains the graves of 5000 Indians who died in two measles epidemics in 1804 and 1826. The Mission will be familiar to Hitchcock fans, scenes from his film "Vertigo" starring Kim Novak and James Stewart having been shot here.

Haight Ashbury

Anyone with fond memories of the 1960s should be sure to visit the adjoining district of Haight Ashbury (to the west), in whose Victorian villas the Hippies set up their pads. A whiff of the heady "Summer of Love" still pervades many a book – or muesli shop. Buena Vista Park was the scene of amazing happenings and "be-ins"; and no one passes Janis Joplin's house (112 Lyon St.) without observing a minute's silence.

★Twin Peaks

To the south-west are the Twin Peaks (909 ft and 902 ft). In recent years this has become a favoured residential district. From the hills photographers can take the famous "fog views" of San Francisco – colourful little Victorian houses silhouetted against the skyline.

★★Golden Gate Park

This landscaped park (area 1000 acres), laid out from 1887 onwards to the design of the Scottish landscape gardener John McLaren, is still one of the largest and finest municipal parks in the United States, with over 5000 different species of plants. It contains enclosures with bison and various species of deer, a number of lakes and ponds and a variety of monuments.

On the east side of the park is the California Academy of Sciences, with the Natural History Museum, the Steinhart Aquarium and the Morrison Planetarium. Open daily 10am–5pm.

California Academy of Sciences

North-west of the Academy of Sciences is the M.H. de Young Memorial Museum, with a collection of pictures, sculpture, stained glass, including works by Rembrandt, El Greco, Rubens, Tiepolo and many other masters. Open daily 10am–5pm.

★M.H. de Young Memorial Museum

In the west wing of the De Young Museum is the Asian Art Museum, with the Avery Brundage Collection. This contains almost 10,000 works of art from Japan, Korea, China, India, Iran and other Asian cultures. To the south-west is the beautiful Japanese Tea Garden.

★Asian Art Museum

South of Golden Gate Park lies San Francisco Zoo, which was modelled on Hagenbeck Zoo in Hamburg.

★San Francisco Zoo

Presidio/Golden Gate/Seacliff

The Presidio (fort) has been so called since Spanish troops set up their first garrison here in 1776. This military area (1460 acres) extending

Golden Gate Bridge; in the foreground Fort Point

along the northern tip of the San Francisco peninsula to the Pacific is now the headquarters of the US 6th Army. The only building of the Spanish period still surviving in the park, most of which is open to the public (fine views), is the Officers' Club. There is a colours parade daily at 5pm. Within the area of the Presidio are an Army Museum and a large military cemetery. Among those buried in the cemetery is the actress Pauline Tyler, who during the Civil War spied for the Union states.

★★Golden Gate Bridge

The Golden Gate Bridge, one of the largest and handsomest suspension bridges in the world, spans the Golden Gate, the narrow strait between the San Francisco peninsula and the Marin peninsula. It was built in 1933–7 by the Cincinnati-born engineer Joseph B. Strauss (1870–1938) and was then the world's longest suspension bridge (total length 3060 yds). Every week some 2 tons of red lead paint are applied to the bridge to protect it from rust. Tolls are payable only when travelling from north to south (cyclists and pedestrians free; sufferers from vertigo are advised against crossing on foot). Vista Point, in the Golden Gate National Recreation Area at the north end of the bridge, commands magnificent views of both bridge and city.

Fort Point

Fort Point at the south end of the bridge was built in 1853 to guard the strait against a feared British invasion. It is now a military museum.

★Palace of the Legion of Honor

From the Golden Gate Bridge Lincoln Boulevard (wide views) runs south to Lincoln Park, with the little promontory of Land's End. Near the golf course at the east end of the park is the neoclassical Palace of the Legion of Honor, which contains a very fine collection of 18th and 19th c. European art, including works by Degas, Manet, Monet and Renoir.

Cliff House

Below Lincoln Park, to the west, is Cliff House (1858; museum, restaurant), from which there is a fine view of the Seal Rocks. There is bathing near by at Ocean Beach and China Beach.

Surroundings

Oakland

In 1936 the two-level San Francisco to Oakland bridge was completed across San Francisco Bay. At the east end of this 8½ mi. long bridge is the industrial city of Oakland, founded in 1850. The population includes a high proportion of coloured, and the militant Black Panther movement originated here in 1966. In the city centre is Lake Merritt, a small salt-water lake with facilities for recreation. At the south-west end of the lake is the Oakland Museum (natural history, history, art and culture of California).

★Berkeley

North of the bridge is the town of Berkeley, founded in 1841. It is a favoured residential town with major teaching and research institutions, in particular the University of California on the east side of town. The university was in the van of the student movement in the United States and in 1967/68 Berkeley was the scene of bloody confrontations between student protesters and the National Guard.

Of particular interest are the Robert H. Lowie Museum of Anthropology, the University Art Museum, established on the initiative of the German painter Hans Hofmann, the Pacific Film Archive and the Lawrence Berkeley Laboratory, in which the famous atomic physicist Julius Robert Oppenheimer (1904–67) worked. From the Sather Tower or Campanile there are fine views of San Francisco Bay and the Golden Gate Bridge.

Mount Diablo

20 mi. east of Berkeley, beyond Walnut Creek, is Mount Diablo (3849 ft), a hill in the Coast Range. From its summit there are wide views, extending in clear weather for almost 200 mi. There are attractive hiking trails in Mount Diablo State Park.

Once a fishing village on Richardson Bay (the northern part of San Francisco Bay), Sausalito is now a popular resort for the citizens of San Francisco. It is a town of picturesque winding lanes, often linked by flights of wooden steps. In the harbour are numerous brightly painted houseboats, some of them of rather eccentric design. The town is now the home of many artists and prosperous citizens who commute to San Francisco. The ferry from San Francisco to Sausalito affords magnificent backward views of the city.

★Santa Fe   O 19

State: New Mexico
Altitude: 6990 ft
Population: 60,000

Santa Fe, capital of the state of New Mexico and second oldest city in the United States – the oldest being St Augustine (see entry) in Florida – lies on the Santa Fe River, a tributary of the Rio Grande, on the south-western slopes of the very beautiful Sangre de Cristo Mountains. No other town in the south-western United States is as steeped in Indian and Spanish culture as Santa Fe. With eight large museums and a host of art galleries, as well as jewellery and craft shops, the city is also one of the country's leading art and cultural centres. Above all, however, Santa Fe has the richest and best preserved heritage from the Spanish colonial period to be found anywhere in North America, with its adobe buildings

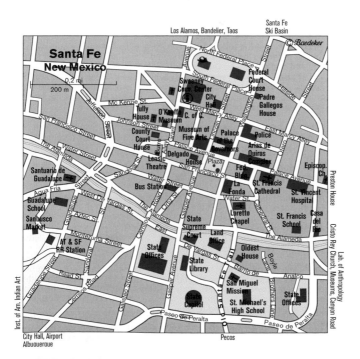

and lovely churches in the superbly restored city centre, and its festivals – the Spanish Market at the end of July, the Indian Market on the third weekend in August, and the Fiesta de Santa Fe on the first Monday in September.

All this, together with the dry mountain climate and magnificent surrounding countryside with its fascinating Indian pueblos, makes Santa Fe a must for anyone visiting the south-west States. It is even possible to ski; winter sports facilities having been introduced on some slopes of the Sangre de Cristo Mountains where snow is guaranteed. So Santa Fe really is one of the best-endowed cities in the United States, a fact well appreciated by those who live there, to whom it is "The City Different".

History In 1542 the first Spaniards to come here found a populous Indian village. In 1609 they founded a town that became the religious and administrative centre of the province of New Mexico. In 1680 the Spaniards were driven out by the Indians, but returned twelve years later. After Mexico broke away from Spain in 1821 Santa Fe remained capital of New Mexico and built up a lively trade with the Americans. The principal transport route was the Santa Fe Trail, which ran through the valley of the Rio Grande to reach the Missouri at Kansas City. Another important route was the Old Spanish Trail, which led to Los Angeles in California. In 1846, during the Spanish–Mexican War, Santa Fe fell to the United States without any serious fighting and later became capital of the US territory of New Mexico. In 1862 the town fell briefly into the hands of the Confederates. The economy of the town and surrounding area was given a boost by the opening of the Santa Fe Railroad in 1880. Then, at the start of the 20th c. it was discovered by artists and writers.

Sights

Plaza

The busy hub of the town's life is the Plaza, a market square built by the Spaniards where the Santa Fe Trail ended. Here Indian traders offer local arts and crafts for sale. On the north side of the square is the fortress-like ★**Palace of the Governors** (1614), which was successively the seat of Spanish, Mexican and American governors and is believed to be the oldest public building in the United States. Here in 1880 Governor Lewis Wallace wrote part of his much-filmed novel "Ben Hur".

Exhibitions in the **Museum of New Mexico** trace the history of Santa Fe from prehistoric times to the present day, with particular emphasis on the Indian heritage.

In an adobe building to the west of the palace is the **Museum of Fine Arts** (sculpture, pottery, woven fabrics).

At the south-east corner of the Plaza is the long-established adobe **La Fonda Hotel**, which marked the end of the Santa Fe Trail.

Georgia O'Keeffe Museum

A little to the west of the Plaza in Johnson Street is a museum with works by the painter Georgia O'Keeffe (1887–1986), who spent a large part of her life near Santa Fe. The museum was opened in 1997.

Palace Avenue

On Palace Avenue, which runs south-east from the Plaza, are a number of imposing buildings, for example the Prince Plaza (1840), once the centre of the town's social life, and the roomy Sena Plaza, once the property of a major who had fought in the Civil War, which is now occupied by attractive boutiques and galleries.

The neo-Romanesque **Cathedral of St Francis** (San Francisco de Asís) was built between 1869 and 1884 on a site occupied by several earlier churches. In a chapel on the north side is La Conquistadora (1625), a figure of the Virgin brought from Spain.

From the Plaza the Old Santa Fe Trail runs south. Immediately beyond the La Fonda Hotel is the Gothic-style Loretto Chapel (1873). The Miraculous Staircase, a spiral staircase leading to the gallery, is said by legend to have been made by St Joseph himself.

Loretto Chapel

Beyond the Rio de Santa Fe is the Barrio de Analco, an old quarter dating from the early 17th c. in which a number of buildings have been lovingly restored. Here too is what is claimed to be the oldest building in the United States, an adobe structure that may have been built around 1200, now housing a restaurant and a number of souvenir shops.

★Barrio de Analco

Immediately south is one of the oldest religious buildings in the United States, the chapel of San Miguel (1636), which contains a number of fine statues and a high altar of 1798 with the likeness of St Gertrude (1256–1302; mystic and abbess of a Benedictine convent in Germany).

★San Miguel

South-west of the chapel is the State Capitol (guided visits), a striking circular building (1966) modelled on an Indian kiva (cult building).

State Capitol

In Guadalupe Street in the west of the town centre stands the church of Nuestra Señora de Guadalupe, the patron saint of Mexico.

Nuestra Señora de Guadalupe

Along picturesque Canyon Road, an old trade route leading to Pecos, and the equally picturesque Camino del Monte Sol that cuts across it are numerous artists' studios and craftsmen's workshops, some of which can be visited. Some 200,000 adobe bricks were used in the building of the Cristo Rey Church at the end of Canyon Road.

★Canyon Road/Camino del Monte Sol

Those with an interest in Indian culture should be sure to visit the three museums brought together to form Museum Plaza in the south-east of the town.

★Museum Plaza

The **Museum of Indian Arts and Culture** (710 Camino Lejo) is devoted to the peoples of New Mexico. It has numerous exhibits relating to the Navajo, Apache, Hopi and Pueblo Indians.

Focussing on both parts of the American continent, the **Museum of International Folk Art** is one of the largest ethnographic museums in the United States, with a corresponding breadth and variety of exhibits, among them a most unusual and rare collection of toys from all over the world (706 Camino Lejo).

Originally devoted to Navajo life and culture – which is why it was built in the shape of a Navajo hogan – the **Museum of the American Indian** is now dedicated to the cultures of all the Indians of North America (704 Camino Lejo).

★★Pueblos

Round Santa Fe are a number of settlements of Pueblo Indians, mostly descendants of the Indians who left the Frijoles Canyon in the 16th c. In these villages old traditions are still maintained, including ritual dances and artistic craft work. They tend to treat strangers with some reserve, and visitors should not photograph or film them except with express permission. Regard should always be had to the particular mentality and sensitivities of the Indians.

The distances and directions of the pueblos listed below are reckoned from Santa Fe.

Santa Fe

Southern pueblos

Cochiti Pueblo (30 mi. SW) is noted for the manufacture of jewellery and pottery. The inhabitants of Santo Domingo Pueblo (32 mi. SW) hold fast to their traditions (particularly ritual dances) but also sell pottery, textiles and silver jewellery. San Felipe Pueblo (34 mi. SW) is one of the oldest settlements in a wide surrounding area; it too has skilled craft workers. Sandia Pueblo (50 mi. SW) shows the influence of the nearby city of Albuquerque (see entry).

Northern pueblos

San Ildefonso Pueblo (22 mi. NW), near Los Alamos, is one of the best known Indian villages, with a lively street market and a very interesting l(no admission). In Santa Clara Pueblo (27 mi. NW) interesting dances are performed around Christmas. The very picturesque San Juan Pueblo (28 mi. NW) is noted for its skilled potters and woodcarvers. The old Picuris (San Lorenzo) Pueblo (55 mi. NE) was built in the 13th c.

Taos

The little town of Taos (pop. 3000), situated in the mountains 70 mi. north-east of Santa Fe, was founded in 1615. It has enjoyed a reputation as an artists' colony since the 1880s, but has now unfortunately become a popular tourist centre.

Downtown

The central feature of the town is the picturesque Plaza, in which the American flag always flies, a privilege accorded to only a few American towns and owed in Taos's case to the legendary pioneer Kit Carson (1809–68) who, following the Confederate withdrawal during the Civil War, rehoisted the Stars and Stripes and stood guard over it. In Ledoux Street, to the south-west, are the adobe house of the artist Ernest Blumenschein, who came here in the 19th c., and the Harwood Museum

Pueblo in the Santa Fe area

(works by members of the local artists' colony, Indian arts and crafts, the sacred figures called santos). To the east of the Plaza is Kit Carson's house, now a museum. North-east of the Plaza is the gallery of the Taos Art Association, displaying works by members of the artist's colony. The Van Vechten-Linberry Art Museum and the Fechin Institute are dedicated to two prominent members of the Taos Artist Society.

3 mi. north-east of Taos is Taos Pueblo, which has been continuously and exclusively occupied by Indians since the 12th c. and has preserved its character as a pueblo in the purest form. Round the central plaza, through which flows a stream, are fortress-like houses in the oldest adobe style, but built only of clay and straw, without fired bricks. Particularly notable are the multi-storey community houses, the *kivas* (cult sites) and the egg-shape ovens. The Pueblo Indians who live here are still strongly attached to their traditions. Tourists are tolerated only during the day and intending visitors should enquire at the Taos Visitor Center before proceeding.

★★Taos Pueblo

To the north of Taos the Rio Grande has gouged out a grandiose gorge 650 ft deep, now spanned by a boldly engineered road bridge.

Rio Grande Gorge Bridge

North-east of Taos, in the Sangre de Cristo Mountains (8900–12,500 ft), is the magically beautiful and excellently equipped winter sports region of the Taos Ski Valley.

★ Ski Valley

20 mi. north of Taos on a poor road is the D.H. Lawrence Ranch, the last resting place of the writer D.H. Lawrence (1885–1930), who lived here in 1922–3. Lawrence died in Vence, in southern France, but his wife Frieda von Richthofen brought his ashes back to Taos and had them mixed with sand, cement and water to make an altar that was then set up on a specially built chapel.

D.H. Lawrence Ranch

Surroundings

For an insight into life on a Spanish colonial hacienda in the 18th and 19th centuries, pay a visit to the Las Golondrinas open-air museum, situated 15 mi. south of the city centre (334 Los Pinos).

El Rancho de las Golondrinas

15 mi. east of Santa Fe on the I 15 is the Pecos National Monument, the remains of a pueblo dating from the 14th c. and of which a description was given by the Spaniard Vásquez de Coronado. There is also a 17th c. mission station here.

Pecos National Monument

34 mi. north-west of Santa Fe is Los Alamos (alt. 7300 ft; pop. 12,000) – "Atomic City" – an atomic research centre established during the Second World War. Here was constructed the first atomic bomb, which was detonated on July 16th 1945 in what is now the White Sands National Park (see entry). In the Bradbury Science Hall in Los Alamos Scientific Laboratory is an exhibition on the development of nuclear weapons.

Los Alamos

45 mi. west north west of Santa Fe, in the volcanic Jemez Mountains, is the wild and romantic Frijoles Canyon, whose principal feature of interest is the Bandelier National Monument. This area, once occupied by Pueblo Indians, was explored by the Swiss–American anthropologist A.F. Bandelier (1840–1914). Between the 13th and 16th centuries the Indians had hewn cave dwellings and cult sites (kivas) out of the easily workable tufa and built multi-storey dwellings, known as talus, against the rock faces. A short distance to the north-west are remains of the pueblo of Tynony, with some 400 rooms and three kivas. In the surrounding area, in country that is difficult of access, are remains of other Indian dwellings and cult sites.

★Frijoles Canyon

In Capulin Canyon is the remarkable **Painted Cave**, with a whole series of Indian wall paintings of different periods.

Savannah   R 44

State: Georgia
Altitude: 43 ft
Population: 137,500

Savannah lies on the Atlantic coast at the mouth of the Savannah River, directly on the border with South Carolina. Once the world's most important cotton port, it suffered a period of decline but is now once again a considerable port (mainly container ships and tankers), with oil refineries. Savannah was founded in 1733 by General James E. Oglethorpe in his newly created colony of Georgia – the first town in North America to be laid out on a regular plan. It developed into the leading port for the shipment of cotton and was thus a place of strategic importance in the Civil War. It was badly damaged during the war, but when it was taken by General Sherman's Union troops in December 1864 it was not set on fire but was preserved intact as a Christmas gift to President Lincoln. It has thus one of the largest historic districts in the United States, which with its green streets and shady squares carries visitors back to the great days of the south.

Sights

Bull Street

The best way of getting to know Savannah's historic district is to take a stroll along Bull Street and the side streets opening off it. The starting point is City Hall (1905), opposite which is the US Customs House, built in 1852 on the site of the colony's first public building. To the south of this is Johnson Square, the first square laid out in the new planned town, with Christ Episcopal Church (1838), on the site of the colony's first church of 1733.

From Wright Square, the next square on Bull Street, it is a short distance west to the **Telfair Mansion and Art Museum** (a very handsome Regency house of 1818) and Art Museum (American and European art of the 18th and 19th centuries). Then south, passing the birthplace (1820) of Juliet Gordon Low, who founded the Girl Scouts of the United States, to Oglethorpe Avenue, the southern boundary of the old town. From here it is possible to continue southwards to Chippewa Square, on which stands Forrest Gump's bench, and then Madison Square with the Green-Meldrim Home (1852). A shorter way back is along Oglethorpe Avenue, turning east into Abercorn Street, which runs north towards the river, passing the Owens-Thomas House (1816–19) and continuing to Reynolds Square, with the Pink House of 1790.

Factors Walk

Factors Walk runs from east to west above the river, with iron steps and bridges linking the old cotton warehouses on the river banks with the streets on a higher level. The most important building is the ★**Cotton Exchange** (1886), the centre of the cotton trade.

Riverfront

One of the flights of iron steps leads down from Factors Walk to Riverfront, a row of 19th c. warehouses now occupied by shops, bars and restaurants. From here there are views, particularly fine in the evening, of the port and the large suspension bridge.

Museums Savannah has a number of interesting museums: the Ships of the Sea Museum (ship models) at 503 East River Street; adjoining the

Cotton Exchange and Factors Walk, Savannah

Visitor Center at 303 Martin Luther King Jr Boulevard, the Savannah History Museum, housed in a large 19th c. engine shed; and the Black History Museum at 514 Huntingdon Street, which organises guided tours of "black Savannah", taking in, for example, the First African Baptist Church (1788), the oldest black church in North America.

Surroundings

Anyone wanting to bathe can do so at the Tybee Island beach, just half hour's drive east of Savannah.   **Tybee Island**

Just off the coast to the south of Savannah are a number of islands, including Sea Island, St Simons Island and Jekyll Island, all linked with the mainland by road, which are now popular holiday resorts.   **Golden Isles**

Forts 15 mi. east of Savannah is Fort Pulaski, which was held by the Confederates from 1861 to 1862, when it was taken by Union forces; it has been restored to its condition at that time. 24 mi. south of Savannah is Fort McAllister, which was built to defend Savannah; its fall in December 1864 marked the end of Sherman's march to the Atlantic.

★Seattle   B 3

State: Washington
Altitude: 0–125 ft
Population: 503,000

Seattle, an important Pacific port and industrial centre and the largest city in Washington State, lies on a narrow strip of land between Puget Sound and Lake Washington, some 140 mi. from the open Pacific, with which it is linked by the Strait of Juan de Fuca. The port on Elliot Bay is the principal supply base for Alaska, plays an important part in American trade with Asia and is the most important fishing port in the United States. As for industry, simply naming the city's two largest companies – Boeing and Microsoft – is enough to indicate the significance of its role.

From being a rather dull port and industrial centre, Seattle has undergone an astonishing transformation. Driven only in part by its flourishing economy – for which Microsoft in particular provides the natural base – it is today an energetic, forward–looking city at the forefront of innovation technologically, culturally and in terms of its easy going lifestyle. It is no accident that Seattle is the "Coffee Capital" of the United States, with an espresso bar on almost every corner – quite something for a country brought up with a rather different idea of coffee. Then in addition there is the city's magnificent mountain setting: to the east is the ice pyramid of Mount Rainier (see Mount Rainier National Park), rising out of the Cascade Mountains, to the west the partly snow-capped peaks of the Olympic National Park (see entry), towering backcloths to a series of ocean inlets and lakes.

History The first white settlers in this area were given a friendly welcome in November 1851 by the famous Chief Seattle, and soon after being incorporated as a town Seattle had a population of over 1000. In the early days logging and fishing formed the basis of the town's economy. In 1889 the town was destroyed in a great fire but was quick to recover. In 1893 the transcontinental railroad reached Seattle. In 1896 the first ocean-going vessel from Japan put in at the port, and in that year also the gold rush in Alaska brought a great flood of immigrants to the town. By the turn of the 19th c. the population had risen to 80,000.

The opening of the Panama Canal in 1914 and the two world wars gave further boosts to the town's economy, and shipbuilding and aircraft construction developed on a tremendous scale. In 1962 a very successful World Fair was held in Seattle. Since the 1990s Seattle has increasingly led the way in expanding American trade with the Asian countries of the Pacific Rim.

Sights

Central Business District

To the north of Pioneer Square is the Central Business District, with City Hall and a number of eye-catching skyscrapers. Among them are the 42-storey Bank of California, the 50-storey First National Bank, the 40-storey circular Washington Plaza Hotel, the two postmodern structures Pacific First Center and Westlake Center, and the Rainier Square Shopping Center. On University Street is the ★**Seattle Art Museum**, with a collection covering the art of many countries round the world. The Palace of Culture, in postmodern style, was designed by Robert Venturi.

Waterfront Park

To the west, on Elliot Bay, is Waterfront Park, from which there are wide views of the habour and bay. An old-fashioned streetcar shuttles back and forth along the waterfront between Piers 48 and 70. Harbour tours depart from Pier 57. On "Gold Rush Strip" are a number of old buildings, now occupied by souvenir shops (fine craft products of the Northwest Indians) and attractive restaurants.

★Seattle Aquarium

On Pier 59 is the Seattle Aquarium, in whose Underwater Dome a variety of Pacific marine creatures (including sea otters, octopuses and dwarf sharks) can be observed. Open daily 10am–5pm, summer to 7pm.

Close by is the **Omnidome**, a circular cinema in which visitors can

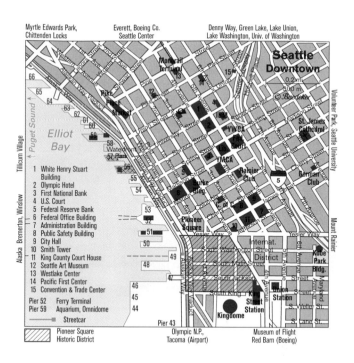

Myrtle Edwards Park, Chittenden Locks

Everett, Boeing Co. Seattle Center

Denny Way, Green Lake, Lake Union, Lake Washington, Univ. of Washington

Seattle Downtown

0.2 mi

300 m

© Baedeker

Puget Sound

Elliot Bay

Tillicum Village

Alaska, Bremerton, Winslow

Volunteer Park, Seattle University

Mount Rainier

1 White Henry Stuart Building
2 Olympic Hotel
3 First National Bank
4 U.S. Court
5 Federal Reserve Bank
6 Federal Office Building
7 Administration Building
8 Public Safety Building
9 City Hall
10 Smith Tower
11 King County Court House
12 Seattle Art Museum
13 Westlake Center
14 Pacific First Center
15 Convention & Trade Center

Pier 52 Ferry Terminal
Pier 59 Aquarium, Omnidome

━━■ Streetcar

▨▨ Pioneer Square Historic District

Pier 43

Olympic N.P., Tacoma (Airport)

Museum of Flight Red Barn (Boeing)

experience on film the 1980 eruption of Mount St Helens. Pier 57 is the departure point of interesting harbour tours.

On the two floors of picturesque Pike Place Market a wide range of wares are offered for sale – fish, fruit, vegetables and all sorts of odds and ends. Here too are a number of cheerful little bars.

★Pike Place Market

The historic core of the city is Pioneer Square, in which stands a 60 ft high totem pole. This was the spot where the first white settlers established themselves in 1852. The old Victorian-style brick buildings (including former department stores and hotels) between the 42-storey Smith Tower (observation platform on 35th floor) in the north and King Street Station to the south were restored some years ago and now cater for tourists, with boutiques, souvenir shops and restaurants. The striking Pioneer Building is the starting point of Bill Speidel's "underground tours", which take visitors round the foundations of buildings destroyed in the 1889 fire.

Pioneer Square Historic District

In the Union Trust Annex Building (117 S Main St.) is the very interesting **Klondike Gold Rush Museum**, which brings to life the wild 1990s of the 19th c. Open daily 9am–5pm.

To the east of Pioneer Square is the colourful International District, in which the street scene is dominated by immigrants from the Far East (mainly Japanese and Chinese) with their shops and restaurants. At 407 7th Avenue are the Wing Luke Museum, which charts the history of Asian immigration, and the Hing Hay Park with a vast mural and a pagoda.

★International District

473

Seattle

The skyline of Seattle, with Mount Rainier in the background

Seattle Center

The futuristic Monorail system carries passengers in 2 min. from the Westlake Center to the Seattle Center (1¼ mi. north-west of the city centre). Built for the 1962 World Fair, it is now a leisure centre. A cableway runs across the main precinct where in the evening the International Fountain is illuminated. The Key Arena, the most recent addition to the Center and home to the Seattle Supersonics, offers professional basketball.

The **Space Needle**, a 605 ft high telecommunications tower, has become the great landmark and emblem of Seattle. From the restaurant and the observation platform there are overwhelming panoramic views. A Rock'n'Roll Museum is due to open at the foot of the Space Needle by 2000 at the latest, designed by the renowned architect Frank Gehry.

To the south-west are the six buildings of the **Pacific Science Center**, designed by Minoru Yamasaki, with excellent presentations of various fields of science and mathematics (including astronomy and space travel). The facilities include an IMAX cinema with a giant screen. Open daily 10am–6pm.

In **Center House** are a Children's Museum (many "hands-on" exhibits), the Food Circus and an International Bazaar selling culinary delights and other products from many different countries.

★Chittenden
Locks

North-west of the Seattle Center is the Myrtle Edwards Park. Farther north are the Hiram M. Chittenden Locks, one of the largest and busiest lock complexes in the United States. Beside the locks is a fish ladder that allows salmon and other fish to make their way upstream from the salt water of Puget Sound to the fresh water of Lake Union and Lake Washington.

Beyond Portage Bay is the campus of the University of Seattle, which was founded in 1861, with the Thomas Burke Memorial Museum (natural history) and the Henry Art Gallery (mainly modern art). To the south are McCurdy Park, with the Museum of History and Industry, and Washington Park, with the Arboretum and a Japanese tea garden.

University of
Washington

Surroundings

Half an hour's drive north of Seattle on US 526, at Everett, is the factory of the Boeing Aircraft Company, with the largest aircraft construction hangar in the world. On a guided tour visitors are shown the latest high-tech aircraft (including the B 747) under construction. Some 20 min. drive south of Seattle is an older Boeing works where the Flying Fortresses of the Second World War were built. Nearby is the Red Barn in which W.E. Boeing constructed his first aircraft in 1916.

★★Boeing
Aircraft Company

To the south of the city, at 9404 Marginal Way, is the Museum of Flight, with over three dozen carefully restored historic aircraft, including one built by the Wright brothers. Open daily 9am–5pm.

★Museum of
Flight

From Pier 56 there are boats (¾ hour) to Tillicum Indian Village, which gives visitors an excellent picture of the culture and way of life of the Northwest Indians.

Tillicum Indian
Village

An excursion to one of the more than 170 islands in Puget Sound is a must; just the ferry trip alone is a delight, the boat slipping smoothly along through this unique seascape. Places out of reach of the ferries can be seen by kayak, the waters being calm.

Puget Sound

To the north of Seattle is **Whidbey Island**, the largest island in Puget Sound, which was reconnoitred by George Vancouver in 1792 and is now a popular summer resort. On the island are the attractive little townships of Coupeville, Langley and Oak Harbor. To the south of Coupeville is the 19th c. Fort Casey.

Also popular with vacationists are the **San Juan Islands**, which preserve a number of buildings dating from the period of British rule. In Friday Harbor is a Whale Museum, and there are boat trips from there to observe whales in the open sea.

Other islands in Puget Sound, all rewarding of a visit, are Orcas Island, Lopez Island, Shaw Island, the virtually unspoiled Vashon Island, a wonderful place to explore by bike, and Blake Island, where Chief Seattle was born and where a Squamish log house has been reconstructed.

Canada too is "just round the corner", with a regular ferry service to the pretty town of Victoria on Vancouver Island.

★Sequoia and Kings Canyon National Park　　M/N 7

State: California
Area: 1350 sq. mi.
Established: 1890 and 1940

Although established at different times, the Sequoia and Kings Canyon National Parks form a single geographical and administrative unit. They take in a large expanse of grand mountain scenery in the southern part of the Sierra Nevada, extending from the foothills on the edge of the Central Valley of California (San Joaquín Valley) in the west to the main ridge of the Sierra Nevada in the east, with Mount Whitney (14,494 ft), the highest peak in the continental United States (excluding Alaska), the

Split Mountain (14,058 ft), Mount Goethe (13,277 ft) and a number of other peaks over 10,000 ft.

Information The National Parks are open throughout the year, though the higher levels can be visited only in summer. There are more than 600 mi. of marked trails. The 7½ mi. long Marble Fork Trail crosses one of the wildest areas while at the same time being relatively undemanding. There are also good winter sports facilities. Visitor Centers in Grant Cove and Lodgepole have information about all aspects of the park. Giant Forest is particularly well provided with motels and cabins; there are also 13 camp sites.

Giant sequoias The two National Parks take in the most impressive part of a 250 mi. long belt of vegetation at altitudes between 4000 and 8000 ft in which there are clumps, groves and forests of giant sequoias or mammoth trees (Sequoiadendron giganteum or Sequoia gigantea). This species and the closely related redwoods of the Pacific coast (Sequoia sempervirens) are the only surviving representatives of a genus of sequoias of the swamp cypress family (Taxodiaceae) that was once widespread in the northern hemisphere. The giant sequoias can reach a height of between 250 and 300 ft and a diameter of 40 ft and can live for up to 3500 years. Their thick bark (up to 18 in.) protects them against fire, and the high tannic acid content of their timber gives them protection against pests and fungal disease. Their only real enemy is man.

Fauna Visitors who spend some time in the National Parks may be lucky enough to see silver foxes, lynxes and pumas. Commoner are raccoons, skunks, red deer and black bears. A careful watch should be kept for the Pacific rattlesnakes that are by no means rare.

History The first inhabitants of this mountain region were Potwisha and Kaweah Indians, who lived by hunting, gathering, fishing and farming. The first whites came here only in 1858. Six years later staff of the Geological Survey explored the Sierra Nevada.

They were followed by settlers, hunters, lumbermen, gold prospectors and adventurers, and the Indian inhabitants were almost exterminated, largely as a result of diseases brought by the incomers. By 1890 there were dozens of sawmills in the area, and the sequoias were decimated, for a single giant sequoia provided enough timber for the construction of forty houses. An energetic fighter against the destruction of the sequoia forests was the Scottish-born John Muir, on whose initiative the Sequoia National Park was established.

Sequoia National Park

★Giant Forest

The Giant Forest in the western part of the Sequoia National Park owes its name to its stands of mammoth trees. The mightiest tree in this area is the General Sherman Tree, which is 275 ft high and has a circumference of 103 ft. It is estimated to be 2800 years old, making it one of the oldest living organisms on earth. Starting at its foot is the 2 mi. Congress Trail, a round walk passing several other groups of trees.

In the little town of Giant Forest, the old market building has been converted into a sequoia museum.

Other impressive groups of mammoth trees are the Senate Group, the Founder's Group and the Cloisters.

Crystal Cave

North-west of the Giant Forest is the very impressive stalactitic cave known as the Crystal Cave.

Moro Rock

A magnificent viewpoint is the 6725 ft high Moro Rock, an isolated granite peak south-east of the Giant Forest.

Crescent Meadow is a very beautiful alpine meadow surrounded by trees. From here there is a road to Tharp's Log, a dwelling contrived by the first white settler in the hollow trunk of a giant sequoia.

Crescent Meadow

Kings Canyon National Park

On the north-west side of Sequoia National Park is Grant Grove, in the northern part of which is the General Grant Tree (266 ft high, circumference at the base 108 ft), which was discovered in 1862.

★Grant Grove

Kings Canyon, carved out of the rock by the southern arm of the Kings River, is flanked by steep rock walls and tall granite peaks. From the Cedar Grove tourist

★Kings Canyon

The 2800-year-old General Sherman Tree in Sequoia National Park

centre there are hiking trails to the very beautiful Zumwalt Meadow and the Roaring River and Mist Falls.

★★Shenandoah National Park   L 47

State: Virginia
Area: 305 sq. mi.
Established: 1936

The National Park lies roughly in the centre of Virginia, taking in a section of the Blue Ridge Mountains (the most easterly ridge of the Appalachians) some 80 mi. long but only between 2 and 13 mi. wide. The Blue Ridge Mountains, which range in height between 2000 and 4000 ft, owe their name to the bluish mist that shrouds the tops of the hills, particularly in the early morning. 95 per cent of the park's area is covered by dense mixed forest, the rest by meadowland.

The National Park is open throughout the year, though in winter some sections of the Skyline Drive may be closed. The flowers and shrubs are at their finest in spring and summer, but the great glory of the park is its autumn colouring. The most popular time for a visit, therefore, is in October.

History The name of the National Park comes from the Indian name of the Shenandoah River ("daughter of the stars"). None of the original inhabitants, the Monacan and Manahoac Indians, survived the settlement of the area by Europeans, which led, particularly during the 19th c., to the almost complete destruction of the mountain forests by deliberate clearance, mining and livestock farming. Finally in the 1930s, in order to save at least part of the landscape and provide work for the remaining inhabitants, the National Park was established and the Skyline Drive constructed.

Flora The most striking feature of the National Park is the density and

477

variety of the forest cover, in which species of oak and pine predominate. In the undergrowth there are ferns and flowers such as the yellow lady's slipper.

Fauna The commonest animal is the Virginian white-tailed deer, the ever-popular Bambi. Much rarer – and distinctly less welcome – is an encounter with one of the five or six hundred black bears who live in the National Park.

★Skyline Drive

Big Meadows Lodge, Skyline Drive

The Skyline Drive, the northern continuation of the Blue Ridge Parkway (see Virginia), runs along the crest of the Blue Ridge Mountains from the north entrance to the National Park at Front Royal (milepost 0.6) to the south entrance at Rockfish (milepost 104.6). Along the road there are numerous stopping points to enjoy the view or see some particular sight. Among them are the Shenandoah Valley Overlook (milepost 17.1), the Swift Run Overlook (milepost 67.2), at an altitude of over 3300 ft, President Hoover's summer residence at the end of the Mill Prong Trail (milepost 52.5) and the old Cave Cemetery below Dark Hollow Falls (milepost 50.7).

Information about hiking trails in the National Park can be obtained at the park entrances or the park office (see Practical Information, National Parks).

★Luray Caverns

The Luray Caves, in the Shenandoah Valley only a short drive west from the Skyline Drive on US 211, contain magnificent formations of stalactites and stalagmites. One of the cave's highlights is the world's only "stalacpipe" or stalactitic organ, the stalactites resonate when struck with rubber covered clappers.

South Carolina (State)   O–R 42–47

Area: 19,530 sq. mi.
Population: 3,699,000
Capital: Columbia
Popular name: Palmetto State

South Carolina (named after King Charles I), one of the thirteen founding states of the Union, lies on the Atlantic coast in the south-eastern United States. The coastal plain has a wet subtropical climate, with summers that can be hot and sultry and mild winters. The climate becomes more temperate towards the north-west as the land rises to the Piedmont Plateau, a well cultivated agricultural region. In the extreme north-west the state takes in part of the Blue Ridge Mountains, a segment of the Appalachians.

History The first Europeans in this area were Spaniards who landed on the coast in 1526. Systematic settlement, however, began only after Charles II granted possession of the Carolinas to eight "proprietors" in 1663. In 1670 the settlement of Charles Towne was founded near present-day Charleston. The Carolinas were divided into North and South Carolina in 1689. On May 23rd 1788 South Carolina became the eighth state to join the Union, and it was the first of the southern states to secede from it on December 20th 1860. The Civil War began with the bombardment by Union forces of Fort Sumter, at the entrance to Charleston harbour, on April 12th 1861. South Carolina suffered severely during the war, when General Sherman marched through the state and almost completely destroyed Columbia and other towns. It was not readmitted to the Union until 1868, and Union troops were stationed in the state until 1877.

Economy The principal industry in South Carolina, one of the classic cotton states, is textiles, followed by chemicals and electronics. The second main source of income is the tourist and holiday trade, mainly on the Atlantic coast. The most important agricultural products after cotton are tobacco and soya beans.

Something of the spirit of the neat little 18th c. plantation town still manifests itself in Beaufort (founded 1710), south-east of Charleston (see entry); especially on the waterfront, in some old villas – many of which now offer bed and breakfast – and in Beaufort Museum.

Beaufort

See entry

Charleston

Columbia (founded 1786), capital of South Carolina, lies roughly in the centre of the state on the Broad and Congaree Rivers. The imposing State House (Main and Gervais Sts.) with its dome and its massive granite columns was built between 1855 and 1907. Bronze stars mark hits by Sherman's artillery during the siege of the town. Opposite State House is Trinity Church (1846), one of the largest Episcopal churches in the United States. To the south is the large campus of the University of South Carolina (founded 1801), the central element in which is the brick complex known as the Horseshoe.

Columbia

A number of antebellum houses have been preserved in the northeast of the town, including the Hampton-Preston Mansion (1818), the Robert Mills Historic House (1823) and the Mann-Simons Cottage (1850). The Woodrow Wilson Boyhood Home, in which the 28th President of the United States spent his early years, was built after the Civil War.

The ★**South Carolina State Museum**, one of the largest museums in the southern states, surveys the history, natural history, science and art of South Carolina.

To the east of Columbia, on the Saluda River, is the ★**Riverbank Zoo**, the terrarium, aquarium and bird house of which are particularly remarkable.

Georgetown, founded in 1729, is built on the spot where the Spaniards landed in 1526. It has an attractive historic district and offers facilities for deep-sea angling.

Georgetown

Hilton Head Island, off the Atlantic coast in the extreme south-east of the state, is now linked with the mainland by a four-lane highway. It is internationally renowned as a fashionable holiday resort, with clean and well-kept beaches, marvellous golf courses and a wide range of other leisure facilities. The sporting highlights of the season are the golf tournament and the ladies' tennis tournament, both of which attract international stars.

★Hilton Head Island

South Dakota

Myrtle Beach, stretching endlessly into the distance

Myrtle Beach

If Hilton Head Island is the resort for the wealthy, Myrtle Beach is its counterpart for ordinary people. Here they will find endless broad sandy beaches – and, immediately beyond the beaches, equally endless lines of hotels. Amusement parks, country music clubs, more than 70 golf courses and almost 200 tennis courts, cater for a range of tastes in entertainment. A more tranquil atmosphere prevails in Brookgreen Gardens (Murrells Inlet).

Ninety Six National Historic Site

Near the little town of Ninety Six on the Piedmont Plateau the first battle of the revolutionary wars in the southern United States was fought in 1775, and, six years later, a British fort was besieged for 28 days. A trail 1 mi. long through the forests takes visitors round the scene of the fighting.

In the far north-west of the state is a lovely stretch of country in the foothills of the Blue Ridge Mountains. The beauty of this relatively unknown part of South Carolina can be enjoyed on a drive on the Cherokee Foothills Scenic Highway (SC 11).

South Dakota (State)   D–F 21–29

Area: 77,115 sq. mi.
Population: 701,000. Capital: Pierre
Popular name: Mount Rushmore State

South Dakota (from the name of a Sioux tribe, the Dakotas, meaning "allies"), a region of continental climate, lies in the north central United States, in the zone of transition between the Central Lowlands

and the Great Plains. It is divided by the Missouri (which is
dammed at several points
within the state) into two
halves. The eastern half is in
the Central Lowlands (lowest
point 968 ft). The western half,
mostly consisting of the
Missouri Plateau, lies in the
Great Plains, a region of grasslands interrupted by tracts of
badlands. In the south-west of

the state are the Black Hills, which reach a height of 7241 ft in Harney
Peak.

History Some 12,000 years ago the territory of South Dakota was
occupied by nomadic bison and mammoth hunters. Later they were
succeeded by hunters and gatherers, who buried their dead in long,
low mounds. Around AD 1200 Mandan and Arikara Indians introduced
farming in the Missouri region; then in the 17th and early 18th centuries they were driven further north by the Sioux. In the 1740s
French fur trappers – the first Europeans in this region – moved into
Sioux territory, which then became part of New France (Louisiana)
and was acquired by the United States in 1803 under the Louisiana
Purchase. Originally the American territory of Dakota also included
large areas of the present-day states of Wyoming and Montana. After
the reorganisation of the territory the present states of North and
South Dakota were formed, and on November 2nd 1889 South Dakota
became the 40th state of the Union. The local Indians put up fierce
resistance to the takeover of their land by whites, and there were frequent bloody encounters with American troops, causing heavy
losses.

The predominant elements in the state's **economy** are agriculture and
the industries processing agricultural produce. Large areas of the grasslands are now pasturage for livestock (cattle, sheep) and arable land on
which grain and fodder crops are grown. Gold and silver mining (Black
Hills) also make important contributions to the economy, along with oil
and brown coal. An increasingly important source of revenue is
tourism. Particular tourist attractions are the Black Hills (Mount
Rushmore), a number of spectacular caves and the Badlands National
Park (see entry).

Mitchell (pop. 15,000), in the valley of the James River, is the chief place
in a predominantly agricultural area. A sight of international renown is
its Moorish-style Corn Palace, which is decorated every year with corn
cobs, mosaics made with different colours of corn (maize) and other
fruits of the earth and grasses – a tradition that has been maintained
since 1892. In mid September there is a large Corn Festival. A permanent
exhibition is devoted to South Dakotan agriculture. Opposite in the
Enchanted World Doll Museum, about 4000 dolls can be seen. The
Balloon and Airship Museum has hot air and captive balloons. To
the north of the town is the site of a 10th c. Indian village that was excavated some years ago.

Mitchell

Pierre (pop. 13,000), capital of South Dakota, lies in the geographical
centre of the state on the Missouri, which is dammed a short distance
above the town to form Lake Oahe. The State Capitol was completed in
1910. The South Dakota Cultural Heritage Center has interesting,
recently redesigned exhibitions on the cultural history of the state. To
the south of the town is the Fort Pierre National Grassland, a stretch of
typical prairie vegetation.

Pierre

Sioux Falls

In the south-east of the state is its largest town, Sioux Falls (pop. 82,000). Originally founded in 1856, it had soon afterwards to be abandoned because of continual Indian attacks and began to develop only after the construction of Fort Dakota to provide protection. The waterfalls from which the town takes it name are situated to the north of Downtown. Also of interest are the Great Plains Zoo and Delbridge Museum of Natural History in Sherman Park and the USS South Dakota Battleship Memorial, as big as the World War II battleship itself and housing a military museum.

Wounded Knee

On December 29th 1890, men of the US Cavalry massacred 153 Indians at Wounded Knee creek. The Indians were adherents of the Ghost Dance cult, which promised the return of the great buffalo herds and the disappearance of the white man. The ignominious military action put an end to the Ghost Dance and finally broke Indian resistance. It has never, however, been forgotten. In 1973 members of the American Indian Movement occupied Wounded Knee in protest at the United States government's Indian policy. Another protest took place in 1993. The site of the massacre, now a hillside cemetery, is in the Pine Ridge Reservation in the far south-west of South Dakota, on the US 18.

Other places of interest

Badlands National Park, Black Hills (see entries)

Tampa   W 43

State: Florida
Altitude: 0–55 ft
Population: 280,000

The city of Tampa, situated on an inlet reaching far into the west coast of Florida, is the economic centre of western Florida. The city centre is an area of high-rise office blocks, but Tampa also has historic old quarters such as Ybor City and Old Hyde Park. On the whole Tampa, and in particular Tampa Bay, make for a more leisurely beach holiday than the more popular Atlantic coast of Florida.

The maps drawn by the Spanish conquistadors show a number of Indian settlements round Tampa Bay. In 1824 the Americans built a fort at the mouth of the Hillsborough River directed against the Seminole Indians. After the Second Seminole War a port and trading centre was established here, and this soon developed into a regional centre. Towards the end of the 19th c. Tampa became a fashionable winter resort.

Sights

Franklin Street Mall

The heart of downtown Tampa, at the mouth of the Hillsborough River, is the Franklin Street Mall. It is a busy pedestrian zone with many shops, attractive restaurants, fountains and trees as well as tall office blocks.

Tampa Museum of Art

To the west of the city centre, at 601 Doyle Arlton Drive, is Tampa Museum of Art, which has one of the finest collections of Greek and Roman antiquities in the United States.

Harbour Island

To the south of the city centre, separated from the mainland by the narrow Garrison Channel, is Harbour Island, with the popular Harbour Island Market (boutiques, fast food stands, restaurants). Along the waterfront runs the Waterwalk, a pleasant promenade with fine views.

★University of Tampa

The University of Tampa occupies a building in the style of a Moorish palace that from 1891 to 1929 was a hotel, with furnishings from Europe and the east. In the south wing is the H.B. Plant Museum (turn of the 19th c. furniture and objets d'art).

Old timber and brick buildings, wrought-iron balconies, arcades and sidewalk cafés are characteristic of Ybor City. In 1886 the Cuban cigar manufacturer Vincente Martinéz Ybor moved his business to Tampa and a new quarter, Ybor City, was built for this Spanish speaking employees. A good starting point for a tour of the district is the State Museum, housed in a former Cuban bakery (restored). Adjoining is Preservation Park, with six renovated cigar-rolling sheds. On Ybor Square, now a small shopping mall with a variety of shops and restaurants, is the Tampa Rico Cigar Company, where visitors can see cigars being rolled by hand.

★★Ybor City

Tampa's best known attraction, in the north-east of the city, is the Busch Gardens, a combination of zoo and theme park (Busch Blvd. and 40th St./SR 580). The themes of this family leisure park centre mainly on the Dark Continent. In addition it seeks to provide entertainments for every taste – animals, an exotic atmosphere, live shows in several theatres, roller coasters and other adventurous rides. The Zoo has gained a reputation for preserving endangered species, and is particularly proud of its success in breeding such rare species as the black rhinoceros. A recent triumph is the rearing of a large family of koalas, and the Zoo is also co-operating with Peking Zoo in the breeding of pandas. There is an impressive herd of Asiatic elephants.

★★Busch Gardens

The Museum of Science and Industry (4801 E Fowler Ave.), notable for its unusual architecture, ranks as one of the best museums of technology and natural history in the United States.

Museum of Science and Industry

On the eastern outskirts of the city, beyond I 4, is the Seminole Cultural Center (5221 N Orient Rd.), which illustrates the history and culture of the Seminoles. In the Seminole village associated with the Center, with the typical *chickees* (open huts), Indian craft skills are demonstrated.

Seminole Cultural Center

Tennessee (State)   N/O 35–44

Area: 42,1433 sq. mi.
Population: 5,320,000
Capital: Nashville
Popular name: Volunteer State

The state of Tennessee (after the name of a Cherokee village), in the south-eastern United States, extends from the Mississippi plain in the west to the Appalachians. The southern range of the Appalachians is formed by the Great Smoky Mountains, with Clingmans Dome (6644 ft). To the west of this are the Great Appalachian Valley, through which flows the Tennessee River, the flat Cumberland Plateau and the Nashville Basin, surrounded by ranges of low hills. To the west of the lower Tennessee River (on which are a number of dams) the gently undulating terrain falls down to the Mississippi. As a result of an energetic programme of reafforestation more than half the state's area is now once again covered with deciduous forest.

History The first Europeans to reach the territory on the Tennessee River, then occupied by Cherokees, were Spaniards, who came here in 1541.

They were followed by Frenchmen and then by British settlers, who in 1663 incorporated the area in the British colony of Carolina. Between 1784 and 1789, when Tennessee was separated from Carolina, there existed on the territory of Tennessee an independent but not officially recognised state called Franklin. On June 1st 1796 Tennessee became the 16th state to adopt the Constitution of the Union. In 1861 it left the Union and joined the Confederation. During the Civil War Tennessee was the scene of much fighting, including the battles of Shiloh and Franklin. In 1866 the state was readmitted to the Union. Thirty years earlier most of the Cherokees had been deported to Oklahoma.

Economy The state's economic rise began with the establishment in 1933, during the great depression, of the Tennessee Valley Authority, charged to develop the valley of the Tennessee, which harnessed the power of the river to produce electricity. Tennessee's industries include chemicals, engineering, automobile construction and mining (coal, zinc, phosphates). Its principal agricultural crops are maize, wheat, tobacco and cotton. The main tourist areas are the Great Smoky Mountains, which attract visitors throughout the year, the valley of the Tennessee River with its numerous artificial lakes (water sports), Nashville and Memphis, home of the Blues and Rock'n Roll.

★Chattanooga

Chattanooga, situated in south-eastern Tennessee on the border with Georgia, was once an outlying settlement of the Cherokee Indians. It is now a city of 150,000 inhabitants in which the first Coca-Cola bottling plant was established and the game of minigolf was invented. The popular song "Chattanooga Choo-Choo" brought it international fame; and visitors can still see the original railroad station of 1909, though it is now converted into a hotel and restaurant arcade. Railway buffs will also find here the largest steam railroad in the south, the Tennessee Valley Railroad. The city has a number of museums, including the Hunter Museum of Art, the Houston Museum of Decorative Arts and the National Knife Museum (knives down the ages). A steep railroad runs up Lookout Mountain, scene of the battle of Chattanooga during the Civil War; on the top, as well as enjoying the view, visitors can study the history of the battle.

The ★**Tennessee Aquarium** displays the freshwater fishes of the southern United States. 6 mi. west of the city, in the Raccoon Mountain recreation area, is one of the largest of the Tennessee Valley Authority's dams.

Knoxville

Knoxville, seat of the University of Tennessee (founded 1794), lies in the east of the state and is a good base from which to explore the Great Smoky Mountains National Park (see entry). It was the first capital of the state, as is evidenced in the Governor William Blount Mansion of 1792; today its emblem is the Sunshine Tower. Other features of interest are General James White's Fort (1786), the Knoxville Museum of Art and the Confederate Memorial Hall, which recalls the siege of the city during the Civil War.

★Museum of
Appalachia

This large open-air museum situated 16 mi. north of Norris, covers every important aspect of Appalachian culture. It has the reputation of being one of the pleasantest heritage villages in the United States.

Oak Ridge

22 mi. west of Knoxville is Oak Ridge, which along with Alamo was involved in the development of the atom bomb. It is still an important centre of nuclear research. The National Laboratory's graphite reactor produced uranium in the form required for the bomb (exhibition). The National Museum of Science and Energy illustrates and explains the development of atomic energy.

Beyond Sweetwater, 46 mi. from Knoxville, there is a cave system with the largest underwater lake yet discovered, the Lost Sea. Guided tours and boat trips.

★**Lost Sea**

The Land between the Lakes, on the border with Kentucky, was developed by the Tennessee Valley Authority as an extensive recreation area with ample scope for hiking, bathing and various sports. Visitors can also observe a herd of bison and see two museum villages of 1800 and 1850.

Land between the Lakes

Cumberland Gap National Historic Park (see Kentucky), Great Smoky Mountains National Park, Memphis, Nashville (see entries).

Other places of interest

Texas (State)

N–Y 19–32

Area: 267,340 sq. mi.
Population: 19,128,000
Capital: Austin
Popular name: Lone Star State

Texas (from an Indian word meaning "friend"), the largest state in the United States after Alaska, consists of three main regions: the Gulf Coast plain, the Great Plains and the Rocky Mountains. The state extends from the Red River in the north to the Rio Grande in the south and the Gulf of Mexico in the south-east. Characteristic features of the 375 mi. long Gulf Coast are the series of coastal lagoons separated from the open sea by long spits of land. To the north-west of the coastal plain are the Great Plains, with hills rising to around 3300 ft, and in the west of the state are the foothills of the Rockies, rising to 8750 ft in the Guadalupe Peak.

While in the eastern part of the state a subtropical climate predominates, the climate in the south-west is desertic. Throughout the state there may be periods of intense heat (over 100°F) in summer and of frost in winter. In the arid regions there are mesquite trees, in the upland areas pines, firs, junipers and oaks; along the rivers, which in their middle and upper courses flow only at certain times of year, there are hickories and cypresses. The characteristic vegetation cover of the Great Plains is grassland, which becomes increasingly scanty towards the west. There are only remnants of the pine and oak forests that once covered the coastal plain.

History The coast of Texas was sighted in 1519 by the Spanish navigator Alonso Alvarez de Piñeda, and in 1528 Alvar Núñez Cabeza de Vaca was shipwrecked at what is now Galveston and spent several years exploring the territory. The first permanent Spanish settlements were established only at the end of the 17th c. In 1821 control of the area passed to Mexico. American settlers led by Moses and Stephen F. Austin rebelled against the Mexican government at the end of 1835 and after their victory at San Jacinto in the following year proclaimed the independent republic of Texas. On December 29th 1845 Texas was admitted to the Union as the 28th state. This led to the American–Mexican War, at the end of which the treaty of Guadalupe Hidalgo (1848) laid down the frontier between Mexico and the United States on broadly the present line. During the Civil War Texas fought on the Confederate side. After the war the cattle barons with their huge herds dominated the region and provided the nation's meat supply. The end of the great cattle-rearing period came with the development of cattle ranching in other states and the discovery of oil in Texas.

Texas

Economy Texas is one of the United States's leading agricultural states. Almost 30 per cent of its cultivated land is planted with cotton. On the irrigated land of the coastal plain the principal crop is rice, grown in the valley of the Rio Grande. Stock farming (cattle, and also pigs) is still important. In output of minerals (oil, natural gas, graphite, sulphur, magnesium chloride, salt, gypsum) Texas takes the leading place among American states, and as a result it also has huge oil refineries and a large petrochemical industry. The existence of space travel research institutes, mainly in Houston, has led to the development of a strong electronics industry. Other important branches of industry are foodstuffs, engineering and automobile construction.

The state's grandiose desert landscapes, forest-covered mountains and steppes, and the Gulf Coast plain with its beaches, lakes and rivers offer endless scope for recreation and holidays, earning Texas a leading position among the states in the tourism statistics.

Amarillo

Texas too has its "pan handle": the state boundary projects northwards towards Oklahoma, incorporating the area around Amarillo. Its history and culture are documented in the outstanding Panhandle Plains Historical Museum in Canyon near Amarillo. In Amarillo itself is the Quarterhouse Museum celebrating the cowboys' legendary steed.

★Palo Duro Canyon

Palo Duro Canyon is to Texas what the Grand Canyon (see entry) is to Arizona. Up to 1313 ft deep and aglow with red and yellow colouring, the gorge is reached from Canyon, south-east of Amarillo. The effortless way to see it is on the 16 mi. long Scenic Drive.

Austin

Austin, capital of Texas, situated 81 mi. north-east of San Antonio at the point where the Colorado River leaves the Edwards Plateau, was founded in 1839 and named after Stephen F. Austin (1793–1836), the "father of Texas". It is an educational centre, with the University of Texas, the Lyndon B. Johnson Library and Museum and the Texas Memorial Museum.

Other features of interest include the red granite State Capitol (1882–88), modelled on the Capitol in Washington, DC, which is the second largest Capitol in the United States; the restored Old Pecan Street (Sixth St.), the town's old main street and still a popular place in the evenings; the museum in the house of the sculptor Elisabeth Ney (1830–1907); and the Governor's Mansion (1010 Colorado St.), a classic Southern mansion dating from 1856.

Anyone wanting exercise in the form of a walk or sport should head for Zilker Park, the adjacent botanical garden or the gardens of the National Wildflower Research Center. A rather more unusual pleasure Austin has to offer is the spectacle every evening of a large flock of bats leaving the Congress Avenue Bridge on their nightly flight.

Brownsville

Brownsville, the most southerly town in Texas, is connected with the Caribbean by a 17 mi. long channel. The American–Mexican War began here on May 8th 1846, as is documented on the Palo Alto Battlefield National Historic Site; and the last battle of the Civil War was fought on the Pallmitto Ranch Battlefield on May 12th and 13th 1865.

Within easy reach of Brownsville, beyond the Rio Grande, is the Mexican town of Matamoros.

Corpus Christi

The little port of Corpus Christi, on an inlet to the north of Brownsville, has two features of interest: the Texas State Aquarium and the Art Museum of South Texas. Moored in the harbour is that legendary of all American aircraft carriers, the "USS Lexington"; also reconstructions of Christopher Columbus's little armada.

★Padre Island National Seashore

Padre Island, to the south of Corpus Christi has very beautiful beaches and dunes that are home to 350 different species of birds.

South-west of Corpus Christi is Kingsville, where visitors can see the ranch established in 1853 by Richard King, one of the cattle barons.

Kingsville

At the western tip of Texas, on the left bank of the Rio Grande, which here forms the frontier with Mexico, is El Paso, the largest American city on the Mexican frontier, with a population of over half a million. As well as separating the two countries, the river also divides El Paso from the Mexican city of Ciudad Juárez, El Paso's San Jacinto Plaza still remains an air of bygone days. The El Paso Museum of Art has a fine collection of pre-Columbian and Indian art and the Kress Collection (works of the Italian Renaissance). The Chamizal National Memorial, a beautiful park on the banks of the Rio Grande, commemorates the settlement of the long-standing dispute over the frontier line between the United States and Mexico. Outside, occupying the site of a military post established in 1846, is Fort Bliss, today one of the largest air defence centres in the world, to which Allied personnel are sent for training. On the base there are three military museums.

El Paso

If visiting El Paso's Mexican sister city the best plan is to take the bus to Santa Fe Bridge, cross the frontier on foot, then make enquiries at the Juárez Tourist Office on the Mexican side. Cheap shopping is one of Ciudad Juárez's chief attractions, all manner of goods being available. The Plaza de la Catedral and Parque Chamizal have an authentic Mexican feel.

Ciuded Juárez

The ★**Mission Trail**, starting from El Paso, leads to a number of former Spanish mission stations in Texas: the Mission Ysleta, the oldest in Texas, established in 1681 as the mission of Nuestra Señora del Carmen; the Mission Socorro, founded in 1682 and moved to its present site after an Indian rising; and San Elizario, with the Spanish garrison church of 1777.

Langtry, on the banks of the Rio Grande in western Texas, exemplifies the wildest of the Wild West. Here for 21 years the self-elected Judge Roy Bean, proprietor of a saloon in the town, applied his ideas of law, advertising in the sign above his saloon "ice-cold beer and the law west of Pecos" – and that's exactly how it was. Nowadays it is tourists rather than outlaws who come to the saloon, which is a museum.

Langtry

This little spot is situated in such a remote corner of the far south-west of Texas (on the US 67/90), that scarcely anyone is likely to stray here unless bound for El Paso. Those who do, though, will meet with a surprise; because on a large former military area nearby, Donald Judd (d. 1994), the best known exponent of Minimal Art, realised his concept of the "ideal museum". Incidentally, part of the film "Giant" starring James Dean, Elizabeth Taylor and Rock Hudson were shot in Marfa.

Marfa

Waco, 2 hour drive south of Fort Worth, was a centre of the secessionists of Texas. The Texas Ranger Hall of Fame and Museum charts the history of this legendary police corps. The town hit the headlines in 1993, when police and troops stormed the stronghold of a militant sect.

Waco

Big Bend National Park, Dallas (see entries), Fort Worth (see Dallas), Galveston (see Houston), Guadalupe Mountains (see Carlsbad Caverns), Houston, San Antonio (see entries).

Other places of interest

Tucson   R 15

State: Arizona
Altitude: 2420 ft
Population: 406,000

Tucson

Tuscon is situated in south-east Arizona, about three or four hour's drive from Phoenix (see entry). It lies in the fertile valley of the Santa Cruz River in the shelter of the Santa Catalina Mountains and because of its mild winter climate and attractive surroundings is a favourite winter destination of many tourists and "snowbirds". Averaging 350 sunny days a year it certainly lives up to its sobriquet "City of Sunshine".

History A Jesuit mission station was established here at the end of the 17th c. In the 18th c. a permanent settlement was founded which in 1857 became a posting station on the route from San Antonio in Texas to San Diego in California. In the second half of the 19th c. Tucson was for a time capital of the territory of Arizona. The construction of the Southern Pacific Railroad increased the importance of the town, in which the University of Arizona was founded in 1891. After the Second World War Tucson developed at an explosive pace, its population rising from 46,000 in 1950 to six times as much in the mid-1970s.

Sights

★El Presidio Historic District

The El Presidio Historic District with its adobe houses dating from the colonial period has been lovingly renovated. The Museum of Art, housed in six restored buildings, has a rich collection that includes contemporary art and applied art. In the Casa Cordova is the Mexican Heritage Museum.

Frémont House

At 151 South Granada Avenue, in the Community Center complex, is

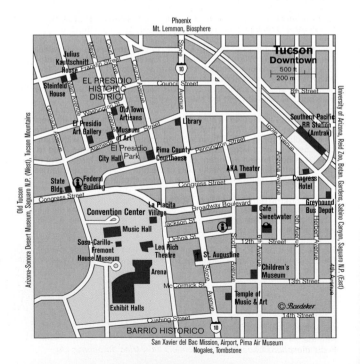

Frémont House, an attractive adobe building of about 1880 that is now a museum run by the Arizona Historical Society.

On the campus of the renowned University of Arizona are the Arizona State Museum, with a large archaeological collection covering 10,000 years of Indian cultural history, the magnificent Mineralogical Museum, the Center for Creative Photography and a fine art collection belonging to the Faculty of Arts. Here too is the Flandreau Planetarium.

University of Arizona

This mission station in the south-west of the city was established by Spanish Jesuits in 1770. The mission buildings, in particular the richly furnished church, are fine examples of the baroque architecture of the colonial period.

★Mission San Xavier del Bac

The Pima Air and Space Museum, on a large site on the edge of town, is well worth visiting, with a display of 200 different aeroplanes, helicopters and other aviation equipment.

Pima Air & Space Museum

Surroundings

The Saguaro National Park part of the Sonora Desert, extends east and west of Tucson (see entry). The characteristic feature of this desert area, the lowest in North America, is the abundant and varied flora and fauna that flourish in spite of the great heat: the typical saguaro or candelabra cactuses, which are the tallest species in North America, birds like the Gila woodpecker and cactus wren that live on the cactuses, rattlesnakes, desert tortoises and the Gila monster (a large lizard).

★Saguaro National Park

13 mi. west of Tucson is Tucson Mountain Park, with a Desert Museum and the reconstructed western town of Old Tucson.

★Tucson Mountain Park

In the Biosphere 2 near Tucson scientists have tried autonomic life

489

Utah

The little town of **Old Tucson**, in the style of the late 19th c., was reconstructed in 1940 as the location for numerous westerns. Wild West shoot-outs are re-enacted here daily.

★**Davis-Monthan Air Force Base**

A quite unreal spectacle greets the eye at the Davis-Monthan Air Force Base, 15 mi. south-east of Tucson. Parked here are as many as 20,000 fighter planes dating from World War II to the present; many look as though they were put there only yesterday, the dry desert climate being excellent for preservation. Open to visitors Jun.–Aug. Mon, Wed.

★**Kitt Peak National Observatory**

45 mi. south-west of Tucson, on Kitt Peak, high in the mountains of the Sonora Desert, is the Kitt Peak Observatory, one of the most important astronomical stations in the world, with 18 telescopes, including a giant solar telescope, and a museum.

Titan Missile Museum

20 mi. south of Tucson, in Green Valley, is the Titan Missile Museum, where visitors can see Titan II missiles, missile mechanisms, helicopters and a missile silo.

Tumacacori National Monument

46 mi. south of Tucson is the Tumacacori National Monument, a Franciscan mission station that was abandoned in 1848, with a beautiful church and patio and an interesting museum.

Utah (State) H–M 12–16

Area: 84,900 sq. mi.
Population: 2,000,000
Capital: Salt Lake City
Popular name: Beehive State

The state of Utah (named after the Ute tribe) lies in the western United States in the intermontane upland region, extending into the cold arid desert of the Great Basin, with the Great Salt Lake. Central Utah is occupied by the western foothills of the Rocky Mountains, the Wasatch Range and the Uinta Mountains (Kings Peak, 13,528 ft). The Colorado Plateau to the south was thrust upward only in geologically recent times, so that the Colorado River and its tributaries were able to cut their way through the rock, forming deep, narrow gorges and steep canyons in which the sedimentary strata with their variegated colouring are exposed. In the desert regions and on the salt soils only plants adapted to the arid conditions, such as the silver-green sagebrush and the creosote bush, can survive. There is forest cover only in the wetter mountain regions.

History The first Europeans to travel through the region, then occupied by the Ute, Paiute and Shoshone Indians, at the end of the 18th c. were Spanish Franciscans, later followed by trappers. Permanent settlement began only in 1847, when the Mormons, led by Brigham Young, reached the Great Salt Lake and founded Salt Lake City. From Salt Lake City they moved out into the surrounding area, cultivating the land and establishing new settlements. The gold rush and the discovery of the region's rich mineral resources led to a sharp increase in population, but it was only on January 4th 1896, after the abolition of polygamy, that the Mormon state was admitted to the Union as its 45th member. Some 70 per cent of all inhabitants of Utah are now Mormons.

Economy The cultivation of the desert steppeland of the Great Salt Lake Valley was made possible only by irrigation. The principal crops are wheat, sugar beet and fruit, and there is also much extensive livestock farming. The rich mineral resources of the region include copper (with the world's largest opencast mine in Bingham Canyon), silver, lead and various other metals. The principal industries are ore smelting, foodstuffs and engineering. The main tourist attractions are the extraordinary landscapes of the various National Parks and ski areas; the towns, apart from Salt Lake City, are of less tourist importance.

55 mi. north of Salt Lake City is Brigham City (named after the Mormon leader Brigham Young), with a Mormon tabernacle of 1897 and an interesting old railway station.

Brigham City

On the north side of the Great Salt Lake is the Golden Spike National Historic Site, the point where the Union Pacific and Central Pacific Railroads, starting respectively from Omaha in Nebraska and Sacramento in California, joined up. This first transcontinental railroad was completed on May 10th 1869, when the last spike (the "Golden Spike") was ceremonially driven in. The event is commemorated by an annual re-enactment of the ceremony. A short stretch of the old track has been reconstructed together with faithful reproductions of the two steam locomotives that met here, a Central Pacific "Jupiter" and Union Pacific "119".

★Golden Spike National Historic Site

The same forces of nature that shaped Bryce Canyon were at work also in Cedar Breaks, in south-western Utah, creating a smaller but even more colourful rocky landscape in the form of a gigantic amphitheatre. The best views are to be had from the Rim Drive.

★Cedar Breaks National Monument

One of the oldest and most spectacular panoramic roads in Utah is the 67 mi. US Highway 191, in the east of the state. Starting at Vernal, it heads north over the wild and unspoilt Uintas Mountains to the Flaming Gorge National Recreation Area on the upper reaches of the Green River. Signs along the road indicate 19 easily recognisable geological features fashioned here over a period of about a billion years. When the sun sinks low, the magnificent Flaming Gorge, cut by the Green River, really lives up to its name.

★Uintas Scenic Byway

Between Bryce Canyon National Park and Capital Reef National Park (see Canyonlands National Park) lie large areas of desert-like landscape distinguished by endless variation. The gorges and canyons cut by the Escalante River and its tributaries are particularly splendid. In addition to the wealth of natural wonders, there are also traces of Old Indian culture – best access is via Scenic Byway UT 12.

★Grand Staircase

Situated in the far south of Utah and extending a little way into Arizona, Lake Powell, 200 mi. long and 1930 sq. mi. in area, is the second largest man-made lake in the United States. Construction of the 709 ft high dam (Visitor Center) across the Colorado River where it passes through **Glen Canyon**, created an all-year recreation area enjoyed by anglers, boating enthusiasts and aficionados of watersports.

★Lake Powell

The best place from which to set out to explore it is the small town of **Page** in Arizona. Several marinas around the lake hire out boats or run boat trips. The Rainbow Bridge National Monument, a 295 ft high natural stone bridge, the second highest of its kind in the world, can be seen on the southern shore.

Rainbow Bridge

Lake Powell – a water lover's paradise in the middle of the Utah Desert

From Page there are excursions to **Antelope Canyon**, a striking, wonderful example of a slot canyon in a remote area to the south (access to it is not easy nor altogether without danger).

Ogden

In Ogden, half an hour's drive north of Salt Lake City, are the Browning Firearms Museum and the Union Pacific Railroad Museum, in the old station, and Fort Buenaventura.

To the east of Ogden are the skiing areas (fine powder snow) of Snow Basin, Nordic Valley and Powder Mountain.

Provo

47 mi. south of Salt Lake City, surrounded by high mountains, is the industrial town of Provo, the second largest in the state of Utah, with the Brigham Young University, founded by the Mormons in 1875, and site of a large ethnographic museum with exhibits from all over the world. There is also an interesting Pioneer Museum. To the west of the town, on the shores of Utah Lake, is a State Park. A cable railway leads to the Bridal Veil Falls in Provo Canyon.

★Sundance Resort & Institute

North-east of Provo lies the Sundance Ski Area where Hollywood star Robert Redford's business interests include a superior hotel, theatre and film institute. Here and in neighbouring Park City, the highly respected Sundance Film Festival is held every year in January.

St George

In the south-west corner of the state is St George, where Brigham Young spent the winter. Some 17,000 tons of sandstone were used in the Mormon Temple here, and timber had to be brought from 80 mi. away. St George owes its popular name of Dixie to the cotton grown in the area. Remains of Indian cave dwellings and rock drawings have been found at Snow Canyon, north-east of St George.

Arches National Park, Bryce Canyon National Park, Canyonlands National Park, Navajo Indian Reservation, Salt Lake City, Zion National Park (see entries).

Other places of interest

Vermont (State)   D–G 52–55

Area: 9610 sq. mi.
Population: 589,000
Capital: Montpelier
Popular name: Green Mountain State

The state of Vermont (from French vert mont, "green mountain") in the north-eastern United States, between New York State and New Hampshire, extends from the valley of Lake Champlain (125 mi. long) in the north-west to the Connecticut River, which forms its eastern boundary. Between them are the Green Mountains that give the state its name – a range in the northern Appalachians, striking from north to south, which reaches its highest point in Mount Mansfield (4393 ft). The cool temperate climate, with heavy snow in the mountains, is continental in character. Almost two-thirds of the state is covered with mixed forests.

History In 1609, during a French campaign against the Iroquois, Samuel de Champlain discovered the lake in north-western Vermont that was later named after him. The first American settlers established themselves in the area in 1724. In 1777 Vermont ratified its first constitution – the first constitution of an American state to ban slavery. On March 4th 1791 it joined the Union as the 14th state (the first "non-founding" state).

Economy Industrial production in Vermont is concentrated mainly on engineering, the manufacture of electronic parts, foodstuffs, woodworking and papermaking. Agriculture (dairy farming, fruit, potatoes and fodder plants) is practised mainly in the river valleys and the Lake Champlain depression. One of the favourite souvenirs brought back from Vermont by visitors is maple syrup.

Tourism is an important source of income, particularly in the mountain regions.

The little town of Bennington lies in the extreme south-west of Vermont. The Bennington Battle Monument commemorates a battle during the War of Independence. Other features of interest are a number of handsome 18th c. buildings and the Bennington Museum (pictures).

Bennington

Burlington (pop. 38,000), the largest town in Vermont and the seat of a university, lies in a beautiful setting on the shores of Lake Champlain. The lively town centre offers excellent shopping facilities (for example in the historic Church St. Marketplace). Other features of interest are a branch of the Vermont State Craft Center, the Discovery Museum for children and young people and the memorial museum for the folk hero Ethan Allen.

★Burlington

Shelburne, 3 mi. south of Burlington, is well worth a visit for the sake of the Shelburne Museum alone. This large and unusual open-air museum is a reconstruction of an old village with all its buildings and services, including a railroad station and a paddle steamer. And if that is not enough, insight into rural life and practices can be gleaned at Shelburne Farms.

★Shelburne

493

Virginia

Killington

The village of Killington, to the west of Rutland, has developed in recent years into one of the largest skiing centres in the southern Green Mountains. The main pistes are on the slopes of Killington Peak and Pico Peak.

Manchester

Manchester, in southern Vermont, is a popular holiday resort (walking in summer and skiing in winter). Anglers should visit the American Museum of Fly Fishing.

Middlebury

19 mi. south of Burlington is Middlebury, which has preserved an attractive old town centre. Features of interest are two small museums on the history of the town, in which the writer Robert Frost figures large; also and in particular, the Vermont State Craft Center. The Sheldon Museum has curiosities from all over North America.

Montpelier

Montpelier is the smallest state capital in the United States, with a population of just under 10,000. Features of interest are the State House, the Vermont Museum (history of the state) and the Kent Museum (local life and lifestyle).

St Johnsbury

In St Johnsbury, the largest township in rural north-eastern Vermont, the famous Vermont maple syrup can be bought from the factory. The Fairbanks Museum of Natural Sciences and Planetarium offers visitors an excursion into the natural history of Vermont – and the universe. St Johnsbury Athenaem is a gem, with superlative wood panels; also a display of photographs by Albert Bierstadt.

Stowe

The attractive old village of Stowe, beautifully situated at the foot of Vermont's highest hill, Mount Mansfield (4393 ft is now the state's leading winter sports centre.

Woodstock

The idyllic village of Woodstock, situated on US 4 between Rutland and White River Junction, attracts many visitors with its old-world beauty. On the northern outskirts of the village is Billings Farm and Museum, which re-creates everyday life on the farm around 1900.

Virginia (State)   K–N 42–50

Area: 40,815 sq.mi.
Population: 6,676,000
Capital: Richmond
Popular name: Old Dominion

Virginia (named after Elizabeth I, the Virgin Queen), one of the 13 founding states, lies on the middle Atlantic coast of the United States. Here the Atlantic, in the form of Chesapeake Bay, advances deep into the mainland, whose rugged coastline is indented by the broad estuaries of the Potomac, Rappahannock, York and James Rivers. To the west the landscape merges into the gently undulating Piedmont Plateau, which in turn rises gradually into the Blue Ridge Mountains. Beyond this range of hills are the valleys of Virginia, including the beautiful Shenandoah Valley. Virginia has an oceanic climate with warm summers.

History Virginia, which was the scene of the first permanent British settlement in North America (Jamestown, founded in 1607) and joined the Union as the tenth state on June 25th 1788, played a unique role in the history of the United States. The great leaders of the independence movement – Patrick Henry, George Washington, Thomas Jefferson, George Mason and James Madison – all came from Virginia, and the Declaration of Independence, the Bill of Rights and the Constitution were written here. But Virginia was also a centre of the movement for secession. Jefferson Davis, President of the Confederation, and the southern General Robert E. Lee also came from Virginia; almost half of all the battles and skirmishes of the Civil War were fought within the state; and finally the surrender of the Confederation was signed here on April 8th 1865.

Economy Virginia's principal industrial products are textiles, automobiles and automobile parts, and electrical and electronic apparatus. Shipbuilding plays a major part in the Norfolk/Portsmouth/ Hampton/Newport News conurbation. The most important elements in the state's economy, however, are commerce and the services sector – largely because of the numerous government departments round the federal capital, Washington, DC. The main crops grown on the Piedmont Plateau are tobacco, soya beans and peanuts; apples are grown on both sides of the Blue Ridge Mountains, where there is also a productive dairy farming industry. For the tourist Virginia offers a great variety of historic towns and sites.

In Appomattox Court House, near the little town of that name in western Virginia, on April 9th 1865, the northern General Ulysses S. Grant and the Confederate leader General Robert E. Lee negotiated the surrender of the southern army and thus ended the Civil War.

Appomattox Court House National Historic Park

The Blue Ridge Parkway winds its way through the states of Virginia and North Carolina along the Blue Ridge Mountains, the southern outliers of the Appalachians, for a distance of 469 mi. This tourist route (maximum speed 45 mph) begins at Rockfish Gap (milepost 0), on the south side of Shenandoah National Park (see entry), and ends on the edge of the Great Smoky Mountains (see entry), in Cherokee territory. All along the route there are overwhelming views of the dense forests with their variety of wild life and of the valley below; some signs of human settlement can also be seen, such as Mabry Mill (milepost 176). For those with time at their disposal there is magnificent walking on waymarked trails along the way.

★Blue Ridge Parkway

Amid the gentle hills of central Virginia is the town of Charlottesville, founded in 1762, the development of which was much influenced by Thomas Jefferson (see Famous People), third President of the United States, who was born near here.
The University of Virginia was founded by Jefferson in 1819, and its red-brick buildings were designed by him. Among students here was Edgar Allan Poe (see Famous People), whose room (No. 13 in the West Building) can be visited.

Charlottesville

One of the finest country houses in the United States (featured on the reverse side of the five-cent coin) is Jefferson's villa of **★★Monticello**. He himself designed the Palladian-style mansion, beautifully situated on a hill, and continued altering and improving it over a period of forty years, from 1768 to 1809. The guided tour through the house shows the versatile genius of its owner, who eased the tasks of domestic life by a variety of inventions. To the rear of the house are the gardens, also designed by Jefferson. Below the gardens is the family cemetery, still in use, in which an obelisk marks Thomas Jefferson's grave.

A short distance from Monticello is **Ash Lawn Highland**, the country house of James Monroe (1758–1831), fifth President of the United States. It too was designed by Thomas Jefferson. There are guided tours of the house.

Virginia

Chesapeake Bay Bridge

The eastern shore of Chesapeake Bay is linked with the Norfolk area by a gigantic feat of engineering, the 17.6 mi. long Chesapeake Bay Bridge and Tunnel.

Colonial National Historical Park

The Colonial Historical Parkway runs along the coast of Virginia, linking three places that played important roles in the history of the United States, namely Yorktown, to Williamsburg and Jamestown.

Yorktown

The victory of Washington's American and French force over Cornwallis's British troops at Yorktown on October 9th–17th 1781 ended the American revolutionary wars. In the Yorktown Victory Center an exhibition of relics of the battle (including Washington's tent) and a film show prepare visitors for a tour of the battlefield.

★★Colonial Williamsburg

One of the most interesting sites in Virginia is Colonial Williamsburg. The town, founded in 1633, was capital of the colony at one time. Its great charm lies not only in the 88 restored and over 50 reconstructed 18th c. buildings but also because it is a living museum, whose "inhabitants", wearing period costume, go about their daily business as cobblers, smiths, barbers, printers, shopkeepers, innkeepers and so on. The handsomest and most historic buildings are the Capitol (1705) and the Governor's Palace (1720). Outside the historic centre is the College of William and Mary (founded 1693), with the oldest academic building in the United States, the Wren Building (1695–9).

If you merely want to stroll about the streets of Colonial Williamsburg (best access on the east side, on North Henry St.) without going into any of the buildings, there is no charge. For admission to the buildings it is necessary to buy a (fairly expensive) ticket at the Visitor Center, which is open daily 8am–8pm.

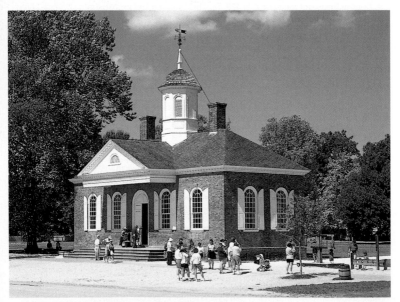

In the Court of Justice of Colonial Williamsburg court sessions are still taking place today – but only for tourists

At the west end of the Colonial Parkway is Jamestown, the oldest British settlement on North American soil. It was established on Jamestown Island on May 13th 1607 by Captain John Smith. Not much is left of the original settlement apart from the foundations of the church tower (1639), the churchyard (probably the oldest British churchyard in North America) and the outlines of a few other buildings.

Jamestown

In the Jamestown Settlement are a re-creation of a Powhatan Indian village and replicas of the three ships that brought the settlers from England.

A memorial stone commemorates Pocahontas (c. 1595–1617), the daughter of an Indian chief who married John Rolfe and contributed to the reconciliation between Indians and Europeans. There is also a very interesting reconstruction of a 17th c. glassblower's workshop, in which glasses are made on old models.

Anyone with a liking for amusement park thrills can enjoy a double helping at Busch Gardens (with the "Alpengeist" super roller coaster) and Water Country, both within a few miles of Williamsburg. Visitor's tastes are also catered for at the Anheuser Busch Brewery.

Busch Gardens

Mary Washington, George Washington's mother, lived and died in Fredericksburg, on the Rappahannock River, and James Monroe, fifth President of the United States, also lived here for some time; they are commemorated in Mary Washington House and the James Monroe Museum. Between December 1862 and May 1864 the four fiercest battles of the Civil War were fought in the surrounding area. The battlefields are part of the Fredericksburg and Spotsylvania National Military Park.

Fredericksburg

George Washington was born in 1732 on the estate of **Popes Creek**, on the banks of the Potomac (east of Fredericksburg on VA 3). The house in which he was born no longer exists, but his life story is vividly presented in an 18th c. farmhouse.

On a tongue of land between the York and James Rivers is Hampton, founded in 1610 – the oldest British foundation in the United States that has remained continuously occupied. Features of particular interest are the Virginia Air and Space Center (aircraft, Apollo 12 capsule), St John's Church (1728; liturgical vessels of 1618) and Fort Monroe (where Jefferson Davis, President of the Confederation, was confined after the Civil War), with the Casemate Museum, in which the first naval battle between steam-powered armourclads (the Northern "Monitor" and the Southern "Virginia", formerly the "Merrimac"), fought during the Civil War in Hampton Roads, between Hampton and Norfolk, is fully documented.

Hampton

Lexington, in the Shenandoah valley, has a long and distinguished military tradition, its Virginia Military Institute having been founded in 1839 (women were first admitted in 1996). Robert E. Lee is buried on the campus of the Washington and Lee University.

Lexington

South of Lexington the US 11 goes over the **Natural Bridge**, an almost 230 ft high natural rock arch formed by erosion.

Norfolk, which is linked with Hampton by a massive bridge and tunnel structure over the Hampton Roads, is one of the most important ports on the eastern seaboard and the largest naval base in the world (bus tours, Apr.–Oct., starting from Tour and Information Office; harbour cruises). Also of interest is the large Naval Museum – and, as a reminder there's more to life than things naval, the Chrysler Museum, with an exhibition not of cars but excellent paintings.

Norfolk

East of the town is the start of **Virginia Beach**, a very popular and hence crowded seaside resort. The Virginia Marine Science Museum at the southern end explores the climate, sea floor and fauna of the coast.

Other places of interest

Alexandria, Arlington, Mount Vernon (see Washington, DC), Richmond, Shenandoah National Park (see entries).

Washington (State)   A–D 1–9

Area: 68,140 sq. mi.
Population: 5,447,000
Capital: Olympia
Popular name: Evergreen State

Washington State, in the extreme north-west of the United States, is divided by the Cascade Range into two differ-ent climatic zones – a wetter western half, with the Coast Range, and a drier eastern half, with the shallow Puget Sound. Numerous snow-covered volcanic peaks, including Mount Rainier (14,410 ft), dominate the Cascade Range, which is flanked on the east by the Columbia Basin and on the north-east by the mighty Rockies. The mountains are covered by forests of spruce and Douglas fir, while the vegetation of the Columbia Plateau is of prairie type.

History The coastal region and the Columbia River were first explored by Spanish and American seamen towards the end of the 18th c. A British captain, John Vancouver, built the fort that bears his name and thus laid the foundations of the profitable fur trade. After the settlement of a dispute between Britain and the United States over the line of the frontier the territory was for a time under joint British-American admin-istration and was finally assigned to the United States in 1848. It was given its present boundaries when Idaho was hived off in 1863, and was admitted to the Union as the 42nd state on November 11th 1889.

Economy The main branches of the manufacturing sector are the aero-space industries (Boeing, in Seattle), foodstuffs, shipbuilding and alu-minium production. The state's agriculture specialises in the growing of wheat, hops, fruit and vegetables and in dairy farming. Thanks to the cool California Current with its abundance of fish the state has a thriving fishing industry. Tourism is concentrated on the Mount Rainier, Olympic and North Cascades National Parks and on the Pacific beaches. The fjord landscape of Puget Sound is particularly attractive.

★Grand Coulee Dam

The 551 ft high Grand Coulee Dam in the north-east of Washington State is the largest cement structure in the United States. It dams the Columbia River at a point where an obstruction created by ice action during the previous glacial period forced the river into a new course, diverting it across the plateau to the south. Some 18,000 years ago the river broke back through the barrier and, within the space of a few weeks, with almost unimaginable power, cut a deep canyon, the Grand Coulee. At first following construction of the dam in the 1940s the canyon was dry, but now it carries water from Roosevelt Lake. At the end of Banks Lake near Coulee City there is an almost 3 mi. long, 394 ft high escarpment known as Dry Falls, over which the river at one time plunged.

Long Beach Peninsula

North of the mouth of the Columbia River a small peninsula separates Willapa Bay from the open Pacific. This sparsely inhabited tongue of land, almost 30 mi. long, is home to great numbers of sea birds, which can be watched in the Leadbetter State Park on the northern tip. At Long Beach itself there is a small amount of beach activity; Oysterville, though, did once live up to its name, oysters having been farmed there.

The eruption of Mount St Helens, in the south-west of Washington State, on May 18th 1980 made headlines around the world. A cloud of ash rose 13 mi. into the air, almost 150 sq. mi. of forest were destroyed, houses were overwhelmed by masses of water and mud, and 57 people lost their lives. The mountain itself lost 1300 ft in height, and in place of its summit there is now a crater over 2000 ft deep, down into which it is possible to look from the Johnston Ridge Observatory. In the area around the volcano, which was declared a National Monument in 1982, visitors are given a unique demonstration of the destructive power of the eruption and can observe the gradual return of animal and plant life. The eruption and its effects are explained in the Information Center in Seaquest State Park.

★★Mount St Helens National Volcanic Monument

The North Cascades are one of the most unspoiled tracts of country in the United States. Anglers, walkers and nature lovers are all well catered for in the North Cascades National Park on the Canadian border. A drive through the National Park on the WA 20 is rewarded with some fantastic views. Anyone wanting to experience highlights like Ross Lake at close quarters however must don their walking boots.

★North Cascades National Park

Starting at the south end of the Park and extending many miles southeastwards, **Lake Chelan** is a paradise for fishing and watersports.

The main features of interest in Olympia, the state capital, situated on Puget Sound, are the State Capitol and the State Museum. The town also has a number of attractive parks.

Olympia

Spokane, in the centre of a farming area, lies in the east of the state, on the border with Idaho. Features of interest are the Cheney Cowles Museum (local history) and the Riverfront Park boasting a hand-carved roundabout made in 1909. There are a number of wineries that offer wine tastings, and there is skiing on Mount Spokane.

Spokane

In the south-eastern corner of the state is Walla Walla, an old Indian hunting ground and later a fur trading fort and a pioneer town. Here Dr Marcus Whitman, the first white settler in the northwest and the only doctor on the Oregon Trail, established himself in 1836. On the site of his house are a memorial and a museum.

Walla Walla

The gorge of Diablo River in the North Cascades National Park

Mount Rainier National Park, Olympic National Park, Seattle (see
entries).

★★Washington, DC   L 48

District of Columbia
Altitude: 0–410 ft
Population: 543,000 (District of Columbia: 607,000)

Roughly half way down the Atlantic coast of North America, at the junction of the Anacostia and Potomac Rivers, is Washington, DC (District of
Columbia), federal capital of the United States, situated on the left bank
of the Potomac. The city is the central element in a conurbation with a
population of 2 million which also includes five counties in Maryland
and five in Virginia, in which the hundreds of thousands of federal
employees live. Almost 70 per cent of the inhabitants of Washington are
African–Americans, who live mainly in the south-western, south-eastern
and north-eastern quadrants of the city, while the north-western quadrant is mainly occupied by whites. Behind the sumptuous façade of
Washington, within a short distance of the Capitol, is another world of
poverty and unemployment.

The city was founded and built for one purpose alone, to provide an
independent place for the work of government. The site selected, 100 mi.
above the outflow of the Potomac into Chesapeake Bay, has a climate
that does not make work particularly agreeable in summer, when it is so
hot and sultry that most of the staff take off their jackets except when
they are working in their air-conditioned offices. Accordingly the best
times for a visit to Washington are spring and autumn.

Washington, DC strikes visitors as an untypical American city, for
there are no skyscrapers, which indeed are prohibited by law. The townscape of Washington is one of classical buildings, some of them giant
size, laid out along the avenues of enormous width that have earned
Washington the name of the "city of magnificent distances". Most of the
20 million people who visit Washington annually are Americans anxious
to see the incarnation of American democracy in stone and the sites that
are so familiar to them from schooldays and television. Foreign visitors
may be surprised to discover how freely accessible – though strictly controlled – even such sensitive areas of government as the Capitol are.
They will also find an abundance of museums, some of which are
among the most important of their kind in the world.

Capital Washington, DC is the seat of Congress (the Senate and the
House of Representatives) and of the President of the United States.
Over 350,000 people – from drivers to the White House Chief of Staff –
are employed by the Administration, and tens of thousands more work
in various national and international organisations (the World Bank, the
Organisation of American States, the International Monetary Fund)
based in Washington, as lobbyists or in various services dependent on
government.

Washington has little industry, but there are in the city, in addition to
five universities, various research institutes and laboratories concerned
with electronics, space travel and armament projects, so that
Washington's population has the highest percentage of qualified
researchers of any American city. The city's second most important
source of revenue – after the work of government – is tourism.

Culture is represented in Washington by theatres like the National
Theatre and orchestras like the National Symphony Orchestra, housed

A prominent landmark: the Washington Monument ▶

in the extensive John F. Kennedy Center for the Performing Arts. More important, and perhaps of more interest to visitors, are the city's numerous museums, headed by the National Gallery and the Smithsonian Institution. Washington also has the National Archives and the Library of Congress, the largest library in the world. Nor should the culinary world be forgotten: the city's eating places range from the hamburger stand by way of a variety of foreign cuisines to gourmet French restaurants. Nightlife is centred on Georgetown and Adams Morgan, where the best shopping streets are too.

History After breaking away from Britain in 1776 the young United States had at first no capital and in consequence Congress met in eight different places. In 1789 New York became the capital, but a year later gave place to Philadelphia. Congress then passed the Residence Act, which provided for the establishment of a 10 mi. square Federal District responsible only to Congress, and authorised President George Washington to select a site for the new capital. Washington chose an area on the Potomac River near his country house of Mount Vernon and commissioned Major Pierre-Charles L'Enfant (1754–1825), an officer of French origin who had been dismissed for insubordination, to prepare a plan.

L'Enfant's plan provided for two commanding buildings as "poles" of

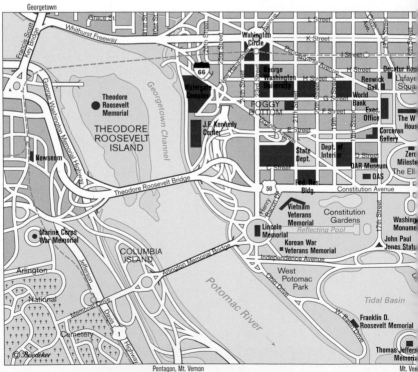

the layout, the Congress House (Capitol) and the Presidential Palace (White House), to be linked by a wide avenue. By 1800 the Presidential Palace and the Capitol were so far advanced that Congress was able to meet and President John Adams to take up residence in the new buildings in August. Washington suffered a severe setback, however, in 1814, during the British–American war, when British troops took the city and burned down the Capitol and the White House. For many years the new capital was to remain a wish rather than a reality, and Virginia was able to take back the land that it had made over on the right bank of the Potomac.

It was only after the Civil War and the influx of tens of thousands of former slaves that fresh stimulus was given to the development of the capital, mainly due to the energy of Alexander "Boss" Shepherd, and L'Enfant's plans were brought out again. The Washington Memorial, which had been begun in 1848, was completed in 1884, and the much derided city, less than half finished, gradually became the imposing capital of the United States. The appointment in 1901 of the MacMillan Commission on the development of Washington, an Act of 1915 that laid down limits on the height of buildings, the Public Building Act of 1926 (which provided for the construction of magnificent new government buildings), the influx of government officials during the two world wars, the restoration of Pennsylvania Avenue during the Presidency of John F.

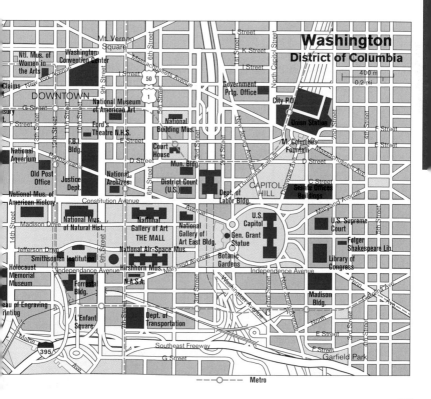

Kennedy and the opening of the Metrorail system in 1976 were further milestones in the development of the city. Since 1961 citizens of Washington have been able to take part in the election of the President.

Today the District faces immense problems; there is insufficient money in the coffers even to repair all the holes in the roads, the infrastructure suffers, the crime rate is one of the highest in the United States. By confining themselves to the magnificent government quarter, and to Georgetown, Foggy Bottom or Adams Morgan, visitors though, scarcely notice any crisis.

Sights

The **townscape** of Washington today largely reflects L'Enfant's ideas. The Capitol and the White House are set in a network of streets intersecting at right angles, across which cut thirteen diagonal avenues named after the thirteen founding states. From the Capitol four streets radiate to the points of the compass, dividing the city into four quadrants – North-west (NW), North-east (NE), South-west (SW) and South-east (SE). The north–south streets are numbered, the east–west streets named after the letters of the alphabet. A special position is occupied by the wide Mall running between Capitol Hill and the Lincoln Memorial, which was designed to open up the layout of the capital.

The principal tourist sights lie almost exclusively in the north-western quadrant, along the Mall and in the immediately surrounding area, and can be seen on foot. The three other quadrants are of little interest and are areas not without danger, certainly not to be visited after dark.

Capitol Hill

★★Capitol

At the east end of the Mall, commandingly situated on the 100 ft high Capitol Hill, is the United States Capitol, seat of the House of Representatives and the Senate. The first building erected by William

Principal Floor

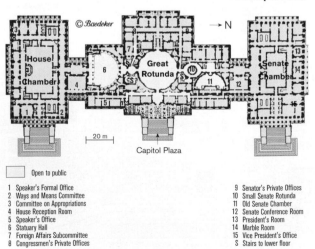

Capitol Plaza

| | Open to public |

1 Speaker's Formal Office
2 Ways and Means Committee
3 Committee on Appropriations
4 House Reception Room
5 Speaker's Office
6 Statuary Hall
7 Foreign Affairs Subcommittee
8 Congressmen's Private Offices

9 Senator's Private Offices
10 Small Senate Rotunda
11 Old Senate Chamber
12 Senate Conference Room
13 President's Room
14 Marble Room
15 Vice President's Office
S Stairs to lower floor

Thornton between 1793 and 1812, the present Senate Wing, was burned down by the British in 1814. Reconstruction was carried out in several stages: the central block was rebuilt by Latrobe and Bulfinch in 1829, following Thornton's plans; the side wings and the 270 ft high dome, modelled on the dome of St Peter's in Rome and crowned by an allegory of Freedom, were built between 1851 and 1865 to the design of Thomas Walter; and finally in 1958–62 the main façade, in front of which each President takes the oath, was enlarged. The Capitol faces east, since it was originally thought that the city would develop in that direction. As a result the Capitol turns its back on the main part of the present city – though it is perhaps some compensation that there is a splendid marble terrace on the rear front that affords a marvellous view of the Mall. Open daily 9am–4.30pm, Easter–Labor Day to 8pm; tours every half-hour from the Rotunda.

The **interior** of the Capitol is as busy as an antheap, swarming with Congressmen, lobbyists, security officers and tourists. The entrance on the main floor leads through heavy bronze doors with scenes from the life of Columbus into the Rotunda, under the great cast-iron dome with a ceiling painting of the Apotheosis of Washington (by Constantino Brumidi, 1865). On the walls are huge paintings of scenes from the history of North America. On the south side of the Rotunda is the former Chamber of the House of Representatives, since 1864 the National Hall of Statuary, in which each state has the right to set up statues of two of its leading citizens (some now displayed on the lower floor).

On the north side of the central Rotunda is the small Senate Rotunda, leading into the finely restored Old Senate Chamber in which the Senate met from 1810 to 1859, followed until 1935 by the Supreme Court. Spiral staircases lead down to the lower floor, on which are an interesting exhibition on the history of the Capitol and the old Chamber of the Supreme Court.

On the eastern end of the Mall stands the Capitol

505

★Library of
Congress

Beyond the gardens on the main front of the Capitol is the Thomas Jefferson Building, the main building of the Library of Congress, which was modelled on the Paris Opera House. The library is the largest in the world, with some 90 million volumes. Among its principal treasures are one of the three surviving complete Gutenberg Bibles and Thomas Jefferson's manuscript draft of the Declaration of Independence (illustration, p. 67). The guided tours of the Library show visitors these and other rarities, as well as the magnificent rooms (daily except Sun. 11.30am, 1, 2.30 and 4pm).

Folger
Shakespeare
Library

Fans of Shakespeare should not forgo a visit to the Folger Shakespeare Library, behind the library of Congress. It possesses the world's largest collection of Shakespeariana and has a permanent exhibition.

Supreme Court

On the north side of the Library of Congress is the Supreme Court of the United States (illustration, p. 50). Designed by Cass Gilbert in the form of an ancient temple, this gleaming white building, built between 1929 and 1935, contains the large courtroom in which the nine judges of the Supreme Court hold their sessions.

Union Station

A short walk north along 1st Street is the huge Union Station of 1908, the concourse of which has been converted into an exclusive shopping and restaurant arcade.

National Postal
Museum

In the adjoining City Post Office is the National Postal Museum, opened in 1993.

East Mall

The eastern half of the Mall, between 15th and 1st Streets, is flanked by

The National Museum of Natural History

a number of museums of outstanding interest. Open daily 10am–5.30pm; admission free.

Washington's youngest museum is the National Holocaust Memorial Museum, opened in 1993 and mainly privately financed, which lies just off the south side of the Mall on 14th Street. In this lavishly designed building the history of the extermination of European Jews by Nazi Germany is impressively – and depressingly – documented. On four floors into which no daylight enters, using the latest methods of presentation, are displayed a great range of original items and other documentation following the development of the Holocaust from the Nazi seizure of power in 1933 and the first measures of discrimination against Jews to planned mass murder and the liberation of the death camps by the Allies. In their tour of the museum visitors enter one of the goods wagons in which so many people were transported to Auschwitz or Treblinka and the high room known as the Stetl whose walls are covered with portraits and family groups of an exterminated Jewish community in Poland. At the end of the route is a light room, intended for meditation and reflection, in which burns an eternal flame.

★★National Holocaust Memorial Museum

Adjoining the Holocaust Museum is the Bureau of Engraving and Printing, the federal printing office in which banknotes, stamps and state documents are printed (guided tours daily 2pm, or by appointment in morning until noon).

Bureau of Engraving and Printing

Most of the museums along the Mall belong to the Smithsonian Institution, founded in 1846 by the bequest of a British scientist, James Smithson (1765–1829). A total of 14 museums in Washington, together with the Zoo, are run by the Smithsonian, whose headquarters (and an Information Center) are in the Castle, a striking building of 1856 in the style of a Norman castle on the south side of the Mall.

Smithsonian Institution

To the right of the main front is the Freer Gallery of Art (reopened in 1993), with a collection of outstanding works of art from Asia and the Far East, together with 19th and 20th American art, including an excellent collection of Whistler.

★Freer Gallery

On the south side of the garden is the Arthur M. Sackler Gallery, whose underground rooms supplement the Freer Gallery with another fine collection of Asian art, including a notable collection of jade.

★Arthur M. Sackler Gallery

The National Museum of African Art, also underground, is devoted to the art of Africa south of the Sahara.

★National Museum of African Art

To the left of the Castle is the Arts and Industries Building, which contains reconstructed exhibits and displays (including the steam engine "Jupiter" and various impressively large engines and drive mechanisms) from the Philadelphia World's Fair of 1876 marking the 100th anniversary of the United States.

Arts and Industries Building

The adjoining Hirshhorn Museum is notable for the striking architecture (by Gordon Bunshaft) of its circular main building, the "Doughnut of the Mall", as well as for its fine collection of modern European and American art (Picasso, Miró, Archipenko, Mondrian, Hopper, Max Weber, Pop Art). The Sculpture Garden has a number of works by Rodin.

★Hirshhorn Museum

One of the most popular museums of all is the huge National Air and Space Museum. The main entrance hall displays a series of milestones in the history of air and space travel, all originals: the Wright brothers' "Kitty Hawk Flyer", Lindbergh's "Spirit of St Louis", the X 1 (the first supersonic aircraft), the X 15 (the fastest aircraft of all time), the Apollo 11 command module, a piece of genuine moon rock and, another sort of

★★National Air and Space Museum

The Air Transportation Hall in the National Air and Space Museum

milestone, the fuselage of the "Enola Gay", the B 29 that dropped the world's first atom bomb on Hiroshima.

The other rooms and galleries are devoted to a variety of themes, including the history of civil aviation (with some very fine original aircraft), the pioneers of flight (Lilienthal's glider, Amelia Earhart's Lockheed Vega), military aviation (First and Second World Wars, aircraft carrier) and space travel (the Apollo lunar module, astronauts' clothing, a walk-in model of Skylab). In addition to the large number of original aircraft there are film shows, recordings, diagrams and displays of all kinds.

The newest room has as its motto "What next, Columbus?" and is concerned with future research in space and on earth. The Albert Einstein Planetarium introduces visitors to the wonders of the universe, and the Langley Theater displays films on a huge five-storey-high screen.

★★National
Gallery of Art

On the north side of the East Mall, opposite the Air and Space Museum, rises the white dome of the National Gallery of Art, one of the world's largest and finest art galleries. It does not belong to the Smithsonian Institution. Open Mon.–Sat. 10am–5pm, Sun. 11am–6pm.

This sumptuous marble building houses works by masters of the 13th to the 19th c., including Leonardo da Vinci ("Ginevra de' Benci", 1474), Raphael ("Madonna Alba", c. 1510), Titian ("Doge Andrea Gritti", 1534–40), van Eyck ("Annunciation", 1435), Dürer ("Portrait of a Priest", c. 1516), Grünewald ("Crucifixion", c. 1510), Rembrandt (more works than in the Rijksmuseum in Amsterdam), Vermeer ("Woman by Gold Cradle", 1664), El Greco ("Laocoon", 1610), Watteau ("Italian Actors", c. 1720), Cézanne ("Pot of Flowers", c. 1876) and many more. American painting is represented by Whistler ("The White Girl", 1862), John Singer Sargent ("Repose", 1911) and many others.

The East Building (by I.M. Pei, 1978) is devoted to 20th c. art, with works by Matisse, Picasso, Miró, Kandinsky, Max Ernst, Mark Rothko.

To the east of the National Gallery is the large National Museum of Natural History, which presents all aspects of natural history on its two floors. Among the most notable exhibits are a huge stuffed African elephant, a large model of a blue whale, skeletons of saurians, an insect zoo and – the pride of the mineralogy department – the famous and legendary Hope Diamond.

★National Museum of Natural History

The last museum on the north side of the Mall is the National Museum of American History. The ground floor is devoted to science and technology, including the automobile industry (Model T Ford) and the development of the oil industry. The second floor (European-style first floor) deals with the life and development of the United States, with exhibits that cover a wide range, including the original Star Spangled Banner of 1814 from Fort Henry, George Washington's false teeth and the dresses of First Ladies. The third floor covers a great variety of subjects, including military history and American elections.

★National Museum of American

West Mall

The city's dominant landmark, the Washington Monument, stands at the near end of the West Mall, which is laid out in gardens. This 555 ft high obelisk of Maryland marble, built to the design of Robert Mills in two phases (1848–55 and 1876–88), is a fitting memorial to George Washington, "father of the nation". A lift (or a flight of 898 steps) takes visitors up to the observation platform at a height of 500 ft, from which there are superb views of the capital and the surrounding area (no tickets required 8pm–midnight). Open daily 9am–5pm, Apr.–Labor Day to midnight.

★★Washington Monument

To the west of the Washington Memorial, at the far end of the Reflecting Pool, in which the obelisk is beautifully mirrored, is the Lincoln Memorial, which stands at the end of the Mall. It was designed by Henry Bacon on the model of the Parthenon in Athens and completed in 1922. The interior is dominated by a 20 ft high seated figure (by Chester French) of Lincoln, looking rather sternly past the Washington Monument towards the Capitol. On the walls are extracts from Lincoln's most celebrated speeches.

★Lincoln Memorial

Leaving the Lincoln Memorial and turning left, we come to the Vietnam Veterans Memorial, at the entrance to which is a realistic piece of bronze sculpture, "Three Servicemen". This simple but impressive memorial, designed by a 21-year-old architectural student, Abraham Lincoln Memorial Maya Ying Lin, in 1982 and completed in 1984, commemorates the Americans who died in the Vietnam War. On a 500 ft long wall faced with marble slabs are inscribed in chronological order the names of the 58,156 American citizens who were killed or reported missing in Vietnam between 1959 and 1975.

★Vietnam Veterans Memorial

Erected in 1995, the memorial honours the more than 54,000 Americans who lost their lives in the Korean War. Seen to the right of the Lincoln Memorial, it comprises 19 sculptures of personnel from all sections of the armed forces, together with more than 2500 photographs of participants etched into a granite wall.

Korean War Veterans Memorial

South of the Reflecting Pool and the Washington Monument lies the Tiday Basin. It is surrounded by Japanese cherry trees, whose flowering each year is marked with a celebratory festival.

Tidal Basin

509

Franklin D.
Roosevelt
Memorial

The Vietnam Veterans Memorial

On the west side of the Tidal Basin stands Washington's most recent memorial to a president, in this case Franklin D. Roosevelt. The likeness of the legendary leader, shown seated, was from a photograph taken at the Yalta Conference.

Jefferson
Memorial

Beyond the large Tidal Basin, is the Jefferson Memorial, a circular building reminiscent of the Pantheon in Rome that was erected in 1943 on the 200th anniversary of the birth of Thomas Jefferson, one of the authors of the Declaration of Independence.

White House area

★★White House

On Pennsylvania Avenue, to the north of the Washington Monument, is the White House, the official residence of the President. As with the Capitol, the best-known aspect of the White House, familiar from many television reports, is the rear front: the main façade is on the far side, facing Lafayette Square. The White House, with two main storeys, was originally built by James Hoban in 1792, and after being burned down by British forces in 1814 was rebuilt in 1818. On the guided tours visitors do not see a great deal of the interior – a few small rooms in period styles, the East Room, the Ballroom, the State Dining Room and the entrance hall: the rooms where government policy is made, such as the Oval Office, are not open to the public.

Tickets for the guided tour are available from 7.30am at the **White House Visitor Center** in the Eclipse (corner of 15th and E Sts.). They specify the exact time at which visitors should join the queue at the visitors' entrance. It is essential to obtain tickets very early in the day as visiting times are limited (10am to noon). Tickets are only issued on the day and once the allocation is exhausted the ticket desk closes.

Lafayette Square

At the corners of Lafayette Square, in front of the entrance to the White House, are statues of four heroes of the Revolution who came from Europe to aid the American cause: Friedrich Wilhelm von Steuben (1730–94), Tadeusz Kósciuszko (1746–1817), the Marquis de Lafayette (1757–1843) and the Comte de Rochambeau (1725–1807). In the centre of the square is an equestrian statue of Andrew Jackson, seventh American President (1767–1845).

At the north-east corner of Lafayette Square is Decatur House (1818–19), and on the north side is St John's Church (1816), the "President's church".

Treasury Building

On the east side of the White House grounds is the neoclassical Treasury Building (by Robert Mills, 1838–42).

South-west of the White House, on 17th Street, are the headquarters of the Daughters of the American Revolution, an association of women belonging to the families of well-known revolutionary heroes founded in 1890, with 33 rooms in 17th, 18th and 19th c. styles.

Daughters of the American Revolution

To the north is the Corcoran Gallery of Art, with an excellent collection of American and European art, including works by Frederic Edwin Church and Albert Bierstadt as well as by Rembrandt and Degas.

★Corcoran Gallery of Art

Still further north is one of the most striking old government buildings in Washington, the Old Executive Building, erected in 1871–88 to house the State Department and the Army and Navy Departments. It is now occupied by White House offices.

Old Executive Building

To the north of the Old Executive Building is the Renwick Gallery, Washington's oldest art gallery. It is now devoted to American (including Indian) art.

Renwick Gallery

Downtown Washington

The triangular area to the north of the Mall that is bounded by Pennsylvania Avenue, Constitution Avenue and 15th Street is known as the Federal Triangle because of the numerous government agencies in this area. The most recent addition is the massive J. Edgar Hoover Building, headquarters of the legendary FBI (Federal Bureau of Investigation) and home of the notorious G-men ("government's men"). There are guided tours on which visitors can see a variety of items from the rich history of crime in the United States. Open Mon.–Fri. 8.45am–4.15pm.

Federal Triangle

The handsome rear front of the White House

511

At the east angle of the Federal Triangle, opposite the National Gallery, are the **National Archives**, which display the "charters of freedom", the icons of American democracy: the Declaration of Independence, two pages (the preamble and the signatures) of the Constitution and the Bill of Rights.

The northern boundary of the Federal Triangle, **Pennsylvania Avenue**, runs diagonally from the Capitol by way of the spacious Freedom Plaza to the White House. The replanning of the avenue began in the time of President Kennedy. Its most striking feature is the Old Post Office, a massive granite structure built in 1889 that after thorough renovation has been converted into a shopping and restaurant arcade.

★Ford's Theatre

At 511 10th Street NW is Ford's Theatre (opened in 1863), in which President Lincoln was shot during a performance by John Wilkes Booth on April 14th 1865, five days after the surrender of the southern states. Performances are still regularly given in the theatre, in which Lincoln's box is preserved as it was on the evening of his murder. Open daily 9am–5pm.
The Lincoln Museum commemorates the murder. Lincoln died in Peterson House, opposite the theatre.

★National
Museum
of Women in the
Arts

North of Ford's Theatre and east of the large Washington Convention Center, is the National Museum of Women in the Arts (1250 New York Ave. NW), which is devoted exclusively to the work of women artists from the 16th c. to the present day, from Indian pottery by way of 19th c. portraits to modern sculpture.

★National Portrait
Gallery

In the north-east of downtown Washington, housed in the old Patent Office Building, is the National Portrait Gallery (8th and F Sts.; run by the Smithsonian Institution), with a very fine collection of portraits of great Americans. In the same complex is the **National Museum of American Art**, with a large collection that includes works by the famous painter of Indian life George Catlin, Frederic Remington, Whistler and John Singer Sargent.

National Building
Museum

To the east of these two galleries, on the north side of Judiciary Square, is the massive brick Pension Building, built in 1887 to house the department responsible for paying war veterans' pensions. One of the veterans, General Sherman, thought that the worst thing about it was that it couldn't burn down. The building now houses a museum on the history of American architecture.

MCI Center

Situated between the Portrait Gallery and Building Museum is the MCI Center. Opened in 1997, it is a major venue for concerts and sporting events (basketball, ice hockey) as well as housing the National Sports Gallery and a large interactive exhibition on technology and the natural world.

Other sights

Foggy Bottom

Foggy Bottom, the area to the west of the White House extending to the Potomac, was once the site of a German settlement called Hamburg. It is now occupied by government buildings and, round Washington Circle, the campus of George Washington University. After Georgetown, Foggy Bottom is one of the most attractive restaurant and shopping districts in the city.

Octagon

South-west of the White House, on New York Avenue, is the Octagon, a finely appointed house built in 1798–1800 that in spite of its name has only six sides. After the burning of the White House in 1814 President James Madison made this his official residence.

Behind the 1960s façade of the State Department (23rd and C/D Sts.) are concealed the very elegant and finely furnished 18th c. Diplomatic Reception Rooms.

State Department

The focal point of Washington's cultural life, on the banks of the Potomac, is the John F. Kennedy Center for the Performing Arts (1971), with an opera house, a concert hall, three theatres and a movie house.

John F. Kennedy Center

To the north of the John F. Kennedy Center is the Watergate Complex, infamously associated with the late President Nixon. Within the complex are restaurants, a hotel and a marina.

Watergate Complex

The Dupont Circle district north of Foggy Bottom is home to yet another premier art collection. The Phillips Collection (1600 21st St.) brings together works by lesser-known artists such as A.G. Dove and J. Martin (who enjoyed Duncan Phillip's patronage), with those of celebrated masters including El Greco, Cézanne, Renoir, Bonnard, Klee and Mondrian.

★Phillips Collection

This district adjoins Dupont Circle to the north. Around Columbia Road there are boutiques to catch the eye during the day and a large choice of restaurants for an evening meal. Washington Zoo is situated next to Adams Morgan.

Adams Morgan

Further west, towering on the highest point in the city, stands the massive Washington National Cathedral on which construction work continued from 1907 to 1990. A lift goes up to the observation platform from which the view of the city can be enjoyed.

Washington National Cathedral

Surroundings

Beyond the Potomac in the state of Virginia, reached by way of the Arlington Memorial Bridge, is Arlington, with the **National Cemetery** of the United States, which can be visited either on foot or by minibus. The Visitor Center has an exhibition on the history of the cemetery, which was established – on land belonging to the Custis and Lee families that was occupied by Union troops during the Civil War – as a burial place for citizens of the United States, particularly soldiers, who had deserved well of their country. Most visitors will find their way past the endless rows of white headstones to the grave of John F. Kennedy and his wife Jacqueline, and that of his brother Robert close by.

★★Arlington

Above the cemetery is Arlington House, now the Robert E. Lee Memorial, from the terrace of which there is a fantastic view of Washington. Here in April 1861 Lee was faced with the choice between taking command of the Confederate army and remaining loyal to the Union. He opted for the south and left Arlington House, which was occupied in May 1861 by Union forces. From the hill on which the house stands it is a short distance to another hill on which is the Tomb of the Unknown Soldier. The changing of the very smart guard takes place every half hour in summer and every hour in winter, accompanied by a consummate display of arms drill.

Located in the Rosslyn district north of the cemetery is the truly amazing Newseum. Opened in 1997 and spread over three storeys, it traces the evolution of the news media. Visitors can play at being a television reporter, see the very latest televised news from all over the world and have daily access to the first pages of 70 American and foreign newspapers. Open Wed.–Mon. 10am–5pm.

★Newseum

To the south of the Arlington Cemetery is the famous Pentagon, headquarters of the Department of Defense and the United States armed forces (guided tours every half-hour Mon.–Fri. 9.30am–3.30pm).

Pentagon

The cemetery of Arlington

★Alexandria

South of Washington on the George Washington Memorial Parkway is Alexandria, a port town founded by Scottish merchants and laid out on a regular grid plan. It has many fine old buildings, including the Stabler-Leadbeater Apothecary of 1792 (107 S Fairfax St.), Carlyle House of 1752 (121 N Fairfax St.) and the house in which Robert E. Lee spent his early years (607 Oronoco St.). The finest church is Christ Church (Cameron and N Washington Sts.), in which the seats occupied by Washington and Lee are marked with silver plaques.

★★Mount Vernon

From Alexandria the George Washington Memorial Parkway continues south through green residential suburbs along the Potomac to Mount Vernon, Washington's beautifully situated country house. The property had belonged to the family since 1674, and when George Washington took it over in 1752 he planned the present house, in which he lived with his family in 1759–74, 1783–9 and from 1797 until his death. The Georgian-style house has 19 rooms filled with mementoes of the first President. Among the rooms shown to visitors are Washington's library and study and the room in which he died. Near the house are the kitchen, the secretary's house, stables and workshops. From the terrace there is a marvellous view of the Potomac.

In the spacious grounds are the family vault in which George Washington and his wife Martha are buried and the cemetery of his slaves. In the Orangery is a memorial exhibition with many items that belonged to the family. Open Apr.–Aug. daily 8am–5pm; Nov.–Feb. 9am–4pm; Mar., Sep., Oct. 9am–3pm.

Hillwood Museum

Those interested in Russian art will find an excursion to Hillwood, north of Washington, well worth while. Here can be seen the collection assembled in 1937–8 by Marjorie Post Davies, wife of the American ambassador to the Soviet Union – the largest collection of Russian art outside

Russia, including Fabergé eggs that once belonged to the Tsar, icons and furniture.

In the opposite direction, south-east, on the Anacostia River, lies the **Navy Yard**, with the Navy Museum, the Marine Corps Historical Museum and a decommissioned destroyer, the "USS Barry". This part of the city is not without its dangers, so it is definitely advisable to take a taxi.

Georgetown, north-west of Washington, must be visited twice – during the day and at night. By day, visitors will be surprised to discover what an idyllic place much of this old town, founded in 1751 and incorporated in Washington in 1871, still remains. Walking through the streets of the little town, the seat of Georgetown University, they will come across attractive old houses dating from the early days of the United States, like Cox Row and Smith Row in N Street, where the Kennedys once lived, or find a secluded spot on the quiet Ohio and Chesapeake Canal, on which they can take a trip in a narrow boat. In the evening Georgetown – particularly in M Street and Wisconsin Avenue – offers a profusion of excellent restaurants, bars and music clubs with a lively night life.

★★Georgetown

Dumbarton Oaks (1703 32nd St. NW) is a sumptuous mansion built in 1800–1 by Senator William Dowsey. Surrounded by marvellous gardens, it now houses a unique collection of Byzantine art, including over 20,000 coins, and a collection of pre-Columbian artefacts. The Music Room has hosted concerts and recitals by leading musicians, among them Igor Stravinsky.

George Washington enjoyed the views on the Potomac in peace from the veranda of Mount Vernon

Washington has its quiet spots too: here the Ohio and Shesapeake Canal in Georgetown

★Waterton-Glacier International Peace Park   A 11/12

State: Montana
Area: 1788 sq. mi.
Established: 1895 (Waterton), 1910 (Glacier)

Glacier National Park in the United States and Waterton Lakes National Park in Canada have joined since 1932 in the Waterton-Glacier International Peace Park. Although separated by the frontier, the two National Parks form a geographical unit, taking in a relatively unspoiled part of the Rocky Mountains in the area of the Continental Divide (Watershed). This grandiose mountain region, the "crown of the continent", is for the most part an empty wilderness with steep rock faces, more than 50 glaciers and over 200 lakes. Here, in the Lewis and Livingston Ranges, the Rockies have a markedly alpine character. The highest peak is Mount Cleveland (10,470 ft). The landscape of this region was transformed during the ice ages.

Information The two constituent parks are administered separately. Visitor centres for the Glacier National Park – much the bigger of the two – are located in St Mary (at the east entrance), Apgar (at the west entrance) and at the Logan Pass. The Waterton Visitors Centre is on Highway 5 inside the Park. Both Parks have hotels, motels and sufficient camping sites. Anyone who can afford it should spend at least one night at the luxurious Prince of Wales Hotel on the Canadian side. The fantastic setting alone is worth the expense.

The park is open throughout the year, though many roads are closed from November to April. Most visitors come in the summer months, but it is also very pleasant in autumn (until mid-Oct.).

The **flora and fauna** of both National Parks are still largely intact. During the short summer when the snow has gone the alpine meadows are a magnificent sea of blossom. The marshland areas (water birches, willows, reeds) are a refuge for beavers, mink, muskrats, ducks, geese and even elk. The narrow prairie zone in the east is the home of coyotes and bison. In the mountain valleys and in the pine and Douglas fir forests on the lower slopes there are red deer, black bears and pumas. The subalpine zone, the most important plants in which are spruce. Engelmann fir, larch, white pine, bear grass and gentian, is the habitat of grizzly bears, and higher up, in the mountain pine zone, there are marmots, Rocky Mountain goats and bighorn sheep. In recent years wolves have been heard howling again in remote mountain valleys. Prior to setting out on foot it is essential to take instruction from the park rangers about what to do in the event of meeting a bear.

The 50 mi. long road (completed in 1932) from St Mary over the Logan Pass (7747 ft) to West Glacier is rated one of the most beautiful mountain roads in North America. Narrow and with many bends, it is normally closed to vehicles over 8 ft wide and 29 ft long. From St Mary the road follows the north side of St Mary Lake (coming in 3 mi., on the south side, to the Triple Divide, the watershed between three drainage systems – to the Pacific, the North Atlantic and the Gulf of Mexico). The view of St Mary Lake and the surrounding peaks from the wide bend beyond Rising Sun is probably the most photographed scene in the park. From the lake the road climbs steeply to the Logan Pass, with the Logan Pass Visitor Center, above which tower the imposing peaks of Reynolds (9128 ft) and Clements Mountain (8773 ft).

★Going-to-the-Sun Road

From the Visitor Center a **nature trail** (1¼ mi.) runs through the Hanging Gardens, which are gay with colour during the short summer season. In

A grand mountain landscape in the Waterton-Glacier International Peace Park

this alpine ecosystem marmots and Rocky Mountain goats can some-times be observed. There are rewarding mountain hikes to the Hidden Lake and the Granite Park Chalet. The section of the road between Logan Pass and McDonald Valley is a masterpiece of engineering, winding its way down into the valley in a series of sharp bends and a large loop.

9 mi. before St Mary, at Babb, a road (closed in winter) goes off to the **Many Glacier**, a region of great scenic beauty in which Rocky Mountain goats and black bears can be seen. On the shores of Swiftcurrent Lake is the Many Glacier Hotel (built in 1914), from which there are a variety of walks and climbs – to the Grinnell Glacier, the Granite Park area, Iceberg Lake, on whose shimmering green water there are ice floes even in the height of summer, and the Red Rock Falls.

★Chief Mountain International Highway

The American and Canadian National Parks are linked by the Chief Mountain International Highway (Hwy 6/SR 17), opened in 1935, which runs partly through the Canadian park and partly through the Blackfoot Indian Reservation, with fine views of the Waterton Valley. Prominently visible is Chief Mountain (9065 ft), a holy mountain to the Indians. From the frontier there is a view of Mount Cleveland, the highest peak in Glacier National Park.

West Virginia (State)   J–M 43–47

Area: 24,180 sq. mi.
Population: 1,826,000
Capital: Charleston
Popular name: Mountain State

West Virginia's popular name, the Mountain State, charac-terises its topography. Two-thirds of its area is occupied by the Alleghenies in the east of the state, which fall down westward into the Allegheny Plateau, with the Ohio River. Its tourist attractions, therefore, lie in a variety of outdoor activities – hiking, fishing, rafting, winter sports. Some parts of West Virginia evoke an America straight from a 1930s or 40s movie.

History The local Indians lived undisturbed by white settlers until 1670. The state of West Virginia came into being when the western counties of Virginia, which did not wish to secede from the Union in 1860, broke away from the rest of the state. It was admitted to the Union on June 20th 1863 as the 35th state.

Economy West Virginia's industrial base is mining (particularly coal mining), but this branch of the economy has been badly hit by rational-isation measures and falling demand, and West Virginia is now one of the poorest states in the United States. Other traditional activities are agriculture (fruit, grain), woodworking and glass-blowing. Tourism is now the state's main source of revenue however, and in particular winter sports. At least compared with the Rocky Mountains, ski resorts in the Alleghenies such as Winterplace, Snowshoe, Canaan Valley and Timberline, are neither overcrowded nor overcommercialised.

Berkeley Springs

Berkeley Springs, in the extreme north-eastern tip of the state, is the oldest spa in the United States. George Washington established its repu-tation by his frequent visits to the springs. Today quite a lot still goes on here centred on the spa, though of a quiet sort.

Charleston, the state capital, lies on the Kanawha River. The Capitol with its golden dome ranks as one of the finest in the United States. In the adjoining Cultural Center, the State Museum documents West Virginia's history. In the evening people congregate at the Riverfront.

Charleston

On October 16th 1859 the fanatical opponent of slavery John Brown (see Famous People) attacked the Union arsenal at Harpers Ferry, in the north-eastern tip of West Virginia, with the idea of establishing a base there and gathering former slaves round him. American troops commanded by Robert E. Lee overwhelmed his small force, and Brown was carried off to Charles Town and hanged in December 1859. His story is retold in the John Brown Wax Museum in Harpers Ferry and the Jefferson County Courthouse in Charlestown.

★Harpers Ferry National Historical Park

The marvellous lonely mountain world of the Alleghenies can be experienced in the Monongahela National Forest (reached by way of US 33). Here both the Potomac and the Ohio rise. There are breathtaking views from the Seneca Rocks.

★Monongahela National Forest

White Sulphur Springs, at the south end of the forest, is an elegant spa, whose warm springs were already known to the Indians.

In **Lewisburg**, a little to the west of White Sulphur Springs, gas lamps burning in the streets at night lend an air of the 18th c.

In the hill country in the south-west of the state, the New River has cut through the rock to form a gorge up to 1000 ft deep. The 52 mi. long stretch of the river between Hinton and Fayetteville, with a whole series of rapids, offers good walking and rafting and magnificent views. The gorge is spanned by the longest steel arch in the world.

★New River Gorge National Park

★★White Sands National Monument   R 19

State: New Mexico
Area: 230 sq. mi.
Established: 1933

The White Sands National Monument, a unique area of gleaming white gypsum sand dunes, lies in the Tularosa basin, a mountainous northern offshoot of the Chihuahua Desert (Visitors Centre 16 mi. south-west of Alamogordo). Despite its location in the middle of a vast missile testing range, this extraordinary landscape of constantly shifting, wind-blown dunes up to 60 ft high, must be a highlight of any visit to New Mexico.

Origins Some 250 million years ago this area was occupied by a shallow sea on the bottom of which gypsum was deposited. The present hills were created by the upthrusting and folding of marine sediments. A large section of the earth's crust fell in and the Tularosa basin was formed. In the hills round the basin the deposits of gypsum were dissolved by rain, and water with a high gypsum content gathered in the Tularosa basin, which had no outlet, and formed a lake, now known as Lake Lucero. The lake repeatedly dried out and the gypsum crystallised; and finally small grains of gypsum were blown by wind into the remarkable dunes we see today.

The 16 mi. Heart of Sands Drive goes deep into the midst of the gypsum dunes. The experience is breathtaking. It is a strange feeling climbing one of the dunes and finding that, despite the searing heat, the sand stays relatively cool.

★Heart of Sands Drive

Wisconsin

White and and prickly shrubs, White Sands

All the life forms characteristic of the gypsum desert can be seen on the **Big Dune Nature Trail**, which branches off some 3 mi. from the start of the Drive. Caution: keep to the trail. It is easy to become disorientated when walking aming the dunes.

Surroundings

White Sands Missile Range

The White Sands National Monument is surrounded on all sides by the White Sands Missile Range, on which captured German missiles were tested during the Second World War. On July 16th 1945 the very first atomic bomb was exploded on the remote Trinity Site. The range area is only open to the public twice a year (Apr. Oct; information tel. (505) 6781134).

Alamogordo

Alamogordo's history is intimately bound up with that of the first atomic bomb and it remains one of the most important armament and space technology research and production centres in the United States. The town's main attraction is the International Space Hall of Fame, where the story of American manned space flight from "Mercury" to "Apollo" is recorded.

Wisconsin (State)   C–G 33–39

Area: 56,155 sq. mi.
Population: 5,160,000
Capital: Madison
Popular name: Badger State

Wisconsin (from the Indian term ouisconsin, "where the waters meet") lies in the northern Middle West, bounded by Lake Michigan, Lake Superior and the Mississippi. The scarped and lake-strewn region to the north, part of the Canadian Shield, gives place further south to the sandy Central Lowlands. In this continental climate influenced by the Great Lakes, with its long

cold winters and short warm summers, forest is the natural vegetation form, and more than 40 per cent of the state's area is still forested. The steppe country of the Central Lowlands is now for the most part under cultivation.

History The first European to reach the region round Green Bay on Lake Michigan, then occupied by Algonquin tribes, was a Frenchman, Jean Nicolet, in 1634. The area was under French control until 1763, when it passed to Britain. Although after 1783, following the Revolution, it officially belonged to the United States, it continued to be controlled by Britain until the outbreak of the British–American War in 1812. The mass immigration of farmers and miners began after the Black Hawk War ended the conflict with the Indians. Wisconsin ratified the Constitution on May 29th 1848 as the 30th state, and during the Civil War remained loyal to the Union.

Economy The predominant form of agriculture is dairy farming: Wisconsin, the "Dairy State", supplies fully 45 per cent of the country's production of cheese. Other agricultural products are maize, potatoes and other vegetables, and tobacco. Logging and mining (zinc, copper, iron) supply important raw materials for industry (mainly engineering, metalworking, papermaking and brewing). There is a particular concentration of industry on the shores of Lake Michigan and in the Milwaukee area. Wisconsin has a flourishing tourist industry, centred mainly on water sports on Lakes Michigan and Superior, winter sports (particularly on Mount Telemark, near Cable) and the summer holiday trade.

These 22 picturesque little islands in Lake Superior can be reached by ferry from Bayfield (south of which on the WI 13 there is a pretty beach). A museum on Madeline Island traces the history of the local Indians and fur traders. Glorious sunsets can be seen at the appropriately named Sunset Bay. **Apostle Islands**

Door County, a peninsula projecting into Lake Michigan to the north of Milwaukee (see entry), is a land of apple and cherry trees, trout streams and romantic strands well supplied with marinas and diving schools. A tasty local speciality is a fish stew of trout, onions and potatoes. One of the most stimulating ways of exploring this delightful stretch of country is by bicycle. **★Door County**

The chief places on the peninsula are Sturgeon Bay (with the Door Couny Museum) and Baileys Harbor on Lake Michigan, Ephraim (originally founded by Moravian Brethren from Norway), and Egg Harbor and Ellison Bay on Green Bay. From Ellison Bay there is a ferry to Washington Island (originally settled by Icelanders), with Rock Island State Park.

Hayward, in north-western Wisconsin, is the scene of the lumberjacks' world championship, held annually on the last weekend in July. **Hayward**

The Land o' Lakes is the region between Boulder Junction, Eagle River **★Land o' Lakes**

Madison

The state capital, Madison, lies in southern Wisconsin. More interesting, perhaps, than the Capitol and the State Museum are the many buildings designed by Frank Lloyd Wright (see Famous People), including the headquarters of the First Unitarian Society and several private houses.

Baraboo

Baraboo (37 mi. north-west) will be of interest particularly to circus enthusiasts. This is the home of the world-famous Ringling Brothers' Circus, whose winter quarters open their doors to the public in summer as the Circus World Museum.

Wisconsin Dells

A few miles north of Baraboo is Wisconsin Dells, the chief place in the state's most popular holiday region, centred on the gorges carved out by the Wisconsin River. Cruises on the river, good hiking country and a number of amusement parks are among the attractions that draw tens of thousands of visitors every year.

Taliesin

Anyone familiar with the work of Frank Lloyd Wright will almost certainly know of Taliesin, his house and architectural school situated at the farming community of Spring Green about 35 mi. west of Madison.

Milwaukee

See entry

★Oshkosh

The town of Oshkosh on Lake Winnebago, north-west of Milwaukee, would be unknown to fame but for the world's largest meet of aviators held here annually in July/August. The total number of aircraft that have attended these meets is now over 10,000. There is an Air Adventure Museum in the town.

Prairie du Chien

Prairie du Chien, in the far south-west of Wisconsin at the confluence of the Wisconsin and Mississippi Rivers, was founded in 1673 by the Frenchman Marquette and Joliet and was for a long time an important fur trading post. Today it is a river station for the big Mississippi paddle steamers, with the added attraction of the Kickapoo Indian Caverns and the Villa Louis Mansion, former home of a wealthy fur trader.

Wyoming (State)   E–H 14–21

Area: 90,085 sq. mi.
Population: 481,000
Capital: Cheyenne
Popular names: Equality State, Cowboy State

The thinly populated state of Wyoming (from an Indian term meaning "change between mountain and valley") lies in the north-western United States.

The eastern part of the state, which has a climate of continental type, is occupied by the dry grassland, interspersed with areas of badlands, of the High Plains, at altitudes of between 3300 ft and 5900 ft. To the north-east the Black Hills (6660 ft) and the spectacular Devil's Tower rise out of the prairies. The heart of the state is the desert-like Wyoming Basin, a depression some 250 mi. wide lying at an average altitude of 6500 ft that is surrounded by various ranges of the Rocky Mountains (Bighorn

Mountains, Wind River Range). In the extreme north-west of the state is the Yellowstone Plateau, with numerous post-volcanic features (including spectacular geysers). To the south is the beautiful Teton Range, which is of almost Alpine character. The highest point in the state is the Gannett Peak (13,806 ft) in the Wind River Range, its lowest point on the Belle Fourche River (3101 ft) in the extreme north-east.

History The first Europeans to reach the territory of Wyoming, then occupied by Arapaho and Shoshone Indians, were French prospectors, who came here in the middle of the 18th c. Subsequently a number of French settlements were established. A hundred years later thousands of settlers travelling north-west passed through Wyoming on the Oregon Trail. The Union Pacific Railroad reached the area in 1867, and this led to the establishment of larger settlements and large ranches run by the "cattle barons". Violent clashes between the local Indians and the new white settlers continued into the 1890s. In 1868 Wyoming was officially established as a United States territory. In 1869 the women of Wyoming were given the vote (the first in the United States to receive it). On July 10th 1890 Wyoming became the 44th state of the Union. The first oil well in the state had been drilled in 1884, and by 1908 it experienced its first oil boom.

Economy Wyoming's coal, oil and natural gas reserves are among the richest in the world. Some 90 per cent of the soda needed by American chemical and glass industries comes from Wyoming. Stock farming plays an important part in the state's agricultural economy (1.3 million cattle and huge numbers of sheep). More than 5 million visitors are attracted to Wyoming every year by its spectacular National Parks (Yellowstone, Grand Teton) and the lure of the Wild West (e.g. in Buffalo Bill's town of Cody).

In northern Wyoming are the beautiful Bighorn Mountains (13,186 ft). On their eastern slopes are the two little cattle-ranching towns of Buffalo and Sheridan, now tourist centres. For a drive through awe-inspiring mountain scenery, leave Buffalo on US 16, which runs over the Powder River Pass (9666 ft) and then, in Ten Sleep Canyon, through millions of years of the earth's history. The journey ends in Ten Sleep (pop. 400), which still retains something of the atmosphere of the Wild West.

★**Bighorn Mountains**

Casper, on the North Platte River, is now the chief town in an area given up to agriculture and the oil industry. It is named after Lieutenant Caspar Collins, who tried to rescue a group of settlers beset by Indians on the Oregon Trail in 1865. Something of the period lives on in the reconstructed Fort Caspar on the western outskirts of the town.

Casper

Towering above the Sweetwater River about 53 mi. south-west of Casper is the monolithic ★**Independence Rock** on which settlers heading west left their marks for prosperity. A mile further south-west is an impressive natural monument known as Devil's Gate.

The capital of the state of Wyoming, named after the Cheyenne Indians, was founded in 1867 as a station on the Union Pacific Railroad, and two years later became the chief town in the territory of Wyoming. The town was the largest outpost of the United States Cavalry. The town's principal sights are the prominently situated State Capitol, the Wyoming State Museum and the Union Pacific Railroad Depot, a notable example of industrial architecture built in 1886. North-east of the Depot is a Big Boy locomotive, one of the largest steam engines ever built.

★**Cheyenne**

In the north of the town, in Frontier Park (adjoining the rodeo arena), is the interesting **Frontier Days Old West Museum**, with much information

A hands-on experience of the Wild West: in Cody everything tells the tale of Buffalo Bill

about rodeos and a number of the old coaches and wagons in which the first settlers came to the Wild West.

In the Frontier Days festival, held annually in the last week in July, the Wild West comes to life again. Hundreds of thousands of spectators come to watch spectacular rodeos, cowboy shows, chuckwagon races, parades and a mock battle between Sioux Indians and the United States Cavalry.

On the western outskirts of the town (west of Frontier Park) is the extensive area occupied by the **F.E. Warren Air Force Base**. The site was originally occupied by a 19th c. fort. During the Second World War it was a prisoner of war camp. Since 1958 it has been an intercontinental ballistic missile base. There is an informative Air Base Museum.

★Cody

The little town of Cody, founded by "Buffalo Bill" (Colonel William F. Cody; see Famous People), lies on the western edge of the Bighorn Basin in Wyoming, an area rich in raw materials, where the land begins to rise to the Absaroka Range in the Rockies. It is a good base from which to visit Yellowstone National Park (see entry). The well preserved old town centre, once the domain of cowboys and prospectors, is now crowded, particularly in summer, with tourists anxious to experience something of the atmosphere of the old Wild West.

One of the oldest buildings in the town centre is the Irma Hotel (12th and Sheridan Sts.), built by Buffalo Bill in 1902 for his daughter.

On the west side of the town (West Yellowtone Highway) is the Old Trail Town, with 24 old buildings dating from the 1980s and 90s of the 19th c. that give some impression of Wild West life.

Cody's main sight is the **Buffalo Bill Historical Center** at 720 Sheridan Avenue (variable opening times), a four-part museum complex that gives a lively impression of the history of the Wild West. The Buffalo Bill Museum displays saddles, guns, photographs and other personal possessions of Buffalo Bill. The Cody Fire Arms Museum has the largest collection of hand guns in the world. The Whitney Gallery of Western Art possesses what must be one of the finest collections of pictures on Wild West themes. The Plains Indian Museum contains tepees, implements, weapons, clothing and cult objects of the Prairie Indians.

Close by is the arena for the wild rodeos, held every evening at 8.30pm from the first Saturday in June to the last Saturday in August, in which the best cowboys of the Wild West compete.

Half an hour's drive south of the mining town of Rock Springs is the Flaming Gorge National Recreation Area (water sports, fishing), which extends into the neighbouring state of Utah. The Green River is dammed here.

Flaming Gorge

Two hours' drive north-east of Cheyenne, at the junction of the Laramie River with the North Platte River, is Fort Laramie, founded in 1834 as a fur-trading post. The fort was taken over by the United States Army in 1849 in order to protect the Oregon Trail. Throughout the next 40 years Fort Laramie played a key role in the Indian Wars. From there troops could be sent out against the Indians, and there too treaties were signed with them. In the late 1880s the fort increasingly lost its military import-ance, and finally was abandoned. Some of the buildings are well pre-served or have been restored, including the guardhouse, the cavalry barracks, the bakery and some officers' houses. On some summer weekends, particularly around July 4th, there are "living history" presentations.

Fort Laramie

Just under an hour's drive west of Cheyenne is Laramie, named after a French trapper who was murdered in this area in 1821. A military post was built here in 1866 to protect workers building the transcon-tinental railroad, and two years later the first Union Pacific train reached the town. For a time Laramie was reputedly the "wildest town in the Wild West", frequented by robbers, cattle rustlers, gam-blers, prostitutes and other dubious characters. Violent crime was an everyday matter, and it seemed at times that the life of a steer was worth more than the life of a man. On the other side of the coin, Laramie was the first place in the United States where women were elected to public office. It is also the seat of the University of Wyoming, founded in 1886. The University has a rich Geology Museum (remains of *Tyrannosaurus rex*), an Anthropology Museum and a new American Heritage and Art Museum (architect Antoine Predock). Other features of interest in the town are the Laramie Plains Museum, the Rocky Mountains Herbarium and the Wyoming Territorial Park, with the Territorial Prison in which Butch Cassidy was once confined.

★Laramie

The Medicine Row Mountains west of Laramie were sacred to the Indians. Now they are a popular winter sports area, especially in the vicinity of the Snowy Range.

★Medicine Bow Mountains

Two hours' drive south-east of Cody is the spa of Thermopolis (pop. 5000), founded in 1896, with one of the most abundant hot springs in the western hemisphere (36 gallons per second; 135°F).

Thermopolis

In west central Wyoming is the Wind River Indian Reservation, in which a few thousand Shoshone and Arapaho Indians live. The landscape is patterned by Indian villages, great expanses of pasture – and oil der-

Wind River Indian Reservation

Rodeo: Cowboys and Commercialism

Rodeo: a round up of cattle; a place where cattle are rounded up – this much can be learnt from any dictionary. But what rich imagery the magical word rodeo also invokes: marvellous spectacle, the Wild West, jousting cowboys and big business.

The rodeo of today grew out of the working lives of the "cowpokes", who for a period of some 20 to 25 years at the end of the 19th c., were instrumental in creating the myth of the Wild West. Huge herds of cattle were driven great distances to the railheads in order to supply the eastern United States and Europe with meat. It was a dangerous job, a job for the fearless, a job for those prepared to live rough and to do without. Because it demanded such qualities, it was also a job in which a man could take pride; it was not a job for just anybody. Equally important to the cowboy's self-esteem was the opportunity to demonstrate his prowess, at rounding up and corralling cattle, breaking in horses and wielding the cowhand's tools. Anyone especially good at it could earn himself more than the otherwise starvation wages of 20 to 30 dollars a month.

Rivalry on the range was extended to showpiece confrontations, which in turn attracted spectators. In time such contests took on the character of local festivals. Different "disciplines" emerged, and rules of competition were laid down. In bareback riding the challenge was to stay mounted for at least eight seconds astride a specially selected bucking bronco, typically an unbroken mustang or wild horse. Bull riding operated to the same rules. Calf roping, lassoing and tying up a calf, most closely mirrored the everyday work of the cowhand, testing the speed and coordination of rider and horse.

Though there are still traditional small-time rodeos, the major events have long since become huge, money-spinning spectacles with millions of dollars at stake. Cowboys have turned into rodeo professionals, risking life and limb for megabucks. The horses and bulls continue to be drawn from special breeds, selected and reared with an eye to their combativeness. So now there is a new kind of Western legend – like the 1 ton bull "Bodacious", let loose in the arena 135 times. Only seven riders managed to stay on his back for the statutory 8 seconds; 50 refused even to have a go, while others lasted just two or three what must have seemed very long seconds. They were lucky if they escaped without broken bones.

More than anything else, the real cowboy had to be able to trust his horse,

ricks. The chief place in the reservation is Fort Washakie (headquarters of the Bureau of Indian Affairs), near which are the graves of Washakie, a Shoshone chief whose memory is still revered, and Sacajawea. the Indian girl who acted as a guide to the surveyors Lewis and Clark.

Other places of interest

Badlands National Park, Black Hills (see entries), Grand Teton National Park, Yellowstone National Park (see entries).

his companion of the limitless prairie, his equine friend. The traditional American cowboy horse is a unique animal, very different from its European counterpart, not simply in terms of appearance but specifically in the way it was ridden. Whereas in Europe the requirement was for a hunter or cavalry horse, for riding the American range a horse of immense stamina was needed. It had to be sure-footed, fast and nimble. And to be of use on a cattle ranch, it also had to be a quick learner, the complicated tasks it had to perform necessitating a demanding training. In consequence, certain types of horse were favoured and their qualities refined through breeding. This has resulted in three varieties of Western horse that all have one thing in common: with a good rider in the saddle they have no equal among work animals.

Racing over a distance of quarter of a mile (440 yds), the quarter horse is the fastest horse in the world. It is the most widely distributed of the western breeds, numbering in the region of 2½ million. Appaloosas, tough, quiet, creatures distinguished by their mottled colouring, have much the same qualities as the quarter horse. The other Western horse, the skew-bald Paint Horse, has quarter horse ancestry. Quarter and Paint horses are routinely bred by the American Quarter Horse and American Paint Horse Associations. Appaloosas, on the other hand, are bred by the Nez Percé, a Prairie Indian tribe from the north-west United States.

Quarter horses, Appaloosas and Paint Horses are still very much in evidence at any rodeo worthy of the name. By far the biggest such event worldwide, the Cheyenne Frontier Days, is staged in July every year in Cheyenne, Wyoming. The American Royal Livestock, Horse Show and Rodeo, held in November in Kansas City, Missouri, is also among the leading rodeo events in the United States. At a more homespun level, rodeos large and small take place regularly during the summer months in towns across the cattle-rearing states.

Eight seconds already ...

★★Yellowstone National Park   E 14/15

States: Wyoming, Idaho, Montana
Area: 3457 sq. mi.
Established: 1872

Yellowstone, the oldest National Park in the United States, lies on a basalt plateau (average altitude 6600–8200 ft in the north-western corner of Wyoming, extending a little way into the neighbouring states of Idaho and Montana. The Park is one of the most visited in the United States, and for good reason: where else, after all, is it possible to experience, at such close quarters, phenomena manifesting the powerful forces at work in the earth's interior – geysers, thermal springs, fumaroles and mud volcanoes – while at the same time enjoying scenery of such grandeur and the equally fascinating wildlife.

Information The National Park is open throughout the year, but many roads are closed from November to April. Most visitors come in summer when, as a result, the Grand Loop can reach saturation point and most overnight accommodation is booked. But autumn (until mid Oct.) and late spring, when a lot of young animals are being born, are also good times to visit.

There are five Visitor Centers in the Park and a good supply of overnight accommodation in hotels and camping sites (though in summer advance booking is advisable). Budget accommodation is available in places near the Park entrances, e.g. Gardiner or Cooke City, both in Montana.

Origins There were violent volcanic eruptions in the area now occupied by the Yellowstone National Park some 2 million years ago,

again 1.2 million years ago and finally 600,000 years ago. After the last eruption and the collapse of the crater a huge caldera was formed. The magma chamber (the "hot spot") that brought about these eruptions still generates a great deal of heat, as is shown by innumerable post-volcanic, which, amid constant seething and hissing, shroud the landscape in a thick veil of steam. The continuing

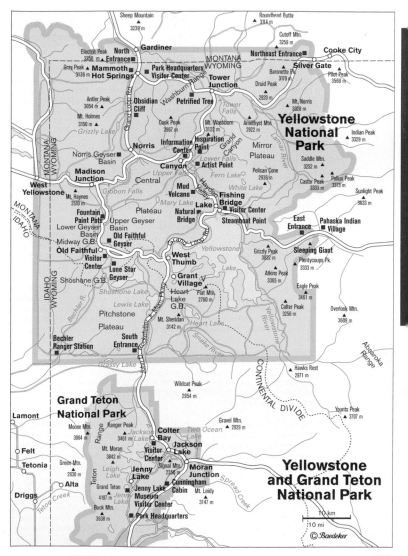

instability of the ground is shown by the frequency of earth tremors in the area.

The forests of Yellowstone had long been familiar territory to the Indians when John Colter led a first expedition here in 1807. The American government recognised the unique nature of the area very early on and in 1872 it was declared a National Park, the first in the United States.

The National Park has a varied range of **flora**, from desertic vegetation at the north entrance to sub-alpine meadows and forests.

There are from time to time devastating forest fires in the National Park, most recently in the summer of 1988, when large areas of forest in the north-western part of the park were destroyed.

Fauna In this relatively intact natural region there is an abundance of wild life. In addition to bison, various species of deer (red deer, wapiti, mule deer), bighorn sheep, beavers and marmots, there are also elk, pronghorn antelopes, black bears, grizzlies and coyotes. In the air swoop ospreys and on water there are pelicans, various species of ducks and geese, and trumpeter swans. The reintroduction of wolves in recent years has had a mixed reception.

Grand Loop Road

The 142 mi. long Grand Loop Road runs round the park in a figure of eight, taking in the most striking of the natural features. The round tour described below starts and finishes at Mammoth Hot Springs, where the National Park offices are located.

Before entering the geyser area you should enquire in the Old Faithful Inn or the Visitor Center at the National Park offices about the times of eruption of the various geysers and should check that the paths are safe to use. You must keep exclusively to the marked paths.

★★Mammoth Hot Springs

On the east flank of Terrace Mountain (8012 ft) are the Mammoth Hot Springs, which have formed magnificent sinter terraces. They consist of ten sinter basins from 35 ft to 200 ft high, ranged in "steps" one above the other. There are some 60 hot springs at temperatures of between 64°F and 165°F. There is a marvellous play of colour in the evening and early morning.

★Norris Geyser Basin

Further south is the very impressive Norris Geyser Basin. The hottest place in this area is the Porcelain Basin (with boardwalk). The Echinus Geyser spouts approximately every hour. Here too is the Steamboat Geyser, the largest in the world, which erupts only very irregularly. It can shoot water up to a height of 425 ft. In the Norris Museum the operation of geysers is explained.

★Lower Geyser Basin

To the south-west is the Lower Geyser Basin, with the Paint Pot Fountain, in which hot reddish mud simmers. A little way south of this, on the Firehole Lake Drive, is the Great Fountain Geyser, which is a magnificent spectacle every 11 hours or so. On the lush green of Fountain Flat bison and deer can be seen grazing, particularly in the early morning and the evening.

Midway Geyser Basin

The most striking feature in the Midway Geyser Basin (boardwalk) is the mighty crater of the Excelsior Geyser, with a flow of 55 gallons of hot water per second. Nearby is the Grand Prismatic Spring (diameter 360 ft), one of the finest hot springs in the Yellowstone National Park.

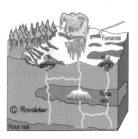

Most of the geysers are in the Upper Geyser Basin, which is only 1 mi. long. A 2 hour trail (boardwalk) through the area takes visitors past Old Faithful, the Giantess Geyser, the Beehive Geyser, the Castle Geyser, the Grand Geyser and fountain basins shimmering in a rainbow of colours.

★★Upper Geyser Basin

On the north edge of the geyser area is the magically beautiful **Morning Glory Pool**, named after the flower of that name.

One of the star attractions of the Yellowstone is the geyser familiarly known as Old Faithful, famed for the regularity with which it used to shoot columns of water up to a height of 115–165 ft – though since the last earthquake it has not been so dependable as before. The intervals between eruptions range between half an hour and two hours (at present about 80 min.); for the approximate times enquire in the Visitor Center or the Old Faithful Inn. The Old Faithful Inn was originally built in log-cabin style in 1904 and has since been several times enlarged. Many famous people have signed the visitors' book.

★★Old Faithful

In the southern half of the National Park, at an altitude of 7737 ft, is Yellowstone Lake (area 137 sq. mi.; depth up to 320 ft. Well stocked with

★Yellowstone Lake

Awsome: the Yellowstone River thunders down into the gorge

fish, it is an angler's paradise. Here too can be seen many species of waterfowl that have become rare elsewhere.

The West Thumb, an offshoot on the west side of Yellowstone Lake, is a water-filled caldera that came into being some 150,000 years ago. On its western edge is the little West Thumb. On the north-west shore of Yellowstone Lake are the little townships of Bridge Bay, Lake Village and Fishing Bridge, with a number of motels, campgrounds and various leisure facilities.

★★Yellowstone
River

Emerging from the lake, the Yellowstone River flows through a quiet valley, with bison grazing on the meadows; then, to the north of Hayden Valley, it plunges over two spectacular waterfalls into a wild and roman- tic canyon.

There is a fascinating walk along the river that introduces visitors to the geology of the region, passing old lava flows and less well known zones of geothermal activity.

A few miles below Fishing Bridge are the striking mud volcanoes of the **Mud Volcano** Area and the simmering Sulphur Caldron. Visitors must take care to stay on the boardwalks.

In **Hayden Valley**, a western side valley of almost genial aspect, a variety of wild life can be observed, including bison, deer and sometimes grizzly bears.

The easily accessible **Upper Falls** on the Yellowstone River drop 110 ft. A few hundred yards lower down the river plunges 310 ft into a gorge with a deafening roar. As a result of chemical reactions in the rhyolite which outcrops here the walls of the gorge shimmer in reddish to yellow tones. There are very fine views of the falls from Lookout Point and Grandview Point on the north side of the valley, near the holiday settle- ment of Canyon Village.

Tower-Roosevelt

On the northern edge of the National Park is the little holiday resort of Tower-Roosevelt (alt. 6270 ft), With Roosevelt Lodge. Notable features are the Tower Fall (130 ft high) and the Petrified Tree. To the south-east is the Specimen Ridge, with the remains of a number of fossil forests superimposed on one another.

★★Yosemite National Park   L/M 6

State: California
Area: 1190 sq. mi.
Established: 1890

The Yosemite National Park in eastern California takes in a section of the western Sierra Nevada that has a particularly rich forest cover and numerous rivers and lakes. Over 4 million visitors a year throng to the most beautiful parts of the park, with its almost vertical granite walls, imposing waterfalls, alpine meadows, mountain lakes, snowfields and giant sequoias.

Information Part of the National Park (the Yosemite Valley) is open throughout the year. The Tioga Road running through the High Sierra is only open in summer (from early Jul.). The best time to visit the park is in spring, when the waterfalls, fed by melt water, are particularly impressive. From June to September the park tends to

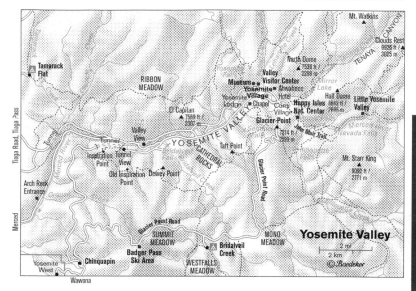

be overcrowded. The Visitor Center is located in the Yosemite Valley. Since the accommodation available within the National Park and immediately outside it is very limited, it is essential to make reservations well in advance – at least a year beforehand in the case of hotels (tel. (219) 2524848) and five months for camping sites (tel. (301) 7221257).

History More than 4000 years ago men were living in the Yosemite Valley, and many years later they were followed by the Miwok and Ahwahneechee tribes. The first Europeans – fur trappers – turned up in the area around 1833. Thereafter there were clashes between the local Indians and gold prospectors. The first whites to reach the Yosemite Valley, in 1851, were members of a military unit pursuing Indians. Although they did not catch the Indians, they reported to the outside world the extraordinary beauty of this valley, which takes its name from the Indian word for the grizzly bear, a native of this area, "u-zu-ma-ta". In 1855 the first large expedition arrived in the valley, and in 1864 President Lincoln signed the Yosemite Agreement transferring the Yosemite Valley and Mariposa Grove to the state of California with an obligation to preserve its natural beauty. The Scottish naturalist John Muir, who visited the Yosemite Valley for the first time four years later, became the leading proponent for the creation of a National Park. When in 1890 the Yosemite National Park was established, the area reverted to federal control. In 1926 the all-weather road to Merced was completed. In January 1997 heavy rain caused severe flooding; Yosemite Village was particularly badly affected as camp sites, huts, trails and small roads were inundated.

The **flora and fauna** of the park are rich and varied. In addition to the giant sequoias there are incense cedars, live oaks, laurels, azaleas, acanthus and rare species of thistle. A variety of animals, including black and brown bears, mule deer, chipmunks and raccoons, are quite frequently to be seen, together with more than 200 species of birds and over two dozen species of reptiles.

Walking The National Park is a splendid place for walkers, not least because the vast majority of visitors venture no further than the Yosemite Valley itself, which represents just 6 per cent of the total area. Anyone planning to walk should be properly equipped and prepared, and should notify the park rangers of their intentions. El Capitán and the Half Dome in the Yosemite Valley are without doubt the two most famous climbs in the whole of California. It was on their rock faces that the technique of free climbing was first tried out and the Alpine scale of difficulty extended beyond grade 6.

Sights

★★Yosemite Valley

The central feature of the National Park is the Yosemite Valley, through which flows the Merced River: a high valley lying at an altitude of around 4265 ft, 8 mi. long and up to 2 mi. wide. Huge granite crags rear up another 4600 ft. 3000 ft above the valley rises El Capitán (7569 ft), the western buttress of the valley. On the other side of the valley are the Three Brothers, Eagle Peak (8530 ft), Sentinel Rock, the two Cathedral Rocks (first climbed only in the 1940s) and the mighty Half Dome (8842 ft), a monolith closing the east end of the valley in the shape of one half of a dome; whether the missing half ever existed is not known.

A breathtaking view of the Yosemite Falls

At the mouth of the valley is the little settlement of **Yosemite Village**, from which there is a free shuttle bus up the valley. Here too are the National Park offices, a Visitor Center and the Yosemite Museum, with an exhibition on the culture of the local Indians and a fine picture gallery. In the Indian Village visitors can see something of the life of the Ahwahneechee Indians.

The renowned Yosemite Falls, half way along the valley, drop down 2425 ft in three stages. Well equipped walkers can cover the 7 mi. round trip to the Upper Falls in half a day. However, the Falls usually dry out between June and October, and other falls in the National Park, such as the Bridal Veil Falls, which in full flow are magically beautiful, are reduced in summer to a meagre trickle.

★Yosemite Falls

2 mi. from the south end of the valley is the (fairly easily accessible) Mariposa Grove with its gigantic redwoods. Here there are some 500 of these giant trees, the most striking of which is the Giant Grizzly. In spite of the fact that its crown has been broken off by the weight of snow this huge tree still stands 210 ft high and has a diameter of 30 ft at the base; and some branches – which start only at a height of 100 ft – have a diameter of 6½ ft. The tree is estimated to be 2700 years old. Less easily accessible are the redwoods in the remoter but highly interesting biotopes of Merced Grove and Tuolumne Grove.

★Mariposa Grove

A climb to Glacier Point (7200 ft) is rewarded by breathtaking views of the peaks in the National Park.

★Glacier Point

To the east of El Capitán and the Yosemite Falls is Indian Canyon. The monumental rock wall on the opposite side is known as the Royal Arches because of the recesses in the rock face. Further east is the Washington Column, a granite pillar over which looms the bare summit of the North Dome (7545 ft). Below this peak the Yosemite Valley divides into the valleys of the Merced River and Tenya Creek, the latter of which flows into the beautifully situated Mirror Lake. In Merced Canyon are two impressive waterfalls, the Vernon Fall and the Nevada Fall.

★Indian Canyon

In contrast to the Yosemite Valley road that runs in a loop from the western edge of the Park, the Tioga Road (CA 120), traversing the Park a little further north, crosses from the west side to the Tioga Pass entrance on the east. This road is only passable in summer, i.e. no earlier than the end of July, and it is essential to enquire in the Park about conditions on the road before setting out. When the road is clear there are exceptional views to be enjoyed and several delightful mountain lakes to be discovered, the loveliest undoubtedly being May Lake, situated approximately 8205 ft above sea level.

Tioga Road

Surroundings

To the east of the National Park, in a beautiful setting, is Mono Lake (alt. 6235 ft; 13 mi. long, 8 mi. across), an alkaline lake of volcanic origin with no outlet, on whose shores many hundreds of thousands of migrant birds find a resting place in spring and autumn. On the south side of the lake are a number of bizarrely shaped limestone sinter pinnacles, formed as a result of variations in water level and geochemical reactions produced by the meeting of alkaline water and fresh spring water containing lime.
    The ecosystem of Mono Lake is in grave danger from the enormous

★**Mono Lake**

water requirements of the Los Angeles conurbation. Several of its tributaries have already been tapped. In recent years the salt content of the water of the lake has been rising dramatically and the water level has been steadily falling.

Mammoth Lakes   The region south-east of the National Park around the town of Mammoth Lakes is one of California's most popular ski areas. Attractions apart from skiing include the basalt columns of the Devil's Postpile, the Rainbow Falls and Mammoth Mountain (cablecar) from the summit of which there are fine views.

★★Zion National Park   M 12/13

State: Utah
Area: 230 sq. mi.
Established: 1919

Zion National Park takes in the imposing canyons of the often tumultuous Virgin River, a tributary of the Colorado River, and its tributaries, which in the course of millions of years have carved their way through

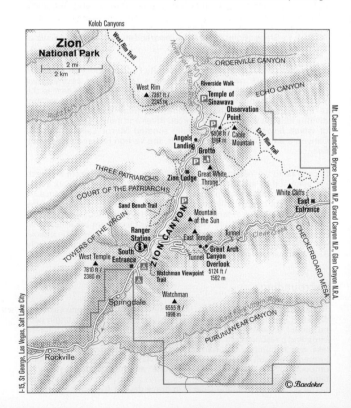

the horizontally bedded sandstones, limestones and slates of the Markagunt plateau, an offshoot of the Colorado Plateau, creating a magnificent landscape of sheer gorges up to 3000 ft deep, mesas (isolated tablelands), rock domes and battlements, in a play of colours ranging from whitish-grey by way of orange and red to deep purple. The predominant colouring of the park is red, in many shades and tones: even the roads are rust red. A number of Indian cultures (Basketmaker, Anasazi, Paiute) have left their traces in Zion Canyon. When the Mormons came here in 1858 they gave the valley and its most striking features the names they now bear, many of them Biblical.

Information The National Park is open throughout the year, but from December to March there are no bus services to the park and no accommodation for visitors. Between May and October temperatures frequently rise above 99°F, and there are often short, violent thunderstorms during the afternoon in July and August. The best times for a visit to the National Park, therefore, are spring and autumn.

The Park is divided into south-eastern Zion Canyon Section, which includes the principal sights, and the north-westerly Kolob Canyons Section, comprising about a third of the total area but still relatively inaccessible to the public. Each section has a visitors' centre. The only places to spend the night inside the Park are several camp sites and the Sion Canyon Lodge on the road through the Park. There are reasonably priced hotels and motels in the small towns near by.

There are guided pony treks from Zion Lodge. Information on these and other activities in the National Park can be obtained from the park offices (see Practical Information, National Parks).

Flora and fauna Ashes, poplars, Douglas firs, spruces, golden aquilegias and maidenhair ferns are only a few of the many species of plants to be found in the National Park. The commonest animals are mule deer, and bighorn sheep are occasionally seen. Small bats flit about in the twilight. Frequent visitors to campgrounds and picnic sites are the comical ground squirrels. Rattlesnakes and cougars, whose main habitat is the Kolob Canyons section, are very rarely seen.

From the south entrance of the National Park at Springdale the park road runs past the Watchman (6546 ft; on right) and the West Temple (7809 ft; on left) and up the deeply indented valley of the Virgin River. A short distance from the entrance are the campgrounds (on right) and the Visitor Center (on left).

★Zion Canyon

The 7½ mi. long Zion Canyon **Scenic Drive** begins after the Zion-Mount Carmel Highway (see below) goes off on the right. On the left are the Sentinel (7156 ft) and the Three Patriarchs (6890 ft), on the right the Mountain of the Sun (6723 ft). Beyond Zion Lodge the road continues up the canyon, passing on the right the Red Arch Mountain (5929 ft) and the Great White Throne (6746 ft) and on the left Angels Landing (5791 ft) and the Organ (5099 ft), to end at the Temple of Sinawava (6014 ft). Open buses take visitors to the main sights on the Zion Canyon Scenic Drive.

The 11 mi. long **Zion-Mount Carmel Highway** goes off on the right at the junction of Pine Creek with the Virgin River, heading for the east entrance to the National Park. It winds its way up the side of Pine Creek Canyon with many sharp bends and then runs through the 1 mi. long (unlighted) Zion Tunnel. Shortly before reaching the east entrance it

In Zion National Park

passes on the right the Checkerboard Mesa, eroded into the chessboard pattern that gives it its name.

Hiking trails At the end of the Watchman Trail (2 mi.) there are fine views of the lower part of Zion Canyon and into Oak Creek Canyon. The Emerald Pools Trail (2 mi.) leads to the Emerald Pools, which are fed by waterfalls. The short Canyon Overlook Trail (1¼ mi.) offers a magnificent prospect of Pine Creek Canyon and the Towers of the Virgin on the west rim of Zion Canyon. The Angels Landing Trail (5 mi.) is an extremely strenuous route. The steep final section up to Angels Landing calls for a good head for heights; but even without climbing up all the way it is a very rewarding hike.

On the Weeping Rock Trail an unusual natural phenomenon can be observed. A nature trail (1¼ mi.) leads to the Weeping Rock, a rock over-hang overgrown with plants known as the Hanging Gardens. Water seeping down through the rock encounters an impervious stratum and emerges from the rock above the plants; the rock thus "weeps". Other rewarding trails are the Gateway to the Narrows Trail (3 mi.), the Sand Bench Trail (3¾ mi.), the Hidden Canyon Trail (2½ mi.) and the East Rim Trail (8 mi.). On the West Rim Trail (27 mi.) a tent should be taken for an overnight halt.

Kolob Canyons

From Highway I 15 the Kolob Canyons Road runs past the Visitor Center in the north-west of the park (closed in winter). An unsurfaced mountain road runs from the township of Virgin (to the west of the National Park) by way of the Kolob Terrace Road to Cedar City (65 mi.). Although scenically magnificent, this road is negotiable only in dry weather and with an all-terrain vehicle.

Hiking Trails The arduous La Verkin Trail starts at Lee Pass at an altitude of 6082 ft and goes round the 8057 ft Timber Top Mountain and 7706 ft Gregory Butte to the Kolob Arch. The massive 79 ft rock arch with a span of 308 ft across a gorge some 328 ft deep, is the largest natural bridge in the world. It appears at its most impressive in the morning sun.

**Practical
Information
from A to Z**

Practical Information from A to Z

Accommodation

The range of accommodation for visitors in the United States is enormous, with many hundreds of thousands of rooms in hotels, motels and other forms of accommodation; and more are being built every year. Much of this accommodation is round the coasts, offering the highest standards of comfort and amenity at correspondingly high prices, but there are plenty of hotels and other establishments in more modest price ranges, though they will usually tend to be further away from bathing beaches and other attractions. Children can stay in their parents' rooms free of charge in most hotels and motels, so find out beforehand about age limits (these can be surprisingly high) and other terms and conditions.

Bed and Breakfast

Bed and Breakfast accommodation in the United States is by no means the type of cheaper option that is customary in Britain and Ireland. Prices usually start at around $70 and can go up to as much as $200. Although the accommodation is a small hotel, often in a renovated heritage building, which has only a few albeit very tastefully appointed rooms. Early booking is necessary since, despite the relatively high prices, this kind of accommodation is very popular.

Other addresses are available from local tourist offices (see Information). For further information about 7000 B & Bs in Canada and the United States contact: The National Network of Reservation Services, Box 4616, Springfield, MA 01101; tel. (1800) 8844288, fax (401) 8474309, www.tnn4bnb.com.

Holiday homes

The range of holiday apartments in the vacation centres of the United States extends from luxury villas with their own landing stage to more modest high-rise apartments with a view of the sea. These condominiums are usually small furnished apartments with fully equipped kitchens and accommodation for three or four people; the minimum length of stay is between 2 and 5 nights. Annually updated lists of properties are available at local and regional tourist offices (see Information).

North American Vacation Homes also have an office in the UK: 32A The Broadway, Haywards Heath, West Sussex RH16 1NJ; tel. (01444) 450034, fax (01444) 441691, www.usahomes.co.uk.

Hotels

Hotels are mostly in the central area of cities and in tourist centres. The larger establishments run courtesy bus services from the nearest airport. In the large hotels there are usually restaurants, coffee shops, snack bars, small shops, beauty parlours, hairdressers and car rental and airline offices.

Resorts

Resorts are luxurious holiday complexes equipped with a wide range of leisure and sports facilities. Often run in the style of country clubs, they

◀ *New York City – the skyline sparkles at night*

have their own bathing beaches, tennis courts, golf courses, horse paddocks, and are usually very expensive.

Motels are geared to the requirements of motorised tourists. They are
usually situated on main roads out of town, have free parking near the rooms
and may sometimes have their own swimming pools and sports facilities.
The standard of service sometimes leaves something to be desired.

Motels

The rate for a double room for one night ranges roughly as follows:

Price categories

Luxury hotels: over $200
Hotels and motels with a high standard of comfort and amenity:
$130–200
Establishments with a good standard of comfort and amenity: $100–150
Value-for-money hotels and motels: $60–100
Modest establishments: $30–80

State taxes may add up to 15 per cent on the cost of a room. There is no
additional charge for children occupying the same room as their parents; for an additional adult the charge will range between $5 and $20.
  Breakfast is not usually included in the price, and there may also be an
additional charge for car parking.
  Many hotels, including luxury hotels, offer weekend rates at considerable reductions.
  Most hotel rooms have their own bath or shower, air-conditioning,
telephone, radio and television. Many hotels, particularly the larger and
more luxurious, have one or more restaurants, with prices related to the
category of the hotel.
  Room keys are normally kept by the guest, not handed in at reception.
All hotels have safes (either at reception or in the room) in which objects
of value can be deposited.

It is advisable to reserve hotel and motel rooms in advance, using the
1800-code toll-free hotlines operated by most hotels; as a rule room
bookings will be taken up until 6pm. Accommodation guides can be
obtained from local tourist information offices (see Information).

Reservation

Hotel and motel chains

Pre-paid accommodation vouchers – at cheaper rates – for some of the
big American hotel chains can be bought direct from companies in
Britain. They can also be acquired – and reservations can be made –
through travel agents. To obtain vouchers for Days Inn, Howard
Johnson, Ramada, Travelodge and Wingate accommodation contact:
Liberty Hotel Pass/TourAmerica Hotel Pass; tel. (01483) 440470, fax
(01483) 451361.

Adam's Mark Hotels: 4442326
Best Western International: 5281234
Budgetel Inns: 4283438
Clarion Hotels & Resorts: 2527466
Comfort Inn: 2285150
Courtyard by Marriott: 3212211
Days Inn: 3252525
Doubletree: 5280444
Econo Lodge: 4466900
Embassy Suites: 3622779
Exel Inn of America: 3568013
Fairfield Inn: 2282800
Fairmont Hotels: 5274727
Four Seasons Hotels & Resorts: 3323442

Toll-free hotlines
(all 1800 code)

Accommodation

Friendship Inn: 4534511
Hampton Inn: 4267866
Hilton Hotels: 4458667
Holiday Inn: 4654329
Howard Johnson: 6544656
Hyatt: 2331234
Inter-Continental: 3270200
La Quinta: 5315900
Loews Hotels: 2356397
Marriott Hotels & Resorts: 2289290
Meridien: 5434300
Motel 6: 4668356
Omni Hotels: 8436664
Quality Inn: 2285151
Radisson: 3333333
Ramada Inn: 2282828
Red Lion Inn: 5478010
Red Roof Inn: 8437663
Renaissance: 4683571
Residence Inn by Marriott: 3313131
The Ritz-Carlton: 2413333
Rodeway Inns: 2282000
Sheraton Hotels & Motor Inns: 3253535
Shilo Inn: 2222244
Super 8 Motels: 8488888
Suisse Chalet: 2581980
TraveLodge & Viscount Hotels: 2553050
Vagabond Inns Inc.: 5221555
West Coast Hotels: 4260670
Westin Hotels & Resorts: 9378461
Wyndham Hotels & Resorts: 8224200

Hotels (selection)

The United States has accommodation of every class and to suit every purse, which is why the following selection only lists hotels and motels in or near cities and visitor attractions covered by entries in this guide. Mostly these are included because their standards, location, atmosphere or service warrant more than an overnight stay. This means they are often on the more expensive side, but some cheaper accommodation that is worth recommending is included as well. The prices are indications of the usual rate for a double room.

Albuquerque

Amberly Suite Hotel
7620 Pan American Freeway NE; tel. (505) 8231300, fax 8232896; 170 r., $100–120, restaurant
This simple but comfortable hotel is a good place for a relatively cheap overnight stay; it is popular with skiers in winter since it is only a few miles from the nearest piste.

Atlanta

Lennox Inn
3387 Lennox Rd.; tel. (404) 2615500, fax 2616140; 174 r., $79–215
Unassuming but cheap and comfortably appointed annex to the grander Terrace Garden Inn in Buckhead, Atlanta's trendy quarter.

Marriott Marquis
265 Peachtree Center Ave.; tel. (404) 5210000, fax 5866299; 1674 r., $220–240, restaurants, bar
Luxury reigns supreme in the hotel with the biggest lobby in the world; the atrium is 48 floors high.

Westin Peachtree Plaza
210 Peachtree St./International Blvd.; tel. (404) 6591400, fax 5897424; 1068 r., $185–205
The 53-storey glass and steel high-rise is America's tallest hotel, with a pool on the roof and waterfalls in the atrium.

Bally's Park Place Casino Hotel
Atlantic City

Park Place; tel. (609) 3402000, fax 3404713; 1870 r., $150, eight restaurants
A night club and many sporting and swimming facilities. Spoilt for choice: either the 1860 Dennis hotel or the modern 37-storey high-rise.

Quality Inn
South Carolina & Pacific Aves.; tel. (609) 3457070, fax 3450633; 200 r., $75–125, restaurant
Among the best places in Atlantic City in terms of value for money.

Days Inn Inner Harbor
Baltimore

100 Hopkins Place; tel. (410) 5761000, fax 5769437; 251 r., $70–150, restaurant
This hotel, with the chain's usual standards, offers good budget accommodation in the Inner Harbor.

Harbor Court Hotel
550 Light St.; tel. (410) 2340550, fax 6595925; 203 r., $300–600, restaurant, café
Some of the spacious rooms in this supremely traditional hotel – with prices to match – have fantastic views of the Inner Harbor; plenty of fitness facilities.

Boston Harbor Hotel
Boston

70 Roves Wharf/Atlantic Ave.; tel. (617) 4397000, fax 3456799; 230 r., $235–385, two restaurants
One of the best places to stay in Boston; ideal location for the waterfront and downtown, fitness club and beauty salon.

Chandler Inn
26 Chandler St.; tel. (617) 4823450, fax 5423428; 56 r., $80–100
Although none too close to Back Bay and with no special facilities the Chandler still has no equal for cleanliness and reliability at these prices.

Copley Square Hotel
47 Huntington Ave.; tel. (617) 5369000, fax 2360351; 143 r., $155–185, three restaurants
Overshadowed by the surrounding mega hotels the smaller Copley Square, which is relatively low priced for Boston, is still outstanding on account of its individually furnished rooms and excellent service.

Fairbanks Inn
Cape Cod

90 Bradford St., Provincetown; tel. (508) 4870386; 13 r., $75–200
The main building dates from 1776 but the rooms in the annex are also stylishly furnished with antiques.

The Masthead
31–41 Commercial St., Provincetown; tel. (508) 4870523, fax 4879251; 8 r., 6 apartments, 4 cottages, $75–200
Solid, no frills but above all very family-friendly accommodation at the tip of Cape Cod.

Anchorage Inn
Charleston

26 Vendue Range; tel. (843) 7238300, fax 7239543; 17 r., $90–180

A rustic atmosphere prevails in this timbered inn converted from an old cotton warehouse dating back to 1840.

Hampton Inn Historic District
345 Meeting St.; tel. (843) 7234000, fax 7223725; 171 r., from $90
New hotel on the edge of the historic district next to the tourist office, pleasing heritage decor and low cost; walking distance from all the sights.

Chicago

The Drake
140 E Walton Place; tel. (312) 7872200, fax 7872549; 535 r., $225–265, three restaurants
One of the most highly recommended places to stay in Chicago; generously furnished rooms, view of the lake and smart ambience.

Motel 6 Chicago Downtown
162 E Ontario St.; tel. (312) 7873580, fax 7871299; 191 r., $90–100
Very cheap, clean and central.

Ohio House Motel
600 N La Salle St.; tel. (312) 9436000, fax 9436063; 50 r., $75–100
Ideal for night owls, this well-kept motel is right in the jazz club and dining quarter.

The Raphael
201 E Delaware Place; tel. (312) 9435000, fax 9439483; 513 r., $240–380, restaurant
European hotel elegance not far from the Magnificent Mile.

Cincinnatti

Best Western Mariemont Inn
6880 Wooster Pike (I 71 Exit 9); tel. (513) 2712100, fax 2711057; 60 r., $60–70
Good, very cheap accommodation in a 1916 Tudor hotel.

Regal Cincinnatti Hotel
150 W 5th St.; tel. (513) 3522100, fax 3522148; 872 r., $130–140
This very large hotel is extremely central and quite close to Fountain Square. Recently renovated, it also has a very good fish restaurant and extensive sports facilities.

Cleveland

Glidden House
1901 Ford Dr.; tel. (216) 2318900, fax 2312130: 62 r., $105–130
Close to Cleveland Garden Center, this 1910 hotel has the stylish decor of its period.

Holiday Inn Lakeside
111 Lakeside Ave.; tel. (216) 2415100, fax 2417437; 370 r., $110, restaurant, sauna
Frill-free accommodation by a lake, very close to Cleveland's biggest attraction, the Rock'n Roll Hall of Fame.

Dallas

Adam's Mark Resort & Hotel
400 N Olive St.; tel. (214) 922800, fax 9220308; 1500 r., $135–155.
Completely renovated and at the some time considerably expanded, the Adam's Mark is on an intersection of the city's subway and skywalk system.

Holiday Inn Aristocrat
1933 Main St.; tel. (214) 6881010, fax 6385215; 172 r., $160–170
This was opened in 1925 as the first Hilton Hotel. Its new owner (since 1992) Holiday Inn has succeeded in retaining the old elegance; individualistic stylishly furnished rooms; fitness centre.

Mansion on Turtle Creek
2821 Turtle Creek Blvd.; tel. (214) 5592100, fax 5284187; 141 r., $290–350
For people who want to stay in one of the best hotels in town: generously appointed rooms, some with panoramic windows, outstanding
restaurant, free limo service to the nearby financial and arts district.

Brown Palace   Denver
321 17th St.; tel. (303) 2973111, fax 3125900; 230 r., $185–205, several
exquisite restaurants (inc. Palace Arms), fitness centre, beauty salon,
boutiques
The venerable grand hotel was opened in 1892 and is listed as a national
monument. The rooms and suites are tastefully furnished in Victorian
and even art-deco style; President Eisenhower often stayed here in the
Fifties.

Loews Giorgio
4150 E Mississippi Ave.; tel. (303) 7829300, fax 7586542; 180 r., $195–295,
excellent restaurant ("Tuscany"), fitness centre
On Cherry Creek just east of downtown Denver, some of the west rooms
in this luxury hotel enjoy wonderful views of the "blue wall" of the Front
Range; the decor of this family-friendly hotel is out and out Italian.

Queen Anne B & B Inn
2147 Tremont Place; tel. (303) 2966666, fax 2962151; 41 r., $75–125
This small and consequently very cosy inn is in two lovingly restored
Victorian houses dating from the 1880s; excellent service – and breakfast!

Westin Hotel   Detroit
Renaissance Center, Jefferson Ave./Randolph St.; tel. (313) 5688000, fax
5688146; $200 plus, restaurant, fitness facilities
The 73-floor Westin is just right for anyone who favours high-rise luxury
in the heart of the city; every room has a view over the Detroit River and
to Canada beyond.

Dearborn Inn and Marriott Hotel
20301 Oakwood Blvd.; tel. (313) 2712700, fax 2717464; 200 r., $125–420,
restaurants
Near a museum and a museum in its own right, the Dearborn Inn opposite the Ford Museum also has models of the homes of famous
Americans such as Edgar Allan Poe.

El Tovar Hotel   Grand Canyon,
US 180; tel. (303) 2972757, fax 2973175; 76 r., $110–160   South Rim
Many famous guests have enjoyed the traditional hospitality of this venerable hotel that dates from 1905; the dining room has a magnificent
view of the Grand Canyon.

Grand Canyon Lodge   Grand Canyon,
On the AZ 67; tel. (520) 6382611; 200 r. and cabins, $75–125, restaurant   North Rim
The hospitable lodge, built in 1928, is particularly popular in summer, so
early reservation is essential; fantastic view of the Canyon from the
lounge.

Hyatt Regency Houston   Houston
1200 Louisiana St.; tel. (713) 6541234, fax 9510934; 939 r., $170–210, 4
restaurants, fitness suite
A typical steel and glass super hotel, with 30-storey lobby.

Lancaster Hotel
701 Texas Ave.; tel. (713) 2289500, fax 2234528: 93 r., $120–220
Charming, intimate old hotel amidst the skyscrapers.

Accommodation

Wyndham Warwick
5701 Main St.; tel. (713) 5261991, fax 6394545; 308 r., $115–155
In the heart of the museum district, the Warwick is relatively cheap despite being furnished with genuine antiques.

Indianapolis

Brickyard Resort & Inn
4400 W 16th St.; tel. (317) 2412500, fax 2412133; 108 r., $60–65, restaurant
"Only" a motel but in an unbeatable location for all "Indy 500" fans, close to the Indianapolis Speedway, plus an excellent 18-hole golf course.

Canterbury
123 S Illinois St.; tel. (317) 6343000, fax 6852519: 99 r., $190–220, restaurant
This stylish hotel on the southern end of the Circle Center Mall has done its best to bring the English lifestyle to Indiana, hence the way the rooms are furnished and, above all, its "tea time".

Kansas City

Crowne Plaza
4445 Main St.; tel. (816) 5313000, fax 5313007; 296 r., $120–150, restaurant
Very comfortable, value-for-money hotel, decorated with marble and flowers.

Hotel Savoy
219 W 9th St.; tel./fax (816) 8423575; 14 suites, $80–120
The oldest hotel in town, in the old textile quarter, the atmosphere under the massive glass dome of the lobby still harks back to the old pioneer days; more of a B & B than a hotel.

Key West

Marquesa Hotel
600 Fleming St.; tel. (305) 2921919, fax 2942121; 27 r., $150–200
Elegant accommodation in a restored Victorian (1884) villa; lovely garden and pool.

Las Vegas

Staying in Las Vegas will certainly not break the bank: although the super hotels listed in the entry for Las Vegas can offer unadulterated luxury at several thousand dollars a night, most of their rooms are eminently affordable since the management wants customers to have plenty of money left to spend in the casino. Hence in the MGM, for example, rooms cost between $70 and $130, depending on location and the day of the week, while in the Circus Circus, which mainly caters for families with children, no room costs more than $130. Still, here are a couple of smaller, more modest hotels close to the big casinos:

Center Strip Inn
3688 Las Vegas Blvd.; tel. (702) 7396066; $70–85

Somerset House Motel
294 Convention Center Dr.; tel. (702) 7384411; $50

Los Angeles

Los Angeles Athletic Club
431 W Seventh St., Downtown; tel. (213) 6252211; 72 r., $150–200
The highly traditional Athletic Club with tastefully appointed hotel rooms (some deluxe) on the upper floors has a well-equipped fitness centre, sports facilities, two swimming pools and several restaurants.

Regal Biltmore Hotel
506 S Grand Ave.; tel. (213) 6241011, fax 6121545; 683 r., $225–235, two restaurants, health club
The Biltmore, in the Beaux Arts style of 1923, was where the Oscar

ceremony was held in the 1930s and 40s, and has aged well to become one of the sights in its own right.

Kawada Hotel
200 S Hill St., Downtown; tel. (213) 6214455, 6874455; 117 r., $75–125, acclaimed restaurant
Cheap alternative for those who find the luxury of most LA hotels too extreme.

Château Marmont Hotel
8221 Sunset Blvd., Hollywood; tel. (213) 6561010, fax 6555311; 116 r., from $200.
At one time this 1927 château numbered Greta Garbo among its guests; the affectionate restoration has retained the patina of times gone by; some rooms with small kitchen.

Beverly Hills Hotel
9641 Sunset Blvd., Hollywood; tel. (310) 2762251, fax 2812905; 270 r., $300–350, several restaurants, gym
The luxurious "pink palace" has become symbolic of the hedonistic Beverly Hills lifestyle; surrounded by tropical vegetation this historic hotel offers every conceivable service to be expected of a (very expensive) luxury hotel.

The Peabody
Memphis

149 Union Ave.; tel. (901) 5294000, fax 5293600; 486 r., $160–320
Legendary downtown hotel opened in 1889: its most famous residents are the ducks that are brought down from their penthouse suite by lift at 11 every morning to waddle across the red carpet, to a piano accompaniment, to their pool in the lobby, where they stay until their return to the roof at 5pm.

Radisson Hotel Memphis
185 Union Ave.; tel. (901) 5281800, fax 5258509; 283 r., from $100–110
Value for money behind its historic facade; very well placed for the sights of Memphis.

Inter-Continental Miami
Miami

100 Chopin Plaza; tel. (305) 5771000, fax 5770384; 676 r., $190–290, three restaurants, lounge, spa
Postmodern skyscraper with a lot of marble and Henry Moore's "The Spindle" in its monumental lobby; a breathtaking view of the city and port from the pool deck.

Biltmore Hotel Coral Gables
1200 Anastasia Ave.; tel. (305) 4451926, fax 9133158; 280 r., $190–260, restaurant, lounge, spa, sports facilities
Miami's top building from the Twenties (a masterpiece by architect George Merrick), the Biltmore has seen the former splendour of its Moorish architecture fully restored.

Sonesta Beach Hotel & Tennis Club Key Biscayne
350 Ocean Dr.; tel. (305) 3612021, fax 3653096; 195 r., two villas, five restaurants, bar, disco, tennis, health club, bathing beach
The height of luxury, on one of Florida's finest beaches: its modern art, including drawings by Andy Warhol, is particularly worth seeing.

Alexander All Suite Luxury Hotel
Miami Beach

5225 Collins Ave.; tel. (305) 8656500, fax 8648525; 137 suites, $225–420, restaurant, spa, bathing beach
First-class accommodation with perfect service.

Fontainebleau Hilton
4441 Collins Ave.; tel. (305) 5382000, fax 6474607; 1200 r., $235–395, 10 restaurants, several lounges and bars, spa, health club, sauna, tennis, bathing beach, water sports, parasailing
Famous as the vast hotel in the James Bond movie "Goldfinger", this is where Sean Connery and Gert Frobe lounged by the pool.

Minneapolis/St Paul

Nicollet Island Inn
95 Merriam St., Minneapolis; tel. (612) 3311800, fax 3316258; 24 r., $115–130
When it comes to location, there is nowhere better in the twin cities – right in the Mississippi, between the St Anthony Center and Downtown; housed in an old factory building, it also has an excellent restaurant.

Whitney Hotel
150 Portland Ave., Minneapolis; tel. (612) 3399300, fax 3391333; 97 r., $160–200
This hotel is another conversion, this time from a flourmill built in 1880: nowadays it boasts an opulent wood-panelled and marble lobby and welcoming rooms. When booking, ask for south-facing rooms since these have the view of the Mississippi.

St Paul Hotel
350 Market St.; tel. (612) 2929292, fax 2289506; 254 r., $200
Built on Rice Park in 1910 the St Paul offers European-style comfort.

Nashville

Opryland Hotel
2800 Opryland Dr.; tel. (615) 8891000, fax 8715728; 1891 r., $200–250
For died-in-the-wool country music fans: a night in the heart of Opryland.

Union Station
1001 Broadway; tel. (615) 7261001, fax 2483554; 124 r., $130–215
A really atmospheric quarter in the old station from 1887.

New Orleans

Bienville House Hotel
320 Decatur St.; tel. (504) 5292345, fax 5256079; 83 r., $115–175
With a historic ambience and individualistic rooms this hotel is well positioned between the French Quarter and River Front; very good Italian restaurant.

Le Richelieu
1234 Chartres St.; tel. (504) 5292492, fax 5248179; 86 r., $95–150
Highly acclaimed for the best value-for-money in the French Quarter.

The Pontchartrain
2031 St Charles Ave.; tel. (504) 5240581, fax 5291165; 102 r., $95–380
Very fine 1927 hotel in the Garden District, still with many of its original period features; its restaurant, "The Caribbean Room", is internationally renowned.

New York City

Algonquin
59 W 44th St.; tel. (212) 8406800, fax 9441419; 165 r., $130–220
The legendary Algonquin, opened in 1902, was where Dorothy Parker, Robert Benchley, James Thurber and others met in the Twenties and Thirties at the famous round table; the rooms are tiny but pretty and the wood-panelled lobby feels like a living room.

Carlyle
35 E 76th St./Madison Ave.; tel. (212) 7441600, fax 7174682; 198 r., $355–525, fitness centre
New York's best-run hotel according to many reviewers; since it opened

in 1930 the five-star hotel has hosted innumerable celebrities. Only about 20 per cent of the luxurious rooms are available to tourists and other travellers; the rest is let all year round.

Lexington
511 Lexington Ave./48th St.; tel. (212) 7554400, fax 7514091; 750 r., $130–220
Its central location near Grand Central Station and the United Nations make this 27-storey hotel a particular favourite with shoppers and business travellers; it has two restaurants – Italian and Chinese.

The Plaza
768 5th Ave./59th St.; tel. (212) 7593000, fax 5465324; 800 r., $235–475
The 19-storey Plaza, opened in 1907 and one of New York's achitectural landmarks, has bright, comfortable and spacious rooms, some with a fantastic view of Central Park. Though an overnight stay in this home from home for many of the world's top people may be beyond your means, you can still try the seafood in the Oyster Bar or get a drink in the Oak Bar.

De Hirsch Residence
1395 Lexington Ave./92nd St.; tel. (212) 4155650, fax 4155578; 370 beds, under $100
Although this is a Hebrew Association hostel for Young Men and Women, you need not be either young or Jewish to stay here. The rooms are roomy, there is a kitchen on every floor and the fitness suite is free of charge.

Days Inn Falls View — Niagara Falls
201 Rainbow Blvd.; tel. (716) 2859321, fax 2859760; 193 r., from $150
A classic among the hotels by the Falls; if you want to see them properly you need to get a room on a high floor – and pay extra.

Clarion Hotel — Oklahoma City
4345 N Lincoln Blvd.; tel. (405) 5282741, fax 2720369; 68 r., $125–200, restaurant
Central location and unusual decor – the fittings are from a bankrupt Christian theme park.

If you want to be in the heart of the Disney experience you need to stay — Orlando
in one of the theme park hotels such as Disney's Boardwalk (Twenties beach hotel), Beach Club Resort (Victorian beach hotel), All Star Music Resort (music down the ages), Polynesian Resort (South Seas romance) or in Wilderness Lodge (safari park style). Prices range between $100 and $365; bookings through Walt Disney World Central Reservations: tel. (407) 9347639; or with travel agents. If you want a good hotel:

Days Inn
4104 & 4125 W Irlo Bronson Memorial Hwy. (US 192); tel. (407) 8464714, fax 9322699; 236 r., $30–75
Value for money, with supermarket and shopping mall.

The Breakers — Palm Beach
1 South County Rd.; tel. (561) 6556611, fax 6598403; 572 r., $200 plus, five gourmet restaurants, night club, shopping arcade, bathing beach, beach club, water sports (inc. diving), golf, 21 tennis courts, fitness centre, beauty salon
This historic hotel in a millionaires' playground with the flamboyance of an Italian Renaissance palace continues to be first in Florida for comfort and service.

Korman Suites Hotel — Philadelphia

Accommodation

2001 Hamilton St.; tel. (215) 5697300, fax 5690584; 182 r., $170–230, restaurant, spa, fitness suite
Large choice of rooms in the Korman's steel and glass tower: double rooms with kitchen, double bedded suites, ordinary double rooms at relatively cheap prices.

Rittenhouse Hotel
210 W Rittenhouse Square; tel. (215) 5469000, fax 7323364; 98 r., $285 plus, two restaurants, fitness suite
Luxury on Philadelphia's finest park.

Thomas Bond House
129 S 2nd St.; tel. (215) 9238523, fax 9238504; 12 r., $75–125
Given that this is Philadelphia, why not try a B & B in the historic district: Thomas Bond House, built in 1769, offers colonial atmosphere complete with open hearth.

Phoenix

Arizona Biltmore
24th St. & Missouri Ave.; tel. (602) 9556600, fax 3817600; 500 r., $280–360, restaurants, golf, tennis, kindergarten
The top hotel in the place, the Arizona Biltmore was opened in 1929 in a wonderful park full of sub-tropical plants; rare woods, marble and expanses of glass lend elegant grandeur to the interior.

Marriott's Camelback Inn Resort Golf Club & Spa
5402 E Lincoln Dr.; tel. (602) 9481700, fax 9518469; 460 r., $110–380, restaurants, health spa, fitness suite
This amazing holiday oasis, north-east of Phoenix city centre, offers virtually every conceivable amenity, both in terms of its furnishings and its perfect service.

Pittsburgh

Ramada Plaza Suites
1 Bigelow Sq.; tel. (412) 2815800, fax 2818467; 311 suites with kitchen facility, restaurant, $75–125
Centrally located in the Golden Triangle, practical accommodation.

Portland

Riverplace Hotel
1510 SW Harbor Way; tel. (503) 2283233, fax 2956161; 131 r., $185–225, very good restaurant
The striking feature of the Riverplace is its lovely location on the Williamette River and Waterfront Park.

Richmond

Madad House Hotel
11 N 4th St.; tel. (804) 6482893, fax 7800647; 62 r., from $75
A pleasant hotel in the Business District.

St Augustine

St Francis Inn
279 St George St.; tel. (904) 8246068; 16 suites, $60–120
Comfortable and prettily furnished old guesthouse that has been run on these lines since the 1840s.

St Petersburg

Don CeSar Resort
3400 Gulf Blvd.; tel. (813) 3601881, fax 3676952; 275 r., $200 plus, three restaurants
The venerable pink primadonna of hotels on the Gulf Coast has managed to retain its charm and elegance despite extensive modernisation.

Salt Lake City

Brigham Street Inn
1135 E South Temple St.; tel. (801) 3644461, fax 5213201; 9 r., $115–135
This small but smart establishment is in a lovingly restored Victorian villa; all the rooms are extremely tastefully furnished.

Salt Lake Hilton
150 W 500 South St.; tel. (801) 5323344, fax 5310705; 350 r., $130–175, restaurant, fitness centre with sauna
This luxurious Hilton is one of the best places in town; free transfer to the airport.

Hotel del Coronado   San Diego
1500 Orange Ave., Coronado; tel. (619) 4356611, fax 5228238; 692 r., $200 plus, three restaurants, fitness suite, hotel beaches
Made famous by "Some Like It Hot" with Marilyn Monroe, Jack Lemmon and Tony Curtis, the château-style hotel by the sea, with its white walls and red towers, has accommodated many Presidents and VIPs in its time.

Hotel Bedford   San Francisco
761 Post St.; tel. (415) 6736040, fax 5636739; 144 r., $110–130
It would be hard to find anywhere cheaper in this central location.

Hotel Majestic
1500 Sutter St.; tel. (415) 4411100, fax 6737331; 57 r., $135–170
For this relatively acceptable price the Majestic, opened in 1902, offers the elegance of a European-style hotel.

Westin St Francis
Union Square, 335 Powell St.; tel. (415) 3977000; 1192 r., $210–375, four restaurants
Period grand hotel in the heart of the city with the charm of days gone by. The rooms, furnished with genuine antiques, in the old building have a superb view of the skyline of the Financial District, while from the 32nd floor of the new hotel tower you can look out over the entire inner city as far as Fisherman's Wharf.

Inn of the Anasazi   Santa Fe
113 Washington Ave.; tel. (505) 9883030, fax 9883277; 60 r., $200 plus, restaurant, health club
Not far from the Plaza the hotel is built in the adobe style and very tastefully furnished; it makes a special feature of the beautiful products of local artists and native American craftsmanship.

Inn of the Governors
234 Don Gaspar Ave.; tel. (505) 9824333, fax 9899149; 100 r., $125–200, restaurant
A well-run middle category hotel in the Mexican style, this comes highly recommended for anyone who enjoys good food: its "Mañana" restaurant is guaranteed not to let you down.

Gastonian   Savannah
220 E Gaston St.; tel. (912) 2322869, fax 2320710; 16 r., $175–300
The most luxurious B & B in Savannah offers pure Southern comfort in an establishment dating back to 1868. The very tasteful rooms have wonderful baths; smashing breakfasts – but all this is for non-smokers only.

River Street Inn
115 E River St.; tel. (912) 2346400, fax 2341478; 86 r., $90–150
Low cost and right on the Savannah River, so best to take a room with a river view.

The Edgewater   Seattle
Pier 67, 2411 Alaska Way; tel. (206) 7287000, fax 4414119; 243 r., $130–220, restaurant

The only hotel in Seattle right on the waterfront; rustic interior with lots of natural wood.

Inn at the Market
86 Pine St.; tel. (206) 4433600, fax 4480631; 71 r., $130–190, French restaurant
Small elegant hotel with French flair by the Pike Place Market with a view of Elliott Bay.

Tampa   **Holiday Inn Busch Gardens**
2701 E Fowler St.; tel. (813) 9714710, fax 9770155; 400 r., $60–120, restaurant
Family-friendly motel close to Tampa's biggest shopping Mall (University Square) and the world-famous amusement park.

Tucson   **Arizona Inn**
2200 E Elm St.; tel. (520) 3251541, fax 7815830; 81 r., $80–195
Since its opening in 1930 the hotel still emanates the classic elegance of the pre-War period, with rooms that are often spacious, though with small bathrooms – but where else can you find a hotel with its own croquet lawn?

Washington, DC   **Hotel Harrington**
11th & E Sts.; tel. (202) 6288140, fax 3433924; 269 r., $80–90
Value for money in every sense, as much for its location as its prices since all the main sights are in walking distance.

Latham
3000 Main St.; tel. (202) 7265000, fax 2952003; 143 r., $175–195, very good restaurant with West Coast cuisine
The right choice for anyone who wants a pleasant – and peaceful – stay in trendy Georgetown.

Willard Inter-Continental
1401 Pennsylvania Ave.; tel. (202) 6289100, fax 6377326; 341 r., $200–380, two restaurants, health club
Here you can reside expensively and opulently in a luxurious listed Second Empire setting that even the austere Abraham Lincoln found to his taste.

Air Travel

Most visitors to the United States go by air. There are numerous scheduled flights from London and other European airports, many of them flying non-stop to major American cities.

There are also frequent charter flights, chiefly during the main holiday season and to favourite holiday destinations.

Special rates   Some American airlines (e.g. USAir, American Airlines, Continental, Delta) offer combined air tickets at advantageous rates, covering the transatlantic crossing and onward flights to other American cities or to the Bahamas, the Caribbean or even Hawaii. Information can be obtained from travel agencies.

Airports

The most important airports for visitors arriving in the United States are New York, Boston, Washington, Chicago, Miami, Atlanta, Los Angeles and San Francisco.

Service facilities at American airports are in line with international standards. On arrival from abroad there may be quite long waits at passport control, baggage claim and customs.

Not surprisingly in view of the great distances to be covered, flying is a very popular means of travel in the United States, and by European standards it is relatively cheap. The busiest airports for travel within the United States are New York, Chicago, Miami, Atlanta, Charlotte, Denver, Houston and Los Angeles, followed by Dallas/Fort Worth, Orlando, Cincinnati, Detroit, Minneapolis/St Paul, Kansas City and San Francisco. From these "hub" airports there are services, usually several times daily, to all major American airports.

Domestic flights

There are numerous regional airports and local airstrips linked with the domestic network of services. They are also convenient for private and charter flying.

Regional airports

Airlines

The main airports are served by all the major American airlines and their associates. Airlines that fly international services may be able to offer convenient connections and advantageous fares on domestic flights.
American airlines flying non-stop from the UK to the United States: American Airlines (to Boston, Chicago, Dallas/Fort Worth, Los Angeles, Miami, Nashville, New York and Raleigh/Durham), Continental (to Denver, Houston and New York), Delta (to Atlanta, Cincinnati, Detroit and Miami), Northwest (to Boston and Minneapolis), TWA (to St Louis), United (to Los Angeles, New York, San Francisco, Seattle and Washington, DC), USAir (to Charlotte).

American airlines

British Airways fly non-stop from London to Atlanta, Baltimore, Boston, Charlotte, Chicago, Dallas/Fort Worth, Houston, Los Angeles, Miami, New York, Orlando, Philadelphia, San Francisco, Seattle and Washington, DC, and also from Glasgow and Manchester to New York.
Virgin Atlantic fly non-stop from London to Boston, Los Angeles, Miami, New York, Orlando and San Francisco.

British airlines

Fares within the United States tend to be higher during the main holiday season, at weekends and around public holidays. Passengers flying the Atlantic on American airlines may be able to get cheap round trip or excursion rates on domestic flights.

Fares

Information

American Airlines: tel. (0845) 7789789, www.americanair.com
British Airways: tel. (0345) 222111, www.british-airways.com
Continental Airlines: tel. (01293) 776464, www.flycontinental.com
Delta Air Lines: tel. (0800) 414767, www.delta-air.com
Icelandair: tel. (0207) 8741019, www.icelandair.co.uk
KLM/Northwest Airlines: tel. (0870) 5074074, www.nwa.com
TWA Trans World Airlines: tel. (0208) 8140707, www.twa.com
United Airlines: tel. (0845) 8444777, www.ual.com
USAirways: tel. (0800) 7835556, www.usairways.com
Virgin Atlantic Airways: tel. (01293) 747747, www.fly.virgin.com

Airline offices in the UK

Toll-free calls for airline enquiries from anywhere in the United States (all 1800 code):
Air Canada: 7763000
American Airlines/American Eagle: 4337300
American West: 2359292

Toll-free calls

Austrian/Lauda Air: 8430002
British Airways: 2479297
Canadian Airlines: 4267000
Continental: 5250280
Delta: 2414141
KLM: 4385000
Lufthansa/Condor: 6453880
Northwest: 4474747
Sabena: 9552000
Southwest: 4359792
Swissair: 2218125
TWA: 2212000
United: 2416522
USAirways: 4284322

Taxes

Transport and airport taxes are payable by passengers on international flights leaving the United States (and Canada).

Private pilots

Holders of a pilot's licence and English radiotelephony certificate are allowed to hire an aircraft after passing a test. Further information can be obtained locally.

Alcohol

Statutory restrictions on the consumption of alcohol are a matter for individual states and counties, and thus differ considerably from place to place. In most states alcohol may not be sold to anyone under 21. Wine, beer and other drinks with a low alcohol content are sold in many supermarkets and foodshops; spirits can usually be bought only in special liquor stores. The sale of alcohol on Sundays is restricted or prohibited, depending on the regulations in each state.

The consumption of alcohol is prohibited in public recreation areas (such as bathing beaches, state parks) and on the street. There are heavy penalties for driving under the influence of alcohol: the permitted level of blood alcohol ranges according to state and county. Opened or empty bottles and cans of alcohol must be stowed away in the boot (i.e. trunk) of a car, since it is forbidden to carry them in the interior.

Amusement Parks

Needless to say for many children the United States is the country of their dreams, with the prospect of visiting theme parks like Disneyland and Walt Disney World and even the chance actually to encounter real cowboys and Indians. In fact this is truly a family-friendly country, with reductions for children and families and special children's facilities virtually everywhere.

The United States has a great many amusement parks and theme parks, large and small, and a major attraction for young and old alike. The following selection lists just a few of the main ones.

California

Disneyland
1313 Harbor Blvd., Anaheim, CA; tel. (714) 7814500. Open (mainly) daily 9am–10pm.

Knott's Berry Farm
Buena Park, CA; tel. (714) 2205200. Open (mainly) daily 9am–11pm.

Paramount's Great America

2401 Agnew Rd., Santa Clara, CA; tel. (408) 9881776. Open Jun.–Aug. daily, Mar.–May, Sep., Oct. weekends only.

Sea World
Sea World Dr. & I 5, San Diego, CA; tel. (619) 2263901. Open high season daily 9am–10pm (longer at weekends); low season shorter opening hours.

Six Flags Magic Mountain
Magic Mountain Pkway., Valencia, CA; tel. (661) 2554111. Open May–Sep. daily 10am 10pm (Fri.–Sun. midnight), Oct.–Apr. Sat., Sun. only.

Universal Studios
100 Universal Dr., Los Angeles, Hollywood, CA; tel. (818) 5089600. Open daily 9am–6.30pm, longer Jul., Aug.

Busch Gardens/The Dark Continent   Florida
3000 Busch Blvd., Tampa, FL; tel. (813) 9875082. Open summer daily 9am–7pm (Fri.–Sun. 8pm); winter daily 10am–5pm.

Sea World Aventure Park of Orlando
7007 Sea World Dr., Orlando, FL; tel. (407) 3513600. Open summer daily 9am–10pm; winter daily 9am–7pm.

Walt Disney World Resort
Lake Buena Vista, FL; tel. (407) 8244321. Open (mainly) daily 9am–10pm.

Six Flags Over Georgia   Georgia
7561 Six Flags Rd., Mapleton/Atlanta, GA; tel. (678) 9454444. Open mid-Jun. to mid-Aug. daily 10am–10pm (Fri.–Sun. midnight); other months Sat., Sun. only.

Six Flags Great America   Illinois
Grand Ave., Gurnee, IL; tel. (847) 2491776. Open May–Sep. daily 10am–10pm; spring and autumn Sat., Sun.

Silver Dollar City   Missouri
Branson, MO; tel. (417) 3382611. Open mid-May to Oct. daily; Apr. to mid-May Wed.–Sun.

Worlds of Fun/Oceans of Fun
4545 Worlds of Fun Dr., Kansas City, MO; tel. (816) 4544545. Open late May–late Aug. daily 10am–10pm; Apr., May, Sep., Oct. Sat. Sun.

Canobia Lake Park   New Hampshire
North Policy St., Salem, NH; tel. (603) 8933506. Open Memorial Day–Labor Day daily; Apr., May Sat., Sun.

Six Flags Great Adventure   New Jersey
Rte. 537, Jackson, NJ; tel. (732) 9282000. Open mid-Apr. to Oct., daily from 10am.

The Great Escape   New York
US 9, Lake George, NY; tel. (518) 7923500. Open Memorial Day–Labor Day daily 9.30am–6pm.

Paramount's Carowinds   North Carolina
Carowinds Blvd., Charlotte, NC; tel. (704) 5882600. Open Mar.–Oct. daily 10am–8pm.

Cedar Point   Ohio

Sandusky, OH; tel. (419) 6272350. Open mid-May to early Sep. daily from 10am; late Sep.–Oct. Sat., Sun.

Pennsylvania **Hersheypark**
100 W Hersheypark Dr., Hershey, PA; tel. (717) 5343900. Open May–Sep. daily from 10am.

Philadelphia **Sesame Street**
100 Sesame Rd., Langhorne, PA; tel. (215) 7571100. Seasonal opening hours.

Tennessee **Dollywood**
700 Dollywood Lane, Pigeon Forge, TN; tel. (1800) 3655996. Open (mainly) daily 10am–6pm.

Opryland USA
2802 Opryland Dr., Nashville, TN; tel. (615) 8896611. Open late May–early Oct. daily; Apr.–early May Sat., Sun.

Texas **Sea World of Texas**
Ellison Dr.,/Westover Hills Blvd., San Antonio, TX; tel. (210) 5233000. Open Memorial Day–Labor Day daily, Mar.–May, Aug.–Oct. Sat., Sun.

Six Flags AstroWorld/WaterWorld
8400 Kirby Dr., Houston, TX; tel. (713) 7991234. Open summer daily; spring, autumn Sat., Sun.

Six Flags Fiesta Texas
I 10 W/Loop 1604, San Antonio, TX; tel. (210) 6975050. Open Memorial Day–Labor Day daily; Mar–May, Sep.–Nov. Sat., Sun.

Six Flags Over Texas
2201 Road to Six Flags, Arlington, TX; tel. (817) 6408900. Open Jun.–early Sep. daily from 10am; Mar.–May, Sep.–Dec. Sat., Sun.

Virginia **Busch Gardens/Water Country**
7901 Pocahontas Trail, Williamsburg, VA; tel. (757) 2533350. Open May–Sep. daily 9am–7pm.

Beaches

Water sports of all kinds are popular in the United States. Particularly renowned are the crystal-clear water and beaches of fine sand round the Florida peninsula and the Gulf coasts of Alabama (Gulf Islands), Mississippi (Biloxi), Louisiana and Texas (Texas Gulf Coast, Padre Island National Seashore). There are also beautiful beaches on a number of islands off the coast of Georgia, in South Carolina (Hilton Head Island, Myrtle Beach) and North Carolina (particularly the Outer Banks and Cape Hatteras), and on the Pacific coast of southern California. For those who do not mind cooler water there are good beaches on the Atlantic coasts of Maryland (Assateague Island), New Jersey (e.g. Atlantic City), Pennsylvania (Long Beach Island, Beach Island State Park), Massachusetts (particularly Cape Cod, Nantucket Island and Martha's Vineyard) and at various points on the coast of Maine (famed for its lobsters), as well as on the cooler shores of the Pacific (e.g. in the Oregon Dunes National Recreation Area). Many beaches are equipped with parking areas, showers and lifeguards. Beaches within easy reach of cities, or with large hotel complexes, tend to be crowded, particularly at weekends, but it is often possible to reach more secluded spots by boat.

Both on the Atlantic and Pacific coasts there can be very heavy swells.

In many of the larger tourist centres and in beach hotels boats and equipment for water-skiing can be hired.

Water-skiing

There are good snorkelling areas on the Atlantic coasts of the south-eastern United States, on the Gulf Coast and on the Pacific coast of southern California. At many places snorkellers will discover a colourful underwater world with a great variety of marine creatures – denizens of coral reefs, molluscs, crustaceans and fish of many different species. Round some of the islands where there has been water pollution and over fishing certain areas have been closed to snorkellers and divers in order to avoid further damage to marine life.

Snorkelling

It is easy to forget that salt water and a tropical sun can quickly cause severe sunburn: it is a good idea, therefore, to wear a cotton shirt or T-shirt when snorkelling. Caution is required in touching unknown sea creatures (possible danger of a rash): protection can be provided by stout rubber gloves. It is inadvisable to feel into cavities in a coral reef.

In many places the taking of marine organisms is prohibited, and should not be done even where there is no official prohibition, in order to avoid endangering the delicate biological balance of this habitat.

Windsurfing is very popular in the United States and is practised wherever bathing is possible. Favourite windsurfing areas are the waters round Florida, on the coasts of Georgia and South Carolina, along the Gulf of Mexico and at various points on the Pacific coasts of California and in Hawaii. The heavy swell on some coasts offers a challenge to surfboarders, many of whom are to be seen on the Californian coast and in Hawaii.

Windsurfing

Nude bathing is frowned on in the United States, and offenders caught by the police face a heavy fine. A degree of tolerance prevails on certain stretches of beach in Florida and California.

Nude bathing

On the beach, Fort Lauderdale

Diving   See Water Sports

Camping

There are innumerable campgrounds all over the United States. The standard provision is an area to pitch a tent or park a trailer or motorhome, a table, a bench and a place to light a fire. On private campgrounds good sanitary facilities can be taken for granted, and there are frequently additional facilities such as food stores, snack bars, laundry rooms, television rooms, swimming pools and saunas. On many campgrounds small "log cabins" can be hired.

State-run campgrounds (for example in National Parks and State Parks) offer not only very reasonable rates but usually a beautiful setting as well, though the equipment and amenities may sometimes leave something to be desired.

Reservations   Many campgrounds – mainly in popular destinations such as National Parks – get very crowded, particularly in the peak holiday periods and at long weekends: this means that advance booking is a must.

Information   The American Automobile Association (see Motoring; Motoring Organizations) publishes an annual directory of selected sites. Over 3000 private campgrounds are listed in the directory published by:
National Association of RV Parks and Campgrounds
113 Park Ave., Falls Church, Virginia, VA 22046; tel. (703) 2421004

Kampgrounds of America, the largest chain of private sites, has campgrounds throughout the United States. For information, contact:
KOA, PO Box 30558
Billings, MT 59114-0558; tel. (406) 2523104, toll-free fax from abroad (0800) 895024

KOA also has an office in the UK that can supply details of over 700 campgrounds and a directory of sites (fee charged):
KOA Kampgrounds of America
PO Box 9, Burgess Hill, West Sussex RH15 8YJ; tel. (08705) 143610, fax 168309

Unofficial   In the National Parks camping is only allowed on official campsites.
camping   Otherwise, although in principle camping is allowed outside official sites, if you want to camp on private land you should politely ask for permission beforehand.

Car Rental

Tariffs   Renting a car is a good way of seeing the United States on your own. Numerous rental firms offer automobiles at attractive rates, weekly hire being particularly good value-for-money. But prospective hirers should not allow themselves to be misled by basic rentals that are sometimes temptingly low: it is also necessary to consider the cost of adequate insurance cover (third party – in the United States called liability insurance – or comprehensive, excess allowance), which can be high. In addition account must be taken of state taxes and, where an airport shuttle bus is taken from the airport to the car rental office, airport taxes.

In general it is cheaper to hire a car before leaving home than after arrival. There is a substantial charge for returning the car to a different place. There is also additional charges for children's car seats (c. $3 a day) and having second driver (c. $2 a day).

If the car ordered is not available the person hiring the car is entitled to a vehicle in the next higher category. It is also possible to move up a category with the "upgrade coupons" issued by some travel agencies and airlines.

Before taking over the car you should check that it is in good condition and draw attention to any defects.

In some states there are special regulations on car hire. You should check up on these in advance.

The car rental firm will ask for a deposit before handing over the car. Usually it is necessary only to present a credit card. Payment in cash is not normal, and if accepted at all is likely to be a substantial amount.

Rental firms offer a confusing variety of insurance cover. The main forms are:
CDW: collision damage waiver (for damage to vehicle; desirable)
LDW: loss damage waiver (for loss of vehicle)
PAI: personal accident insurance
PEC: personal effect insurance (baggage insurance)
SLI: supplementary liability insurance (third party insurance additional to the legal minimum requirement)

Anyone wanting to hire a car must be able to produce a national or international driver's licence and be at least 21. Persons aged 21–24 should check with some companies (e.g. Avis, Budget) beforehand or expect to pay a higher rate (e.g. Alamo); Hertz do not rant cars to anyone under 25.

Car-hire companies can usually provide children's car seats but it is advisable to book them in advance.

All the reputable rental companies have a toll-free telephone number (code 1800) for making reservations, which can be found in the local telephone directory. Almost all of them have offices at airports, in larger hotels, and in city and tourist centres. If you want a hire car on a budget you can also try Rent-a-Wreck – the cars will be older but will only cost about $25 a day.

Alamo: 3279633
Avis: 3311212
Budget: 5270700
Dollar: 8004000
Hertz: 6543131
National: 3284567
Rent-a-Wreck: 3982544
Thrifty: 3672277
Value: 3272501

Anyone who plans to spend some considerable time on the road in the United States may find it worthwhile to buy a car with a buy-back guarantee.

Cruises

The two leading cruise ports on the Atlantic coast of the United States are Miami and New York. From New York passenger liners sail north by way of Boston and Cape Cod into Canadian waters. Popular destinations are Halifax, Nova Scotia, and the two French-speaking metropolises of Québec and Montréal on the St Lawrence. There are short cruises from New York to the Bermudas several times weekly.

The "American Queen" cruises the Mississippi

Florida, Bahamas, Caribbean, Gulf of Mexico

Many visitors to Florida take short cruises to the Bahamas or longer ones to the West Indies or the Gulf of Mexico. Favourite destinations are Nassau and Freeport in the Bahamas, the United States Virgin Islands of St Thomas, St Croix and St John, Puerto Rico in the Greater Antilles and the Mexican peninsula of Yucatán with its two offshore islands of Cancún and Cozumel. The "cruise capital of the world" is Miami, which handles well over 3 million passengers a year. Other important cruise ports in Florida are Port Everglades, Palm Beach, Port Canaveral and Tampa.

Pacific

Important cruise ports on the Pacific coast of the United States are Seattle, San Francisco and Los Angeles. Some ships call in at San Diego and the Mexican tourist resort of Acapulco. Many cruise companies operating in the Pacific run cruises to ports in Alaska and the Hawaiian archipelago.

Mississippi, Missouri, Tennessee, Ohio rivers

A special experience for visitors to the United States is a cruise on the Mississippi in the venerable sternwheel paddle steamers "Delta Queen" and "Mississippi Queen", which sail upstream from New Orleans to Vicksburg, Memphis, Cairo and St Louis and vice versa. There are also cruises on the Tennessee River and Kentucky Lake to Florence, Decatur and Chattanooga, on the Cumberland River and Lake Barkley to Nashville, and on the Ohio River to Louisville, home of the Kentucky Derby, and on via Madison and Cincinnati to Pittsburgh. Information can be obtained from a travel agency or from: Delta Queen Steamboat Co., 30 Robin Street Wharf, New Orleans; tel. (1800) 2150805.

Currency

The unit of American currency is the dollar ($), which contains 100 cents.

There are bills (banknotes) for 1, 2, 5, 10, 20, 50 and 100 dollars (and for larger amounts in internal bank use) and coins in denominations of 1 cent (a penny), 5 cents (a nickel), 10 cents (a dime) and 25 cents (a quarter); there are also 50 cent and 1 dollar coins, more rarely seen.

The exchange rate of the dollar against most other currencies is subject to fluctuation. It is best to change money before leaving home (and to have plenty of small change in coin and low-denomination bills), since the exchange rate is usually better in Europe than in the United States. Foreign currency, however, is not particularly welcome in the United States, and it is better to depend on credit cards, dollar traveller's cheques and a sufficient supply of dollars for the early days of your stay.

There are no restrictions on either the import or the export of foreign or American currency. If you are taking in more than 10,000 US$ the amount must be declared in the customs declaration filled in on the aircraft.

Currency regulations

Money can be changed in the banks at international airports, and there is no difficulty about changing money in tourist centres. It is best to avoid changing money in hotels, which give much poorer rates than the banks.

Exchange

It is best to come provided with dollar traveller's cheques, which are treated like cash and are normally accepted without question in hotels, restaurants and shops on presentation of your passport. If traveller's cheques are lost or stolen they will be replaced at once by local branches of the issuing agency on production of the receipt for their purchase.

Traveller's cheques

The commonest method of payment in hotels, restaurants and all kinds of shops is the credit/debit card, and it is essential for putting down the deposit on a rented car. Visitors should therefore be sure to have one or more of the generally recognised cards. The commonest are Mastercard (Eurocard), Visa, American Express, Diners Club and Carte Blanche. Using a credit card with a PIN (personal identity number), it is possible to obtain money from ATMs; and cash can also be obtained at bank counters on presentation of credit cards and passport.

Credit cards

See Opening Hours

Banks

Customs Regulations

The customs regulations governing travel to and from the United States are constantly being revised. It is therefore advisable to check beforehand with the relevant customs authority or the nearest US consulate.

Visitors arriving in the United States must fill in a customs declaration and an immigration form. These will normally be handed out on the aircraft.

Personal effects (clothing, toilet articles, jewellery, hunting, fishing and photographic equipment) may be taken in duty-free. The duty-free allowances for adults over 21 are: 33 (American) fluid ounces alcohol, 200 cigarettes or 100 cigars or 3 pounds of tobacco, plus gifts up to a value of $100 (including, for adults, up to 100 cigars). There are special regulations on the import of animals, meat and plants (information from Customs Office, American Embassy, Grosvenor Square, London W1A 1AE).

Entry to the USA

The duty-free allowances on re-entry to EU countries are: 200 cigarettes or 100 cigarillos or 50 cigars or 250 grams tobacco; 1 l spirits over 22 per cent proof or 2 l spirits below 22 per cent proof or 2 l sparkling wine, plus

Re-entry to EU countries

563

2 l wine; 50 grams perfume, 0.25 l toilet water. (Tobacco and alcoholic products persons aged over 17 only.)

Electricity

Electricity in the United States is 110 volts AC, with a frequency of 60 cycles. Electrical appliances must therefore be adjustable to that voltage; and adaptors will be required, since American plugs and sockets are different from British or European types.

Embassies and Consulates

United States embassies and consulates

United Kingdom

Embassy
5 Upper Grosvenor St.
London W1A 2JB
Tel. (0171) 4999000

Consulates
3 Regent Terrace
Edinburgh EH7 5BW
Tel. (0131) 5568315

Queen's House, 14 Queen St.
Belfast BT1 6EQ
Tel. (01232) 328239

Ireland

Embassy
42 Elgin Rd.
Ballsbridge, Dublin
Tel. (01) 6688777

Canada

Embassy
100 Wellington St.
Ottawa, Ontario K1P 5T1
Tel. (613) 2385335

Also consulates in Calgary, Halifax, Montréal, Québec City, Toronto and Vancouver.

Embassies and consulates in the United States

United Kingdom

Embassy
3100 Massachusetts Ave. NW
Washington, DC 20008
Tel. (202) 4621340

Consulates
Suite 2700, Marquis Tower One
245 Peachtree Center Ave.
Atlanta, GA 30303
Tel. (404) 5245856

Federal Reserve Plaza, 25th floor
600 Atlantic Ave.
Boston, MA 02210

Tel. (617) 2489555

33 N Michigan Ave.
Chicago, IL 60611
Tel. (312) 3461810

1100 Milam Building, Suite 2260
Houston, TX 77002
Tel. (713) 6596270

11766 Wilshire Blvd., Suite 400
Los Angeles, CA 90025
Tel. (310) 4773322

845 Third Ave.
New York, NY 10022
Tel. (212) 7450200

1 Sansome St., Suite 850
San Francisco, CA 94104
Tel. (415) 9813030

Also consulates in Anchorage, Cleveland, Dallas, Kansas City, Miami,
New Orleans, Norfolk, Philadelphia, Portland, Puerto Rico, St Louis and
Seattle.

Embassy   Ireland
2234 Massachusetts Ave. NW
Washington, DC 20008
Tel. (202) 4623939

Embassy   Canada
501 Pennsylvania Ave. NW
Washington, DC 20001
Tel. (202) 6821740

Also consulates in Atlanta, Boston, Buffalo, Chicago, Cleveland, Dallas,
Detroit, Honolulu, Los Angeles, Minneapolis, New York, San Francisco
and Seattle.

Emergencies

Police, ambulance, fire: tel. 911
If there is no response dial 0 for the operator.
Vehicle breakdown: (toll free) tel. (1800) AAAHELP
There are emergency telephones along many highways.

Events

The tourist offices of the various states (see Information) and the
tourist information offices of counties, cities and precincts and
organisation can usually supply detailed programmes of events
month by month. Regional events are also published in the daily
press.

Breckenridge (CO), Ullr Festival (festival in honour of the Nordic snow   January
god Ullr); Los Angeles (CA), Super Bowl; McCall (ID) and St Paul (MN),
Winter Carnival; Miami Beach (FL), Art-Deco Weekend; Pasadena (CA),

Events

Tournament of Roses Parade; Philadelphia (PA), Mummers' Parade; Tarpon Springs (FL), Greek Epiphany.

February
Apache Junction (AZ), Arizona Renaissance Festival; Daytona (FL), 500 Miles (car race); Miami (FL), Miami Film Festival; Miami Beach (FL), International Boat Show; New Orleans (LA) and Pensacola (FL), Mardi Gras (Carnival); Newport (OR), Seafood and Wine Festival; St Martinsville (LA), La Grande Boucherie des Cajuns (festival of the French speaking Cajuns); Steamboat Springs (CO), Winter Carnival.

March
Boston (MA), New England Spring Flower Show; Charleston (SC), Festival of Houses and Gardens; Columbus (MS), Spring Pilgrimage; Philadelphia (PA), Flower Show; Sarasota (FL), Medieval Fair; Sebring (FL), Twelve Hours of Sebring (car race); Stone Mountain (GA), Antebellum Jubilee; Westport/Grayland (WA), Whale Fest; Maple Sugar events at many places in Vermont.

April
Atlanta (GA), Dogwood Festival; Birmingham (AL), Festival of Arts; Juneau (AK), Alaska Folk Festival; Key West (FL), Conch Republic Festival; Knoxville (TN), Dogwood Arts Festival; Mountain View (AR), Arkansas Folk Festival; New Orleans (LA), Jazz and Heritage Festival; Richmond (VA), Historic Garden Week; Sarasota (FL), Sailor Circus; Tucson (AZ), Tucson Festival; Washington, DC, National Cherry Blossom Festival; Winchester (VA), Shenandoah Apple Blossom Festival.

May
Baltimore (MD), Preakness Stakes; Biloxi (MI), Shrimp Festival and Blessing of the Fleet; Chicago (IL), International Art Expo; Covington (KY), May Festival in Mainstrasse Village; Fernandina Beach (FL), Isle of Eight Flags Shrimps Festival; Hermann (MO), May Festival; Holland (MI), Tulip Time Festival; Indianapolis (IN), Indianapolis 500 (car race); Louisville (KY), Kentucky Derby; Memphis (TN), International Festival; Meridian (MI), Jimmie Rodgers Memorial Festival; Pensacola (FL), Five Flags Festival; Portland (OR), Rose Festival; Tulsa (OK), International May Festival; Walla Walla (WA), Hot Air Balloon Stampede.

June
Boston (MA), Harbor Festival; Boulder (CO), Shakespeare Festival; Clarinda (IO), Glenn Miller Festival; Detroit (MI), International Freedom Festival; Fort Sisseton (SD), Historical Festival; Frankenmuth (MI), Bavarian Festival; Gettysburg (PA), Civil War Heritage Days; Hannibal (MO), National Tom Sawyer Days; Hardin (MT), Custer's Last Stand Re-enactment; Helena (MT), Montana Traditional Jazz Festival; Honolulu (HI), King Kamehameha Celebration; Jacksonport State Park (AR), Rollin' on the River; Milwaukee (WI), Summer Festival, the Big Gig; Myrtle Beach (SC), Sun and Fun Festival.

July
In all states, Independence Day celebrations; Aspen (CO), Music Festival; Bath (ME), Bath Heritage Days; Cedar City (UT), Utah Shakespeare Festival; Cheyenne (WY), Frontier Days; Driggs (ID), Cowboy Festival; Fairbanks (AK), Golden Days; Key West (FL), Hemingway Days; Logan (UT), Festival of the American West; Manti (UT), Mormon Miracle Pageant; Milwaukee (WI), Great Circus Parade; Newport (RI), Newport Music Festival; New Ulm (NM), Heritage Festival; Sturges (WY), Harley Davidson Meeting; Wheeling (WV), Jamboree in the Hills (country music festival).

August
Abingdon (VA), Virginia Highlands Festival; Bethlehem (PA), Music Festival; Charleston (WV), Sternwheel Regatta; Chicago (IL), Jazz Festival; Des Moines (IA), Iowa State Fair; Glenns Ferry (ID), Three Island Crossing; Hugo (OK), Grant's Bluegrass Festival; Middletown (OH), Hot Air Balloon Championship; Rockland (ME), Maine Lobster Festival; Santa Barbara (CA), Old Spanish Days Fiesta; Savannah (GA), Maritime Festival; Hardin (MT), Crow Fair; Sturgis (SD), Harley Davidson Midwest.

Albuquerque (NM), New Mexico State Fair; Bismarck (ND), United Tribes International Pow Wow; Cincinnati (OH), Oktoberfest; Dallas (TX), Texas State Fair; Fort Worth (TX), Pioneer Days Celebration and Rodeo; Geneva (OH), Grape Jamboree; Honolulu (HI), Aloha Festival; Knoxville (TN), Tennessee Valley Fair; Lincoln (NH), New Hampshire Highland Games; New Glarus (WI), Wilhelm Tell Festival; Norwalk (CT), Oyster Festival; Ocean City (NJ), Sun Festival; Virginia City (WV), International Camel Race; West Danville (VT), Northeast Kingdom Fall Foliage Festival.

Albuquerque (NM), International Balloon Fiesta; Cape May (NJ), Victorian Week; Custer State Park (SD), Buffalo Roundup; Lexington (KY), EquiFestival; Minot (ND), Norsk Hostfest (Nordic Autumn Festival); Rehoboth Beach (DE), Sea Witch Festival; Vienna (GA), Big Pig Jig; Vincetown (NJ), Chatsworth Cranberry Festival; Dallas (TX), State Fair.

Kansas City (MS), American Royal Livestock Horse Show and Rodeo; New York (NY), Thanksgiving Day Parade, New York Marathon; Richmond (VA), Thanksgiving Festival; Wheeling (WV), Winter Festival of Lights; Winterthur (DE), Yuletide.

Boston (MA), First Night Celebration (New Year's Night festival); Fort Lauderdale (FL), WinterFest; Hollywood (CA), Christmas Parade on Sunset Boulevard (carriage parade, with many show business personalities); Las Vegas (NV), National Finals Rodeo; Miami (FL), Orange Bowl Festival; Newport (RI), Christmas in Newport; St Augustine (FL), Christmas Regatta; Salt Lake City (UT), Christmas Lights in Temple Square; Walt Disney World (FL), Christmas Parade; Washington, DC, Pageant of Peace.

September

October

November

December

Food and Drink

It is sometimes thought that the main specialities of American cuisine are hamburgers and ketchup, hot dogs and chips; but this is very far from the truth. Restaurants serving "American" food are often excellent, and meat and fish dishes are particularly good. There are also tempting regional specialities such as Virginia ham and the Creole and Cajun dishes of the south; and in a good bar even the humble hamburger, freshly made, makes a very appetising meal. And for those who want to look beyond American cuisine there is a wide range of ethnic restaurants.

Meals

Breakfast is best taken in a coffee shop ("America at its best") or in one of the innumerable fast food restaurants. It can be quite a substantial meal, consisting of a glass of pineapple, grapefruit or orange juice, coffee, eggs (boiled, scrambled, fried – "sunny side up" – or an omelette), fried bacon or sausages, sauté potatoes ("hashed browns"), grits, pancakes with maple syrup and toast with butter and various kinds of jam. Many breakfast buffets offer corn flakes and milk, freshly prepared muesli, fresh fruit and different kinds of yoghurt.

Breakfast

On Sundays and holidays brunch – a combination of breakfast and lunch – is a popular meal, usually eaten from around 11 o'clock. This will usually be a buffet offering a wide choice of dishes.

Brunch

Lunch is usually a light meal, which might include salads, fried food, and vegetables.

Lunch

Food and Drink

Dinner | The main meal of the day is dinner, which can be a very substantial meal, with fish and meat and a variety of side dishes. Some restaurants put on "dinner shows" to entertain their guests.

Food

Meat dishes | Not surprisingly, in view of the great expanses occupied by stock farms and ranches in the United States, meat features prominently on the American menu – T-bone steak, porterhouse steak, sirloin steak and of course the ever-present hamburger. Also very popular are chicken (e.g. fried chicken fingers) and pork (especially prime rib of pork). The main dish is almost always accompanied by a choice of baked potatoes or French fries (chips). Turkey is a meal for a special occasion, particularly Thanksgiving Day.

Fish | The choice of fish dishes includes not only fish and seafood from the Atlantic and Pacific but also a variety of freshwater fish from the country's many lakes and rivers. Particularly tasty are prawns, shrimps, shellfish, oysters, lobsters, grayling, perch and snapper. Stone crabs and conchs are prized as particular delicacies.

Ethnic cuisines | In addition to the all-American steaks, chicken and chef's salad visitors can sample the varied cuisines of all the different races represented in the United States. The range extends from Italian cuisine by way of Greek and Spanish/Cuban to Mexican, Caribbean and Far Eastern, with the specialities of many different countries. Kosher cooking is also, of course, well represented.

Sweets | Favourite sweets are cheesecake, blueberry cake, and Key lime pie (made with the juice of home-grown limes and cream). Doughnuts are ubiquitous.

Fruit, vegetables | The United States has fresh fruit and vegetables throughout the year. This is true particularly of citrus fruits and easily prepared vegetables (e.g. cucumbers, tomatoes, avocados).

Drink

Coffee | American coffee is usually lightly roasted and often served very weak. It is available everywhere and generously supplied: you need only order it once and your cup will be constantly refilled. In areas where there are many Italians or Latinos you can look forward to getting a cup of strong espresso.

Beer | American beers – always served ice-cold – have a relatively low alcohol content (3–3.5 per cent vol), and "light" beers with only 1–1.5 per cent vol are becoming increasingly popular. Bars usually offer a choice of several brands of both bottled and draught beer. Favourite American brands are Budweiser, Busch, Miller, Coors, Michelob and Schlitz. In New England and the Middle West there are numbers of small breweries producing excellent beer. Imported European beer is much dearer than American brands.

Wine | In recent years the United States has developed into one of the world's leading winemakers. Some four-fifths of the total area of vineyards in the United States is in California, where the growing of vines was introduced by Spanish missionaries in the 18th c. The best known Californian wine-growing areas are Santa Rosa, the Napa Valley, the Sonoma Valley, Mendocino, Livermore, Santa Clara, Monterey, San Benito and the San Joaquín Valley. There is another large wine area in the Finger Lakes region in New York State, an area with a not particularly favoured climate, and smaller areas in the states of Maryland, Virginia, Florida, Ohio, Missouri, Oregon and Washington.

The best known Californian red wines, mostly dry and full-bodied, are Zinfandel, Cabernet, Barbera, Ruby Cabernet, Grenache and Gamay. Predominant among Californian white wines are Chardonnay, French Colombard, Chenin Blanc, Sauvignon Blanc, Pinot Blanc, Semillon, Riesling and Gewürztraminer. Well known red wines from the Finger Lakes area are Concord, Isabella, Baco Noir, Chelois and Delaware; white wines include Duchess, Moore's Diamond, Niagara, Seibel, Vergennes and Elvira.

In the United States red wine as well as white wine is often served chilled.

Popular spirits – which can be bought only in special liquor stores and can be served in bars only at certain hours – are Scotch whisky and other whiskeys (bourbon, rye, Canadian, Irish), gin, vodka, brandy, rum, vermouth and cordial. *Spirits*

Fruit juices made from home-grown fruit (oranges, grapefruit, pineapples) are available everywhere. Other popular thirst quenchers are various colas and other soft drinks, root beer (made from water, sugar, dye and various herbs) and iced tea. *Soft drinks*

A glass of iced water is served with every meal. This is ordinary tap water with added ice: if you want bottled mineral water, ask for "spring water". *Water*

Health

The standard of medical care in the United States is very high. The only problem for visitors is likely to be the high cost: a hospital stay in particular is extremely expensive. It is essential, therefore, to make sure that you have adequate insurance cover before leaving home.

The supply of medicines is also well organised. Visitors who regularly need a particular medicine should take a copy of the prescription with them so that it can be reissued by an American doctor if necessary. *Medicines*

Chemists

American drugstores and pharmacies offer a wider range of goods than is usual in a British chemist, beyond just medicines and toiletries. Many department stores and supermarkets (e.g. Kroger, Wal Mart, Biggs, Safeway and K-Mart) have their own pharmacies. A wide range of medicines that are available only on prescription in the UK can be bought freely over the counter in the United States.

There is no night service for the supply of medicines outside normal hours. In case of emergency application should be made to the nearest hospital, which is open round the clock and has its own pharmacy.

Drugstores and pharmacies are usually open 9am–6pm; some stay open until 9pm or later. Pharmacies in supermarkets are open 24 hrs. a day.

Information

Surprisingly, the United States has no national tourist authority and no longer maintains any national tourist offices abroad, although efforts are being made to set up a successor.

Internet   www.usacitylink.com provides access to many cities throughout the United States and is highly recommended as a source of information about sights, accommodation and events.

www.usa.tourism.com offers general information about the Federal States.

The entries under the heading Information Offices of Each State give the web sites for the individual states and these usually also contain tourist information or details of how to access it.

Tourist information in the United Kingdom

Some regional travel associations, states and cities maintain offices in the United Kingdom. They can be contacted on the following telephone numbers or via the internet (see also web sites under Information Offices of Each State).

Regional travel associations

Discover New England (Connecticut, Maine, Massachusetts, New Hampshire, Rhode Island, Vermont); tel. (01732) 742777, www.discovernewengland.com

Great Lakes of North America (Illinois, Michigan, Minnesota, Ohio, Wisconsin, and Ontario, Canada); tel. (0171) 3797526, www.cglg.org/greatlakestourism

Rocky Mountain International (Idaho, Montana, South Dakota, Wyoming); tel. (0171) 8350928

States, cities and areas

Alabama: (0121) 4454994

Alaska: (0891) 100727

Arizona: (01426) 946334 (brochureline)

California, Long Beach : tel. (0208) 2418435, www.golongbeach.org

Colorado: (0870) 0109009

Florida, central: tel. (0207) 9357756, www.cfdc.org/tourism
  Daytona Beach: tel. (0207) 9357756, www.daytonabeach.com
  Keys & Key West: tel. (01564) 794555, www.fla-keys.com
  Greater Fort Lauderdale: tel. (0207) 6309442, www.sunny.org
  Miami: tel. (01444) 250048, www.tropicoolmiami.com
  Kissimmee-St Cloud: tel. (0207) 6301105, www.floridakiss.com
  Lee Island Coast: tel. (0207) 6308825, www.leeislandcoast.com
  Orlando: (09001) 600220 (brochure/infoline)
  Palm Beach County: tel. (01462) 458378, www.palmbeachfl.com
  St Petersburg/Clearwater: tel. (0208) 6514742

Georgia: tel. (0121) 4454554, www.gomm.com

Hawaii: tel. (0181) 9414009, www.gohawaii.com

Illinois: (01564) 794999, www.enjoyillinois.com

Kentucky: tel. (0207) 2280782, www.kentuckytourism.com

Louisiana: (01462) 458696

Maryland: (01295) 750789

Massachusetts: (0207) 9787429

Mississippi: (01462) 440787

Missouri: tel. (01564) 794999, www.missouritourism.org

Nevada: tel. (01564) 794999, www.lasvegas24hours.com

New York City: tel. (0207) 4378300, www.nycvisit.com

North Carolina: (01564) 794999

Pennsylvania: (0207) 7389422

Rhode Island Newport: tel. (01564) 794999, www.gonewport.com

South Carolina: (01462) 458028

Tennessee: (01462) 440784

Texas: (0207) 9785233, www.traveltex.com

Utah: (0207) 7717011

Vermont: tel. (0207) 8367190, www.travel-vermont.com

Virgin Islands (US): tel. (0207) 9785262, www.usvi.net

Virginia: (0208) 6514743

Washington, DC: (0208) 8774521

Washington State: (0207) 9785233, www.tourism.wa.gov

West Virginia: (0207) 9785822, www.wv.us/tourism

Information offices (State)

Each state has Welcome Centers on the interstate highways at the entrance to their state. These act as information centres that can provide maps, leaflets, and other forms of assistance.

Alabama Bureau of Tourism & Travel, Box 4927, Montgomery AL 361036-4927; tel. (334) 2620013, fax 2611111, www.state.al.us, http://alaweb.asc.edu — Alabama

Alaska Division of Tourism, Box 110801, Juneau, AK 99811-0801; tel. (907) 4652010, fax 5868399, www.state.ak.us, www.alaskanet.com/tourism — Alaska

Arizona Office of Tourism, 1100 W Washington St., Phoenix, AZ 85007; tel. (602) 2307733, fax 8428257, www.state.az.us, www.arizonaguide.com — Arizona

Arkansas Department of Parks & Tourism, One Capitol Mall, Dept. 7701, Little Rock, AR 72201; tel. (501) 6827777, fax 6821364, www.state.ar.us, www.ono.com/arkansas/tourhq.htm — Arkansas

California Division of Tourism, 1303 J St., Suite 600, Sacramento, CA — California

Information

95814; tel. (916) 2647777, fax 2647788, www.ca.gov/s/.,
www.gocalif.ca.gov

Colorado
Colorado Travel & Tourism Authority, Box 3524, Englewood, CO 80155;
tel. (1800) 2656723, www.state.co.us, www.colorado.com

Connecticut
Connecticut Department of Economic Development, 865 Brook St.
Rocky Hill, CT 06067; tel. (203) 2584355, fax 2584275, www.state.ct.us

Delaware
Delaware Tourism Office, 99 Kings Highway, Box 1401, Dept. TIA,
Dover, DE 19903; tel. (302) 7394271, fax 7395749, www.state.de.us

District of
Columbia/
Washington, DC
Washington, DC, Convention & Visitors Association, 1212 New York
Ave., Washington, DC 20005; tel. (202) 7897000, fax 7897037,
www.washington.org,dcpages.net

Florida
Florida Tourism Industry Marketing Group, 661 E Jefferson St.,
Tallahassee, FL 32301; tel. (850) 4885607, fax 4870132, www.state.fl.us,
www.florida.de, www.goflorida.com

Georgia
Georgia Department of Industry, Trade & Tourism, Box 1776, Atlanta,
GA 30301-1776; tel. (404) 6563571, fax 6516505; www.state.ga.us,
www.georgia.org

Hawaii
Hawaii Dept. of Business, Economic Development & Tourism, Box 2359
Honolulu, HI 96804; tel. (808) 5762550, fax 5862549, www.hawaii.gov,
www.visithawaii.org

Idaho
Idaho Division Tourism Development, Dept. of Commerce, 700 W State
St. Boise, ID 83720; tel. (208) 3342470, fax 3342631, www.state.id.us

Illinois
Illinois Bureau of Tourism, 100 W Randolph St. Chicago, IL 60601; tel.
(312) 8144732, fax 3146581, www.state.il.us, www.enjoyillinois.com

Indiana
Indiana Dept/Tourism, One North Capital, Suite 700, Indianapolis, IN
46204-2288; tel. (317) 2328860, fax 2324146, www.state.in.us

Iowa
Iowa Division of Tourism, 200 E Grand Ave. Des Moines, IA 50309; tel.
(515) 2424705, fax 2424749, www.state.ia.us

Kansas
Kansas Travel & Tourism Division, 700 SW Harrison, Suite 1300 Topeka,
KS 66601; tel. (785) 2962009, fax 2965055, www.ink.org

Kentucky
Kentucky Department of Travel, 2200 Capitol Plaza Tower, 500 Mero St.,
Frankfort, KY 40601; tel. (502) 5644930, fax 5645695, www.state.ky.us

Louisiana
Louisiana Office of Tourism, Box 94291, Baton Rouge, LA 70804-9291;
tel. (225) 3428119, fax 3428390, www.state.la.us,
www.louisianatravel.com

Maine
Maine Office of Tourism, 189 State St., Augusta, ME 04333; tel. (207)
2875710, fax 2878070, www.state.me.us, www.visitmaine.com

Maryland
Maryland Office of Tourism Development, 217 E Redwood, 9th Floor,
Baltimore, MD 21202; tel. (410) 7673400, fax 3336643,
www.state.md.us, www.mdisfun.com

Massachusetts
Massachusetts Office of Travel & Tourism, 100 Cambridge St., 13th
Floor, Boston, MA 02202; tel. (617) 7273201, fax 7276525,
www.state.ma.us, www.mass-vacation.com

Michigan Travel Bureau, Box 3393, Livonia, MI 48151-3393; tel. (888) 7847328, www.state.mi.us, www.michigan.org   Michigan

Minnesota Office of Tourism, 121 Seventh Place E, St Paul, MN 55101; tel. (651) 2976985, fax 2967995, www.state.mn.us   Minnesota

Mississippi Division of Tourism Development, Box 1705, Ocean Springs, MS 39566-1705; tel. (228) 2144493, fax 2144494, www.state.ms.us, www.mississippi.org   Mississippi

Missouri Division of Tourism, Box 1055, Jefferson City, MO 65102; tel. (573) 7514133, fax 7515160, www.state.mo.us   Missouri

Travel Montana, Box 200533, Helena, MT 59620-00533; tel. (406) 4442654, fax 4442808, www.state.mt.us, www.travel.mt.gov   Montana

Nebraska Division of Travel & Tourism, Box 94666, Lincoln, NE 68509; tel. (402) 4713796, fax 7413778, www.state.ne.us   Nebraska

Nevada Commission on Tourism, Capital Complex, Carson City, NV 89710; tel. (775) 6874322, fax 6876779, www.state.nv.us, www.travel-nevada.com   Nevada

New Hampshire Office of Travel & Tourism Development, Box 856, Concord, NH 03302-0856; tel. (603) 2712665, fax 2716784, www.state.nh.us, www.visitnh.gov   New Hampshire

New Jersey Division of Travel & Tourism, 20 West State St., Trenton, NJ 08625; tel. (609) 2922470, fax 6337418, www.state.nj.us   New Jersey

New Mexico Department of Tourism, 491 Old Santa Fe Trail, Santa Fe, NM 87503; tel. (505) 8277400, fax 8277402, www.state.nm.us, www.newmexico.org   New Mexico

New York State Travel Information Center, One Commerce Plaza, Albany, NY 12245; tel. (518) 4744116, fax 4866446, www.state.ny.us   New York State

North Carolina Division of Travel & Tourism Division, 430 N Salisbury St., Raleigh, NC 27603; tel. (919) 7334171, fax 7338582, www.state.nc.us, www.visitnc.com   North Carolina

North Dakota Tourism Department, Liberty Memorial Bldg., 604 E Blvd., Bismarck, ND 58505; tel. (701) 3282525, fax 3284878, www.state.nd.us   North Dakota

Ohio Division of Travel & Tourism, Box 1001, Columbus, OH 43266-1001; tel. (614) 4668844, fax 4666744, www.travel.state.oh.us   Ohio

Oklahoma Tourism & Recreation Dept., 15 N Robinson, Oklahoma City, OK 73102; tel. (405) 5213981, fax 5213992, www.state.ok.us   Oklahoma

Oregon Economic Development Dept., 775 Summer St., NE, Salem, OR 97310; tel. (503) 9860000, fax 9860001, www.state.or.us, www.traveloregon.com   Oregon

Pennsylvania Office of Travel Marketing, 453 Forum Bldg., Harrisburg, PA 17120; tel. (717) 7875453, fax 7870687, www.state.pa.us   Pennsylvania

Rhode Island Tourism Division, 7 Jackson Walkway Providence, RI 02903; tel. (401) 7511177, fax 4217675, www.state.ri.us, www.visitrhodeisland.com   Rhode Island

South Carolina Department of Parks, Recreation & Tourism, Box 71,   South Carolina

Columbia, SC 29202; tel. (803) 7341700, fax 7340138, www.prt.state.sc.us, www.travelsc.com

South Dakota — South Dakota Department of Tourism, 711 E Well Ave., Pierre, SD 57501-3369; tel. (605) 7733301, fax 7733256, www.state.sd.us

Tennessee — Tennessee Dept. of Tourist Development, 320 Sixth Ave., Nashville, TN 37243; tel. (615) 7418299, fax 7417225, www.state.tn.us

Texas — Texas Dept. of Transportation, Tourism Division, Box 5064, Austin, TX 78763-5064; tel. (512) 4629191, fax 9360088, www.state.tx.us, travel-tex.com

Utah — Utah Travel Council, Capitol Hall, 300 North State St., Salt Lake City, UT 84114; tel. (801) 5381030, fax 5381399, www.state.ut.us, www.utah.com

Vermont — Vermont Dept. of Tourism, Box 1471, Montpelier, VT 05601-1471; tel. (802) 8283237, fax 8283233, www.state.vt.us, www.discover-vermont.com

Virginia — Virginia Tourism Corp., 901 E Byrd St., Richmond, VA 23219-4048; tel. (804) 7862051, fax 7861919, www.state.va.us, www.virginia.org

Washington State — Washington State Tourism, Box 42500, Olympia, WA 98504-2500; tel. (360) 7535600, fax 7534470, www.state.wa.us, www.tourism.wa.gov

West Virginia — West Virginia Division of Tourism, 2101 Washington St. E, Charleston, WV 25305; tel. (304) 3482766, fax 3480108, www.state.wv.us

Wisconsin — Wisconsin Division of Tourism, Box 7606, Madison, WI 53707; tel. (608) 2662161, fax 2663403, www.badger.state.wi.us

Wyoming — Wyoming Division of Tourism, I 25 & College Dr., Cheyenne, WY 82002; tel. (307) 7777777, fax 7776904, www.state.wy.us

Language

It may be helpful to list some of the differences between American and UK English.

American	English
aisle	gangway
apartment	flat
bathrobe	dressing gown
bathroom	toilet
check (in restaurant)	bill
checkroom	cloakroom
closet	cupboard
collect call	reversed charges
cookies, crackers	biscuits
corn	maize
divided highway	dual carriageway
downtown	town centre
drugstore	chemist
elevator	lift
fall	autumn
faucet	tap
flashlight	torch
freeway	motorway

American	English
French fries	chips
gas(oline)	petrol
hood (of car)	bonnet
icebox	refrigerator
license plate (of car)	number plate
line	queue
long distance call	trunk call
mail	post
mailman	postman
movic house	cinema
one way ticket	single ticket
pants	trousers
panty hose	tights
parking lot	car park
potato chips	potato crisps
purse	handbag
restroom	toilet
round trip ticket	return ticket
sedan (car)	saloon
sidewalk	pavement
store	shop
stove	cooker
streetcar	tram
subway	underground
thread	cotton
traffic circle	roundabout
American	English
trunk (of car)	bootwash
cloth	face cloth
wholewheat bread	brown bread
wrench	spanner
zip code	post code

It should also be remembered that the numbering of the floors of a building starts from the ground floor, which in the United States is called the first floor. What in the UK is called the first floor is the second floor in the United States, and so on.

Media

News-stands in the United States offer a very wide range of news-papers and periodicals. The weekend editions of newspapers contain detailed calendars of events and full television, radio and cinema programmes.

Newspapers

The leading newspaper that can be called national is "USA Today". Most papers, including such important journals as the "Boston Globe", the "New York Times", the "Washington Post" and the "Miami Herald", have a mainly regional circulation.

Motoring

To drive a car in the United States visitors must have a valid national driving licence. An international driving licence is not essential but may on occasion be helpful; it is accepted only when accompanied by a national driving licence.

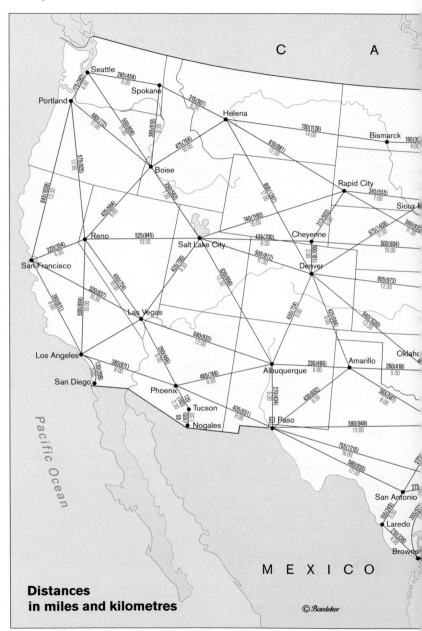

Distances in miles and kilometres

© Baedeker

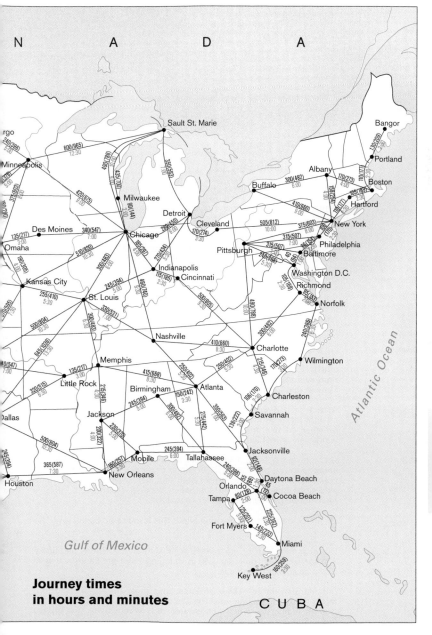

**Journey times
in hours and minutes**

Motoring

<table>
<tr><td>AAA motoring
organisation</td><td>American Automobile Association (AAA, "Triple A")
1000 AAA Dr.
Heathrow, FL 32746-5063
Tel. (407) 4447000</td></tr>
</table>

The AAA is the largest motoring organisation in the United States, with the widest network of branches. For assistance in the event of a breakdown or information tel. (1800) AAAHELP.

Breakdown
Assistance

There are emergency telephones along many highways. If assistance of any kind is required the first thing to do is to call (1800) 336HELP. Otherwise call the AAA (above).

If you have a breakdown in a hired car you should call the rental firm. Tel. 911 for Highway Patrol.

Traffic regulations

Priority

At uncontrolled intersections the vehicle that gets there first has priority.

Speed limits

Traffic-calmed areas in town centres, residential districts, near schools, hospitals and access roads: 15–35 m.p.h.

Arterial roads and highways with traffic in both directions: 45 m.p.h. (35 m.p.h. in areas where game may be crossing at night)

Multi-lane highways and motorways (interstates): 55 m.p.h. (65 m.p.h. on sections of motorway in remote areas with little traffic)

School buses

On a road with traffic in both directions all vehicles must stop when a yellow school bus is taking on or discharging passengers. Where a school bus stops on a carriageway that is separated from traffic coming in the other direction by a broad green strip or an impassable barrier this regulation applies only to traffic going in the same direction as the bus. Disregard of the regulation is subject to severe penalties.

Traffic lights

Traffic lights are situated on the far side of an intersection. It is permissible to turn right against the red provided that you come to a dead stop and give way to any vehicle with priority. At intersections where turning right against the red is not permitted this is indicated by the sign "No Turn on Red".

Headlights

At sunrise and sunset, when visibility is less than 900 ft and on long straight roads with traffic in both directions dipped headlights must be switched on. In some states dipped headlights must be used when the windscreen wipers are in use.

Parking

On highways outside built-up areas and on many roads within built-up areas parking is prohibited. If it becomes necessary to stop on a highway you must pull on to the verge or hard shoulder. There are usually roadside signs indicating where and when parking is permitted. Vehicles must not be parked within 15 ft of a hydrant.

U turns

On many roads U turns are prohibited. This is indicated by the sign "No Turns".

Overtaking

On roads with four or more lanes overtaking on the right is permitted. The same caution must be used in changing to a right-hand lane as in changing to a left-hand one.

Continuous lines

Continuous double yellow or white lines must not be crossed; nor must continuous single lines on the driver's side. Many roads have turn-off lanes, which may be entered only where there is a broken line.

On multi-lane roads in heavily populated areas one lane may be marked with the sign "HOV 2" or "HOV 3". This means that the lane may be used during the morning and evening rush hours only by cars carrying at least two or three people ("HOV" = "high occupancy vehicle"). Some states use different terms. Improper use of an HOV lane is a punishable offence.

Rush-hour lanes

The word "crossing" is frequently abbreviated to "Xing". Thus "Ped Xing" indicates a pedestrian crossing, while "Cattle Xing" is a warning that cattle may be crossing; and in the swamplands of Florida the sign "Gator Xing" invites drivers to keep a lookout for alligators crossing.

Crossings

Cars parked in a prohibited area or in front of an exit may be towed away, and can be recovered only on payment of a heavy penalty.

Tow removal

Hitch-hiking is permitted in the United States, except on motorways (interstates) and their access roads.

Hitch-hiking

Highways and interstate highways

In a country like the United States that depends on the automobile the road system is necessarily extensive and magnificently engineered. Most roads are toll free. Important trunk roads and city motorways are multi-lane and without intersections, permitting a smooth flow of traffic.

The multi-lane interstate highways, without intersections, are the equivalent of the European motorways. They are distinguished from ordinary highways by their blue-white-red signposting. Interstates with even two-digit numbers run east–west; those with odd numbers north–south. Interstates with three-digit numbers are ring roads or bypasses round cities.

Interstate

Highways are main roads, usually with several lanes. They are identified by white signs, and may be either federal (e.g. US 17) or state roads (e.g. SR 14 or VA 14). Again odd-numbered roads run broadly north–south and even-numbered roads east–west. The addition of ALT ("alternative") or BUS ("business") to the number indicates that the road is a bypass. Unlike the interstates, highways have intersections. Great care is necessary, therefore, at road junctions and when turning left.

Highways

On roads with separate carriageways exits are normally on the right. Where the road narrows the exit may well be on the left.

Exits

Filling stations

The United States is covered by a dense network of filling stations (gas stations, service stations). On interstate highways filling stations are signposted well in advance. Filling stations now supply almost exclusively lead-free petrol in "regular" and "premium" grades; leaded petrol is rarely available.

At many filling stations, particularly in the evening and at night, payment in advance is required. If payment is made by credit card there is occasionally an additional charge of a few cents per gallon. There are often separate pumps for attendant service and self-service (which is cheaper).

Museums

Before visiting a museum it is advisable to check the opening hours either with the museum itself or through the local tourist office. Many museums are closed on Monday, and some also on Sunday morning or on another weekday. Admission charges can be high, though at some museums there are reductions for children, students and senior citizens.

Children's
museums

American museums are much more suited to young visitors than many of their European counterparts, and many of them have "Hands On" or "Please Touch" sections where children can try out all kinds of scientific experiments and puzzle solving for themselves. Many cities also have special children's museums, usually designed to introduce them to natural sciences and technology in a child-friendly way.

National Parks and Reserves

Many areas in the United States are under special statutory protection. They fall into three main categories: National and State Parks, National and State Forests, National Seashores; heritage sites such as National and State Monuments, archaeological sites; and Recreation Areas. Land use in all these parks and other areas – which are usually well signed – is strictly controlled and visitors are regulated accordingly. Conservation areas are watched over by specially trained park rangers. To explore them on your own you either need the ranger's permission or the ranger must accompany you.

Admission charges, which vary according to the vehicle and the number of passengers, can be quite high, so if you intend to visit several national parks it is worth buying a Golden Eagle Pass. This currently costs $50 and gives free entry to all national parks for a year; it is available from park entrances and visitor centres.

National parks provide accommodation in motels, lodges, cabins and campsites, but it is always advisable to book in advance. For reservation call (800) 3652267 toll free.

Code of conduct

Visitors must keep to the official trails and roads in National Parks and other protected areas. You will only be allowed to camp or light fires on sites set apart for the purpose. It is forbidden to leave litter or feed wild animals. It goes without saying that you are not allowed to remove plants or wildlife.

Information on National Parks and National Monuments

For details of all National Parks, including information, pictures, maps and reservation options, contact:

National Park Service Office of Public Inquiries
Box 37127, Room 1013
Washington, DC 20013-7127
Tel. (202) 2084747; www.nps.gov

The sites listed below are shown in red or green on the large map of the United States at the back of this guide and so can be easily located.

Alabama

Horseshoe Bend National Military Park, 11238 Horseshoe Bend Rd., Daviston
Little River Canyon National Preserve, Fort Payne

Russell Cave National Monument, 3279 County Rd. 98, Bridgeport
Tuskegee Institute National Historic Site, Tuskegee Institute

Alagnak Wild River, c/o Katmal National Park and Preserve, King Salmon   Alaska
Aniakchak National Monument and Preserve, King Salmon
Bering Land Bridge National Preserve, Nome
Cape Krusenstern National Monument, Kotzebue
Denali National Park and Preserve, McKinley Park
Gates of the Arctic National Park and Preserve, Fairbanks
Glacier Bay National Park and Preserve, Gustavus
Katmal National Park and Preserve, KIng Salmon
Kenai Fjords National Park, Seward
Klondike Gold Rush National Historical Park, Skagway
Kobuk Valley National Park, Kotzebue
Lake Clark National Park and Preserve, Anchorage
Noatak National Preserve, Kotzebue
Sitka National Historical Park, Sitka
Wrangell-St Elias National Park and Preserve, Glennallen
Yukon-Charley Rivers National Preserve, Eagle

Canyon de Chelly National Monument, Chinle   Arizona
Casa Grande National Monument, 1100 Ruins Dr., Coolidge
Chiricahua National Monument, Dos Cabezas Route, Willcox
Coronada National Monument, 4101 E Montezuma Canyon Rd.,
Hereford
Fort Bowie National Historic Site, Bowie
Grand Canyon National Park, Grand Canyon
Hubbell Trading Post National Historic Site, Ganado
Montezuma Castle National Monument, Camp Verde
Navajo National Monument, HC 71, Tonalea

Arizona: Grand Canyon country

581

National Parks and Reserves

Organ Pipe Cactus National Monument, Route 1, Ajo
Petrified Forest National Park
Pipe Spring National Monument, Moccasin
Saguaro National Park, Tucson
Sunset Crater National Monument, Route 3, Flagstaff
Tonto National Monument, Roosevelt
Tumacacori National Park, Tumacacori
Tuzigoot National Monument, Camp Verde
Walnut Canyon National Monument, Walnut Canyon Rd., Flagstaff
Wupatki National Monument, HC 33, Flagstaff

Arkansas
Arkansas Post National Memorial, Route 1, Gillet
Buffalo National River, Harrison
Fort Smith National Historic Site, Fort Smith
Hot Springs National Park, Hot Springs
Pea Ridge National Military Park, Pea Ridge

California
Cabrillo National Monument, San Diego
Channel Islands National Park, Ventura
Death Valley National Park, Death Valley
Daveils Postpile National Monument, Three Rivers
Eugene O'Neill National Historic Site, 1000 Kuss Rd., Danville
Fort Point National Historic Site, Presidio of San Francisco
Golden Gate National Recreation Area, Fort Mason, San Francisco
John Muir National Historic Site, 4202 Alhambra Ave., Martinez
Joshua Tree National Park, Twentynine Palms
Kings Canyon National Park, Three Rivers
Lassen Volcanic National Park, Mineral
Lava Beds National Monument, Tulelake

Indian settlement in Mesa Verde National Park, Colorado

Manzanar National Historic Site, c/o Death Valley National Monument, Death Valley
Mojave National Preserve, Barstow
Muir Woods National Monument, Mill Valley
Pinnacles National Monument, Paicines
Point Reyes National Seashore, Point Reyes
Redwood National Park, Crescent City
San Francisco Martime National Historical Park, Fort Mason, San Francisco
Santa Monica Mountains National Recreation Area, Agoura Hills
Sequoia National Park, Three Rivers
Whiskeytown-Shasta Trinity National Recreation Area, Whiskeytown
Yosemite National Park

Bent's Old Fort National Historic Site, 35110 Highway 194 E, La Junta   Colorado
Black Canyon of the Gunnison National Monument, 2233 E Main, Montrose
Colorado National Monument, Fruita
Curecanti National Recreation Area, Gunnison
Dinosaur National Monument (CO, UT), Dinosaur
Florissant Fossil Beds National Monument, Florissant
Great Sand Dunes National Monument, 11500 Highway 150, Mosca
Hovenweep National Monument, McElmo Route, Cortez
Mesa Verde National Park
Rocky Mountains National Park, Estes Park
Yucca House National Monument, c/o Mesa Verde National Park

Weir Farm National Historic Site, 735 Nod Hill Rd., Wilton   Connecticut

Constitution Gardens, Washington, DC   District of
Ford's Theatre National Historic Site, Washington, DC   Columbia
Frederick Douglass National Historic Site, Washington, DC
Lyndon B. Johnson Memorial Grove on the Potomac, c/o George Washington Memorial Parkway, Turkey Run Park, McLean
Mary McLeod Bethune Council House National Historic Site, Washington, DC
National Capital Parks, National Capital Region, 1100 Ohio Dr., SW, Washington, DC
National Mall, Washington, DC
Pennsylvania Avenue National Historic Site, Washington, DC
Rock Creek Park, Washington, DC
Theodore Roosevelt Island, c/o George Washington Memorial Parkway, Turkey Run Park, McLean

Big Cypress National Preserve, HCR 61, Ochopee   Florida
Biscayne National Park, Homestead
Canaveral National Seashore, Titusville
Castillo de San Marcos National Monument, 1 Castillo Dr., St Augustine
De Soto National Memorial, Bradenton
Everglades National Park, Homestead
Fort Caroline National Memorial, 12713 Fort Caroline Rd., Jacksonville
Fort Matanzas National Monument, c/o Castillo de San Marcos
Gulf Islands National Seashore, 1801 Gulf Breeze Parkway, Gulf Breeze
Timucuan Ecological and Historic Preserve, Jacksonville

Andersonville National Historic Site, Route 1, Andersonville   Georgia
Chattahoochee River National Recreation Area, 1978 Island Ford Parkway, Dunwoody
Chickamauga and Chattanooga National Military Park (GA, TN), Fort Oglethorpe
Cumberland Island National Seashore, St Marys

National Parks and Reserves

Fort Frederica National Monument, Route 9, St Simons Island, GA 31522-9710
Fort Pulaski National Monument, Savannah
Jimmy Carter National Historic Site, 100 Main St., Plains
Kennesaw Mountain National Battlefield Park, 900 Kennesaw Mountain Dr., Kennesaw
Martin Luther King Jr National Historic Site, 522 Auburn Ave., NE, Atlanta
Ocmulgee National Monument, 1207 Emery Highway, Macon

Hawaii
Haleakala National Park, Makawao
Hawaii Volcanoes National Park, Hawaii National Park
Kalaupapa National Historical Park, Kalaupapa
Kaloko-Honokohau National Historical Park, Kailua, Kona
Pu'uhonua o Honaunau National Historical Park, Honaunau, Kona
Puukohola Heiau National Historic Site, Kawaihae
USS Arizona Memorial, 1 Arizona Memorial Place, Honolulu

Idaho
City of Rocks National Reserve, Almo
Craters of the Moon National Monument, Arco
Hagerman Fossil Beds National Monument, 221 N State St., Hagerman
Nez Perce National Historical Park, Highway 95, Spalding

Illinois
Lincoln Home National Historic Site, 413 S Eighth St., Springfield

Indiana
George Rogers Clark National Historical Park, Vincennes
Indiana Dunes National Lakeshore, Porter
Lincoln Boyhood National Memorial, Lincoln City

Iowa
Effigy Mounds National Monument, 151 Highway 76, Harpers Ferry
Herbert Hoover National Historic Site, West Branch

Kansas
Brown v. Board of Education National Historic Site, Omaha
Fort Larned, National Historic Site, Route 3, Larned
Fort Scott National Historic Site, Old Fort Blvd., Fort Scott

Kentucky
Abraham Lincoln Birthplace National Historic Site, 2995 Lincoln Farm Rd., Hodgenville
Cumberland Gap National Historical Park, Middlesboro
Mammoth Cave National Park, Mammoth Cave

Louisiana
Cane River Creole National Historical Park and Heritage Area, New Orleans
Poverty Point National Monument, c/o Poverty Point State Commemorative Area, Epps

Maine
Acadia National Park, Bar Harbor
Appalachian National Scienic Trail, c/o Harpers Ferry Center, Harpers Ferry
Saint Croix Island International Historic Site, c/o Acadia NP

Maryland
Antietam National Battlefield, Sharpsburg
Assateague Island National Seashore, 7206 National Seashore Lane, Berlin
Catoctin Mountain Park, Thurmont
Chesapeake and Ohio Canal National Historical Park, Sharpsburg
Clare Barton National Historic Site, 5801 Oxford Rd., Glen Echo
Fort McHenry National Monument and Historic Shrine, E Fort Ave., Baltimore
Fort Washington Park, Washington, DC
Greenbelt Park, 6565 Greenbelt Road, Greenbelt
Hampton National Historic Site, 535 Hampton Lane, Towson

Monocacy National Battlefield, 4801 Urbana Pike, Frederick
Piscataway Park, Washington, DC
Potomac Heritage National Scenic Trail, Washington, DC
Thomas Stone National Historic Site, 6655 Rosehill Rd., Port Tobacco

Adams National Historic Site, 135 Adams St., Quincy   Massachusetts
Boston African-American National Historic Site, 46 Joy St., Boston
Boston National Historical Park, Charlestown Navy Yard, Boston
Cape Cod National Seashore, South Wellfleet
Frederick Law Olmstead National Historic Site, 99 Warren St., Brookline
John F. Kennedy National Historic Site, 83 Beals St., Brookline
Longfellow National Historic Site, 105 Brattle St., Cambridge
Lowell National Historical Park, 169 Merrimack St., Lowell
Minute Man National Historical Park, Concord
Salem Maritime National Historic Site, Custom House, 174 Derby St., Salem
Saugus Iron Works National Historic Site, 244 Central St., Saugus
Springfield Armory National Historic Site, 1 Armory Square, Springfield

Isle Royale National Park, Houghton   Michigan
Keweenaw National Historical Park, Calumet
Pictured Rocks National Lakeshore, Munising
Sleeping Bear Dunes National Lakeshore, 9922 Front St., Empire

Grand Portage National Monument, Grand Marais   Minnesota
Mississippi National River and Recreation Area, St Paul
Pipestone National Monument, Pipestone
Voyageurs National Park, 3131 Highway 53, International Falls

Brices Crossroads National Battlefield Site, c/o Natchez Trace Parkway,   Mississippi
Tupelo
Gulf Islands National Seashore, Ocean Springs
Natchez National Historical Park, Natchez
Natchez Trace National Scenic Trail, c/o Natchez Trace Parkway, Tupelo
Natchez Trace Parkway, Rural Route 1, Tupelo
Tupelo National Battlefield, c/o Natchez Trace Parkway
Vicksburg National Military Park, Vicksburg

George Washington Carver National Monument, Carver Rd., Diamond   Missouri
Harry S. Truman National Historic Site, 223 N Main St., Independence
Jefferson National Expansion Memorial, 11 N 4th St., St Louis
Ozark National Scenic Riverways, Van Buren
Ulysses S. Grant National Historic Site, 7400 Grant St., St Louis
Wilson's Creek National Battlefield, Route 2, Republic

Big Hole National Battlefield, Wisdom   Montana
Bighorn Canyon National Recreation Area, Fort Smith
Glacier National Park, West Glacier
Grant-Kohrs Ranch National Historic Site, Deer Lodge
Little Bighorn Battlefield National Monument, c/o Crow Agency

Agate Fossil Beds National Monument, Gering   Nebraska
Homestead National Monument of America, Route 3, Beatrice
Missouri National Recreation River, O'Neill
Niobrara National Scenic River, c/o Missouri National Recreation River
Scotts Bluff National Monument, Gering

Great Basin National Park, Baker   Nevada
Lake Mead National Recreation Area, 601 Nevada Highway, Boulder
City

Saint-Gaudens National Historic Site, Rural Route 3, Cornish   New Hampshire

National Parks and Reserves

New Jersey
Edison National Historic Site, Main St. and Lakeside Ave., West Orange
Great Egg Harbor Scenic and Recreation Area, Philadelphia
Morristown National Historical Park, Morristown

New Mexico
Aztec Ruins National Monument, Aztec
Bandelier National Monument, HCR 1, Los Alamos
Capulin Volcano National Monument, Capulin
Carlsbad Caverns National Park, 3225 National Parks Highway, Carlsbad
Chaco Culture National Historical Park, Star Route 4, Bloomfield
El Malpais National Monument, Grants
El Morro National Monument, Route 2, Ramah
Fort Union National Monument, Watrous
Gila Cliff Dwellings National Monument, Route 11, Silver City
Pecos National Historical Park, Pecos
Petroglyph National Monument, 123 Fourth St. SW, Albuquerque
Salinas Pueblo Missions National Monument, Mountainair
White Sands National Monument, Holloman

New York
Castle Clinton National Monument, Manhattan Sites, New York
Eleanor Roosevelt National Historic Site, 519 Albany Post Rd., Hyde Park
Federal Hall National Memorial, New York
Fire Island National Seashore, 120 Laurel St., Patchogue
Fort Stanwix National Monument, 112 E Park St., Rome
Gateway National Recreation Area, Brooklyn
General Grant National Memorial, 122nd St. and Riverside Dr., New York
Hamilton Grange National Memorial, 287 Convent Ave., New York
Home of Franklin D. Roosevelt National Historic Site, 519 Albany Post Rd., Hyde Park
Martin Van Buren National Historic Site, Kinderhook
Sagamore Hill National Historic Site, 20 Sagamore Hill Rd., Oyster Bay

Mabry Mill, an idyllic spot in the Blue Ridge Parkway, North Carolina

St Paul's Church National Historic Site, 897 S Columbus Ave., Mount Vernon
Saratoga National Historical Park, Stillwater
Statue of Liberty National Monument (NY, NJ), Liberty Island, New York
Theodore Roosevelt Birthplace National Historic Site, 28 E 20th St., New York
Theodore Roosevelt Inaugural National Historic Site, 641 Delaware Ave., Buffalo
Vanderbilt Mansion National Historic Site, 519 Albany Post Rd., Hyde Park
Women's Rights National Historical Park, 136 Fall St., Seneca Falls

Blue Ridge Parkway, Asheville   North Carolina
Cape Hatteras National Seashore, Route 1, Manteo
Cape Lookout National Seashore, Harkers Island
Carl Sandburg Home National Historic Site, 1928 Little River Rd., Flat Rock
Fort Raleigh National Historic Site, c/o Cape Hatteras National Seashore
Guilford Courthouse National Military Park, Greensboro
Moores Creek National Battlefield, Currie
Wright Brothers National Memorial, c/o Cape Hatteras National Seashore

Fort Union Trading Post National Historic Site, Rural Route 3, Williston   North Dakota
Knife River Indian Villages National Historic Site, Rural Route 1, Stanton
Theodore Roosevelt National Park, Medora

Cuyahoga Valley National Recreation Area, Brecksville   Ohio
Dayton Aviation Heritage National Historic Park, Wright Brothers Station, Dayton
Hopewell Culture National Historical Park, 16062 State Route 104, Chillicothe
James A. Garfield National Historic Site, 8095 Mentor Ave., Mentor
Perry's Victory and International Peace Memorial, 93 Delaware Ave., Put-in-Bay
William Howard Taft National Historic Site, 2038 Auburn Ave., Cincinnati

Chickasaw National Recreation Area, Sulphur   Oklahoma

Crater Lake National Park, Crater Lake   Oregon
Fort Clatsop National Memorial, Route 3, Astoria
John Day Fossil Beds National Monument, 420 W Main St., John Day
Oregon Caves National Monument, 19000 Caves Highway, Cave Junction

Allegheny Portage Railroad National Historic Site, Cresson   Pennsylvania
Delaware Water Gap National Recreation Area, Bushkill
Edgar Allan Poe National Historic Site, c/o Independence NHP
Eisenhower National Historic Site, Gettysburg
Fort Necessity National Battlefield, The National Pike, RD 2, Farmington
Friendship Hill National Historic Site, c/o Fort Necessity National Battlefield
Gettysburg National Military Park, Gettysburg
Hopewell Furnace National Historic Site, 2 Mark Bird Lane, Elverson
Independence National Historical Park, Philadelphia
Johnstown Flood National Memorial, c/o Allegheny Portage Railroad NHS
Thaddeus Kosciuszko National Memorial, c/o Independence NHP
Middle Delaware National Scenic River, c/o Delaware Water Gap National Recreation Area, Bushkill
Steamtown National Historic Site, 150 S Washington Ave., Scranton
Upper Delaware Scenic and Recreational River, Narrowsburg

National Parks and Reserves

Valley Forge National Historical Park, Valley Forge

Rhode Island   Roger Williams National Memorial, 282 N Main St., Providence

South Carolina   Charles Pinckney National Historic Site, c/o Fort Sumter National Monument
Congaree Swamp National Monument, 200 Caroline Sims Rd., Hopkins
Cowpens National Battlefield, Chesnee
Fort Sumter National Monument, 1214 Middle St., Sullivans Island
Kings Mountain National Military Park, Kings Mountain
Ninety Six National Historic Site, Ninety Six

South Dakota   Badlands National Park, Interior
Jewel Cave National Monument, Rural Route 1, Custer
Mount Rushmore National Memorial, Keystone
Wind Cave National Park, Rural Route 1, Hot Springs

Tennessee   Andrew Johnson National Historic Site, Greeneville
Big South Fork National River and Recreation Area, Route 3, Oneida
Fort Donelson National Battlefield, Dover
Great Smoky Mountains National Park, Gatlinburg
Obed Wild and Scenic River, Wartburg
Shiloh National Military Park, Route 1, Shiloh
Stones River National Battlefield, 3501 Old Nashville Highway, Murfreesboro

Texas   Alibates Flint Quarries National Monument, c/o Lake Meredith Recreation Area
Amistad Recreation Area, Del Rio
Big Bend National Park
Big Thicket National Preserve, Beaumont
Chamizal National Memorial, 800 S San Marcial, El Paso
Fort Davis National Historic Site, Fort Davis
Guadalupe Mountains National Park, HC 60, Salt Flat
Lake Meredith Recreation Area, Fritch
Lyndon B. Johnson National Historical Park, Johnson City
Padre Island National Seashore, 9405 S Padre Island Drive, Corpus Christi
Palo Alto Battlefield National Historic Site, Brownsville
Rio Grande Wild and Scenic River, c/o Big Bend National Park
San Antonio Missions National Historical Park, San Antonio

Utah   Arches National Park, Moab
Bryce Canyon National Park, Bryce Canyon
Canyonlands National Park, Moab
Capitol Reef National Park, Torrey
Cedar Breaks National Monument, 82 N 100 E St., Cedar City
Glen Canyon National Recreation Area, Page
Golden Spike National Historic Site, Brigham City
Natural Bridges National Monument, Lake Powell
Rainbow Bridge National Monument, c/o Glen Canyon NRA
Timpanogos Cave National Historic Site, Rural Route 3, American Fork
Zion National Park, Springdale

Vermont   Marsh-Billings National Historical Park

Virginia   Appomattox Court House National Historical Park, Appomattox
Arlington House, Robert E. Lee Memorial, c/o George Washington Memorial Parkway
Booker T. Washington National Monument, Route 3, Hardy
Colonial National Historical Park, Yorktown
Fredericksburg and Spotsylvania County Battlefield Memorial National Military Park, Fredericksburg

George Washington Birthplace National Monument, Rural Route 1, Washington's Birthplace
George Washington Memorial Parkway, Turkey Run Park, McLean
Maggie L. Walker National Historic Site, c/o Richmond National Battlefield Park
Manassas National Battlefield Park, 12521 Lee Highway, Manassas
Petersburg National Battlefield, Route 36 E, Petersburg
Prince William Forest Park, Triangle
Richmond National Battlefield Park, 3215 E Broad St., Richmond
Shenandoah National Park, Route 4, Luray
Wolf Trap Farm Park for the Performing Arts, 1551 Trap Rd., Vienna

Coulee Dam National Recreation Area, Coulee Dam   Washington
Ebey's Landing National Historical Reserve, Coupeville
Fort Vancouver National Historic Site, 612 E Reserve St., Vancouver
Klondike Gold Rush National Historical Park, Seattle
Lake Chelan National Recreation Area, 2105 Highway 20, Sedro Woolley
Mount Rainier National Park, Tahoma Woods, Star Route, Ashford
North Cascades National Park, 2105 Highway 20, Sedro Woolley
Olympic National Park, Port Angeles
Ross Lake National Recreation Area, 2105 Highway 20, Sedro Woolley
San Juan Island National Historical Park, Friday Harbor
Whitman Mission National Historic Site, Route 2, Walla Walla

Bluestone National Scenic River, c/o New River Gorge National River   West Virginia
Gauley River National Scenic River, c/o Bluestone National Scenic River
Harpers Ferry National Historical Park, Harpers Ferry
New River Gorge National River, Glen Jean

Apostle Islands National Lakeshore, Route 1, Bayfield   Wisconsin
St Croix National Scenic Riverways, St Croix Falls

The historic birthplace of George Washington, Virginia

Wyoming

Devils Tower National Monument, Devils Tower
Fort Laramie National Historic Site, Fort Laramie
Fossil Butte National Monument, Kemmerer
Grand Teton National Park, Moose
John D. Rockefeller Jr Memorial Parkway, c/o Grand Teton NP
Yellowstone National Park

Opening Hours

Banks

In almost every shopping centre and at airports there is at least one bank as well as ATMs. Banks are usually open Mon.–Thu. 8.30am–3 or 3.30pm, Fri. 6pm. At weekends and on public holidays only the banks at international airports are open.

Post offices

See Post

Shops

Retail hours are much more flexible than in some parts of Europe. Most stores open Mon.–Sat. 9am–5pm. Shopping malls are usually open seven days a week until around 9pm (except Sundays). Many stores – especially along highways and in the big cities – also open on Sundays (until 6pm at the latest) or stay open round the clock.

Post

The United States Mail is responsible for postal services (including letters, parcels and the remittance of money) in the United States. Telephone and telegraph services are provided by private companies.

Post offices

Post offices – identified by the American flag – are open Mon.–Fri. 9am–5 or 6pm, Sat. 8am–noon. Small offices close for lunch. In large cities there are post offices open round the clock.

Postboxes

American postboxes are blue, with "US Mail" in white and a stylised eagle.

Public Holidays

There are relatively few public holidays in the United States, and many shops are open on holidays other than Thanksgiving Day, Easter Day, Christmas and New Year, though banks, government offices, schools and even some restaurants are closed. On the great Christian festivals (Easter, Whitsun, Christmas) there is no second day's holiday.

Most official holidays are fixed afresh each year and, in order to produce a long weekend, moved to a Monday before or after the actual day.

Public holidays

January 1st: New Year
Third Monday in January: Martin Luther King Jr's Birthday
Third Monday in February: President's Day
Shrove Tuesday: Mardi Gras (Carnival; only regional, mainly in the Panhandle)
Good Friday (only local)
April 26th: Confederate Memorial Day
Last Monday in May: Memorial Day
July 4th: Independence Day
First Monday in September: Labor Day
Second Monday in October: Columbus Day

November 11th: Veterans' Day
Fourth Thursday in November: Thanksgiving Day
December 25th: Christmas Day

Public Transport

Greyhound

Greyhound Inc. operates services between all the main American cities and tourist centres; their buses are usually comfortable and well equipped.

Information about Greyhound fares and timetables is available from: fax (212) 9672239, or, in the United States, on the toll-free hotline (1800) 2312222.

Greyhound's International Ameripass entitles non-US citizens to cheap travel over the whole network for 7, 10, 15, 30, 45 or 60 days, prices vary according to the season from $149 for a 7 day pass to $499 for a 60 day. It is advisable to buy it from a travel agent before you leave home since in the United States the Ameripass costs more and can only be bought from:

International
Ameripass

Greyhound International Office
625 Eighth Ave.
New York, NY 10018
Tel. (1800) 2468572, (212) 9710492

Amtrak

Although America's economic history, and with it the growth of tourism, was inextricably linked with the railroad, nowadays this is very much a subsidiary means of transport. Amtrak has had to reduce its number of lines and some of its routes are now covered by buses. Even so, a train journey on one of the great railroad routes – with the "City of New Orleans", say, from Chicago on the Great Lakes to New Orleans on the Gulf of Mexico – is still something to remember.

Amtrak, America's National Railroad Passenger Corporation, is responsible for timetabling and operating Inter City rail services in the United States. Accommodation includes coach class (ordinary seating) and sleepers. Children under two usually travel free, and children aged from 2 to 15 pay half fare.

Amtrak offers six different rail passes, valid for either 15 or 30 days, which can be bought outside the United States at very advantageous rates. The national USA Rail Pass covers their whole rail network: peak season (1 June–6 Sept.) $440/15 days, $550/30 days; low season $295/15 days, $385/30 days. The other cheaper passes, which also have to be bought before departure for the United States, are for different regions: Eastern Region, Western Region, Far Western Region, Coastal Region, and Northeast Region. Amtrak Passes are available from US travel specialists, travel agents and some tour operators.

Rail pass

In the United Kingdom from:

Information

Destination Marketing Ltd; tel. (0207) 4007099
LEISURAIL; tel. (0870) 7500222
Trailfinders Ltd.; tel. (0207) 9375400

In the United States from:

591

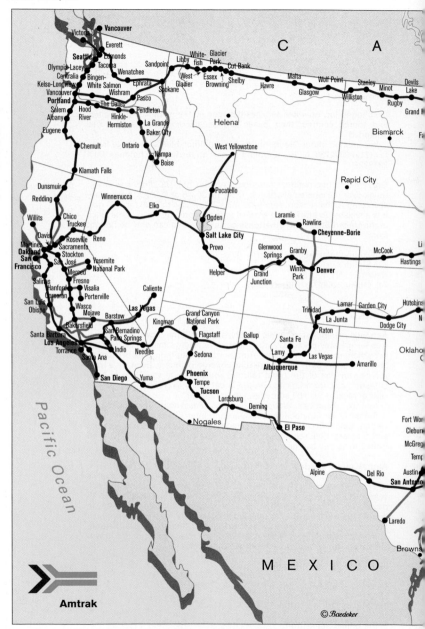

Amtrak

Public Transport

Amtrak, Union Station, 60 Massachusetts Ave., NE, Washington, DC 20002; tel. (202) 4847540, fax (202) 9062211, www.amtrak.com
New York; tel. (212) 5826875
Philadelphia; (215) 8241600

Amtrak hotline throughout the United States: (1800) 8727245

Inter City trains

Metroliner: New York–Washington, DC
Northeast Direct: main routes Newport News–Washington, DC, New York–Boston
Twilight Shoreliner: Newport News–Boston
Keystone: New York–Philadelphia–Harrisburg
Empire Service: New York–Albany–Niagara Falls–Toronto
Adirondack: New York–Montreal
Vermonter: New York–St Albans, VT
Ethan Allen Express: New York– Rutland, VT
Silver Service: New York–Tampa/Miami
Carolinian & Piedmont: New York–Charlotte
Crescent: New York–New Orleans
Lake Shore Limited: Boston/New York–Chicago
Three Rivers: New York–Philadelphia–Pittsburgh–Chiacgo
Capitol Limited: Washington, DC–Pittsburgh–Cleveland–Chicago
Cardinal: Washington, DC–Charleston, WV–Chicago
Midwest Corridor: several routes by different operators fanning out from Chicago, including to Kansas City, Cincinnati and Toronto
City of New Orleans: Chicago–New Orleans
Texas Eagle: Chicago–Houston/San Antonio
Southwest Chief: Chicago–Albuquerque–Los Angeles
California Zephyr: Chicago–Denver–Salt Lake City–Emeryville/San Francisco
Empire Builder: Chicago–Minneapolis/St Paul–Seattle/Portland
Sunset Limited: Los Angeles–New Orleans–Orlando
Coast Starlight: Seattle–Emeryville/San Francisco–Santa Barbara–Los Angeles
Cascades Service: Eugene–Portland–Seattle–Vancouver
California Corridors: several routes by various operators in California and to Nevada

Autorail

A train carrying cars runs daily in each direction between Lorton (VA, near Washington, DC) and Sanford (FL, near Orlando).

Steam railways

In the United States as in other countries there is a great nostalgia for steam trains. All over the country old lines, either standard or narrow gauge, have been brought back into use, mining and lumbering lines have been restored and small railway museums have been established. On some longer stretches of line there are excursions on "dinner trains", sometimes made up of a curious medley of rolling stock. The following is a selection of old-time lines, with the point of departure.

Alaska

White Pass and Yukon Route, Skagway

Arizona

Grand Canyon Railway, Williams

Arkansas

Eureka Springs and North Arkansas Railway, Eureka Springs

California

Napa Valley Railroad; Roaring Camp and Big Trees Narrow Gauge Railroad; Santa Cruz Big Trees and Pacific Railway, Felton

Connecticut

Valley Railroad Co., North Cove Express Dinner Train, Essex

Durango and Silverton Narrow Gauge Railroad, Durango; Georgetown Loop Railroad, Georgetown	Colorado
Seminole Gulf Railway, Fort Myers-Bonita Springs	Florida
Lahaina, Kaanapali and Pacific Railroad, Maui Island	Hawaii
The Enter-train-ment Line, Union Bridge	Maryland
Kalamazoo, Lake Shore and Chicago Railway, Paw Paw	Michigan
Osceola and St Croix Valley Railway; Minnesota Zephir Dinner Train, Stillwater	Minnesota
Fremont and Elkhorn Valley Railroad, Fremont	Nebraska
Nevada Northern Railway, East Ely	Nevada
New York and Lake Erie Railroad, Gowanda	New York
Great Smoky Mountains Railway, Dillsboro	North Carolina
Sumpter Valley Railroad, Baker City	Oregon
Strasburg Railroad, Strasburg	Pennsylvania
Black Hills Central Railroad, Hill City	South Dakota
Broadway Dinner Train, Nashville	Tennessee
Texas State Railroad, Rusk-Palestine	Texas
Spirit of Washington Dinner Train, Renton	Washington
Cass Scenic Railroad State Park, Cass	West Virginia

Restaurants

In the tourist regions of the United States there are not only an enormous choice of restaurants but also a surprisingly wide range of ethnic cuisines. In addition to restaurants serving "American" cuisine – which has a great deal more to offer than hamburgers and hot dogs, influenced as it has been by the cuisine of many other countries – there are many Italian and Chinese restaurants, "Tex-Mex" restaurants offering Texan and Mexican specialities, gourmet temples of French cuisine and innumerable German, Swiss, Austrian, Korean, Vietnamese, Thai, Japanese, Brazilian, Argentinian and Arab restaurants. Kosher and vegetarian food is increasingly popular. On the coast there are numerous restaurants specialising in fish and seafood. And visitors will not want to miss the opportunity of sampling the excellent wines produced in the United States.

Restaurants in the United States cover a wide price range, but a good meal need not cost a fortune. Many bars serve tasty snacks such as chilli con carne, chicken fingers, sandwiches and hamburgers. To eat at reasonable cost it is not necessary to patronise restaurant chains such as Taco Bell, Pizza Hut, McDonald's, Burger King and Kentucky Fried Chicken, which are cheap but not always entirely satisfying (though Denny's and Friday's are exceptions). There are better – and not necessarily too expensive – restaurants in areas frequented by tourists, in old

Prices

town centres that have been regenerated, in holiday resorts and round large hotel complexes.

Almost all restaurants accept payment by credit card or traveller's cheque as well as in cash.

Children

Eating out with children is made easy; all family restaurant chains provide children's menus, high chairs and reasonable prices; the Chuck E. Cheese diners are specially designed for children. Some steak-house chains and Chinese restaurants cater for family budgets too, although more upmarket restaurants are less likely to cater for children.

If you have to watch your budget, look out for places that offer "all you can eat": if junior cannot manage to eat up you can often get the leftovers in a "doggie pack" to take away with you.

Reservations

In the more expensive restaurants, particularly at long weekends and during the main holiday season, it is advisable to book a table in advance.

In good restaurants it is usual to wait to be shown to your table by one of the staff. Guests will often be asked "smoking or non-smoking?".

Tipping

See entry

Restaurants (selection)

The prices given are the average cost of a main course in the evening, not including drinks.

Albuquerque

Conrad's
2nd St. (in the historic La Posada Hotel); tel. (505) 2429090; from $25
One of the best (and most expensive) restaurants in town; delicious Spanish and Mexican cuisine.

66 Diner
1405 Central Ave.; tel. (505) 2471421; from $10
Here the Fifties live on, as when Route 66 ran right through the town; the menu features ham and eggs, all sorts of burgers, and grilled liver and onions.

Atlanta

Patio by the River
4199 Paces Ferry Rd. NW; tel. (404) 4322808; $15–20
French cooking southern style; lovely location on the Chattahochee River.

Pittypat's Porch
25 International Blvd.; tel. (404) 5258228; from $20
One of the best soul-food restaurants in town.

Varsity Drive Inn
61 North Ave.
This really is something else: big fast-food drive-in with the whole range from burgers and chicken breast to chili dog, but so good that it is always crowded.

Atlantic City

Angelo's Fairmount Tavern
2300 Fairmount Ave.; tel. (609) 3442439; $10–15
Atlantic City's favourite Italian restaurant.

Dock's Oyster House
2405 Atlantic Ave.; tel. (609) 3450092; $25–30
Tops for seafood since 1897, and still owned by the Dougherty family.

Baltimore

Obrycki's Crab House

1727 E Pratt St.; tel. (410) 7326399, from $20
Obrycki's, in trendy Fells Point, specialises in crabs from Chesapeake
Bay, but its steaks and chicken dishes are not to be despised.

Women's Industrial Exchange Tea Room
333 N Charles St.; tel. (410) 6854388; $5–10
Something special: the (mature) ladies serve good plain fare such as
soups, salads, omelettes in an authentic 19th c. atmosphere; closed after
teatime.

Hamersley's Bistro
Boston

553 Tremont St.; tel. (617) 4232700; $20–30
Gordon Hamersley is reckoned to be a trendsetter with a refreshingly
nouvelle approach to New England cuisine.

Ye Olde Union Oyster House
41 Union St.; tel. (617) 2272750; from $30
Boston's oldest restaurant (1826) is the leading authority on seafood,
particularly lobster.

Eastham Lobster Pool
Cape Cod

US 6, North Eastham; tel. (508) 8963640; $10–15
One of the best places to eat out in Cape Cod – lashings of good seafood
at moderate prices.

Front Street
230 Commercial St., Provincetown; tel. (508) 4879715; $20–30
Sophisticated bistro famed far and wide for its wonderful lamb.

Carolina's
Charleston

10 Exchange St.; tel. (843) 7243800; $10–25
First-class southern cooking in a smart but relaxed atmosphere.

Magnolia
185 E Bay St.; tel. (843) 5777771; $10–20
In an old warehouse, specialities include hominy grits (polenta-style maize).

The Berghoff
Chicago

17 W Adams St.; tel. (312) 427170; $10–20
Home from home for Chicago's German community.

Carson's
612 N Wells St.; tel. (312) 2809200; $10–25
When it comes to prime ribs, this is a Chicago institution.

Charlie Trotter's
816 W Armitage (Lincoln Park); tel. (773) 2486228; $70
Very expensive but also good enough for star rating: Charlie Trotter is
one of the United State's most innovative chefs, the gourmet menu runs
to 8 or 10 courses.

Pizzeria Uno and Pizzeria Due
29 E Ohio St./619 N Wabash Ave.; tel. (312) 3211000, 9432400; $5–20
The ultimate place to try their own invention, authentic "Chicago Deep
Dish Pizza".

Prairie
500 S Dearborn St. (Hyatt); tel. (312) 6631143; $20–30
Mid-West cuisine such as a gourmet version of buffalo steak; the back
dining room was designed by Frank Lloyd Wright.

La Normandie
Cincinnatti

Restaurants

118 E 6th St.; tel. (513) 7212761; $15–30
Not French, but steaks in an easygoing atmosphere.

Rookwood Pottery
1077 Celestial St.; tel. (513) 7215456; $5–10
Everything you imagine of American food, in the rustic setting of the old pottery: jumbo burgers, hot dogs, chili, spare ribs and more.

Cleveland

Sammy's
1400 W 10th St.; tel. (216) 5235560; $20–30
This "in" restaurant offers modern, light American cuisine and superb views of the Cuyhoga River.

Dallas

Calle Doce
415 W 12th St.; (214) 9414304; from $20
Dishes from the Mexican port of Veracruz.

Javier's
4912 Cole Ave.; tel. (214) 5214211; $5–10
This little restaurant is always full thanks to its sensationally good Latin American food at unbeatable prices.

Seventeen-Seventeen
Dallas Museum of Art; tel. (214) 8800158; $20–30
Innovative Texas/Southwest cuisine in the Dallas Museum of Art.

Denver

The Fort
19192 Colorado Hwy 8/US 285; tel. (303) 6974471; $15–30
Buffalo and moose steak, served by trappers and Indians to the sound of fiddles and mandolins.

La Bonne Soupe
1512 Larimer St.; tel. (303) 5959169; from $15
Not just good soup but all kinds of other dishes á la française on Writer Square; the prices are surprisingly moderate.

Detroit

Elwood Bar & Grill
2100 Woodward Ave.; tel. (313) 9617485; $10–15
Good plain American fare in a lovely art-deco bar, with Swing accompaniment.

Lelli's Inn
7618 Woodward Ave.; tel. (313) 8711590; from $15
Detroit's best Italian.

Houston

Brennan's
3300 Smith St.; tel. (713) 5229223; $25–30
This elegant restaurant serves New Orleans cuisine with a light Texan touch; popular Sunday brunch.

Goode Company Texas Barbecue
5109 Kirby Dr.; tel. (713) 5222530; from $10
In the biggest city in Texas you must try at least one genuine Texas BBQ, and this is just the place for it.

Indianapolis

St Elmo Steak House
127 S Illinois St.; tel. (317) 6371811; $25–30
The oldest steak house in town still has the same bar from 90 years ago; the restaurant provides high-quality service.

Shapiro's Delicatessen & Cafeteria
2370 W 86th St.; tel. (317) 6314041; $5–10

A classic deli: burgers, mammoth sandwiches, cheesecake.

Stroud's   Kansas City
5410 NE Oak Ridge Dr.; tel. (816) 4549600; from $20
Solid American fare in the old mailcoach staging post.

Westside Café
723 Southwest Blvd.; tel. (816) 4720010; from $20
You would think the chef cannot make up his mind: Greek, Indian and
North African dishes, cooked in the tandoori oven, but they taste wonderful.

Louie's Backyard   Key West
700 Waddell Ave.; tel. (305) 2941061; from $30
Here you sit outdoors and savour dishes influenced by Southeast Asia
and the Pacific.

Alpine Village   Las Vegas
3003 Paradise R.; tel. (702) 7346888; $10–20
Las Vegas at its best in a jolly German-Swiss kitsch setting.

Big Sky
Stratosphere Las Vegas Hotel, 2000 Las Vegas Blvd.; tel. (775) 7807777;
$10–15
Here you get very affordable "all you can eat" with plenty of grills and
salads but a big variety of other dishes as well.

Dive!
3200 Las Vegas Blvd.; tel. (702) 3693483; from $10
One of the gambling city's most original theme restaurants; proprietor
Steven Spielberg. It may be as cramped as a submarine but the many
genuine American delicacies make up for that.

El Cholo   Los Angeles
1121 S Western Ave.; tel. (323) 7342773; $10–15
This big adobe restaurant is a favourite with families who enjoy Mexican
food LA style.

Spago
1114 Horn Ave., West Hollywood; tel. (310) 6524025; from $25
Spago has long been an LA institution, where the rich and famous
gather to try out Wolfgang Puck's latest Californian creations; reservation essential.

Matsuhisa
129 N La Cienega Blvd.; tel. (310) 6599639; $25–30
Like nowhere else: Japanese cuisine with a Peruvian accent, and of a
standard to tempt VIPs.

Café Roux   Memphis
94 S Front St.; tel. (901) 5257689; from $10
Cajun cooking with blues accompaniment.

Justines
919 Coward Place; tel. (901) 5273815; from $35
Top place in town, Creole-French cuisine.

Chef Allen's   Miami
Aventura, 19088 NE 29th Ave.; tel. (305) 9352900; $20–30
Masterchef Allen Susser prepares excellent fish – in an art-deco setting
– as his diners look on.

Restaurants

Garcia's Seafood Grill & Fish Market
398 NW North River Dr.; tel. (305) 3750765 $10–15
Not at all expensive, good fish restaurant in Little Havanna; it closes early evening so best to go there for lunch.

Miami Beach

Wolfie Cohen's
17190 Collins Ave.; tel. (305) 9474581; $5–15
For decades the best for Jewish food: corned beef, pastrami, chopped liver sandwiches.

Yuca
501 Lincoln Rd.; tel. (305) 5329822; $20–30
Subtle Cuban-central American nouvelle cuisine in this rendezvous for the Cuban exile glitterati; their own ice cream is superb too.

Minneapolis/St Paul

Café Brenda
300 1st Ave., Minneapolis; tel. (612) 3429230; from $10
Unpretentious chic but inexpensive restaurant in the Warehouse District for vegetarians and lovers of fish.

Famous Dave's BBQ & Blues Club
Calhoun Sq., Minneapolis; tel. (612) 8229900; $10–20
For anyone unfazed by the decibel level, since live Blues usually goes along with the massive helpings from the barbecue.

Dakota Bar and Grill
1021 E Bandana Blvd., St Paul; tel. (612) 6421442; $10–20
Jazz club with restaurant serving Midwest cuisine.

Nashville

Arthur's
1001 Broadway; tel. (615) 2551494; from $45
Grand restaurant in the Union Station Hotel.

New Orleans

Alex Patout's
221 Royal St.; tel. (504) 5257788; from $20
Chef Alex Patout serves the very best of Louisiana cuisine.

Antoine's
713 St Louis St., (504) 5814422; $20–50
This legendary French-Creole restaurant – said to have created Oysters Rockefeller – was founded in 1840.

Johnny's Po-Boys
511 St Louis St.; tel. (504) 5248129; from $5
Cheap snack restaurant: 35 different very good Po-Boys (filled baguettes), seafood, gumbo, breakfast.

New York City

Chart House
Pier D-T, Lincoln Harbor, Weehawken, NJ; tel. (201) 3486628; from $20
The Chart House is not in New York but on the other side of the Hudson in New Jersey; along with typically American jumbo steaks and lots of salad at moderate prices you get a fantastic view of the Manhattan skyline.

Daniel
20 E 76th St./Madison Ave.; tel. (212) 2880033; $30–40
Subtle seafood, phenomenal wine list; highly romantic, with no word spoken above a whisper. One of the best places in town – book two months ahead.

Gotham
12 E 12th St.; tel. (212) 6204020; $25–30

Greenwich Village's gourmet heaven, American food exquisitely prepared. Certainly deluxe, but the fixed price lunch menu is only $20.

Katz's
205 E Houston St.; tel. (212) 2542246; from $10
Katz's kosher deli, opened in 1888, is a New York institution, specialising in 6" deep pastrami sandwiches – a real feat to eat without making a mess.

Lucky Cheng's
24 1st Ave.; tel. (212) 4730516; $10–20
Light Chinese cuisine, Californian style.

Nobu
105 Hudson St./Franklin St.; tel. (212) 2190500; $20–30
One of New York's most popular Japanese restaurants; high-priced cuisine, all kinds of rice wine.

Osteria del Circo
120 W 55th St.; tel. (212) 2653636; $20–30
Esteemed by New York gourmets for its fine Tuscan cuisine with wonderful dishes, substantial and light; reservation required.

Oyster Bar
Grand Central Station; tel. (212) 4906650; $10–30
The elegant restaurant in the station basement is a New York institution; specialities: fish and 24 kinds of oyster.

Windows on the World
1 World Trade Center; tel. (212) 9381111; $25–35
Only one of 22 restaurants in the World Trade Center, but definitely the one with the best view of Manhattan; modern American cuisine served on the 107th floor of the Northern Tower.

Red Coach Inn
Niagara Falls
2 Buffalo Ave.; tel. (716) 1459; from $25
East Coast cuisine in sterling olde English surroundings with a view of the Upper Falls.

Walt Disney World has several restaurants in Orlando where you can eat out with the youngsters and share a table with Disney characters. Book in advance: tel. (407) 9393463.
Orlando
Parents who would rather dine without the children might prefer:

Chatham's Place
7575 Dr. Philipps Blvd. Orlando; tel. (407) 3452992; from $30
Small but charming restaurant with international cuisine.

City Tavern
Philadelphia
138 S 2nd St.; tel. (215) 4131443; $15–25
Modelled on the tavern where the fathers of the Constitution took their ease, here nowadays you can get the best of Philadelphia cuisine.

Jake Oliver's House of Brews
22 S 3rd St.; tel. (215) 6274825; $10–15
Bar, night club and restaurant combined in a former church, serving fish, pork and beef (grilled and roast), pizzas and over thirty beers from small breweries.

Susanna Foo
1512 Walnut St.; tel. (215) 5452666; $15–25
Here East meets West, with the best of both cuisines, but at a price.

Restaurants

Phoenix

Vincent Guerithault on Camelback
3930 E Camelback Rd.; tel. (602) 2240225; from $25
Vincent Guerithault, masterchef of the new Southwestern cuisine, serves wonderful lamb and poultry.

Such is Life
3602 N 24th St.; tel. (602) 9557822; from $20
Probably the best Mexican food in Phoenix.

Portland

Southpark Seafood Grill & Wine Bar
901 W Salmon St.; tel. (503) 2275700; from $10
One of Portland's many local breweries; very lively and usually full. Good plain fare such as pizza from the oven, chilli, burgers and sandwiches.

Jake Famous Crawfish
401 SW 12th St.; tel. (503) 2261419; $15–30
A seafood institution since 1909.

Salt Lake City

Market Street Grill
50 Market St.; tel. (801) 3224668; $15–25
The best place for fresh and excellently cooked fish, but if you prefer a hearty steak or grilled chicken these are of course also on the menu.

Marianne's
149 W 200 South St.; tel. (801) 3640513; $5–10
A favourite with visitors from Germany and Central Europe who still hanker after sausage and sauerkraut, goulash soup.

San Diego

Hob Nob Hill
2271 1st Ave.; tel. (619) 2398176; from $20
This restaurant near Balboa Park offers imaginative meat and fish dishes at acceptable prices.

San Francisco

Harbor Village Restaurant
4 Embarcadero Center; tel. (415) 7818833; from $20
Chinese restaurant on the waterfront serving classic Cantonese food, with a view of San Francisco Bay.

Hong Kong Flower Lounge
5322 Geary Blvd.; tel. (415) 6688998; $5–15
The best dim-sum restaurant in town, often very full, but worth the wait.

Pane e Vino
3011 Steiner St.; tel. (415) 3462111; $10–20
Super straightforward Italian fare at acceptable prices.

Postrio
545 Post St.; tel. (415) 7767825; $25–30
Another of masterchef Wolfgang Puck's restaurants; light Californian cuisine and still one of the best in town.

Santa Fe/Taos

The Pink Adobe
406 Old Santa Fe Trail, Santa Fe; tel. (505) 9837712; $15–20
In the lovely setting of a 17th c. adobe building you can enjoy Steak Dunnigan, Porc Napoléon, Poulet Marengo, or the delicious creations of modern Southwestern cuisine.

Doc Martin's
In the old Taos Inn, 125 Paseo del Norte, Taos; tel. (505) 7581977; from $15
This restaurant recalls artists like Bert Philips and Ernest Blumenschein;

the menu offers all kinds of often very original variations of modern Southwestern cuisine.

Savannah
Elizabeth on 37th
105 E 37th St.; tel. (912) 2365547; $20–25
One of the best restuarants in Georgia; regional cuisine.

Mrs Wilkes Dining Room
107 W Jones St.; tel. (912) 2325997; from $10
Southern soulfood at its best by the legendary cookbook writer Mrs. Wilkes; very much a family atmosphere, lunch only, so get there early.

Emmett Watson's Oyster Bar
1916 Pike Place No.16; tel. (206) 4487721; $5–10
Just right for anyone who likes oysters, since this snack bar hidden away in the Pike Place Market has the best in town, plus locally brewed beers.

Seattle

Wild Ginger
1400 Western Ave.; tel. (206) 6234450; from $20
Northwestern cuisine (especially seafood) with an oriental touch.

Bern's
1208 S Howard Ave.; tel. (813) 2512421; $20–30
Bern Lexer's steak house is one of the best in the southeast, serving only their own home-grown meat and vegetables; exceptional prime rib.

Tampa

Café Poca Cosa
88 E Broadway Blvd.; tel. (520) 6226400; from $15
The menu, which changes daily, includes unusual Mexican cuisine.

Tucson

Citronelle
3000 M St. NW; tel. (202) 6252150; from $50
Californian light cuisine at Georgetown's top restaurant.

Washington, DC

Meskerem
2434 18th St. NW; tel. (202) 4624100; $10–15
There are many Ethiopian restaurants in the Adams Morgan district, and this is one of the best.

Pizzeria Paradiso
2029 P St. NW; tel. (202) 2231245; $5–15
Very popular pizzeria, so often full; great panini too.

Red Sage
605 14th St.; tel. (202) 6384444; $20–30
First-class south-western dishes; the Red Sage also has the Chilli Bar, where the imaginative snacks and meals are somewhat cheaper.

Safety

The activities of gangsters like Al Capone and, more recently, "Miami Vice" have made the world familiar with the existence of organised crime in the United States. This is particularly true of the densely populated cities – New York, Washington, Chicago, Los Angeles, Miami – with their sharp social divides, where the financial aristocracy of the United States and the international jet set live side by side with dropouts and castaways and prosperous yuppies cavort in brilliantly neon-lit discos alongside hostels for the old and destitute. Pimps, arms dealers, drug bosses and those who aspire to become so are driven around in luxuri-

Crime

ous limousines, while round the corner poor blacks, Latinos and Asians compete for the lowest-paid jobs.

Drug-related crime

Drug-related crime presents serious problems for the security forces. The country's long coastline and its nearness to the drug-producing countries of Central and South America have made the United States, and the state of Florida in particular, the centre of a large and dangerous drug trade.

Advice

Visitors should be careful and watchful, particularly in large cities and tourist centres but sometimes also in less populous areas. The danger of criminal attack is greater after dark. In any emergency tel. 911 (police).

After dark it is advisable to avoid certain areas, particularly parks, bus stations and shady districts in towns. Public transport in the late evening, with few passengers, may also be a possible source of danger. It is worth asking your hotel or a local acquaintance what parts of the town are better avoided. To get back to your hotel at a late hour it is best to take a taxi: it is not advisable to walk about alone after dark.

You should try not to look like a tourist in appearance or behaviour. Keep your camera concealed, and do not think of taking photographs in doubtful areas. It should be remembered that for those concerned poverty has nothing romantic or interesting about it.

You should never carry objects of value or large sums of money, which should be deposited in the hotel safe. Instead of cash it is better to have dollar traveller's cheques and credit cards – though there is something to be said for having a small sum in cash, say 20–50 dollars, which may serve to "buy off" a possible attacker. Showy jewellery should not be worn, and a purse attached to the belt is better than a shoulder or wrist bag.

In your hotel you should lock the door on the inside and not open it to persons unknown to you. On leaving the room take the key with you, and do not leave any objects of value in the room.

In airports and railway stations, at bus stops, in the car parks of car rental firms and in hotels never leave your baggage unattended or give it to anyone who volunteers to take it to a taxi or to your room.

If you feel you are being followed you should call the police from the nearest place of safety.

If travelling in a car study the route in advance. If you lose your way and want help the best plan is to stop in a parking place outside a filling station or a shop.

If your car is run into from behind or from the side it is better not to stop at once but to make for the nearest well-lighted parking place at a filling station or a shop and call the police from there; tel. 911.

You should not on any account give a lift to hitch-hikers.

You should park your car only in well-lighted and easily visible places. It is inadvisable to spend the night in your car.

Shopping

Shopping streets in the European sense are to be found only in large cities and tourist centres; elsewhere there are only limited shopping facilities in downtown areas. Every town of any consequence, however, has one or more shopping malls, a Marketplace, a Galleria and a flea market. For information apply to the local tourist information office or chamber of commerce. When shopping in the United States it should be remembered that many goods are subject to a sales tax ranging between 3 per cent and 9 per cent from state to state.

Malls

Shopping malls, sometimes of enormous size, with parking for cars, are to be found on the outskirts of all large and medium-size towns. They usually contain branches of a number of department stores (such as Sears, J.C. Penney, McAlpine), together with a variety of smaller shops, boutiques, services and restaurants under the same roof. In these shopping malls you can buy practically everything you are likely to want and can compare the price and quality of goods in different shops.

The most exclusive shops are to be found only in places where the necessary purchasing power is available – in the famous bathing resorts of California and Florida, in some tourist centres in the mountains and in world-famous cities like New York, Boston, Chicago, San Francisco and New Orleans. Elsewhere shops of this quality are much more difficult to find.

Exclusive boutiques

Bargains can often be found in factory outlet shops; but these too are usually to be found only in areas where there is likely to be a sufficient demand from tourists – for example round such tourist magnets as Disneyworld. In some cities there are regular "outlet centers" where several dozen manufacturers offer their products straight from the factory. As a rule these factory shops are run separately from the factories themselves.

Factory shops

Popular souvenirs are those sold in the large theme parks (e.g. Mickey Mouse T-shirts) and in National Parks and museums. Many visitors like to take home Indian craft products, sold mainly in the reservations but also in some tourist resorts.

Souvenirs

Among items that are relatively cheap in the United States are electronic apparatus, cameras and photographic accessories, telephones, answering machines and computers. Other good buys are clothing (especially jeans), underwear, leather goods (particularly shoes) and sports articles (e.g. baseball equipment), since well-known brands cost much less in the United States than in Europe.

Social Customs

Smoking is nowadays rather frowned on in the United States. Some airlines have banned it, and it is also prohibited (e.g. in the states of Arizona and Florida) in many public places. Many restaurants have separate sections for smokers and non-smokers.

Smoking

Sport

Spectator sports

The most popular – and most telegenic – spectator sports are American football, baseball, basketball and ice hockey. In spite of the fact that the United States hosted the World Cup in 1994 association football is very far from being a mass-spectator sport.

The favourite sport, by a long way, is American football. The rules of the game, which originally developed out of rugby, are complicated and difficult for an outsider to understand: what is fascinating is the dynamism of the play and the tactical refinements to which it lends itself. It is played in the National Football League (NFL) in two "conferences", the American Football Conference and the National Football Conference, each of which in turn consists of three divisions (East, Central and West). The high point of the season, in January, is the match between the leaders of the two conferences for the Super Bowl, the supreme football trophy. Among the strongest teams in recent years have been the

American football

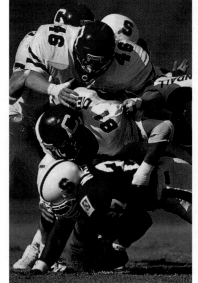

Battle of the Giants

Baseball

Basketball

Ice hockey

Other sports

Angling

Washington Redskins, the Dallas Cowboys, the New York Giants, the San Francisco 49ers and the Buffalo Bills. The second football league is the College Football League. This is the talent nursery of the NFL.

Second place in the popularity stakes is taken by baseball, a game that evolved from rounders and which is even more difficult to follow than American football. There are two leagues, the National League and the American League (each with two divisions), in which Canadian teams are also included. There is no trophy comparable to the Super Bowl. The leading teams are the Pittsburgh Pirates, the Atlanta Braves, the Toronto Blue Jays and the Oakland A's.

Thanks to superstars like Charles Barkley, Shaquille O'Neal and above all Michael "Air" Jordan, Americans flock to the matches of the National Basketball Association (NBA), which has two "conferences" of two divisions each. It is the ambition of all basketball professionals to play in the NBA with teams such as the Chicago Bulls, the Los Angeles Lakers, the Orlando Magics and the Phoenix Suns. High School and University teams play in the NCAA, on which the professional clubs draw for their new talent, as in American football.

Ice hockey also has two "conferences", each with two divisions. The National Hockey League (NHL) is formed by American and Canadian teams, reinforced by Scandinavian, Czech and Russian players. The two teams that reach the final after a series of playoffs play for the Stanley Cup, ice hockey's highest trophy, which is of such importance to the North American professional teams that only second- and third-level players compete in the ice hockey world championships. In recent years the Stanley Cup has been won by the Pittsburgh Penguins, the Edmonton Oilers, the Calgary Flames and the Canadiens of Montréal.

Other popular spectator sports include motor racing (Daytona 500, Indianapolis "Indy" 500), horse racing (Kentucky Derby), tennis, boxing, wrestling, golf, lacrosse, and, of course, rodeo (see Baedeker Special p. 000).

Activity sports

Angling is one of the United State's most popular leisure pursuits, which should come as no surprise given the country's many superb fishing waters. Local tourist offices often have very useful brochures listing the best places for angling in their area. Tackle shops can be a mine of useful information as well.

In some states anglers need a fishing permit. These can be obtained – usually on payment of a fee – from tackle shops.

Boats for big-game fishing (for swordfish, sailfish, shark, barracuda, tuna) can be chartered from many ports on the Atlantic, in the Gulf of Mexico and on the Pacific; they come complete with bait and fishing tackle.

Golf

The United States is a Mecca for golfers. Golf is a popular American sport; it is not, as in some other countries, a select and expensive one, and there are large numbers of golf courses all over the country: in Florida alone, where golf can be played practically all the year round, there are over a thousand courses. Many American courses, for example the Seminole Golf Club in Palm Beach, are internationally renowned. The stars of the golfing world are frequently to be found playing somewhere in the United States.

Many American golf courses are open to the public, and many golf clubs welcome golfers who are members of foreign clubs. Many hotels and holiday resorts that have their own golf courses or can offer guests the opportunity of playing in a neighbouring golf or country club offer attractive all-in rates.

The tourist offices of the various states (see Information) issue brochures on golfing facilities in their areas.

Riding

In the land of cowboys and Indians there are naturally plenty of opportunities for holidaying on horseback. To get the real feel of the Westerns you can try trail riding, which involves several days hiking cross-country, or vacationing on a dude ranch. These package holidays include the horses and the necessary equipment. For further information contact the state tourist offices (see Information).

Tennis

The United States is the Promised Land for tennis fans; this is where tennis stars from all over the world come to train and win their spurs, delighting enthusiastic TV audiences with appearances in tournaments at Flushing Meadows, Amelia Island, Boca Raton and Key Biscayne. Some parents send their young hopefuls from Europe to train in Florida which has been the springboard for many of today's rising stars.

It is possible to play tennis here practically all year round, often on a hotel's own courts. Many places also provide an opportunity to watch top qualifying rounds as well. Travel agents can supply information about which hotels have tennis courts, where to find tennis resorts and schools, and how to book.

Walking

The numerous National and State Parks and Recreation Areas offer endless scope for walking. There are numerous trails of varying lengths (sometimes on boardwalks over swampy ground) that make exploration of their natural beauties easy and offer magnificent views.

The various parks and forests have their own visitor centres and information bureaux, where visitors can get detailed information on the trails. In many parks there are guided walks led by park rangers.

Information about these and other trails – including the 2000 mi. Appalachian Trail, which runs along the crest of the Appalachians from Maine to Georgia – can be obtained from:

American Hiking Society
1015 31st St. NW
Washington, DC 20007

Taxis

In all cities and tourist centres there are sufficient numbers of taxis. They can be hailed in the street.

The basic fare for the first mile is $1–3, plus $1.50 for each additional mile. Since distances in cities and tourist centres are often considerable, the fare can very quickly mount up. In some areas the fares are fixed by zone.

As a tip the driver should be given about 15 per cent of the amount on the meter.

Telephone

America's telephone network is operated by private companies. The only effect this has for the visitor is that when making international calls from payphones you have to go through the operator.

The buttons on American phones have letters as well as digits, so many numbers spell out easy-to-remember key words.

Payphones

Public payphones takes coins (25, 10 and 5 cents) and phonecards.

Toll-free numbers

Calls to 1800 or 1888 numbers can only be made inside the United States. They are toll-free calls and should not be confused with 1900-code premium-rate numbers that can be very expensive.

Calls within the US

For trunk calls within the United States dial 1 followed by the area code and the subscriber's number.

The American phone companies provide telephone cards (Calling Cards) that can be used for making cheaper calls from many public payphones. These cards are available from gas stations and drugstores, and can also be purchased through credit card companies. They are easy to use and work out much cheaper than making overseas calls from hotels.

International dialling codes

The international dialling code for the United States is 001 then the local code and the subsciber's number.

Calling from the United States, the international code to the United Kingdom is 01144. From private phones dial 011 and the country code 44, then, dropping the first 0, the area code followed by the subscriber's number. On public payphones dial 0 to get the operator for instructions for a call.

Rates are slightly cheaper 5–11pm, and considerably cheaper 11pm–8am, and at weekends.

Time

Time zones

The continental United States extend over four time zones: Eastern Time (5 hours behind GMT), Central Time (6 hours behind GMT), Mountain Time (7 hours behind GMT) and Pacific Time (8 hours behind GMT). Alaska and Hawaii have their own time zones, 9 and 10 hours behind GMT.

Summer Time

Summer Time (Daylight Saving Time), when clocks are moved one hour forward, is normally in force from the last Sunday in April to the last Sunday in October.

Tipping

In contrast to the general practice in Europe, a service charge is not normally included in hotel and restaurant bills, and tips must be given separately. The staff of hotels and restaurants are often very poorly paid and depend on tips to make up their income.

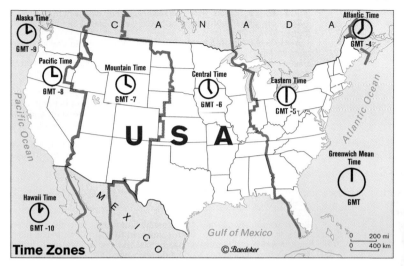

Time Zones

It is usual to give the boy who takes your luggage to or from your room a tip of 50 cents or $1 dollar per item, and to leave $2 per day for the room maid. Staff in reception expect no special tip for normal services. It is usual to give the hotel porter $1 for fetching a taxi. If a hotel or restaurant offers "valet parking" – that is, if a member of the staff parks your car for you – a tip of $1 should be offered for taking it away and again for bringing it back.

Hotels

The normal tip is 15 per cent of the bill (before the addition of sales tax). The money is usually left on the table. In the better restaurants the head waiter and wine waiter will also expect a tip. When paying by credit card add the amount of the tip to the bill.

Restaurants

Both men's and women's hairdressers expect a 15–20 per cent tip.

Hairdressers

For a shoeshine a tip of between 50 cents and $1 is usual.

Shoeshines

Usherettes are not normally tipped.

Theatres, cinemas

On an organised coach tour the bus driver receives $2–3 per person per day.

Drivers and tour guides

Travel Documents

British visitors to the United States must have a full 10-year passport valid for at least 90 days from the date of entry, and stating that the holder is a British citizen (if it states British Subject the holder must apply for a visa).

Passports

Nominally all visitors are required to have a visa but this requirement is currently waived for, amongst others, citizens of EU states, Australia and New Zealand, who are travelling on an unexpired passport for holiday, transit or business purposes for a stay not exceeding 90 days and who

Visas

hold a return or onward ticket. Nevertheless they will have to fill in form 1-94 before arrival (normally distributed on the plane) and hand it in to immigration control.

A visa is still required for the following groups: people staying longer than 90 days, students, journalists, exchange visits, government officials, fiancés of American citizens, and air crew. Applications should be made to American embassies and consulates (see Diplomatic and Consular Offices).

Financial status

Visitors to the United States must have a return or onward ticket, or be able to prove they have enough money to buy a return ticket and support themselves during their stay.

Innoculations

Evidence of innoculation is only required for visitors coming from an infected country. It is advisable, however, to check up on current regulations at a US consulate.

Visitors with Disabilities

Building regulations vary considerably from state to state. In recent years the authorities have been concerned to ensure that public buildings, airports, railroad stations, hotels and restaurants have proper facilities for disabled people. Theme parks and other entertainment also try to cater for the disabled, and everywhere there are special parking lots for them.

Information in the UK

The main organisations for information and advice for travellers with disabilities are:

Royal Association for Disability and Rehabilitation (RADAR), 12 City Forum, 250 City Rd., London EC1V 8AF; tel. (0207) 2503222, fax 2500212

Mobility Information Service, National Mobility Centre, Unit 2A, Atcham Industrial Estate, Shrewsbury SY4 4UG; tel. 4106297, fax 4106874

Information in the United States

Twin Peaks Press publishes directories of tour operators, car-hire companies and holidays for the disabled: Twin Peaks Press, Box 129, Vancouver, WA 98666; tel. (360) 6942462, fax 6963210.

Water Sports

Diving

For diving enthusiasts the United States is indeed the "land of unlimited possibilities". The long Atlantic seaboard, extending from the tropical shores of the Florida Keys to the cool waters of Maine, the coasts of the Gulf of Mexico, the Pacific coast from California to Canada and great expanses of inland waters offer unrivalled diving opportunities. Much the most inviting diving grounds, however, are to be found in and around Florida, in the Hawaiian archipelago and off the coast of California.

There are numerous well equipped diving centres where all necessary equipment can be hired. If you bring your own aqualung you may need an adaptor for air cylinders of a different type. When hiring an aqualung you will usually be asked to show evidence of your competence.

Diving grounds

The coastal waters of **Florida** are a diver's paradise. The turquoise water is of extraordinary clarity, particularly round the more thinly populated islands. Many islands are partly or completely sheltered by coral reefs, home to a colourful underwater world. Off some islands are regular underwater gardens. Round the coasts, too, there are numerous wrecks – including ships of the Spanish silver fleet – that attract treasure hunters from far and wide.

The best diving grounds are round the Florida Keys. There are well equipped diving stations on Big Pine Key and Cudjoe Key, Islamorada, Key Largo, Key West, Looe Key and Tavernier. Of particular interest are the marine zone of Key Biscayne National Park, Key Largo Coral Reef Preserve, the John Pennekamp Underwater Park and the little islands of coral limestone between Marathon and Key West. There is also good diving off the Gulf Island National Seashore, on the Gulf coast of the Panhandle. There are large diving stations at Destin, Fort Walton Beach, Panama City and Pensacola.

A special diving experience is diving in some of the freshwater spring pools in the interior of Florida, in company with manatees and alligators. On some of these (e.g. Live Oak, High Springs) there are diving stations.

Although the waters off **California** are relatively cool as well as rough and subject to currents, they offer interesting diving opportunities. Here underwater forests of seaweed swarm with life – sealions, sea otters, groupers, Garibaldi fish, abalones, colourful purple shells and a host of other sea creatures. Off Monterey the underwater world is on a giant scale, with bizarre rock formations. Round Point Lobos is an underwater nature reserve, access to which is very strictly regulated. There are other interesting diving grounds off the Californian coast round the Channel Islands, Catalina Island the San Clemente Islands. The wild cliff coastline of Salt Point State Park to the north of San Francisco will tempt experienced divers.

The islands of **Hawaii**, particularly the waters round the largest island, Hawaii itself, have also come into favour with divers in recent years. Among the varied range of marine creatures to be seen here are whales, sharks, mantas, turtles, colourful prawns and squids. An unusual spectacle is provided by the glowing red lava from the volcano Kilauea that is continually flowing down into the sea. The best diving grounds are on the west side of the island of Hawaii between Kailua-Kona and Honaunau. There is relatively safe and easy diving in sheltered Kealakekua Bay.

Canoeing, kayaking, rafting

Anyone who enjoys canoeing, kayaking or rafting will find ideal conditions in the United States. The Atlantic, Gulf and Pacific coasts, and the many rivers and lakes in the interior offer endless scope for boating activities of all kinds.

The tourist offices of the individual states and tourist resorts (see Information; Chambers of Commerce, Visitor Centers, Welcome Centers) and the National Park offices (see National Parks) can supply information about the navigability of particular stretches of water, and keep up-to-date lists of reliable boat hirers.

Many inland water routes in the United States lend themselves to canoe trekking. These include the Adirondacks region in New York State, the rivers of Maine and West Virginia, the swamplands in Georgia, Florida and Louisiana, the National Parks and Nature Reserves in North Minnesota, and the Ozarks in Missouri. When embarking on this kind of trip, though, you need to go really well prepared, especially for dealing with insects and other wilderness hazards. It is also easy to get lost in the dense network of channels in some waterways, so be sure to inform the canoe-hire company or the local park administration (if you are in a

Canoe trekking

National or State Park) of your destination and the route you are taking. Information is also available from: American Canoe Association, 7432 Alban Station Blvd., Suite 232b, Springfield, VA 22150; tel. (703) 4510141.

Rafting

Rafting (usually in an inflatable or paddle boat) is increasingly popular, and new routes are being opened up all the time. There are all kinds of trips to choose from, ranging in difficulty from family-friendly floating trips up to thrilling whitewater rafting through spectacular canyons. The organizers of these trips usually supply all the necessary equipment as well as the provisions. The programme often includes other adventure-holiday activities such as riding, climbing, and mountain biking. Rafting trips are reckoned to be very safe but you need to be aware that the operators disclaim any liability, and it is up to participants to take out their own insurance.

The best rivers for whitewater rafting are in the mountain country of , particularly Arizona, California, Colorado, Idaho (Salmon), Montana, Utah (Cataract Canyon) and Wyoming, but there is also good whitewa-ter rafting to be had in West Virginia (New River) and Georgia (Chattooga). The most popular rivers for more straightforward rafting include the Colorado (inc. Grand Canyon) and some of its tributaries (inc. Green River), the upper stretch of the Snake River (near Jackson) and the Shoshone River at Cody. Information is available from: American River Touring Association, 24000 Casa Loma Rd., Groveland, CA 95222; tel. (209) 9627873.

Sailing

There are numerous marinas where sailing boats can be hired on some stretches of the Atlantic coast (particularly Maine, Cape Cod and the Outer Banks), round the Florida peninsula, along the Gulf Coast and on the Pacific coast of California. There are also good sailing waters on the Great Lakes, a number of smaller lakes and the numerous artificial lakes formed by dams on the great rivers. Fuller information can be obtained from the tourist offices of the states concerned (see Information).

When to Go

In a country of such enormous extent it might be supposed that the best time for a visit would be different for each region; but in fact, because of the general north–south orientation of the mountain ranges, which oppose no barrier to the southward movement of cold air masses from the north in winter or to the warm south winds that blow north in summer, this is not entirely true. The coastal ranges prevent the moder-ating influence of the Pacific from reaching more than a relatively narrow coastal zone, while the influence of the Atlantic, with the warm Gulf Stream and the cold Labrador Current, is felt to a varying extent in different areas.

Much of the United States has a continental climate (see Climate, p. 20), with very cold winters and heavy snow, particularly in the north-east and round the Great Lakes, and hot summers, which in the wet coastal regions in the east and south can be extremely oppressive. The summer heat is more tolerable in the drier west.

For much of the United States the best time for a visit is spring, which quickly gives place to the hot summer. It can also be very pleasant in autumn, which is long and usually dry. From early September to November there is a beautiful Indian summer, when the mountain forests are in the full glory of their autumn colouring. At higher altitudes (above 5000 ft or so), for example in the Rockies, on the rim of the Grand

Canyon, in the Coastal Range in the west and the Appalachians in the east, and on the cooler coastal strip of California reaching up to the Canadian frontier, under the influence of cold marine currents, warm clothing may be needed even in summer.

For a winter holiday there is Florida, usually warm at this time of year, and at the other climatic extreme the winter sports regions in the mountains (Rockies, Front Range, Sierra Nevada, Cascade Range, Adirondacks, White Mountains).

The best time to visit Alaska is from May to the end of September. With their equable tropical climates, Hawaii, Puerto Rico and the Virgin Islands offer a pleasant holiday at any time of year.

The main holiday season in the United States is between Memorial Day (end of May) and Labor Day (beginning of September).

Main holiday season

Winter Sports

In recent decades extensive winter sports areas have been developed in the United States – in the mountains of the north-east with their abundance of snow, in the Rocky Mountains, famed for their "champagne snow", in California's Sierra Nevada and even in the desert states of Arizona, Nevada and New Mexico.

In the main skiing areas there are frequently dozens of pistes, well equipped with lifts (cabin cableways, chairlifts, ski-tows). In some areas there are facilities for heli-skiing. Experienced skiers can then be taken by helicopter to remote and beautiful mountain regions – though from the point of view of the environment this is not a wholly desirable development.

Alpine skiing

Cross-country skiing has become very fashionable in recent years, and many areas – especially National and State Parks, and Recreation Areas – have designated cross-country ski-trails. Information from: USA Cross Country Ski Areas Association, 259 Bolton Rd., Winchester, NH 03470; tel. (603) 2394341.

Cross-country skiing

Also very popular, though not environment friendly, are trips in snowmobiles (motor sledges).

Snowmobiles

Regions

In the Northern Appalachians, which are famed for their abundance of snow, there are a number of fine skiing areas, though because of their nearness to the great cities of the north-east they are frequently overcrowded. As a result the access roads to the most popular areas are often closed quite early in the day.

Northern Appalachians

The Adirondacks, in the north-east of New York State, are a very popular skiing area. A major skiing centre in this area is Lake Placid, which has twice (in 1932 and again in 1980) hosted the Winter Olympics.

Adirondacks

The main skiing areas in the state of Vermont are Killington, Mount Snow, Stowe and Sugarbrush.

Vermont

In New Hampshire are the White Mountains, with excellent skiing facilities on Mount Washington.

New Hampshire

In the extreme north-east of the United States, in the state of Maine, a number of winter sports areas are still in course of development.

Maine

613

Winter Sports

Rocky Mountains

There are superb skiing areas in the Rocky Mountains. Here are some of the oldest, largest and best known winter sports resorts in the United States, well able to stand comparison with Garmisch, Davos and St Moritz.

Round Denver and its neighbouring city of Colorado Springs to the south are numerous excellently equipped skiing areas, all in the Front Range, which rises like an alpine wall to the west of the two cities. Within easy reach of Denver are the pistes above Golden and Boulder, at Idaho Springs (Mount Evans), Arapahoe, Hot Sulphur Springs and in the Rocky Mountain National Park (with the resort of Estes Park). Round Colorado Springs are the beautiful pistes above Manitou Springs and on Pikes Peak.

A 2 hour drive west of Denver is the internationally famed resort of Vail. Within easy reach of Vail are other skiing areas (Beaver Creek, Copper Mountain).

The skiing resort in the Rockies, easily reached from Denver, is Aspen, the meeting place of the international jet set. Round the town are a number of recently developed skiing areas (including Aspen Mountain, Aspen Highlands, Snowmass, Buttermilk).

Among other winter sports in Colorado that have come to the fore in recent years are Breckenridge, Keystone, Steamboat Springs, Telluride, Gunnison, Grand Junction, Dolores and Durango.

Wyoming

The most popular winter sports resort in Wyoming by a long way is Jackson, from which other skiing areas in the Grand Teton and Yellowstone National Parks are easily reached.

Other skiing areas in course of development are Pinedale (south-east of Jackson), the Bighorn Mountains (above Buffalo and Sheridan) and the Medicine Bow Range (west of Laramie).

Utah

There is particularly good powder snow in some skiing areas in the state of Utah. Well-known resorts are Alta, Brighton and Snowbird. Two hours' drive south of Salt Lake City, in the Wasatch Range, is the still relatively undiscovered resort of Sundance.

Idaho

In Idaho is the oldest skiing resort in the United States, Sun Valley. There are other good skiing areas at Boise, Grangeville and McCall, and at Montpelier and Soda Springs in the Wasatch Range.

New Mexico

The best skiing areas in New Mexico are in the Sangre de Cristo Mountains and the Sacramento Mountains. Particularly popular are the Taos Ski Valley, the Santa Fe Ski Basin and the Sierra Blanca.

Sierra Nevada

In California's Sierra Nevada there are a number of magnificent skiing areas, best reached by way of San Francisco or Reno (Nevada).

The best known skiing region in the west is Squaw Valley, where some events in the 1960 Winter Olympics were staged. There are other smaller skiing areas round Lake Tahoe and to the south of South Lake Tahoe.

The other large skiing region in California is the Yosemite National Park, where the winter sports season lasts into late spring.

In the Mammoth Lakes/June Mountain area, 300 mi. from Los Angeles, there are over 180 pistes, with some three dozen lifts.

Other skiing areas

There are good skiing areas, still not overcrowded, in the states of Oregon and Washington. There are excellent facilities in some areas in the Cascade Range (on the Upper Klamath Lake and Crescent Lake, round Timberlin Lodge and on Mount Baker, near the Canadian frontier) and the Olympic National Park.

Youth Hostels

Accommodation specially designed for young people is generally to be found only in areas where there are likely to be numbers of young visitors: that is, mainly in the large cities, in towns with colleges and universities, in the beach resorts of Florida and California favoured by young people and in certain winter sports centres.

There are in the United States only some 150 youth hostels run by the American Youth Hostels (AYH) organisation, together with 100 other hostels. It is evidently not possible, therefore, to tour the United States going from hostel to hostel; but there are some areas – in New England and southern Pennsylvania, round the Great Lakes, in the Colorado Rockies, on Puget Sound in the state of Washington and on the Californian Pacific coast – in which it is possible to make shorter tours round a chain of youth hostels. Early book is recommended. Information from:

American Youth Hostels
733 15th St. NW
Washington, DC 20005
Tel. (202) 7836161, fax (202) 7836171, www.hiayh.org

The International Youth Hostel Handbook, containing a comprehensive list of hostels, is available in the UK from:

Youth Hostel Adventure Shop
14 Southampton St.
London WC2
Tel. (0207) 8368541)

Reservations cannot be taken at this number but can be made from the YHA headquarters; tel. (01629) 581418. Further information is given by the official AYH Hostelling Handbook, annually updated, which is available at AYH hostels or from the AYH headquarters (above). *Advice*

Some youth hostels not run by the AYH organisation fall short of an adequate standard. Genuine youth hostels can be identified by the triangular AYH logo or the internationally recognised "house and tree" symbol. *YMCA and YWCA*

In all the larger American cities young people can find accommodation in YMCA and YWCA hostels – though these tend to be fully booked and are sometimes relatively expensive for the accommodation they provide. *Student residences*

Information: Y'Ways International, 224 E 47th St.

During university vacations accommodation is often available at reasonable rates in student residences. Information can be obtained from local information offices (see Information) or from the universities and colleges concerned.

Index

Index

Index

Source of Illustrations

Front cover: Tony Stone Images
Back cover: AA Photo Library (P. Wood)

Ariv für Kunst und Geschichte: 74, 80, 85, 87, 88, 90, 93, 95 (B), 96, 108, 125, 385
AP: 86, 95 (T), 96, 118, 196
Isolde Bacher/Albert Maier: 3 (B), 7 (B), 13, 154, 339, 348, 538, 581
Baedeker-Archiv: 46, 67, 88, 99, 100, 106, 124, 147, 314
Heinz Burger: 203, 333, 356
Coca-Cola GmbH: 164, 165
dpa: 54
Carin Drechsler-Marx: 29, 297, 410, 452, 463
Eichmüller: 562
Rainer Eisenschmid/Gabriele Maier: 6 (×2), 50, 58, 91, 207, 293, 390, 407, 471, 478, 480, 496,
501, 506, 508, 510, 511, 514, 515, 516, 531, 589
Astrid Feltes-Peter: 299, 460
Florida Department of Tourism: 320
Franz Marc Frei: 115, 307, 344
Frick: 284
Rainer Hackenberg: 158, 193, 347, 444
Rainer Hamberger: 150, 258, 492, 517
HB-Verlag: 26, 44, 52, 103, 114, 189, 206, 210, 214, 218, 222, 243, 244, 270, 302, 323, 327, 382,
392, 398, 499, 505
Ole Helmhausen: 199, 308, 430
Sabine Hofmann: 273
IFA: 8, 21, 132, 170, 286, 291, 425, 468, 489
Helmut Linde: 134, 173, 175, 225, 239, 277, 283, 384, 433
Nico Linde: 17, 185, 254
Lindenmuseum Stuttgart: 35, 39, 41
Dr Ruth Nestvold: 229, 447
New Orleans Convention and Vistors Bureau: 358
Pinellas Suncoast Chamber of Commerce: 441
Dr Madeleine Reincke: 247, 338, 379, 454, 534, 559
Schapowalow: 368, 412, 414, 527
Anja Schliebitz: 371
Schröder: 341, 474
Schuster-Bildagentur: 183, 208
Manfred Strobel: 157, 458
USTTA: 415
Verlag Der Spiegel: 117
Martin vogel: 62, 163, 235, 264, 280, 362, 438, 477, 520
The Delta Steamboat Company: 3, 562
The Walt Disney Company: 7 (T), 403
Wiechmann Tourism Services: 524
ZEFA: 6 (M), 16, 60, 166, 180, 375, 538, 606

622

Imprint

184 illustrations, 116 maps and plans, 1 large map at end of book

Editorial work: Baedeker-Redaktion (Rainer Eisenschmid)

Cartography: Franz Huber, Munich; Christoph Gallus, Hohberg (Niederschopfheim); Mairs Geographischer Verlag GmbH & Co., Ostfildern (panoramic map, fold-map of USA)

Original German text: Isolde Bacher and Albert Maier, Dr Peter H. Baumgarten, Annette Bickel, Dr Helmut Blume, Gisela Bockamp, Rainer Eisenschmid, Rolf Eisenschmid, Heidi Engelmann, Christine Gebhardt, Dr Winfried Heinzler, Dr Cornelia Hermanns, Rupert Koppold, Dr Heinrich Lang, Heribert Langen, Helmut Linde, Dr Christina Melk-Haen, Dr Ruth Nestvold-Mack, Dr Madeleine Reincke, Inge and Dr Georg Scherm, Lydia Störmer, Manfred Strobel, Martin Vogel, Werner Voran, Andrea Wurth, Dagmar Zimmermann

General direction: Rainer Eisenschmid, Baedeker Stuttgart

English translation: James Hogarth, Margaret Court, David Cocking, Brenda Ferris, Rosemary Quinton.

Editor English edition: Jackie Staddon

3rd English edition 2000

© Karl Baedeker GmbH, Ostfildern
Original German edition 2000

© Automobile Association Developments Limited 2000
English language edition worldwide

Published by AA Publishing (a trading name of Automobile Association Developments Limited, whose registered office is Norfolk House, Priestley Road, Basingstoke, Hampshire RG24 9NY. Registered number 1878835).

Distributed in the United States and Canada by:
Fodor's Travel Publications, Inc.
201 East 50th Street
New York, NY 10022

A CIP catalogue record of this book is available from the British Library.

Licensed user:
Mairs Geographischer Verlag GmbH & Co., Ostfildern

Tyepset by Fakenham Photosetting Ltd, Fakenham, UK

Printed in Italy by G. Canale & C. S.p.A., Turin

ISBN 0 7495 2086 8

Principal Sights of Tourist Interest

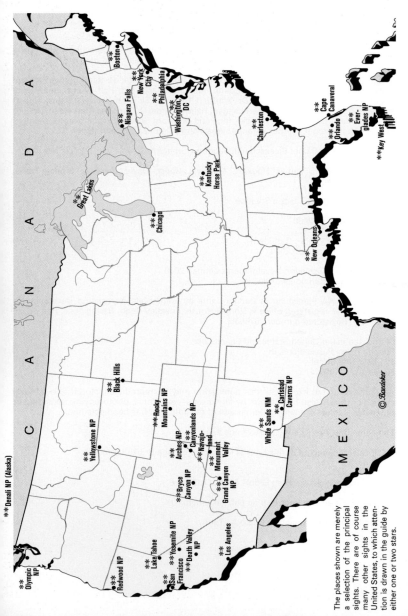

The places shown are merely a selection of the principal sights. There are of course many other sights in the United States, to which attention is drawn in the guide by either one or two stars.

**Denali NP (Alaska)

**Olympic NP
**Redwood NP
**San Francisco
**Lake Tahoe
**Yosemite NP
**Death Valley NP
**Los Angeles

**Bryce Canyon NP
**Grand Canyon NP
**Zion
**Monument Valley
**Navajo-land
**Arches NP
**Canyonlands NP
**Rocky Mountains NP
**Yellowstone NP
**Black Hills
**White Sands NM
**Carlsbad Caverns NP

**Chicago
**Great Lakes
Kentucky Horse Park
**Niagara Falls
**Boston
**New York City
**Philadelphia
**Washington, DC
**Charleston
**New Orleans
**Cape Canaveral
Orlando
**Everglades NP
**Key West

C A N A D A

M E X I C O

© Baedeker

624